Microsoft®

Microsoft® Windows® Small Business Server 2003 R2 Administrator's Companion

Charlie Russel and
Sharon Crawford

PUBLISHED BY
Microsoft Press
A Division of Microsoft Corporation
One Microsoft Way
Redmond, Washington 98052-6399

Library of Congress Control Number 2006924472
978-0-7356-2280-7
0-7356-2280-9

Printed and bound in the United States of America.

1 2 3 4 5 6 7 8 9   QWT   1 0 9 8 7 6

Distributed in Canada by H.B. Fenn and Company Ltd.

A CIP catalogue record for this book is available from the British Library.

Microsoft Press books are available through booksellers and distributors worldwide. For further information about international editions, contact your local Microsoft Corporation office or contact Microsoft Press International directly at fax (425) 936-7329. Visit our Web site at www.microsoft.com/mspress. Send comments to *mspinput@microsoft.com*.

Microsoft, Active Directory, ActiveSync, Entourage, Excel, FrontPage, Hotmail, Internet Explorer, JScript, Microsoft Press, MS-DOS, Outlook, SharePoint, Windows, Windows Mobile, Windows NT, Windows Server, and Windows Vista are either registered trademarks or trademarks of Microsoft Corporation in the United States and/or other countries. Other product and company names mentioned herein may be the trademarks of their respective owners.

The example companies, organizations, products, domain names, e-mail addresses, logos, people, places, and events depicted herein are fictitious. No association with any real company, organization, product, domain name, e-mail address, logo, person, place, or event is intended or should be inferred.

This book expresses the author's views and opinions. The information contained in this book is provided without any express, statutory, or implied warranties. Neither the authors, Microsoft Corporation, nor its resellers, or distributors will be held liable for any damages caused or alleged to be caused either directly or indirectly by this book.

Acquisitions Editor: Martin DelRe
Project Editor: Melissa von Tschudi-Sutton
Production: Custom Editorial Production, Inc.

Body Part No. X12-21114

Dedication

When you are labouring for others let it be with the same zeal as if it were for yourself.

Confucius

Dedicated to the SBS MVPs--Confucians whether they know it or not.

Contents at a Glance

Part I
Preparation and Planning

1   Looking at the Big Picture 3
2   Planning Your SBS Network. 13

Part II
Installation and Setup

3   Installing Windows Small Business Server 2003 39
4   Upgrading or Migrating to Windows Small Business Server 2003 . . 55
5   Completing the To Do List and Other Post-Installation Tasks 71

Part III
Performing the Basic Tasks

6   Disk Management 99
7   Storage Management 131
8   Managing Users and Groups 147
9   Shares and Permissions 175
10 Installing and Managing Printers 205
11 Managing Computers on the Network 235
12 Patch Management 269
13 Backing Up and Restoring Data 291

Part IV
Performing Advanced Tasks

14 Using Exchange Server 315
15 Managing Connectivity 363
16 Using ISA Server 2004 409
17 Using Group Policy 443
18 Customizing a SharePoint Web Site 465

19 Managing an Intranet Web Server 495
20 Using SQL Server 2005 515

Part V
Maintenance and Troubleshooting

21 Monitoring and Fine-Tuning Performance 541
22 Disaster Planning 581
23 Planning Fault Tolerance and Avoidance 601

Part VI
Appendices

A Introduction to Networks 621
B Partially Automating Installation 627
C Using the Transition Pack 637
D Using File Server Resource Manager 647

Table of Contents

Acknowledgments xvii

Introduction. xix

Part I   Preparation and Planning

1   Looking at the Big Picture. 3
  Features of Windows Small Business Server 4
    Internet and E-Mail Made Easy 4
    Ready-Made Intranet 5
    Quickly Add Users and Computers to the Network. 5
    Effortless Remote Access 6
    Services for Mobile Devices. 6
    Simple Administration and Management 6
    Fax with Fewer Phone Lines 7
    Enhanced Security. 8
    Manage Data Effectively 8
    Manage Storage Resources 9
    Create Advanced Web Pages. 9
    Online Licensing 9
    Growth Is Good 10
  Restrictions on Windows Small Business Server 10
    A Single Domain Controller 10
    A Single Domain 11
    Client Limit 11
  Summary 12
2   Planning Your SBS Network 13
  Planning the Network Infrastructure 13
    Determining Your Needs 15
    Choosing an Internet Connection 16
    Choosing a Network Type 19
    Choosing Network Devices 22
    Choosing Server Hardware 28
    Choosing Client Hardware and Software 29

Choosing Naming Conventions 30
    Choosing a Domain Name for the Network 31
    Naming Computers 32
Planning for Security 32
    Ensuring Physical Security 33
    Securing Client Computers 33
    Securing Wireless Networks 35
    Securing Internet Firewalls 36
Summary 36

Part II   Installation and Setup

3   **Installing Windows Small Business Server 2003** 39
Planning Partitions 40
Preparing the Server 41
Installing Windows Small Business Server 42
    Installing the Operating System 42
    Using the Windows Small Business Server Setup Wizard 48
Summary 53

4   **Upgrading or Migrating to Windows Small Business Server 2003** 55
Choosing Between Upgrading and Migrating 55
What's Involved in a Conventional Migration 57
What's Involved in a Swing Migration 58
    Advantages of Swing Migration 59
Preparing for an Upgrade 60
    Checking for Compatibility Issues 60
    Preparing for the Worst 61
    Preparing the Server 62
    Preparing Client Computers 64
    Final Preparation 65
Performing the Upgrade 66
Migrating User Permissions 69
Summary 70

5   **Completing the To Do List and Other Post-Installation Tasks** 71
Security Best Practices 72
Connecting to the Internet 73
    Setting Up a Broadband Connection with a Local Router 76
    Setting Up a Direct Broadband Connection 77
    Setting Up a Broadband Connection with User Authentication (PPPoE) 78
    Setting Up a Dial-Up Connection 79
    Configuring the Firewall 80

Configuring Remote Access 85
        Remote Access via Virtual Private Networking 86
        Remote Access via Dial-Up 87
Activating Your Server 88
Adding Client Access Licenses 89
Adding Printers 90
Adding Users and Computers 90
Configuring Fax Services 91
        Changing Fax Sending and Receiving 92
        Setting Fax Service Properties 93
Configuring Monitoring 94
Configuring Backup 95
Security Basics 95
Updating Windows Small Business Server 95
        Updating Client Computers 96
Summary 96

Part III   Performing the Basic Tasks

6   Disk Management 99
The Search for Disaster Protection 100
Understanding Disk Terminology 100
Choosing the Storage Solution for Your Network 103
        Storage Connection Technologies 104
Managing Disks 105
Using Disk Management 105
        Dynamic Disks 107
        Adding a Partition or Volume 108
        Converting a Disk to a Dynamic Disk 120
        Extending a Volume 121
        Adding a Mirror 123
        Drive Failure in a Mirrored Volume 124
        Removing a Mirror 126
        Breaking a Mirror 127
        RAID-5 Volumes 127
        Mounting a Volume 128
Summary 129
7   Storage Management 131
Disk Quotas 132
        Enabling Disk Quotas 132
        Setting Quota Entries for Users 134

Exporting and Importing Quotas 136
Creating Quota Reports 136
Encrypting Files 137
Enabling Encryption 138
Shadow Copies of Shared Folders 140
Configuring Shadow Copies 140
Enabling Shadow Copies 140
Setting Up Clients to Use Shadow Copies 143
Accessing Shadow Copies 143
Disabling Shadow Copies 145
Summary 146

8   **Managing Users and Groups** **147**
Understanding Groups 147
Assigning Group Scopes 149
Managing Built-in Groups 149
Built-in Universal Groups 150
Built-in Local Groups 151
Built-in Domain Local Groups 152
Built-in Global Groups 153
Creating Security Groups 153
Creating Distribution Groups 154
Understanding User Accounts 155
Creating User Accounts 155
Configuring Password Policy 159
Managing User Templates 162
Creating a New User Template 162
Applying a Template to Existing Users 162
Managing User Accounts 164
Redirecting My Documents to the Default Server Folder 165
Redirecting My Documents to a Network Folder 165
Maintaining User Profiles 167
Local Profiles 168
Roaming Profiles 169
Assigning a Logon Script to a User Profile 171
Using the Run As Command 172
Making Shortcuts to Run As 173
Summary 174

9   **Shares and Permissions** **175**
Sharing Resources 175
Folder Sharing 176

Removing a Share 177
Moving or Renaming a Shared Folder 178
Creating a New Share for a Shared Folder 179
Setting Offline File Rules 180
Synchronizing Offline Files 182
Making Shares Available Offline 182
Share Permissions vs. File Permissions 183
How Permissions Work 183
Working with NTFS File and Folder Permissions 184
Considering Inheritance 185
Configuring NTFS Folder Permissions 187
Assigning NTFS Permissions to Files 188
Configuring Special Permissions 189
Ownership and How It Works 191
Determining Effective Permissions 195
Privileges and Logon Rights 196
Encrypting Sensitive Data. 198
Creating a Recovery Policy 199
Encrypting Files and Folders 200
Decrypting Files and Folders 201
Sharing Encrypted Files 202
Recovering Files 202
Summary 204

10   Installing and Managing Printers 205
Understanding Print Servers 205
Choosing Printers 207
Installing Printers 208
Adding Locally Attached Printers 208
Adding Printers with Network Interfaces 211
Changing Printer Driver Settings 216
Sharing a Printer and Adding Client Drivers 217
Specifying a Color Profile 220
Changing Printer Availability and Priorities 221
Determining Group Printer Priorities 221
Setting Up Printer Pools and Changing Port Settings 222
Changing Spool Settings 223
Setting Print Server Options 224
Managing Printers 225
Managing Printers from Windows 226
Managing Printers from a Web Browser 227

Managing Printers from a Command Line 228

Using Printer Migrator to Back Up or Migrate Print Servers 229

Troubleshooting Printing Problems 230

Document Fails to Print 231

Document Prints Incorrectly 232

Deleting Stuck Documents 232

Summary 234

11   **Managing Computers on the Network** 235

Connecting Computers to the Network 236

Creating Computer Accounts for Client Computers 236

Creating Computer Accounts for Server Computers 238

Establishing Basic Network Connectivity 239

Using the Small Business Server Network Configuration Wizard 243

Connecting Alternate Clients 249

Using the Remote Web Workplace 254

Managing Computers from the Server 258

Assigning Applications to Client Computers 259

Creating a Remote Connection Disk 263

Viewing and Modifying Client Computer Settings 265

Remotely Managing Computers and Viewing Event Logs 266

Removing Computers from the Network 267

Summary 268

12   **Patch Management** 269

Why Patching Is Important 270

The Patching Cycle 272

Assess 272

Identify 273

Evaluate and Plan 275

Deploy 276

Repeat 276

Installing SBS 2003 R2 WSUS 277

Using WSUS 280

Reviewing Errors 283

Review Pending Updates 284

Review Status of Updates Installation 286

Change Update Services Settings 288

Third-Party Solutions 289

Summary 290

13   **Backing Up and Restoring Data** **291**

    Backup Terminology and Methods 291

        Backup Devices 292

        Backup Media 293

    Designing a Backup Strategy 294

        Backup Schedules 295

        Using Shadow Copies to Supplement Backups 297

    Backing Up Your Data 298

        Configuring the Backup Utility 298

        Running a Backup Manually 302

        Modifying the Backup Configuration 306

    Restoring Data 307

        Using the Backup Utility to Restore Files and Folders 307

        Using the Previous Versions Client to Restore Files and Folders 309

    Summary 311

Part IV   Performing Advanced Tasks

14   **Using Exchange Server** **315**

    Basic E-Mail Configuration 315

    POP3 E-Mail 322

        Configuring POP3 E-Mail 322

        Adding, Removing, and Editing POP3 E-Mail Boxes 322

        Setting a POP3 Delivery Schedule 325

        Routing POP3 E-Mail 326

        Troubleshooting POP3 329

    Advanced E-Mail Configuration and Management 331

        Changing E-Mail Password 331

        Synchronize E-Mail 332

        Managing E-Mail Distribution Lists 332

        Setting the Reply To Address 339

    Managing E-Mail Delivery 342

        Setting an Individual User's Message Properties 343

        SMTP Filtering 345

        Managing Queues 355

    Exchange 2003 SP2 359

    Summary 361

15   **Managing Connectivity** **363**

    Administering TCP/IP Services 363

        Managing DHCP 364

        Viewing DNS Records 368

Administering Routing and Remote Access 370

Viewing Remote Access Clients 371

Configuring Ports 372

Advanced Network Security 372

Using Internet Authentication Service to Increase VPN Security 373

Deploying Certificate Services 375

Creating L2TP VPN Connections 381

Using 802.1X Authentication for Wireless Security 388

Using Group Policy to Automatically Configure 802.11
and Certificate Settings 403

Summary 407

16   Using ISA Server 2004 . . . . **409**

Concepts 410

Network Address Translation 410

Packet Filtering and Application Layer Filtering 412

Caching 412

Client Types 413

ISA Server Firewall Policies 413

Installing ISA Server 2004 414

Installing the Firewall Client 419

Adding the Firewall Client to Client Applications 419

Deploying the Firewall Client 421

Administering ISA Server 2004 421

Changing Your Broadband or Dial-Up Connection 422

Enabling or Disabling Services Through the ISA Server 422

Enabling or Disabling Web Services 424

Enabling L2TP With ISA Server 2004 425

Advanced Configuration. 429

Create Firewall Policy Rules 429

Recommended Initial Configuration Steps 433

Backing Up the ISA Server Configuration 434

Import, Export, Backup, and Restore 434

Monitoring ISA Server 437

Summary 441

17   Using Group Policy **443**

Group Policy Objects 444

Managing Group Policies 444

Order of Inheritance 447

Overriding Inheritance 447

Order of Implementation 448

Creating a Group Policy Object 450
Deleting a Group Policy Object 451
Managing Group Policy Links 452
    Setting the Scope of the GPO 453
    Enabling and Disabling GPO Links 454
    Disabling a Branch of a GPO 455
Refreshing Group Policy 455
Backing Up a Group Policy Object 456
 Restoring a Group Policy Object 457
Delegating Permissions on a GPO 457
Predicting Group Policy Outcomes 459
    Group Policy Modeling 459
    Group Policy Results 461
Summary 463

18   Customizing a SharePoint Web Site **465**
Getting Familiar with Windows SharePoint Services 466
    Understanding SharePoint Items 467
    Interacting with a SharePoint Site 469
Changing the Appearance of the Site 471
Changing Home Page Content 472
Customizing Pages 474
Administering a SharePoint Web Site 477
    Managing Site Users 478
    Managing Site Groups and Access Permissions 480
    Managing Templates, Usage Data, and Other Settings 481
Administering SharePoint Virtual Servers 482
Using FrontPage 2003 to Customize Windows SharePoint Services 485
    Customizing Existing SharePoint Sites 485
    Creating New SharePoint Web Sites 490
Backup and Restore of a SharePoint Site 491
    Using Stsadm 492
    Using Smigrate 492
Summary 493

19   Managing an Intranet Web Server **495**
Creating New Virtual Directories 496
Using Web Sharing 498
Changing Security Settings 499
    Changing Which Sites Are Externally Accessible 500
    Enabling or Disabling Anonymous Access 503
    Changing Server Certificates and SSL Settings 505

Limiting Network Usage by Web Sites 508
Setting Up an FTP Server 509
    Installing FTP 510
    Configuring FTP 510
Configuring the Indexing Service 511
Backing Up and Restoring the IIS Configuration 512
Reinstalling IIS 513
Summary 514

20   **Using SQL Server 2005** **515**
Installing SQL Server 2005 515
Upgrading Windows SharePoint Services to SQL Server 2005 522
    Before You Upgrade 523
    Upgrading Companyweb to SQL Server 2005 525
Architecture 532
Administration 532
    Start, Stop, and Pause 533
    Backup 534
Summary 538

Part V   Maintenance and Troubleshooting

21   **Monitoring and Fine-Tuning Performance** **541**
Enabling Auditing And Monitoring 541
    Predefined Performance and Usage Reports 542
    Auditing Events 542
    Viewing Event Logs 543
    Searching Event Logs 543
    Setting the Size of Event Logs 545
Selecting A Monitoring Method 546
Using System Monitor 546
    System Monitor Items 546
    Running System Monitor 547
    Monitoring Another Computer 553
Performance Logs and Alerts 553
    Counter Logs 554
    Trace Logs 554
    Creating Counter and Trace Logs 554
Using Alerts 558
    Creating an Alert 558
    Configuring an Alert 559
Permissions for Counter Logs, Trace Logs, and Alerts 561

Monitoring Memory Usage 562

 Recommended Counters 563

Monitoring Processor Activity 565

 Minimum Recommended Counters 565

Monitoring Disk Activity 567

 Minimum Recommended Counters 567

Using Health Monitor 568

 Modifying an Existing Threshold 570

 Adding a Threshold 571

 Configuring Actions 571

 Using Data Collectors 574

Summary 579

22 Disaster Planning **581**

Planning for Disaster 581

 Identifying the Risks 583

 Identifying the Resources 584

 Developing the Responses 585

 Testing the Responses 589

 Iterating 589

Preparing for a Disaster 590

 Setting Up a Fault-Tolerant System 591

 Backing Up the System 591

 Creating an Automated System Recovery Disk 591

 Creating a Boot Disk 595

 Installing the Recovery Console 597

 Specifying Recovery Options 598

 Creating and Using a Recovery Drive 599

Summary 600

23 Planning Fault Tolerance and Avoidance **601**

Mean Time to Failure and Mean Time to Recover 602

Protecting the Power Supply 603

 Local Power Supply Failure 604

 Voltage Variations 606

 Short-Term Power Outages 608

 Long-Term Power Outages 609

Disk Arrays 610

 Hardware vs. Software 610

 RAID Levels for Fault Tolerance 611

 Hot-Swap and Hot-Spare Disk Systems 616

Other Spare Parts 616

Summary 617

Part VI Appendices

A   **Introduction to Networks** **621**

Servers 621

Clients 622

Media Connecting Servers and Clients 622

Features of the Windows Operating System 622

Domains and Workgroups 623

Do Workgroups Work? 623

Defining Domains 624

Domain Components 625

B   **Partially Automating Installation** **627**

Automating CD-Based Installations 627

Using the System Preparation Tool to Image Windows Server 2003 633

C   **Using the Transition Pack** **637**

What's in a Transition Pack? 637

Why Convert? 638

Handling Business Growth 638

Handling Multiple Domains 638

Will I Lose RWW? 639

Preparing to Run the Transition Pack 640

Performing the Transition 641

Post-Transition 644

Post-Transition Tasks 644

D   **Using File Server Resource Manager** **647**

Installing FSRM 647

Setting Global Options 648

Using Folder Quotas 650

Creating Quotas 650

Creating and Editing Quota Templates 653

Screening Files 655

Creating File Screens 656

Scheduling Storage Reports 658

Glossary **661**

Index **677**

Acknowledgments

No book happens in a vacuum, and certainly no book is ever the work of just the authors, and this even less so than many. We're deeply indebted to all who have helped with this very demanding project.

The SBS MVPs give of their expertise and skills unstintingly to the entire community, and to us on this book as well. When we had questions, they had answers! As did the Inside SBS Podcast team, the SBS Product Support team, and the SBS Product team. We truly appreciate all the help we got from you. We had specific answers and support from Eric Ligman, Damian Leibashoff, Mark Stanfill, Marie McFadden, Kevin Beares, Paul Fitzgerald, Peter Gallagher, John Bay, and David Copeland, and we thank them sincerely, but we had support and answers from many others in these teams as well, and we greatly appreciated all you did.

An SBS MVP who had an impact on every single page of this book was Susan Bradley, our Peer Reviewer. She not only read every single word, but offered invaluable insights, suggestions, technical expertise and just plain old *help* at every turn. Thank you, Susan.

The SBS community has many great resources. The MVPs are obviously one, but another that we've enjoyed the support and help of is the User Group community. Locally, the VanSBS User Group is an excellent resource for us, and your local user group should be for you as well. When we needed a critical piece of hardware, Jasminder Rai, the leader of VanSBS, pulled a brand new one off his shelves and loaned it to us without question. We can't repay that, we can only say thank you.

Over the years, we've worked with good and less good editorial teams. The teams at Microsoft Press are among the very best in the business, and this time was no exception. Product planner Martin DelRe contributed mightily to the planning and execution of this book and helped us at several critical junctures. Thank you, Martin—you really came through on this one. Melissa von Tschudi-Sutton was our Project Editor, and a joy to work with. It was our first time working with you, Melissa, but we sincerely hope not our last. Mitch Tulloch was our Tech Editor, and he is simply the best Tech Editor we've ever worked with. Megan Smith-Creed at Custom Editorial Productions and the copy editor Becka McKay did an excellent job making our sentences actually readable. As authors, we truly appreciate good editors. Thank you. And to the proofreader, indexer, and composition team: we never really know your names but we sincerely appreciate your efforts.

As always, we thank past collaborators Rudolph S. Langer, David J. Clark, and Karen Szall. Valued friends and true scholars.

Introduction

The first time you noticed Microsoft Windows Small Business Server 2003, it might have been because it's such a remarkable bargain. For about the price of a mid-level desktop copier, you get Microsoft Windows Server 2003, Windows SharePoint Services, Microsoft Exchange Server 2003, Microsoft Office Outlook 2003, and Routing and Remote Access firewall technology. And that is just the Standard Edition.

In Windows Small Business Server 2003 R2, you now have all that, plus enhanced security; Microsoft Windows Small Business Server Update Services for automated, network-wide patch and update management; Exchange Server 2003 updated to SP2 with increased mailbox limits to 75 GB; the File Server Resource Manager, which allows you to set quotas and file screens by folder; and expanded client access license (CAL) rights.

The Premium Edition has all that, plus Microsoft SQL Server 2005 Workgroup Edition, Microsoft Internet and Security Acceleration (ISA) Server 2004, and Microsoft Office FrontPage 2003. In both editions, the technologies are optimized to work as a package for the small business user.

Windows Small Business Server has always been a bargain, and each new version has been easier to install and much easier to configure and use. The various applications are better integrated than ever before. New tools have centralized and simplified server management, and dozens of wizards are available to help with just about every conceivable task. Best of all, Windows Small Business Server allows companies with as few as 3 or as many as 75 computers to have an affordable, real, client/server network with all the security and efficiency that implies.

How to Use this Book

Microsoft Windows Small Business Server 2003 R2 Administrator's Companion is a handy reference and assistant for the busy network administrator, whether the administrator is on the scene or accessing the network from another location.

Even though Windows Small Business Server 2003 has automated many, many of the tasks associated with configuring and securing a network, this book is required when you want to do something slightly out of the ordinary—or when you need additional understanding of what a wizard is doing.

Look for book elements such as the following:

Under the Hood Because wizards are so efficient at what they do, it can be very difficult to know what's going on in the background. Sidebars titled "Under the Hood" describe the technical operations being performed by the wizard. These sidebars also include methodological information to help you understand Windows Small Business Server.

Real World Everyone can benefit from the experiences of others. "Real World" sidebars contain elaboration on a particular theme or background based on the adventures of other users of Windows Small Business Server.

Note Notes include tips, alternative ways to perform a task, or some information that needs to be highlighted.

Security Alert Nothing is more important than security when it comes to a computer network. Security elements should be carefully noted and acted on.

Planning As we stress throughout the book, proper planning is fundamental to the smooth operation of any network. These boxes contain specific and useful hints to make that process go smoothly.

Important Boxes marked Important shouldn't be skipped. (That's why they're called Important.) Here you'll find security notes, cautions, and warnings to keep you and your network out of trouble.

More Info Often there are excellent sources for additional information on key topics. We'll use these boxes to point you to a recommended resource.

What's in This Book

Microsoft Windows Small Business Server 2003 R2 Administrator's Companion is divided into six parts. The first five parts roughly correspond to the developmental phases of a

Windows Small Business Server network. The last part has appendixes with helpful information.

■ **Part I: Preparation and Planning**   Planning and preparation are the *sine qua non* for any kind of network. It comes down to the old saying, "If you don't have the time to do it right, how will you find the time to do it over?" Chapters 1 and 2 are all about doing it right the first time.

■ **Part II: Installation and Setup**   Chapters 3 through 5 take you through the process of installing or upgrading Windows Small Business Server and performing initial configurations using the To Do List (a great feature new in Windows Small Business Server 2003).

■ **Part III: Performing the Basic Tasks**   Chapters 6 through 13 cover the day-to-day tasks in running a network: configuring disks, setting up user accounts, arranging the sharing of information among users, adding and removing computers and printers, and backing up and restoring data.

■ **Part IV: Performing Advanced Tasks**   Chapters 14 through 20 provide insight and information about using Exchange Server, connectivity technologies, and Internet Security and Acceleration Server (Premium Edition). In this part, you'll also find chapters about setting up and managing an intranet plus the basics of Microsoft SQL Server (Premium Edition).

■ **Part V: Tuning and Troubleshooting**   Chapter 21 covers the extensive library of monitoring tools available in Windows Small Business Server, and Chapter 22 is all about how to save your business, your network, and yourself in the face of the many varieties of disaster that can afflict networks. Chapter 23, the final chapter in this section, will help with planning fault tolerance to enable your network to avoid problems, or survive them with minimal disruption.

■ **Part VI: Appendices**   At the end of the book, Appendices A through D deal with network basics, using the transition pack to move from Small Business Server 2003 to R2, using the new File Server Resource Manager, and other useful subjects.

System Requirements

This book is designed to be used with either of the following software editions:

■ Microsoft Windows Small Business Server 2003, Standard Edition, SP1 or later

■ Microsoft Windows Small Business Server 2003, Premium Edition, SP1 or later

Windows Small Business Server R2 is required for specific R2 features.

For information on Windows Small Business Server 2003, visit

http://www.microsoft.com/Windowsserver2003/sbs/

The following are the minimum system requirements to run the companion CD provided with this book:

- Microsoft Windows 2000 or later

- CD-ROM drive

- Internet connection

- Display monitor capable of 800 x 600 resolution or higher

- Microsoft Mouse or compatible pointing device

- Adobe Reader for viewing the eBook (Adobe Reader is available as a download at *http://www.adobe.com*)

About the Companion CD

The companion CD contains the fully searchable electronic version of this book and additional materials you might find useful. We've included the current versions of important Microsoft Knowledge Base Articles that we referenced in the book, as well as several whitepapers we found useful in our research. Also included are links to other resources that didn't lend themselves to inclusion on the CD.

Support

Every effort has been made to ensure the accuracy of this book and companion CD content. Microsoft Press provides corrections for books through the Web at the following address:

http://www.microsoft.com/learning/support/

To connect directly to the Microsoft Knowledge Base and enter a query regarding a question or issue that you may have, go to the following address:

http://www.microsoft.com/learning/support/search.asp

If you have comments, questions, or ideas regarding the book or companion CD content, or if you have questions that are not answered by querying the Knowledge Base, please send them to Microsoft Press using either of the following methods:

E-Mail:
mspinput@microsoft.com

Postal Mail:
Microsoft Press
Attn: Microsoft Windows Small Business Server R2 Administrator's Companion Editor
One Microsoft Way
Redmond, WA 98052-6399

Please note that product support is not offered through the preceding mail addresses. For support information, please visit the Microsoft Product Support Web site at the following address:

http://support.microsoft.com

Talk to Us

We've done our best to make this book as accurate and complete as a single-volume reference can be. However, Windows Small Business Server 2003 is large and we are mere humans, so we're sure that alert readers will find omissions and even errors (though we fervently hope not too many of those). If you have suggestions, corrections, or tips, please write and let us know at SBS2003R2@scribes.com.

We really do appreciate hearing from you.

Part I
Preparation and Planning

Chapter 1 Looking at the Big Picture. 3
Chapter 2 Planning Your SBS Network 13

Chapter 1
Looking at the Big Picture

Features of Windows Small Business Server 4

Restrictions on Windows Small Business Server 10

Summary 12

Owners of small businesses say key factors for producing fiscal growth include acquiring new customers, minimizing customer turnover, marketing products and services, and keeping ahead of competitors. You need technology to realize all those factors, but technology is not your business—your business is making a product, selling a product, or providing a service. Every minute that you have to spend doing something else is time taken away from the real business of your business. Plus, the desire to be competitive frequently runs up against the fact of real-world budgets. You need to do more with less—less money, less time, and fewer resources.

Microsoft Windows Small Business Server (SBS) 2003 is a comprehensive, easy-to-use, and inexpensive solution. Microsoft has taken all the components necessary to run a business and combined them into a single, integrated, made-to-work-together package. Easy to set up and even easier to manage, Windows Small Business Server allows you to concentrate more time on what you went into business for.

Windows Small Business Server is available in two versions, so you don't have to pay for what you don't need. Since both versions include Microsoft products that would be considerably more expensive if bought individually, you get a fully developed business solution that's a bargain to boot. The R2 release adds additional and updated functionality to both versions.

Windows Small Business Server 2003, Standard Edition, includes Microsoft Windows Server 2003, Standard Edition; Microsoft Windows SharePoint Services; Microsoft Exchange Server 2003; and Microsoft Shared Fax Service. The R2 release of SBS 2003 adds Windows Server Update Services (WSUS) to provide a fully integrated and comprehensive update management package to help ensure that your entire network stays up to date and fully patched, along with the latest updates to Microsoft Exchange Server 2003 and SharePoint Services. It also adds a new tool and new capabilities with the addition of the File Server Resource Manager (FSRM) to manage quotas and filter what types of files are allowed to be stored on the server. These products give you a fully developed business solution that includes all the essentials: e-mail, Internet connectivity, a preconfigured internal Web site, a shared fax service, services for remote users and mobile users, and wizards to make configuration easy.

Note   Microsoft's official terminology does not use the word "patch," but rather uses "update," "security update," and several other terms, as detailed in Microsoft Knowledge Base Article 824684 found at *http://support.microsoft.com/kb/824684/*. The industry as a whole, however, still uses the more general term, "patch," to describe a broad range of security and non-security updates, as does the general public. In most cases in this book, except when we want to be very specific about a particular type of update, we will use the industry's standard term: patch. It was a patch when I was first supporting UNIX systems 20 years ago, and as far as I'm concerned, it still is.

Windows Small Business Server 2003, Premium Edition, includes all the preceding features plus Microsoft Internet Security and Acceleration (ISA) Server 2004 for firewall and Web caching services, Microsoft SQL Server 2000 to handle databases, and Microsoft Office FrontPage 2003. The R2 release replaces SQL Server 2000 with SQL Server 2005.

Features of Windows Small Business Server

Although a list of components is impressive—especially when considering the package price—it doesn't really convey the full extent of SBS capabilities. The next sections describe those capabilities and what's special about their use in Windows Small Business Server 2003.

Internet and E-Mail Made Easy

Everyone needs e-mail today and a business without Internet connectivity is viewed as absolutely antiquated. Unfortunately, under normal circumstances, setting up e-mail and an Internet connection is just about as daunting as it ever was. SBS changes all that with tools to make both processes quite painless. For example, the Configure E-mail and Internet Connection Wizard (known hereafter as the CEICW) allows you to easily configure the network, set up a shared Internet broadband or dial-up connection, configure firewall services, and customize Exchange Server for e-mail. Use Exchange Server 2003 with Microsoft Office Outlook 2003 and add numerous features, including the ability to schedule meetings and hold online conferences.

Chapter 5, "Completing the To Do List and Other Post-Installation Tasks," covers the use of the CEICW for the initial set up of e-mail. Details on Exchange Server are provided in Chapter 14, "Using Exchange Server."

Ready-Made Intranet

Most businesspeople know the value of an intranet as a centralized location for users to collaborate and share documents, providing a friendly and easy-to-use framework for teamwork. However, many of those same people have been forced to retreat when faced with the costs of building and maintaining an internal Web site. This particular problem vanishes when Windows Small Business Server is deployed because the product includes a pre-built, internal Web site based on Windows SharePoint Services.

The internal Web site comes with preconfigured document and picture libraries, shared lists, and sample content. The site can easily be set up so that users can share documents, read announcements, respond to surveys, make requests to the Help desk, and view the vacation calendar. If the preconfigured elements don't meet your needs, you can remove them or add new ones.

More Info   Chapter 18, "Customizing a SharePoint Web Site," and Chapter 19, "Managing an Intranet Web Server," are all about customizing and maintaining an intranet site for your business.

Quickly Add Users and Computers to the Network

The Add User Wizard in Windows Small Business Server allows you to add a single user or multiple users. The wizard sets up everything a user will need: a mailbox in Exchange; access to shared printers, files, and folders; access to the intranet; a home folder on the server; and a user account in Active Directory. Use a predefined template to add multiple users with settings in common, or create your own template with the Add Template Wizard.

More Info   Adding users with or without a template is covered in Chapter 8, "Managing Users and Groups."

Client computers can be added to the network simply by browsing to a Web site that contains all the tools for configuring network settings. Client applications included with SBS are installed with the Set Up Computer Wizard, and other software can be set up to deploy to client computers using the Set Up Client Applications Wizard.

> **More Info**   The Set Up Computer Wizard is described in Chapter 5. Configuring client software is covered in Chapter 11, "Managing Computers on the Network."

Effortless Remote Access

The number of workers who telecommute at least part of the time continues to grow. Whether an organization has a few or many remote users, the mechanisms for access have to be reliable, secure, and easy to use. Unfortunately, this is honored more in theory than in practice. In many places, problems with remote access make up the largest single category of calls to the Help desk.

To improve this situation, SBS includes the Remote Web Workplace (RWW). RWW is a feature of SBS that many larger organizations will wish they had. Using any device that can connect to the Internet, authorized users can access this dynamically created Web site using a simple Internet address. These users can then read their e-mail, access the company intranet, and connect to their own computers' desktops. Users can download Connection Manager, which automates the process of connecting their remote computers to the company's network, making the whole process quite easy.

> **More Info**   See Chapter 5 for information on configuring remote access. Chapter 15, "Managing Connectivity," discusses remote access administration.

Services for Mobile Devices

Client computers are added to the network using the Setup Computer Wizard. This wizard also configures client computers to support mobile devices. Users of Windows Small Business Server just connect a mobile device to the client computer to access their e-mail, schedule, and task information. See Chapter 5 for more information.

Simple Administration and Management

All the most common network management tasks are made simpler than ever before. As a result, you can spend more time on what you do best (your business) and much less time managing your network.

Set up automatic backups with the Backup Configuration Wizard. This tool, along with Volume Shadow Copy, offers powerful ways to protect your data's integrity. You create a backup strategy and Windows Small Business Server takes it from there—on any computer, backup to tape, network hard drive, or shared folder. The program will report the success or failure of each backup and even remind the appropriate person when a hard drive is full or it's time to change the tape.

More Info   See Chapter 13, "Backing Up and Restoring Data," for the essentials of backing up and restoring data.

Monitoring and usage tools are easy to set up and reports are easy to read. The Monitoring Configuration Wizard sets up alert notifications, performance reports, and usage updates. You choose when and to whom reports are sent. Authorized recipients can receive notices in e-mail or on a secure Web page on your intranet.

More Info   Chapter 21 "Monitoring and Fine-Tuning Performance," covers monitoring and fine-tuning your network.

You can grant power users rights and privileges ranging from the very specific to the very general. These users can then take over management chores such as backing up the server, adding new users, or monitoring network performance, or they can perform any other task you want to get out of your hair.

More Info   Chapter 9 "Shares and Permissions," is all about granting and restricting rights.

Keeping the computers on your network up to date with all the latest security updates is a daunting task if you have to do it manually—and not a task you dare ignore. SBS 2003 R2 adds all the tools you need to simplify and manage the whole process.

More Info   Chapter 12, "Patch Management," is all about keeping your computers secured with the latest updates.

Fax with Fewer Phone Lines

Windows Small Business Server includes a shared fax service that allows faxing from the users' desktops. Faxes can be delivered through e-mail, Windows SharePoint Services, or to a printer. No matter how many or how few faxes your business receives, the ability to share phone lines will reduce the total number of lines needed.

More Info   See Chapter 5 for information about fax services.

Enhanced Security

Of course you want your network to be secure—everyone knows about the menace of hackers, viruses, worms, and other vermin. But how to go about it? Windows Small Business Server includes an internal firewall to protect your network and supports external firewalls as well. The Premium Edition includes Internet Security and Acceleration (ISA) Server, which provides improved security and ease of use beyond that of traditional firewalls. ISA Server includes built-in intelligent filtering of HTTP, FTP, Simple Mail Transport Protocol (SMTP), streaming media, and remote procedure calls (RPC). Third-party programs can add the ability to scan for malicious viruses, detect intrusions in real time, improve ISA Server caching, and use additional user-authentication methods.

Group Policy allows you to restrict unauthorized software installations, require strong passwords, and ensure that users receive access only to resources they need.

More Info   Chapter 2, "Designing a Network," includes information about planning for security. Chapter 5 has details about adjusting security policies. Chapter 17, "Using Group Policy," covers how to effectively use Group Policy to manage your network, and Chapter 16, "Using ISA Server 2004," covers installing and configuring ISA Server 2004 if you have SBS, Premium Edition.

Manage Data Effectively

If you have a lot of business information to manage, such as inventory, e-commerce, and data warehousing, you need a way to organize the data to make it useful. The Premium Edition of SBS comes with Microsoft SQL Server, a fast, extremely reliable database that grows with your business.

Manipulate your data in simple ways, for example, by conducting full-text searches. You can search not only plaintext data stored in relational tables, but also formatted documents such as Office and HTML (HyperText Markup Language) documents. Do more complex operations such as developing profiles of your most valued customers and what those customers want. Analyze data, construct business models, and get personalized, real-time reports that can be delivered anywhere, anytime, on any device.

SQL Server will fit your business now and, more important, can be scaled up to whatever your future needs might be.

More Info   Chapter 20, "Using SQL Server 2005," covers installing and configuring SQL Server 2005 (part of the R2 release of SBS) on your SBS Premium Edition network.

Manage Storage Resources

Managing storage resources and ensuring that only appropriate file types are stored on the server is a problem that many system administrators struggle with. In R2, SBS adds the File System Resource Manager (FSRM) to enable administrators to better manage quotas, and to enable file system filtering that blocks saving files with specific extensions, such as .mp3, on the SBS server.

More Info   Appendix D, "Using the File System Resource Manager" covers the enhanced file system management and reporting capabilities in SBS 2003 R2.

Create Advanced Web Pages

Microsoft Office FrontPage has long been the preferred application for easy Web page creation. It has been offered as a standalone application and as part of Microsoft Office, adding ever more sophisticated capabilities with each version. A single copy of Microsoft Office FrontPage 2003 is included in the Premium Edition of SBS.

The delight of FrontPage is that it can be (and is) used by everyone from true beginners to professional Web developers. Use the pre-made templates and the scripting features in FrontPage 2003 to quickly implement a site with simple interactivity. Create your own templates, each containing multiple content regions, and apply these to pages in your Web site. In fact, you can build, update, and maintain a whole site—even an e-commerce one—without knowing a word of HTML, DHTML (Dynamic HyperText Markup Language), or XML (Extensible Markup Language).

On the other hand, a developer accustomed to writing HTML code will feel equally at home using FrontPage. Complicated, interactive Web sites with precise layouts, imported graphics, scripts, dynamic updating, and other features are cost-effectively constructed using FrontPage. Integration with Windows SharePoint Services and SQL Server makes editing and presenting live data possible—it even allows users to post to the Web using just their browsers.

More Info   Chapter 18 covers using FrontPage 2003.

Online Licensing

Both versions of Windows Small Business Server include five client licenses. If you have more than five client computers, you must purchase additional licenses. You'll receive a paper license from Microsoft (instead of a floppy disk, as in the past), and licenses can be activated over the Internet.

Client access licenses can be device-based (one license for each computer) or user-based (one license for each user). The two types of licenses are priced the same. You can even have a mixture of license types, but it's best to choose one type and stick with it to make tracking easier. Chapter 5 covers how to add client access licenses.

Growth Is Good

If you intend to expand your business by leaps and bounds, you might be wondering what happens to Windows Small Business Server when you're no longer a Small Business. In this context, a small business is one with fewer than 75 PCs or fewer than 100 employees.

If it turns out that Windows Small Business Server can't keep pace with the growth of your business, you'll be able to convert to Windows Server 2003 with only minimal business disruption by using the SBS Transition Pack. We cover the use of the Transition Pack to grow your network beyond the bounds of SBS in Appendix C, "Using the Transition Pack."

Another reason you might need to use the Transition Pack is if you need to merge another network into yours. Since SBS doesn't allow you to have multiple domains, you'll need to move to full Windows Server 2003 if you have to support another domain.

Because Windows Server 2003 is the underlying operating system in Windows Small Business Server, all files, records, and configurations are migrated without change. You lose nothing and gain all the abilities of a Windows Server 2003 domain.

Restrictions on Windows Small Business Server

Because Windows Small Business Server is designed for smaller organizations—and because of its bargain price—you will face specific limits when working with the package. These limits are not recommendations—they're boundaries that can't be transcended.

A Single Domain Controller

All the components of Windows Small Business Server must be loaded on a single machine—the domain controller. You can have other servers, such as file servers and print servers, but none of the components of Windows Small Business Server can be run on a computer other than the domain controller.

> ## Under the Hood   The Additional Domain Controller
>
> Only one Windows Small Business Server installation is allowed per domain, but it is technically possible to have one or more additional domain controllers on an SBS network. An additional domain controller running Windows Server 2003 provides load balancing and logon capability when the Windows Small Business Server machine is out of service.
>
> You cannot transfer any of the Operation Master roles to the additional domain controller.

Because the server does so much work, you'll need a powerful computer with lots of capacity on which to install Windows Small Business Server.

More Info   Chapter 2 provides information about choosing suitable hardware for your network.

Note   If you must have a component of Windows Small Business Server on a separate computer, you can purchase a license for, say, Exchange Server or SQL Server, and install it on a computer other than the domain controller. It will still integrate smoothly with Windows Small Business Server. And, beginning with SBS R2, your SBS Client Access Licenses (CALs) are valid CALs for the server application, so all you need is the actual server application license.

A Single Domain

Windows Small Business Server and its clients constitute a single domain. The domain is based on Active Directory, just as any other Windows Server 2003 domain, except that it cannot form trust relationships.

Client Limit

Windows Small Business Server comes with five client access licenses (CALs). You can purchase additional licenses up to a maximum of 75, though Windows Small Business Server is designed to work best with no more than 50 users/devices.

The client limit shouldn't restrict you except in the sense that 50 or more clients working off a single server is limiting. You are likely to want to change to a Windows Server 2003 network because of its greater flexibility in distributing the load across multiple servers long before you reach the client limit. While SBS allows multiple servers, the core components all need to run on the primary SBS server unless you buy fully licensed standalone versions of the components.

Summary

To be competitive in today's world of commerce, you need the power of technology. You need to find and retain customers, market and sell to those customers, and do all of it better than anyone else. Small businesses have big needs but small budgets.

Windows Small Business Server 2003 integrates e-mail, shared Internet access, fax services, database, remote access, security, Web development and collaboration, and other features into a single package that is easy to deploy and easy to maintain.

The next chapter provides an overview of networks and specifics on how to design a network that will work for you.

Chapter 2
Planning Your SBS Network

Planning the Network Infrastructure 13

Choosing Naming Conventions. 30

Planning for Security. 32

Summary 36

Before you actually start installing Microsoft Windows Small Business Server 2003, you should spend some time and thought planning what your network will look like. Time spent now, *before* you actually start installing anything, will save you time, energy, and complications later. By designing your network infrastructure, naming conventions, and network security now, you'll prevent having to modify or rebuild your network later.

Planning the Network Infrastructure

The first tasks in designing a network for your company are evaluating the computing needs of the organization, choosing an Internet connection method and local network type, and selecting network devices. You also need to choose server hardware as well as client hardware and software.

Under the Hood   Network Operating Systems

On an ordinary PC, the role of the operating system is to manage the file system, handle the running of applications, manage the computer's memory, and control the input and output to attached devices such as cameras, printers, and scanners. A network operating system (NOS) expands that role, managing the following:

- Centralized security
- Remote file systems
- Running shared applications
- Input and output to shared network devices
- CPU scheduling of networked processes

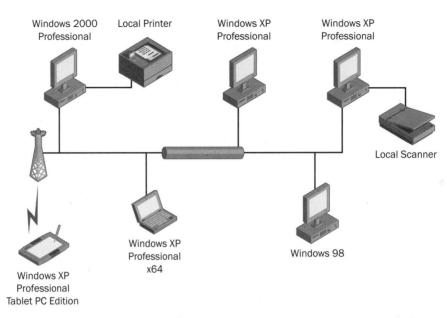

Windows 2000 Professional

Local Printer

Windows XP Professional

Windows XP Professional

Local Scanner

Windows XP Professional Tablet PC Edition

Windows XP Professional x64

Windows 98

Figure 2-1   A peer-to-peer network, which has no central server or management.

When multiple computers are connected in a *workgroup*, as shown in Figure 2-1, the result is called a *peer-to-peer network:* a network without a central server and with no network operating system.

Adding one or more servers running Windows Server 2003, or Windows Small Business Server 2003, as shown in Figure 2-2, is a *client/server-based network*—one or more servers and multiple clients, all sharing a single security policy. The servers provide both the resources and the security policy for the network, and the clients are the computers that use the resources managed by the server.

Servers Use Network Operating Systems

Because the Windows Small Business Server has to supply services to as many as 75 users, and you're depending on it to run your business, a high-powered, robust operating system and highly reliable hardware are essential. When your users rely on a server to get their work done and keep your business running, you certainly don't want frequent failures—you don't even want to reboot!

In addition to supplying print, file, or other services, the network operating system has to provide network security. Different businesses and organizations have varying security needs, but *all* must have some level of data protection. Therefore, the system must offer a range of configurable security levels, from the relatively non-intrusive to the very stringent.

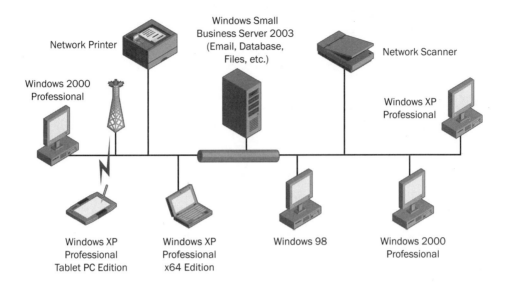

Figure 2-2 A client/server network, which has a central management and resource server.

Clients Use Workstation Operating Systems

Like other computers, client machines on a network need an operating system. However, a client operating system doesn't need to manage the resources for other computers, or manage security for the network. Rebooting a workstation can be a pain for the user but doesn't usually disrupt anyone else's work.

On a Windows Small Business Server network, clients can run Windows 98, Windows Me, Microsoft Windows 2000 Professional, and Microsoft Windows XP Professional as their supported operating systems. And business editions of Windows Vista will be supported when Windows Vista ships. However, for best performance and security, and for support of Remote Web Workplace, only Windows XP Service Pack 2 or later—or Windows Vista—should be deployed on clients.

Determining Your Needs

Before designing a network, decide which features of Windows Small Business Server 2003 R2 your business needs; doing so helps ensure that the network design is dictated by business needs instead of by fancy technology. Key needs to consider include:

- Centralized user account management
- Centralized update management

- Web and e-mail access for employees
- File sharing and centralized file storage
- Database storage using Microsoft SQL Server
- Printer sharing
- Centralized backup
- Centralized fax server
- Remote access to the internal network via the Internet, including remote access directly to the user's desktop from the Web.
- Facilitation of group projects via a Windows SharePoint Services intranet or "team" Web site

You also must decide how important the following factors are, as well as what resources (money and personnel, for example) are available to support your choices:

- Performance
- Reliability
- Security

Planning   Get a thorough idea of what kind of work will be done on the network, when and where it will be done, and by whom. For example, your organization might need to do payroll every other Friday, during which time the file server and printers are under a heavy load.

Choosing an Internet Connection

To choose an Internet connection method, you must balance an organization's bandwidth needs and budget against the available Internet connection methods. The following sections discuss how to do this, as well as how to choose an Internet Service Provider (ISP).

Determining Bandwidth Needs

First, determine the baseline level of bandwidth you require. You can then balance this against the organization's budget and performance goals. Allow for 100 kilobits per second (Kbps) of download bandwidth and 50 Kbps of upload bandwidth for each simultaneous user of e-mail and the Web. If remote access via Virtual Private Network (VPN) is important, allow for a minimum of 100 Kbps of upload bandwidth for each simultaneous remote access user. Table 2-1 lists a number of Internet connection speeds and the number of users supported for each speed, assuming that users will be browsing the Web and using e-mail. This table does not include requirements for VPN connections.

Important   Running an Internet-accessible Web server on your network requires at least 50 Kbps of upload bandwidth or more per simultaneous visitor, depending on the size of images or files. This can quickly swamp your Internet connection, which is why most small businesses pay for Web hosting.

Table 2-1   Bandwidth requirements for Web browsing and e-mail

Download/Upload Speed	Number of Users
256/128 Kbps	1–5
512/256 Kbps	5–10
768/384 Kbps	5–15
1024/512 Kbps	10–20
1536/768 Kbps	15–30

Important   These bandwidth numbers are not intended to be definitive – they are a planning baseline. Each organization and its users has different usage patterns and needs, and you should evaluate your needs accordingly. Be prepared to add additional bandwidth if necessary. Your users will never complain that the Internet connection is too fast, but they will definitely complain if it's too slow!

Note   Users of Windows Small Business Server 2003, Premium Edition, can wring extra Web browsing performance out of their connection by using Microsoft ISA Server, which is discussed in Chapter 16, "Using ISA Server 2004." Similarly, using Microsoft Exchange Server for company e-mail enhances e-mail performance without requiring a faster connection.

Under the Hood   Bits and Bytes

Network speeds are measured in either kilobits per second (Kbps) or megabits per second (Mbps), whereas download speed and hard disks are rated in kilobytes per second (KBps) or megabytes per second (MBps). For example, a 640-Kbps DSL connection might download files at 60 KBps from a fast Web site, but a 1.5-Mbps cable Internet connection might download at 180 KBps from the same site. (Some of the bandwidth is used by transmission overhead and inefficiencies.)

Types of Internet Connections

To choose an Internet connection method, you need to know which methods are available as well as their performance characteristics. Table 2-2 lists the most common connection methods and their speeds.

Table 2-2   Internet connection types

Type of Connection	Download Speed	Upload Speed	Notes
Dial-up	28.8–53 Kbps	28.8–40 Kbps	Analog telephone line. Sometimes referred to as Plain Old Telephone Service (POTS).
ISDN (Integrated Services Digital Network)	64–128 Kbps (one channel or two)	64–128 Kbps (one channel or two)	Must be within 50,000 feet of a telephone company central office (CO). Connection is dial-up (not persistent).
ADSL (Asynchronous Digital Subscriber Line)	256 Kbps–8 Mbps	128 Kbps–1 Mbps	Must be within 18,000 feet of a CO.
IDSL (ISDN over DSL)	128–144 Kbps	128–144 Kbps	Works at greater distances from a CO than other DSL variants.
SDSL (Synchronous DSL)	128 Kbps–2.3 Mbps	128 Kbps–2.3 Mbps	Must be within 20,000 feet of a CO.
Cable	128 Kbps–8 Mbps	128 Kbps–1 Mbps	Must have access to broadband cable service; speed can fluctuate.
Microwave wireless	256 Kbps–10+ Mbps	256 Kbps–10+ Mbps	Must be in line of sight to ISP's antenna; maximum distance 10 miles.
Frame relay/T1	56 Kbps–1.54 Mbps	56 Kbps–1.54 Mbps	Good availability; very reliable; consistent throughput; expensive.
802.11b (WiFi)	Up to 11 Mbps	Up to 11 Mbps	Speed decreases with increasing distance from access point.
802.11g	Up to 54 Mbps	Up to 54 Mbps	Speed decreases with increasing distance from access point
Geosynchronous satellite	150 Kbps–3 Mbps	33.6 Kbps–128 Kbps	Requires line of sight to satellite (southern sky in North America). Unsuitable for real-time multimedia because of high latency.
Ethernet	10 to 1000 Mbps	10 to 1000 Mbps	Limited availability. Backbone connection might be DSL or T1, limiting actual bandwidth.

Choosing ISPs

After determining the preferred connection type and bandwidth, it's time to actually find ISPs. Three Web sites to check are *http://www.cnet.com/internet/*, *http://www.dslreports.com*, and *http://www.isp.com*. In addition to speed and cost, look for the following features:

- **Static IP address**   To host any kind of Internet-accessible service such as e-mail, Microsoft Outlook Web Access, VPNs, or Web sites, you need a static IP address and an ISP that supports the Dynamic DNS service, or you need to manage your external DNS with a DNS service that supports dynamic updates such as *www.zoneedit.com*.

- **Transfer limitations**   If the ISP has a monthly data transfer limit, make sure that limit isn't lower than your anticipated usage—charges for going beyond the limit can be significant.

- **Web hosting**   If you want the ISP to host the organization's Internet Web site, look for virtual hosting (so that your organization can use its own domain name) with enough disk space on the ISP's Web servers. If the organization uses Microsoft FrontPage, look for FrontPage Server Extensions support.

- **Backup Internet connection**   If your business is dependent on always being connected to the Internet, choose a secondary Internet connection with sufficient bandwidth to allow you to limp along in case the primary Internet connection fails. This second Internet connection should use a different ISP and a different connection technology. You can use a dual WAN router to use both connections simultaneously.

Choosing a Network Type

The next step in designing a network is to choose a network type (see Table 2-3). Start by looking at where your computers are physically located. If you can easily run cable between all computers, the choices are simple: Gigabit Ethernet or Fast Ethernet. Choose Gigabit Ethernet if your budget can afford it and your wiring supports it; otherwise, stick to Fast Ethernet. If you're installing new cabling, hire a professional cabling expert. Spending money on good wiring now can save you a *lot* of problems in the future.

If the computers are widely scattered or mobile, consider including some wireless *access points* (APs), which are network devices that permit wireless clients access to a wired network. Fast Ethernet is more than twice as fast as the current wireless standards, more reliable, more secure, and cheaper as well. For these reasons, use wireless networks to supplement wired networks, not to replace them.

More Info   For more information about wireless access points, see the section "Choosing a Wireless Standard: 802.11a/b/g" later in this chapter.

Important   All wireless technologies have the potential to introduce security risks. When using wireless networking, always use appropriate security measures, such as 802.11i, Wireless Protected Access (WPA), 802.1x, or a VPN. For more information, see the section titled "Planning for Security" later in this chapter.

Table 2-3   Common network types

Technology	Speed	Speed (Real World)	Cabling	Maximum Distance	Other Hardware Requirements
Fast Ethernet	100 Mbps	94 Mbps	Cat 5, Cat 5e, Cat 6	328 feet from hub or switch	Fast Ethernet hub or switch
Gigabit Ethernet	1000 Mbps	327 Mbps	Cat 5e or Cat 6	328 feet from hub or switch	Gigabit hub or switch
802.11b (WiFi)	11 Mbps	4.5 Mbps	Wireless	1800 feet (60–150 feet typical indoors)	802.11b or 802.11g access point (AP), 32 users per AP
802.11a	54 Mbps	19 Mbps	Wireless	1650 feet (50–100 feet typical indoors)	802.11a AP, 64users per AP
802.11g	54 Mbps	13 Mbps	Wireless	1800 feet (60–150 feet typical indoors)	802.11g AP, 32users per AP

Note   Wireless speeds vary greatly depending on distance from the access point, and the number and type of walls, floors and other interferences between the access point and the client device.

Note   Avoid the consumer-focused HomePNA and HomePlug network types. They're more expensive, slower, less secure, and less reliable than Ethernet or a properly configured 802.11a/b/g wireless network.

Choosing the Right Network Cable

Choosing the right cable for a wired Fast Ethernet (100 Mbps) network is easy—Cat 5 cable. However, there are exceptions to this rule that pertain to existing installations and new construction.

Cables in an existing network might not be usable. In general, Token Ring equipment should be replaced. 10-megabit Ethernet equipment can be used until convenient to replace or until the utilization of the network segment becomes too high (but don't wait until the segment is saturated). Coaxial (thinnet) Ethernet and Cat 3 Unshielded Twisted Pair (UTP) cables are unreliable and slow, and should be replaced.

New construction should run several strands of Cat 5e or, ideally, Cat 6. Although Cat 5 cable can be used with Gigabit Ethernet, it is marginal at best. Cat 5e and Cat 6 cables are more reliable and provide headroom for possible 10-Gigabit Ethernet standards. Cables should converge at a reasonably clean, centrally located wiring closet with adequate power, ventilation, and security for all servers and network devices. (Be sure to leave room for future growth.)

Shielded Cat 5, Cat 5e, and Cat 6 cables are available for situations that potentially involve high levels of electromagnetic interference (such as antennas). Plenum-grade cable should be used any time wiring is placed in a drop ceiling. (Before running cable in a drop ceiling, talk to the building manager.)

Choosing a Wireless Standard: 802.11a/b/g

Currently you can choose from three wireless standards: 802.11b, 802.11a, and 802.11g. Here's what you need to know about each (also see Table 2-3):

- **802.11b** 802.11b is the most widely deployed standard, though the speed is limited (11 Mbps theoretical; 5 Mbps or even less in the real world). 802.11b supports a maximum of 32 users per AP, and a maximum of 3 simultaneous channels in use in the same location. *Channels* separate wireless networks, with each channel providing 11 Mbps of bandwidth. You should not buy new equipment that only supports 802.11b, but you can use existing equipment.

- **802.11g** 802.11g is faster than 802.11b (54 Mbps theoretical; 13 Mbps real-world), and backward-compatible with 802.11b, making it the best choice for most organizations. 802.11g supports a maximum of 32 users per AP, and a maximum of 3 simultaneous channels in use in the same location.

- **802.11a** 802.11a is the fastest standard (54 Mbps theoretical; 19 Mbps real-world) and is more tolerant of microwave interference and network congestion. 802.11a supports a maximum of 64 users per AP, and a maximum of 8 channels in use simultaneously in the same location. 802.11a is not compatible with either 802.11b or 802.11g.

  If you decide to use 802.11a network devices, stick with devices from the same vendor and consider a tri-mode 802.11a/b/g device that will allow other devices, such as laptops with built-in 802.11b/g connectivity, to work on the wireless network. (This strategy also permits the highest network density, with 11 channels available simultaneously for wireless networks.)

Choosing Network Devices

After selecting a network type and Internet connection method, create a network diagram to visually show which network devices are needed, and then select the necessary devices for the network, such as switches, wireless access points, firewalls, and network adapters.

Note   Choose a single brand of network hardware, if possible. This ensures greater hardware compatibility, simplifies administration, and makes obtaining vendor support easier.

Diagramming the Network

Creating a diagram of the network can quickly show which devices you need and where they should be located, as shown in Figure 2-3.

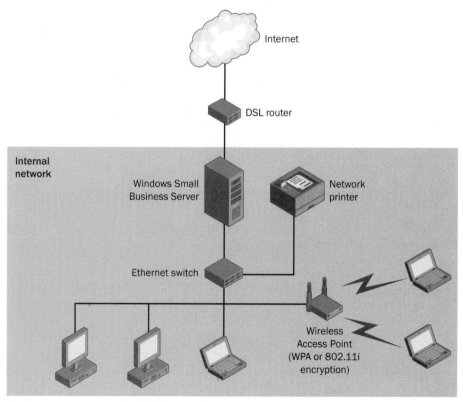

Figure 2-3   A network with the Windows Small Business Server computer connected directly to the Internet.

Use the following list as a guide when creating the network diagram:

- **Internet connection** The Internet connection usually comes in the form of a telephone or coaxial cable that connects to a DSL or cable router. It is traditionally represented by a cloud at the top of the drawing and a line that connects to the router or firewall.

- **DSL or cable modem** The Internet usually enters the organization in the form of a telephone or cable line that plugs into a DSL or cable modem.

- **Firewall** The DSL or cable modem is then plugged into the firewall, which can either be the Windows Small Business Server computer, or a stand-alone firewall or router. Some modems are combined with built in routers that have basic firewall capabilities.

- **Perimeter network** This is an optional area of the network between the external firewall (if present) and the Windows Small Business Server computer, where low-security devices such as wireless access points can be placed.

- **Internal network** The Windows Small Business Server computer's second network card connects to the internal network via an Ethernet switch. This is where all other computers and other network devices are located.

Planning   Networks with a small number of wireless clients (1 to 10) should place their access points on the internal network and use 802.11i (WPA2) or WPA encryption. Access points can be placed in the perimeter network when you want to provide Internet access to the general public (such as in a coffee shop or lobby).

Larger networks should place access points on the internal network and use 802.1x authentication, as described in Chapter 15, "Managing Connectivity."

Choosing a Network Switch

Ethernet networks use the *star* network topology (also known as *hub and spoke*), which means that all network devices must be plugged into a central hub or switch. Choosing the right switch requires evaluating the following factors:

- **Switch or hub** Don't buy a hub unless you have a specialized need and understand why you're doing it. Get a switch instead. Switches are inexpensive, provide additional performance, and facilitate mixing 10-Mbps, 100-Mbps, and 1-Gbps devices on the same network segment.

- **Number of ports** Make sure that the switch provides more than enough ports for all computers, access points, network printers, and Network Attached Storage (NAS) devices on the network.

- **Speed** Fast Ethernet (100/10 Mbps) switches offer sufficient performance for most small businesses, but Gigabit (1000/100/10 Mbps) switches are dropping in price and provide extra bandwidth for heavily used file servers and high-quality streaming video.

- **Management** Managed switches provide the ability to view the status of attached devices from a remote connection, which can be useful for off-site technicians. In general, save the cash and stick with an unmanaged switch unless the cost difference is slight or the organization uses an off-site consultant who wants the ability to remotely administer switches.

Choosing Wireless Access Points

As you learned earlier in the chapter, wireless access points permit clients to wirelessly connect to a wired network. Access points are often integrated into routers, but they are also available as stand-alone devices that must be plugged into a switch like any other network device. Avoid wireless "gateway" or router products for connecting to your internal network—they will complicate your network management and TCP/IP configuration. They're fine for externally connected wireless access points.

Business-grade access points are more expensive than consumer-oriented access points; however, they are usually more reliable and full-featured.

When choosing an access point, consider the following features:

- Routers with built-in access points are often no more expensive than stand-alone access points and are useful when creating a perimeter network. But be sure that they can be used as a pure access point—many can only function as a router, which will complicate your network setup.

- Access points should support 802.11i (WPA2) or WPA encryption. WEP is only appropriate when combined with 802.1x.

- Access points should support 802.1x (RADIUS) authentication if you want to provide the highest level of security and ease-of-use to a wireless network. This is the best method of authenticating wireless clients, though it does require setting up a RADIUS server, as discussed in Chapter 15.

Important Don't bother disabling SSID broadcasting and enabling Media Access Control (MAC) address filtering—they provide an added administrative burden, and a hacker with a port scanner can easily defeat them anyway.

- Some access points have two antennas that can be adjusted for better coverage; others have external antennas that can be mounted on a wall for better placement.

- Stand-alone wireless bridges (often referred to as wireless Ethernet bridges) and some access points provide the ability to wirelessly bridge (connect) two wired networks that can't be connected via cables. There are a number of different types of bridging modes, including Point-to-Point, which uses two wireless bridges to link two wired networks, and AP Client, which uses an AP on the main network (to which wireless clients can connect) and a wireless bridge in AP Client mode on the remote network segment, acting as a wireless client.

  Clients on the other side of a wireless bridge will experience slower performance to the main network segment because of the shared wireless link, so use wireless bridges with discretion, and always use bridges and APs made by the same manufacturer.

- Don't include "turbo" or other high-speed modes offered by some manufacturers in your buying criteria. They provide little performance gain, if any, in the real world.

Real World   Placing Access Points for the Best Coverage

Wireless access points have a limited range, especially in the environment of a typical office. The indoor range of 802.11b, 802.11g, and tri-mode 802.11a access points is usually around 60–100 feet at the highest connection speed, and 25–75 feet for first-generation, single-mode 802.11a access points. That said, 2.4-GHz cordless phones, microwave ovens, and Bluetooth devices can cause serious interference with 802.11b and 802.11g networks (but not with 802.11a networks) when they are turned on. Fluorescent lights, metal walls, computer equipment, furniture, and standing too close to the access point can also reduce the range of wireless networks. Unfortunately, there is no reliable way to quantify these variables, leaving trial and error as the best way to position access points. However, you can follow some guidelines when selecting access point locations:

- Place the access point and wireless network card antennas as high as possible to get them above objects that might attenuate the signal.

- If you place access points in the plenum (the space inside a drop ceiling or raised floor), make sure you obtain access points or enclosures certified for plenum installation.

- Place the access point in the center of the desired coverage area to provide the best coverage while also reducing the publicly exposed "surface area" of the network.

- Use multiple access points as necessary to cover multiple floors or large offices, or to service a large number of clients simultaneously. Twenty clients per 802.11b or 802.11g AP is a reasonable maximum, with an average of no more than two to four simultaneously active users per AP yielding the best network performance.

■ Wireless bridges can be used to place another Ethernet network segment (or another wireless access point) in a location unreachable by cables. Wired clients on this segment communicate with other wired devices on this segment at the speed of the wired network (1000/100/10 Mbps); however, communication with the main network segment takes place at the speed of the wireless network (4–20 Mbps real-world bandwidth).

■ When selecting channels for access points, *sniff* (look for by using a wireless client) for the presence of other networks and then choose an unused channel, preferably one that is four or more channels separated from other channels in use. For example, channels 1, 6, and 11 can all be used without interference.

Choosing a Firewall Device or Router

Windows Small Business Server 2003 is designed to connect directly to the Internet and act as a router and firewall for internal clients. However, many companies don't want to expose such a critical server directly to Internet-based attacks and prefer to place the Windows Small Business Server behind a separate firewall. This location provides an extra layer of security.

Note   The firewall included in Windows Small Business Server contains the same basic features as small office/home office (SOHO) firewall devices or routers, and provides a roughly equivalent level of security to clients (although data stored on the Windows Small Business Server computer is exposed to greater risk). However, Internet Security and Acceleration (ISA) Server, included in Windows Small Business Server, Premium Edition, provides industrial-strength firewall capabilities rivaled only by enterprise-level, dedicated firewall devices.

If you decide to use an external firewall device (or a router serving this function) as a first layer of protection, evaluate the following features:

■ **Packet filtering**   Firewalls should support inbound packet filtering and Stateful Packet Inspection (SPI).

■ **Protection from specific attacks**   Firewalls should support protection from the denial-of-service (DoS) attacks and other common attacks such as Ping of Death, SYN Flood, LAND Attack, and IP Spoofing.

■ **Network Address Translation (NAT)**   NAT is the backbone of most firewall devices, providing basic security and Internet connectivity to internal clients.

- **VPN pass-through**   To permit properly authenticated Internet users to establish VPN connections with a Windows Small Business Server computer behind a firewall, the firewall must support VPN pass-through of the desired VPN protocol (PPTP, L2TP, and/or IPSec).

- **VPN tunnels**   Some firewall devices themselves support establishing VPN connections. Although there are many fans of this approach, it doesn't work well when the Windows Small Business Server computer is acting as a second-layer firewall, because clients still need to tunnel through the Windows Small Business Server computer. If you do choose to use a firewall device to establish VPN connections with clients and servers in remote offices, make sure the firewall supports the necessary number of simultaneous VPN tunnels.

- **UPnP support**   Windows Small Business Server can automatically configure firewalls that support Universal Plug and Play (UPnP) to work with Windows Small Business Server services such as Exchange Server and remote access (by opening the necessary ports on the firewall). UPnP support can be found in most consumer firewall devices as well as in some business firewalls.

Note   Enabling UPnP on a dedicated firewall device makes configuring the device to work with Windows Small Business Server easy and doesn't significantly increase the security risk to the Windows Small Business Server computer or clients behind it. Although pre-SP1 Windows XP clients did have a significant UPnP vulnerability, this was resolved in SP1. Pre-SP1 Windows XP is no longer supported for client workstations on Windows Small Business Server. For more information on this vulnerability, see Microsoft Security Bulletin MS01-059, available at *http://www.microsoft.com/technet/security/bulletin/MS01-059.mspx.*

- **Dual-WAN support**   Some firewalls come with support for two WAN connections to increase speed and reliability, which is a great solution for networks looking for a reliable Internet connection. Other firewalls provide a serial port so that an external dial-up modem can be used as a backup connection, but this connection is much slower.

- **Content filtering**   Most firewalls make blocking certain Web sites possible, such as Web sites containing specified keywords. Many businesses use this feature to reduce the employees' ability to visit objectionable Web sites, although most content filters are largely ineffective.

- **ICSA certification**   ICSA Labs (*http://www.icsalabs.com*), a division of the private security corporation Cybertrust, certifies computer security products that meet its stringent security standards. Firewalls with ICSA certification are known to be secure; others might or might not be.

■ **Built-in wireless access point**   Firewalls with built-in access points and switched wired ports can make setting up a perimeter network easy and can be used to provide non-secured wireless access to clients or customers.

Choosing Server Hardware

If you have a server that can meet the capacity needs of the network or can be upgraded to do so while allowing for future growth, by all means use this server, particularly if it happens to be your existing Small Business Server 2000 computer.

More Info   See Chapter 4, "Upgrading or Migrating to Windows Small Business Server 2003," for more information about upgrading and migrating to Windows Small Business Server 2003.

Note   For the highest level of compatibility with Windows Small Business Server 2003, make sure that the server and all devices are listed in the Windows Server Catalog (formerly known as the Hardware Compatibility List), which you can access at *http://www.microsoft.com/windows/catalog/server.*

When evaluating server hardware, refer to Table 2-4, which lists the minimum configurations necessary for adequate performance at different load levels.

More Info   The sidebar "Determining Server Load," appearing later in this chapter, provides more information about configuration and performance.

Table 2-4   Minimum server configurations for different load levels

Component	Light Load	Medium Load	Heavy Load
CPU	Pentium III 1 GHz or dual Pentium III 500 MHz	Pentium IV 1.7 GHz or dual Pentium III 1.0 GHz	Xeon 3 GHz, dual Xeon 2 GHz, Opteron, or dual Opteron
Memory	1 GB	1.5 GB	2 GB
Storage	2 or more hard drives with 30 GB available for Windows Small Business Server 2003	3-drive hardware-based RAID using SATA or SCSI drives	4 or more drive hardware-based SCSI or SAS RAID
WAN Network Adapter (for Internet access)	100/10 Mbps PCI card	100/10 Mbps PCI card	100/10 Mbps PCI card
LAN Network Adapter	100/10 Mbps card	100/10 Mbps card	Gigabit LAN card

More Info See Chapter 6, "Disk Management" for more information on RAID, Chapter 7, "Storage Management," for more information about choosing the appropriate storage solution, and Chapter 13, "Backing Up and Restoring Data," for more information about creating a backup strategy and choosing backup devices.

Note Although Windows Small Business Server 2003 runs on servers using the x64 processors, including AMD Opteron and Athlon 64, and Intel Xeon with EM64T, Windows Small Business Server 2003 is a 32-bit operating system and can't take advantage of any 64-bit features such as large memory support. Because the next version of Windows Small Business Server will definitely require an x64 processor, you should not buy a new server that doesn't support x64.

Under the Hood   Determining Server Load

The appropriate hardware for a Windows Small Business Server 2003 server depends on the load you place it under. Think of load as equal to the number of requests per unit of time multiplied by the difficulty of fulfilling each request.

The easiest way to determine load is to sample the performance of the existing server over a range of conditions. Of course, this is tricky when you're constructing a new network or restructuring an existing network. Consider the following factors:

- **The usage pattern over time (number of requests per unit of time)** A server that handles an average load can easily become swamped at key times, such as at the beginning and end of a work day, when many users simultaneously log on or log off; during lunch, when users might browse the Internet for personal use; or around deadlines, when many users make heavy use of file, e-mail, or database services.

- **The kinds of user requests (the complexity of each request)** This determines which server subsystems are stressed most heavily. Database serving stresses storage, memory, and possibly CPU; file serving stresses mostly storage and I/O; Internet access places some load on storage and memory (if using ISA Server); Exchange Server stresses storage, memory, and to some extent CPU.

Choosing Client Hardware and Software

When selecting client computers for use on a network, choose systems that are fast enough to perform adequately Windows XP Professional or Windows Vista. (See Table 2-2 for recommended configurations.) Other operating systems such as Windows 2000,

Mac OS X, and Linux can be made to work on a Windows Small Business Server 2003 network; however, they won't provide full support for such features as automatic application and service pack installations, shared fax and modem services, and Outlook 2003.

Table 2-5   Recommended client computer configurations

Component	Minimum Configuration	Better Configuration
Operating System	Windows 2000 Professional	Windows XP Professional or Windows Vista
CPU	Pentium II 300 MHz or faster	Pentium 4 2.0 GHz or faster
RAM	128 MB	512 MB
Hard drive	10 GB	40 GB
Network Adapter	Ethernet or 802.11b	Fast Ethernet, 802.11g, or 802.11a
Display	15-inch monitor running at 800 x 600 resolution	17-inch monitor running at 1024 x 768 resolution

Under the Hood   Terminal Server

Computers too slow to adequately run a Windows XP or Windows 2000 operating system can be put to use as Terminal Server clients. In this configuration, users connect to a separate Windows Server 2003 computer running Terminal Server that displays a standard Windows desktop in which users can run any installed program. This server can *not* be the Windows Small Business Server computer. All processing is done on the server, and the display is sent back to the client machine, which can run any supported Terminal Server client operating system.

This approach can make more efficient use of resources, and make central management easier, although it's inappropriate for graphics-intensive applications. For more information on Terminal Server, see *Microsoft Windows Server 2003 Administrator's Companion,* 2nd *Edition* (Microsoft Press) and the "Deploying Windows Server 2003 Terminal Server to Host User Desktops" whitepaper at: *http:// www.microsoft.com/technet/prodtechnol/sbs/2003/deploy/adstrmsr.mspx.*

Choosing Naming Conventions

Creating naming conventions makes choosing names for computers, shared folders, and users easier and lends consistency to the network. This consistency results in a more user-friendly network.

More Info   For help with naming users, see Chapter 8, "Managing Users and Groups." For help with naming shared folders, see Chapter 9, "Shares and Permissions."

Choosing a Domain Name for the Network

The domain name is the most important and politically sensitive name on the network. Do not make this decision without consulting everyone who has a stake in the result. By getting others involved in the process, you'll have a much greater chance of acceptance. Some questions to ask when choosing a domain name include:

- Is the name easy to remember and does it make sense for the company? This could be the company name in its most common form or an abbreviation.

- Is the name 15 characters or shorter? Use only letters, numbers, the underscore, and a hyphen in the name to ensure DNS and NetBIOS compatibility.

- Is the name available? If the name is already in use as an Internet domain name for another company, you'll have to choose a different name.

- If you already have an Internet Web site, use the same domain name with the .local, .lan, or .office at the end of the domain, instead of .com. For example, if the company uses *www.example.com* for its Internet Web site, use example.local for the domain name.

Note   If you have older Mac clients (prior to version 10.3 of Mac OS X), don't choose a top-level domain of .local.

- Once you choose a domain name, register it (preferably with .com, .net, or .org) on the Internet so that another company can't purchase it.

Important   Changing a domain name is difficult and can cause numerous problems on a network, so picking a name that will last is important.

Real World   Internal Domain Name vs. Internet Domain Name

There are two domain names you need to worry about when setting up your network: the Internet domain name that the outside world sees for your company and e-mail, and the internal domain name that Windows Small Business Server uses. They are usually related but not identical. The public, Internet domain name needs to be globally unique, officially registered with a Domain Naming Service, and clearly identifiable as your company. The internal, Windows name should be the same as the external, public one, but with a different top-level domain. So if your company is "Example Widgets," and your public Internet domain name is "example.com," your internal Windows domain name should be something like "example.local" or "example.lan." This makes it easy to keep track of, and gives you complete control over managing the internal DNS of your Windows Small Business Server network while allowing you to have a reliable third party manage your public DNS records.

While it is technically possible to change either your public name or your internal name, neither is particularly easy or painless, so it's worth spending time up front to make sure you're choosing a name that is appropriate and has the support of all parties.

Naming Computers

It's easy for *you* to keep a map of what the different clients and servers are called and where they are on the network, but if you make life hard on users, you pay in the long run. So naming all the computers after Shakespearean characters or Norse gods might make sense to you, but it isn't going to help users figure out that "Puck" is the Windows Small Business Server computer and "Hermes" is the desktop used for payroll. On the other hand, using "Srv1" for the Windows Small Business Server computer tells everyone immediately which machine it is. When naming computers, use a consistent convention and sensible names, such as the following:

- SRV1 or SBSSRV for the Windows Small Business Server 2003 computer
- FrontDesk for the receptionist's computer

Planning for Security

It is far easier to implement effective security measures to protect your Windows Small Business Server network if you plan for security *before* you actually start installing software. In the following sections, we'll cover some of the most common attack vectors and the preliminary steps you can take in this planning stage to prepare your defenses.

- **Careless or disgruntled employees and former employees**   Internal users and former users are the biggest risk factors to data loss and data theft on most computer networks. Whether from laziness, disregard of security policies, or outright malice, the internal user is often the most dangerous on your network. To help prevent this, refer to the "Ensuring Physical Security" section of this chapter as well as to Chapter 5, "Completing the To Do List and Other Post-Installation Tasks."

- **Internet hackers** All computers and devices attached directly to the Internet are subject to random attacks by hackers. According to the Cooperative Association for Internet Data Analysis (CAIDA), during a random 3-week time period in 2001 there were more than 12,000 DoS attacks: 1200–2400 were against home machines and the rest were against businesses. If your organization has a high profile, it might also be subject to targeted attack by hackers who don't like your organization or who are engaging in corporate espionage.

  For more information about securing a network against Internet hackers, see the "Securing Internet Firewalls" section of this chapter. Also review the "Updating Windows Small Business Server" section of Chapter 5.

- **Wireless hackers and theft of service** Wireless access points are exposed to the general public looking for free Internet access and to mobile hackers. To reduce this risk, refer to the "Securing Wireless Networks" section in this chapter.

- **Viruses and worms** Networks are subject to virus exposure from e-mail attachments, infected documents, and worms such as CodeRed and Blaster that automatically attack vulnerable servers and clients. Look at the "Securing Client Computers" section of this chapter along with the "Updating Windows Small Business Server" section of Chapter 5 for help with this.

Ensuring Physical Security

Although security is not something that can be achieved in absolute terms, it should be a clearly defined goal. The most secure operating system and network in the world is defenseless against someone with physical access to a computer. Evaluate your physical environment to decide what additional security measures you should take, including:

- Place servers in a locked server room. And control who has keys!
- Use case locks on your servers and don't leave the keys in them.
- Place network hubs, routers, and switches in a locked cable room or wiring closet.
- Install case locks on client systems or publicly accessible systems.
- Use laptop locks when using laptops in public.

Securing Client Computers

Even a highly secure network can be quickly compromised by a poorly secured client computer—for example, a laptop running Windows 98 with sensitive data stored on the hard drive. To maximize the security of client computers, use the following guidelines (refer to Chapter 5 and Chapter 11, "Managing Computers on the Network," for more security procedures):

- **Use a secure operating system**   Use Windows XP Professional or Windows Vista on all client computers (particularly laptops).

- **Use NTFS, file permissions, and possibly EFS**   Use NTFS for all hard drives, and apply appropriate file permissions so that only valid users can read sensitive data. Encrypt sensitive files on laptop computers using Encrypting File System (EFS).

- **Keep clients updated**   Use the Automatic Updates feature of Windows XP Service Pack 2 and Windows 2000 Professional Service Pack 4 or later to keep client systems updated automatically, or use Windows Update. Ideally, use the Windows Software Update Service, integrated into Windows Small Business Server 2003 R2, to centrally control which updates are installed, as described in Chapter 12.

- **Use MBSA v2 to check clients for security problems**   The Microsoft Baseline Security Analyzer version 2.0 (MBSA2) makes it easy to check all computers running Windows Server 2003 (including Windows Small Business Server 2003), Windows Vista, Windows XP, and Windows 2000 for missing service packs, hot fixes, security updates, and other security problems. See Chapter 5 for more information.

- **Enable password policies**   Password Policies is a feature of Windows Small Business Server 2003 that requires user passwords to meet certain complexity, length, and uniqueness requirements, ensuring that users choose passwords that aren't trivial to crack.

More Info   For more information about enabling the password policies feature during the initial Windows Small Business Server 2003 server setup process, see Chapter 5.

Note   Remembering passwords has become an increasingly difficult prospect, leading to the resurgence of the yellow-sticky-note method of recalling them. It's important to discourage this practice.

- **Install antivirus software**   Antivirus software should be installed on the Windows Small Business Server 2003 server as well as on all clients. The best way to do this is to purchase a small-business antivirus package that includes client, server, and Exchange Server virus scanning. This package is often no more expensive than purchasing consumer antivirus software for each client, and it provides additional scanning and management capabilities. Companies that provide these solutions include Trend Micro (*http://www.trendmicro.com*), Sophos (*http://www.sophos.com*), Symantec (*http://www.symantec.com*), and McAfee (*http://www.mcafee.com*).

■ **Install antispyware software**   Antispyware software should be installed on all client computers on the network and configured for real-time monitoring and daily full scans.

■ **Sign and encrypt e-mail**   Companies with the need to send secure e-mail should set up users to send digitally signed and possibly encrypted e-mail. If a small number of users need this capability, purchase digital IDs from an Internet Certificate Authority such as VeriSign (*http://www.verisign.com*) or Thawte (*http://www.thawte.com*). If a large number of users require this ability, consider installing Certificate Services (included in Windows Small Business Server 2003) and creating your own digital IDs.

■ **Keep Web browsers secure**   Unpatched Web browsers are a significant security issue. Always keep Web browsers patched with the latest security updates.

Securing Wireless Networks

Wireless networks using the 802.11b, 802.11a, and 802.11g standards are very convenient but also introduce significant security vulnerabilities if not properly secured. To properly secure wireless networks, follow these recommendations:

■ Change the default password of all access points.

■ Change the default SSID. Pick a name that doesn't reveal the identity or location of your network.

■ Enable 802.11i (WPA2) or WPA encryption on the access points.

Note   If the access points don't support 802.11i or WPA2, use WPA. WPA and WPA2 provide two methods of authentication: an "Enterprise" method that makes use of a RADIUS server, and a "SOHO" method known as WPA-PSK (Pre-Shared Key) that makes use of an 8–63 character network key, similar to WEP. Using a network key is easier to set up and provides adequate security for most small networks. Some WPA devices also provide the option of using the stronger, hardware-accelerated (and thus faster) AES encryption method used by the 802.11i standard.

■ Companies with many wireless clients should consider installing Internet Authentication Services (IAS) and Certificate Services on the Windows Small Business

Server 2003 server and using 802.1x Authentication (using IAS as a RADIUS server). This procedure is discussed in Chapter 15.

■ Disable the ability to administer access points from across the wireless network.

Securing Internet Firewalls

Most external firewall devices are secure by default, but you can take some additional steps to maximize the security of a firewall:

■ Change the default password for the firewall device! We know this seems obvious, but unfortunately, it is all too often ignored.

■ Disable remote administration, or limit it to responding to a single IP address (that of your network consultant).

■ Disable the firewall from responding to Internet pings. OK, I admit, this is controversial. It's certainly a best practice, but it can also make it a lot harder to troubleshoot a connectivity issue remotely.

■ Enable Stateful Packet Inspection (SPI) and protection from specific attacks such as the Ping of Death, Smurf, and IP Spoofing.

■ Leave all ports on the firewall closed except those needed by the Windows Small Business Server 2003 server. Alternatively, enable UPnP so that Windows Small Business Server 2003 can automatically configure ports as needed.

■ Regularly check for open ports using trusted port scanning sites. We use *www.dsl-reports.com*.

■ Keep the firewall updated with the latest firmware versions, available for download from the manufacturer's Web site.

Summary

In this chapter we've covered how to design or prepare a network prior to installing Windows Small Business Server. We've also covered basic naming conventions and how to plan for adequate network security. The next chapter starts the coverage of installation and initial setup by showing how to install Windows Small Business Server 2003 on a blank server, including automated installation procedures for network consultants.

Part II
Installation and Setup

Chapter 3 Installing Windows Small Business Server 2003 39
Chapter 4 Upgrading or Migrating to Windows Small Business Server
           2003 55
Chapter 5 Completing the To Do List and Other Post-Installation Tasks 71

Chapter 3

Installing Windows Small Business Server 2003

Planning Partitions. 40

Preparing the Server 41

Installing Windows Small Business Server 42

Summary 53

This chapter covers performing a clean installation of Microsoft Windows Small Business Server 2003 Service Pack 1. A clean installation provides the best performance and stability; however, it wipes out any existing data and settings on the server.

Note   The steps in this chapter assume you are installing an integrated version of SBS 2003 SP1. If you're working from an older set of pre-SP1 media, the overall process is the same, but the actual steps might be slightly different. And, of course, once you get SBS installed, you'll then need to apply SP1 as a separate step. SP1 is a prerequisite for installation of R2, and the installation of R2 requires that you have completed the initial installation, and at least the Connect to the Internet portion of the To Do list .We'll cover installation of R2 in Chapter 12, "Patch Management," since that's the first chapter in which you'll see any difference between SP1 and R2.

More Info   If you have a server with Windows Small Business Server preinstalled, you're not in the clear yet—skip ahead to the "Using the Windows Small Business Server Setup Wizard" section of this chapter for more information.

More Info   If you already have a server running a previous version of Windows Small Business Server or Windows Server and want to maintain existing settings and data, see Chapter 4, "Upgrading or Migrating to Windows Small Business Server 2003," for more information.

Planning Partitions

It's a good idea to decide how you want your server storage to look *before* you start installing SBS. You're not required to create partitions on your hard disks during the installation phase beyond the partition where SBS is installed, but you certainly can do so. And by creating all the partitions ahead of time, you have additional options for where some of the components of SBS are placed. To create your initial storage during installation, follow these recommendations:

- Create a partition during the initial text installation screens for the operating system and log files that is at *least* 16 gigabytes (GB) in size. (32 GB is a more realistic minimum, especially if you're installing R2 later.)

- Optionally, create the other partitions you'll be using.

- If you're using hardware-based RAID, you must create the volume for the operating system using the manufacturer's tools *before* you start the installation of SBS. Also, it's a good idea to create any other volumes you'll be using, even if you don't partition them yet.

- If you'll be using software RAID for some or all of your drives, create these after Setup completes processing.

Note   For more detailed information about planning a storage solution, see Chapter 7, "Storage Management."

Under the Hood   Dividing Storage

While you can have one, single, large partition and put everything on it, there are compelling reasons to divide hard-drive space into at least three different partitions, even if you are using hardware RAID. The three partitions are:

- The primary operating system partition.

- A partition for static storage, such as programs.

- A partition for data, logs, and other volatile information. This will be the most active partition and should have a storage technology optimized accordingly.

Dividing your storage space into logical partitions in this way makes backups and disaster recovery easier and allows you to focus your efforts on the critical data partition.

Preparing the Server

After planning partitions and gathering network information, perform the following preparations before launching Setup:

- Make sure the server is sized appropriately for the load under which you plan to place it. For more information on server sizing, see Chapter 2, "Designing a Network."

- If installing on an existing server, back up all data and record any important settings.

- Remove the Uninterruptible Power Supply (UPS) management cable from the server (even if it's USB).

- Upgrade the system BIOS to the latest version available.

- Set the boot order in the BIOS to boot from the CD-ROM before the hard disk.

- Locate any mass storage drivers or custom hardware abstraction layer (HAL) files necessary for the system.

- Disconnect the server from the Internet (unless protected by a firewall).

Under the Hood   Active Directory and Domain Name System

As part of installation, Setup installs Active Directory and promotes the computer to a domain controller, creating a domain. Active Directory is a requirement for Windows Small Business Server and is leveraged by several of the components in SBS.

The SBS network is TCP/IP-based, so a Domain Name System (DNS) server provides name resolution. Although Active Directory can be made to work with any DNS server that complies with the appropriate standards, stick with the DNS server provided with SBS—it works great and is configured automatically by SBS—and you'll have fewer problems.

During Setup, the DNS service is configured to listen only to DNS queries from the local network. In addition, the DNS server is unbound from the external network adapter so that your internal DNS information is not available to outsiders.

If you think that you need to host your own Internet-accessible DNS server (to host the DNS records for your company Web site and e-mail server), re-examine that assumption. You are far better off using a commercial DNS host such as *www.zoneedit.com* to host public DNS records. Trying to host both an Internet DNS server and an internal DNS server on the same computer results in a security vulnerability and will probably break DNS resolution for client computers. If you absolutely must host your own public DNS records, do so on a separate server from the SBS server, and place this server in a perimeter network.

Note   See Appendix B, "Partially Automating Installation," for details about automating the operating system portion of the installation using the answer file.

Installing Windows Small Business Server

The Windows Small Business Server 2003 installation process takes place in two phases. The first phase installs a slightly modified version of Windows Server 2003, Standard Edition. The second phase occurs after Windows Server 2003 is installed. In this second phase, the Windows Small Business Server Setup Wizard installs Active Directory and other server applications.

If you purchased a server with Windows Small Business Server 2003 preinstalled, skip ahead to the "Using the Windows Small Business Server Setup Wizard" section of this chapter; otherwise, read on.

Under the Hood   Text-Mode and Graphical Setup

The installation of the operating system has two major phases of its own: text-mode setup and Graphical User Interface (GUI)–based setup. Text-mode setup begins after booting from the Windows Small Business Server 2003 Disk 1. You select the partition on which to install Windows. Setup then copies a minimal version of Windows to the hard drive and boots into GUI-based setup, which is home to the familiar Windows Setup Wizard. Setup then detects and installs devices, configures the network, and finishes installing files to the computer.

Finally, the computer restarts a second time, booting into Windows Server 2003. After logging on, you then launch the Windows Small Business Server 2003 Setup Wizard to begin the final phase of the Windows Small Business Server setup process.

Installing the Operating System

When installing Windows Small Business Server on a server that didn't ship with Windows Small Business Server 2003 preinstalled, the process starts by installing a special version of Windows Server 2003 Standard Edition as the underlying operating system for SBS, and then continue by installing the SBS-specific components. The Windows Server portion can be automated (see Appendix B for details), but the SBS portion needs to be done interactively.

Under the Hood   RAID Controllers and F6

The SBS installation starts with the basic Windows Server 2003 installation, which is still based on the venerable Windows NT installation that we've been using for many years. The very early part of the installation process loads the storage controller drivers that allow Windows Server 2003 to connect to the hard drives on your server. Standard SCSI and IDE controllers are included on the SBS CD1, but *not* most RAID controller drivers, and only some of the more basic SATA controller drivers. The mechanism for adding drivers during the installation process is to press the F6 key during the initial loading of files. Windows even prompts you at the bottom of the screen, as shown in Figure 3-1.

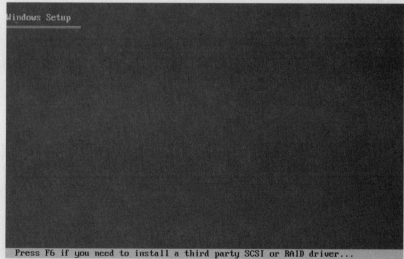

Figure 3-1   Windows Server 2003 installation prompting for storage drivers.

Once you've pressed F6, you'll be prompted for any additional drivers you want to load, as shown in Figure 3-2. *These drivers must be on a floppy disk.*

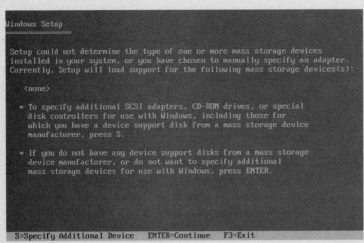

Figure 3-2 The Specify Additional Device prompt of Windows Setup.

Insert the floppy disk with the drivers into your floppy drive and press the S key. I know, most of us don't even buy servers with floppy drives any more. The good news is that most computers will successfully load these drivers from a USB floppy drive, though you may have to change a setting in the BIOS to enable "legacy" USB support. You'll be prompted to insert the floppy disk. Do so if you haven't already, and press Enter. Once the floppy has been read, you'll be prompted again to choose the correct driver from the ones on the floppy, as shown in Figure 3-3. Many manufacturers combine several driver versions into a single entity, thereby simplifying distribution.

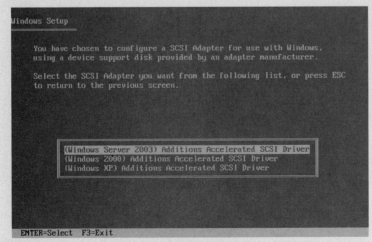

Figure 3-3 Choosing the correct driver during Windows Setup.

Another problem with storage drivers that can occur later in the installation process is that some controllers will let you complete the text-mode phase of Setup, but then fail when the computer first boots into the graphical phase. When this occurs, it will issue a Stop 0x0000007B error, indicating that it couldn't find the boot hard drive. This happens because there are two very different mechanisms for loading storage drivers: the text-mode mechanism, and the Plug-and-Play mechanism used during graphical installation and operation. If you have this problem, check with your computer manufacturer or RAID controller manufacturer for updated drivers.

For additional information on F6 and storage drivers, see the Microsoft Knowledge Base article 314859 at *http://support.microsoft.com/kb/314859*.

To install the underlying operating system, complete the following steps:

1. Insert Windows Small Business Server 2003 Disk 1 into the CD-ROM drive of the server and turn on or restart the computer. When prompted, press any key to boot from the CD.

2. To use a hard-drive controller for which SBS has no built-in support, press F6 when prompted, as described in the sidebar "RAID Controllers and F6." To use a HAL provided by the server manufacturer, press F5.

3. When the Welcome To Setup screen appears, press Enter.

4. Read the licensing agreement and, if you agree, press F8. (If you don't agree, you can't install SBS, so you don't really have a choice.)

5. On the next screen, shown in Figure 3-4, select a disk partition. If no suitable disk partition for Windows Small Business Server 2003 exists, create one:

    ❑ To delete a partition, select it using the arrow keys and then press D. Deleting a partition permanently erases all information on that partition.

    ❑ To create a new partition, select some free space, press C, specify how large to make the partition, and then press Enter.

    Important   If the first partition on the disk is under 50 MB in size, it's probably a utility partition. Leave it alone. The system might not boot or function properly without it.

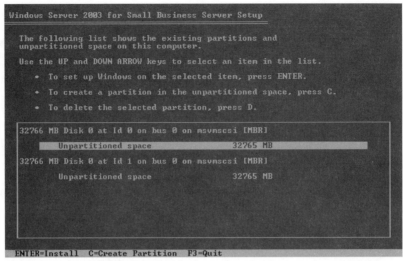

Figure 3-4   Choosing a disk partition.

6.   Select the partition or free space in which you want to install Windows Small Business Server and then press Enter.

7.   If you selected free space or a new partition, choose a formatting option on the next screen. NTFS Quick Format is the fastest way to format, but NTFS Full Format ensures that any bad sectors are properly marked and also wipes out the information on the disk, which is useful if that disk once contained sensitive data. If the selected partition is already formatted as FAT32, choose to convert the partition to NTFS. *You must format the system drive for SBS as NTFS.*

8.   Press Enter after making your formatting choice and, if necessary, press C on the next screen to confirm that you want to convert to NTFS. Setup copies files, which will take several minutes, and then reboots the server. (If Setup needs to convert the hard drive partition to NTFS, an additional reboot will be required.) After the reboot, GUI-based Setup runs and the installation continues for several minutes.

9.   When the Regional And Language Options page (shown in Figure 3-5) appears, change the regional and language options, if necessary, and then click Next. You can use the Regional And Language Options tool in Control Panel to change regional settings after you install Windows Small Business Server, so you probably don't need to linger here.

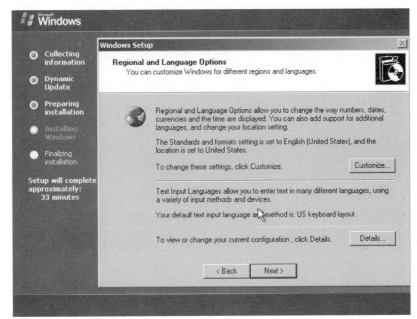

Figure 3-5 Specifying regional options.

10. On the Personalize Your Software page, type the name and organization under which the computer should be registered.

11. On the Your Product Key page, type the product key from the Windows Small Business Server 2003 packaging, and then click Next.

12. On the Computer Name And Administrator Password page, type the name for the computer in the Computer Name text box.

> **More Info**   See Chapter 2 for help with naming computers.

13. Type an administrator account password in the Administrator Password text box, and type it again in the Confirm Password text box. Click Next.

> **Important**   As a best practice for security, use passwords that are greater than seven characters in length and include a mixture of uppercase and lowercase letters, numbers, and special characters. Use acronyms for phrases that are meaningful to you, easy to remember, and unlikely to be meaningful or memorable to anyone else, such as Uk,Ur?Ue! (You know, you are what you eat!)

> Choose a good password for the Administrator account. Please. And then follow the guidelines in Chapter 8, "Managing Users and Groups," for protecting the Administrator account password.

14. If Setup detects a modem, use the Dialing Location page to select the country, type the area code of the telephone line, and type any digits needed to get an outside line. Click Next to move on. You can choose additional locations or modify the current location after Setup completes using the Phone And Modem Options tool in Control Panel.

15. On the Date And Time Settings page, review the date, time, and time zone information; make any necessary corrections; and then click Next. After several minutes, Setup finishes the installation and then reboots. After you log on, the Windows Small Business Server Setup Wizard launches, as discussed in the next section.

Using the Windows Small Business Server Setup Wizard

The second major phase of the SBS setup process is the Windows Small Business Server Setup Wizard. During this phase, Active Directory, Exchange Server, and the rest of the SBS Standard Edition server applications are installed. If you purchased a server with SBS preinstalled, this is the only phase of Setup you'll see, and it will probably be a few steps shorter than the following procedure, so don't be alarmed.

Note   If you happen to have an old copy of Windows Small Business Server 2003 that was manufactured before February 1, 2004, be aware that there is a bug on CD 3 that causes an error during setup. To resolve the issue, use a newer version of the CD or see the FAQ at http://www.microsoft.com/windowsserver2003/sbs/techinfo/sharepointinstall.mspx. Also see Microsoft Knowledge Base Article 832880 for more information.

Under the Hood   Configuring Network Settings

During Setup, all network cards on the server are disabled except the one identified as connecting to your internal network. Settings on the disabled adapters are retained. SBS only supports using one or two network adapters. If your server has more than two adapters, you should remove all but the two you will use for the internal and external SBS networks.

During installation, network cards are enabled and configured to use Transmission Control Protocol/Internet Protocol (TCP/IP). As part of installation, you select the network adapter that connects to your local network (also called your private or internal network). It's a good idea to unplug the network cable to the adapter that will be your Internet connection during the initial setup, and make sure that your internal side is properly connected to your internal network so that SBS will detect which network adapter is which. Setup will prompt you to supply a static IP address (the default value is 192.168.16.2). The internal network address of SBS must be a fixed IP address.

The Windows Small Business Server Setup Wizard launches automatically the first time you log into SBS after the underlying operating system is installed. To use this wizard, complete the following steps:

1. Make sure that all network adapters have the correct drivers installed and are functioning properly (but plug in the external Internet-connected network adapter). Also, plug in any UPS devices that you unplugged during the first phase of Setup. When you're ready, click Next on the first page of the Windows Small Business Server 2003 Setup Wizard, shown in Figure 3-6.

Figure 3-6   The Windows Small Business Server Setup Wizard lists what's left to be done.

2. If the requirements for Setup are not met, a Setup Requirements page appears. Review the requirements and, if necessary, take further action to correct.

3. On the Company Information page, provide the phone, fax, and address for your company or organization and then click Next. Setup uses this information to configure server tools.

4. On the Internal Domain Information page, set the default DNS and NetBIOS names. SBS uses a default based on your company name provided earlier in the setup. Click Next.

Security Alert   Your internal domain is kept isolated from the Internet as the first step in the defense of your network. Using a top-level domain such as *.local* or *.lan* that isn't in use on the Internet is part of that process. The default top-level domain is .local, but if your network will include Mac clients running Mac OS X versions prior to 10.4, you should change this to .lan or another top-level domain that isn't used on the Internet.

The NetBIOS name is used for backward compatibility and to create the organization name for Exchange Server.

5. If there are two network adapters in your Windows Small Business Server computer, specify which one connects to the local network, as shown in Figure 3-7, and then click Next.

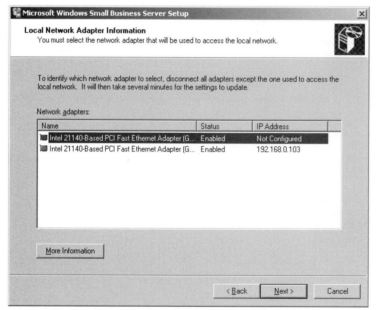

Figure 3-7   Specify which network adapter is for the local (internal) network.

6. If Setup detects an existing DHCP server on the network the dialog shown in Figure 3-8 will appear. Click Yes to use the SBS DHCP Server service, and then manually disable the existing DHCP server. See the Under the Hood sidebar, "DHCP," for more information.

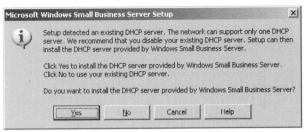

Figure 3-8   What happens when an existing DHCP server is detected.

7. On the Local Network Adapter Configuration page, confirm or change the default settings for the internal network adapter card and then click Next.

8. During the remaining parts of Setup, the computer will reboot several times. To save time logging on, provide your password on the Logon Information page. This saves your password only until Setup is completed.

9. Follow the screen prompts as the operating system is configured, the system reboots, and components are loaded. This process will take several minutes.

10. The next page is Component Selection, shown in Figure 3-9. By default all components are selected and will be installed on drive C:. Click the arrows to select items not to install, and make any changes to installation locations. Click Next.

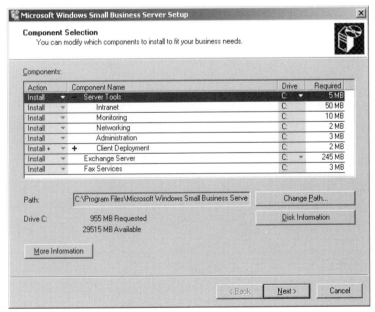

Figure 3-9   The Component Selection page.

11. The Data Folders page displays components and the folders in which they'll be placed. To make changes, select the item and click Change Folder. Click Next to continue.

12. The Component Summary page provides an opportunity to review your choices and modify them.

Note   In general terms, we favor installing as few components as possible to the system drive (usually C:), but in the case of SBS, we prefer to put all the core components on the C drive. But by all means feel free to move the data folders off of C drive, especially the Users Shared Folders.

From this point on, the installation requires no further input except the changing of CDs. Any errors are reported on a Component Messages page. After the final reboot, you'll see the To Do List. To tackle the chores on the list, go directly to Chapter 5, "Completing the To Do List and Other Post-Installation Tasks."

Under the Hood   DHCP

Dynamic Host Configuration Protocol (DHCP) is a method of assigning dynamic IP addresses to devices on a network. With dynamic addressing, clients boot up and automatically receive an IP address and other TCP/IP settings, such as DNS servers, WINS servers, and the default gateway.

Although you can assign static IP address settings to your client computers rather than use a DHCP service, it's not a good idea. With DHCP, the network automatically allocates and keeps track of IP addresses, ensuring that there are no conflicts. With static addresses, the administrator becomes the keeper of the list, resulting in more management overhead and room for error. Also, without DHCP you won't be able to use the network Setup to configure clients automatically.

SBS can be made to work satisfactorily with a non-Microsoft DHCP server, but you'll have to manually manage and configure it. Given that SBS includes a perfectly good DHCP server that it will automatically configure correctly for you, we strongly recommend using the built-in DCHP server.

Setup can configure DHCP server settings on devices that support Universal Plug and Play (UPnP), but some devices can't take advantage of all the settings that Setup can configure.

Summary

This chapter discussed how to prepare and perform a clean installation of Windows Small Business Server 2003. After installation, additional configuration specific to your environment is done using the To Do list, as discussed in Chapter 5.

Chapter 4, which follows, describes how to upgrade a computer running Windows Small Business Server 2000 and how to migrate from Windows 2000 Server or Windows Server 2003.

Upgrading or Migrating to Windows Small Business Server 2003

Choosing Between Upgrading and Migrating 55

What's Involved in a Conventional Migration. 57

What's Involved in a Swing Migration 58

Preparing for an Upgrade. 60

Performing the Upgrade. 66

Migrating User Permissions 69

Summary 70

Building a new network from scratch and installing a fresh new copy of Microsoft Windows Small Business Server 2003—which we covered in the preceding chapters—is a straightforward exercise. But if you have an existing Windows or SBS network, you're probably going to want to upgrade or migrate that network to SBS 2003 to preserve your existing data and settings. In this chapter, we'll cover how to upgrade your existing SBS server or migrate to a new server without losing your existing settings. We'll also discuss an innovative approach to migration—"swing migration"—which isn't an official, Microsoft-supported solution, but is our preferred migration strategy.

Choosing Between Upgrading and Migrating

First, decide whether you want to upgrade an existing server or migrate to a new server. Upgrading an existing server is relatively easy and causes substantially less disruption to the network than a conventional migration. You save time and money on your hardware, and the whole process is well defined and fully supported by Microsoft. There are some downsides to a pure upgrade, however. Often the existing server really needs a major hardware upgrade itself, and you are dependent on your backup of the server if something goes wrong in the middle of the process and you have to revert to your old SBS installation. And, of course, any upgrade always brings along some legacy stuff that isn't part of a pure, clean, new installation. In this case, there will be some permissions differences between an upgraded system and a fresh installation.

Conventional, Microsoft-defined migration to a new server is a complex process that requires a new domain (hosted by the new server) and moving all data and accounts. When you migrate, the new server is unencumbered by old programs, unused accounts, and incorrect settings. However, all existing client connections and mapped drives will be broken and must be replaced with connections to the new server.

An alternative to the Microsoft method of migration is *swing migration*, a technique that takes advantage of well documented and tested disaster recovery techniques to quickly and safely migrate an SBS domain to a new server—or back to the original server—with all accounts, connections, drive mappings, and names unchanged. Swing migration techniques can also be used instead of direct, in-place upgrades to reduce the risk and downtime.

Migration, either conventional or swing, is the only practical option when the current server is too slow or isn't running Microsoft Windows Small Business Server 2000, Windows 2000 Server, or Windows Server 2003.

Note   You can enhance the performance of a current server by upgrading the RAM to 1 GB or more, adding a SCSI-based RAID, and even upgrading the processor. You can also offload some tasks to another server on the network—file sharing and printer sharing are both good candidates. However, the Windows Small Business Server 2003 computer must host Microsoft Exchange Server 2003, Active Directory, and the Premium Technologies components (ISA Server 2000 and SQL Server 2000).

Planning   You can back up the existing server and restore the software to a new server that shares the same motherboard chipset, number of processors, and mass storage controller. However, minuscule hardware differences often lead to large problems, and you should restore a backup set to a different server only when the original server can't be repaired—not because you want to migrate to a faster server. For additional information, see Chapter 13, "Backing Up and Restoring Data," and the Restrdoc.htm file on the Windows Small Business Server 2003 CD 1.

What's Involved in a Conventional Migration

A conventional, official, Microsoft migration is better-documented and automated on SBS 2003 than it was on SBS 2000, but there are still major problems with the process, including:

- Exchange Mailbox rules, the Administrator account mailbox, and public folders aren't migrated and must be manually exported using the Exchange Mailbox Merge Wizard (ExMerge.exe).

- Custom settings such as DHCP scope options and Exchange server SMTP connector settings aren't migrated.

- Group Policy Objects (GPOs) aren't migrated, and must be manually exported from the existing domain using the Group Policy Management Console in Windows Small Business Server 2003.

- Custom Web sites aren't automatically migrated—you must copy the Web site files to the new server and re-create the site in Microsoft Internet Information Services (IIS), or use the IIS 6.0 Migration Tool.

- All references to the original server break during the migration (shortcuts, mapped drives, and so forth).

- The final result is a different domain name, and a different server name.

The following steps provide an overview of the conventional migration process:

1. Disable the DHCP Server service on the source server (the existing server).

2. Install Windows Small Business Server 2003 on the destination computer (creating the new domain) and perform the tasks on the To Do List.

3. Disconnect the destination server from the Internet and disable real-time antivirus software on both servers.

4. Prepare client computers for migration by removing unnecessary software and deleting any shortcuts to the existing server.

5. Use the Active Directory Migration Tool (ADMT) on the destination server to migrate users, groups, and computer accounts to the new domain.

6. Use the Exchange Migration Wizard in Windows Small Business Server 2003 to migrate Exchange mailboxes to the new server.

7. Use ExMerge on the Windows Small Business Server 2003 computer to export Exchange public folders and the Administrator account mailbox from the existing

server. ExMerge is available for download at *http://www.microsoft.com/downloads/ details.aspx?familyid=429163ec-dcdf-47dc-96da-1c12d67327d5&displaylang=en*.

8. Move shared folders and application data to the destination server.

9. Migrate any SQL Server databases to the destination server, as discussed in Microsoft Knowledge Base article 314546, "HOW TO: Move Databases Between Computers That Are Running SQL Server" found at *http://support.microsoft.com/ kb/314546/*.

10. Assign migrated user accounts to Windows Small Business Server 2003 templates and assign applications to client computers.

11. Import Exchange server public folders and configure Exchange distribution lists, custom recipient policies, and the Microsoft Connector for POP3 Mailboxes.

12. Connect client computers to the new domain. (See Chapter 11, "Managing Computers on the Network.")

13. Remove permissions used for migration, uninstall ADMT, and then retire the source server.

Note   For complete information about conventional migration to Windows Small Business Server 2003, see: *http://www.microsoft.com/windowsserver2003/sbs/ upgrade/default.mspx*. The two migration white papers are "Migrating from Small Business Server 4.5 or Windows NT Server 4.0 to Windows Small Business Server 2003" and "Migrating from Small Business Server 2000 or Windows 2000 Server to Windows Small Business Server 2003."

If this all seems like a dangerous, messy, and overly complicated process that will disrupt your network, your users, and your life, you're not alone—it seems like that to us as well. In fact, we simply cannot recommend this process except in the specific case of wanting to change the underlying domain name.

When we moved our own network to SBS 2003, we chose to do a swing migration. Total downtime was about an hour and a half, and there were no lost connections, drive mappings, accounts, or e-mail. Even our public folders came through without an issue.

What's Involved in a Swing Migration

A swing migration is not an official Microsoft migration, but it does use well-documented and Microsoft-supported disaster recovery techniques on an SBS server. Swing migration uses a temporary domain controller to hold the Active Directory information while the new server is created, and then the account information and other settings are migrated to the new server. The domain name remains the same, the SBS server name remains the same, and even the IP address of the server stays the same. This means that your users will experience virtually no disruption in their normal work except for the hour or so that you actually have the network down for the final switchover.

To perform a swing migration, you will need at least one additional computer that can be temporarily used as the swing domain controller. This can be any client machine, since it will only be used temporarily.

The basic steps that are performed in a swing migration are:

1. Windows Server 2003 is installed as a fresh, new installation on the computer that will serve as the temporary domain controller.

2. This temporary server is joined to the existing domain, DNS is installed, and the server is promoted to be a domain controller and Global Catalog server.

3. Wait for the new temporary domain controller to completely replicate from the existing domain. This shouldn't take more than about 15 minutes, assuming that you have a good connection and no firewall interference.

4. The temporary server, now a domain controller, is physically removed from the SBS network and all Flexible Single Master Operation (FSMO) roles are seized.

5. The Active Directory and DNS databases on the temporary server are cleaned up to remove all references to the original SBS server.

6. The new, final SBS server is installed and configured as a domain controller *at the same IP address and with the same server name as the original SBS server* but on the domain hosted by the temporary domain controller. Once replication has completed, the temporary domain controller is shut down and removed from the network. The seizure of roles and cleanup of AD and DNS is repeated.

7. Normal SBS setup is completed, and the data from the original server is migrated to the new server. The intact Exchange data store can then be mounted on the new server, or migrated using ExMerge.

8. The new server is inserted in the original network in place of the original SBS server.

Advantages of Swing Migration

There are three key advantages to this process. First, there is almost no risk at all. If at any time you encounter a problem, you simply go back and start again, since your original server is untouched and still happily working away. This is an important concept. Because the original server remains untouched throughout the process, there's always a safe fallback position.

Second, all the work and preparation happens offline, at your time and your pace. There's no hurry, and your users won't even know it's happening. The only actual downtime is during the final switchover when the original server is taken offline and the new one put in its place.

Finally, there is the absolute minimum of disruption to your network. Not only is the downtime minimal, but when the new server comes online and your users connect to it, they'll still have all their shortcuts, mapped drives, e-mail—everything they expect to see.

I wish I could say that we thought up swing migration, but we didn't. It's the creation of Jeff Middleton, a fellow Microsoft Most Valuable Professional (MVP). For complete details on swing migration, including tools, documentation, and support options, see Jeff's Web site: *http://www.sbsmigration.com.*

Preparing for an Upgrade

If you do decide to upgrade your existing SBS server instead of migrating to new hardware, you should start preparing for the upgrade by checking for compatibility issues, creating a disaster recovery plan, and updating the server and clients. Complete final preparations the day before the upgrade. Perform the actual upgrade outside of business hours and with a realistic deadline that minimizes disruption to the business. (In other words, calculate how long the process will take and then double it.)

Checking for Compatibility Issues

Windows Small Business Server 2003 is very compatible with earlier versions of Windows, but it's a good idea to check for possible compatibility issues ahead of time.

- **System requirements**   To complete the upgrade, the existing server must be running Small Business Server 2000, Windows 2000 Server, or Windows Server 2003; have a minimum of 2 GB of free disk space; and meet all the system requirements listed in Chapter 2, "Designing a Network." Realistically, it should have at least twice that amount of free disk space, however.

- **Third-party applications**   Verify that your third-party applications are compatible with Windows Server 2003. If you have any that are incompatible, you should uninstall them prior to the upgrade.

- **Device drivers**   Verify that all your hardware is supported by Windows Server 2003—especially older network cards. Make sure you have the correct drivers for your RAID controller before starting the upgrade. Visit the Windows Server Catalog at *http://www.microsoft.com/windows/catalog/server* for a listing of certified devices.

- **Client computers**   Computers running Microsoft Windows NT, Windows 95, Windows 98, Windows Me, or older operating systems should be upgraded or replaced. These operating systems are no longer supported, and don't receive even critical security updates.

- **Language**   The Windows Small Business Server 2003 upgrade software must be the same language edition as the existing operating system.

Server applications that aren't compatible with Windows Small Business Server 2003 can be run in a virtual machine using Microsoft Virtual Server, or moved to another server on the network.

Preparing for the Worst

SBS is the virtual brain of a small business network, and even when other domain controllers are on the network, the failure of the SBS server constitutes a disaster. Users lose access to the Internet, Exchange Server e-mail, fax services, and any resources shared by the SBS server, such as shared folders and printers.

Therefore, it's extremely important to have a fallback plan if the upgrade doesn't go smoothly. Start by planning how you can restore from a current backup set and estimating how much time is required. (A major failure during the upgrade could require a basic installation of Windows to access backup sets.)

The upgrade meets an acceptable level of functionality when users can:

- Log on successfully
- Access their Exchange server accounts
- Browse the Internet
- Access their usual resources (files and printers)
- Access vital business applications

You might have additional criteria to add to this list.

If the network doesn't meet the minimum level of functionality by the deadline you've set, implement the recovery plan, restore the existing server from backup, and verify proper server functioning. Then evaluate the problems and redesign the upgrade plan to compensate for them (and possibly allow more time to deal with unanticipated issues).

More Info   For more information about disaster preparation and recovery, see Chapter 22, "Disaster Planning."

Preparing the Server

To prepare a server for upgrading to Windows Small Business Server 2003, fix any current problems, install required service packs, remove unnecessary software, and check the items in this list:

- **Check Event Viewer**   Fix problems reported in Event Viewer *before* the upgrade.

- **Collect Internet setup information**   Although Internet settings are preserved during an upgrade, you should have the following information available: the server's Internet IP address and subnet mask, the host name, the default gateway, DNS server addresses, any PPP Over Ethernet (PPPoE) user names and passwords, and external mail server addresses used by your company.

- **Uninstall unnecessary software**   Unless you need a software package on the server, uninstall it. This is especially applicable for end user applications such as Microsoft Office—these have no place on a server.

- **Remove Windows 2000 Administration Tools**   These tools are incompatible with Windows Small Business Server 2003 and must be uninstalled before upgrading.

- **Install the latest system BIOS**   This reduces the likelihood of device errors or BIOS issues causing stability problems in Windows.

> **Note**   You should also update the firmware on your firewall device (especially if it supports UPnP) and any wireless access points (especially if you plan on using WPA or 802.1X authentication).

- **Install all necessary service packs and updates**   Install the service packs that are relevant to the existing server:

  1. Small Business Server 2000 Service Pack 1

  2. Windows 2000 Service Pack 4 (included in Small Business Server Service Pack 1a)

  3. Exchange 2000 Service Pack 3 (included in Small Business Server Service Pack 1)

  4. ISA Server 2000 Service Pack 1

  5. ISA Server 2000 Required Updates For Windows Server 2003 (see Microsoft Knowledge Base article 331062, "Running ISA Server on Windows Server 2003")

  6. SQL Server 2000 Service Pack 3a

■ **Remove discontinued Exchange components**   Using Add Or Remove Programs, select Microsoft Small Business Server 2000, click Change/Remove, and then use the Microsoft Small Business Server 2000 Setup Wizard to remove the following Exchange components (if installed):

1. Microsoft Exchange MSMail Connector
2. Microsoft Exchange Connector for Lotus cc:Mail
3. Microsoft Exchange Instant Messaging Service
4. Microsoft Exchange Chat Service
5. Microsoft Exchange Key Management Service

> **More Info**   Microsoft Exchange Instant Messaging Service and Microsoft Exchange Chat Service have been replaced by Microsoft Live Communications Server 2003. See *http://office.microsoft.com* for more information.

■ **Remove Remote Storage**   If you're using the Remote Storage service, use the Windows Components Wizard (available from the Add Or Remove Programs tool) to remove it before upgrading.

■ **Remove any trust relationships**   Windows Small Business Server supports only a single domain, so if you have any trust relationships established with other domains, disable them before upgrading.

■ **Remove CALs**   If you're running Windows 2000 Server or Windows Server 2003, reset the number of installed CALs to five. After installing Windows Small Business Server 2003, you can install additional Windows Small Business Server CALs.

■ **Remove the Windows Server 2003 POP3 service**   If the Windows Server 2003 POP3 service is installed, you must remove it using the Windows Components Wizard, available from Add Or Remove Programs.

■ **Make sure that all domain controllers are online**   Windows Small Business Server can't install if it can't contact all domain controllers in the domain, so don't take any domain controllers offline during the upgrade.

■ **Assign all FSMO roles to the Small Business Server computer**   If you have multiple domain controllers, make sure that the SBS server holds *all* the FSMO roles. There are five roles: schema master, domain master, relative identifier (RID) master, primary domain controller (PDC) emulator, and infrastructure master.

> **More Info**   For information about transferring operations master roles, see the "Transferring Operations Master Roles" page in Windows Help, or see Microsoft Knowledge Base article 255504 found at *http://support.microsoft.com/kb/255504/*.

- **Upgrade or retire any Windows NT 4.0 BDCs**   Windows NT 4.0 backup domain controllers (BDCs) cause the upgrade to halt at the end of the operating system installation phase because Windows Small Business Server 2003 needs to convert the domain to Windows 2000 native functional level. To avert this, upgrade any BDCs to Windows 2000 with SP3 or later, or retire them.

Real World   Upgrading Remote Domain Controllers

To reduce the amount of replication traffic generated when upgrading or deploying a new domain controller in a remote office, back up the system state information from the SBS 2003 server and physically ship the backup media to the remote site. Next, upgrade the remote domain controller to Windows Server 2003, or perform a clean install, and restore the system state files to a local hard drive *before* running the Active Directory Installation Wizard (by specifying Restore Files To: Alternate Location in Backup). Then run the Active Directory Installation Wizard (Dcpromo.exe) with the */adv* switch and specify the location of the restored files. This seeds the new or upgraded domain controller with slightly out-of-date Active Directory data, which is updated during the first replication. This first replication is significantly faster than transferring the entire Active Directory.

Preparing Client Computers

Windows 95 and Windows NT 4.0 computers must be updated before they can communicate with an SBS 2003 server, and since they are no longer supported by Microsoft, they should be upgraded to Windows 2000 or Windows XP Professional, or retired.

> **Planning**   Besides preparing client computers, you must also prepare users as far ahead of time as possible. Tell users when the upgrade will occur, how long the network will be down, and how the upgrade will benefit them.

Final Preparation

The day before you upgrade to Windows Small Business Server 2003, perform the following tasks:

1. Check all hard drives for errors using chkdsk c: at a command prompt (where c is the drive letter you want to check). If any errors are detected, run chkdsk c: /f to correct the errors.

2. Use the Disk Cleanup Wizard to find and delete unnecessary files.

3. Defragment the system drive.

4. Update virus definitions and perform a complete virus scan. Then uninstall the antivirus program. If you know that the program works under Windows Server 2003 without modification, you can simply disable it.

Important   Do not attempt to perform an upgrade with an antivirus program running. Disable it, or better yet, uninstall it prior to beginning the upgrade process.

Important   Don't back up or scan the Exchange M drive for viruses. Doing so can lead to Exchange database corruption.

5. Locate all drivers and operating system CD-ROMs.

6. Reboot into Safe Mode (unless you're running Windows Server 2003) and then perform a full backup, including the system state. Test the backup set by restoring some randomly selected files to an alternate location and comparing the files with the originals. If you don't have a satisfactory backup solution, implement one before performing the upgrade.

Note   In a normal backup, many files aren't backed up because the system is using them. Backing up the system in Safe Mode increases the number of files that are backed up because fewer are in use. Windows Server 2003 systems allow backing up open files using shadow copies, making a Safe Mode reboot unnecessary.

---

7. Stop and disable third-party services that are using the Local System account. Open Services in the Administrative Tools folder, double-click third-party services that

show Local System in the Log On As column, stop the service, write down the start-up types so that you can restore the settings after the upgrade is complete, and then change the startup type to Disabled. Repeat until all third-party services are disabled. (There's no easy way to identify third-party services—you'll just have to read their names and descriptions.)

Performing the Upgrade

When all preparations are complete, complete the following steps outside of normal business hours to upgrade a server running Small Business Server 2000, Windows 2000 Server, or Windows Server 2003 to Windows Small Business Server 2003:

1. Disable disk utilities such as backup programs and antivirus programs.

2. Disconnect any uninterruptible power supply (UPS) devices, including USB models.

3. Disconnect any USB or FireWire storage devices, or any USB device except a keyboard and mouse.

4. Warn your users, again. If there are any users still logged on or with open files, you'll need to do whatever it takes to get them logged off and their files closed, including going from office to office and shutting down their computers.

5. Unless you have a hardware firewall, disconnect the Internet connection device from the Internet.

6. Log on using an Administrator account and insert the Windows Small Business Server 2003 DVD or CD 1. The Microsoft Windows Small Business Server Setup window appears automatically.

7. Click Set Up Windows Small Business Server.

8. On the first page of the Microsoft Windows Small Business Server Setup Wizard, click Next, review the upgrade information, and then click Next again.

9. On the Setup Requirements page, review any warnings, select the I Acknowledge All Warnings check box, and then click Next.

10. On the License Agreement page, review the license agreement, choose I Agree, and then click Next.

11. On the Product Key page, type the product key from the Windows Small Business Server 2003 packaging, and then click Next.

12. On the Required Components page, click Next. Setup installs Windows Small Business Server 2003 and reboots the computer several times.

13. Log on using an Administrator account and then click Next on the first page of the Microsoft Windows Small Business Server Setup Wizard. (Double-click the Continue Setup icon on the desktop if the wizard doesn't appear automatically.)

14. If the Setup Requirements page appears, address any requirements and then click Next.

15. On the Company Information page, type the phone, fax, and address for your company or organization, and then click Next. This information is used by Setup to configure server tools.

16. If the Internal Domain Information page appears, enter the DNS domain name, NetBIOS domain name, and computer name, and then click Next.

17. On the Local Network Adapter Information page, shown in Figure 4-1, select the network adapter connected to the local network and then click Next.

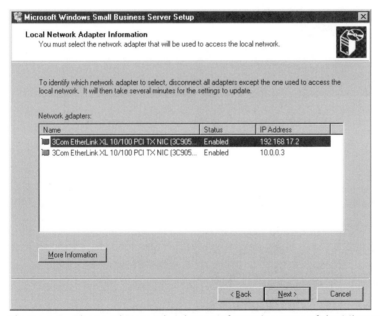

Figure 4-1   The Local Network Adapter Information page of the Microsoft Windows Small Business Server Setup Wizard.

18. If the Local Network Adapter Configuration page appears, specify the IP address and subnet mask for the network adapter that connects to the local network and then click Next.

19. During the remaining parts of Setup, the computer reboots several times. To save time logging on, provide your password on the Logon Information page and then click Next. (This saves your password only until Setup is complete.) Click Next again to continue Setup.

20. On the Component Selection page, shown in Figure 4-2, all components are selected by default. Specify any items you do not want to install and then click Next.

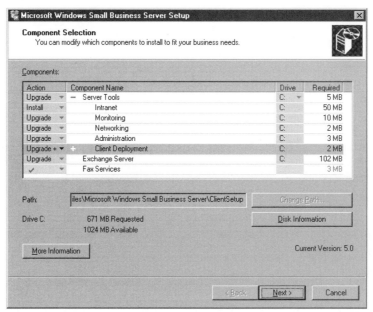

Figure 4-2   The Component Selection page.

21. The Data Folders page displays components and the folders in which they'll be placed. To make changes, select the item and click Change Folder. Click Next to continue.

22. The Component Summary page provides an opportunity to review your choices and modify them. Click Next to continue. Windows installs the specified components and then reboots the computer.

From this point on, the installation requires no further input except the changing of CDs. Errors are reported on a Component Messages page. After the final reboot, you see the To Do List, covered in Chapter 5, "Completing the To Do List and Other Post-Installation Tasks." However, there's one more task to complete—migrating user permissions, which we'll discuss next. Users of Windows Small Business Server 2003, Premium Edition should follow the steps in Chapter 16, "Using ISA Server 2004," for installing ISA Server

2004 and Chapter 20, "Using SQL Server 2005," for installing SQL Server 2005. Once any Premium Edition components have been installed, you should proceed to Chapter 12, "Patch Management," to install the R2 components, including Windows Server Update Services (WSUS).

Important   We say this in several places, but that's because we think it's really, really important. The very first thing you should do once you've completed the Configure E-Mail and Internet Connection Wizard (CEICW) on the To Do list is to connect to Microsoft Update and download any and all security updates for SBS.

Migrating User Permissions

After upgrading to Windows Small Business Server 2003, run the Change User Permissions Wizard to apply appropriate permissions to existing user accounts. This ensures that users can access domain resources, use the Internet, and connect to the internal network from across the Internet using the Remote Web Workplace and VPN connections (if you apply the Mobile Users template to the users). The wizard also configures disk quotas and creates Exchange mailboxes and home folders for users that don't already have them.

To use the Change User Permissions Wizard, complete the following steps:

1. In the To Do List, click Migrate Users to launch the Change User Permissions Wizard, and then click Next.

2. On the Template Selection page, shown in Figure 4-3, select the user template to apply to a group of existing users and choose whether to replace existing permissions, which provides the most consistent results, or to add to existing permissions. Click Next to continue.

Note   To apply different permissions to groups of users, run the Change User Permissions Wizard multiple times, each time choosing a different template and group of users.

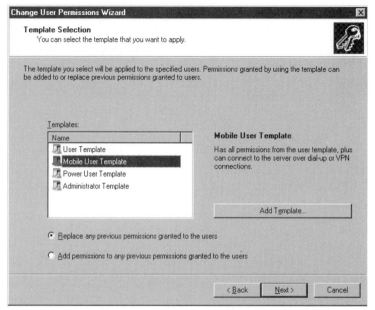

Figure 4-3   The Template Selection page of the Change User Permissions Wizard.

3. On the User Selection page, select the users whose permissions you want to change, click Add, and then click Next.

4. Review the settings and then click Finish to apply the new permissions.

    Existing permissions applied directly to user accounts are preserved—only group permissions are changed.

Summary

Upgrading an existing server to Windows Small Business Server 2003 is one way to install Windows Small Business Server while preserving existing settings and data. The alternative is a migration, either conventional or swing. A conventional migration is a major disruption to your network and your users, and should be undertaken only as a last resort. Whatever method of upgrading or migration you perform, it's important to adequately prepare the server and clients for the process.

The next chapter covers how to complete the To Do List and Windows Small Business Server 2003 configuration.

Chapter 5

Completing the To Do List and Other Post-Installation Tasks

Security Best Practices. 72

Connecting to the Internet. 73

Configuring Remote Access 85

Activating Your Server. 88

Adding Client Access Licenses 89

Adding Printers 90

Adding Users and Computers 90

Configuring Fax Services. 91

Configuring Monitoring 94

Configuring Backup. 95

Security Basics 95

Updating Windows Small Business Server. 95

Summary 96

When the initial installation of Microsoft Windows Small Business Server 2003 is complete, you need to tweak several components to fit your unique situation. The To Do List and an assortment of helpful wizards make these chores considerably easier. This chapter covers the settings needed to make your system work properly.

Note Installation of Premium Edition components and R2 components are separate processes that are run after the initial installation of SBS is complete. We'll cover installation of the Premium components in their individual chapters, and we'll cover the R2 components in Chapter 12, "Patch Management."

After installation of Windows Small Business Server, the first thing you see when you log on is the Windows Small Business Server To Do List. If the To Do List is not displayed, select Server Management from the Start menu. In the Server Management console, click To Do List, as shown in Figure 5-1.

Figure 5-1   The To Do List, which you can summon easily.

Security Best Practices

It's best to tackle the items on the To Do List in the order they're listed, and the very first item is View Security Best Practices. This is not mere happenstance. Implementing and maintaining the best security practices are the most crucial tasks on a network. Click Start next to View Security Best Practices to open Security Best Practices help.

Security strategies are of three types:

- Protecting your network against external assault in the form of hackers and malicious code.

- Protecting against internal threats. Internal threats are more likely the result of accidents than malice, but it's necessary to be protected from both kinds.

- Monitoring the network for security issues and keeping current on security information.

Completing the To Do List configures some of all three elements.

Connecting to the Internet

The first action item on the To Do List is Connect To The Internet. Click Start next to Connect To The Internet to launch the Configure E-Mail And Internet Connection Wizard, better known among SBS users as the CEICW. On the first page, click the link for Required Information For Connecting To The Internet. This link connects to a help file (see Figure 5-2) that tells you what you need for your network.

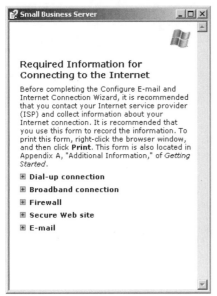

Figure 5-2   The help file that determines what information you'll need for your connection to the Internet.

> **Note**   Determining the information you need to connect to the Internet can be one of the more complicated tasks required by Windows Small Business Server, so you might want to print this help file, which you can do by right-clicking inside the help window and then selecting Print.
>
> Determine which details you need and note the answers on the printed form. And don't hesitate to press your Internet Service Provider (ISP) for all the assistance you can get.

The information you collect depends on your Internet connection type. SBS supports four Internet connection types:

- Broadband connection with a local router

- Direct broadband connection

- Broadband connection with user authentication (PPPoE)
- Dial-up connection

To complete the CEICW, select one of these Internet connection types. The following sections describe setting up each connection type.

Real World   Internet Connection Choices

Many options are available for connecting to the Internet. Not all of them will be available in every location, but wherever you are, balancing budget restrictions with performance needs will be the thorniest issue. Before making a decision, do your research. Contact the local telephone company, cable company, and ISPs to determine the availability of different connections and the costs and hardware requirements associated with each. Some of the usual types of connections are described here.

Dial-Up

A dial-up connection uses a standard analog modem over regular telephone lines. Dial-up connections are easy to configure, though data transmission speed depends on the quality of the line. Most dial-up connections provide bandwidth of 56 kilobits per second (Kbps) or less. Dial-up connections are the slowest and (usually) least expensive way to connect to the Internet, but provide bandwidth to support only a few users. Choose this option only if there is no alternative available.

Integrated Services Digital Network

Integrated Services Digital Network (ISDN) is a telephone company technology that provides digital service typically in increments of 64 Kbps. An ISDN line is similar to an analog telephone line except that it connects faster and transmits data much faster. Basic Rate ISDN can be more than twice as fast as an ordinary dial-up connection, with two 64-Kbps channels and a total bandwidth of 128 Kbps. Primary Rate ISDN, with 23 B-channels and one D-channel (U.S.) or 30 B-channels and one D-channel (Europe) can rival the 1.544 megabits per second (Mbps) speed of a T1 line.

In the United States, ISDN calls (including local calls) are frequently charged by the minute. This varies from provider to provider, but if your ISDN provider uses this method, charging by the minute will make a very large difference in the cost of your connection.

ISDN has been largely eclipsed by other broadband technologies, but it's a viable option in areas where DSL or other fast connections aren't available, since it is not as limited by distance from the phone company's central office.

Digital Subscriber Line

A Digital Subscriber Line (DSL) is similar to ISDN in that both operate over existing copper telephone lines. However, DSL speeds start at about 128 Kbps and go up to 1.5 Mbps, and some connections can go as fast as 50 Mbps depending on equipment used, distance to the telephone office, cabling quality, and other factors.

DSL is available only in some areas and is often available in one part of a city but not in others. (Nevertheless, the availability of DSL is spreading rapidly.) DSL is an always-on connection and as such is fast and convenient to use.

Cable Modem

A cable modem connection is a fast connection provided by your cable company, which also functions as your ISP. Cable modems are primarily used by home customers, but many cable companies offer businesses transmission speeds up to 10 Mbps, though speeds up to 3.5 Mbps download and 384 Kbps upload are more typical even on business class cable connections. Cable connections to the Internet can be a viable alternative for a small business but are sometimes expensive, depending on the locality. However, it's important to check the Terms of Service for the cable company's ISP division. Many cable ISPs do not allow business services such as an e-mail server or a Web server on their lines.

Satellite

If you live in a seriously broadband-challenged area, your only option for broadband may be satellite. Generally, these use a small satellite dish for download and a dedicated phone line for upload, though there are bidirectional satellite systems as well. Overall, this option is quite expensive, slow because of the signal transit delays, and not very satisfactory. But if you have no other choice, it's worth a look. But read the Terms of Service carefully.

T1

A full T1 line (E1 is the European near-equivalent) supports up to 1.544 Mbps of total bandwidth. T1/E1 cabling requirements are more rigorous than those for DSL and the setup costs are correspondingly high. T1 is a more expensive option than DSL or cable modems but the service level for T1 lines is typically superior. T1 lines provide identical upload and download speeds, making them ideal for companies who host their own Web servers, or with large numbers of remote users.

Fractional T1

The T1 bandwidth of 1.544 Mbps actually consists of 24 separate 64-Kbps channels. A fractional T1 line lets you purchase as many of these channels as you need. For example, if you need 512 Kbps of total bandwidth, you can make a cost comparison between eight channels of a fractional T1 and a 512-Kbps DSL line.

Setting Up a Broadband Connection with a Local Router

A broadband connection using a local router can be set up with either one or two network adapters in the server. Figure 5-3 shows the arrangement when you have two network adapters. In this setup, your server is the default gateway and default firewall.

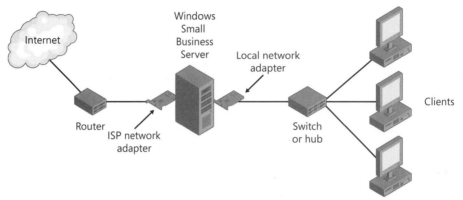

Figure 5-3   How the network is connected using two network adapters on your Windows Small Business Server computer.

Note   Using one network adapter, the router becomes the default gateway and the Windows Small Business Server firewall can't be configured. The ISA Server 2004 from the Premium Edition is also not an option. Because you won't have the firewall capabilities of SBS or ISA, you also won't have information from them in your daily e-mail report on the health of your system. Given the cost of network adapters, and the additional security that a second network adapter provides, get one. Please.

To set up a broadband connection to the Internet using a local router, complete the following steps:

1. On the To Do List, click Start next to Connect To The Internet.

2. On the Connection Type page, select Broadband and click Next.

3. On the Broadband Connection page, select A Local Router Device With An IP Address from the drop-down list and click Next.

Note   If your router supports UPnP, the CEICW will recognize that it does, and offer to configure the router for you. You can choose to have SBS control your router directly, or do the router configuration manually.

4. On the Router Connection page, type the DNS server addresses and the IP address for the router. This is the external DNS server your ISP has provided. Clear the check box for using a single network connection and click Next.

5. If the adapter obtains an IP address using DHCP, select that option on the Network Connection page. Otherwise, select Use The Following ISP Address and provide the addresses. When you click Next, the ISP network configuration is completed.

6. On the second Network Connection page, verify that the ISP network connection and the server local connection are correct and click Next.

7. Follow the steps in the "Configuring the Firewall" section (appearing later in this chapter) to complete the Configure E-Mail And Internet Connection Wizard.

Setting Up a Direct Broadband Connection

A connection to the Internet made through a DSL modem or cable modem is a *direct broadband connection*. Figure 5-4 shows the arrangement for a direct broadband connection.

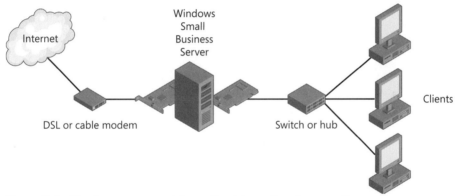

Figure 5-4   Hardware arranged for a direct broadband connection.

To set up a direct broadband connection, complete the following steps:

1. On the To Do List, click Start next to Connect To The Internet. Click the link for Required Information For Connecting To The Internet. When you're ready to proceed, click Next.

2. On the Connection Type page, select Broadband and click Next.

3. On the Broadband Connection page, select A Direct Broadband Connection from the drop-down list and click Next.

4. On the Network Connection page, verify that the ISP network connection and the local network connection are correct and click Next.

5. On the Direct Broadband Connection page, supply the IP addresses for the default gateway and DNS servers. (Your ISP provides these addresses.) Click Next.

Security Alert   Leaving the DNS server information blank on your Internet-facing connection will force SBS to use *root hints* to resolve DNS queries. While this can slightly slow down DNS queries, it provides an extra layer of protection against DNS poisoning attacks. If your ISP is very conscientious about keeping their DNS servers fully and completely updated, and you absolutely trust them to get it right, point to their DNS servers. If you have any doubts at all, leave this field blank. We leave it blank on our SBS server.

6. Follow the steps in the "Configuring the Firewall" section (appearing later in this chapter) to complete the Configure E-Mail And Internet Connection Wizard.

Setting Up a Broadband Connection with User Authentication (PPPoE)

If your broadband connection requires user authentication and uses a device such as a DSL or cable modem, you need two network adapters in the Windows Small Business Server computer, and the firewall is configured on the server. To set up a Point to Point Protocol over Ethernet (PPPoE) connection, complete the following steps:

1. On the To Do List, click Start next to Connect To The Internet. Click the link for Required Information For Connecting To The Internet. When you're ready to proceed, click Next.

2. On the Connection Type page, select Broadband and click Next.

3. On the Broadband Connection page, select A Connection That Requires A User Name And Password (PPPoE) from the drop-down list and click Next.

4. On the PPPoE Connection page, select the PPPoE connection from the drop-down list. (If the connection isn't listed, click the New button and type the name for the connection and the service name.)

5. Type the ISP user name and password (that is, the user name and password that the ISP associates with your connection). If your ISP has assigned a static IP address to the connection, select that check box and supply that IP address and the IP addresses for the DNS servers for name resolution. Click Next.

6. On the Local Network Connection page, select the local connection, verify the IP address, and click Next.

7. Follow the steps in the "Configuring the Firewall" section (appearing later in this chapter) to complete the Configure E-Mail And Internet Connection Wizard.

Setting Up a Dial-Up Connection

To set up a connection to the Internet using a modem or an ISDN adapter, complete the following steps:

1. On the To Do List, click Start next to Connect To The Internet. Click the link for Required Information for Connecting to the Internet. When you're ready to proceed, click Next.

2. On the Connection Type page, select Dial-up and click Next.

3. On the Dial-Up Connection page, select the dial-up connection. If the connection hasn't been configured, click New and provide a name for the connection and the telephone number for connecting to your ISP.

4. Type the ISP user name and password (that is, the user name and password that the ISP associates with your connection), as shown in Figure 5-5. If your ISP has assigned a static IP address to the connection, select that check box and supply the IP address and the IP addresses for the DNS servers on the Internet for name resolution. Click Next.

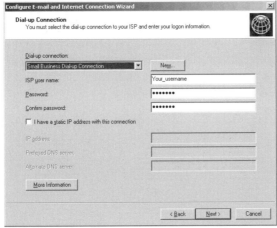

Figure 5-5   Providing the logon information for your dial-up connection.

5. On the Local Network Connection page, select the local connection, verify the IP address, and click Next.

6. Follow the steps in the "Configuring the Firewall" section to complete the Configure E-Mail And Internet Connection Wizard.

Under the Hood   E-Mail Delivery and Retrieval

When you have a choice (and with some ISPs you may not), always use DNS for delivering your e-mail. When you use DNS, you are responsible for deciding where e-mail goes. The e-mail headers are correct and you're actually being a good Internet citizen. When you forward e-mail to what's called a "smart host," the headers will show that the e-mail was forwarded or relayed, and in today's world, where people are being swamped with spam, that alone is enough to get your e-mail blocked from many servers.

E-mail is retrieved either directly from Post Office Protocol 3 (POP3) mailboxes and then routed to Exchange, or the e-mail is delivered directly to Exchange. POP3 mailboxes are the easiest to manage. They will have addresses such as user@YourISP.com. Many ISPs include 5 or 10 free POP3 e-mail accounts with their service.

How your ISP handles incoming e-mail determines the configuration of e-mail delivered directly to Exchange. Either it's delivered to Exchange as soon as it's received, or it's held until your server sends a signal to the ISP. Two types of signal are in use:

- ETRN, which requires that you use a static IP address supplied by the ISP.

- TURN After Authentication, which allows the ISP to deliver to a dynamic IP address. If you choose this option, the TURN Authentication Information page of the wizard will prompt for the user name and password used to authenticate your server to the ISP.

If you're using a fixed IP address, you'll usually use ETRN, but for a dynamic IP address, TURN is used. If in doubt, contact your ISP to confirm which option to choose.

Configuring the Firewall

Unless you have another firewall (hardware or ISA), you must use the SBS Routing and Remote Access (RRAS) based firewall or your network will be completely vulnerable to attack from the Internet. When running the CEICW, you are prompted to enable the firewall and then configure the services. Complete the following steps to configure the firewall:

1. On the Firewall page, click Enable Firewall and then click Next.

2. On the Services Configuration page (see Figure 5-6), select the services that you'll need and then click Next.

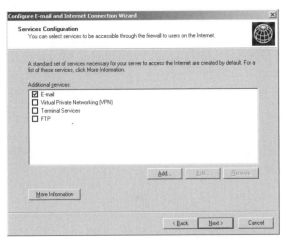

Figure 5-6   Selecting the services to pass through the firewall.

Note   If you select Virtual Private Networking (VPN), the system will warn you that your server isn't configured for remote access. Click OK. Remote access is enabled in the next To Do List item.

3. On the Web Services Configuration page, shown in Figure 5-7, select the Web services you want available to users connecting from the Internet.

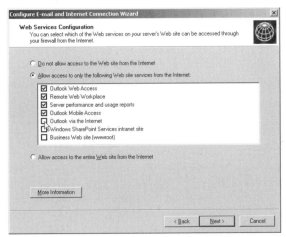

Figure 5-7   The Web Services Configuration page of the CEICW.

4. If you don't allow any access, you'll have maximum security but you won't be able to use some of the best features of Windows Small Business Server, including Remote Web Workplace and Outlook Mobile Access. On the other hand, allowing

access to the entire Web site will allow users to access all the Web site directories. So it's advisable to pick and choose specific services:

- ❏ Outlook Web Access is a component of the Web-based messaging client in Microsoft Exchange Server that gives users secure access to their e-mail, a personal calendar, and group scheduling from any browser.

- ❏ Remote Web Workplace allows authorized users to connect through an Internet address to Outlook Web Access, your SharePoint Services intranet site, and their own desktops. If you select this option, you must also select Outlook Web Access, SharePoint Services, and Server Performance And Usage Reports if you want users to be able to use these services.

- ❏ Server Performance And Usage Reports allows authorized users to receive scheduled performance and usage statistics and to receive immediate alerts when an issue arises on the server.

- ❏ Outlook Mobile Access allows users to read and send e-mail from a mobile device.

- ❏ Outlook Via The Internet allows a user with an Outlook profile on the server to access e-mail from a computer on the Internet without creating a VPN connection. The client computer must be running Microsoft Windows XP Professional with the latest Service Pack and Microsoft Office Outlook 2003 or later.

- ❏ Windows SharePoint Services Intranet Site allows users to make use of the intranet site from the Internet.

- ❏ Business Web Site permits user to access your Internet Web site from the Internet.

5. Click Next.

Note   If your network adapter for the Internet has a dynamically assigned IP address via DHCP, a warning message will appear. If your server is assigned a new IP address, your Internet domain name might not be resolved properly, causing your Web services to be inaccessible from the Internet. If your IP address is dynamically assigned, ensure that your ISP supports dynamic DNS, or consider getting a static IP address. Or use a DNS service, such as ZoneEdit.com, that supports dynamic DNS updates. See Chapter 15, "Managing Connectivity" for more on DNS management.

6. If you choose to allow access to some or all of your Web site, the Web Server Certificate page appears, prompting you to specify a Web certificate, which is necessary to configure Secure Sockets Layer (SSL).

Security Alert   A Web certificate is a security tool for ensuring safe communications on the Web. A site certificate ensures that the server is the one it claims to be, not an imposter, and that data sent to the server will not be intercepted.

A self-signed certificate will work perfectly well for internal clients that need access to Outlook Web Access and Remote Web Workplace, but if you're hosting a public site that requires a certificate, you should use a commercial certificate. If you use a self-signed certificate, your customers—and visitors who access your Internet site—are notified that the site certificate is not signed by a third-party Certification Authority (if their browser security settings are what they should be).

A commercial certificate can cost from $150 to $900 (USD) per year, but is a good investment in security for your customers and visitors. VeriSign (*http://www.verisign.com*), Thawte (*http://www.thawte.com*), and GeoTrust (*http://www.geotrust.com*) are the best-known commercial providers. Although some providers sell 40-bit as well as 128-bit encryption, 40 bits is too weak to offer adequate protection.

---

7. On the Internet E-Mail page, select Enable Internet E-Mail to use Exchange for Internet e-mail and click Next.

8. On the E-Mail Delivery Method page, select how to deliver your Internet e-mail and click Next.

9. On the E-Mail Retrieval Method page, specify how e-mail is retrieved from the Internet. Select Use The Microsoft Connector For POP3 Mailboxes if your organization's e-mail accounts are at your ISP. If you are using Exchange, select Use Exchange, specify how the e-mail is delivered to Exchange, and click Next. For more information about e-mail delivery and retrieval, see the Under the Hood sidebar, "E-Mail Delivery and Retrieval," earlier in this chapter.

10. On the E-Mail Domain Name page, enter your e-mail domain name. This must be a registered Internet domain. Click Next.

11. If you chose to retrieve e-mail using POP3, the POP3 Mailbox Accounts page appears, allowing you to configure your POP3 mailbox accounts and how e-mail is routed to your Exchange server. Since you probably haven't created user accounts yet, you won't be able to specify Exchange accounts where the e-mail should be

routed to. E-mail configuration is discussed in Chapter 14, "Using Exchange Server," so you can leave this until later.

12. If you chose to retrieve e-mail using POP3, the Mail Schedule page appears. Select a frequency for how often to send and receive e-mail.

13. On the Remove E-Mail Attachments page, you can specify the e-mail attachments you want Exchange to remove automatically (see Figure 5-8). If you want, you can save attachments in a folder—preferably one available to administrators only. Click Next.

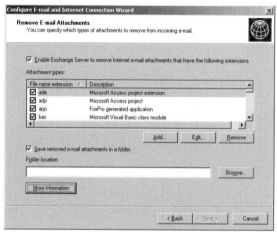

Figure 5-8   Configuring the automatic removal of e-mail attachments.

Note   Attachments sent with internal e-mail on the local network aren't affected by these settings.

---

14. The final page of the CEICW summarizes all of the steps in the configuration, beginning with the type of connection selected and ending with the settings for e-mail attachments. Click the link at the bottom of the page for detailed information. Save, print, or e-mail the details for your records (see Figure 5-9).

After the wizard has completed, you're prompted to enable password policies. You can do this now or later. You will also be connected to the Windows Update Web site to obtain any critical updates. Keeping Windows Small Business Server up to date is discussed in the "Updating Windows Small Business Server" section later in this chapter.

More Info   See Chapter 8, "Managing Users and Groups," for details about establishing strong passwords.

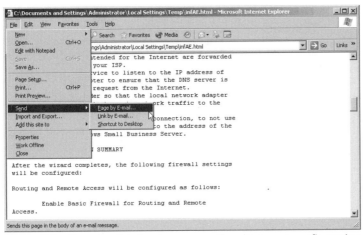

Figure 5-9 Save the details of your e-mail and Internet configuration.

Configuring Remote Access

The next item on the To Do List is Configure Remote Access. With remote access, users—on the road, at home, just about anywhere—can connect to the local network and use the resources as if they were physically present in the office. A mobile user can connect a laptop to the local network and then take it on the road and connect remotely. The user experience will be the same in either scenario. Remote access can be configured in two ways: virtual private networking or dial-up.

Under the Hood   Virtual Private Networking or Remote Web Workplace?

Virtual private networks are geographically isolated from remote users and other private networks by insecure communication lines such as the Internet. A VPN creates a tunnel between two separate networks that provides a private connection. Both ends of the tunnel—the requestor and the authenticator—see the connection as a private dedicated line. Each packet that passes through the tunnel is encrypted before entering the tunnel and decrypted at the other end. Because encryption protects the data packet, any in-transit interception results in unreadable data.

Before you can establish a VPN connection, the client must be authorized. The policies established in Configure Remote Access, the user's group membership, and the client computer's settings determine authorization.

Once the client establishes a VPN connection, the user appears to be accessing the private network directly, as shown in the following illustration.

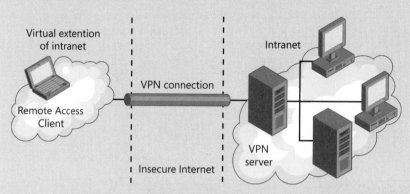

Remote Web Workplace (RWW) offers many of the advantages of a VPN with a lot less overhead and configuration. Your users don't need to know how to do anything except connect to a Web page, they have full access to their desktops and e-mail, and they even have the ability to change their passwords. This is actually one of the best features of Windows Small Business Server 2003 – and it isn't available with any other Microsoft product.

So, which to choose? Both have their place. For the user whose only desktop is a mobile laptop, or who always works remotely from home and doesn't maintain a desktop at work, a VPN is probably a better option. But for everyone else, even the mostly mobile user, RWW is clearly superior. It's easy to set up, doesn't have problems with hotel broadband connections, and provides your users with a simple-to-use experience.

Remote Access via Virtual Private Networking

To configure remote access via virtual private networking, complete the following steps:

1. Click Start next to Configure Remote Access on the To Do List to launch the Remote Access Wizard. Click Next on the Welcome page.

2. On the Remote Access Method page, select Enable Remote Access and VPN (Virtual Private Networking) access. (See the Under the Hood sidebar, "Virtual Private Networking," earlier in this chapter for additional information.) Click Next.

3. If the Client Addressing page appears, specify that the DHCP server assigns IP addresses to remote clients, or designate a range of addresses. Click Next.

Important   If you assign a specific range of IP addresses, make sure the number of addresses is large enough to provide connections for the number of clients likely to connect at any given time, plus one for the server. If all the IP addresses in the range are in use, any additional remote clients will not be able to connect.

4. On the VPN Server Name page, supply the full Internet name for your VPN server. This is the name of your server with your registered Internet domain name, as shown in Figure 5-10. Click Next.

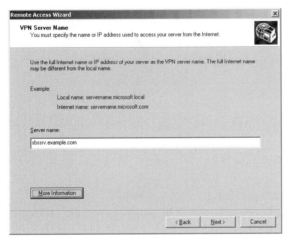

Figure 5-10   Supplying the full name of the VPN server.

5. The last page of the Configure Remote Access Wizard displays a summary of the settings you've made. Click the link at the bottom of the page to save, print, or e-mail the details for your records.

Remote Access via Dial-Up

To configure dial-up remote access, complete the following steps:

1. On the To Do List, click Start next to Configure Remote Access to launch the Remote Access Wizard.

2. On the Remote Access Method page, select Enable Remote Access And Dial-in Access and click Next.

3. If the Client Addressing page appears, specify that the DHCP server assigns IP addresses to remote clients, or designate a range of addresses. Click Next.

> **Important**   If you assign a specific range of IP addresses, make sure the number of addresses is large enough to provide connections for the number of clients likely to connect at any given time, plus one for the server. If all the IP addresses or all the modems are in use, any additional remote clients will not be able to connect.

4. On the Modem Selection page, select the modems designated for remote users. As with the range of IP addresses, make sure there are enough for the number of remote users that will connect at one time. Click Next.

5. On the Dial-Up Phone Numbers page, type the primary and alternate telephone numbers that remote users will dial to connect to the server and click Next.

6. The last page of the Configure Remote Access Wizard displays a summary of the settings you've made. Click the link at the bottom of the page to save, print, or e-mail the details for your records.

7. After the wizard has completed, you're prompted to enable password policies. You can do this now or later.

> **More Info**   See Chapter 8 for details about establishing strong passwords.

The big issue with remote access isn't configuring the server. As you've seen, doing that is relatively simple. The difficulty arises when users in the field attempt to connect to the server. To help in this process, Windows Small Business Server includes Connection Manager.

> **More Info**   See Chapter 11, "Managing Computers on the Network," for details about installing Connection Manager on networked and remote computers.

Activating Your Server

The Activate Your Server item on the To Do List is refreshingly easy to take care of. Click Start next to Activate Your Server to open the Let's Activate Windows page shown in Figure 5-11. Select the first option to activate over the Internet (there's no reason to put it off) and click Next.

Choose to register (or not) at the same time as activation and click Next again. The system connects using the method you configured while completing the Connect To The Internet item on the To Do List.

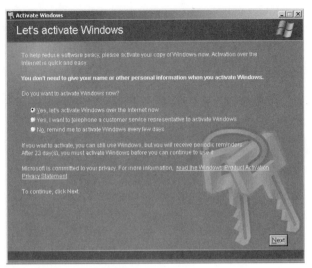

Figure 5-11   Activating your server.

Adding Client Access Licenses

The next task on the To Do List is to activate new licenses for the network's client computers or reissue existing licenses after reinstalling Windows Small Business Server. To perform this task, complete the following steps:

1. Click Start next to Add Additional Client Licenses to launch the Add License Wizard and click Next on the Welcome page.

2. On the License Agreement page, review the license agreement and, if you agree, select I Agree. Click Next.

3. On the Contact Method page, select the Internet or telephone as a method of connecting. Click Next.

4. On the License Code Information page, type the license codes that were provided when you purchased Windows Small Business Server or the license codes you purchased later.

    Note   To transfer licenses from one computer to another, use the Transfer License Wizard. Launch Server Management from the Start menu, click Licensing, and then click Transfer Licenses in the details pane.

5. Check that each code is correct and then click Next.

6. If you're connecting through the Internet, the wizard will continue and the license codes will be activated. If connecting by telephone, call the number the wizard provides and provide the Installation IDs from the Telephone Information page. Write down the confirmation IDs and type them in when requested.

7. If the licenses are accepted, you'll see a finish page like the one shown in Figure 5-12. Don't forget to click the To Print, Save Or Email This Information, Click Here link at the bottom of the page to save your licensing information in a safe place.

Figure 5-12   The Add License Wizard final confirmation page.

Adding Printers

The Add A Printer item on the To Do List allows you to set up a local or network printer.

More Info   For more than you ever wanted to know about installing, configuring, or sharing every sort of printer, see Chapter 10, "Installing and Managing Printers."

Adding Users and Computers

The Add User Wizard is available from the To Do List, or you can launch Server Management from the Start menu, click Users, and click Add A User or Add Multiple Users in the details pane.

> **More Info** See Chapter 8 for all the details about adding and configuring user accounts, managing groups, and managing user profiles. Managing client computers is the subject of Chapter 11.

Configuring Fax Services

Every organization has to cope with faxes—but you no longer have to cope with a fax *machine* and the daily stack of junk faxes (what we used to complain about before we complained about spam). Windows Small Business Server 2003 will send, receive, and route faxes. Faxes can be printed, sent to an e-mail address, stored in a folder (shared or not), or stored in a document library on your intranet Web site. Or you can install multiple modems and set fax routing differently on each one.

To set up the fax service, complete the following steps:

1. On the To Do List, click Start next to Configure Fax to launch the Fax Configuration Wizard. Click Next on the Welcome page.

2. The Provide Company Information page should show the name, the telephone and fax numbers, and the address that you provided during installation of SBS. Enter any missing information and click Next.

3. The Outbound Fax Device page lists the fax modems installed on the server. If you have more than one, use the arrows to set the order in which the devices are used. Click Next.

4. On the Inbound Fax Device page, select which modems will receive faxes. Check the option for all devices using the same routing information, or choose to have each device route independently.

5. On the Inbound Fax Routing page, select the routing methods. As you check an option, a Configure link prompts you for the e-mail address, folder, document library, or printer to use, as shown in Figure 5-13.

6. On the final page of the wizard is a summary of all the settings made. Click the link at the bottom of the page to save this information.

> **More Info** For information about connecting to the Shared Fax Service from client systems, see Chapter 11.

Planning Windows Small Business Server 2003 supports up to four fax modems to increase the number of simultaneous faxes the server can send and receive. It does *not* support Internet fax services, unfortunately.

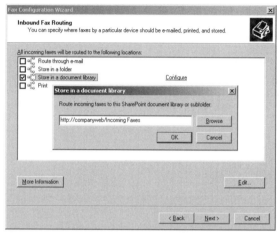

Figure 5-13 Selecting methods of fax routing.

Changing Fax Sending and Receiving

To change how faxes are sent and received, complete the following steps:

1. In the Server Management console, expand the Fax container, expand Devices And Providers, and then select Devices to view a list of fax modems installed on your system.

2. To change the attributes for a device, right-click the device and choose Properties from the shortcut menu. Use the Properties dialog box to configure the device's send and receive settings:

   ❑ Select the Send Faxes and Receive Faxes check boxes to enable the device to send and receive faxes.

   ❑ If you chose to enable the receipt of faxes, choose how many rings to allow before the fax modem answers the line and attempts to receive the fax.

   ❑ Type the sender ID text (usually your company name and telephone number) that you want to appear on outgoing faxes in the Transmitting Subscriber ID (TSID) box.

   ❑ Type the ID text you want to provide to callers who send you faxes in the Called Subscriber ID (CSID) box. (This is usually the same text.)

3. Select Outgoing Routing in the console tree and then use the Groups and Rules containers to optionally route outgoing faxes to different fax devices based on the recipient's fax number. (This can be useful to send all international faxes using a specific telephone line, for example.)

4. To work with cover pages, select Cover Pages in the console tree. Double-click a cover sheet to edit it in the Fax Cover Page Editor.

Setting Fax Service Properties

To change fax service properties such as delivery receipts, archiving, permissions, and logging, right-click Fax in the Server Management console, choose Properties from the shortcut menu, and then use the Fax Properties dialog box to change the server settings:

- Select the Receipts tab to specify how to notify clients when faxes are sent successfully.

- The Event Reports and Activity Logging tabs control what will be reported in Event Viewer.

- Select the Outbox tab as shown in Figure 5-14 to make settings for the outgoing fax queue.

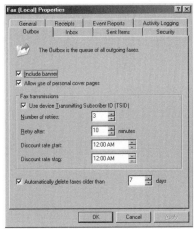

Figure 5-14   The Outbox tab of the Fax Properties dialog box.

- Use the Inbox and Sent Items tabs to control how faxes are archived. (Archiving is done separately from the normal delivery of faxes.)

- Select the Security tab to set fax server management permissions so that only the users and groups you select can send faxes, manage the fax service, or manage fax documents. (If you're going to mess around with default fax permissions, do so either here or in the Printers And Faxes folder in Control Panel—not in both places.) Click OK when you're finished.

Configuring Monitoring

Monitoring the performance and usage of the network is an important, nay a critical, component of security. On the To Do List, click Start next to Configure Monitoring to launch (what else?) the Monitoring Configuration Wizard. Chapter 21, "Monitoring and Fine-Tuning Performance," covers more advanced monitoring and alerting topics, but for now you should set up the basic predefined reports that are included with SBS. These reports will give you a daily e-mail with a quick overview of the health of your network and server, and a weekly report that covers the e-mail, fax, and Internet usage in your organization.

Windows Small Business Server 2003 includes predefined monitoring reports. To enable these reports, complete the following steps:

1. From the To Do List, click Configure Monitoring to start the Monitoring Configuration Wizard

2. On the Reporting Options page, make report choices:

   ❑ **Performance Report** After the wizard completes, the performance report is viewable (by a member of the Domain Admins group) in Server Management. Select the option, and receive a daily report in e-mail as well. Performance reports include information about the server specifications, the processes being run, and any critical errors in critical logs.

   ❑ **Usage Report** The Usage Report includes information about Internet, fax, and e-mail use. You can select just the option to view the report in Server Management, or you can also specify that you want to receive the report in an e-mail.

3. If you chose an e-mail option, supply the destination e-mail address (or addresses) on the E-mail Options page.

4. On the Business Owner Usage Report, which is perhaps not the most unambiguous title, you can specify users (other than members of the Domain Admins group) who should receive reports. These users receive an e-mail telling them where to view the reports on the intranet.

5. On the Alerts page, click the option to receive notification of performance alerts by e-mail. Because these alerts warn of system problems that can be serious, someone with an administrative account should receive them. Supply one or more destination e-mail addresses.

6. The final page of the wizard summarizes the choices made. Click Finish to set up the reports.

   The wizard performs the configuration, and a dialog box keeps you apprised of its progress.

   Note   Neither Performance nor Usage Reports are available instantly. The first Usage Report can take up to 24 hours to assemble and Performance data is gathered just once per hour.

Configuring Backup

Regular backups are essential, which is why this item is on the To Do List. Launch the Backup Configuration Wizard from here, but first read Chapter 13, "Backing Up and Restoring Data," to develop the optimal backup strategy.

Security Basics

Before leaving the To Do List, be sure that security basics are taken care of. This includes configuring automatic updates and setting up a method to regularly scan the network for security flaws. Our preferred tool for scanning our SBS networks is the Microsoft Baseline Security Analyzer version 2.0 (MBSA v2), available from *http://www.microsoft.com/technet/security/tools/mbsahome.mspx*.

Updating Windows Small Business Server

A key part of security is keeping your SBS server current on updates. When vulnerabilities are exposed, Microsoft makes fixes available almost instantly. And "almost instantly" is none too soon for your network. Click the globe icon in the notification areas of the Taskbar to start the Automatic Updates Setup Wizard.

On the Notification Settings page, select the updating method you want. Essentially, the three methods are:

- Don't do anything without telling me.
- Download updates but don't install automatically.
- Download and install. Don't bother me with the details.

The first option lends itself too much to delay. The third option is a bit aggressive for us because some updates require a reboot, and with this option the reboot occurs no matter what the server is doing or who is using it. There have also been some issues when SBS servers needed special versions or instructions when applying a security update. The second option is an effective choice. Updates are downloaded when they become available, but you can choose when to install them—important when a server reboot is required to complete the installation.

Note   When you install Windows Small Business Server 2003 R2, you're also installing the Windows Server Update Services (WSUS). WSUS will allow you to directly configure and control updates on your SBS network, keeping both clients and server fully patched and up to date.

Updating Client Computers

Automatically updating your server with Windows Automatic Updates is easy enough, but what about client machines? You can't count on users to consistently update their own machines, nor do you want to have to deal with it manually. Windows Small Business Server 2003 R2 includes a special, integrated version of Windows Server Update Services (WSUS). We'll cover how to configure and manage WSUS in Chapter 12.

Summary

When you finish this chapter, the basic installation and configuration of Windows Small Business Server 2003 is complete, with the exception of the programs on the Premium Edition CD if you have Premium Edition, and the R2 components. We'll cover those additional features later in Chapters 12, 16, 18, and 20. Of course, there's more you can do to polish your SBS network to a high gloss. In the next chapters, you'll find information on disk management and storage alternatives.

Part III
Performing the Basic Tasks

Chapter 6   Disk Management 99

Chapter 7   Storage Management 131

Chapter 8   Managing Users and Groups 147

Chapter 9   Shares and Permissions 175

Chapter 10   Installing and Managing Printers. 205

Chapter 11   Managing Computers on the Network. 235

Chapter 12   Patch Management 269

Chapter 13   Backing Up and Restoring Data. 291

Chapter 6
Disk Management

The Search for Disaster Protection 100

Understanding Disk Terminology 100

Choosing the Storage Solution for Your Network 103

Managing Disks 105

Using Disk Management. 105

Summary 129

Arguably the single most important function that a server provides to the rest of the network is to be a central, secure, managed file storage area. By centralizing file storage on a server, it becomes an order of magnitude easier to ensure the safety, integrity, recoverability, and availability of the core files of your business. Instead of having files spread all across the network on individual users' computers, you have them in a single place—easier to share among collaborators, easier to back up, easier to recover in the event of a disaster, and easier to secure so that only those people who *should* have access to a file, do. The downside to having all your important files in a single location is the potential for a single point of failure. You need to make sure that your files are seriously protected and always available, since your business depends on them. This makes it imperative that you carefully manage the underlying disks that support your file storage and that those disks be both redundant and thoroughly backed up.

Storing, securing, backing up, and making available the core files of your business is a bigger topic than we could fit in a single chapter, so we've spread it out and organized it according to the various functions involved. But we can't stress this enough: *All* of the pieces are essential to a safe, secure, and available network. Don't shortchange any of them. In this chapter, we'll cover the underlying disk management that makes it possible to store your files and protect against loss, corruption, or disaster. In Chapter 7, "Storage Management," we'll cover some of the new features of Microsoft Windows Small Business Server 2003 that enable you to manage storage, protect critical files, and provide versioning of shared files to protect against corruption or misadventure. Additional backup and recovery details are covered in Chapter 13, "Backing Up and Restoring Data." Finally, in Chapter 22, "Disaster Planning" and Chapter 23 "Planning Fault Tolerance and

Avoidance," we'll go over the steps to ensuring that your data systems and network are both highly available and can be recovered in the event of a serious disaster.

The Search for Disaster Protection

Traditionally, large businesses have used a variety of techniques to ensure that files stored on a server were both secure and safe. These solutions tend to be expensive, but, when spread across all the supported workstations and buried in a large MIS budget, they are feasible. The same solutions would *not* be feasible or acceptable in most small businesses, but that doesn't change our very real need to protect ourselves from disaster. Fortunately, there are both hardware and software solutions that can provide a very high level of security and safety. However, before we can talk about those solutions, let's make sure we all understand the terminology of disk management.

Understanding Disk Terminology

Before going into the details of managing disks and storage, let's review some definitions.

- **Physical drive**   The actual hard disk itself, including the case, electronics, platters, and all that stuff. Not terribly important to the disk administrator.

- **Partition**   A portion of the hard disk. In many cases, this will be the entire hard disk space, but it needn't be.

- **Allocation unit**   The smallest unit of managed disk space on a hard disk or logical volume. Also called a cluster.

- **Primary partition**   A portion of the hard disk that's been marked as a potentially bootable logical drive by an operating system. MS-DOS could support only a single primary partition, but Microsoft Windows NT, Windows 2000, Windows XP, and Windows Server 2003 can support multiple ones. Only four primary partitions can be on any hard disk.

- **Extended partition**   A non-bootable portion of the hard disk that can be subdivided into logical drives. There can be only a single extended partition per hard disk, but this partition can be divided into multiple logical drives.

- **Volume**   A unit of disk space composed of one or more sections of one or more dynamic disks.

- **Simple volume**   The dynamic equivalent of a partition. A portion of a single dynamic disk, it can be assigned either a single drive letter or no drive letter and can be attached (mounted) on zero or more mount points.

- **Extended volume** Similar to, and sometimes synonymous with, a spanned volume, this is any dynamic volume that has been extended to make it larger than its original size. When it uses portions of more than one physical disk, it is more properly referred to as a spanned volume.

- **Logical drive** A section or partition of a hard disk that acts as a single unit. An extended partition can be divided, for example, into multiple logical drives.

- **Logical volume** Another name for a logical drive.

- **Basic disk** A traditional disk drive that is divided into one or more partitions up to a maximum of four partitions, with a logical drive in each primary partition, if present, and one or more logical drives in any extended partition. Basic disks do not support the more advanced functions of disk management, but they can be converted to dynamic disks in many cases.

- **Dynamic disk** A managed hard disk that can be used to create various volumes.

- **RAID (redundant array of independent [formerly "inexpensive"] disks)** The use of multiple hard disks in an array to provide for larger volume size, fault tolerance, and increased performance. RAID comes in different levels, such as RAID-0, RAID-1, and RAID-5. Higher numbers don't necessarily indicate greater performance or fault tolerance, just different methods of doing the job.

- **Spanned volume** A collection of portions of hard disks combined into a single addressable unit. A spanned volume is formatted like a single drive and can have a drive letter assigned to it, but it will span multiple physical drives. A spanned volume—occasionally referred to as an extended volume—provides no fault tolerance and increases your exposure to failure but does permit you to make more efficient use of the available hard disk space.

- **Striped volume** Like a spanned volume, a striped volume combines multiple hard disk portions into a single entity. A striped volume uses special formatting to write to each of the portions equally in a stripe to increase performance. A striped volume provides no fault tolerance and actually increases your exposure to failure, but it is faster than either a spanned volume or a single drive. A stripe set is often referred to as RAID-0, although this is a misnomer because plain striping includes no redundancy.

- **Mirror volume** A pair of dynamic volumes that contain identical data and appear to the world as a single entity. Disk mirroring can use two drives on the same hard disk controller or use separate controllers, in which case it is sometimes referred to as duplexing. In case of failure on the part of either drive, the other hard disk can be split off so that it continues to provide complete access to the data stored on the drive, providing a high degree of fault tolerance. This technique is called RAID-1.

■ **RAID-5 volume**   Like a striped volume, this combines portions of multiple hard disks into a single entity with data written across all portions equally. However, it also writes parity information for each stripe onto a different portion, providing the ability to recover in the case of a single drive failure. A RAID-5 volume provides excellent throughput for read operations but is substantially slower than all other available options for write operations.

■ **SLED (single large expensive disk)**   Now rarely used, this strategy is the opposite of the RAID strategy. Rather than using several inexpensive hard disks and providing fault tolerance through redundancy, you buy the best hard disk you can and bet your entire network on it. If this doesn't sound like a good idea to you, you're right. It's not.

■ **JBOD**   Just a bunch of disks. The hardware equivalent of a spanned volume, this has all the failings of any spanning scheme. The failure of any one disk will result in catastrophic data failure.

Under the Hood   Disk Technologies for the Server

The first time we wrote a chapter about disk management, there were basically three possible technologies available: Modified Field Modification (MFM), Pulse Frequency Modulation (PFM), and Small Computer System (or Serial) Interface (SCSI). Unless you were a total geek (and had oodles of money), your systems used either MFM or PFM, and RAID wasn't even an option. Over time, SCSI became the only real choice for the vast majority of servers and even became mainstream on high-end workstations. Servers at the high end might use fiber, but SCSI had the vast majority of the server disk market.

Integrated Device Electronics (IDE), later called Advanced Technology Attachment (ATA), became the standard on the personal computer. However, IDE never made a serious inroad into the server market because while fast for single tasks, it lacked the inherent multitasking support and bus mastering that a server disk interface technology required, and there were no real hardware RAID solutions that supported it. Avoid it on your server except as secondary storage.

Recently, the introduction of Serial ATA (SATA) technology has made serious inroads into the lower end of the server marketplace. With SATA RAID controllers built into many motherboards, and stand-alone SATA RAID boards that support eight or more SATA drives and have substantial battery-backed RAM cache onboard, many low- to mid-range servers are finding SATA RAID solutions to provide a cost effective alternative to SCSI. While most SATA RAID controllers lack the ability to hot-swap a failed drive, and generally don't have the ultimate performance potential of SCSI, they are still quite attractive alternatives where cost is a primary factor.

On the horizon are newer and even faster technologies for interfacing with disks. We think that Serially Attached SCSI (SAS) is the most interesting addition to the server market, but it's still early in the adoption cycle for SAS, and therefore very expensive. With the main bottleneck for servers continuing to be I/O in general, and especially disk I/O, there will continue to be pressure to find new and faster methods to access disk-based storage.

Choosing the Storage Solution for Your Network

The first decision you need to make when planning your storage solution for Windows Small Business Server is really made when you specify your main server. If your budget can afford it, you should definitely consider choosing a hardware RAID solution that lets you add disks "on the fly" and reconfigure the array without powering down the server or rebooting. This is absolutely the best and most flexible storage solution for protecting your data, and could take the form of hot-swappable SCSI hard drives, or even a Storage Area Network (SAN). None of the possible solutions comes cheap, and in most cases you need to make at least some portion of the decision as part of the original server purchase.

Real World   Network Attached Storage

Although most hardware storage solutions require you to make decisions very early in the buying process, a growing number of Network Attached Storage (NAS) solutions can provide a cost-effective way to increase the storage flexibility of your Windows Small Business Server network. When these NAS solutions are based on Microsoft Windows Storage Server 2003, they support all the features of Windows Small Business Server and will easily integrate into your Windows Small Business Server network. For more on Windows Storage Server 2003–powered NAS servers, see *http://www.microsoft.com/windowsserversystem/ wss2003*.

Once the server is actually in place and is being used, you can't really make a change to the underlying hardware that would allow you to use a hardware RAID solution—at least not easily. But you *can* use the built-in facilities of Windows Small Business Server to make your existing disk subsystem more fault-tolerant by using dynamic disks and the software RAID of Windows Small Business Server as described in "RAID-5 Volumes" later in the chapter.

Storage Connection Technologies

If you're reading this chapter before you buy your server, congratulations on being a thorough person. If not, some of these decisions have already been made, but you may well find that you will have to add storage. If you do, you'll want to focus on storage solutions designed and optimized for servers—a very different set of needs from the typical workstation. Your choices are:

- **Integrated Device Electronics (IDE)**   Primarily a client solution. Inexpensive, but not really best on a server.

- **Serial Advanced Technology Attachment (SATA)**   A newer, and faster, version of IDE. Still primarily a workstation solution, but acceptable when combined with hardware RAID for smaller servers.

- **External Serial Advanced Technology Attachment (eSATA)**   A way to use SATA for external, secondary, or backup storage.

- **Small Computer System Interface (SCSI)**   Perfect for servers and high-end workstations, but significantly more expensive than IDE. Ability to have up to 13 drives per SCSI channel.

- **Serially Attached SCSI (SAS)**   Perfect for large servers. This is a relatively new technology that could become the mainstream server storage interface if the prices come down to something reasonable.

- **Internet SCSI (iSCSI)**   Important for Network Attached Storage, but not for internal storage.

- **FireWire**   Hot-pluggable. A good choice as a backup storage device.

- **Universal Serial Bus (USB)**   Only appropriate if you use USB 2.0. Good for CD and DVD drives. Hot-pluggable. A good choice as a backup storage device.

- **Fiber Channel**   Great if you have large amounts of money to spend.

- **Network Attached Storage (NAS)**   A good way to provide large amounts of storage that can be flexible to meet your needs. Specify Windows Storage Server 2003–based NAS for the greatest flexibility and compatibility.

- **Storage Area Networks (SAN)**   Faster and more robust than the typical NAS, but also much more expensive and difficult to configure.

Managing Disks

There are two different kinds of disks in Windows Small Business Server: basic disks and dynamic disks. *Basic disks* are the conventional disks we're used to. *Dynamic disks* were introduced in Windows 2000 Server, and support additional management and agglomeration options.

Basic disks support two different kinds of partitions: primary and extended. They cannot be used with the advanced disk management techniques that are supported by SBS. They can, however, be seen by other operating systems if you have your SBS server configured for dual booting, as you might in a test environment.

Dynamic disks use volumes instead of partitions, and support the additional management, redundancy, and agglomeration features of Windows Small Business Server, including Spanned Volumes, Striped Volumes (RAID-0), Mirrored Volumes (RAID-1), and RAID-5.

Using Disk Management

The primary method for managing disks on an SBS server is the Disk Management snap-in. This can be used as a stand-alone, from the Computer Management console, or from the Server Management console, as shown in Figure 6-1.

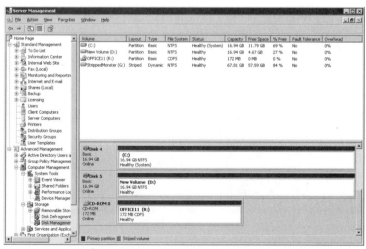

Figure 6-1   The Disk Management snap-in from inside the Server Management console.

The Disk Management snap-in is divided into two panes. The top pane shows the drive letters (volumes) associated with the local disks and gives their properties and status; the bottom pane has a graphical representation organized by physical drive.

Real World   Hardware RAID

Although Disk Management provides an excellent software RAID solution, hardware RAID is also now widely available, from either the original server vendor or from third parties, and it provides substantial advantages over software RAID. Hardware RAID solutions range from a simple RAID controller to fully integrated, stand-alone subsystems. Their features vary, as does their cost, but all claim to provide superior performance and reliability over a simple software RAID solution such as that included in Windows Small Business Server. In general, they do. Some of the advantages they can offer include:

- Hot-swap and hot-spare drives, allowing for virtually instantaneous replacement of failed drives

- Integrated, battery-protected disk caching for improved disk performance

- A separate, dedicated system that handles all processing, for improved overall performance

- Increased flexibility and additional RAID levels, such as RAID-10 (also called RAID 0+1), which is a combination of striping (RAID-0) and mirroring (RAID-1) that provides for fast read and write disk access with full redundancy

Single Server

Although not all hardware RAID systems provide all the possible features, they all have the potential to improve the overall reliability and performance of your hard disk subsystem. With SBS being predominantly a single-server environment, you have your entire business running on that single server. This makes hardware RAID a particularly sound investment for your SBS server.

NAS and SAN

Many NAS systems are built on hardware RAID, providing an easy and cost-effective way to expand your original server storage in a highly fault-tolerant way. However, it pays to look closely at exactly what you are buying—some are built on RAID-0, which is *not* fault tolerant at all and actually increases your risk.

We only briefly mentioned Storage Area Networks (SANs) earlier, and we won't mention them again. Although they are excellent, fast, flexible, and highly fault tolerant, they are only for those with really large IT budgets at this point. Plus they can be rather tricky to implement and configure. Given the strong advances in NAS, we think it provides a better solution for those running on realistic budgets.

Dynamic Disks

Windows Small Business Server supports dynamic disks. A basic disk can be converted to a dynamic disk, allowing you to use Disk Management to manage it in new ways, *without requiring a reboot* in most cases. You can extend a disk volume, span a volume across multiple physical disks, stripe the volume for improved performance, mirror it, or add it to a RAID-5 array—all from the Server Management console and all without a reboot, after the disk is converted to a dynamic disk. The initial creation or conversion of the first of your basic disks to a dynamic disk requires a reboot, unfortunately, but when you get over that hurdle, you'll breeze through the remaining tasks. Dynamic disks give the system administrator powerful tools for managing the type and configuration of hard disk storage across the enterprise.

Note Recovering or rebuilding a server that has a dynamic disk for the boot disk can be tricky. We suggest keeping your boot disk (C:) a basic disk and use hardware mirroring (RAID-1) to safeguard its contents, and then use dynamic disks for other disks on your server.

Under the Hood   Command Line

Windows Small Business Server adds to the system administrator's toolkit a complete command-line interface for managing disks—Diskpart.exe. This command-line utility is scriptable or it can be used interactively. Here is a simple script to create a volume on an existing dynamic disk and assign it to the next available drive letter:

```
REM Filename: MakeVol.txt
REM
REM This is a DiskPart.exe Script. Run from the command line
REM or from another script, using the syntax:
REM
REM    diskpart /s MakeVol.txt > logfile.log
REM
REM to run this script and dump the results out to a log file.
REM
REM This script creates a simple volume of 28 Gb on disk #3, and then
REM assigns a drive letter to it. Note that this does NOT format
```

```
REM the volume -- that requires using the format command, not part
REM of diskpart.exe

REM First, list out our disks. Not required for scripting, but useful
REM to show the overall environment if we need to troubleshoot problems
list disk

REM Next, select which disk will have the simple volume created on it.
select disk 3

REM Now, create the volume...
create volume simple size=28672

REM Assign without parameters will choose the next available HD letter.
Assign
```

Adding a Partition or Volume

Adding a new drive or partition to an SBS server is straightforward. First, obviously, you need to physically install and connect the drive. If you have a hot-swappable backplane and array, you don't even have to shut the system down to accomplish this task. If you're using conventional drives, however, you need to shut down and power off the system.

After the drive is installed and the system is powered up again, SBS automatically recognizes the new hardware and makes it available. If the disk is a basic disk that is already partitioned and formatted, you're able to use it immediately. If it's a brand new disk that has never been partitioned or formatted, you need to prepare it first. If it's a dynamic disk or disks, but from another computer, you can use it as soon as you import it. If the disk is a basic disk that has already been formatted, you don't get prompted to upgrade it to a dynamic disk. If the disk has never been used before, the Initialize and Convert Disk Wizard prompts you.

Adding a New Disk Using the Initialize and Convert Disk Wizard

When you install a new hard drive, the drive is automatically recognized, and the Initialize and Convert Disk Wizard starts when you open Disk Management. To add a new disk, complete the following steps:

1. Open the Server Management console.

2. In the console tree, expand Advanced Management, Computer Management, Storage, and then click Disk Management. If the disk is new, you see the first page of the Initialize and Convert Disk Wizard, shown in Figure 6-2. This wizard allows you to both initialize the disk so it can be recognized by SBS, and also upgrade the new disk to a dynamic disk. Click Next.

Figure 6-2   The first page of the Initialize and Convert Disk Wizard.

3. On the Select Disks To Initialize page, you see a confirmation of the disk (or disks, if you added more than one) that can be selected for initializing, as shown in Figure 6-3.

Figure 6-3   The Select Disks To Convert page of the Initialize and Convert Disk Wizard.

4. Make sure a check mark appears to the left of the disk or disks to be initialized and then click Next again.

5. On the Select Disks To Convert page, select from the list the disks you want to convert to dynamic disks, as shown in Figure 6-4, and then click Next.

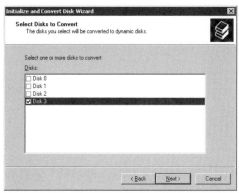

Figure 6-4   The Select Disks To Initialize page of the Initialize and Convert Disk Wizard.

6. You get a confirmation message. If all the options are correct, click Finish. The disk is initialized and converted to a dynamic disk.

When the wizard finishes, you're at the main Disk Management console, shown in Figure 6-5. Notice that the disk is still not formatted or allocated and is highlighted in black (if you haven't changed the default color settings for the Disk Management console).

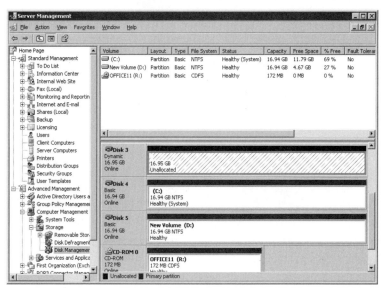

Figure 6-5   The main Disk Management console, showing the new disk (Disk 3).

Creating a Volume

To create a new volume (the dynamic disk equivalent of a partition), complete the following steps:

1. In the Disk Management console, right-click the unallocated disk and choose New Volume from the shortcut menu. The New Volume Wizard opens to guide you through the process of creating the new volume on the dynamic disk. Click Next.

2. On the Select Volume Type page, select the type of volume you'll be creating, as shown in Figure 6-6. Depending on the number of available unallocated volumes, you see one or more options for the type of volume. These options include Simple, Spanned, Striped (RAID-0), Mirrored (RAID-1), and RAID-5. Click Next.

3. On the Select Disks page, select the dynamic disks to use for the new volume. The choices available and the selections you need to make depend on the type of volume you're creating and the number of available unallocated disks. Figure 6-7 shows a RAID-5 volume being created.

4. On the same page, adjust the size of the new volume. By default, the new volume will use the maximum available space from each of the selected disks. For spanned volumes, this will be the sum of the free space on the selected disks; for other types of volumes, it will be the number of disks multiplied by the available space on the smallest of the selected disks multiplied by the factor for the type of volume. Mirror is 50 percent of the smallest volume; RAID-5 is $n-1$ multiplied by the size of the smallest volume in the group. All others are 100 percent of the size of the smallest volume multiplied by the number of disks in the group. Click Next.

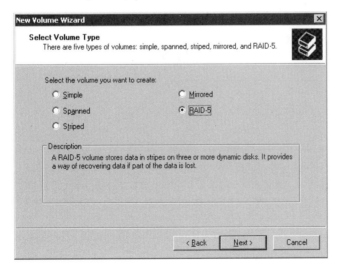

Figure 6-6   Select the type of dynamic volume you want to create.

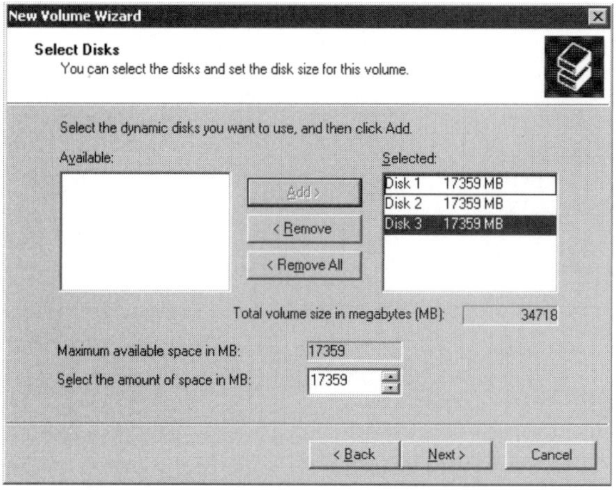

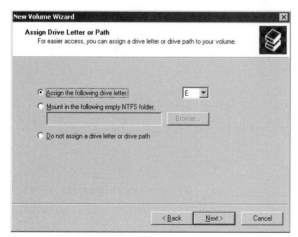

Figure 6-7   Select the dynamic disks that will be part of this volume.

5. On the Assign Drive Letter Or Path page, select either a drive letter or a mount point for the new volume, as shown in Figure 6-8. You could opt not to assign a drive letter or path now, but why? You can't use the disk until you do. With Windows Small Business Server, you can mount a volume on an empty subdirectory, minimizing the number of drive letters and reducing the complexity of the storage that is displayed to the user. If you want to take advantage of this feature, click Browse to locate the directory where you will mount the new volume. Click Next.

More Info   For more information about mounting a volume, see the Real World sidebar "Mounted Volumes" later in this chapter.

Figure 6-8   Select a drive letter or mount point for the new volume.

6. On the Format Volume page, select the formatting options you want, as shown in Figure 6-9. Even when mounting the volume rather than creating a new drive, you can choose your format type without regard to the underlying format of the mount point. Click Next.

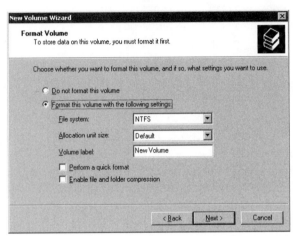

Figure 6-9   Set the formatting options for the new volume.

7. You see a confirmation page. If all the options are correct, click Finish to create and format the volume, which will take a few minutes depending on the size of the disk. You return to the Disk Management console, where you see the new volume, as shown in Figure 6-10.

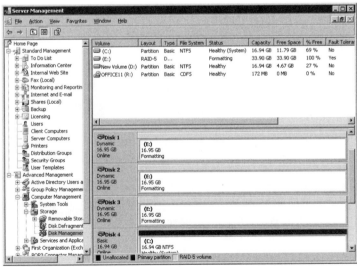

Figure 6-10   The new RAID volume being generated and formatted.

Real World   Mounted Volumes

Windows Small Business Server borrows a concept from the UNIX world by adding the ability to mount a volume or partition on a subfolder of an existing drive letter. A mounted volume can also have a drive letter associated with it, although it does not need to, and it can be mounted at more than one point, giving multiple entry points into the same storage.

A volume must be mounted on an empty subfolder of an existing NTFS volume or drive. FAT and FAT32 drives do not support mounted volumes. You can, however, mount a FAT or FAT32 volume at any mount point, though with Windows Small Business Server, the use of FAT and FAT32 file systems is strongly discouraged (and not supported for the system drive). You can mount only a single volume at a given mount point, but you can then mount further volumes on top of an existing mounted volume, with the same rules and restrictions as any other mount. An important caution, however—the properties of a drive do not show all the available disk space for that drive, because they do not reflect any volumes mounted on the drive. Further, mounted volumes are not supported with Windows Services for UNIX on shared Network File System (NFS) exports.

Mounted volumes can be used to provide a mix of redundant and non-redundant storage in a logical structure that meets the business needs of the business while hiding the complexities of the physical structure from the users.

Creating a Partition

You can create partitions only on basic disks, not on dynamic disks. To create a new partition, complete the following steps:

1. In the Disk Management console, right-click the unallocated basic disk and select New Partition. The New Partition Wizard, shown in Figure 6-11, opens to guide you through the process of creating the new partition on the basic disk. Click Next.

2. On the Select Partition Type page, select the type of partition you'll be creating, as shown in Figure 6-12. If this is a removable drive, you see only an option for a primary partition, but if this is a nonremovable disk, you're able to choose either a primary or an extended partition. A basic disk can hold up to four primary partitions or three primary partitions and one extended partition. Click Next.

Figure 6-11   The first page of the New Partition Wizard.

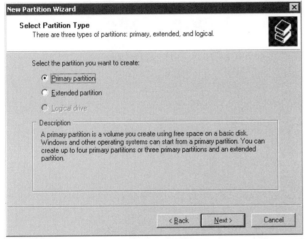

Figure 6-12   Select the type of partition you want to create.

3. On the Specify Partition Size page, specify how much of the available space on the disk you want to use for this partition, as shown in Figure 6-13. Click Next.

4. If you're creating an extended partition, continue with Step 6. If you're creating a primary partition, the Assign Drive Letter Or Path page appears. Select either a drive letter, as shown in Figure 6-14, or a mount point for the new partition. You can also choose to defer giving the new partition a mount point or drive letter until later. However, this partition is unavailable to your users until you do. Click Next.

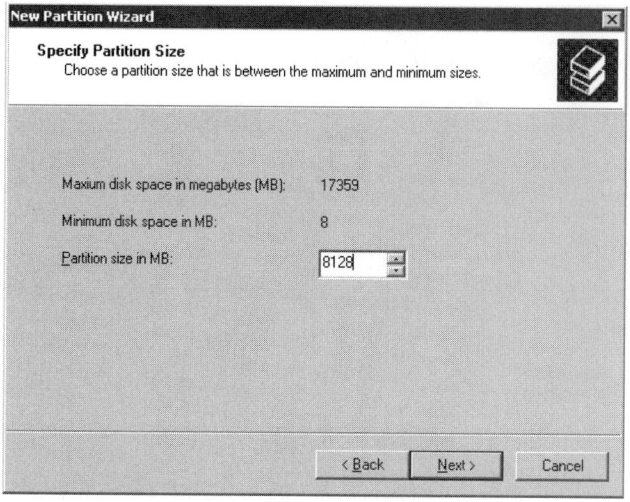

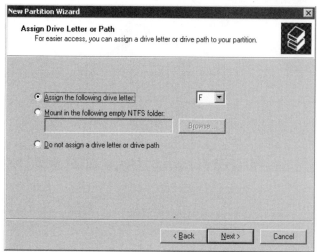

Figure 6-13   Specify how much of the disk will be used by this partition.

Figure 6-14   Select a drive letter or a mount point for the new partition.

5. On the Format Partition pages, select the formatting options you want, or opt to defer formatting until later. Click Next.

6. You see a confirmation page. If all the options are correct, click Finish to create the partition. If it is a primary partition, it will be formatted and the drive letter or mount point assigned. If it is an extended partition, you'll need to format it and choose the drive letters and mount points for it, as discussed in the next section, "Creating Logical Drives in an Extended Partition."

Under the Hood   Formatting Options

Windows Server 2003 can recognize hard drives that are formatted in any of the three file system formats: FAT, FAT32, and NTFS. Only NTFS is supported by Windows Small Business Server. Although it is technically possible to format any drive except the system drive as FAT or FAT32, it is not recommended.

You can choose to quick-format a drive to make it available more quickly, but this option simply removes the file entries from the disk and does no checking for bad sectors. Chose quick formatting only when recycling a disk that has already been formatted and when you are confident it hasn't been damaged.

On an NTFS volume or partition, you can specify the allocation unit size. This option lets you tune the disk for a particular purpose, depending on the disk's size and intended function. A database storage volume that will contain large database files managed by the database program might lend itself to large allocation units (also called *clusters*), whereas a disk that must hold many small files is a candidate for smaller clusters. However, the default sizes are an excellent compromise for most situations—modify them only with caution and with a clear understanding of the consequences for your environment.

You can also choose to enable disk and folder compression on NTFS volumes and partitions. This causes all files and folders on the volume (as opposed to individual files or folders you select) to be compressed. Compression can minimize the amount of hard disk space used by files but can have a negative impact on performance and makes recovery more problematic. Given the cost of hard drive space today, it hardly seems worth it and is certainly not a good idea for frequently updated data.

Creating Logical Drives in an Extended Partition

If you created a new extended partition, the next step is to create logical drives in the partition. You can assign one or more logical drives in an extended partition, and each of those logical drives can be assigned a drive letter and one or more mount points. Each of the logical drives can be formatted with any of the supported file systems, regardless of the format of other logical drives. To create a logical drive, complete the following steps:

1. In the Disk Management console, right-click the Free Space portion of the extended partition and select New Logical Drive from the shortcut menu to open the New Partition Wizard (shown earlier in Figure 6-11). Click Next.

2. On the Select Partition Type page, shown in Figure 6-15, you see the Logical Drive option selected and the only choice active. Click Next.

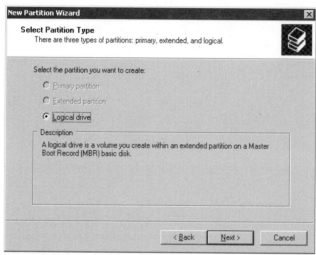

Figure 6-15   The Select Partition Type page of the New Partition Wizard.

3. On the Specify Partition Size page (shown in Figure 6-16), specify the size of the logical drive you'll be creating. You can specify the entire partition for a single drive, or you can divide the partition into multiple logical drives. Click Next.

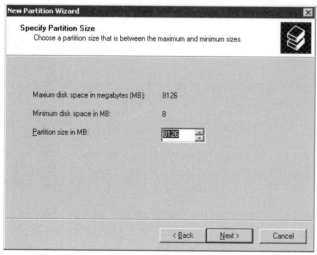

Figure 6-16   Adjusting the size of the logical drive.

4. On the Assign Drive Letter Or Path page, select the drive letter or mount point for the new logical drive, as shown in Figure 6-17. You can also choose not to assign a letter or mount point at this time. Click Next.

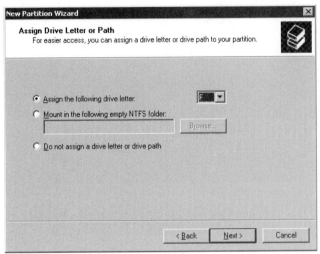

Figure 6-17   Assigning a drive letter or mount point for the logical drive.

5. On the Format Partition page, select the formatting options you want. Click Next, and you see the final confirmation page. If all the options are correct, click Finish to create and format the new logical drive. If you need to create additional logical drives on the partition, you can repeat these steps as many times as required to create the number of logical drives desired.

Deleting a Partition, Volume, or Logical Drive

Deleting a partition, deleting a logical drive, and deleting a volume are essentially the same task, with one important exception. When you delete a logical drive, you end up with free space in the partition, but other logical drives in the partition are untouched. When you delete a partition or volume, the entire volume or partition is deleted. You cannot, however, delete an extended partition until all the logical drives in the partition have first been deleted. You can directly delete a primary partition or a volume.

In all cases, when you delete a volume, logical drive, or partition, you end up with free or unallocated space and no data on the volume, drive, or partition when you're done, so make sure you have a good backup if there's a chance you might later need any of the data. To delete a partition, logical drive, or volume, follow these steps:

1. Right-click the partition, logical drive, or volume and choose Delete Partition, Delete Logical Drive, or Delete Volume.

2. If you're deleting a volume or partition, you see a warning message similar to the one shown in Figure 6-18. Deleting an extended partition involves extra steps, because you must first delete the logical drives in the partition before you can delete the partition itself.

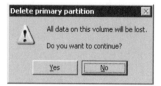

Figure 6-18 Confirmation message for deleting a partition.

When the volume or partition is completely deleted, the space it occupied will be unallocated. Space that is unallocated on dynamic disks can be used to create mirrors, extend an existing volume, create a RAID array, or otherwise manage the storage on your server. Space that is unallocated on basic disks can be partitioned.

Converting a Disk to a Dynamic Disk

The advantages of dynamic disks are substantial. Even if you use hardware RAID controllers and hot-swappable disks to manage your hard disks, you'll probably find it a good idea to use dynamic disks. There is a caveat, however. Because you can't boot from or even see a dynamic disk from any other operating system released prior to Windows 2000 Server, you might want to consider leaving at least your boot drive as a basic drive. Doing so makes working with it somewhat easier, especially when troubleshooting boot problems. If you need to provide for redundancy on that drive, and if hardware RAID is an option, use RAID level 1 to make recovery from a failed hard disk or other disaster as painless as possible. To convert a basic disk to a dynamic disk, complete the following steps:

1. Right-click the disk's icon on the left side of the Disk Management console, and choose Convert To Dynamic Disk from the shortcut menu.

2. You see a Convert To Dynamic Disk dialog box like the one shown in Figure 6-19, listing the available basic disks on your computer. The disk you clicked is checked, and you can select other disks to upgrade at the same time. Click OK to continue with the upgrade.

3. You see a Disks To Convert dialog box that shows the disks that will be converted. Click Convert if all is correct.

4. You get a warning message stating that no other version of Windows can use these disks. Click Yes to continue.

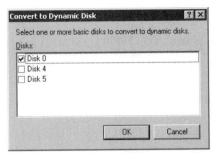

Figure 6-19   You can select more than one disk to convert.

5. If there are no file systems on the disks you chose to upgrade, that's all there is to it. However, if there are file systems on any of the disks, you get a warning message stating that the file systems will be dismounted. Click Yes and the upgrade proceeds. Existing partitions will be converted into Simple volumes. You can now manage the disks dynamically, and they can be part of mirrors, RAID-5 arrays, or other enhanced disk configurations that aren't supported by basic disks.

> **Important**   If there are any open files on the disk to be upgraded, you might experience data loss. Perform disk upgrades only during quiet times when no users are logged on to or using the server.

Extending a Volume

You can add space to a volume without having to back up, reboot, and restore your files if the volume is on a dynamic disk and if it is a simple volume or a spanned volume. You do this by converting the volume to a spanned or extended volume that incorporates unallocated space on any dynamic disk. Unfortunately, you can't increase the size of a RAID-5 or RAID-0 (striped) volume simply by adding disks to the array, unless you're using a version of hardware RAID that supports this functionality. To extend a volume, complete the following steps:

1. In the Disk Management console, right-click the volume you want to extend. Choose Extend Volume from the shortcut menu to open the Extend Volume Wizard. Click Next.

2. On the Select Disks page, select one or more disks from the list of dynamic disks that are available and have unallocated space. Click Add to add the selected disk or disks, and indicate the amount of space you want to add, as shown in Figure 6-20. Click Next.

3. The Extend Volume Wizard displays a final confirmation page before extending the volume. Click Finish to extend the volume, or click Cancel if you change your mind.

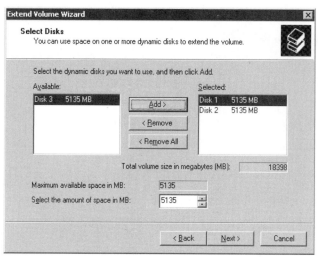

Figure 6-20   Selecting the disks to use to extend the volume.

Important   A spanned (extended) volume is actually less reliable than a simple disk. Unlike a mirror or RAID-5 volume, in which there is built-in redundancy, a spanned or striped volume will be broken and all its data lost if any disk in the volume fails.

Real World   Extending—Friend or Foe?

Most people responsible for supporting a busy server have wished at some point that they could simply increase the space of a particular volume or drive on the fly when it got low on space—preferably without having to bring the system offline for several hours while the entire volume is backed up and reformatted to add the additional hard disks, the backup is restored, and the share points are recreated. Fun? Hardly. Risky? Certainly. And definitely a job that means coming in on the weekend or staying late at night—in other words, something to be avoided if at all possible.

All this makes Windows Small Business Server's ability to create additional space on a volume without the need to back up the volume, reformat the disks, and recreate the volume a seductive feature. However, unless you're running hardware RAID, you should think twice before jumping in. Only spanned or stripped volumes allow you to add additional storage on the fly, and because neither is redundant, using them exposes your users to the risks of a failed drive. Yes, you have a backup, but even under the best of circumstances, you'll lose some data if you need to restore a backup. Further, using spanned volumes actually *increases* your risk of a hard disk failure. If any disk used as part of the spanned volume fails, the entire volume is toast and will need to be restored from backup.

Why, then, would anyone use spanning? Because they have hardware RAID to provide the redundancy. This combination offers the best of both worlds—redundancy provided by the hardware RAID controller and flexibility to expand volumes as needed, using Windows Small Business Server Disk Management. Yet another compelling argument for hardware RAID, as if you needed any more.

Note   Windows Small Business Server uses the terms "extended" and "spanned" nearly interchangeably when describing volumes. Technically, however, a spanned volume must include more than one physical disk, whereas an extended volume can also refer to a volume that has had additional space added to the original simple volume on the same disk.

Adding a Mirror

When your data is mission-critical and you want to make sure that the data is protected and always available no matter what happens to one of your hard disks, consider mirroring the data onto a second drive. Windows Small Business Server can mirror a dynamic disk onto a second dynamic disk so that the failure of either disk does not result in loss of data. To mirror a volume, you can either select a mirrored volume when you create the volume or you can add a mirror to an existing volume. To add a mirror to an existing volume, complete the following steps:

1.   In the Disk Management console, right-click the volume you want to mirror. If a potential mirror is available, the shortcut menu lists the Add Mirror command.

2.   Choose Add Mirror to display the Add Mirror dialog box, shown in Figure 6-21, where you can select the disk to be used for the mirror.

Figure 6-21   The Add Mirror dialog box.

3. Select the disk that will be the mirror, and click Add Mirror. The mirror is created immediately and starts duplicating the data from the original disk to the second half of the mirror, as shown in Figure 6-22. This process is called *regeneration*, or sometimes *resynching*. (The process of regeneration is also used to distribute data across the disks when a RAID-5 volume is created.)

Note   Regeneration is both CPU-intensive and disk-intensive. When possible, create mirrors during slack times or during normally scheduled downtime. Balance this goal, however, with the equally important goal of providing redundancy and failure protection as expeditiously as possible.

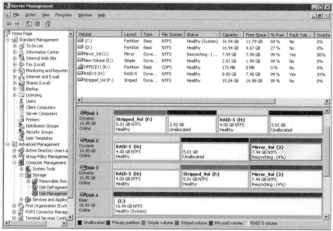

Figure 6-22   A newly created mirrored disk in the process of regeneration.

Note   To improve your overall data security and reliability, mirror your volumes onto disks that use separate controllers whenever possible. This process is known as duplexing and eliminates the disk controller as a single point of failure. It can also speeding up both reading and writing to the mirror, because the controller and bus are no longer potential bottlenecks.

Drive Failure in a Mirrored Volume

If one of the disks in a mirrored volume fails, you continue to have full access to all your data without loss. Windows Small Business Server marks the failed disk as missing and takes it offline, as shown in Figure 6-23, while sending alerts to the alert log and popping up a balloon on the server console, as shown in Figure 6-24. It continues, however, to read and write from the other half of the mirrored volume as though nothing had happened. Be warned, however. You no longer have any fault tolerance on that volume, and any additional failure will result in catastrophic data loss.

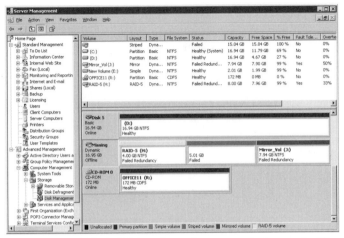

Figure 6-23   Failed disk in mirror shown as missing and offline.

> **⚠ Windows - FT Orphaning**   **☒**
> A disk that is part of a fault-tolerant volume can no longer be accessed.

Figure 6-24   Balloon opens on the console to warn of a failed drive in a fault tolerant volume.

After you replace the failed disk or correct the problem and reactivate it, the mirror automatically starts regenerating. If the problem can be solved without powering down the system, you can regenerate the mirror on the fly. To reactivate the failed disk, complete the following steps:

1.   Right-click the icon for the failed disk on the left of the Disk Management console, shown in Figure 6-25.

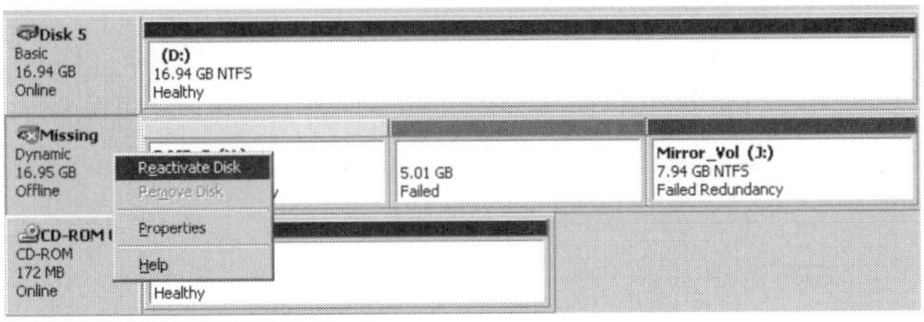

Figure 6-25   Reactivating a failed disk that is part of a mirrored volume.

2. Choose Reactivate Disk. Windows Small Business Server warns you about running Chkdsk on any affected volumes, and then brings the disk back online and starts regenerating the failed mirror, as shown in Figure 6-26. When the mirror has been regenerated, the disk status changes from Regenerating to Healthy.

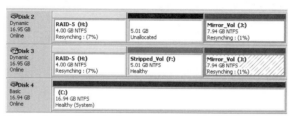

Figure 6-26 Data being regenerated on a reactivated mirrored disk.

Removing a Mirror

If you need to make additional disk space available on your system and you have no additional disks available, you can remove the mirror from a mirrored volume. When you remove a mirror, the data on one of the disks is untouched, but the other disk becomes unallocated space. Of course, you will have lost all redundancy and protection for the data, so you need to take steps to restore the mirror as soon as possible. Until then you might want to modify your backup schedule for the remaining disk. To remove a mirror, complete the following steps:

1. In the Disk Management console, right-click either half of the mirror. Choose Remove Mirror from the shortcut menu, and the Remove Mirror dialog box opens, shown in Figure 6-27.

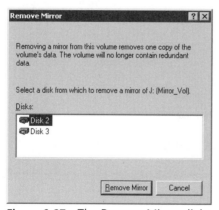

Figure 6-27 The Remove Mirror dialog box.

2. Select the disk you want to remove from the mirror. Click Remove Mirror. You get one last chance to change your mind. Click OK, and the disk you highlighted becomes unallocated space.

Breaking a Mirror

If a disk fails and you can't replace it with an identical one, break the mirror until a replacement becomes available. Breaking a mirror severs the connection between the two disks, allowing the remaining disk to continue to function normally until a replacement disk becomes available. Once the replacement disk is available, the mirror can be re-created.

You might also find it useful to break a mirror even when both disks are still functioning, because you then end up with two identical copies of the same data. One half of the broken mirror continues to have the same drive letter or mount point, while the second half of the broken mirror is assigned the next available drive letter. To break a mirror, complete the following steps:

1. In the Disk Management console, right-click either disk of the mirrored volume.

2. Choose Break Mirror from the shortcut menu. You're asked to confirm that you really want to break it.

3. Click Yes, and the mirror is broken. You'll have two volumes. One retains the drive letter or mount point of the original mirror, and the other is assigned the next available drive letter. They will both contain exact duplicates of the data at the instant of the break but will immediately start to diverge as they are modified.

RAID-5 Volumes

Windows Small Business Server 2003 supports a software implementation of RAID-5 that allows you to have a redundant file system without the 50 percent capacity overhead of using mirrored volumes. The overhead on a RAID-5 volume decreases for each additional disk you add to the volume, making this the most space efficient method of providing redundancy in Windows Small Business Server.

Unfortunately, this efficiency doesn't come without some costs. RAID-5 arrays are inherently slower at write operations than even a plain old stand-alone drive. You also don't have the flexibility that you have with mirrored volumes in Windows Small Business Server. You can't simply remove a drive from a RAID-5 volume, nor can you break a failed drive out of the volume, allowing the remaining drives to regenerate. Further, when a disk fails on a RAID-5 volume, not only is the volume no longer redundant, but it also gets a lot slower because both read and write operations must calculate the correct value for every byte read or written.

Some of the tasks you do with a mirror also apply to a RAID-5 volume. You can:

- Create the RAID-5 volume.

- Assign a mount point or drive letter to the RAID-5 volume.

- Format the RAID-5 volume.

- Continue to use the RAID-5 volume after the failure of one of the disks in the volume.

What you can't do with the software RAID in SBS is add or remove disks from the RAID-5 volume once you have created it, except for replacing a failed disk. To be able to dynamically add and remove disks from a RAID-5 array, the solution is a to choose a hardware RAID array that supports dynamic reconfiguration.

Real World   Assigning Volume Names

The name you assign to a volume, partition, or drive should tell you something about it rather than simply mimicking the drive letter. A volume name like "Big70GBSCSI" tells you pretty conclusively that it's that big new SCSI drive you just bought, unless, of course, you already have a half dozen of them on your server, in which case you're going to need to come up with a more effective name. On the other hand, a volume name of "C_DRIVE" is just about useless, because the drive letter is available from anywhere that the volume name is. A common scheme is to assign volume names based on the primary use of the volume, so "UserHome" or "DB_STORE" make it pretty clear which volume it is from a logical (but not necessarily physical) view.

Mounting a Volume

Windows Small Business Server allows you to mount a dynamic volume—or any partition or logical drive in an extended partition—on an empty directory of a nonremovable NTFS drive. The volume being mounted appears to users as a simple directory. This feature makes it possible to create larger file systems that use multiple hard disks without the inherent risks of using spanned volumes, because the failure of any one of the mounted volumes affects only the directories that were part of that volume. To mount a volume, complete the following steps:

1. From the Disk Management console, right-click a volume or partition. Choose Change Drive Letter And Paths from the shortcut menu. The Change Drive Letter And Paths dialog box opens.

2. Click Add. The Add Drive Letter Or Path dialog box (see Figure 6-28) opens.

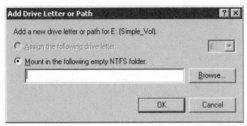

Figure 6-28   The Add Drive Letter Or Path dialog box, used to mount a volume.

3. You can type the mount point or click Browse to select or create a mount point. Any empty directory that resides on a nonremovable NTFS volume or drive can be the mount point.

4. After you select or type the mount point, click OK, and the volume or partition is mounted.

> **Important**   It's actually easy to get yourself into trouble with this new feature. Disk Management lets you make multiple levels of mounted volumes, including ones that are recursive. You're well advised to mount volumes *only* at the root level of a drive. Trying to mount below that point can lead to confusion and make management and documentation difficult.

Summary

In this chapter, we covered the details of how to manage the hard disks on your Windows Small Business Server computer, and how to configure them for data integrity and redundancy. In the next chapter, we'll cover the configuration and management of file storage on your SBS server.

Chapter 7
Storage Management

Disk Quotas. 132

Encrypting Files 137

Shadow Copies of Shared Folders. 140

Summary 146

Whereas disk management is all about the mechanics of configuring disks, storage management is where you actually get to use those disks for something. In this chapter, we'll cover some of the features of Microsoft Windows Small Business Server 2003 that enable you to manage storage, protect critical files, and provide versioning of shared files to protect against corruption or misadventure. (Note that the File Server Resource Manager (FSRM) from Windows Server 2003 R2 was added to SBS too late to be covered in this chapter, so we've added it as Appendix D, "Using the File Server Resource Manager." FSRM enables folder level quotas, file type screening, and advanced reporting capabilities to help manage storage on your SBS server.) Additional backup and recovery details are covered in Chapter 13, "Backing Up and Restoring Data." But first, a word about file systems and why we care.

Under the Hood   NTFS

The underlying file system format for Windows Small Business Server is the Microsoft Windows NT File System, or NTFS. Originally introduced with the first version of Windows NT and essentially unchanged until Microsoft Windows 2000, NTFS was substantially enhanced for Windows 2000 and then again for Microsoft Windows Server 2003. While it is technically possible to use the old File Access Table (FAT or FAT32) file system for some of your storage with Windows Small Business Server 2003, by attaching or installing disks that have already been formatted with FAT, this is not supported. NTFS is the only supported file system and is necessary to support disk quotas, shadow copies, and encryption.

Disk Quotas

SBS uses *disk quotas* to limit the amount of disk space individual users can have for file storage on the server. By default, all non-administrative users are limited to the amount of disk space they are allowed to use on the drive that contains the Users shared folder. This is a good thing and allows the Windows Small Business Server administrator to take advantage of some of the special features of SBS such as My Documents Redirection (more on that in just a moment) without having to worry about any one user grabbing all the storage space on the server to store a bunch of home videos.

What happens when users reach the quota limit? As they get close, they will reach the warning level and be reminded that they're close to using up all their allocated space on the drive. If you've chosen to use *hard quotas*—that is, to deny disk space to users who exceed their limits—users will get an error message that their disks are full when they reach that limit. And for them, it is. Other users or groups of users who have not exceeded their quota will continue to be able to use the volume for storage, but any users who are over their quota will get a "disk full" message until they delete enough files to get below the limit. Note also that just like with any other disk operation, files in the Recycle Bin count just as much as regular files, so users not only have to delete files to get below the limit, but they also need to remove them from the Recycle Bin.

An alternative to the default hard quotas are *soft quotas*. These aren't really quotas at all—just warnings. A user subject to soft quotas can continue to store files on a drive until the entire drive is full, at which point no one can store any more files on the drive. The user will get some annoying messages about reaching his or her limits, but nothing will actually stop the user from storing more files on the drive. Generally, we think soft quotas don't make much sense—though you may need to use soft quotas for certain key personnel. Putting hard quotas on the CEO isn't usually something that you want to do, for example.

Enabling Disk Quotas

By default, disk quotas are turned off for all partitions and volumes except the volume that includes the Users shared folder. You must enable disk quotas for each additional volume on which you want a quota. Quotas are available only for volumes that are assigned a drive letter. You can set different quotas for individual users or for groups of users, or you can set them to be the same for all users. To enable quotas on each volume where you want them, complete the following steps:

1. Right-click the drive letter in Microsoft Windows Explorer and choose Properties.

2. Click the Quota tab, as shown in Figure 7-1.

3. Select the Enable Quota Management option.

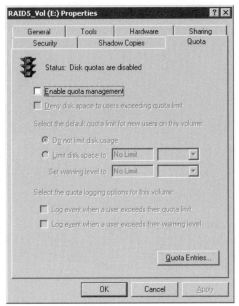

Figure 7-1   The Quota tab of the Properties window for a logical drive.

4. Define the limits on disk usage for this drive letter. The available choices are:

- ❑ **Deny Disk Space To Users Exceeding Quota Limit**   When this option is selected, the quotas are enforced for all disk usage. When it is cleared, the limits are advisory only—that is, soft quotas.

- ❑ **Limit Disk Space To**   Here you can specify the limits of disk space usage for new users on the volume.

- ❑ **Set Warning Level To**   This option indicates the limit at which users will receive a warning message.

- ❑ **Logging Options**   You can choose to log when users exceed their warning level or their usage limit, or you can leave these options blank when you don't want logging.

5. You see a confirmation message. If everything is correct, click OK to scan the drive and enable quotas.

Setting Quota Entries for Users

There's one catch with quotas that are enabled as described in the previous procedure: They apply only to users. Domain administrators slip by without having quotas enforced unless you explicitly set them in a separate quota entry. To set quotas for administrators, or to tweak the quotas for individual users, you need do some additional steps:

1. In Windows Explorer, right-click the drive you want to set quota entries for and choose Properties. Click the Quota tab to display the dialog box shown previously in Figure 7-1.

2. Click Quota Entries to display the quota entries for the volume. You see the window shown in Figure 7-2. This window contains entries for everyone who has ever stored files on the volume, unless you have explicitly removed the entries for users who no longer store files there.

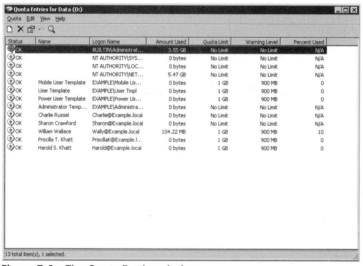

Figure 7-2 The Quota Entries window.

3. You can change the properties for any entry by double-clicking the entry, which displays the dialog box shown in Figure 7-3. The figure shows a user whose quota has been lowered so that he is now exceeding his disk space limit. He will be unable to store any additional data on the volume until he is below the limit.

The Quota Entries window lets you sort by any of the columns to make it easy to quickly identify problem areas or to locate an individual entry. You can also use the Find function to locate a specific entry.

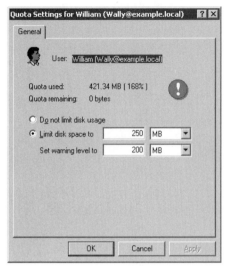

Figure 7-3   Quota settings and status for a user.

Under the Hood   Managing Quotas from the Command Line

Managing quotas from the GUI can be tiresome, especially if you're managing quotas separately for each user. Most quota tasks, however, can easily be automated using scripts and the command-line utility "fsutil.exe". The syntax for fsutil is:

```
fsutil quota [disable|enforce|query|track|violations] volume
      quota modify volume threshold limit [user]
```

So, for example, to enable quotas on the E: drive, and assign a warning threshold of 1 GB and a limit of 2 GB to user "wally@example.local" on that drive, you'd type the following at the command prompt:

```
fsutil quota enforce e:
fsutil quota modify e: 1073741824 2147483648 wally@example.local
```

Real World   Avoid Individual Quotas

Resist the temptation to fine-tune a disk's quotas for each individual. Giving in will lead to an administrative nightmare, especially because you then cannot manage quotas for the all-users audience, only for individual users. Make changes to the quotas for an individual only when there is a compelling reason to do so, and then keep careful records so that all administrators have ready access to the information. The one

> exception to this that we think makes sense is to add entries for any users who are also Domain Administrators. And you should have very few users who have that right. If you do enable quotas for any such users, make them soft quotas.

Exporting and Importing Quotas

If you have a complicated quota system set up so that some users get more space than others, implementing that system on a new volume can be a pain. But SBS lets you export the quotas from one volume to another – simply highlight the entry or entries and select Export from the Quota menu. If there isn't an entry for a user on the new volume yet, one will be created. If a user already has a quota entry, you're asked whether you want to over-write it with the imported quota entry for that user, as shown in Figure 7-4.

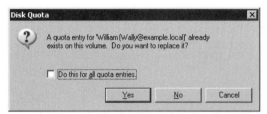

Figure 7-4   Confirmation message for overwriting a quota entry with an imported entry.

Avoid importing quota settings to an existing drive unless you're changing your overall quo-tas across the entire server. Any customizations you made on the current drive could be lost, and having to acknowledge each change that affects an existing user lends itself to mistakes. Or worse, you could check the Do This For All Quota Entries check box, now overwriting the current quota settings with no warning or confirmation at all. Finally, any special limits set for specific users on the source volume will be applied to the target volume.

There are two ways to import quotas from one volume to another. You can open the Quota Entries window for the source volume, highlight the entry or entries you want to export, click Quota and choose Export to save the entry to a file, and then open the Quota Entries window for the target volume and choose Import from the Quota menu.

Creating Quota Reports

You can use the Quota Entries window to create reports about disk usage. Select the accounts you want to include in the report and drag them into the reporting tool you'll be using. The supported formats include Rich Text Format, Comma Separated Value, CF_UNICODETEXT, and CF_TEXT. If you drag the entries into Microsoft Excel, for example, you get not only the entries but also the column headings. This makes whipping out a disk usage report pretty trivial.

Encrypting Files

Windows Small Business Server includes the ability to encrypt individual files or entire subdirectories in a totally transparent way. To their creator, encrypted files look exactly like regular files—they can be opened, read, modified, or deleted just like any other file. No changes to applications are required to use them. However, to anyone except the creator/encryptor, the files are unavailable, and even if someone did manage to gain access to them, the files would be gibberish because they're stored in encrypted form. In this section, we'll cover the basics of how to enable encryption on a folder or file.

> **More Info**   For more details about encryption, including how to share encrypted files and how to unencrypt files in the event an employee leaves, see Chapter 9, "Shares and Permissions."

Encryption is simply an advanced attribute of the file, just as compression is. However, a file cannot be both compressed and encrypted at the same time—the attributes are mutually exclusive. Encrypted files are available only to the encryptor or to those individuals who are explicitly granted access, but the files can be recovered by the domain recovery agent if necessary. Encrypted files can be backed up by normal Windows Small Business Server backup procedures, and the files remain encrypted. Restoring encrypted files retains their encryption.

By default, no user except the actual creator of an encrypted file has access to the file. Even a change of ownership does not remove the encryption. This prevents sensitive data, such as payroll and annual reviews, from being accessed by the wrong users, even if those users have administrative rights. The catch is that encryption is enabled for an individual user, not for a group of users, which limits its effectiveness. Although you can add individual users with the appropriate certificates to the list of users who can access a file, you can't add groups of users to the list. On our wish list for the Encrypting File System (EFS) is the ability to make the encryption transparent to either a group of users or any user with a specific key, smartcard, or other security identifier or combination of security identifiers.

> **Note**   Encryption is available only on NTFS and only on versions of NTFS beginning with Windows 2000. If the owner/encryptor of an encrypted file copies it to a disk or to another computer that doesn't support encryption, the encryption will be removed.

Enabling Encryption

When you encrypt a folder, all new files created in that folder are encrypted from that point forward. You can also elect to encrypt the current contents when you perform the encryption. Be warned, however: If you choose to encrypt the contents of a folder when it already contains files or subfolders, those files and subfolders are encrypted *for the user performing the encryption only*. This means that even files that are owned by another user are encrypted and are thus available for your use only—the owner of the files will no longer be able to access them. Of course, if you don't have the Modify privilege on the file owned by someone else, you won't be able to encrypt it.

When new files are created in an encrypted folder, the files are encrypted for use by the creator of the file, *not the user who first enabled encryption on the folder*. Unencrypted files in an encrypted folder can be used by all users who have security rights to use files in that folder, and the encryption status of the files does not change unless the file names themselves are changed. Users can read, modify, and save the files without converting them to encrypted files, but any changes in the name of the files triggers an encryption, and the encryption makes the files available only to the person who triggers the encryption.

To encrypt a file or folder, complete the following steps:

1. In Windows Explorer, right-click the folder or files you want to encrypt, and choose Properties from the shortcut menu.

2. Click Advanced on the General tab to open the Advanced Attributes dialog box shown in Figure 7-5.

Figure 7-5 The Advanced Attributes dialog box.

3. Select the Encrypt Contents To Secure Data option, and click OK to return to the main Properties window for the folder or file. Click OK or Apply to enable the

encryption. If any files or subfolders are already in the folder, you're presented with the dialog box shown in Figure 7-6.

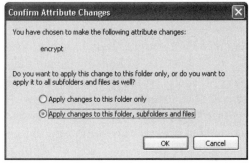

Figure 7-6   Choosing whether to encrypt the files already in a folder or just new files.

4.   If you choose Apply Changes To This Folder Only, all the current files and subfolders in the folder remain unencrypted, but any new files and folders are encrypted by the creator as they are created. If you choose Apply Changes To This Folder, Subfolders, And Files, all the files and folders below this folder are encrypted so that only you can use them, regardless of the original creator or owner of the file.

5.   Click OK and the encryption occurs.

Users can choose to have files that are encrypted appear in a different color in Windows Explorer. When they do, the file will appear in green text, as shown in Figure 7-7, for the file Encrypted.txt. Notice that even though all new files in this folder are encrypted, the files that were already in the folder have not been encrypted.

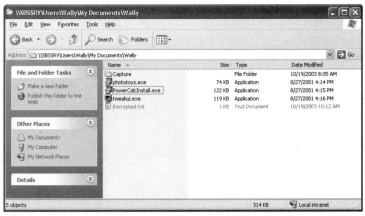

Figure 7-7   Encrypted file is shown in green.

Shadow Copies of Shared Folders

New to SBS 2003 is the ability to create shadow copies of shared folders. A *shadow copy* is a backup snapshot of the files in a shared folder. Snapshots are created automatically on a schedule you control, enabling easy fallback to older versions of a particular file in the event of corruption, deletion, or inadvertent and undesired changes. Considering that a file deletion from a network share would otherwise be both immediate and permanent, with no intervening Recycle Bin, shadow copies are highly recommended. But even when you're not dealing with the deletion of a file, shadow copies are a really useful tool. How many times have you inadvertently saved the wrong version of a file? With shadow copies, you can retrieve an earlier version and recover it quickly without having to restore from a backup tape. Best of all, users can directly recover earlier versions of files without having to involve an administrator at all.

Configuring Shadow Copies

Shadow copies provide a sort of "network Recycle Bin" by taking snapshots of shared folders at a set interval. This allows you to go back and look at earlier versions of files stored in network shares, even if the original files are modified or deleted. This also permits you to recover deleted or overwritten files, or compare modified files to earlier versions (up to 64 versions can be kept). You'll still need to perform regular backups, but shadow copies can be a great way to supplement your backup strategy.

Enabling Shadow Copies

Shadow copies are enabled by default on Windows Small Business Server on the volume that houses the Users shared folder, so you don't need to do anything at all to enable them. However, you do need to think about your overall strategy for shadow copies and how you want to use them. You should consider the total amount of storage you'll use for shadow copies, where the shadow copy storage will reside, how often automatic shadow copies will be made and how many versions you're going to keep.

If you want to enable shadow copies on other volumes, you will need to manually enable them, as described in this section.

Important If you're storing shadow copies on a different volume from the source files, you should make any disk changes to that volume before you enable it for storage. If you convert from a basic disk to a dynamic disk, you might lose the shadow copy data.

If the source volume is a dynamic disk, you can get around this problem by first taking the source volume offline, and then converting the volume storing the shadow copies to a dynamic disk and bringing the source volume back online. (This must be performed in fewer than 20 minutes to preserve the existing shadow copies.) But much better to configure all your disks first.

Important   If your backup device is a hard drive instead of a tape drive, do *not* enable shadow copies on the target drive.

To enable shadow copies, complete the following steps:

1. In Windows Explorer, right-click the volume on which you want to enable shadow copies and select Properties.

2. Click the Tools tab, and click the Defragment Now button to open the Disk Defragmenter tool and defragment the volume.

3. When defragmentation is done, return to the main volume Properties page and click the Shadow Copies tab.

4. Select a volume on which to enable shadow copies, as shown in Figure 7-8.

5. Click Settings.

6. If you're going to store your shadow copies on a separate volume, select the target volume from the Located On This Volume drop-down list.

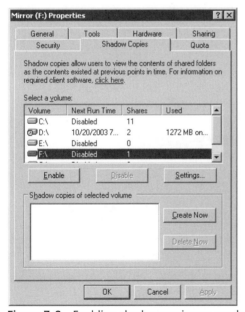

Figure 7-8   Enabling shadow copies on a volume.

7. Type in the maximum amount of storage to allocate in the Use Limit box, as shown in Figure 7-9.

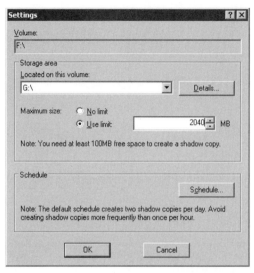

Figure 7-9   Setting storage location and limits for shadow copies.

8. Click Schedule and specify the schedule for shadow copy creation. The default is twice a day.

9. Click OK in the Settings dialog box to return to the Shadow Copies tab.

10. Click Enable to display the Enable Shadow Copies dialog box, shown in Figure 7-10. Even though it says that Windows will use the default settings, the settings you just made will actually be used.

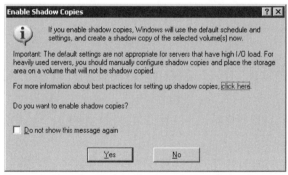

Figure 7-10   The Enable Shadow Copies dialog box.

11. Configure any additional volumes and click OK when you're finished.

Real World   Disk Defragmentation and Volume Shadow Copy

Running disk defragmentation software, including the disk defragmentation built into SBS, can cause the volume shadow copy service to think that the files are being changed on the drive, even though they're only being moved to defragment them. When this happens, the volume shadow copies can be lost on that volume, potentially creating problems for any users who need to recover a file or files. There are a couple of ways you can work around this issue, but they take some planning and forethought.

The first way to work around the problem is to format the drive in question using 16K or larger clusters. This allows the volume shadow copy to correctly recognize that a disk defragmentation program is running and act accordingly. Unfortunately, that solution could cause more wasted space on the drive, but we still think it's a good idea.

The second solution is to have your volume shadow copies stored on a separate drive that isn't subject to disk defragmentation. This is has a second advantage—if the second drive is on a physically separate hard disk, you'll distribute the I/O load on your disk subsystem and improve the overall efficiency of your disk access.

For more information on disk defragmentation and volume shadow copy, see Microsoft Knowledge Base article 312067 at: *http://support.microsoft.com/ default.aspx?scid=kb;en-us;312067.*

Setting Up Clients to Use Shadow Copies

To access stored shadow copies, clients need to have the Previous Versions Client software installed. The Previous Versions Client software is automatically installed on Windows 2000 (SP3 or later) and Microsoft Windows XP clients when you configure a new client computer in Windows Small Business Server. The software is located in the Client-Apps\ShadowCopy folder on the server. For Microsoft Windows 98 Second Edition and Windows Me, the client must be installed manually, as discussed in Chapter 11, "Managing Computers on the Network."

Accessing Shadow Copies

To access shadow copies from a client using the Previous Versions Client software, complete the following steps:

1. In Windows Explorer, right-click the network share and choose Properties from the shortcut menu.

2. Click the Previous Versions tab, shown in Figure 7-11.

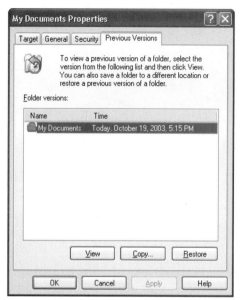

Figure 7-11   Accessing previous versions of a file.

Note   For the Previous Versions tab to show up, at least one shadow copy on the server must be created. To create a shadow copy on the server immediately, open the Properties dialog box for the volume, click the Shadow Copies tab, and click Create Now.

---

3. Select the folder version and then click the button corresponding to the action you want to perform:

   ❏ **View**   Opens the shadow copy in Windows Explorer. You can then open or copy the files just like in a normal folder (although you can't delete anything or save to these folders).

   ❏ **Copy**   Copies the shadow copy to the location you specify.

   ❏ **Restore**   Rolls back the shared folder to its state as of the snapshot image you selected.

Note   To access shadow copies from the server, connect to the shared folder using its UNC path (for example, \\sbssrv\Users\Wally) instead of using a local path.

Disabling Shadow Copies

To disable shadow copies on a volume, complete the following steps:

1. In Windows Explorer, right-click the volume you want to disable shadow copies on and select Properties.
2. Select the Shadow Copies tab.
3. Select the volume to disable and click Disable.
4. Click Yes to confirm that Windows will delete all previous shadow copies on the volume.

Important   Disabling shadow copies on a volume deletes all previously saved shadow copies (snapshots) for that volume.

Note   If you want to delete a volume on which shadow copies is enabled, first disable shadow copies for the volume. If you don't first disable shadow copies, the event log will fill up with errors.

Under the Hood   Volume Shadow Copy Command Line

To administer shadow copies from a command line, use the Vssadmin command:

```
vssadmin [Add ShadowStorage] [Create Shadow] [Delete Shadows] [Delete
ShadowStorage] [List Providers] [List Shadows] [List ShadowStorage]
[List Volumes] [List Writers] [Resize ShadowStorage]
```

The available parameters for Vssadmin are:

- **Add ShadowStorage**   Specifies on which volume shadow copies should be stored for the specified source volume
- **Create Shadow**   Manually creates a shadow copy
- **Delete Shadows**   Deletes all shadow copies for the specified source volume
- **Delete ShadowStorage**   Deletes the association between a source volume and the volume on which the shadow copies are stored
- **List Providers**   Displays the installed shadow copy providers (Windows Server 2003 ships with only one.)
- **List Shadows**   Displays the complete list of stored shadow copies
- **List ShadowStorage**   Displays all associations between source volumes and the volumes on which shadow copies are stored
- **List Volumes**   Displays all volumes on which shadow copies can be enabled

- **List Writers**   Displays a list of all applications that make use of shadow copies
- **Resize ShadowStorage**   Changes the maximum size allocated to storing shadow copies

For additional help with individual parameters, type:

vssadmin <parameter> /?

Summary

In this chapter, we covered the features of Windows Small Business Server 2003 that give it a flexible, robust, and recoverable storage system. With a pure NTFS file system as a requirement, Windows Small Business Server uses volume shadow copies, disk quotas, and file and folder encryption—the tools for handling the storage needs of your business.

In the next chapter, we'll cover users, groups, and managing the security and accounts of your Windows Small Business Server.

Chapter 8
Managing Users and Groups

Understanding Groups 147

Managing Built-in Groups 149

Creating Security Groups 153

Creating Distribution Groups. 154

Understanding User Accounts 155

Managing User Templates 162

Managing User Accounts 164

Maintaining User Profiles 167

Using the Run As Command 172

Summary 174

The whole purpose behind a network is to provide users with everything they need and clear away the clutter that hampers their progress. What they need includes *reliable* access to the files, folders, applications, printers, and Internet connections required to do their jobs. What they don't need is any trouble getting at what they *do* need.

The person in charge of the network has his or her own needs, such as shielding need-to-know material from those who don't need to know and protecting the users from themselves. The key to all these needs is the configuration of groups and users—the topic of this chapter.

More Info See Chapter 17, "Using Group Policy," for information about Group Policy.

Understanding Groups

By definition, Microsoft Windows Small Business Server groups are Active Directory directory service or local computer objects that can contain users, contacts, computers, or other groups. In practice, though, a *group* is usually a collection of user accounts. The point of groups is to simplify administration by allowing the network administrator to assign rights and permissions to groups rather than to individual users.

SBS allows two group types: security and distribution. Almost all groups are *security groups* because they're the only groups through which permissions can be assigned. Each security group is also assigned a *group scope*, which defines how permissions are assigned to the group's members. Programs that can search Active Directory can also use security groups for nonsecurity purposes, such as sending e-mail to a group of users. *Distribution groups,* on the other hand, are not security-enabled and can be used *only* with e-mail applications to send e-mail to sets of users.

User rights are assigned to security groups to establish what members of the group can or cannot do. Some rights are automatically assigned to some groups—for example, a user who is a member of the Print Operators group has the ability to administer the printers in the domain.

Note   Permissions and user rights are different. Permissions determine what resources members of a group can access. User rights determine what members of a group can or cannot do. See the Under the Hood sidebar "Rights and Permissions" later in this chapter for additional information.

Real World   Why Use Groups at All?

Groups are an effective way of simplifying administration. If you have only a handful of users, it's possible to manage permissions for each user manually, though we certainly wouldn't want to do it. And with SBS, you'd have nothing but problems trying to make sure you got everything right, since SBS controls access to many features based on group membership. You can easily use SBS without changing any of the default groups or adding to them at all. Just use the built-in templates to add users and you'll end up with the correct permissions and rights.

The real strength of groups is that when you change the rights of the group, you change them for everyone in the group, without having to do anything else. This makes it easy to update the rights of users on your network without having to go in and change every single account. For example, when you have a number of people who travel or telecommute, you don't need to keep track of which users have the right to log on remotely if you add them all to the Mobile Users group. If you need to ensure that all mobile users have access to a special share or automatically get a set of programs installed, you only have to make the changes for the Mobile Users group. Everyone who is a member of the group sees the change.

Assigning Group Scopes

When a group is created, it is assigned a group scope that in turn defines how permissions are assigned. There are three possible group scopes: global, domain local, and universal.

Global Scope

A group with a global scope is actually a bit of an anomaly in an SBS domain, since it is designed to provide global scope across multiple domains, something that SBS doesn't support. Global groups can be members of universal and domain local groups, and they can have the following members:

■ Other global groups

■ Individual accounts

Domain Local Scope

A domain local group controls access to specific local resources, and can have one or more of the following members:

■ Other domain local groups

■ Global groups

■ Universal groups

■ Individual accounts

Universal Scope

A universal security group is another concept that is a bit awkward in the single-domain environment of SBS. Universal groups can have the following members:

■ Other universal groups

■ Global groups

■ Individual accounts

Managing Built-in Groups

Because Microsoft Windows Server 2003 is the underlying operating system for SBS 2003, all the built-in security groups integral to Windows Server 2003 still exist. However, many of these groups are focused on a much larger, multidomain network, so the designers of Windows Small Business Server created a subset of organizational units to simplify administration.

To view a list of groups (Figure 8-1), select Server Management from the Start menu and then click Security Groups in the console tree.

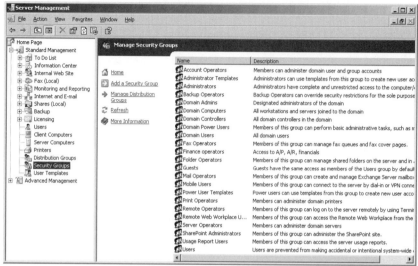

Figure 8-1   The security groups built in to Windows Small Business Server.

> **Note**   Some built-in groups, such as DHCP Administrators and DHCP Users, are listed only in Active Directory Users and Computers.

Built-in Universal Groups

All the built-in universal groups listed in Table 8-1 are specific to Windows Small Business Server. With few exceptions, these are the groups that all users belong to and that are used to make templates. Templates are discussed in more detail later in the chapter.

Table 8-1   Universal groups in Windows Small Business Server

Universal Group	Description
Administrator Templates	Members of this group are the templates that an Administrator can use to create new user accounts. The built-in user templates are default members.
Domain Power Users	Members can create and modify user accounts and install programs on the local computer but cannot view other users' files. This group is a default member of Fax Operators, Folder Operators, Mail Operators, Remote Operators, and SharePoint Administrators—all other built-in universal groups. Domain Power Users is also a member of Account Operators and Print Operators, which are built-in local groups.

Table 8-1   Universal groups in Windows Small Business Server (Continued)

Universal Group	Description
Fax Operators	Members of this group can manage fax cover pages and queues. The Domain Power Users group is a member by default.
Folder Operators	Members can manage shared folders in the domain. The Domain Power Users group is a member by default.
Mail Operators	Members can create and manage Microsoft Exchange Server mailboxes. The Domain Power Users group is a member by default.
Mobile Users	Members can connect to the server remotely. Default members are the Administrator account, Administrator Template, Mobile User Template, and Power User Template.
Power User Templates	Members of this group are the templates that power users utilize to create new user accounts. Default members are the built-in Mobile User Template and the User Template.
Remote Operators	Members can log on to the server remotely but not locally. The Domain Power Users group is a member by default.
Remote Web Workplace Users	Members can access the Remote Web Workplace from the Internet. The built-in templates are default members.
SharePoint Administra-tors	Members can administer the Microsoft SharePoint Web site. Default members are the Domain Power Users group and the STS Worker account (used by the Windows Small Business Server to route faxes).
Usage Report Users	Members can view server usage reports. The Domain Admins group is a member by default.

Built-in Local Groups

Built-in local groups are created when Windows Small Business Server is installed. These groups can't be members of other groups and their group scope can't be changed. Table 8-2 shows the built-in local groups.

Table 8-2   Built-in local groups in Windows Small Business Server

Group	Description
Account Operators	Members can add, change, or delete user and group accounts. The Domain Power Users group is a member of this group.
Administrators	Members can perform all administrative tasks on the computer. The built-in Administrator account that is created when the operating system is installed is a member of the group. When a member server or a client running Microsoft Windows XP Professional or Microsoft Windows 2000 Professional joins a domain, the Domain Admins group (see Table 8-4) is made part of this group.

Table 8-2   Built-in local groups in Windows Small Business Server (Continued)

Group	Description
Backup Operators	Members can log on to the computer, back up and restore the computer's data, and shut down the computer. Members cannot change security settings but can override them for purposes of backup and restore.
Guests	Members have the same access as members of the Users group. The Guest account has fewer rights and is a default member of this group.
Print Operators	Members can manage printers and print queues on domain printers. The Domain Power Users group is an automatic member.
Server Operators	Members can administer servers. No default members.
Users	Members of this group can log on to the computer, access the network, save documents, and shut down the computer. Members cannot install programs or make system changes. When a member server, Windows 2000 Professional, or Windows XP Professional machine joins a domain, the Domain Users group is added to this group.

If you don't want members of the Domain Users group to have access to a particular workstation or member server, remove Domain Users from that computer's local Users group. Similarly, if you don't want the members of Domain Admins to administer a particular workstation or member server, remove Domain Admins from the local Administrators group.

Built-in Domain Local Groups

The built-in domain local groups provide users with rights and permissions to perform tasks on domain controllers and in Active Directory. The domain local groups have predefined rights and permissions that are granted to users and global groups that you add as members. Table 8-3 shows the commonly used built-in domain local groups used in Windows Small Business Server.

Table 8-3   Domain local groups used in Windows Small Business Server 2003

Domain Local Group	Description
DHCP Users (installed with DHCP Server service)	Members of this group can read DHCP information stored on a specific server for troubleshooting purposes. No default members.
DHCP Administrators	Members of this group can administer DHCP Server service but do not have access to other parts of the server.

Security Alert   On Microsoft Windows NT Server networks, all domain users, in addition to any anonymous or guest users, were members of the Everyone group. This group was controlled by the operating system and appeared on any network with Windows NT servers. In Windows Small Business Server 2003, all domain users are members of the Authenticated Users group. Unlike the Windows NT Everyone group, Authenticated Users contains no anonymous users or guests. The Everyone group survives as a *special identity, but one that no longer includes anonymous or guest users*. You don't see it when you administer groups, and it cannot be placed in a group. When a user logs on to the network, the user is automatically added to Everyone. You can't see or change the membership of the special identities, which also includes the Network and Interactive groups.

Built-in Global Groups

Built-in global groups are created to encompass common types of accounts. By default, these groups do not have inherent rights; an administrator must assign all rights to the group. However, some members are added to these groups automatically, and you can add more members based on the rights and permissions you assign to the groups. Rights can be assigned directly to the groups or by adding the built-in global groups to domain local groups. Table 8-4 describes the built-in global groups that are commonly used.

Table 8-4 Commonly used built-in global groups

Global Group	Description
Domain Admins	This group is automatically a member of the built-in local Administrators group, so members of Domain Admins can perform administrative tasks on any computer in the domain. The Administrator account is a member of this group by default.
Domain Computers	All servers and workstations in the domain are members.
Domain Controllers	The Windows Small Business Server.
Domain Users	All domain users are members. The Domain Users group is automatically a member of the built-in local Users group.

Creating Security Groups

The security groups built in to Windows Small Business Server 2003 are sufficient for most operations. Changing the options for the built-in templates can cover a lot of variation among companies. One conspicuous lack is a security group granting access to personnel and financial information. Every company has confidential information that must be accessed by only a limited number of people. To handle needs of this type, create a new security group by following these steps:

1. Select Server Management from the Start menu. Click Security Groups and then click Add A Security Group to launch the Add Security Group Wizard.

2. On the Security Group Information page, provide a name and description for the group.

3. On the Group Membership page, select members. You can add individual users or another security group. You can also make a template (see "Managing User Templates" later in this chapter) to create user accounts specific to the new group.

4. On the final page of the wizard, the settings are summarized. Click the link at the bottom of the page to save the summary.

Creating Distribution Groups

Distribution groups are mechanisms for managing the delivery of information. They have no security implications, and are not restricted to members of the domain. SBS creates a default distribution group that includes all users of the network. Messages sent to the distribution group's e-mail address go to all members of the group. You can create additional distribution groups for subsets of your users, or even for external addresses that you add as Contacts in Exchange.

To create a distribution group, complete the following steps:

1. Launch Server Management from the Start Menu. Click Distribution Groups in the console tree and then click Add A Distribution Group to launch the Add Distribution Group Wizard.

2. On the Distribution Group Information page, provide a name, description, and e-mail alias for the distribution group. (See Chapter 14, "Using Exchange Server," for more information about creating e-mail aliases.)

3. On the Group Membership page, select members.

4. On the Group Manager page, you can specify a group manager from the distribution group. The group manager can change the membership of the group using Microsoft Office Outlook 2003.

    On the Group Options page, select the group options to enable (Figure 8-2).

    a. **Create A Public Folder To Archive E-Mail Messages Sent To This Group.** Depending on the nature of the distribution group, you might want all messages sent to the group saved in an Exchange public folder. Select this option and a public folder named Distribution_Group_Name Archive will be added as a member of this group.

    b. **Enable This Group To Receive E-Mail Messages From Users Outside Of Your Network.** Select this option when part of this distribution group's role is communicating with people outside the network. If the group is strictly internal, clear this check box.

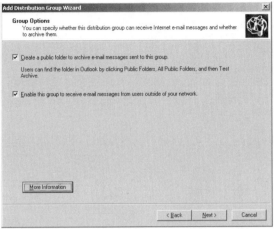

Figure 8-2 Selecting options for a new distribution group.

5. On the final page of the wizard, the settings are summarized. Click the link at the bottom of the page to save the summary.

Understanding User Accounts

Gaining access to the network requires a domain user account, which authenticates the identity of the person making the connection and controls what resources a user has a right to access.

Windows Small Business Server 2003 creates two predefined accounts: the Administrator account, which is granted all rights and permissions, and the Guest account, which has limited rights and is disabled by default. All other accounts are created by an administrator and are either domain accounts (valid throughout the domain by default) or local accounts (usable only on the computer on which they are created).

Creating User Accounts

Adding user accounts could scarcely be easier than it is in SBS. Using the templates provided or templates of your own devising, you can add all users at once, in bunches, or one at a time.

Under the Hood   Naming User Accounts

In Active Directory, each user account has a *principal name*. This name consists of two parts, the *security principal name* and the *principal name suffix*. For Windows Small Business Server user accounts, the administrator assigns the security principal name. The principal name suffix is the DNS name of the root domain in the domain tree. So, for example, Active Directory sees CharlieR@example.local as the user's principal name. The security principal name is CharlieR and the principal name suffix is example.local.

Assign the security principal name using a consistent naming convention so that you and your users can remember user names and find them in lists. The Add User Wizard proposes the following conventions:

- Entire name without spaces
- Last name followed by first name
- First initial plus last name
- First name plus last initial

You can overrule the wizard and type in your own choice for a logon and e-mail name. In a smaller organization, there's no need for long names. Users type their logon names and e-mail addresses every day. The simpler you can make it, the happier everyone will be. (Save the complexity for passwords.)

Adding a Single User

To add a user account to the network, complete the following steps:

1. Select Server Management from the Start menu, click Users in the console tree, and click Add A User to launch the Add User Wizard.

2. On the User Account Information page, add the user information. As you type in the user's name, the Add User Wizard automatically proposes a corresponding logon name and e-mail alias. Logon name variations are available in the drop-down list (Figure 8-3).

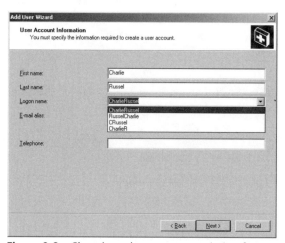

Figure 8-3 Choosing a logon name variation for a user account.

3. On the User Password page, provide a password. This is a temporary password that the user will be required to change when logging on for the first time and at whatever intervals you've specified in password policies.

4. On the Template Selection page, choose a template to define user rights. (For more information about templates, see "Managing User Templates" later in this chapter.) Select the check box to display the template's default settings.

> **Note**   Use templates whenever possible. Without a template, you must configure all the user's groups and other rights manually. It's very easy to slip up while doing this and create problems that are very difficult to trace. Templates provide a consistent and uniform assignment of rights and privileges appropriate to each type of user.

5. On the Security Groups page, the default group memberships assigned by the template (in this case, the Mobile User template) are listed (Figure 8-4). As shown, these memberships allow the user to log on to the domain locally, log on to the domain from a remote location, and use the Remote Web Workplace. Add other group memberships if they are required.

Security Alert   The default templates do not include Domain Admins membership except for the Administrator Template. Don't add Domain Admins membership to any additional templates, even for users who need to be Administrators on their local machine. Instead, change the memberships on that local machine only. This way, even if the user's account is compromised, you've restricted the damage.

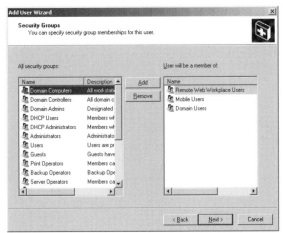

Figure 8-4   Mobile users are members of three groups by default.

6. On the Distribution Groups page, you can make the user a member of any other distribution groups that you've created. All users are members of the default distribution group. (See "Creating Distribution Groups," earlier in this chapter.)

7. On the SharePoint Access page, specify the user's roles on your SharePoint site.

8. On the Address Information page, supply address information.

9. On the Disk Quotas page, set a limit of hard drive space that the user can fill on the SBS server. (See Chapter 7, "Storage Management," for more about the pros and cons of disk quotas.)

10. On the Set Up Client Computer page, specify whether to set up a client computer for the user. The wizard creates a computer account with the user's name plus a number—though you can type in a different name. (If you choose not to set up a computer, the configuration of the user account is summarized and the wizard is complete.)

11. On the Client Applications page, select the applications you want installed on the client computer. (See Chapter 11, "Managing Computers on the Network," for details about assigning applications to client computers.)

12. On the Mobile Client And Offline Use page, shown in Figure 8-5, select the options to install on this client. If the client computer is going to travel, install Connection Manager so that the user can connect to the Windows Small Business Server remotely. Install Microsoft ActiveSync to allow devices such as Windows Mobile Pocket PC Phone Edition to synchronize with the client computer and with SBS.

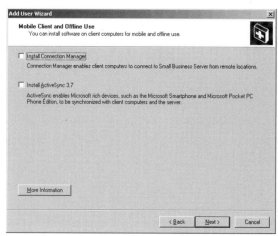

Figure 8-5 Options for mobile clients.

13. The final page of the Add User Wizard summarizes all your settings. Click the link at the bottom of the page to save the information.

Adding Multiple Users

The ability to add several user accounts at once is a new and highly helpful feature in Windows Small Business Server 2003. The process works much like adding a single user. To add multiple user accounts, complete the following steps:

1. Select Server Management from the Start menu, click Users in the console tree, and click Add Multiple Users to launch the Add User Wizard.

2. On the Template Selection page, choose a template that will define the users' rights. (For more information about templates, see "Managing User Templates" later in this chapter.)

3. On the User Information page, click the Add button. Specify the first user's information. As you type in the user's name, the Add User Wizard automatically proposes a corresponding logon name and e-mail alias. Logon name variations are available in the drop-down list. Click OK after each user. When the User Information page is complete (Figure 8-6), click Next.

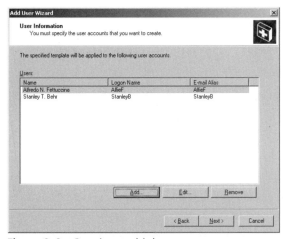

Figure 8-6   Creating multiple user accounts.

4. On the Set Up Client Computers page, if you want to set up client computers for these users, select the Set Up Computers Now option, specify computer names on the Client Computer Names page, and follow Steps 11 through 13 in the preceding section, "Adding a Single User."

Configuring Password Policy

Passwords are a critical line of defense in the security wars. Passwords must be sufficiently complex and changed often. SBS will prompt you at several points in the configuration and initial setup of SBS to enable Password Policies, including every time you run the CEICW. If you haven't set Password Policies yet, open Server Management from the Start menu, click Users in the console tree, and then click Configure Password Policies to open the Configure Password Policies dialog box (Figure 8-7).

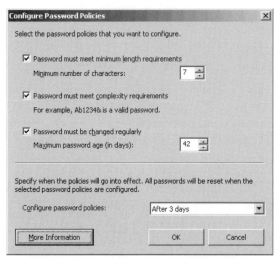

Figure 8-7   Setting password requirements.

Set the minimum password length (at least seven characters). Select the second check box to require that the password be of sufficient complexity—that is, it meets three of the following four conditions:

- It includes at least one capital letter.
- It includes at least one lowercase letter.
- It includes at least one numeral.
- It includes at least one nonalphanumeric character (such as +, *, ^, $, and @).

Select the third check box to set the number of days that a password can be used before the system requires a change. The default setting is 42 days. Resist the temptation to make the number smaller. If users are required to change passwords too often, it won't be long before passwords start appearing on sticky notes in desk drawers or attached to monitors.

At the bottom of the dialog box, specify when these password policies go into effect. If your Windows Small Business Server is new, postpone activating strong passwords until after you configure the clients but before users log on for the first time.

Under the Hood   Rules for Good Passwords

A good password has the following characteristics:

- It is not a rotation of the characters in a logon name.

- It contains at least two alphabetic characters and one nonalphabetic character.

- It is at least seven characters long.

- It isn't the user's name or initials, the initials of his or her children or significant other, or any of these items combined with other commonly available personal data such as a birth date, telephone number, or license plate number.

- It isn't the name of a pet or a favorite sport, drink, television show, or any other personal term that could be easily guessed.

Among the best passwords are alphanumeric acronyms of phrases that have a meaning to the user but are not likely to be known to others. This makes the password easy for the user to remember while at the same time making it hard for an outsider to guess. For example, you could use a catch phrase such as "too good to be true" and change it into the password *Twogood2bTru*. Or "forever and a day" could be transformed into the password *4ever+24*. It just takes a little imagination.

Another good password strategy is a *passphrase*—from several words to an entire sentence, including punctuation, spaces, numbers, and letters. Something like "The price of a latté is up to $3.95!" Passphrases have the advantage of being considerably longer and yet easy to remember.

Security Alert   It pays to educate your users about passwords and password privacy, but most of all, it pays to heed your own advice: Make sure the password you select for administration is a strong password, and change it frequently. Doing so will help you avoid the consequences of having somebody break into your system and wreak havoc in your own kingdom.

Administrators should have two accounts on the system: one administrative account and one normal user account. Use the normal user account unless you are performing administrative tasks. Because administrative accounts have virtually unlimited privileges, they are a prime target for intruders.

The actual Administrator account is an especially tempting target for attack and should not be used remotely, nor for any day to day administration. Make sure you give it a long, strong, and complex password, and use it *only* for tasks that can't be run from another account.

Managing User Templates

User rights, privileges, permissions, and shares are some of the mechanisms that make Windows Server 2003 quite daunting to many. Windows Small Business Server can shield you from these details with user templates. When you create or modify user accounts, you can apply templates to the accounts. By using templates, many of the account properties and permissions will already be specified, making account management easier.

Creating a New User Template

Most organizations can use the supplied user templates with or without modification. However, it's a simple matter to make your own templates when you follow these steps:

1. Select Server Management from the Start Menu. Click User Templates in the console tree and then Add A Template to launch the Add Template Wizard.

2. On the Template Account Information page, provide a name for the template and specify whether it is to be the default template for the Add User Wizard and whether power users will be able to use it.

3. On the Security Groups page, select the security group memberships for user accounts created with this template.

4. On the Distribution Groups page, select the distribution groups for user accounts created with this template.

5. On the SharePoint Access page, specify the roles that user accounts created with this template will have on your SharePoint site.

6. On the Address Information page, type in address information that will be applied to all the users created with this template. When address information will be different for different user accounts, leave the fields empty and click Next.

7. On the Disk Quotas page, specify disk quotas if they are to be applied to the user accounts.

8. On the final page of the wizard, the settings you made for this template are summarized. Click the link at the bottom of the page to print, save, or e-mail the summary.

Applying a Template to Existing Users

When you create a new template, modify an existing one, or just want to make changes to users' permissions, you can apply a template to one or more user accounts by completing these steps:

1. Select Server Management from the Start menu then click Users in the console tree. Click Change User Permissions to launch the Change User Permissions Wizard.

2. On the Template Selection page, select the template to apply, as shown in Figure 8-8.

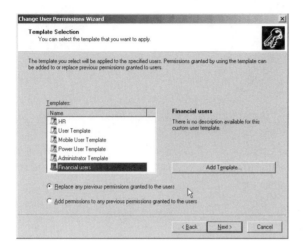

Figure 8-8   Choosing a template to apply to existing user accounts.

3. Select the option to replace existing permissions or to add this template's permissions to the existing ones.

4. On the User Selection page, select the users to whom this template will apply. (Note that you can use this template to change other templates.)

5. The final page of the Change User Permissions Wizard displays a summary of the operations the wizard will complete. Click the link at the bottom of the page to select a method of saving this information.

Important   Previous group memberships will be replaced by group memberships in the new template. But explicit permissions previously granted directly to a user account remain unchanged after applying the template. Yet another reason to use group memberships to apply permissions and rights.

Under the Hood   Rights and Permissions

What users can and cannot do depends on the rights and permissions that have been granted to them. *Rights* generally apply to the system as a whole. The ability to back up files or to log on to a server, for example, is a right that the administrator can assign or remove. Rights can be assigned individually, but most often they are characteristics of groups, and a user is assigned to a particular group on the basis of the rights that the user needs.

Permissions indicate the access that a user (or group) has to specific objects such as files, directories, and printers. For example, a user's ability to read a particular directory or access a network printer is a permission.

Rights, in turn, are divided into two types: privileges and logon rights. *Privileges* include such things as the ability to run security audits or force shutdown from a remote system—obviously not things that are handled by most users. *Logon rights* are self-explanatory: They involve the ability to connect to a computer in specific ways. Rights are automatically assigned to the built-in groups in Windows Small Business Server, although they can be assigned to individual users as well as groups. Assignment by group is preferred, so whenever possible, you should assign rights by group membership to keep administration simple. When membership in groups defines rights, rights can be removed from a user by simply removing the user from the group.

Managing User Accounts

Disabling, enabling, deleting, and renaming user accounts are tasks easily done from the Manage Users taskpad. Launch Server Management and click Users in the console tree. Select a user account to expand the options, as shown in Figure 8-9.

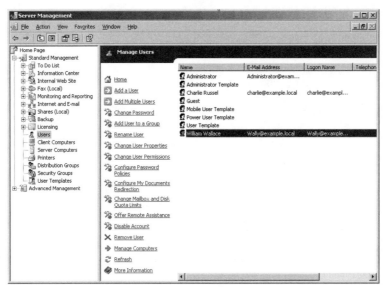

Figure 8-9   Using the Manage Users taskpad to make changes to user accounts.

Click the task you want to perform. Most of these are completely self-explanatory but a few require more explanation.

For documents to be safest, they should be stored on the Windows Small Business Server, but users are not always conscientious about storing important files on the server rather than on the local hard drive.

Redirecting My Documents to the Default Server Folder

Windows Server 2003 has the capacity to redirect users' folders by applying Group Policy. SBS leverages this feature to give you a single setting that implements the redirection of each user's My Documents folder to the server.

Note   Redirecting all My Documents folders to the server will take up a lot of disk space. Make sure you have sufficient room. The partition on which the Users Shared Folder is created has default disk quotas of 1 GB per new user.

To redirect all My Documents folders, complete the following steps:

1. Select Server Management from the Start menu and click Users. Click Configure My Documents Redirection. The Client Document Redirection dialog box appears.

2. Select the option to Redirect All My Documents Folders To The Default Shared Folder For Users On The Small Business Server. This option will automatically send all the documents saved to users' My Documents folders to Users Shared Folder, a built-in shared folder on the server.

3. Click OK.

A copy of the My Documents folder remains on the user's computer. When a user logs on or logs off the network, the copy on the client computer synchronizes with the copy on the server. This can be a problem on slower wireless networks. If your users are primarily connected wirelessly, you might find it better to not redirect folders.

Redirecting My Documents to a Network Folder

Although redirecting the My Documents folder to the default server folder is the simplest approach, you might want to use a shared folder at a different location. This requires setting several types of permissions on the shared folder to be sure that the user's My Documents folder is accessible to the user but not to the world at large. To redirect all users' My Documents folder to a network folder, complete the following steps:

1. In Windows Explorer, create the folder you want to use and give it a descriptive name.

2. Right-click the folder and select Sharing And Security from the shortcut menu. The Properties dialog box appears.

3. On the Sharing tab, select Share This Folder, and then click the Permissions button.

4. Click the Add button and add the groups Domain Users, Domain Admins, and Folder Operators. Assign all three groups Full Control. (Remove the Everyone group.) Click OK.

5. On the Security tab, click the Advanced button, and then clear the check box for Allow Inheritable Permissions. A security prompt appears asking how to assign permissions. Click Remove.

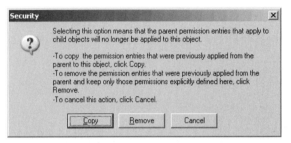

6. Click the Add button and add the Creator Owner group. In the Permission Entry dialog box, select This Folder Only from the Apply Onto drop-down list. Then select the options to allow List Folder/Read Data, Read Attributes, and Create Folders/Append Data. Click OK.

7. Repeat Step 6, adding Domain Admins, Folder Operators, and SYSTEM. When finished, close the open dialog boxes.

8. Launch System Management and click Users in the console tree. Click Configure My Documents Redirection. The Client Document Redirection dialog box appears.

9. Select the option to redirect to a network folder, and type in or browse to the network folder you created (Figure 8-10). Click OK.

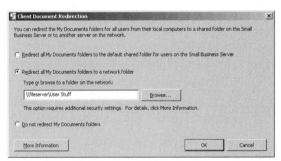

Figure 8-10   Redirecting the My Documents folder to a shared folder on the network.

When completed, all the My Documents folders are redirected to the new folder. Admittedly, this is a tedious process, but fortunately it has to be done only once.

Note   To stop redirecting folders, select Server Management from the Start menu and click Users. Click Configure My Documents Redirection and select the option Do Not Redirect My Documents Folders.

Note   In addition to My Documents, other special folders are Application Data, Desktop, and Start Menu on Windows 2000 or later systems. These folders can also be redirected either to a single location or to locations based on group membership. To configure this form of redirection, see "Redirecting Special Folders Using Group Policy" in Chapter 9, "Shares and Permissions."

Maintaining User Profiles

A *profile* is an environment specifically customized for a user. The profile contains the desktop and program settings for the user. Every user has a profile, whether the administrator configures one or not, because a default profile is automatically created for each user who logs on to a computer. Profiles offer a number of advantages:

- Multiple users can use the same computer, with the settings for each user restored at logon time to the same state as when he or she logged off.

- Desktop changes made by one user do not affect any other user.

- If user profiles are stored on a server, they can follow users to any computer on the network running Windows Server 2003, Windows XP Professional, or Windows 2000.

Administrators can also set up *mandatory* profiles that allow a user to make changes to the desktop while logged on but not to save any of the changes. A mandatory profile always looks exactly the same every time a user logs on. There are three types of profiles:

- **Local profiles**   Profiles created on a computer when a user logs on. The profile is specific to a user, local to that computer, and stored on the local computer's hard disk.

- **Roaming profiles**   Profiles created by an administrator and stored on a server. These profiles follow a user to any computer on the network running Windows Server 2003, Windows XP Professional, or Windows 2000.

- **Mandatory profiles**   Roaming profiles that can be changed only by an administrator.

Real World   What's Stored in a Profile?

All profiles start out as a copy of the Default User profile that is installed on every computer running Windows Server 2003, Windows XP Professional, and Windows 2000. Registry data for Default User is in the Ntuser.dat file contained in the Default User profile. Profiles contain some or all of the following folders:

- **Application Data**   Program-specific settings determined by the program manufacturer plus specific user security settings

- **Cookies**   Messages sent to a Web browser by a Web server and stored locally to track user information and preferences

- **Desktop**   Desktop files, folders, shortcuts, and the desktop appearance

- **Favorites**   Shortcuts to favorite locations, particularly Web sites

- **Local Settings**   Application data, History, and Temporary files

- **My Documents**   User documents and My Pictures, which contains user graphics files

- **NetHood**   Shortcuts to My Network Places

- **PrintHood**   Shortcuts to items in the Printers folder

- **My Recent Documents**   Shortcuts to the most recently accessed folders and files

- **SendTo**   Items on the Send To menu

- **Start Menu**   Items on the user's Start menu

- **Templates**   Application templates

By default, only the Cookies, Desktop, Favorites, My Documents, and Start Menu folders are visible in Microsoft Windows Explorer. The other folders are hidden; to see them in Windows Explorer - from the Tools menu, click Folder Options, View tab, and then select Show Hidden Files And Folders.

Local Profiles

Local profiles are created on computers when individual users log on. On a computer with a new installation of Windows Server 2003, Windows XP Professional, or Windows 2000, the user profile is in the Documents And Settings folder.

The first time a user logs on to a computer, a profile folder is generated for the user, and the contents of the Default User folder are copied into it. Any changes made to the desktop by the user are saved in that user's profile when he or she logs off.

If a user has a local account on the computer as well as a domain account and logs on at different times using both accounts, the user will have two profile folders on the local computer: one for when the user logs on to the domain using the domain user account, and one for when the user logs on locally to the computer. The local profile is shown with the logon name. The domain profile is also shown with the logon name but has the domain name appended to it.

Roaming Profiles

Roaming profiles are a great advantage for users who frequently use more than one computer. A *roaming profile* is stored on a server and, after the user's logon attempt is authenticated in the directory service, is copied to the local computer. This allows a user to have the same desktop, application configuration, and local settings at any machine running Windows Server 2003, Windows XP Professional, or Windows 2000.

Here's how it works. You assign a location on a server for user profiles and create a folder shared with users who are to have roaming profiles. You type a path to that folder on the Profile page of the user's account properties. The next time the user logs on to a computer, the profile from the server is downloaded to the local computer. When the user logs off, the profile is saved both locally and in the user profile path location. Specifying the user profile path is all it takes to turn a local profile into a roaming profile, available anywhere in the domain.

When the user logs on again, the profile on the server is compared to the copy on the local computer, and the more recent copy is loaded for the user. If the server isn't available, the local copy is used. If the server isn't available and this is the first time the user has logged on to the computer, a user profile is created locally using the Default User profile. When a profile isn't downloaded to a local computer because of server problems, the roaming profile is not updated when the user logs off.

Setting Up Roaming Profiles

To set up a roaming profile, you assign a location on a server and complete the following steps:

1. In Windows Explorer, create a shared folder for the profiles on the server.

2. In Server Management, open the Properties dialog box for a user account.

3. On the Profile tab, provide a path to the shared folder, such as **\\SBS_server_name \shared_profile_folder**%*username*%.

Figure 8-11 shows an example of a path for a roaming profile. When you use the variable %*username*%, the operating system automatically replaces the variable with the user account name.

After you create a shared profile folder on a server and supply a profile path in the user account, a roaming profile is enabled. The user's configuration of his or her desktop is copied and stored on the server and is available to the user from any computer. Most of the time, though, you don't want to send off your users to fend for themselves. Life is easier for users, and for you, when they are assigned a customized profile that is already set up with appropriate shortcuts, network connections, and Start menu items. For this, you need to set up customized profiles.

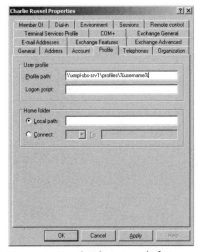

Figure 8-11   Setting a path for a roaming profile.

Creating Customized Roaming Profiles
Creating customized roaming profiles is a simple—albeit multistep—process:

1. Create a user account that will be used to develop the roaming profile. This is a "dummy" account that will be used just for this purpose.

2. Log on to the server using the dummy account and create the desktop settings you want, including applications, shortcuts, appearance, network connections, and printers.

3. Log off the account. Windows Small Business Server creates a user profile on the system root drive in the Documents And Settings folder.

4. Log on again using an administrator account. Find the accounts that are going to have this customized roaming profile.

5. Open the Properties dialog box for each account, click the Profile tab, and in the Profile Path box, type **SBS_server_name profile_folder**\%*username*%. Click OK.

6. In Control Panel, open System.

7. Click the Advanced tab, and then in the User Profiles section, click Settings. Select the dummy account and click Copy To.

8. In the Copy To dialog box, type the path of the profiles folder on the server, **\\SBS_server_name\profile_folder***username*. Note that this time you must use the actual name of the roaming profile or the profile will be stored under the name of whoever is logged on.

9. In the Permitted To Use area, click Change. Give the appropriate permissions for the user to use the profile. Click OK to copy the template profile.

Under the Hood   On Mandatory Profiles

If you're going to all the trouble of assigning customized profiles, perhaps you'd like to make the profiles mandatory. To change a profile into a mandatory profile, you need only rename the hidden file Ntuser.dat to Ntuser.man.

If you don't see the Ntuser file in the individual's profiles folder, choose Folder Options from the Tools menu and click the View tab. In Advanced Settings, select Show Hidden Files And Folders.

Mandatory profiles allow the user to change the desktop, but the changes aren't saved when the user logs off.

Note   Don't create a mandatory user profile for a group of users unless all the users use computers with the same video hardware, because the profiles won't work consistently when the hardware isn't consistent.

Assigning a Logon Script to a User Profile

Logon scripts can be assigned by profile or through Group Policy. (Group Policy is covered in Chapter 17.) The following steps describe how to assign a script to a profile:

1. Select Server Management from the Start menu.

2. In the console tree, click Users. Right-click the user account and choose Properties.

3. Click the Profile tab and type the name of the logon script in the Logon Script box.

4. Click OK when you're finished.

Windows Small Business Server always looks for logon scripts in the same place—on the server at %SystemRoot%\SYSVOL\sysvol*domain_name*\scripts. Scripts in this folder can be typed in the Logon Script path by name only. If you use folders inside the Scripts folder, you must show that part of the path in the Logon Script path. Table 8-5 shows some of the environment variables that can be used when creating logon scripts. Logon scripts can also be created in VBScript and JScript.

Table 8-5 Logon script variables

Variable	Description
%homedrive%	Letter of the drive containing the user's home directory on the user's local workstation
%homepath%	Full path of the user's home directory
%os%	User's operating system
%processor_architecture%	Processor type on the user's workstation
%processor_level%	Processor level of the user's workstation
%userdomain%	Domain where the user's account is defined
%username%	Account user name

Using the Run As Command

Recommended administrative practice dictates that an administrator be logged on to a privileged account (one with administrative rights) only while doing chores that require privileges. For ordinary work, the administrator is supposed to log off from the privileged account and then log on again to an ordinary account. Of course, 10 minutes later a situation again arises requiring use of the privileged account. So then it's necessary to log off from the ordinary account and log back on to the administrator account, with the process reversed again a few minutes later.

After a few days of this, even the most security-conscious person begins to toy with the idea of logging on to the administrator account and staying there. Using an administrator account for day-to-day computing increases your susceptibility to Trojan horse attacks. Just running Microsoft Internet Explorer and accessing a non-trusted Web site can be risky when done from an administrator account. A Web page with Trojan code that uses an unpatched exploit can be downloaded to the system and executed. The execution, done in the context of administrative privileges, can do considerable mischief, including such things as installing a root kit, reformatting a hard disk, deleting all files, or creating a new user with administrative access.

The Run As service allows you to work in a normal, nonprivileged account and launch applications or tools using the credentials of a different account without logging off and then logging back on again.

To use the Run As feature, create an ordinary user account for your own use (if you don't have one already). Make sure that the user account has the right to log on locally at the machine you want to use. Log on using that account. When you need to perform a task requiring administrative privileges, complete the following steps:

1. Hold down the Shift key and right-click the desired program, Control Panel tool, or Administrative Tools icon.

2. Choose Run As from the shortcut menu. The Run As dialog box appears.

> **Note**   After using the Shift key to display the Run As option on the shortcut menu, Run As is permanently available in the shortcut menu for that user.

3. Enter the user name and password of an administrator account to use.

4. Click OK to open the program or tool using the specified account's credentials.

> **Note**   Some administrative tasks, such as setting system parameters, require an interactive logon and do not support Run As.

Making Shortcuts to Run As

Run As is meant to encourage administrators to work outside the administrator's account, and the configuring of useful shortcuts makes this more likely. Create the shortcuts while logged on with an account without administrative rights. Right-click an open area of the desktop, choose New, and then choose Shortcut. Table 8-6 shows examples of useful shortcuts.

Table 8-6   Useful Run As shortcuts

A Shortcut To	Enter
A command prompt with local administrative privileges	**runas/user:**AdministratorAccountName **cmd**
A command prompt with domain administrative privileges	**runas/user:**DomainAdminAccountName@Domain **cmd**
Active Directory Users and Computers with domain administrative credentials	**runas/user:**DomainAdminAccountName@Domain "mmc %windir%\system32\dsa.msc"
Performance Monitor with domain administrative credentials	**runas/user:**DomainAdminAccountName@Domain "mmc %windir%\system32\perfmon.msc"
Group Policy Management Console with administrative credentials	**runas/user:**AdministratorAccountName@Domain "%windir%\system32\gpmc.msc"

After you open one of the shortcuts in Table 8-6, you're prompted for the administrative account's password. Keep a few of the most used shortcuts on your desktop and you'll find it easier to stay in your less-privileged account most of the time.

Summary

This chapter explored the options available to the administrator for configuring groups, group scope, and user accounts in Windows Small Business Server. The next chapter covers shares and permissions—additional tools to provide accessibility and security for your network.

Chapter 9
Shares and Permissions

Sharing Resources 175

Setting Offline File Rules 180

Share Permissions vs. File Permissions 183

Configuring Special Permissions 189

Ownership and How It Works 191

Determining Effective Permissions 195

Privileges and Logon Rights. 196

Encrypting Sensitive Data. 198

Summary 204

If you think all this talk of shares, permissions, rights, and privileges is confusing—you're right. All the terms appear to be nearly synonymous. However, just as you learned that words like inflammable and sanction can mean completely opposite things depending on context, you can also learn to distinguish among these words.

> **More Info** See Chapter 8, "Managing Users and Groups," for more information about rights and permissions assigned to users and groups.

Sharing Resources

Shared resources are folders, files, printers, devices, or applications that are available to users over a network. Until a drive or folder is shared over the network, users can't see it or gain access to it. After a folder is shared, authenticated users on the network have, by default, read access to all files in the folder, and to all subfolders of that folder, and so on. After a drive or folder is shared, restrictions can be added or removed in the form of *share permissions*. These permissions apply only at the drive or folder level—not at the file level—and are limited to allowing or denying Full Control, Read, and Change. Table 9-1 summarizes the three types of access, from most restrictive to least restrictive.

Table 9-1   Types of share permissions

Share Permission	Type of Access
Read	Allows viewing of file and subfolder names, viewing data in files, running programs
Change	Allows the access under Read, plus allows adding files and subdirectories to the shared folder, changing data in files, and deleting files and subdirectories
Full Control	Allows all the access under Change, plus allows changing permissions (NTFS volumes only) and taking ownership (NTFS volumes only)

Folder Sharing

To share a folder, you have only to open Server Management and select Shares (Local) in the console tree, and then complete the following steps:

1.   Click Add A Shared Folder to launch the Share a Folder Wizard.

2.   On the Folder Path page, type in the path to the folder you want to share. Better yet, click Browse and navigate to the folder, as shown in Figure 9-1.

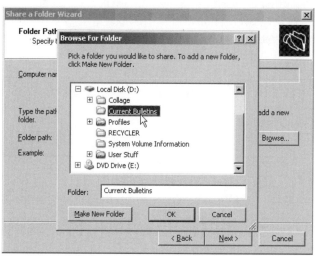

Figure 9-1   Specifying a folder to be shared.

> **Note**   You can create a new folder to share in this process. Just click Browse, navigate to the location for the new folder, and click Make New Folder.

3. On the Name, Description, And Settings page, you can change the default settings for the share. For example, if the original name of the folder isn't helpful, type in a more comprehensible Share Name that will appear to users as the name of the folder. You can also add a description (always useful) and change the settings for offline use. (See "Setting Offline File Rules" later in this chapter for more information.)

4. On the Permissions page, you can select one of the three preconfigured settings or click the option to Use Custom Share And Folder Permissions and click Customize. (See "Working with NTFS File and Folder Permissions" later in this chapter for details about setting permissions.)

5. The final page of the wizard shows the details of the share and includes an option to run the wizard again to share another folder.

> **Note**   You can also create shares and configure their permissions and offline file settings from the command line. The command to use is net share, and the full syntax for it is:

```
NET SHARE   sharename=drive:path
                [/GRANT:user,[READ | CHANGE | FULL]]
                [/USERS:number | /UNLIMITED]
                [/REMARK:"text"]
                [/CACHE:Manual | Documents| Programs | None ]
          sharename [/USERS:number | /UNLIMITED]
                [/REMARK:"text"]
                [/CACHE:Manual | Documents | Programs | None]
          {sharename | devicename | drive:path} /DELETE
```

Removing a Share

To turn a shared folder into an unshared one, open Server Management and select Shares (Local) and find the folder in the details pane. Right-click the folder and select Stop Sharing from the shortcut menu. Or, from the command line:

```
net share sharename /delete
```

Moving or Renaming a Shared Folder

After a folder has been shared, if you move or rename it, it loses its shared status. You need to run the Share a Folder Wizard to make the folder shared again.

Under the Hood   Using Special Shares

In addition to shares created by a user or administrator, the system creates a number of special shares that shouldn't be modified or deleted. The special share you're most likely to see is the ADMIN$ share and the drive shares: C$, D$, E$, and so on. These shares allow administrators to connect to drives that are otherwise not shared.

Special shares exist as part of the operating system's installation. Depending on the computer's configuration, some or all of the following special shares could be present. These shares are essential in a networked environment for control and management of the workstations in the domain, and should not be modified or deleted.

- **ADMIN$**   Used during the remote administration of a computer. The path is always the location of the folder in which Windows was installed (that is, the system root).

- **driveletter$**   The root folder of the named drive. Only Administrators, Backup Operators, and Server Operators can connect to these shares on SBS 2003. On Microsoft Windows XP Professional and Windows 2000 Professional computers, only Administrators and Backup Operators can connect to these shares.

- **IPC$**   Used during remote administration and when viewing shared resources. This share is essential to communication and can't be deleted.

- **NETLOGON, SYSVOL**   Essential to all domain controllers. Do not remove.

- **FsxSrvCp$**   A shared folder used by fax clients while sending a fax. The folder is used to store shared cover pages and to cache files.

- **Resources$**   Contains Event Log files.

- **PRINT$**   A resource that supports shared printers.

To connect to an unshared drive on another computer, you need to be logged on using an account with the necessary rights. Use the address bar in any window and type the address using this syntax:

\\computer_name\[driveletter]$

To connect to the system root folder (the folder in which Windows Small Business Server is installed) on another computer, use this syntax:

\\computer_name\admin$

Other special shares such as IPC$ and PRINT$ are created and used solely by the system. NETLOGON is a special share used while processing domain logon requests. NETLOGON is on Windows Small Business Server, Windows Server 2003, Windows 2000, and Windows NT servers.

Adding a $ character to the end of a share name hides the share from *all* users. To access a hidden share, you need to specify it explicitly; you can't browse the network for the share.

Creating a New Share for a Shared Folder

A single folder might be shared more than once. For example, one share might include Full Control for Administrators and another share for users might be more restricted. To add a new share, complete the following steps:

1. Right-click the Start button and select Explore. Navigate to the shared folder.

2. Right-click the folder and select Sharing And Security from the shortcut menu.

3. On the Sharing tab, click the New Share button.

4. In the New Share dialog box, enter a new Share Name. (Each share must have a unique name.) Set a user limit, if necessary.

5. Click Permissions to set permissions for this new share. As you can see in Figure 9-2, only Administrators and members of the Finance Operators group can connect to this new share.

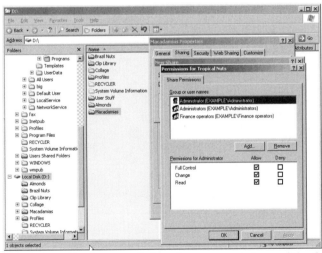

Figure 9-2   Setting permissions for a second share of the folder.

The original share of the Macadamias folder (Hawaiian Nuts) now has an additional share called Tropical Nuts—though both shares access the same folder (Figure 9-3).

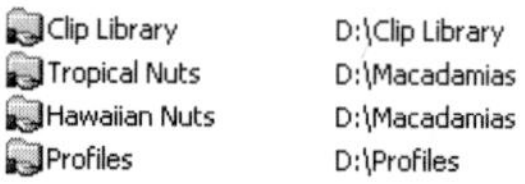

Clip Library	D:\Clip Library
Tropical Nuts	D:\Macadamias
Hawaiian Nuts	D:\Macadamias
Profiles	D:\Profiles

Figure 9-3   A shared folder can be shared under more than one name.

> **Note**   A second share can't be added through Shares (Local) in Server Management because the option isn't available. You must find the folder through My Computer or Windows Explorer and add the share directly.

Setting Offline File Rules

When you share a folder in SBS, you can also set rules for accessing the folder when users are offline. The default setting is to allow users to access files that they manually specify. To set offline rules on a folder, complete the following steps:

1. Select Server Management from the Start menu.

2. In the console tree, right-click Shares (Local) and select New Share to launch the Share a Folder Wizard.

3. On the Folder Path page, shown in Figure 9-4, type in the path to the folder or click Browse and select a folder or create a new one.

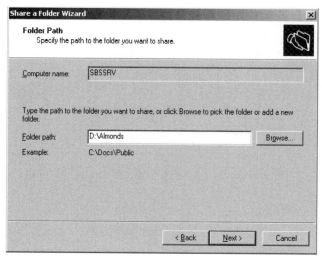

Figure 9-4   Selecting a folder for which to set offline files.

4. On the Name, Description, And Settings page, click Change to open the Offline
   Settings dialog box shown in Figure 9-5.

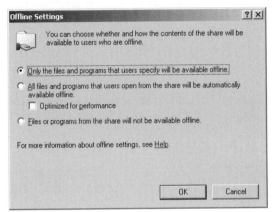

Figure 9-5   Choosing how offline users can access this share.

Choose the setting you want:

- ❏ **Only The Files And Programs That Users Specify Will Be Available Offline**
  With this setting, users must identify the shared files that they want to be able
  to use while offline. For most folders, this is the best setting.

- ❏ **All Files And Programs That Users Open From The Share Will Be**
  Automatically Available Offline   If programs are to be available to run
  offline, select the Optimized For Performance check box. Programs are
  cached at the local user's computer to minimize network traffic. If the shared
  folder contains files that might change, don't use this option unless the files
  can first be made read-only.

- ❏ **Files Or Programs From The Share Are Not Available Offline**   With this setting, users cannot use the shared files offline. Choose this option for folders
  that should *not* be used offline under any circumstances, such as folders containing database files.

5. Click OK and then click Next.

   Note   If the folder is already shared, it's easiest to right-click it and select
   Sharing And Security from the shortcut menu. On the Sharing tab, click
   Offline Settings and select the option you want.

6. On the Permissions page, you can choose from one of the three commonplace permission settings. Or select Use Custom Share And Folder Permissions, then click

Customize and set up the permissions you want. When you click Finish, the settings are applied.

Synchronizing Offline Files

Users choose when to synchronize their files. The default settings are to synchronize at log on and log off, so changes made to an offline file are synchronized with the network version when the user first connects to the network and again when the user logs off. In most cases, the default settings are fine, but to make a change, open a folder window, and select Synchronize from the Tools menu to display the Items To Synchronize dialog box, shown in Figure 9-6.

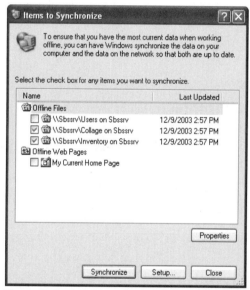

Figure 9-6   Selecting the items to synchronize.

In the Items To Synchronize dialog box, select the check boxes next to items that you want to synchronize and clear the others.

Making Shares Available Offline

Users who want to use a shared folder on the server offline just have to right-click the folder and select Make Available Offline from the shortcut menu.

Share Permissions vs. File Permissions

There are two kinds of permissions involved in any shared folder—those on the actual share and those imposed by the underlying file system. These permissions are *subtractive*. This means that only the most restrictive permission will win. Managing permissions on both the share and the file system at the same time can often be quite confusing, and it's difficult to keep track of the details of both. We generally recommend using the underlying NTFS file permissions to control access and setting the share permissions to Full Control for everyone for most normal shares. The NTFS file permissions give much greater granularity and control over exactly what level of access is granted. However, there are cases in which using a more restrictive share permission is useful. We suggest, however, that when you do use a more restrictive share permission, you indicate in the share name that the share is restricted.

Microsoft Windows Server 2003 (and therefore Windows Small Business Server) uses the default share permission of Everyone = Read. (Microsoft Windows 2000 and Windows NT uses a default share permission of Everyone = Full Control.) You can change the share permission to Everyone = Full Control or Domain Users = Full Control (for more security) and use NTFS permissions for more granular control.

> **Note** In SBS 2003, the Everyone group is a bit different than in previous versions, and is essentially the same as the Authenticated Users group. It does *not*, by default, include anonymous users. However, if you're running Microsoft Services for UNIX, you might need to modify this setting by adding anonymous users to the Everyone group. See the Microsoft TechNet article: *http://technet2.microsoft.com/WindowsServer/en/Library/7c2373bd-b2c2-4392-ad26-ffdd89ef8c741033.mspx*.

Whatever your choice, avoid configuring both share permissions *and* NTFS permissions because the result can be unpredictable and hard to troubleshoot.

How Permissions Work

If you take no action at all, the files and folders inside a shared folder have the same permissions as the share. Permissions for both directories and files can be assigned to the following:

- Groups and individual users on this domain
- Global groups, universal groups, and individual users from domains that this domain trusts
- Special identities such as Everyone and Authenticated Users

The important rules for permissions can be summarized as follows:

■ By default, a folder inherits permissions from its parent folder. Files inherit their permissions from the folder in which they reside.

■ Users can access a folder or file only when they are granted permission to do so or they belong to a group that has been granted permission.

■ Permissions are cumulative, but the Deny permission trumps all others. For example, if the Sales group has Read access to a folder and the Finance group has Modify permission for the same folder, and Wally is a member of both groups, Wally has the higher level of permission, which is Modify. However, if the Sales group permission is changed to explicitly Deny, Wally is unable to use the folder, despite his membership—and ostensibly higher level of access—in the Finance group.

■ The user who creates a file or folder owns the object and can set permissions to control access.

■ An administrator can take ownership of any file or folder.

■ Members of the Administrators, Backup Operators, and Server Operators built-in security groups can take ownership and reassign ownership.

Working with NTFS File and Folder Permissions

Windows Small Business Server has a set of standard NTFS permissions that are combinations of specific kinds of access. The individual permissions are Full Control, Modify, Read & Execute, List Folder Contents, Read, and Write. Each of these permissions consists of a group of special permissions. Table 9-2 shows what special permissions are included with each standard permission.

Table 9-2   Special permissions for folders

Special Permission	Full Control	Modify	Read & Execute	List Folder Contents	Read	Write
Traverse Folder/Execute File	Yes	Yes	Yes	Yes	No	No
List Folder/Read Data	Yes	Yes	Yes	Yes	Yes	No
Read Attributes	Yes	Yes	Yes	Yes	Yes	No
Read Extended Attributes	Yes	Yes	Yes	Yes	Yes	No
Create Files/Write Data	Yes	Yes	No	No	No	Yes
Create Folders/Append Data	Yes	Yes	No	No	No	Yes
Write Attributes	Yes	Yes	No	No	No	Yes
Write Extended Attributes	Yes	Yes	No	No	No	Yes
Delete Subfolders and Files	Yes	No	No	No	No	No

Table 9-2 Special permissions for folders (Continued)

Special Permission	Full Control	Modify	Read & Execute	List Folder Contents	Read	Write
Delete	Yes	Yes	No	No	No	No
Read Permissions	Yes	Yes	Yes	Yes	Yes	Yes
Change Permissions	Yes	No	No	No	No	No
Take Ownership	Yes	No	No	No	No	No

File permissions include Full Control, Modify, Read & Execute, Read, and Write. As with folders, each of these permissions controls a group of special permissions. Table 9-3 shows the special permissions associated with each standard permission.

Table 9-3 Special permissions for files

Special Permission	Full Control	Modify	Read & Execute	Read	Write
Traverse Folder/Execute File	Yes	Yes	Yes	No	No
List Folder/Read Data	Yes	Yes	Yes	Yes	No
Read Attributes	Yes	Yes	Yes	Yes	No
Read Extended Attributes	Yes	Yes	Yes	Yes	No
Create Files/Write Data	Yes	Yes	No	No	Yes
Create Folders/Append Data	Yes	Yes	No	No	Yes
Write Attributes	Yes	Yes	No	No	Yes
Write Extended Attributes	Yes	Yes	No	No	Yes
Delete Subfolders and Files	Yes	No	No	No	No
Delete	Yes	Yes	No	No	No
Read Permissions	Yes	Yes	Yes	Yes	Yes
Change Permissions	Yes	No	No	No	No
Take Ownership	Yes	No	No	No	No

Important Any user or group assigned Full Control on a folder can delete files and subfolders no matter what the permissions are on the individual files or subfolders.

Considering Inheritance

Just to complicate matters a bit more, there are two types of permissions: explicit and inherited. *Explicit permissions* are the ones you set on folders you create. *Inherited permissions* are those that flow from a parent object to a child object. By default, when you create a sub-folder, it inherits the permissions of the parent folder.

If you don't want the child objects to inherit the permissions of the parent, you can block inheritance at the parent level or at the child level. Where you block inheritance is impor-tant. Block at the parent level and no subfolders inherit permissions. Block selectively at the child level and some folders inherit permissions but others do not.

To block a file or folder from inheriting permissions, right-click the folder, select Proper-ties, and then click the Security tab. Click Advanced and clear the check box for Allow Inheritable Permissions From The Parent To Propagate To This Object And All Child Objects, as shown in Figure 9-7.

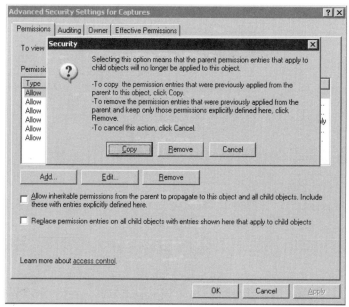

Figure 9-7   Blocking inheritance on a folder.

Important   An additional check box is shown on the Advanced Security Set-tings page: Replace Permission Entries On All Child Objects With Entries Shown Here That Apply To Child Objects. If you select this option, subfolders and files have their permissions reset to those they inherit from a parent object. Once you select this item and click Apply or OK, you can't go back and undo it.

When the check boxes for permissions appear shaded, it means the permissions are inherited from a parent object. When the check boxes are shaded *and* have a check mark, as in Figure 9-8, some permissions are inherited and others have been added. There are three ways to change this situation:

- Clear the check box for Allow Inheritable Permissions From the Parent To Propagate To This Object And All Child Objects. When the check box is cleared, you can make changes to the permissions or change the users or groups in the list.

- Change the permissions of the parent folder.

- Select the opposite permission—Allow or Deny—to override the inherited permission.

    If neither Allow nor Deny is selected, the users or groups might have acquired the permission through a group membership. Otherwise, failure to explicitly configure Allow effectively denies the permission.

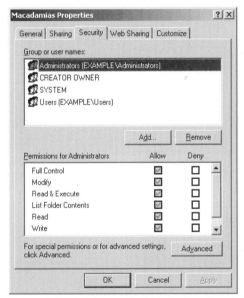

Figure 9-8   A folder with inherited and noninherited permissions.

Configuring NTFS Folder Permissions

Before sharing a folder on an NTFS volume, set all the permissions on the folder. When you set folder permissions, you're also setting permissions on all the files and subfolders in the folder. To assign permissions to a folder, right-click the folder in Windows Explorer, choose Properties from the shortcut menu, and then click the Security tab.

- To remove an individual or group from the list, select the name and click Remove.

■ To add to the list of those with permissions, click Add. This opens the Select Users, Computers, Or Groups dialog box. Or click Advanced to perform a more sophisticated search, as shown in Figure 9-9. Click OK when you're finished.

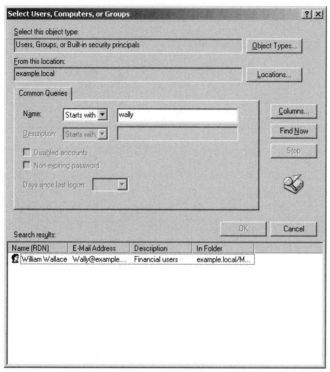

Figure 9-9   Selecting users and groups.

Assigning NTFS Permissions to Files

Permissions for individual files are assigned in the same way as folders. There are, however, some special considerations:

■ Remember to grant permissions to groups, rather than to individuals.

■ Create universal groups and assign file permissions to them rather than assign permissions directly to local groups.

■ Think carefully about alternatives. Trying to manage individual file permissions is major administrative overhead you really don't need or want.

Important   Groups or users who have Full Control for a folder can delete
files and subfolders, no matter what protective permissions are assigned to
the files and folders.

Configuring Special Permissions

In some circumstances, you might find it necessary to set, change, or remove special permissions on either a file or folder. To access special permissions, complete the following steps:

1. Right-click the file or folder and choose Properties from the shortcut menu.

2. Click the Security tab, and then click Advanced.

    ❑   To add a user or group, click Add. Supply the name of the user or group. Click OK to open the Permission Entry dialog box.

    ❑   To view or modify existing special permissions, select the name of the user or group and click Edit.

    ❑   To remove special permissions, select the name of the user or group and click Remove. If the Remove button is unavailable, clear the check box for Allow Inheritable Permissions From Parent To Propagate To This Object, and skip to Step 6.

3. In the Permission Entry dialog box, shown in Figure 9-10, select where you want the permissions applied in the Apply Onto box. (See Table 9-4 and Table 9-5 for explanations of the choices in this drop-down box.) Apply Onto is available when configuring folders only. You can choose to apply permissions to all the files in the folder, but different settings for different files require configuring each file separately.

Figure 9-10   Setting special permissions for a folder.

4. In Permissions, select Allow or Deny for each permission.

5. To prevent subfolders and files from inheriting these permissions, select Apply These Permissions To Objects And/Or Containers Within This Container Only.

6. Click OK to close the dialog box.

In the Permission Entry dialog box for folders, you can choose how and where the special permissions are applied. Table 9-4 and Table 9-5 demonstrate the application of the special permissions depending on whether Apply These Permissions To Objects And/Or Containers Within This Container Only is selected.

Table 9-4   Application of special permissions when Apply These Permissions To Objects And/Or Containers Within This Container Only is selected

Selected in Apply Onto	Applies to Current Folder?	Applies to Subfolders in Current Folder?	Applies to Files in Current Folder?	Applies to Subsequent Subfolders?	Applies to Files in Subsequent Subfolders?
This folder only	Yes	No	No	No	No
This folder, sub-folders and files	Yes	Yes	Yes	No	No
This folder and subfolders	Yes	Yes	No	No	No
This folder and files	Yes	No	Yes	No	No
Subfolders and files only	No	Yes	Yes	No	No
Subfolders only	No	Yes	No	No	No
Files only	No	No	Yes	No	No

Table 9-5   Application of special permissions when Apply These Permissions To Objects And/Or Containers Within This Container Only is not selected

Selected in Apply Onto	Applies to Current Folder?	Applies to Subfolders in Current Folder?	Applies to Files in Current Folder?	Applies to Subsequent Subfolders?	Applies to Files in Subsequent Subfolders?
This folder only	Yes	No	No	No	No
This folder, subfolders, and files	Yes	Yes	Yes	Yes	Yes
This folder and subfolders	Yes	Yes	No	Yes	No
This folder and files	Yes	No	Yes	No	Yes

Table 9-5 Application of special permissions when Apply These Permissions To Objects And/Or Containers Within This Container Only is not selected (Continued)

Selected in Apply Onto	Applies to Current Folder?	Applies to Subfolders in Current Folder?	Applies to Files in Current Folder?	Applies to Subsequent Subfolders?	Applies to Files in Subsequent Subfolders?
Subfolders and files only	No	Yes	Yes	Yes	Yes
Subfolders only	No	Yes	No	Yes	No
Files only	No	No	Yes	No	Yes

Ownership and How It Works

As you've seen, Administrators and members of a few other select groups are the only ones who can grant and change permissions. The exception is when a user is the owner of the folder or file in question. Every object on an NTFS partition has an owner, and the owner is the person who created the file or folder. Or, if that user is a member of the Administrators group, the file is owned by the Administrators group. The owner controls access to the file or folder and can keep out anyone he or she chooses.

For example, Wally (a user) creates a folder on his computer called My Private Stuff. After creating the folder, he right-clicks the folder, chooses Properties, and then clicks the Security tab, as shown in Figure 9-11.

Figure 9-11 Viewing the NTFS permissions for a new folder.

Wally sees that the Administrators group has full access to his folder, but because he is the owner of the folder, he can change the permissions so that he has the folder all to himself. He clicks Advanced to open the Advanced Security Settings dialog box and clears the Inherit From Parent check box. When the Security dialog box appears, Wally clicks Remove to remove the permission entries that were previously applied from the parent, as shown in Figure 9-12.

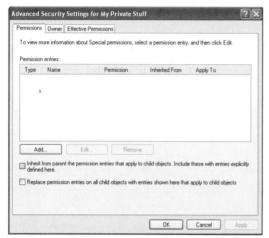

Figure 9-12   Removing inheritance from a permission entry.

After clicking Remove and accepting the security warning, Wally clicks OK and a Security warning appears indicating that everyone has been denied access to the folder. Wally clicks Yes to continue and returns to the Properties dialog box. He clicks the Add button and adds his user account with Full Control. After this is done, even the administrator receives an Access Denied message when trying to open the folder.

Of course, nothing on the network can be *completely* beyond the reach of administrators, so an administrator can change the ownership by following these steps:

1. Right-click the My Private Stuff folder and choose Properties from the shortcut menu to open the Properties dialog box. Select the Security tab. A Security warning appears indicating that you don't have permissions to the folder but can take ownership. As shown in Figure 9-13, no changes can be made on the Security tab and only the Advanced button is enabled.

2. Click Advanced to open the Advanced Security Settings dialog box and then click the Owner tab, as shown in Figure 9-14.

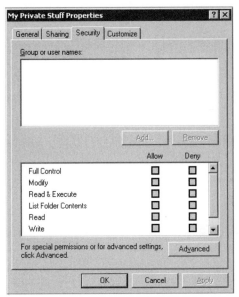

Figure 9-13   The administrator viewing permissions for a folder owned by a user.

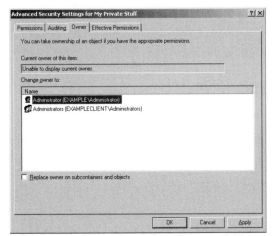

Figure 9-14   Changing the ownership of a folder.

3. No matter what the status of the folder is, the administrator can take ownership. Select the new owner and click OK.

4. Close the Properties dialog box. Then right-click the folder again and select Properties and then the Security tab. The Properties dialog box now reveals Wally as the only user with permission to use the folder.

5. Click Advanced and on the Permissions tab, select the check box for Inherit From Parent The Permission Entries That Apply To Child Objects. Click Apply, as shown in Figure 9-15, and all the previously removed permissions are reinstated.

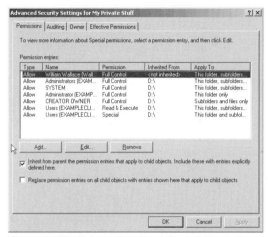

Figure 9-15   Reinstating the default inherited permissions.

6. Click OK twice to close the dialog boxes.

When Wally logs on the next time, he still has access to My Private Stuff. If he opens the Properties dialog box, clicks the Security tab, clicks Advanced, and then clicks the Owner tab, he sees that he's no longer the only user with Full Control. Changing the ownership of the folder doesn't automatically give administrators access to the contents of the folder, but ownership does grant the ability to read and change permissions. With that, an administrator can change permissions and attain access to the folder contents.

Note   The owner of a file or folder can also grant the Take Ownership special permission to others, allowing those users to take ownership at any time.

Real World   Keep It Simple

Windows Small Business Server goes to considerable lengths and offers many tools to simplify the running of a network. However, there are several different ways to turn administration into a tangled mess, and one of them is to get too deeply into setting lots of specific permissions.

SBS has a rich and highly granular permission set that gives you the ability to manage permissions on individual files for each individual in your organization, giving everyone a different level of access and control. But just because you *can* do something, doesn't mean you should. Give yourself, your network and your users a break–keep it simple.

Always try to operate with the simplest possible permissions. Set as few restrictions as possible. Assign permissions to groups, not individuals. Don't set file-by-file permissions unless it is unavoidable. Managing the minutiae of permissions can quickly soak up all your time and much of your life's blood as well, unless you guard against it.

Determining Effective Permissions

What with the complexities of inheritance and the nested nature of groups, it's no small chore to find out exactly what permissions a user or group has. Windows Small Business Server 2003 includes a tool to help determine which permissions are in effect for a given object. Follow these steps:

1. Log on as a member of Domain Administrators.

2. Right-click a file or folder and select Properties from the shortcut menu.

3. Click Security, and then click the Advanced button.

4. In the Advanced Security Settings dialog box, click the Effective Permissions tab.

5. Click Select and locate the user or group you have questions about in the Select User, Computer, Or Group dialog box. Click OK. The effective permissions are displayed, as shown in Figure 9-16.

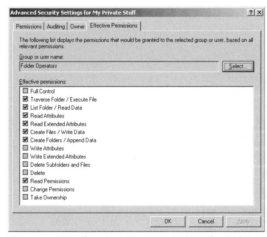

Figure 9-16   Showing the permissions for Folder Operators on an object.

Note The effective permissions result is more an estimation than a precise determination. Included in the calculation of effective permissions are memberships in global and local groups, local permissions, and local privileges.

Not included are share permissions and any permissions based on how the user logs on. If you're viewing effective permissions remotely, membership in local groups and local privileges are not part of the formula for determining effective permissions.

Privileges and Logon Rights

In addition to permissions, Windows Small Business Server includes assignable rights, which are of two types: *privileges* and *logon rights*. *Privileges* include such things as the ability to run security audits or force shutdown from a remote system—obviously not things that are handled by most users. *Logon rights* are self-explanatory; they involve the ability to connect to a computer in specific ways. Rights are automatically assigned to the built-in groups in Windows Small Business Server, although they can be assigned to individual users as well as groups. Whenever possible, you should assign rights by group membership to keep administration simple. When membership in groups defines rights, rights can be removed from a user by simply removing the user from the group. Tables 9-6 and 9-7 list the most-used logon rights and privileges and the groups to which they are assigned by default.

Important The default settings for rights and privileges in SBS have been carefully thought out and adjusted to work correctly in an SBS environment. Changing them is certainly possible, but doing so should only be done with full understanding of the consequences and a good backup. We think you're better off leaving well enough alone.

Table 9-6   Logon rights assigned to groups by default

Name	Description	Groups Assigned the Right by Default
Access Windows Small Business Server from the network	Permits connection to the computer through the network.	Administrators, Domain Power Users, Everyone.
Log on as a service	Allows logging on as a service using a specific user account and security context.	None.

Table 9-6   Logon rights assigned to groups by default (Continued)

Name	Description	Groups Assigned the Right by Default
Log on to Windows Small Business Server locally	Permits logon at the computer's keyboard.	Administrators, Account Operators, Backup Operators, Print Operators, Server Operators.
Allow Logon through Terminal Services	Permits logon as a Terminal Services client.	Administrators on Domain Controllers. Administrators and Remote Desktop Users on workstations and stand-alone servers.

Table 9-7   Privileges assigned to groups by default

Privilege	Description	Groups Assigned the Privilege by Default
Act as part of the operating system	Allows a process to authenticate as any user. A process that requires this privilege should use the LocalSystem account, which already includes this privilege.	None.
Add workstations to domain	Allows a user to add new workstations to an existing domain.	Authenticated Users on domain controllers.
Backup files and directories	Allows backing up the system; overrides specific file and folder permissions.	Administrators, Backup Operators.
Change the system time	Allows the setting of the computer's internal clock.	Administrators and Service Operators on domain controllers. Administrators, Domain Power Users on workstations and stand-alone servers.
Force shutdown from a remote system	Allows the shutdown of a computer from a remote location on the network.	Administrators and Server Operators on domain controllers. Administrators on workstations and stand-alone servers.
Generate security audits	Sets which accounts can use a process to make entries in a security log.	None.
Increase scheduling priority	Allows the use of Task Manager to change the scheduling priority of a process.	Administrators.

Table 9-7   Privileges assigned to groups by default (Continued)

Privilege	Description	Groups Assigned the Privilege by Default
Lock pages in memory	Allows a process to keep data in physical memory. This is an obsolete privilege that can have a seriously negative effect on system performance. Avoid assigning it.	None.
Restore files and directories	Allows restoring files and folders to a system; overrules specific file and folder permissions.	Administrators, Backup Operators, and Server Operators on domain controllers. Administrators and Backup Operators on workstations and stand-alone servers.
Take ownership of files or other objects	Allows a user to take ownership of any security object including files and folders, printers, registry keys, and processes. Overrules specified permissions.	Administrators.

Important Privileges can sometimes override permission settings. For example, a user can create a file and set permissions that deny access to all users, but members of the Backup Operators group can still access the file and back it up, and Administrators (as we saw earlier in this chapter) can take ownership of the file.

Encrypting Sensitive Data

It's deceptively simple to encrypt and decrypt files in Windows Small Business Server 2003. Of course, anything that's sensitive enough to be encrypted should be treated very carefully, so take time to plan before implementing file and folder encryption. You need to have a clear and well-understood recovery policy, as described in this section, to prevent irreversible data loss. Make sure also that your vendors for any affected line of business applications will fully support encryption.

Encryption of stored files in SBS is accomplished through the use of the Encrypting File System (EFS). Using public-key encryption, EFS allows files and directories stored on NTFS partitions to be encrypted and decrypted transparently. The user's EFS public and private keys are used to perform self-encryption transparently to the user, whose access to the files is the same as if they weren't encrypted. Other users, however, are denied access to the file. If files that are encrypted with EFS are saved to another computer, the user's key information must be imported to that computer for decryption to occur.

Files' encryption keys are automatically encrypted by the recovery agent key. In the event of the loss of the user's encrypting key, the recovery agent can decrypt the files. EFS encrypts the bulk of the file with a single symmetric key. The symmetric key is then encrypted twice: once with the user's EFS public key to allow decryption, and once with the recovery agent's public key to allow data recovery.

Creating a Recovery Policy

The recovery policy provides a way to recover an encrypted file when its key has been lost. To recover the file, the recovery certificate for the recovery agent (a specially desig-nated user account) is used. On an SBS domain, the recovery agent is set automatically to the Administrator account of the domain.

> **Note**   We suggest that you create a special account just for the recovery agent role, and then assign the recovery agent role to this account. Because the recov-ery agent is such a sensitive role (specifically, it's capable of decrypting any file on the domain), it's imperative that you take proper precautions with it.

The following steps take you through adding extra recovery agents, backing up the recov-ery certificate to a floppy disk or USB key, and deleting the locally stored recovery key for extra security:

1. Launch the Active Directory Users and Computers snap-in.

2. Right-click the SBS domain, and choose Properties from the shortcut menu.

3. On the Group Policy tab, select the appropriate policy and click Edit.

4. In the console tree, select Computer Configuration, select Windows Settings, select Security Settings, and finally select Public Key Policies.

5. Under Public Key Policies, select Encrypting File System.

6. Right-click the Encrypted Data Recovery Agents folder, and choose Add Data Recovery Agent from the shortcut menu.

7. Use the Add Recovery Agent Wizard to add another recovery agent to the domain, It's a good practice to have at least two recovery agents for your SBS domain.

> **Note**   Create recovery agent accounts specifically for the recovery agent role, and do not use them for anything else. Replace the default Adminis-trator recovery agent with one of the new, specially created recovery agent

accounts to minimize the impact of the Administrator account getting compromised.

8. Right-click a recovery agent, and choose All Tasks and then Export from the shortcut menu.

9. Use the Certificate Export Wizard to export the recovery key to an external storage device, such as a USB key or floppy disk. Store it in a highly secure location (preferably off-site).

10. Log on using the recovery agent's account, and then open the Certificates MMC snap-in. (If prompted, select My User Account and click OK.) You might have to open a blank MMC console and add the Certificates snap-in to it.

11. From the console tree, select Personal and then Certificates.

12. Select the certificate corresponding to the recovery key that you exported, and then click the Delete toolbar button. Now the only copy of the recovery key is stored separately in a secured location. Even someone with physical access to the computer does not have access to the recovery key and will not be able to decrypt the encrypted files on your network.

Encrypting Files and Folders

Encrypting files with EFS is as easy as setting any other file attribute, such as Hidden or Read-Only. To encrypt a file in Windows Explorer, complete these steps:

1. Right-click the file and choose Properties.

2. On the General tab, click Advanced.

3. Select the Encrypt Contents To Secure Data check box.

Important   Encrypt entire folders only. If you encrypt individual files but not their folders, a program might create a temporary file (which won't be encrypted) and then save the file over the original file, thereby leaving the file decrypted.

Note   Remember that system files, compressed files, and files on partitions other than NTFS can't be encrypted using EFS. Further, a drive's root folder cannot be encrypted using EFS.

Like normal files, encrypted files can be moved and copied with the Edit menu commands Cut, Copy, and Paste. Files moved or copied using drag-and-drop retain their encryption even when moved to an unencrypted folder. However, files which are saved using "Save As" from the File menu, lose their encryption if their save location isn't encrypted. You can rename encrypted files as you would any other file without losing the encryption.

Important   Encrypted files and directories are not immune from deletion. Any user with appropriate rights can delete an encrypted file.

You can use the same method for encrypting a folder as you use for encrypting a file. When encrypting a folder, you are asked whether you want all files and folders contained in the current folder to be encrypted. If you choose to encrypt them, they are immediately encrypted, but if you choose not to, only the folder is encrypted. No matter which you choose, however, any files or folders subsequently added to the encrypted folder are encrypted as well.

Note   To ensure the security of temporary files that have been created by applications, mark your system's Temp folder for encryption.

Real World   Encryption Best Practices

Here are some encryption best practices to consider:

- Encrypt the My Documents folder of sensitive desktops and laptops.

- Encrypt the Temp folders of appropriate user profiles to protect temporary data, or data that was marooned in the Temp folder following a program crash.

- If you use spool files while printing, encrypt the Spool folder.

- Don't tamper with the EFS keys.

- Don't tamper with the RSA folder; this is the repository for EFS keys.

Decrypting Files and Folders

EFS allows a user to reverse the encryption process. However, describing this as a mere decryption operation is a bit misleading. Indeed, removing data encryption from a file does cause the file to be decrypted, but any encrypted file is also decrypted every time a user or application accesses it. What we're describing here is permanent decryption.

To indicate that a file no longer needs to be encrypted or that a folder no longer needs to encrypt its files, complete these steps:

1. Right-click the file or folder in Windows Explorer and choose Properties.

2. Select the General tab and click Advanced.

3. Clear the Encrypt Contents To Secure Data check box.

Sharing Encrypted Files

SBS 2003 permits the sharing of encrypted files, as does Windows XP. This mechanism facilitates data recovery and business collaboration by permitting a specified list of users to access encrypted data.

To share encrypted files complete the following steps:

1. Right-click the encrypted file and select the Properties menu item.

2. Select the General tab and click Advanced.

3. Click Details in the Advanced Attributes dialog box.

4. Click Add and select the users with whom you want to share the item.

There are a couple of limitations you need to be aware of. You can share the encrypted items with users only; that is, sharing with a group is not permitted. Also, the user you want to share the encrypted file with must have a valid certificate for EFS.

More Info   For a description of the specifics of cryptography, including symmetric-key and public-key methods, visit *http://www.microsoft.com/technet/security/ topics/cryptographyetc/cryptpki.mspx*.

Recovering Files

When you encrypt files to protect them from prying eyes, you run the risk of protecting them from yourself and ultimately losing the data. EFS requires the user's private key (associated with the user's EFS public-key certificate) to decrypt a file. As long as this key is available, EFS-protected files are accessed just like a normal file. In the event of key loss, however, a secondary means of retrieving the data is necessary. Another kind of key loss occurs with the voluntary or involuntary departure of a user—for example, a user who encrypts company files might leave the company. Multiuser sharing described in the previous section lessens this problem, but consider the situation where sharing isn't enabled.

The ability to recover files starts when an individual user backs up his or her EFS public-key certificate and associated private key. To back up this information, the user must export the certificate and key through the Certificates snap-in in the MMC. (See the "Exporting Certificates and Private Keys" section earlier in this chapter.) If the private key is ever lost, the user can import the saved EFS private key and certificate and salvage the data. To do so, complete these steps:

1. Launch the Certificates MMC snap-in.

2. Select Personal from the console tree, right-click the Certificates folder, and choose All Tasks and then Import from the shortcut menu.

3. Use the Certificate Import Wizard to restore the backup key, which allows access to the encrypted file again.

> **Note** Exported keys and certificates are stored in a standard PKCS #12 (also known as Personal Information Exchange or PFX) format. This format is understood by a number of security-enhanced applications, allowing exchange of keys between independent computers or applications.

If a user is unable to decrypt lost data, an administrator can salvage the data by using a recovery agent certificate. To do so, complete these steps:

1. Instruct the user with the encrypted files to back up the files using Backup or another Windows Server 2003–compatible backup program, and send the backup file to the recovery agent using e-mail or removable media.

2. Log on using a Recovery Agent account, and restore the recovery key using the previous procedure. (The recovery key is presumably stored in a secure location such as a vault and deleted from the system when not in use.)

3. On the Recovery Agent's computer, use Backup or another backup program to restore the files to a local folder.

4. In Windows Explorer, right-click the folder and choose Properties from the shortcut menu.

5. In the General tab, click Advanced.

6. Clear the Encrypt Contents To Secure Data check box. This decrypts the files using the recovery agent's recovery certificate.

7. Back up the decrypted files and e-mail or deliver them to the user, who can then encrypt them using his or her key (which is probably newly issued after the old key was lost). Consider using e-mail encryption when sending the files, if appropriate.

Real World   Protecting Recovery Agent Certificates

Store recovery agent certificates in a secured storage facility to prevent possible data compromise. (It's important to store to old recovery agent certificates because the associated certificate or recovery policy for encrypted files is updated only when the files are opened.) Upon receiving the recovery agent certificate, the recovery agent exports it to a diskette or other device that can be protected and deletes it from the computer. When data needs to be recovered, the certificate and associated private key can be imported. After the data is recovered, delete the certificate again. For information about exporting certificates, see the "Exporting Certificates and Private Keys" section earlier in this chapter.

Summary

Shares and permissions are the basic elements of file-security management in Windows Small Business Server, and are a basic part of the everyday life of the system administrator. In Chapter 10, "Installing and Managing Printers," you'll find the details about another part of the system administrator's daily life—installing and configuring both printers and the fax service.

Chapter 10

Installing and Managing Printers

Understanding Print Servers 205

Choosing Printers. 207

Installing Printers 208

Changing Printer Driver Settings 216

Setting Print Server Options 224

Managing Printers 225

Troubleshooting Printing Problems 230

Summary 234

One of the early expectations of computers in business was that they would eliminate paper, creating the "paperless office." The reality seems to be the opposite—the ease of printing has meant that we generate more paper, not less. Printing is an essential service on the network, and one that still generates more help desk calls than just about anything else. In this chapter, we'll cover installing and configuring printers, including configuring print drivers to support additional architectures such as x64 Editions of Microsoft Windows. We'll finish up with a troubleshooting section covering some of the most common printing problems.

Understanding Print Servers

Print servers are computers (or sometimes network appliances) that manage the communications between printers and the client computers generating the print jobs.

Generally, there are two approaches to print servers. The Microsoft approach is to use a Windows computer as an "intelligent" print server that handles communication between the printers and the client computers (reducing strain on the clients), and maintains a common print queue for all clients. Microsoft print servers also make it easy to find printers on the network by name (NetBIOS, DNS, or Active Directory), and install the appropriate printer drivers.

Planning   Microsoft Windows XP Professional and Microsoft Windows 2000 Professional can be used as print servers; however, they support a maximum of 10 simultaneous users. Additionally, if the shared printer is connected via a USB or parallel interface, the computer acting as a print server can slow to a crawl while clients print, which will have an impact on any user who is logged on locally.

In contrast, other operating systems, such as Linux, and printers with built-in network interfaces use a relatively "dumb" print server called the Line Printer Daemon (LPD), which acts strictly as an interface between the network and the printer. Each client maintains its own printer queue and performs all preprint processing, increasing the amount of time the computer is partially or completely unavailable for other tasks.

These two approaches aren't in opposition to each other and, in fact, the best way to connect a printer to a Windows print server is via a network connection to a printer, which usually runs the LPD service. The Windows print server connects to the printer using the traditional Line Printer Remote (LPR) service (the client-side equivalent of LPD) or via the higher-performance standard TCP/IP printer port, and shares the printer on the network. The Windows print server holds the printer queue and sends each print job to LPD, which passes the job to the printer.

Printer Terminology

Although the term "printer" is usually used to refer to both the physical device and its software interface, strictly speaking, a *printer* is a device that does the actual printing, and a *logical printer* is the software interface (printer driver) for the printer. You can have one logical printer associated with a single printer, or you can have several logical printers associated with a single printer. In this second arrangement, the logical printers can be configured at different priority levels so that one logical printer handles normal printing and another handles print jobs that should be printed during off-peak hours. For a printer that supports both PostScript and Printer Control Language (PCL), two logical printers allow users to choose which type of printing to do.

A single logical printer can also be associated with multiple physical printers in a printer pool, as long as all the printers work with the same driver. Printer pools distribute printing load more evenly, increasing performance. Because the physical printers in the pools are interchangeable, printer pools also make it possible for an administrator to add or remove physical printers without affecting the users' configurations.

Choosing Printers

Choosing the right printers for an organization is a lot like choosing the right car. There are certain practical matters to look at such as up-front cost, cost of consumables (gas, ink, or toner), and suitability to the task at hand (for example, hauling lumber or printing brochures). Use Table 10-1 to decide which basic category of printer would work best for your company. There's one type of printer we don't list in Table 10-1, primarily because it doesn't quite fit anywhere: the multipurpose copier. Many copiers these days also double as printers and scanners, and can be a cost-effective way to add high-volume printing to your network.

Consumable costs vary widely, especially for inkjet printers, so try to find reviews that list the cost per page for the printer in question. Look for printers with built-in network interfaces because they print faster, require less processing power on the print server, and can be flexibly located anywhere there's a network cable. Printers with a USB connection can be used if print volumes are low (or for backup printers), but steer clear of printers using parallel port connections if possible—they can drastically slow a print server.

Table 10-1   Printer types and suitability to different print volumes

Document Type	Low Volume (100–500 Pages/Month)	High Volume (500+ Pages/Month)
Black-and-white text and graphics	Consumer inkjet or laser printer	Black-and-white laser printer
Color text and graphics	Consumer inkjet printer	Color laser printer
Documents with pictures	Consumer inkjet printer	Business inkjet or color laser printer
Photo prints	Consumer inkjet printer	Inkjet photo printer, business inkjet printer, or high-quality color laser printer

Note Having at least two printers online in an organization is a good idea in case one runs into problems at an inopportune moment. One cost-effective approach is to use a laser printer as the primary printer and an inkjet printer as a backup printer that can also be used for high-quality photo prints.

Installing Printers

Before a Windows print server can share a printer on the network, it must first connect to the printer and install the necessary drivers. The following sections walk you through adding printers that are attached directly to the print server via USB or parallel port interface, as well as connecting to printers with built-in network adapters.

Real World   Local vs. Network Printers

In the consumer world, most printers are directly connected to a computer with a parallel port, USB port, or IEEE 1394 port. This solution—simple to use and to understand—is perfectly adequate and appropriate for individual users, or even most very small offices. But it has some significant disadvantages over a network-attached printer. It seriously limits where the printer can be physically located, since it must be within a few feet of the computer that supports it. And it can seriously slow down the work of the individual whose computer acts as the print server. Printer I/O is not terribly efficient, especially when using the traditional parallel printer port.

A network-attached printer, by comparison, can be located virtually anywhere. If you're using standard Ethernet to connect to the printer, you'll need a network port nearby, but if you use one of the widely available wireless print servers, even that requirement is eliminated. And network printing doesn't have an adverse effect on the server that supports it—you can manage all your print queues directly from the SBS server, thereby simplifying management.

If your printers don't have a network interface, you can use one of the widely available stand-alone print server appliances, either wireless or Ethernet. SBS treats these as if they were a standard network printer, but you don't have to buy a printer with a network card included—the print server appliance has a port or ports to connect to the printer as well as a network interface.

The one exception we'd suggest to the "all printers are network printers" rule is for the user who has a privacy (or other) need for a locally attached printer. Human Resources and hiring managers are two classes of users that this might apply to.

Adding Locally Attached Printers

If you're using a USB or IEEE 1394 (FireWire) connection to the printer, as soon as you plug the printer into the server, Windows automatically detects, installs, and shares the printer on the network, and also publishes it in Active Directory (although you might be prompted for drivers).

To use the Add Printer Wizard to set up a local printer that is physically connected to your system using a legacy parallel port, complete the following steps:

1. Connect the printer to the appropriate port on the server.

2. Click Start, choose Printers And Faxes, and then double-click Add Printer. Alternatively, select Printers from the Standard Management tree in the Server Management console and then click the Add A Printer link.

3. Click Next in the first page to begin using the Add Printer Wizard.

4. On the Local Or Network Printer page, select the Local Printer Attached To This Computer option, select the Automatically Detect And Install My Plug And Play Printer check box (Figure 10-1), and then click Next.

Important   If you're installing a Plug and Play (PnP) printer, always select the Automatically Detect And Install My Plug And Player Printer check box in the Add Printer Wizard. If you don't select this option, Windows detects the printer the next time the system is rebooted and attempts to install the printer a second time.

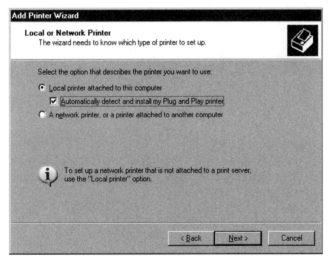

Figure 10-1   The Local Or Network Printer page of the Add Printer Wizard.

5. Windows displays the New Hardware Found dialog box when it locates the printer. If Windows has the appropriate drivers for the device, it installs them automatically.

6. If the printer wasn't detected, click Next to set up the printer manually.

7. On the Select A Printer Port page, shown in Figure 10-2, choose the port the printer is attached to, and then click Next.

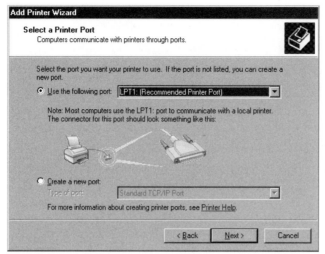

Figure 10-2   The Select A Printer Port page of the Add Printer Wizard.

8.   On the Install Printer Software page, select the manufacturer and model of the printer from the Install Printer Software page. Click Windows Update to search for drivers online, or click Have Disk to provide the location of updated drivers. When finished, click Next.

9.   On the Name Your Printer page, type a name for the printer in the Printer Name text box and click Next. Try to keep the total length of the printer name, including the server's fully qualified domain name (FQDN), to 31 characters or fewer, and don't use spaces or special characters if you want to support non-Windows clients.

10.   On the Printer Sharing page, select Share Name and then type a share name for the printer. Windows automatically creates an 8-letter name for optimal compatibility with MS-DOS and Microsoft Windows 3.x clients, even though these operating systems haven't been supported for years; don't use spaces when you want to maintain compatibility with non-Windows clients and automated Windows installations. Click Next.

11.   On the Location And Comment page, type the location name for the printer in the Location box, describe the capabilities of the printer in the Comment text box, and then click Next.

> **Note**   The Location field was designed for large networks that have the Printer Location Tracking feature enabled; however, on a smaller network, it's still useful for communicating the location of a printer to users.

12. On the Print Test Page, print a test page by clicking Yes, and then click Next to display a summary of the printer installation. To change the installation choices, click Back; otherwise, click Finish to complete the installation.

Adding Printers with Network Interfaces

If you have a printer with a built-in network connection, you can connect to it in two ways: via a standard TCP/IP printer port, or via the slower LPR service if the printer refuses to work with a Standard TCP/IP printer port.

Note   You can also connect Windows Small Business Server to printers shared by other Windows servers or clients, and turn around and share these connections using the Add Printer Wizard (choose the Network Printer option).

Adding Printers on a Standard TCP/IP Printer Port

The best solution for connecting to network printers is to use a standard TCP/IP printer port. The standard TCP/IP printer port in SBS supports network printers that use TCP/IP (most commonly implemented with LPD), as well as printers connected to network devices such as the Hewlett-Packard JetDirect. The standard TCP/IP printer port is easier to set up, provides more printer status information, and is 50 percent faster than an LPR Port Monitor (which is discussed in the next section).

To set up a network-based printer through a standard TCP/IP printer port—which SBS treats as a local port—complete the following steps:

1. Connect the printer to the network and configure the printer with the proper TCP/IP settings for the network. You should either configure the printer with a fixed IP address, or assign a DHCP reservation to the printer's MAC address. Many older printers allowed you to set the IP address manually from the front panel buttons. Newer models often have a Web interface for settings.

2. Click Start, choose Printers And Faxes, and then double-click Add Printer. Alternatively, select Printers from the Standard Management tree in the Server Management console, and then click the Add A Printer link.

3. Click Next on the first page to begin using the Add Printer Wizard.

4. On the Local Or Network Printer page, select the Local Printer Attached To This Computer option, clear the Automatically Detect And Install My Plug And Play Printer check box, and then click Next.

5. On the Select A Printer Port page, select Create A New Port, select Standard TCP/IP Port from the drop-down list (Figure 10-3), and then click Next. Windows launches the Add Standard TCP/IP Printer Port Wizard.

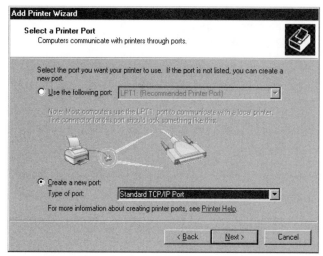

Figure 10-3   The Select A Printer Port page of the Add Printer Wizard.

6. Make sure the printer is turned on and connected to the network, and then click Next on the first page of the Add Standard TCP/IP Printer Port Wizard to begin using the wizard.

7. On the Add Port page, type the printer name or IP address in the first text box, as shown in Figure 10-4.

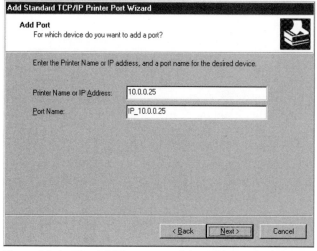

Figure 10-4   The Add Port page of the Add Standard TCP/IP Printer Port Wizard.

8. If necessary, modify the TCP/IP port name that Windows automatically fills in and then click Next. Windows attempts to connect to the printer.

9. If Windows can't detect the printer, the Additional Port Information Required page is displayed. Select the printer type from the Standard list (Figure 10-5), click Next, click Finish, and then skip to Step 15. Or select Custom and click Settings to display the Configure Standard TCP/IP Port Monitor dialog box, shown in Figure 10-6 and discussed in the next steps.

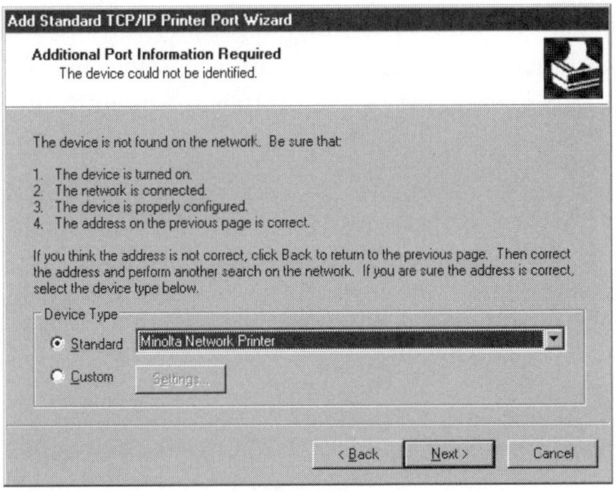

Figure 10-5   The Additional Port Information Required page.

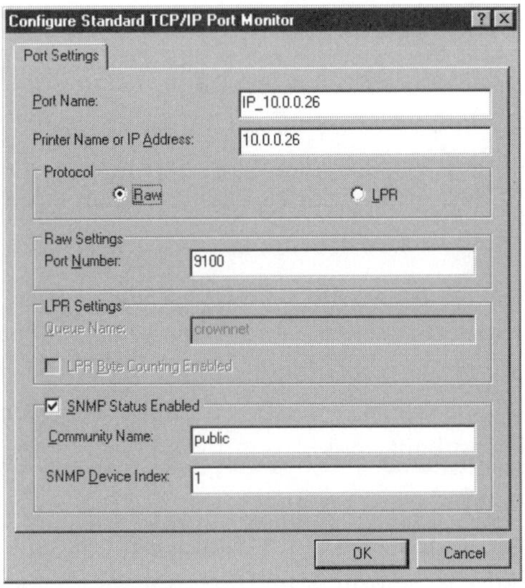

Figure 10-6   The Configure Standard TCP/IP Port Monitor dialog box.

10. Choose the protocol the printer uses, either RAW or LPR. Use RAW if possible; it closes the printer port when finished with a print job, reducing the likelihood of hanging the print spooler.

11. Type the port number for the printer if you're using the raw protocol. Use the default port number (9100) unless the printer documentation specifies that you must use a different port.

12. If using the LPR protocol, type the queue name in the box provided.

13. If the printer supports Simple Network Management Protocol (SNMP), select the SNMP Status Enabled check box, and type the Community Name (usually "public") and SNMP Device Index. SNMP allows the printer to communicate status information to the server.

> **Note**   Select the LPR Byte Counting Enabled check box if you're having problems with incomplete or missing documents. However, be aware that selecting this check box tells the server to count the number of bytes in a document before sending it to the printer, requiring the server to spool the job twice (taking extra time).

14. Click OK when you're finished configuring the TCP/IP port, click Next, and then click Finish.

15. If SBS doesn't detect the printer, the Install Printer Software page is displayed. Choose the manufacturer and printer model and then click Next.

16. On the Name Your Printer page, type a name for the printer in the Printer Name text box. Try to keep the total length of the printer name, including the server's fully qualified domain name (FQDN), to 31 characters or fewer, and don't use spaces or special characters if you want to support non-Windows clients. Specify whether to make the printer the default printer, and then click Next.

17. On the Printer Sharing page, select Share Name and then type a share name for the printer. Windows automatically creates an 8-letter name for optimal compatibility with MS-DOS and Windows 3.x clients even though these operating systems haven't been supported for years; don't use spaces when you want to maintain compatibility with non-Windows clients and automated Windows installations. Click Next.

18. On the Location And Comment page, type the location name for the printer in the Location box, describe the capabilities of the printer in the Comment text box, and then click Next.

19. On Print Test Page, print a test page by clicking Yes, and then click Next to display a summary of the printer installation. To change the installation choices, click Back; otherwise, click Finish to complete the installation.

Adding Printers on an LPR Printer Port

If you have a network printer or print device that doesn't support the Standard TCP/IP printer port, you can use an LPR printer port. You'll probably also have to use an LPR printer port if the printer is being shared by a UNIX or Linux system using the LPD service.

To set up a network-based printer through an LPR port, complete the following steps:

1. Connect the printer to the network and configure the printer with the proper TCP/IP and LPD settings.

2. Install Print Services For Unix: In Control Panel, click Add Or Remove Programs, click Add/Remove Windows Components, select Other Network File And Print Services, click Details, select Print Services For Unix, click OK, and then click Next.

3. Click Start, choose Printers And Faxes, and then double-click Add Printer. Alternatively, select Printers from the Standard Management tree in the Server Management console and then click the Add A Printer link.

4. On the Local Or Network Printer page, select the Local Printer Attached To My Computer option, clear the Automatically Detect And Install My Plug And Play Printer check box, and then click Next.

5. On the Select A Printer Port page, choose Create A New Port, select LPR Port from the drop-down list, and click Next.

6. In the Add LPR Compatible Printer dialog box, type the IP address or DNS name of the printer or print server running LPD in the first text box, shown in Figure 10-7.

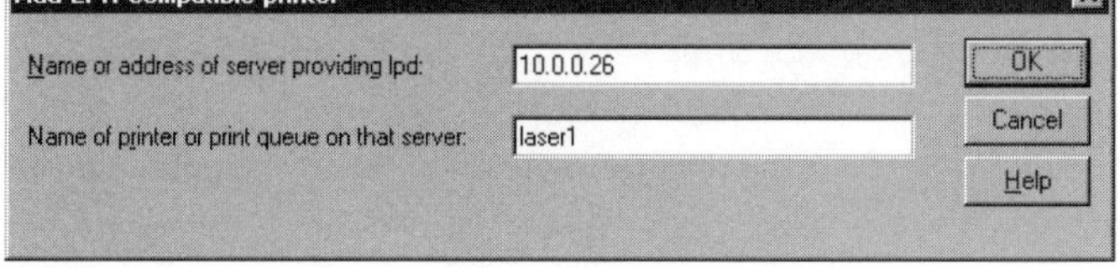

Figure 10-7   The Add LPR Compatible Printer dialog box.

7. In the second text box, type the name of the printer or print queue on the LPD server, and then click OK. Windows adds the port to the list of ports.

8. If Windows doesn't detect the printer, the Install Printer Software page is displayed. Choose the manufacturer and printer model and then click Next.

9. On the Name Your Printer page, type a name for the printer in the Printer Name text box. Try to keep the total length of the printer name, including the server's fully qualified domain name (FQDN), to 31 characters or fewer, and don't use spaces or special characters if you want to support non-Windows clients. Specify whether to make the printer the default printer, and then click Next.

10. On the Printer Sharing page, select Share Name and then type a share name for the printer. Windows automatically creates an 8-letter name for optimal compatibility with MS-DOS and Windows 3.x clients even though these operating systems haven't been supported for years; don't use spaces when you want to maintain compatibility with non-Windows clients and automated Windows installations. Click Next.

11. On the Location And Comment page, type the location name for the printer in the Location box, describe the capabilities of the printer in the Comment text box, and then click Next.

12. On the Print Test Page, print a test page by clicking Yes, and then click Next to display a summary of the printer installation. To change the installation choices, click Back; otherwise, click Finish to complete the installation.

Changing Printer Driver Settings

SBS installs new printers with printer options that are a good choice for most installations. You can change these defaults or add additional features or drivers as appropriate for your environment. Some modifications you might need to make include installing additional client printer drivers, specifying color profiles, changing printer availability, determining group printing priorities, and setting up printer pools. These features might not be available until you actively enable them.

Note Depending on the printer driver you use, the dialog boxes and printer options you have are probably different from those shown here. Printing preferences such as quality and paper types aren't covered here because they are extremely driver-dependent and, for the most part, self-explanatory.

Sharing a Printer and Adding Client Drivers

Before a shared printer can be used by clients of a different architecture, such as x64 Editions of Windows, you need to add the drivers for the printer to SBS. This isn't available in the initial printer sharing wizard, so you'll need to add the necessary client drivers after the shared printer is created.

To change the share name the printer uses on a network, to stop sharing the printer, or to install drivers for clients of different architectures, follow these steps:

1. In the Printers And Faxes folder, right-click the printer you want to modify, and then choose Properties from the shortcut menu.

2. Click the Sharing tab, click the Share This Printer option (if not already selected), and type the share name for the printer in the text box provided (Figure 10-8).

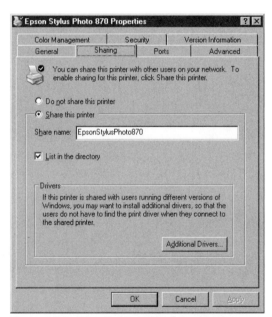

Figure 10-8   The Sharing tab of a printer's Properties dialog box.

3. To publish the printer in Active Directory, select the List In The Directory check box.

4. To add client drivers that are automatically downloaded and installed when a Windows client other than Windows XP, Windows 2000, or Windows Server 2003 connects to the printer, click Additional Drivers.

5. In the Additional Drivers dialog box, shown in Figure 10-9, select the check box next to any client drivers to be installed, and then click OK. To install additional client drivers, you need access to the installation files for the appropriate driver version, either on CD-ROM or across the network. To reinstall a previously installed driver, see the "Setting Print Server Options" section of this chapter.

Figure 10-9 The Additional Drivers dialog box for a shared printer.

6. SBS will prompt you for the location of the appropriate drivers for the printer, as shown in Figure 10-10. For x64 clients, this will normally be the NTPRINT.INF file, located in the \AMD64 directory of the installation CD, as shown in Figure 10-11.

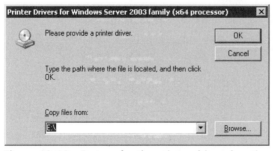

Figure 10-10 Browse for the printer drivers location for the architecture you've chosen.

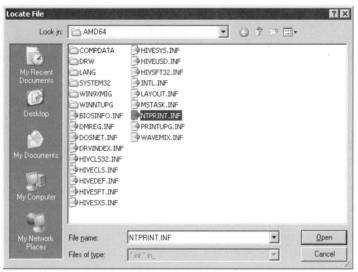

Figure 10-11   Windows x64 Edition drivers are located in the \AMD64 directory.

7. Click OK through the rest of the dialogs and the drivers will be loaded and available for your x64 clients.

Note   To change the driver that the print server uses for a printer, click the Advanced tab and then choose a driver from the Driver drop-down list, or click New Driver to start the Add Printer Driver Wizard.

Real World   Supporting x64 Clients

While the steps we've described in the preceding sections will enable SBS to support any printer that is included in the shipping release of Windows XP Professional x64 Edition or Windows Server 2003 x64 Edition, that list of printers is by no means comprehensive and there very well might not be a perfect match for your printer in the list in NTPRINT.INF. Unfortunately, if the specific model you're sharing in SBS isn't listed in NTPRINT.INF (or in a third-party .INF file for the printer), SBS will refuse to accept and load the driver, even though there may be a related driver that would work acceptably. There two ways to work around this problem: Have the x64 clients print directly to the printer if it's network-connected, or create a second logical printer in SBS that points to the same physical printer but uses a driver that is in the x64 list.

The first solution takes the printer out of direct management and control by your IT staff, and can cause interference if multiple print jobs are being sent to the printer at the same time from different clients, but is the least disruptive or confusing to the rest of your network.

The second solution keeps the printer entirely within the management of SBS, but is more likely to confuse users who know that the printer is a particular model, but then see a second model and don't know which to use. If you're just setting up your network, we suggest using the alternate printer driver as your only logical printer for that printer as long as it provides sufficient functionality. This will provide the least confusion for users. If your SBS network is already set up, and you're just adding the logical printer to support your new x64 clients, use the Description field to make it clear the printer is for x64 clients only.

For additional information about supporting printers in x64, see *http://msmvps.com/blogs/xperts64/search.aspx?q=Printer+support&p=1*.

Specifying a Color Profile

Windows Small Business Server 2003 includes the Integrated Color Management (ICM) 2 API for maintaining consistent colors across monitors, color printers, and scanners. When you need to achieve accurate color reproduction, it's useful to set up the printer—as well as the users' monitors and scanners—with an appropriate color profile. To specify a color profile, complete the following steps:

1. In the Printers And Faxes folder, right-click the printer you want to modify and select Properties from the shortcut menu.

2. Click the Color Management tab. Select the Automatic option to have Windows choose the best color profile.

3. To manually select a color profile, choose the Manual option, and then select a profile from the list or click Add to install an additional color profile from the device manufacturer. Click OK.

Note   Color management in Windows has come a long way, but most graphics professionals still use third-party, hardware-based, color-matching solutions when color accuracy is important. However, ICM provides a good way to attain a reasonable measure of accuracy.

Changing Printer Availability and Priorities

To set up a printer to be available only during certain times—perhaps to discourage after-hours printing—complete the following steps:

1. In the Printers And Faxes folder, right-click the printer you want to modify and select Properties from the shortcut menu.

2. Click the Advanced tab, and then click the Available From option.

3. Select the earliest and latest times the printer is to be available to users, and then click OK.

Determining Group Printer Priorities

To set up user groups to have different priorities on a printer, you need to set up two or more logical printers for the physical printer. Assign each printer a different priority, and give your highest priority groups print permissions to the highest priority logical printer. To do this, follow these steps:

1. In the Printers And Faxes folder, double-click the Add Printer icon and use the Add Printer Wizard to add one or more duplicate logical printers for a physical printer already installed on the print server.

2. Right-click the logical printer for which you want to change the priority, and then select Properties from the shortcut menu. Click the Advanced tab, shown in Figure 10-12.

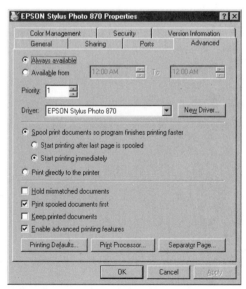

Figure 10-12   The Advanced tab of a printer's Properties dialog box.

3. Change the priority to be assigned to the logical printer for the users and groups who use this printer driver by typing a number in the Priority text box. The priority range goes from 1, which is the lowest priority, through 99, which is the highest priority—the reverse of what you might expect.

4. Click the Security tab and add the users and groups you want to allow to print at this priority level. Remove or deny print permissions to users whose printing should occur at a different priority level. Those users will utilize another printer driver with a different priority level.

5. Click OK, and repeat the process for all other logical printers created for the printer, until you prioritize the user groups.

Setting Up Printer Pools and Changing Port Settings

A printer pool has more than one printer sharing a single driver and appears as one printer to users. The advantage of using a printer pool is that clients don't need to find which printer is available; they simply print to the single logical printer on the print server, which then sends the print job to the first available printer. Administration of the printers is also simplified because all printers in the printer pool are consolidated under one driver. If you modify the properties for the single logical printer, all physical printers in the printer pool use the same settings.

To set up a printer pool or change the port settings for a printer, complete the following steps:

1. In the Printers And Faxes folder, right-click the printer you want to modify and select Properties from the shortcut menu.

2. Click the Ports tab.

3. Select the Enable Printer Pooling check box.

4. To add additional printers to the printer pool, select the ports to which the additional printers are connected.

5. To change the settings for a port, select the port and click Configure Port.

Important   All printers in a printer pool must be able to use the same printer driver. If they are not identical printer models, you can often achieve this by careful selection of a printer driver that will support an acceptable level of functionality for several different, but related, printers.

Changing Spool Settings

Print spooling, or storing a print job on disk before printing, affects the actual printing speed as well as how clients perceive printing performance. You can change the way print spooling works to correct printing problems or to hold printed documents in the printer queue in case a user needs to print the document again. To change the spool settings for a printer, right-click the printer you want to modify, select Properties from the shortcut menu, and then use the Advanced tab to modify the spool settings.

Following is a description of the print spool settings on the Advanced tab:

- **Spool Print Documents So Program Finishes Printing Faster**   Spools the print documents to the print server, freeing the client to perform other tasks more quickly.

    1. To ensure that the entire document is available to the printer when printing begins, select Start Printing After Last Page Is Spooled. This step might correct some printing problems, and also helps high-priority documents print before low-priority documents.

    2. To reduce the time it takes to print a document, select Start Printing Immediately.

- **Print Directly To The Printer**   Turns off spooling, causing a performance hit on the server (though it might fix some printing problems).

- **Hold Mismatched Documents**   Holds documents in the queue that don't match the current printer settings (for example, documents that require legal-size paper when letter paper is currently in the printer). Other documents in the print queue are unaffected by held documents.

- **Print Spooled Documents First**   Prints the highest priority document that is already spooled first, ahead of higher priority documents that are still spooling. This step speeds overall printer throughput by keeping the printer from waiting for documents.

- **Keep Printed Documents**   Keeps a copy of print jobs in the printer queue in case users need to print the document again. In this circumstance, the user can resubmit the document directly from the queue rather than printing from his or her application a second time.

- **Enable Advanced Printing Features**   Enables metafile spooling and printer options such as page order, booklet printing, and pages per sheet (if available on the printer). Disable this when you're experiencing printer problems.

- **Separator Page**   Allows you to specify a separator page to insert between printed documents. Windows Small Business Server 2003 comes with three default separator pages located in the %systemroot%\System32 folder: Pcl.sep for PCL printers, Pscript.sep for PostScript printers that support Printer Job Language (PJL), and Sysprint.sep for PostScript printers that don't support PJL.

Setting Print Server Options

Although most printer configuration occurs in the printer driver for a particular printer, you can also configure print server settings that affect all printers hosted by the print server. These settings include determining which forms are available and which ports and printer drivers are available to use, as well as some spool settings.

1. In the Printers And Faxes folder, choose the Server Properties command from the File menu to open the Print Server Properties dialog box, shown in Figure 10-13.

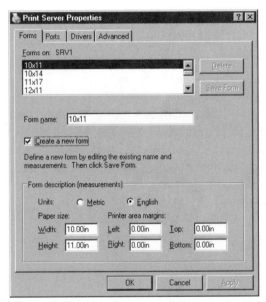

Figure 10-13   The Forms tab of the Print Server Properties dialog box.

2. To create a new form corresponding to a special paper size on which users can print, select the Create A New Form check box, type a name for the form in the Form Name box, use the Form Description (Measurements) section to define the form, and then click Save Form.

3. To view the ports available on the print server, click the Ports tab. Select a port and click Configure Port to modify the port settings, or click Add Port or Delete Port to add or remove a port from the system.

4. Click the Drivers tab to view and modify the list of currently installed drivers on the print server.

   a. To view the driver details for a printer driver, select the driver and then click Properties to display the Driver Properties dialog box.

   b. To reinstall a printer driver, select the driver and click Reinstall.

   c. To add a printer driver that you want to make available to clients to download, click Add to launch the Add Printer Driver Wizard, which guides you through the driver installation process.

   d. To remove a printer driver, select the driver and click Remove.

5. Click the Advanced tab. In the Spool Folder text box, type the location in which you want to store the spool folder. Make sure the drive is big enough to hold all the documents in the print queue. If you choose to enable the holding of printed documents, the drive needs to be big enough to archive all print jobs.

6. Select the check boxes next to the events to be logged.

7. To be notified of errors while printing remote documents, select Beep On Errors Of Remote Documents. Windows XP clients display an unobtrusive balloon tip in the System Tray for 10 seconds (or until clicked) when a document has finished printing. To notify earlier clients when a document has finished printing, select Notify When Remote Documents Are Printed. To display a notification message on the computer the document was printed on (even if the user who printed it is currently logged on elsewhere), select Notify Computer, Not User, When Remote Documents Are Printed.

Note The Notify When Remote Documents Are Printed feature can be useful to earlier clients on busy print servers when a significant delay might occur between the time a client sends a document and the time the document reaches the head of the queue and actually prints. However, in most cases on an SBS network, this feature is just plain annoying, and most of the time you'll have happier users if you turn off this option.

Managing Printers

Windows makes the job of managing printers easy and flexible. You can manage printers from virtually any Windows computer using the standard Windows print queue, you can use a Web browser interface, or you can use the Windows Small Business Server 2003 command-line interface.

Managing Printers from Windows

If you're logged in with an account that has sufficient privileges, you can manage printers shared by the SBS server from any computer running Windows Server 2003, Windows XP, or Windows 2000 (including the SBS computer, of course). To manage printers from within Windows, double-click a printer in the Printers And Faxes folder to view and manage the print queue, as shown in Figure 10-14.

Note To open the Printers And Faxes folder using an account with Administrator privileges without logging off and then logging on again, launch Windows Explorer using the Run As command, display the Address Bar if it's not already present, type Control Panel in the Address Bar, and then double-click Printers And Faxes. For more information about the Run As command, see Chapter 8, "Users and Groups"

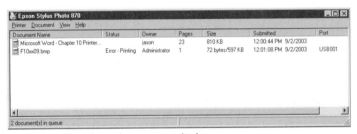

Figure 10-14   The print queue window.

You can manage the print queue using the following simple processes:

- To temporarily stop a *single* document from printing, right-click the selected document and choose Pause from the shortcut menu. To resume printing, right-click the document and choose Resume.

- To temporarily stop *all* documents from printing, choose Pause Printing from the Printer menu. To resume printing all documents, select Pause Printing a second time from the Printer menu.

- To cancel one or more print jobs, select the documents, right-click and choose Cancel from the shortcut menu. (You can also cancel print jobs by selecting them and pressing the Delete key.)

- To cancel *all* print jobs in the print queue, choose Cancel All Documents from the Printer menu.

- To restart a print job (force the document to print from the beginning again), right-click the document and choose Restart from the shortcut menu.

- To change the priority of a print job, right-click the print job, choose Properties from the shortcut menu, and then use the Priority slider to adjust the priority of the document, with 1 being the lowest priority and 99 being the highest priority.

- To specify that a print job should be printed only during a certain period, right-click the print job, choose Properties from the shortcut menu, select the Only From option, and choose the time range to allow the document to print. This feature is useful when you want to set a large document to print only during a time when you anticipate the printer to be free.

Note   Sometimes a print job appears stuck in the queue and cannot be deleted. Try turning the printer off and then on again, or stop the Print Spooler service on the print server and restart it. See the "Deleting Stuck Documents" section of this chapter for more information.

Managing Printers from a Web Browser

SBS lets you manage printers from any browser, provided you have Internet Printing support installed. To install Internet Printing support, double-click Add Or Remove Programs in Control Panel, click Add/Remove Windows Components, select Application Server, click Details, select Internet Information Services (IIS), click Details, select Internet Printing, and then click OK.

Note   Just because you *can* do something, doesn't necessarily mean you *should* do it. This is one feature we just don't like and don't use.

Once Internet Printing support is installed, complete the following steps to manage printers using a Web browser:

1. Type the URL of the print server followed by /**printers** in the browser's Address window.

2. To display a printer's queue, click the hyperlink of the printer you want to manage.

3. Click a hyperlink under the Printer Actions heading to pause, resume, or cancel the printing of all documents in the print queue.

4. To pause or cancel a specific print job, select the option button to the left of the document, and then click the Pause hyperlink or the Cancel hyperlink under the Document Actions heading.

5. To view the properties for the printer, click the Properties hyperlink under the View heading. Note that you can only view properties in the browser. To change properties, you must use the Printers And Faxes folder.

Managing Printers from a Command Line

SBS 2003 makes command-line administration of printers almost practical for administrators who are so inclined. Open the Command Prompt window and then use the following commands to get started. To view a list of parameters, type the command followed by *servername**printername* at a command prompt, or use the Help and Support Center.

- **Print**   Prints the specified text file to the specified printer.
- **Lpr**   Prints the specified text file to the specified LPD print queue.
- **Net print**   Displays information about the specified print queue or print job. Can also hold, release, or delete print jobs.
- **Lpq**   Displays information about the specified LPD print queue.
- **Net start**   Starts the specified service. Can be used to start or stop the spooler service.

SBS also comes with the several print management scripts that you can run from a command line using Cscript:

Important   To run these scripts from the command line, you need to either change your current directory to the %windir%\system32 directory, or use a fully qualified path to the .VBS file. Or, do what we do, and write a little batch file wrapper script for each of them. The one we have for prnmngr.vbs is:

```
@echo off
REM Shell Wrapper to call prnmngr.vbs from anywhere
REM without having to worry about current working directory

cscript %windir%\system32\prnmngr.vbs %*
```

- **Prnmngr.vbs**   Adds, deletes, or lists printers on a Windows print server
- **Prnjobs.vbs**   Lets you view and manage the print jobs of printer shares on a Windows print server
- **Prncfg.vbs**   Allows you to view and change the settings of printers on a Windows print server
- **Prnqctl.vbs**   Pauses or resumes printing, clears the print queue, or prints test pages
- **Prnport.vbs**   Administers all things related to printer ports
- **Prndrvr.vbs**   Adds, deletes, or lists printer drivers on a Windows print server

Using Printer Migrator to Back Up or Migrate Print Servers

You can use the free Microsoft Printer Migrator utility (also called the Print Migrator) to back up, restore, or migrate print server settings, including printer drivers and print queues. This utility makes moving to a new server much easier—simply back up the print server configuration on the old server and restore it to the new one—even when the servers are running different versions of Windows.

To use this program, you can download it from the Microsoft Web site. Then launch the program (Figure 10-15) and choose Backup from the Actions menu. This saves the configuration to a compressed (.cab) file. Move the .cab file to the desired server and run Printer Migrator again, this time choosing Restore from the Actions menu. Voilà! The settings and drivers are restored. (Keep in mind that if you migrate from Windows NT 4.0, you'll want to promptly upgrade the migrated level 2 drivers to native level 3 drivers for maximum stability.)

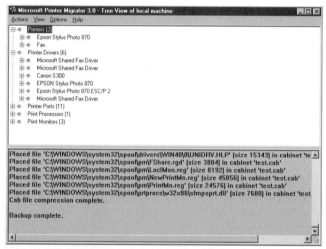

Figure 10-15   The Printer Migrator utility.

Under the Hood   Level 2 and Level 3 Printer Drivers

Windows Small Business Server 2003 can use two types of printer drivers: level 2 printer drivers, which were written for Windows NT 4.0; and level 3 printer drivers, which are written for the Windows 2000, Windows XP, and Windows Server 2003 families. Level 2 drivers run in kernel mode, and can destabilize the operating system or force a reboot when they crash. Level 3 drivers run in protected user mode, where unstable drivers can't cause operating system instability (at worst they can crash the spooler service, which restarts automatically without requiring a reboot). Level 2 drivers can be used only on an upgraded system—they can't be installed on a running Windows Small Business Server 2003 system, except by using the Printer Migrator utility.

Troubleshooting Printing Problems

The following sections address a number of common printing problems. If you're having trouble pinpointing the problem or solution, first use the following steps to troubleshoot the printing process:

- **Print from the client experiencing the problem and pay attention to any errors.**

  If the document prints properly, you probably have a user error, in which case you might need to educate the users as to the proper printing procedure. Otherwise, you might have a problem with a particular program, or the printer driver might be improperly configured for the users.

- **Check the print server status.**   When no errors are listed, check to see whether any documents are printing correctly. If not, check that sufficient free disk space exists on the drive holding the spool folder. If documents print garbled, the printer might be using the wrong data type (EMF or raw). Try using the raw data type to see whether this corrects the problem. You might also want to clear the Enable Advanced Printing Features check box on the Advanced tab of the printer's Properties dialog box. (See "Changing Spool Settings" earlier in this chapter for more information.)

  If some documents in the print queue don't print and you can't delete them, the print spooler might be stalled. Restart the Print Spooler service to see whether this corrects the problem. You might also want to add another logical printer (printer driver) for the printer to try to rule out the possibility of a corrupt printer driver.

  > **Note**   To prevent documents with certain languages from printing slowly, install on the print server the fonts for all languages that the clients will use to print. To do this, copy the fonts to the %*SystemRoot*%\Fonts folder on the print server and open the Fonts folder (or reboot the server).

- **Print from another client computer.**   If the second client prints properly, go back to the original client and perform more in-depth troubleshooting, such as reinstalling the printer drivers and testing the printing subsystem. If the second client can't print to the specified printer, you most likely have a problem with the print server or printer.

■ **Check the printer.**   If no documents are printing, pause the print queue and then go check the actual printer. Are any errors reported on the printer? Make sure that the ready or online light is illuminated and that the printer cable is securely attached, or that the network cable is properly plugged in and the light next to the network port is illuminated (if available). Print a test page directly from the printer. If the test page prints properly and the printer is connected directly to the network, use the Ping.exe program from a command prompt to test the ability to reach the printer. If you still can't print to the printer, try installing the printer on a different computer temporarily to rule out the original print server.

Document Fails to Print

When the document doesn't print, error messages frequently appear that might help you identify the problem. Here are some solutions to try:

■ If you receive an error stating that the appropriate printer driver wasn't available for download, you need to install the appropriate client drivers on the print server (or manually install drivers on the client).

■ Log in as the user having problems at the client having problems. Print a test document from Notepad. If you can print with Notepad but not with the user's application, you've eliminated connectivity and drivers as the problem with one simple test. The application is the likely culprit.

■ If you can't print with Notepad, you can try printing from the command line by typing the following command: **dir** > [printer port name], using the share name of the network printer as the printer port name. The chances of this working when Notepad didn't are small, however.

■ If you receive an error stating that the print device was unavailable, you might have a network connectivity problem, or the client might lack sufficient permissions. Try using the Ping command to test connectivity, or print using a user account with administrative privileges.

■ Determine whether you can see and connect to the print server (usually the SBS server) across the network. Try copying a file to the print server to see whether you can access the print server. (Generally, if you can't access the print server, you can't access any attached printers.)

■ If you experience a lot of disk access and the document fails to print, verify that the drive holding the client's spool folder contains enough free disk space to hold the spooled document.

- If you still can't print at all, run the Add Printer Wizard, choose the Local Printer option, select Create A New Port, choose Local Port, type the share name of the printer (*servername**printername*) for the port name, and complete the rest of the wizard. Then print a test page.

Document Prints Incorrectly

When a document prints but appears garbled or has some other defect, a compatibility problem exists between the client, the printer driver, and the printer. Make sure that the client is using the proper client printer driver and that the server is also using the proper printer driver. If the problem only occurs from a line-of-business application, verify which printer driver it's using.

Install a duplicate logical printer to test whether the printer driver is corrupt. If this isn't the problem, try changing the spool settings on the client driver (or, if multiple clients experience the same problem, try changing the settings on the server's printer driver). Specifically try changing the following options on the Advanced tab of the printer's Properties dialog box:

- To ensure that the entire document is available to the printer when printing begins, select the Start Printing After Last Page Is Spooled option.

- If you continue to have printing problems, choose the Print Directly To The Printer option to turn off spooling. This action causes a performance reduction on the server.

- Clear the Enable Advanced Printing Features check box on the print server to turn off metafile spooling, which disables some printer options such as page order, booklet printing, and pages per sheet (if available on the printer).

More Info   For more information about the Advanced tab options, see the "Changing Spool Settings" section earlier in this chapter.

Deleting Stuck Documents

When you can't delete documents in the print queue or documents don't print, the print spooler might be stalled. This stalling also affects any fax services the server is running. To restart the Print Spooler service, complete the following steps:

1. Launch the Computer Management snap-in from the Administrative Tools folder, expand Services And Applications in the console tree, and then select Services.

2. Select the Print Spooler service in the right pane, shown in Figure 10-16, and then click the Restart Service toolbar button.

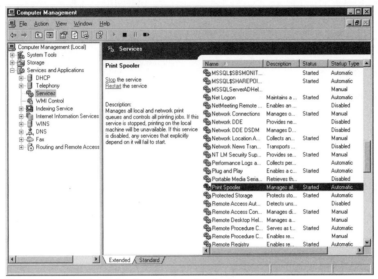

Figure 10-16   The Print Spooler service in Computer Management.

3. To view the services (such as remote procedure call) on which the print spooler depends, double-click the Print Spooler service and then click the Dependencies tab. You can also use this tab to view the services that depend on the print spooler to function properly.

4. To configure a recovery process to take place should the Print Spooler service fail, click the Recovery tab, and then specify whether you want to restart the service, reboot the computer, or run a program after each print spooler failure.

   Restarting the service is usually a good option—it saves time. Automatic rebooting of the computer is a last option.

   Note   To restart the print spooler from a command prompt, type net stop "print spooler", press Enter, and then press Y to stop any dependant services. When all services have stopped, type net start "print spooler", press Enter, and then restart any dependant services using the same method (for example, net start "Fax").

Summary

Printing is a vital service to most networks, and this chapter showed you how to accomplish virtually any printing administration task you might need to accomplish, including installing and managing printers, and troubleshooting print problems. In the next chapter, we discuss an equally important topic—managing computers on a network.

Chapter 11
Managing Computers on the Network

Connecting Computers to the Network. 236

Using the Remote Web Workplace. 254

Managing Computers from the Server. 258

Summary 268

Microsoft Windows Small Business Server 2003 streamlines client management tasks by making it easy to connect computers to the network and manage them remotely from the server. With the R2 release of SBS, Microsoft adds the important ability to directly manage and control Microsoft software updates to all Windows computers on the network with the addition of Windows Server Update Services (WSUS). The installation, configuration, and management of WSUS is covered in Chapter 12, "Patch Management."

SBS supports Microsoft Windows XP Professional (32-bit and 64-bit versions), Microsoft Windows XP Tablet PC Edition, and Microsoft Windows 2000 Professional for all client computers on the network. (Member servers should use Microsoft Windows Server 2003 or Microsoft Windows 2000 Server.) Microsoft Windows NT 4.0, Microsoft Windows 98, and Microsoft Windows Me computers can technically function on an SBS network, but since they are no longer supported operating systems and no longer receive even critical security updates, their use is strongly discouraged. Computers running Microsoft Windows Vista are not yet shipping, so support for Vista computers is experimental only. Computers running other operating systems, such as Linux or Mac OS/X, usually can be made to work with SBS for basic tasks, but have significant limitations and require more work on the part of the administrator.

Connecting Computers to the Network

Connecting computers running Windows XP Professional, Windows Server 2003, or Windows 2000 to an SBS network is easy: just create computer accounts for the computer, establish basic network connectivity, and then use the Small Business Server Network Configuration Wizard to configure the rest of the client's settings.

Note   Mobile or remote computers that routinely connect to the SBS network using VPNs should be added to the domain just as if they were locally connected. This enables computer authentication as well as user authentication, and it eliminates the need for remote users to provide credentials for every domain resource they access. Because VPN client computers that are domain members must authenticate with the domain during logon, remote users can log onto their computers either via a dial-up VPN connection to the domain or by using cached credentials when they don't want to establish a VPN connection.

Creating Computer Accounts for Client Computers

Before you connect a client computer to the network, you need to run the Set Up Computer Wizard on the SBS server. This wizard, which can be started directly or as part of the Add User Wizard, creates computer accounts and optionally assigns software to the computers.

More Info   For information about connecting additional servers to the network, see the next section, "Creating Computer Accounts for Server Computers."

To run the Set Up Computer Wizard, complete the following steps:

1. Log on to the SBS server, click Start, and then click Server Management to open the Server Management console.

2. Click Computers and then click Set Up Client Computers to open the Set Up Computer Wizard.

3. Click Next. On the Client Computer Names page, shown in Figure 11-1, create computer accounts for one or more client computers, and then click Next:

   ❑ To create a new computer account, type the computer name in the Client Computer Name box and click Add.

   ❑ To rename or remove a computer account you added, select the computer account and click Rename or Remove.

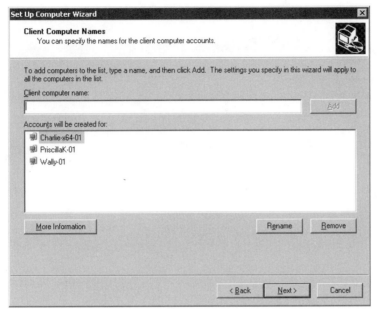

Figure 11-1   The Client Computer Names page of the Set Up Computer Wizard.

4. On the Client Applications page, shown in Figure 11-2, select the applications to install on each client computer. To allow users to change which applications are installed during Client Setup, select the During Client Setup, Allow The Selected Applications To Be Modified check box. To force the client computer to log off after Client Setup completes processing, select the After Client Setup Is Finished, Log Off The Client Computer check box. Click Next to continue.

> **Note**   Users of Windows Small Business Server 2003, Premium Edition, should also assign the ISA Server Firewall Client to client computers. (Unfortunately, it's not assigned by default.) To do so, first add the Firewall Client to the list of available applications, as described in the "Assigning Applications to Client Computers" section of this chapter.

5. On the Mobile Client And Offline Use page, select the Install Connection Manager and Install ActiveSync 3.7 check boxes if the client computers connect remotely via VPN and synchronizing Microsoft Pocket PC and Microsoft SmartPhone devices. Click Next to continue.

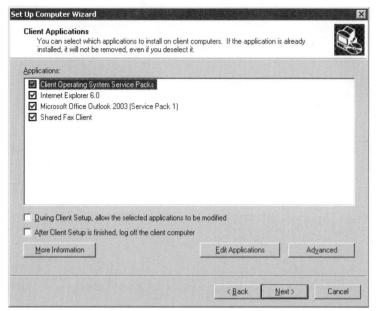

Figure 11-2   The Client Applications page of the Set Up Computer Wizard.

6.   Review the settings and then click Finish. You'll see a final informational dialog titled "Finishing Your Installation" with instructions for connecting the client to a web page to perform the actual details of adding it to the domain.

More Info   To edit the list of applications, see the "Assigning Applications to Client Computers" section of this chapter. To change client computer settings, see the "Viewing and Modifying Client Computer Settings" section of this chapter.

Creating Computer Accounts for Server Computers

SBS supports adding additional servers to the network, either to distribute the application and file sharing load or to act as additional domain controllers. Before connecting an additional server to the network, first run the Set Up Server Wizard on the SBS server to create the computer account and optionally assign software to the computer by completing these steps:

1.   Select Server Management from the Start menu.

2.   Click Server Computers in the console tree, and click Set Up Server Computers to launch the Set Up Server Wizard.

3. Click Next. On the Server Computer Name page, type the computer name you want to use for the server in the Server Name box, and then click Next.

4. On the IP Address Configuration page, shown in Figure 11-3, select Obtain An IP Address Automatically By Using DHCP, or select Use The Following Static IP Address and type the static IP address of the server. For servers, we recommend using a static IP address or creating a DCHP reservation to ensure that the server is always at the same address. Click Next when you're finished.

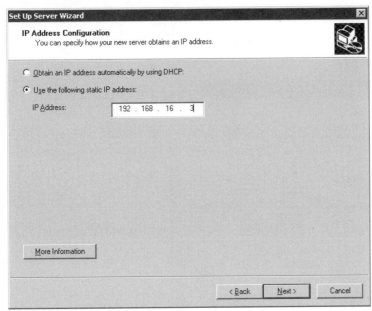

Figure 11-3   The IP Address Configuration page of the Set Up Server Wizard.

5. Review the settings and then click Finish. You'll see a final informational dialog titled "Finishing Your Installation" with instructions for connecting the client to a web page to perform the actual details of adding it to the domain.

Establishing Basic Network Connectivity

The first step in connecting a computer to an SBS network is to connect to the network and obtain a valid IP address. This process is pretty simple: plug the computer into an Ethernet switch on the internal network, and configure the system for Dynamic Host Control Protocol (DHCP). Wireless clients must first associate with an access point and provide a WPA / WEP key.

Configuring Windows XP and Windows Server 2003 to Use DHCP

By default, Windows XP (including x64 Edition) and Windows Server 2003 will use DHCP to configure TCP/IP, and you shouldn't have to change anything. However, if the client has been set to use a fixed IP address, you can change it back to using DHCP by completing the following steps:

1. In the Network Connections folder (available in Control Panel), right-click the appropriate network adapter (most likely Local Area Connection), and choose Properties from the shortcut menu.

2. In the Local Area Connection Properties dialog box, select the Internet Protocol (TCP/IP) component, and click Properties. The Internet Protocol (TCP/IP) Properties dialog box, shown in Figure 11-4, appears.

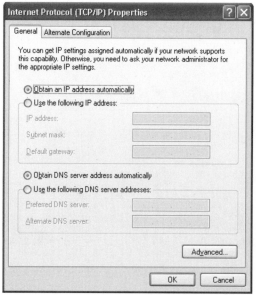

Figure 11-4   The General tab of the Internet Protocol (TCP/IP) Properties dialog box.

3. Verify that the Obtain An IP Address Automatically and Obtain DNS Server Address Automatically options are selected, and then click OK.

> **Note**   If your SBS environment includes more than one server, the secondary servers are good candidates for a static IP address. If you use a static IP address, configure the server with an IP address in the excluded IP address range of 192.168.16.3 through 192.168.16.9, or add an appropriate exclusion in DHCP.

Configuring Windows 2000 to Use DHCP

By default, Windows 2000 will also use DHCP to configure TCP/IP, and you shouldn't have to change anything. However, if the Windows 2000 client has been set to use a fixed IP address, you can change it back to using DHCP by completing the following steps:

1. In the Network And Dial-Up Connections folder (available in Control Panel), right-click the appropriate network adapter (usually Local Area Connection), and choose Properties from the shortcut menu.

2. In the Local Area Connection Properties dialog box, select the Internet Protocol (TCP/IP) component and click Properties. The Internet Protocol (TCP/IP) Properties dialog box, shown in Figure 11-5, appears.

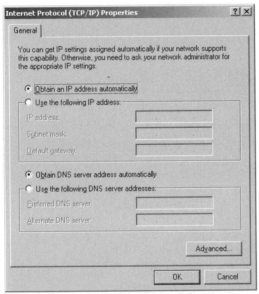

Figure 11-5   The General tab of the Internet Protocol (TCP/IP) Properties dialog box.

3. Verify that both the Obtain An IP Address Automatically and Obtain DNS Server Address Automatically options are selected, and then click OK.

Associating with a Wireless Access Point

Windows XP SP2 clients have a new interface to wireless networking. With SP2 clients and later, do the following:

1. After installing and configuring a wireless network adapter, right-click the Wireless Network Connection icon in the system tray, and choose View Available Networks from the shortcut menu.

2. Select your wireless network in the Choose A Wireless Network dialog box, shown in Figure 11-6, and click Connect.

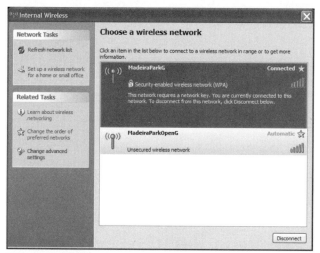

Figure 11-6   The Choose A Wireless Network dialog box.

3. If the network is secured, you'll see the Wireless Network Connection dialog box. Type the network key in the Network Key and Confirm Network Key boxes, and then click Connect.

Note   Pocket PC 2003 devices provide a feature called Zero Configuration Wi-Fi, which works almost identically to the Zero Configuration Wireless feature in Windows XP.

Real World   WPA and WPA2 Authentication

The initial security method for wireless authentication was Wired Equivalent Privacy (WEP). Unfortunately, WEP has been shown to be woefully insecure, and can no longer be considered adequate protection for even the most casual users. The initial replacement for WEP was WiFi Protected Access (WPA), which is now being superseded by WPA2. WPA2 is also known as Institute of Electrical and Electronics Engineers (IEEE) 802.11i.

To use WPA for wireless authentication, clients must run Windows Server 2003 SP1, Windows XP Professional Edition, or Windows XP Professional x64 Edition. For WPA2 support, clients must run Windows XP SP2 and they must have installed the hotfix discussed in Microsoft Knowledge Base article 893357. (See *http://support.microsoft.com/default.aspx?scid=kb;en-us;Q893357.*)

You should enforce a minimum standard of WPA authentication with an initial pre-shared key that is both complex and regularly changed on all wireless networks that are connected to your internal network. If your hardware supports full WPA2, and you don't have to support x64 clients yet, you should definitely use WPA2. WPA2 enforces a higher level of encryption—the Advanced Encryption Standard, or AES—than WPA, but AES encryption requires hardware support for smooth functioning. WPA2 has two modes—WPA2-Personal and WPA2-Enterprise. WPA2-Personal uses a preshared key and is easier to set up for most small businesses, while WPA2-Enterprise supports full 802.1x authentication.

Using the Small Business Server Network Configuration Wizard

After you create a computer account and establish network connectivity, the next steps in connecting a computer to an SBS network are to log on to the computer, open Internet Explorer, and launch the Small Business Server Network Configuration Wizard by logging on to the computer and connecting to *http://sbssrv/ConnectComputer* (where *sbssrv* is the computer name of the SBS server). This wizard configures the computer to run on the network by performing the following actions:

- Changes the computer's workgroup or domain membership to be a member of the Windows Small Business Server's domain.

- Installs operating system service packs and the Previous Versions (Volume Shadow Copy) client.

- Optionally migrates existing local user profiles stored on the computer to new domain user profiles, preserving the data and settings of local user accounts.

- Optionally installs Outlook 2003, the shared fax client, and any other software you assign to computers (as discussed later in this chapter in the "Assigning Applications to Client Computers" section).

- Optionally installs printer drivers and changes various Windows settings, as discussed later in this chapter in the "Viewing and Modifying Client Computer Settings" section.

- Sets the browser home page to *http://companyweb*.

- For Windows XP clients, enables Remote Web Workplace connections.

More Info   Running the Network Configuration Wizard on computers running Windows XP Professional (including x64 Edition), Windows XP Tablet PC Edition, Windows Server 2003, or Windows 2000 automatically configures them to connect properly to the SBS network. Other operating systems, including earlier versions of Windows, must be manually connected to the network, as discussed in the "Connecting Alternate Clients" section of this chapter.

Real World   Connecting Clients Across VPN Links

Clients that frequently connect to the network via a VPN connection, such as telecommuters and wireless clients, should be added to the domain. This makes accessing domain resources easier, and improves security by implementing computer authentication. However, VPN clients can't use the Network Configuration Wizard to join the network, and they can't receive assigned applications either.

Because of this design decision (made so that VPN clients wouldn't swamp a company's Internet connection downloading assigned applications), VPN clients must connect directly to the internal network to join the domain and receive assigned applications. If this approach isn't feasible (as would be the case with many telecommuters), manually add the clients to the domain using the following steps (clients will not receive assigned applications):

1. Connect to the SBS network using a VPN connection.

2. Open the System tool in Control Panel.

3. On Windows XP and Windows Server 2003 clients, click the Computer Name tab and then click Change. On Windows 2000 clients, click the Network Identification tab and then click Properties.

4. Select Domain, type the name of the SBS domain, and then click OK. Reboot the computer when prompted.

To use the Small Business Server Network Configuration Wizard to join a computer to the network, complete the following steps:

1. Log on to the client computer using an account with local administrator privileges.

2. Open Internet Explorer. If the Internet Connection Wizard appears, use the wizard to connect to the Internet via a LAN connection.

3. In the Address bar, type **http://**sbssrv/**ConnectComputer** (where sbssrv is the computer name of the SBS server) and press Enter.

4. On the Network Configuration page, click the Connect To The Network Now link.

5. If a Security Warning dialog box appears asking whether you want to install and run the SBS Network Configuration Wizard, click Yes. After a few moments, the Small Business Server Network Configuration Wizard appears.

6. On the User Account And Password Information page, type the user name and password of a domain user account, and then click Next.

7. On the Assign Users To This Computer And Migrate Their Profiles page of the wizard, shown in Figure 11-7, select all domain user accounts that will use the computer from the Available Users list, and then click Add.

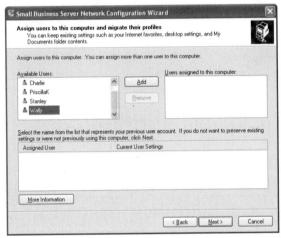

Figure 11-7 The Assign Users To This Computer And Migrate Their Profiles page.

8. To migrate existing documents and program settings that are stored in a local user profile to the new domain user profile, select the domain user account in the Assigned User column, and then select the local user profile to migrate in the Current User Settings box. Click Next when you're finished assigning users to the computer and migrating user accounts.

> **Note**   Use the Files And Settings Transfer Wizard provided with Windows XP to transfer user data and settings from a different computer, or to migrate user settings from an account in an existing domain to the new SBS domain. (See the Real World sidebar "Migrating Profiles from an Existing Domain" for a more thorough procedure.)

9. On the Computer Name page, select the computer name to use and then click Next. Only names created using the Set Up Computer Wizard and not already taken by another computer are listed.

> **More Info**   For more information about the Set Up Computer Wizard,
> see the sections "Creating Computer Accounts for Client Computers" and
> "Creating Computer Accounts for Server Computers" in this chapter.

10. On the Completing The Network Configuration Wizard page, review the settings and
    then click Finish. The Small Business Server Network Configuration Wizard adds the
    computer to the domain and then restarts the computer (typically two times).

11. Log on to the client computer using a domain account assigned to the client. A Cli-
    ent Setup Wizard dialog box will appear automatically.

> **Important**   If clients are running previous versions of Outlook and you
> want to upgrade them to Outlook 2003, disable any COM add-ins before
> running the Client Setup Wizard.

Real World   Client Setup and Local Administrator

Running Client Setup and using */connectcomputer* has an unfortunate side effect that
you may not realize. Regardless of what level of domain user template you use, the
users are placed in the Administrators local group on their computers. This makes it
easy for them to install software (do you really want all your users being able to install
any software they think they might want to use on their computer) and it makes it
easy for them to get infected with whatever malware they happen to be careless about.

Poorly written software can make it difficult to run their program without being a
local administrator—see *http://www.threatcode.com* for some well known examples.
But most programs, even those that don't work well from a simple local user
account by default, can be made to work with some patience and careful investiga-
tion. The basic solution is to install the software as an administrator, then change to
an account that is only a local user account, and try to run the software. Observe
where it fails, and try to correct it. The correction may require change where the
software writes its logs, or changing the permissions on a registry key, for example.
The process isn't simple, but if you're patient you can usually resolve the problems.
And the payback is a much more secure and safe computer.

Susan Bradley (*http://msmvps.com/blogs/bradley*), an SBS MVP and the peer
reviewer for this book, suggests letting */connectcomputer* do the setup. Then set up
Outlook, and the desktop, and any other critical programs, and when things are
as you want them, change the account to no longer be a member of the Local
Administrators group. This seems like an excellent suggestion, and one that will
make your client computers, and your SBS network as a whole, a safer and more

secure place. Just be sure to test all your client applications after you've done this to make sure they still work when the user is no longer a local administrator on his or her computer, and if you can't get one or more applications they need to run properly as non-admin, you'll have to leave them as local admins and find other ways to manage the security hole (for example, by warning them not to install any applications that you haven't approved).

12. In the Client Setup Wizard dialog box, click Start Now to install assigned service packs and software immediately, or click Postpone to do it later.

13. On the first page of the Client Setup Wizard, click Next. On the Assigned Applications page, shown in Figure 11-8, which appears if you selected the During Client Setup, Allow The Selected Applications To Be Modified check box when you created the client computer account, clear the check boxes next to any applications you don't want to install and then click Next.

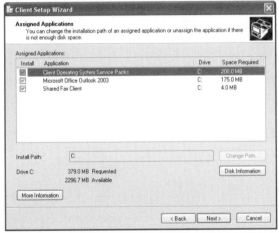

Figure 11-8   The Assigned Applications page of the Client Setup Wizard.

14. If the Automatic Logon Information page appears, either type your password to permit the Client Setup Wizard to automatically log on during the Client Setup Wizard (one or more reboots might be necessary) or select Manual Logon to do it yourself. The automatic logon feature is disabled after Client Setup completes. Click Next when you're finished.

The Application Setup Progress page appears. The Client Setup Wizard installs the specified applications and service packs and reboots the computer a couple of times, if necessary.

Real World   Migrating Profiles from an Existing Domain

Although the Files And Settings Transfer Wizard in Windows XP is the simplest way to preserve settings in a domain account when switching domains or migrating from an old server, it doesn't preserve all settings. To preserve the entire user profile, use the following steps to create a new local user account and copy the domain profile to that account.

1. On the client computer, create a new local user account using the Local Users and Groups MMC snap-in (accessible via the Computer Management snap-in) and add the account to the local Administrators group. (You can make the local group memberships more appropriate after joining the domain.)

2. Log on with the new local user account.

3. Open the System tool in Control Panel, click the Advanced tab, and then click Settings in the User Profiles section.

4. Select the domain account you want to migrate, click Copy To, and in the Copy To Profile box, type the path to a suitable folder on the hard drive (most likely a subfolder of the C:\Documents And Settings folder).

5. Click Change, click Locations, select the local computer in the Locations dialog box, and then click OK. This returns you to the Select User Or Group dialog box.

6. Type the name of the local user account you created and then click OK. Click OK again twice to finish copying the profile.

7. Open the Local Users And Groups snap-in, double-click the local user account you created, click the Profile tab, and then type the location of the folder to which you copied the profile in the Profile Path box. Click OK when you're finished.

8. Open the System tool in Control Panel, click the Computer Name tab, and then click Change (on Windows XP and Windows Server 2003 computers). On Windows 2000 computers, click the Network Identification tab and then click Properties.

9. Select Workgroup, type a workgroup name (**WORKGROUP** is the default), and then click OK. Reboot the computer when prompted, log on using the newly minted local user account, and then use the Network Configuration Wizard to join the domain and migrate the new local user account, which now stores the settings of the domain account you want to migrate.

Connecting Alternate Clients

Windows XP Professional and Windows 2000 clients (and soon, Windows Vista clients) provide the best client experience on an SBS network and take the least amount of time to administer. However, clients running older, unsupported versions of Windows—as well as computers running other operating systems such as Linux or Mac OS X—can be connected to an SBS network. They will not have full functionality, nor can they be managed.

> **Note** Windows XP Home Edition isn't suitable for use on a Windows Small Business Server network and should be upgraded to Windows XP Professional. However, in an emergency, a Windows XP Home Edition computer can be temporarily connected to an SBS network. You must enable DHCP on the computer, join it to a workgroup with the same name as the SBS domain, and provide a domain user name and password when connecting to any shared resource. You cannot join the Windows XP Home Edition computer to the domain, nor can you manage it, assign applications to it, or control who logs on to it. Remote Web Workplace won't work, either.

Connecting Older Windows Clients

Microsoft Windows NT4, Windows 95, Windows 98, and Windows Me clients are no longer Microsoft-supported operating systems and should be replaced with Windows 2000 or Windows XP clients. They no longer receive even critical security updates and pose a significant security hazard to the entire network. While it is still technically possible to connect and use these legacy clients on an SBS network, we strongly discourage it.

Connecting Mac OS X Clients

Mac OS X is more compatible than previous Macintosh operating systems. Mac OS X 10.2 and later versions can connect to file shares and printers hosted by an SBS server Besides the built-in support, Microsoft Office 2004 is available on Mac OS X; Microsoft Entourage has native support for Microsoft Exchange; and there's a free Remote Desktop Connection client for Mac OS X available at *http://www.microsoft.com/mac/otherproducts/otherproducts.aspx?pid=remotedesktopclient.*

There are some caveats. First, if you haven't updated your Mac OS X to 10.4 or later, do so—it will make life easier on an SBS network. But if you haven't, you'll find it's easier to get Macs and SBS working together if the SBS domain doesn't use a top-level domain of .local. The Mac Rendezvous automatic network configuration feature of Mac OS X 10.2 and 10.3 uses a DNS multicast that uses the .local syntax. While Mac OS X computers are still somewhat second-class citizens on an SBS network, they definitely work better with OS X 10.4 and later. There is still no support for the Previous Versions or Shared Fax clients, no remote administration capabilities, and limited support for the Remote Web Workplace.

The following sections show how to use a Mac OS X 10.2 computer with Windows file shares and shared printers and how to disable SMB signing on the Windows Small

Business Server network for Mac OS X 10.2 clients. Mac OS X 10.3 and later clients work fine with SMB signing enabled.

Connecting to Windows File Shares

To connect to a Windows file share from a computer running Mac OS X 10.2.x, use the following steps. (Mac OS X 10.3.x clients look slightly different.)

1. Disable SMB signing on the Windows Small Business Server, as described in the "Disabling SMB Signing" section of this chapter. (This isn't necessary for Mac OS X 10.3 and later clients.)

2. Configure the computer to obtain its IP address using DHCP, if it doesn't already.

3. Select Connect To Server from the Go menu of Finder.

4. In the Connect To Server window, shown in Figure 11-9, browse to the computer or type the address of the Windows file share, using one of the following formats:

   smb://*fullyqualifieddomainname/sharename*

   smb://*domain.name;servername/sharename*

   For example, to connect to the Data share on the dellsrv.example.office computer in the example.office domain, type **smb://dellsrv.example.office/Data.**

Figure 11-9   Connecting to a Windows file share.

5.   Verify the workgroup or domain name, type an appropriate user name and password in the SMB/CIFS Filesystem Authentication dialog box, and then click OK. If you browsed to the computer, select a share and then click OK. The Windows file share appears on the desktop.

Real World   Can't Connect to .local Domains

Apple computers running Mac OS X version 10.2 and 10.3 support automatic network configuration using a technology called Rendezvous. This is all fine and well until you try to use one of these systems on a domain that uses the .local DNS extension (which Windows Small Business Server 2003 uses by default). Simply put, the Mac system isn't able to connect to any Windows systems via Server Message Blocks (SMBs)—the default file sharing protocol of Windows.

To remedy this situation, install Mac OS X 10.4 (it fixes this issue), read article 107800 in Apple's Knowledge Archive (*http://search.info.apple.com*), or use the following procedure:

1.   Open the Terminal program located in the Utilities folder, which opens a full-fledged UNIX command line. (OK, technically it's not UNIX, it's Darwin—an open-source variant of FreeBSD.)

2.   Change to the /etc/resolver/ directory by typing the following commands, pressing Enter after each line:

     cd /

     cd etc/resolver

3.   Log on as the root (administrator) user by typing **sudo tcsh** and then typing the administrator password for the system.

4.   Edit the local file using the text editor of your choice. To use pico (a simple text editor), type **pico local**.

5.   Replace the listed nameserver IP address with the correct IP address of a DNS server on the .local domain that you want the Mac OS X system to access.

6.   Replace the port number with **53**.

7.   Save the file by pressing Ctrl+X, and then Y, and then Enter.

Connecting to Networked Printers

The easiest way to print to a printer shared by a Windows computer from a Mac OS X 10.2.x client is to install Print Services For UNIX on the SBS server and then print using

IP printing. (Mac OS X 10.3 and later clients can connect directly to Windows print servers and don't need this section.) To do so, complete the following steps:

1. On the SBS server, open Add/Remove Programs and then click Add/Remove Windows Components.

2. In the Windows Components Wizard, select the Other Network File And Print Services option, click Details, select Print Services For Unix, and then click OK. Click Next to install the component.

3. On the Mac OS X client, open the Applications folder, and then open the Utilities folder.

4. Double-click Print Center to open the Printer List dialog box.

5. Click Add.

6. Choose IP Printing from the box at the top of the sheet and type the IP address or DNS name of the print server.

7. To specify a printer on the print server, clear the Use Default Queue On Server check box and type the share name of the printer in the Queue Name box.

8. Select the appropriate printer driver from the Printer Model box. If a driver isn't available from the printer manufacturer, try using Gimp-Print (*http://gimp-print.sourceforge.net*), though these drivers are unsupported.

9. Click Add when you're finished. The printer is then added to the list of printers available on the Mac OS X client system.

Disabling SMB Signing

To use Mac OS X 10.2.x on an SBS network, you need to first disable SMB signing on the domain. This is unnecessary for Mac OS X 10.3 and later systems, and is a compelling reason to upgrade. While we present this workaround for completeness, we strongly urge you to upgrade your Mac to the latest release. It will be much happier in an SBS environment.

To disable SMB signing, complete the following steps:

1. Open the Group Policy Management console in the Administrative Tools folder on the Start menu.

2. In the console tree, navigate to Domains, then to example.local (or whatever the domain is called), and then to Group Policy Objects.

3. Create a new Group Policy Object (GPO) for the settings by right-clicking the Group Policy Objects container, choosing New from the shortcut menu, typing a name for the GPO (such as Disable SMB Signing), and then clicking OK.

> **Note** Don't make changes to the default GPOs—instead create new GPOs with your settings. That way you can easily undo your changes by disabling the GPO. Use the Group Policy Results and Group Policy Modeling tools to ensure that your GPO is being applied properly.

4. Link the new GPO to the Domain Controllers container by dragging it from the Group Policy Objects container into the Domain Controllers container. Click OK when asked whether you want to create the link.

5. Select the Domain Controllers container. On the Linked Group Policy Objects tab (Figure 11-10), select the GPO you created and click the Move Link To Top button to ensure that the GPO overrides the settings in the Default Domain Controllers Policy. The GPO you created appears at the top of the list, with a link order of one (the lower the link order, the later the policy is processed, with each policy over-writing any preceding policies that conflict).

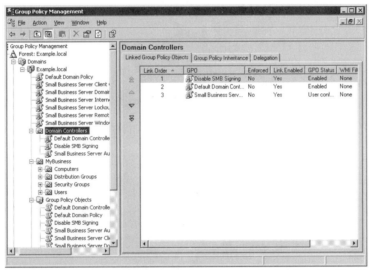

Figure 11-10 The Linked Group Policy Objects tab showing the Disable SMB Signing GPO processed last (and thus having the highest priority).

6. Right-click the GPO you created and choose Edit from the shortcut menu. This opens the Group Policy Object Editor.

7. Navigate to Computer Configuration, Windows Settings, Security Settings, Local Policies, and finally Security Options, as shown in Figure 11-11.

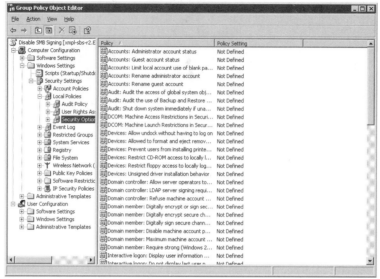

Figure 11-11   The Security Options container of the Group Policy Objects Editor window.

8. Double-click the Microsoft Network Server: Digitally Sign Communications (Always) policy.

9. In the Microsoft Network Server: Digitally Sign Communications (Always) dialog box, select the Define This Policy check box, choose Disabled, and then click OK. Close the Group Policy Object Editor window.

10. Open a command prompt window and type **gpupdate** to refresh Group Policy.

> **Note**   To verify that the policy is being applied to the Windows Small Business Server 2003 computer, right-click the Group Policy Results container in the Group Policy Management console, choose Group Policy Results Wizard from the shortcut menu, and then use the wizard to create a report detailing which settings are applied to the server.

Using the Remote Web Workplace

Windows Small Business Server 2003 automatically creates a special Web site on the server called the Remote Web Workplace (RWW) that provides access to Exchange e-mail (via Outlook Web Access), the SharePoint intranet site, Windows Small Business Server usage reports, Remote Desktop connections, and a couple of methods for connecting to the internal network from across the Internet.

RWW is available on the local network to all clients with correct TCP/IP settings, Internet Explorer 5 or later, and a valid domain user account—no other connection steps are required. RWW can also be accessed by properly authenticated users on the Internet, provided that you selected Remote Web Workplace in the Web Services Configuration page of the CEICW.

More Info   For more information about the CEICW, see Chapter 5, "Completing the To Do List and Other Post-Installation Tasks."

Following is a brief overview of how to use RWW:

1. To open the Remote Web Workplace, launch Internet Explorer and type **https://** *xmpl-sbs-r2.example.local/***Remote** in the Address bar (where xmpl-sbs-r2.example.local is the DNS address of the SBS server). If you're connecting from across the Internet, use the registered domain name used by the public interface of the SBS server (or the IP address of the firewall device if there isn't a registered domain name that refers to the SBS server).

2. On the Remote Web Workplace logon page, shown in Figure 11-12, type your user name and password, select the connection speed, clear the I'm Using A Public Or Shared Computer check box if you're using a secure computer, and then click Log On.

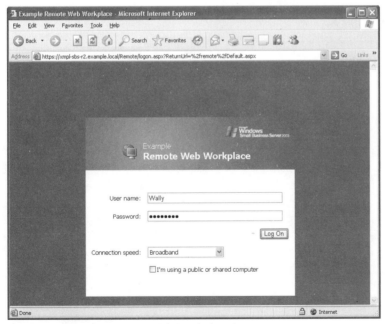

Figure 11-12   The Remote Web Workplace logon page.

Note   You must be a member of the Mobile Users or Remote Web Workplace Users groups to be able to use RWW.

---

3. On the main Remote Web Workplace page, shown in Figure 11-13, click the link that corresponds to the action you want to perform. (Some links might not work over an Internet connection, depending on which services you allow through the firewall.)

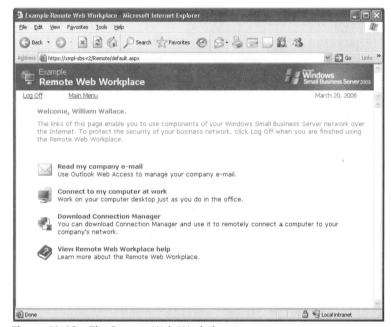

Figure 11-13   The Remote Web Workplace page.

The Remote Web Workplace page can include the following options:

- **Read My Company E-Mail**   This opens Outlook Web Access (OWA) to display your Exchange folders, as shown in Figure 11-14. OWA provides almost all the functionality of the full-fledged Outlook 2003 application, allowing you to work with your Exchange folders as you would normally. You can also log on directly to OWA by typing **https://***xmpl-sbs-r2.example.local*/**Exchange** in the Address bar (where *xmpl-sbs-r2.example.local* is the DNS address of the SBS server). You can connect to OWA even from the Internet, either by connecting first to RWW, or by connecting directly. For a direct connection over the Internet, use the proper Internet domain name of the SBS server or gateway router, for example, *http://www.example.com/ exchange*.

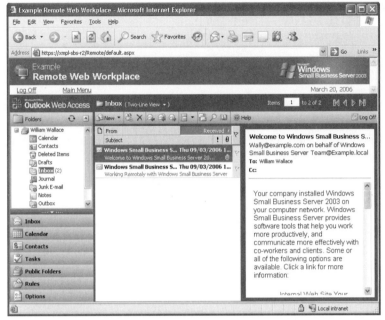

Figure 11-14   Outlook Web Access.

- **Connect to Server Desktops**   This displays a list of servers on the network to which you can connect via Remote Desktop, and is only available if you log on using an account that's a member of the Domain Administrators group. Select a computer (assuming it supports Remote Desktop connections), click Optional Settings to change the connection behavior, and then click Connect.

- **Connect To My Computer At Work**   This displays a list of computers on the network to which you can connect via Remote Desktop. (This option is called Connect To Client Desktops if you log on using an administrator account.) Select your computer (assuming it supports Remote Desktop connections), click Optional Settings to change the connection behavior, and then click Connect.

- **Use My Company's Internal Web Site**   This displays the SharePoint intranet site (accessible to internal clients via *http://companyweb*). For information about Share-Point, see Chapter 18, "Customizing a SharePoint Web Site."

- **View Server Usage Reports**   This displays the current usage data for the server, as discussed in Chapter 21, "Monitoring and Fine-Tuning Performance." (This option is only available if your account is permitted to view reports.)

- **View Server Performance Reports**   This displays the current performance data for the server. (This option is only available if your account is permitted to view reports.)

- **Download Connection Manager**   This downloads Connection Manager, which installs a secure VPN connection to the Windows Small Business Server.

- **Configure Your Computer To Use Outlook Via Internet**   This displays instructions for setting up Outlook 2003 to connect to the Exchange Server over the Internet without a VPN connection (via RPC over HTTP). (This option is only available if you've configured RPC over HTTP in the CEICW.)

- **View Remote Web Workplace Help**   This displays the Help pages for Remote Web Workplace.

Note   Instruct users always to log off when they're finished using Remote Web Workplace by clicking the Log Off link.

Managing Computers from the Server

Most aspects of Windows XP and Windows 2000 clients can be easily managed across the network from an SBS computer using the Server Management console. The following sections cover assigning applications (including the ISA Server firewall client) to computers, creating a Remote Connection disk for VPN access, remotely managing client computers and settings, as well as removing computers from the network.

More Info   For information about using the Microsoft Baseline Security Analyzer tool to scan client systems for security issues and missing updates, see Chapter 5.

Real World   Virus, Malware and Spam Strategies

Viruses, malware, and spam are major headaches and security risks of the modern network. You can't make them go away, but you can take concrete steps to protect your users and your network. Some of the steps you can take to protect yourself include:

- Do consistent backups.

- Configure automatic updates using Windows Server Update Services (WSUS).

- Install antivirus software on your SBS server.

- Install anti-malware software on your clients.

- Enable Intelligent Message Filtering (IMF) on your SBS Exchange server.

The first line of defense is to make sure you do consistent backups of the network and have a solid disaster recovery plan in place. This will ensure that if all else fails, you at least have the option of reverting to an earlier backup.

With the release of SBS 2003 R2, we finally have an integrated update service in SBS. Use it! Keep your clients *and* your servers up to date.

Install self-updating antivirus software on the SBS server as well as on all clients. There are good antivirus packages that are designed (and priced) for SBS networks and include server, client, and Exchange modules. These packages are often no more expensive than purchasing consumer antivirus software for each client, and provide additional scanning and management capabilities. If you're running SBS Premium Edition, you can also use third-party antivirus and spam filtering plug-ins. SharePoint-specific antivirus software packages are also available.

Install self-updating, real-time monitoring, anti-malware software on each client. This doesn't need to be on the server, since you do *not* surf the Web from the server. Ever. Many of the SBS antivirus packages now include an anti-malware module. This may be sufficient for your needs, or consider Microsoft Defender, which is free.

To reduce the effects of spam on your business, install Service Pack 2 for Microsoft Exchange 2003 and enable the Intelligent Message Filter. (See Chapter 14, "Using Exchange Server," for details.) Configure Outlook 2003 to block HTML e-mail messages (the default) and enable spam filtering to supplement the IMF. You can also configure Outlook to read *all* messages in plain text only. While this doesn't look pretty, it definitely makes it harder for malware and phishing attacks to cause problems.

Assigning Applications to Client Computers

SBS lets you easily assign applications to client computers running Windows 2000 Professional, Windows XP Professional, or Windows XP Tablet PC Edition. (Additional servers should install software manually or by using Group Policy.) To do so, complete the following steps:

1. Open the Server Management console.

2. Click Computers to open the Client Computers container, shown in Figure 11-15.

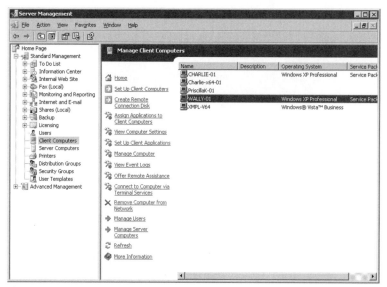

Figure 11-15   The Client Computers container of the Server Management console.

3. Click Assign Applications To Client Computers, and then click Next in the first page of the Assign Applications Wizard.

4. On the Client Computers page, select the computers to which you want to assign applications and then click Add. Click Next to continue.

5. On the Client Applications page, shown in Figure 11-16, select which applications you want to assign to the specified computers. Click Next when you're finished.

   ❑ To allow users to change which applications are installed during Client Setup, select the During Client Setup, Allow The Selected Applications To Be Modi-fied check box.

   ❑ To force the client computer to log off once Client Setup is complete, select the After Client Setup Is Finished, Log Off The Client Computer check box.

   ❑ To change whether SBS configures such settings as Outlook Profiles and Internet Explorer settings, click Advanced.

   ❑ Click Edit Applications to edit or add to the list of available applications. See the Real World sidebar "Adding Your Own Applications" in this chapter for information about how to add other applications to the Client Applications list.

More Info   Refer to the "Viewing and Modifying Client Computer Settings" section later in this chapter for information about changing client settings such as Internet Explorer Favorites.

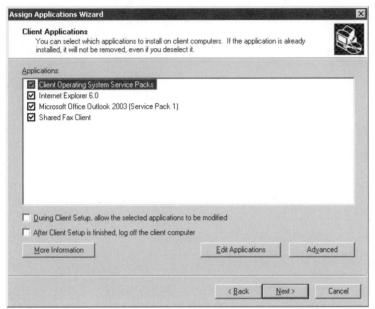

Figure 11-16   The Client Applications page of the Assign Applications Wizard.

6. On the Mobile Client And Offline Use page, check the Install Connection Manager and Install ActiveSync 3.7 check boxes to facilitate the client computers connecting remotely via VPN connection and synchronizing Microsoft Pocket PC and Microsoft SmartPhone devices. (You must run the Remote Connection Wizard before Connection Manager will work.) Click Next to continue.

7. Review the settings and then click Finish. The next time a domain user logs on to the computer to which applications are assigned, the applications automatically install. For programs that you manually added to the list of client applications, a shortcut to the installation program is placed on the desktop instead.

Real World   Adding Your Own Applications

SBS makes it easy to assign service packs, Internet Explorer 6, Outlook 2003, and the Shared Fax Client to client computers, but this isn't exactly a comprehensive list of applications. In fact, there is a very important omission for users of Windows

Small Business Server 2003 Premium Edition—the ISA Server Firewall Client. To add applications to this list, complete the following steps:

1. Perform an administrative installation of the desired program to a new folder in the C:\ClientApps folder on the SBS server, or copy the setup files to a new folder in the C:\ClientApps folder (assuming the \ClientApps folder is located on the C:\ drive). To perform an administrative installation of Microsoft Office, for example, use the setup.exe /a command.

2. Start the Assign Applications Wizard.

3. On the Client Applications page of the Assign Applications Wizard, click Edit Applications, which displays the first page of the Set Up Client Applications Wizard. Click Next.

4. On the Available Applications page, click Add.

5. In the Application Information dialog box, shown in Figure 11-17, type the application name and network path, including any setup parameters (such as those that automate setup), and enclose the path in quotation marks. For the ISA Firewall Client, type *xmpl-sbs-r2***ClientApps\Firewall Client\setup.exe** (where xmpl-sbs-r2 is the computer name of the SBS server). Click OK.

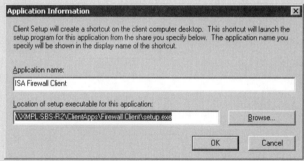

Figure 11-17   The Application Information dialog box.

6. SBS might notify you that the permissions need to be set to Read and Execute on the folder. Click Yes to continue, but don't neglect changing the permissions.

7. Add or remove any additional programs, click Next, and then click Finish to return to the Assign Applications Wizard.

Under the Hood   How Applications Are Assigned

SBS assigns applications to computers using a logon script (SBS_LOGIN_SCRIPT.BAT) that is assigned to all domain users. When a user logs on, the script is run and the Windows Small Business Server client setup program starts (\\sbssrv\Clients\Setup\Setup.exe). The client setup program then parses the XML response file (Apps.dat) located in the *sbssrv*\clients\response*computername* folder (where *sbssrv* is the name of the SBS server and *computername* is the name of the computer the user is logging on to). This XML file provides the location of the setup program for each assigned application, as well as any setup parameters. The Apps.dat file can be edited to force a reboot after an application is installed by changing the *needsReboot="0"* value to *"1"*.

Using the SBS method of application deployment is the most painless way to deploy applications in Windows Small Business Server 2003; however, the Software Installation And Maintenance feature of Group Policy is also present, and can be used by savvy administrators (though be careful when mixing the two). For in-depth coverage of software deployment using Group Policy, refer to *Microsoft Windows Server 2003 Administrator's Companion* 2nd Edition (Microsoft Press).

Creating a Remote Connection Disk

SBS can create a Remote Connection disk to automate the process of connecting a client computer to the SBS network using a VPN connection. (This is the same process as installing Connection Manager on a client.)

> **More Info**   For more information about VPN connections, see Chapter 15, "Managing Connectivity."

To use this feature, you must first run the Remote Access Wizard (if you haven't yet done so) and then complete the following steps:

1. In the Client Computers container of the Server Management console, click Create Remote Connection Disk.

2. Click Next in the first page of the Create Remote Connection Disk Wizard, specify the floppy drive to use as well as the number of disks to create, and then click Next.

3. Insert a blank floppy disk into the SBS server and click Finish.

Note You can turn the Remote Connection disk into a Remote Connection CD, USB key, or e-mail by taking the contents of the disk and putting it on the media of your choice—the total size is less than 600 KB. This is fine if your SBS server has a floppy drive installed. Since many servers no longer have floppy drives (including our SBS server, I might add), you will need to have one you can plug in temporarily to create the initial disk, since the wizard is hard-coded to only go to a floppy. We've found that having a spare USB floppy drive in the server room is quite handy for all sorts of things that expect a floppy drive. But make sure you have the right floppy—some won't work. See Microsoft Knowledge Base article 916196 at *http://support.microsoft.com/?kbid=916196* for details.

When you don't have a floppy available, you can open the Remote Web Workplace from the client computer and click Download Connection Manager to download Connection Manager.

To use the Remote Connection disk on a client computer, insert the floppy disk, run the Setup.exe program, and click Yes when asked whether you want to install the connection to Small Business Server. To use the new VPN connection, double-click the Connect To Small Business Server icon on the desktop, shown in Figure 11-18, type the appropriate user name and password, and then click Connect.

Figure 11-18   The Connect To Small Business Server window.

Viewing and Modifying Client Computer Settings

Windows Small Business Server 2003 makes viewing and changing the settings it applies to client computers on the network easy. To view or change the settings, open the Server Management console, click Computers, and click View Computer Settings. In the View Or Change Client Computer Settings dialog box, perform the appropriate tasks:

- To view the settings for a computer, as shown in Figure 11-19, click the plus sign next to the computer name, and then click the plus sign next to Assigned Applications, Client Setup Settings, or Client Setup Configuration Options.

- To add applications to a specific computer, right-click Assigned Applications under the appropriate computer and choose Run Assigned Applications Wizard.

- To unassign or reinstall an application on a computer, click the plus sign (+) next to Assigned Applications, right-click the application, and choose either Unassign This Application or Reinstall from the shortcut menu. Unassigning an application doesn't uninstall it.

- To toggle Client Setup Settings or Client Setup Configuration Options on or off, right-click the setting or option and choose Change from the shortcut menu.

Figure 11-19   The View Or Change Client Computers Settings dialog box.

Under the Hood   Settings Applied to Client Computers

Besides installing applications, the Small Business Server Network Configuration Wizard configures the following settings:

- **Remote Desktop Connections**   Enables Remote Desktop and Remote Assistance on the client computer.

- **Fax Settings** Configures the client fax software with the default sender information from the server so that cover sheets automatically contain the correct sender information.

- **Printers** If a single printer is published in Active Directory, the printer is installed on the client and made the default printer, unless a local printer is installed on the client. If multiple printers are published in Active Directory, all are installed, but no default printer is specified.

- **Fax Printers** Installs a fax printer so that the client computer can send faxes by "printing" to the Windows Small Business Server Shared Fax service.

- **Desktop** Creates a My Network Places link to the /General Documents folder in the SharePoint Intranet Web site (*http://companyweb/General Documents*).

- **Internet Explorer** Sets the Home Page to *http://companyweb* and adds links to the Favorites menu for an SBS help page, the official Microsoft Small Business Server Web site, a remote server management page, and a remote e-mail access page (Outlook Web Access).

- **Outlook Profile Settings** Configures Outlook to use Exchange Server for the default e-mail account, installs the fax mail transport allowing MAPI applications (including Outlook) to send faxes, and configures manual synchronization of offline folders for computers that are assigned Connection Manager.

Remotely Managing Computers and Viewing Event Logs

Checking the health of client computers can be a time-consuming task when it involves physical visits to each machine. SBS reduces the time involved by allowing you to remotely check event logs, open the Computer Management console, offer Remote Assistance, and even establish a Remote Desktop connection to client computers, all from within the Server Management console.

To perform these tasks, open the Client Computers or Server Computers container in the Server Management console, select the computer, and do one of the following:

- To open Computer Management on the client computer, click Manage Computer. The Computer Management console provides access to event logs, Device Manager, Services, Shared Folders, local users and groups, and other important tools.

- To go straight to the event logs, click View Event Logs.

- To offer to establish a Remote Assistance session, click Offer Remote Assistance.

- To establish a Remote Desktop connection to the computer, click Connect To Computer Via Terminal Services. This feature doesn't work on computers running Windows 2000 Professional.

- To go straight to the Services console of a selected server computer, click View Services. This feature is only available for server computers.

More complex administrative tasks can be accomplished using Windows Management Instrumentation (WMI), although learning WMI is worth the time only if you do a *lot* of remote administration. Use the Scriptomatic Tool (available at *http://www.microsoft.com/technet/scriptcenter*) to get started, which makes it easy to create simple scripts that remotely obtain useful information from client computers running most versions of Windows. You can also use the Windows Management Instrumentation Console (WMIC), a relatively easy-to-use command-line interface for WMI, from within Windows XP or Windows Small Business Server 2003. (Type **wmic /?** at a command prompt for more information.)

Removing Computers from the Network

To permanently remove a computer from the network, delete the associated computer account by completing the following steps:

1. In the Server Management console, click Client Computers or Server Computers.

2. Select the computer you want to remove and then click Remove Computer From Network. Click Yes when prompted. This deletes the computer account in Active Directory.

3. On the client, open System in Control Panel.

4. On Windows XP and Windows Server 2003 clients, click the Computer Name tab and then click Change. On Windows 2000 clients, click the Network Identification tab and then click Properties.

5. Select Workgroup, as shown in Figure 11-20, type a suitable workgroup name, and then click OK. Reboot the computer when prompted.

Deleting the computer account prevents the computer from connecting to the domain. To reinstate the computer on the network, create a new computer account (see the "Connecting Computers to the Network" section of this chapter), and then use the Small Business Server Network Configuration Wizard on the client computer.

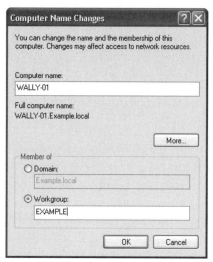

Figure 11-20   The Computer Name Changes dialog box.

Summary

Managing computers on a network can be a lot of work, but Windows Small Business Server 2003 reduces the effort involved by streamlining the process of connecting computers to the network, deploying software, remotely managing computers, and connecting from across the Internet.

In the next chapter, we'll cover installing and using Windows Server Update Services (WSUS). This is a major addition to SBS that was added with the R2 release.

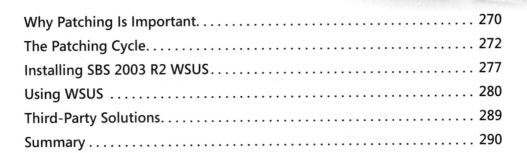

Chapter 12
Patch Management

Why Patching Is Important. 270

The Patching Cycle. 272

Installing SBS 2003 R2 WSUS. 277

Using WSUS 280

Third-Party Solutions. 289

Summary 290

Software updates, or *patches* in the common parlance, are something that everyone hates, but they have become a basic part of life in the modern computing world. We hated them and complained about them when we were UNIX system administrators some 20 years ago, and we still hate them now, even though the overall process of obtaining, testing, and applying them has improved greatly. We doubt that anything we can say will make you like patches any better than we do, but in this chapter we'll try to cover the basics to make the patch management process as straightforward and manageable as possible. We'll also highlight the important addition that the R2 release of SBS 2003 gives us—a fully integrated version of Windows Server Update Services (WSUS) that will help us manage software updates across our SBS networks, and even give us a nice green check mark in our morning Server Performance Report when everyone is patched up.

Real World   Terminology

The first rule of patches is that Microsoft doesn't like that word. Microsoft uses several different terms, each with a slightly different meaning, but the reality is that to the rest of the world, they're still called patches. We call them patches, the magazines and newspapers call them patches, even most Microsoft employees call them patches, unless they're giving a formal presentation. So throughout this chapter, that's what we'll call them. But Microsoft does have official terminology, and we should all be clear on what it is:

- **Critical Update**   A generally available fix for a critical but non-security-related bug. A critical update has an accompanying Knowledge Base article.

- **Security Update**   A generally available fix for a security vulnerability. Security updates have an accompanying Knowledge Base article and a Security Bulletin.

- **Software Update**   A broad term that covers Service Packs, hotfixes, update rollups, security updates, feature packs, and so on. A software update has an accompanying Knowledge Base article.

- **Service Pack**   A generally available collection of fixes and feature enhancements. Service packs are cumulative and contain all currently available updates, update rollups, security updates, critical updates, and hotfixes, and they might contain fixes for problems that were found internally and have not been otherwise released. Service packs also sometimes add new features (Microsoft Windows XP SP2, for example).

- **Hotfix**   A narrowly available fix for a specific issue. Hotfixes are generally available only through Microsoft Product Support Services and cannot be redistributed. Hotfixes are not tested as thoroughly as updates, update rollups, or service packs.

- **Update**   A generally available fix for a specific, nonsecurity, noncritical problem. An update has an accompanying Knowledge Base article.

- **Update rollup**   A generally available and tested collection of hotfixes, security updates, critical updates, and updates that are packaged together. An update rollup has an accompanying Knowledge Base article.

See? All sorts of terms and terminology and not one of them is a patch. For complete, up-to-date details on Microsoft update terminology, see *http://support.microsoft.com/kb/824684/*.

Why Patching Is Important

In the old days, when your network wasn't connected to the Internet, and system administrators were the only people who installed software, and users had only a green screen terminal, deciding when to apply a patch was a fairly straightforward decision. If you were having a specific problem and you wanted a bit of overtime on the weekend, you came in and applied a patch. If no one was complaining and you didn't want to work on the weekend, you threw the tape (patches always came on tapes in those days) in the drawer and waited until you had to come in on the weekend for some other maintenance, or users started complaining about a problem that seemed related. Or you simply never got around to it at all.

Even in the more recent past it was possible to have a more considered and gradual approach to applying patches. When a vulnerability was identified, it often took months before there was any real risk to your network.

Today that approach simply won't work, as Code Red, Nimda, Slammer, and others have all too clearly demonstrated. Within hours or (at most) days of the release of a critical security update, there will almost certainly be sample exploit code posted on the Internet telling anyone and everyone how to exploit the vulnerability. If you ignore critical security updates, you place your entire SBS network—and the data stored on it—at risk.

Applying software updates is only one part of a defense-in-depth strategy to protect your network, but it's a critical part. Don't neglect it.

Real World   Patch Tuesday

In the old days, patches, especially security updates, were released whenever a new vulnerability was identified and corrected. When that happened a few times a year, it wasn't a big problem, and the system administrator dealt with each patch as it came out. In most cases, you could just wait until the Service Pack came out and deal with a whole bunch of them at once. But as more and more security updates and critical updates were released on an almost daily basis, it became increasingly difficult to properly test and identify all the patches that were necessary for your system. The whole process became a serious impediment to productivity.

In direct response to many, many complaints, Microsoft has moved to a monthly update release process. Unless there is a compelling and immediate need for a critical security update to be released off-cycle, all security updates are released once a month, on the second Tuesday of the month. This change has greatly simplified the planning and deployment of patches.

The Patching Cycle

There are (or there should be) four basic phases in the ongoing cycle of maintaining a well-patched, up-to-date network:

- Assess
- Identify
- Evaluate and plan
- Deploy

Each of these phases is essential to the successful management of patches on your network. And in a large, well-run network, each of these phases is quite formal and carefully delineated.

Given the relative simplicity of SBS networks, and the more realistic IT budgets and resources we have, you're going to have to combine and simplify the overall process a bit, and you'll probably even bypass phases on occasion. However, it's good to have an understanding of the phases and to think through the steps involved in each one, even if you're combining them.

Assess

The *assess* phase of patch management is all about understanding what your environment is, where and how it is vulnerable and can be attacked, and what resources and procedures are in place to reduce those vulnerabilities.

When a patch is released, you can't make an informed decision about whether you need to install that patch unless you first know what software is present in your environment and what your critical business assets are that absolutely, positively must be protected. So the first step to an overall patch management process is to figure out *what* software you're running in your environment. All of it, we hope. Whether you build a spreadsheet, have an Access database, or just a keep it all in a chart in Word, you need to get your software environment audited and documented.

Identify your critical business assets. Is there confidential data that you couldn't function without? Are there critical systems that must be available at all times? Are there individuals whose productivity is mission-critical? All of these are business assets that you should factor into your overall patch management strategy.

The next part of the assessment phase is to understand what security threats and vulnerabilities you currently have. Do you have legacy Windows NT 4 systems that are no longer supported? Are there Windows 95 or Windows 98 computers on your network? (Remember, we told you it was time to get rid of them.)

Are you running old versions of software programs that can't be easily updated or replaced? Do you have public-facing Web servers that are not behind your firewall? What are your security policies and how are they enforced? These and many, many more questions need to be asked—and answered.

Finally, you need to assess your patching infrastructure and resources. How do you deploy software and patches now? Who is responsible for identifying, testing, and deploying patches? What resources are available to help with that? How rapidly can you respond to a critical vulnerability that affects your systems? What steps can you take to improve your response time?

SBS Version

If all this information seems a bit much, it's really just a lot of somewhat formal words to say that what you really need to do is know *what* is on your network that you need to keep patched. It's also good to have a record of what kinds of patches have caused trouble for you before—when you see new patches that affect these areas, you'll probably want to do some additional testing before you send the patch out.

Identify

The *identify* phase is about finding out what software updates or patches are available, and how critical it is that they be deployed in your environment. You need to

- Discover the patch.
- Decide whether it's relevant to your environment.
- Download the patch.
- Identify the patch's criticality.

There are many ways to discover patches, but for Microsoft products one of the best ways is to sign up for e-mail alerts. If you do this, Microsoft will send you notifications of security updates before they are actually released. The signup page is at *http://www.microsoft.com/technet/security/bulletin/notify.mspx*. You can tailor the notification method and detail level to suit your environment.

> **Note**   The link above provides alerts only for security-related patches.

Whatever method you use to discover patches, it's important that you have a way to trust the source of the patch information. All Microsoft security update alerts are signed with a publicly available PGP key, for example. And it shouldn't be necessary to say this, but just in case: *Microsoft will never send a security update as an attachment to an e-mail!* Never.

> **Important**   Wait, maybe you missed that. Again, for emphasis: *Microsoft will never send a security update as an attachment to an e-mail!* Never.

Once you know about a patch, you need to decide whether it's relevant to your environment. If all your client computers are running Windows XP Professional SP2 (and they should be!), a patch that applies only to Windows 2000 isn't really relevant to your environment. However, if the patch is a critical security update for Microsoft Office 2003 and you run that in your environment, you'll need to apply it.

When you determine that a patch is relevant to your environment, you need to obtain the patch *from a known and trusted source*. For a Microsoft patch, this generally means downloading it directly from Microsoft. With SBS 2003 R2, this means letting WSUS download the patch by synchronizing, but we'll get to the gory details of WSUS later. Find the relevant Knowledge Base article for the patch, and then cut and paste the link to the download page directly into your browser. Do *not* click the link in an e-mail to get your patch. Even when you have verified that the e-mail is really from Microsoft and is a legitimate e-mail, you shouldn't click the links. Get into the habit of always using cut and paste. When you use cut and paste to put a link into your browser, you greatly reduce the likelihood of a *phishing* attack—being unknowingly redirected to a site that looks *exactly* like the site you expected to go to, but is actually a site designed to steal information from you, or download unwanted spyware onto your computer.

> **Note**   Most e-mail clients today have the ability to force all e-mail to display as plain text. This is a *good* thing, because it prevents unscrupulous people from hiding the real destination of a link. The giveaway for detecting a bogus link will usually be that it's a link to an IP address, not the actual DNS domain name, or if it is a DNS name, it's not exactly the one you think it is. If you make the change and only read your e-mail in plain text, your e-mail won't be as pretty, but you'll give yourself an additional layer of protection from phishing attacks.
>
> To enable plain-text e-mail handling in Outlook 2003, select Options from the Tools menu. Click the Preferences tab, then click E-Mail Options. Select the Read All Standard Mail In Plain Text and Read All Digitally Signed Mail In Plain Text check boxes. Click OK and restart Outlook.

Once you've downloaded the patch and read the associated Knowledge Base article, you are in a position to determine just how critical the patch is in your environment. Is this a patch that needs to be deployed immediately, with limited testing—or even with no testing? Or are there ameliorating factors that allow the patch to be deployed as part of a regular patching schedule after full testing?

SBS Version

Again, if that seemed a bit much, you're probably right. But it's actually what we had to go through before SBS 2003 R2 if we didn't have some method—usually third-party—to automatically download and identify patches for our environment. With R2, you can let WSUS take care of the downloads and the initial analysis of which computers need it. You'll want to do some thinking, though, before you let it fire off an automatic update to every client in the network.

Evaluate and Plan

The *evaluate and plan* phase of patch management flows naturally out of the identify phase, and in many ways is an extension of it. In this phase, you determine how to respond to the software update you've downloaded. Is it critical, or even necessary? How should it be deployed? And to whom? Should interim countermeasures be employed that will minimize your exposure to the vulnerability? What priority does the patch have?

The initial determination of need, suitability, and priority is made during the identify phase, but in the evaluate and plan phase, you should take a closer look at the patch. What priority is the patch? If it affects a critical business asset, and there's no easy or appropriate countermeasure except the patch, it will have a higher priority for testing and deployment than if there's a simple countermeasure that you can implement until the patch can be deployed. If it targets critical business assets, it's going to have a higher priority than if the only computers that are affected are several old Windows 98 computers that aren't running any critical business applications. (But you got rid of those old Windows 98 computers, right?)

Once you've identified the priority of the patch, you need to plan the actual deployment. Which computers need to have the patch deployed to them? Are there any constraints or issues that interfere with the deployment? Who needs to be notified, and what steps need to be taken so that the deployment minimizes the disruption to the environment? If this is an emergency release, will it go through a staged deployment, or is every affected computer going to have the patch deployed as soon as possible?

SBS Version

In any SBS network larger than a few clients, you should have a couple of clients that are designated canaries. In all but emergency patch situations, these computers will have the new patches deployed to them first. If they survive the patch without major issues, you can OK the deployment onto the rest of your clients.

Unfortunately, WSUS—as included with SBS 2003 R2—doesn't support having a special group of client computers that are treated differently from other clients. The workaround we've found is to have one (or two) users who go directly to Microsoft Update every Patch Tuesday and update their computers. This gets the update onto their computers quicker than any other method, and allows some testing time before any automatic deployment can happen. If you go this route, choose a user who has a fairly typical computer and, most important, who is willing to take on this role. Also, make sure that you carefully review the "Caveats" section of the Security Bulletin. This section will detail known issues and interactions that you should be aware of.

Deploy

The *deployment* phase of patch management is in many ways the easiest phase. You've done all your preparatory work; now all you need to do is the actual deployment.

First and foremost, *communicate*. Let everyone who will be affected know that you will be deploying a patch, and what application or area of the operating system it affects. If you know that the deployment will cause changes in behavior, tell your users *before* the deployment. You will have far fewer support calls if you've warned people that a certain behavior is expected than if you surprise them.

SBS Version

With SBS 2003 R2, we have WSUS to do the deployment and track its progress. If your canary user has survived, you should proceed with the deployment. But the same rule applies as for a really large enterprise—*communicate*.

Repeat

Once you've deployed a patch, the process starts over again. It really is a continuous process—or it should be. At a minimum, verify that the patch has been successfully deployed to the affected computers. Update your software map and database so that you know which computers have had the patch applied. Since our assumption is that every patch is on every computer, we only keep track of the exceptions. Once a patch cycle is complete, we make a note of any issues, confirm that deployment has been successful, and get ready for the next round.

Installing SBS 2003 R2 WSUS

The major inclusion in the R2 release of SBS 2003 is our own version of Windows Server Update Services (WSUS): Windows Small Business Server Update Services. Integrated into the main Server Management page, and into SBS reporting, WSUS gives us an easy to use method to manage software updates on SBS. If you're using SBS Premium Edition, you should install the Premium Technologies first, and then install R2, which will include WSUS.

Note In this chapter and throughout the book, we will use WSUS as an abbreviation for the Windows Small Business Server Update Services that are included in the R2 release of SBS 2003. Even though there are some specific customizations that make the SBS version slightly different from the generally available WSUS download, the final result is based on the same program. And frankly, WSBSUS would just be too much for us.

Before you can install WSUS or any of the rest of the R2 release of SBS 2003, you need to install the Exchange Server 2003 Service Pack 2 and Windows SharePoint Services Service Pack 2. Both are included on the R2 Technologies CD, also known as CD6. When you install R2, you will at least need 1GB of free disk space on the system drive, and *at least* 8GB of free disk space on the drive where WSUS will store the updates.

Important You must install SBS 2003 R2 while logged in to the default Administrator account. Any other account will fail.

To install SBS 2003 R2, including WSUS, follow these steps:

1. Insert the R2 Technologies CD into your CD-ROM drive. If it doesn't automatically start the Setup program, double-click setup.exe to open the Windows Small Business Server 2003 R2 Setup Wizard, as shown in Figure 12-1.

2. Read How To Install and the Release Notes for any last-minute changes in the process.

3. Click Install Service Pack 2 For Exchange Server 2003 (if you haven't already installed this update) to open the Microsoft Exchange Installation Wizard, as shown in Figure 12-2. Click Next, agree to the EULA, and click Next again.

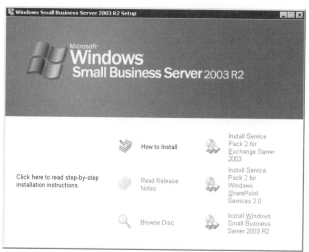

Figure 12-1   The Welcome page of the Windows Small Business Server 2003 R2 Setup Wizard.

Figure 12-2   The Welcome page of the Microsoft Exchange Installation Wizard.

4. On the Component Selection page of the Microsoft Exchange Installation Wizard, you can modify the update selections, but there's usually no reason to do so. Click Next.

5. On the Installation Summary page, you'll see a list of what will be updated and the installation path, as shown in Figure 12-3.

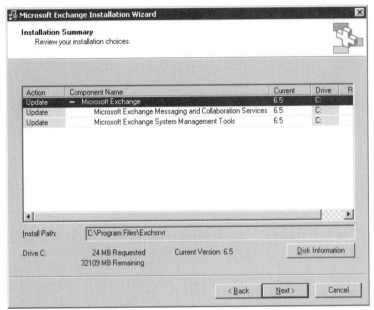

Figure 12-3   The Installation Summary page of the Microsoft Exchange Installation Wizard.

6. Click Next and the installation of Exchange will begin. When the installation is finished, click Finish to return to the main R2 Setup page.

7. If you haven't already installed Service Pack 2 for Windows SharePoint Services 2.0, install it now. Most existing installations will already have this Service Pack installed.

8. Once both Exchange and SharePoint have been updated, click the icon to start the Windows Small Business Server 2003 R2 Setup Wizard.

9. When the Welcome page appears, click Next. If you have met all the requirements for running Setup, you'll see the EULA. If you haven't, or you have the Server Management console open in the background, you'll be politely reminded to correct the problem, as shown in Figure 12-4. Correct the problem, click Check Again, and then click Next.

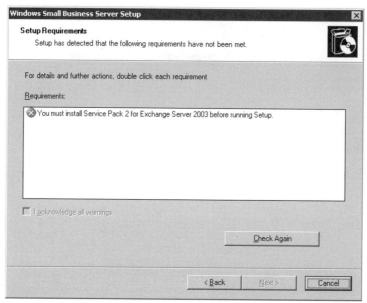

Figure 12-4 The Setup Requirements page of the Windows Small Business Server Setup Wizard.

10. Accept the EULA and click Next.

11. On the Update Services page, shown in Figure 12-5, specify the location for Windows Small Business Server Update Services to store its downloaded updates. This is *not* the location for the actual program files—those must be on the system disk and you won't be offered a chance to change their location. Click Next and then click Next again.

12. Once Setup has completed the installation, click Finish to open the To Do List again.

13. Close the To Do List and open the Server Management console, as shown in Figure 12-6, with the new Update Services section.

Using WSUS

Once WSUS is installed, the next step is to synchronize your installation. This process can take several hours and puts a bit of a strain on your Internet connection, so we recommend waiting until the end of the day to start it. To begin synchronization, open the Server Management console and click Update Services to open the Welcome page of the Update Services Status page, as shown in Figure 12-7. When you're ready to begin the synchronization, click Synchronize Now.

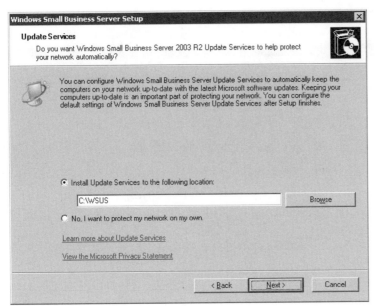

Figure 12-5   The Update Services page of the Windows Small Business Server Setup Wizard.

Figure 12-6   The Server Management console, with the new Update Services icon and section.

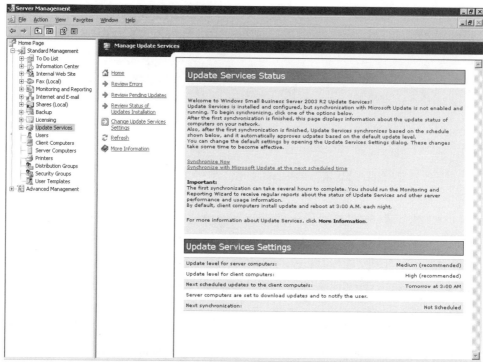

Figure 12-7   The Welcome page of Windows Small Business Server Update Services.

Once the initial synchronization has finished, you'll see a new Welcome page for WSUS in Server Management, as shown in Figure 12-8.

This status page gives you all the information you need about the current patch status of your SBS network in a single page. You can see here that there are updates waiting to be reviewed. You would also see any errors that were present, and you can see what the settings are for WSUS. On the left side of the Update Services page, you can select the various functions of WSUS. The choices are

- Review errors
- Review Pending Updates
- Review Status of Updates Installation
- Change Update Services Settings
- Refresh
- More Information

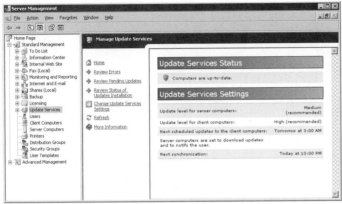

Figure 12-8   The Windows Small Business Server Update Services Welcome page in the Server Management console.

Reviewing Errors

The Review Errors link takes you to the Computers With Update Installation Errors page, which will show any outstanding errors. From here, you can click an error and then click View Details to see the details associated with that error, as shown in Figure 12-9.

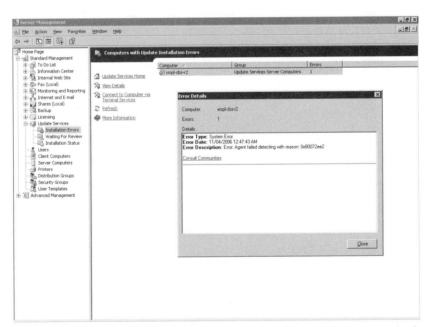

Figure 12-9   The details dialog box for an outstanding installation error in the Computers With Update Installation Errors page.

> **Note** Always click the Refresh link when navigating to a new page in the
> Update Services section. The Update Services Home page reliably refreshes auto-
> matically, but other pages do not.

Another useful link on the Computers With Update Installation Errors page is Connect
To Computer Via Terminal Services. When you've reviewed the error, you can click this
link to open a Remote Desktop session to the computer having the problem, and then
correct the source of the error.

Review Pending Updates

When you click the Review Pending Updates link on the Update Services home page, it
takes you to the Updates Waiting For Review page, shown in Figure 12-10.

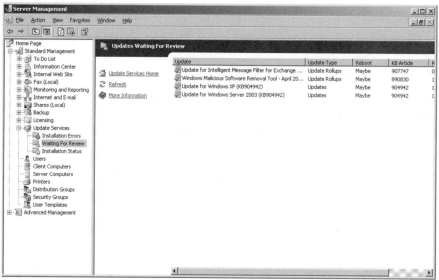

Figure 12-10 The Updates Waiting For Review page of the Update Services section of
Server Management.

When you have pending updates, you have two choices: You can decline the update and it
will not be distributed to computers in your environment, or you can open a window that
shows you the details of the update and lets you approve it for deployment. If you select an
update and click View Details and then click Approve, you'll see a page similar to 12-11.

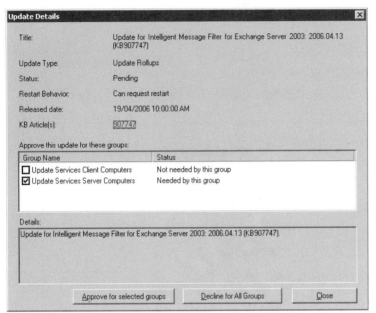

Figure 12-11   The Update Details dialog box for a Microsoft Intelligent Message Filter update.

On the Update Details page, you can choose whether the update is applied to your client computers, your servers, or both—or you can decline the update for both groups of computers by clicking Decline For All Groups.

If the summary of the update given on the Update Details page isn't enough information, there is also a link to the relevant Microsoft Knowledge Base (KB) articles for the patch. By clicking on this link, you'll be taken directly to the KB article that contains full details for the patch, as shown in Figure 12-12.

When you click Approve For Selected Groups, you'll get a fairly useless progress dialog box. Click Closed and you're back at the Updates Waiting For Review page, where you can decide which other updates should be approved.

Some updates will require a separate EULA to be approved. When that happens, you'll get an additional prompt to approve the EULA when you click Approve For Selected Groups.

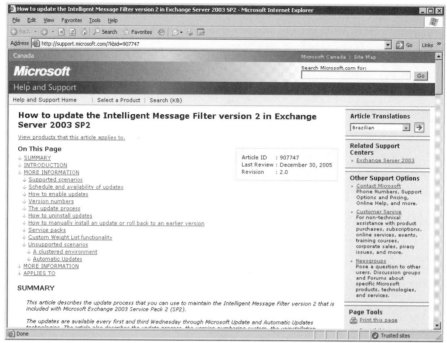

Figure 12-12 The KB article (KB 907747) associated with the IMF filter update.

So, what's wrong with this whole process? Well, when there are one or two updates to approve, all those mouse clicks are a bit annoying but still tolerable. However, if you have 30 or 40 of them waiting for review and approval, as you do with a new installation and a new, unpatched computer on the network, the process becomes not just annoying, but positively obnoxious. There should be a way to approve multiple updates all together, but there isn't, so you'll just have to slog through them. The alternative is to connect new computers directly to Microsoft Update and download and install all the available updates in bulk. Once the computer is current, the process of keeping them up to date with Update Services is at least tolerable.

Review Status of Updates Installation

When you've approved patches for installation, the home page of Update Services will show that there are updates scheduled in the main status page, with a link to the View Installation Status page, or you can go to the View Installation Status page directly by clicking Installation Status in the left-hand pane of Server Management, as shown in Figure 12-13.

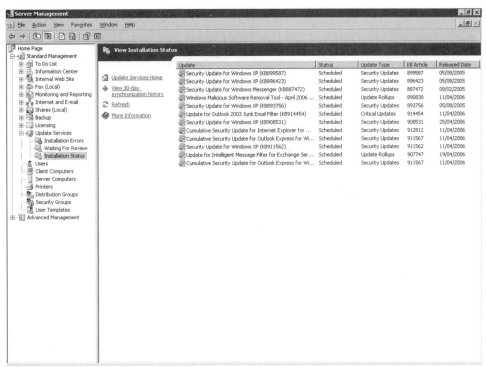

Figure 12-13   The View Installation Status page of the Update Services section of Server Management.

You should always click the Refresh link when you open any page of Update Services—only the home page automatically refreshes.

On the View Installation Status page, you can see all the updates that are scheduled to be downloaded and installed. These will automatically be downloaded and installed on client computers if you haven't changed the default settings, but will only be downloaded to servers—you'll still need to install them manually on your servers unless you change the defaults.

From this page, you can double-click a scheduled patch and decline it for all computers. There is no direct way to force a scheduled patch out early, or fine-tune the specific computers on which the patch will be deployed beyond the two groups that Windows Small Business Server Update Services supports. If your environment requires a more fine-grained management of patches, you'll need to look at alternatives to the version of WSUS built into SBS 2003 R2.

Change Update Services Settings

On the Update Services Settings page, shown in Figure 12-14, you can manage the update level for the two update groups—servers and clients. The default settings are Medium for servers and High for clients.

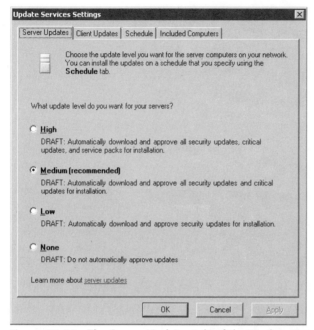

Figure 12-14 The Server Updates tab of the Update Services Settings page.

On the Schedule tab, you can change the default update schedule and action for clients and servers independently. The default actions are for updates to be downloaded to servers but not automatically installed, and to automatically download and install to client computers. Seem like good choices to us.

On the Included Computers tab, you'll see a list of computers that have been included and excluded from automatic updates. By default, all new computers are automatically added to the appropriate group when they're joined to the SBS domain. But you can exclude any on which you want to manually manage patches. Or, if you have a sensitive client computer that you want to treat as a server, you can select it and click Modify to change which group it's in, as shown in Figure 12-15.

Figure 12-15   The Change Update Group Membership dialog box.

Third-Party Solutions

The new Update Services included in the R2 release of SBS 2003 is a big step forward for SBS networks. Update Services provides a single, integrated, and consistent method for patch management that will meet the basic needs of the majority of SBS environments. And it's definitely easier to get set up and working correctly than using the regular Windows Server Update Services download from Microsoft.com. But having said all that, there are limitations. WSUS will only manage updates of Microsoft products, and it doesn't give you the fine-grained control that some SBS networks might need. If your needs go beyond the basics in Windows Small Business Server Update Services, you're going to have to go either to a product such as Systems Management Server (SMS) or to a third-party product. Frankly, SMS is just overkill for SBS networks, and the implementation costs are quite high.

An alternative to the Microsoft patch management solutions that we've used and like a lot is Shavlik's HFNetChkPro (*http://www.shavlik.com/hfnetchkpro.aspx*). This is a full-featured, powerful product that gives you the ability to create multiple patch groups, control the download and deployment actions and schedules for each group differently, and even patch computers that aren't part of your SBS domain but are connected to your network. It also supports patching of some non-Microsoft products that you're likely to have on your SBS network, such as WinZip and Adobe Acrobat.

Other alternatives that we've not used, but that have come recommended by fellow SBS administrators include PatchLink (*http://www.patchlink.com*), BigFix (*http://www.bigfix.com*), and St. Bernard Software's UpdateEXPERT (*http://www.stbernard.com/products/updateexpert/products_updateexpert.asp*).

Summary

In this chapter, we've covered both the process of patch management and the mechanics of using the new Windows Small Business Server Update Services, which is part of the R2 release of SBS 2003. In the next chapter, we'll cover another critical security process—backing up and restoring your SBS network.

Chapter 13
Backing Up and Restoring Data

Backup Terminology and Methods. 291

Designing a Backup Strategy 294

Backing Up Your Data 298

Restoring Data 307

Summary 311

Backing up the data on your network is a chore that everyone knows is important but which all too many ignore or don't take seriously. Ignoring backups is a serious mistake. After all, you're betting your entire business that there won't be a fire, or earthquake, or hurricane, or just a plain-old, everyday hard-drive failure. Does that seem like a good idea? Yeah, we don't think so either. Backups aren't fun, or sexy, or even particularly interesting. But they can mean the difference between having a business and not having a business.

Microsoft Windows Small Business Server 2003 includes a dedicated backup utility that makes the task of doing a regular backup simple and straightforward. Although businesses at the upper end of the range covered by SBS might find they need a more full-featured backup program with all the bells and whistles, most businesses will find the included Backup Utility quite adequate, especially given the integration into the Server Management console.

Backup Terminology and Methods

You'll need to understand a number of different terms when dealing with backups. Here's a short list of the most important ones:

- **Backup device**   The hardware device on which backups are saved.

- **Backup media**   The actual tape, disk, CD, or DVD on which the backup is stored.

- **Full backup**   What it says—this backup includes *all* files in a given selection set.

- **Incremental backup** All the files in a given selection set that have changed since the last full or incremental backup. To restore, you need the last full backup and all the incremental backups since then.

- **Differential backup** All the files in a given selection set that have changed since the last full backup. To restore, you need the last full backup and the latest differential backup.

Backup Devices

Windows Small Business Server supports writing to either a tape device or a hard drive. The hard-drive backup option includes both fixed and removable hard drives. There is no official support, however, for using a CD or DVD writer as a backup device. In theory, you could use a CD or DVD device by using third-party software that makes them appear to be just another hard drive, albeit a removable one. This is a tempting option, but not one that you should use—primarily because it is not supported. Let's face it, when you really, really need help because you're trying to restore a backup in the event of a disaster, you want to be running a supported solution.

Important Windows Small Business Server 2003 does not directly support using writeable CD or DVD drives as backup devices. Using these drives as backup devices requires third-party software that is designed for consumer use to make the CD or DVD drive appear as a hard drive, allowing the Backup Utility to use it. Using consumer-grade software for your backup strategy is not tested on Windows Small Business Server 2003 and is not a supported scenario. Just don't do it.

Traditionally, the preferred backup device has always been tape of one variety or another. Tape drives are not cheap; large, fast tape drives are very definitely not cheap. But tape is a proven technology that has many advantages, including portability, easy off-site storage, and a predictable life span. It does, however, have some very real disadvantages—probably the most important is that it is slower than the alternatives. And tapes are notoriously problematic to restore. Even when buying first-quality tapes and using name-brand tape drives, every system administrator I know has horror stories about failed tape restores because the tape couldn't be read. The slow speed can create a problem with the length of time a backup takes, as well as the time to recover a specific file or files. And a tape failure on a critical backup can present a real problem. Tape is still an appropriate and viable backup method in a small business, but do *not* skimp on hardware or media. Choose a proven, reliable tape technology designed for backing up servers. We like Digital Data Storage (DDS), Advanced Intelligent Tape (AIT), or Digital Linear Tape (DLT). All are proven technologies with good track records.

The alternatives to tape are hard drives or optical media such as CD or DVD. While hard drives, even removable ones, are not ideal for off-site storage, they can be handled by off-site storage companies. And hard drives do have some definite advantages. Because the cost of IDE hard drives has come down, it's possible to afford several of them, which you can rotate for backups using inexpensive USB2 or FireWire external cases. Optical drives are not a viable alternative, in our opinion. CDs simply don't hold enough any more. And even writeable DVDs really don't hold enough for most backups without having to span multiple DVDs and, most important, they are not a supported solution.

The solution we've come up with for our SBS environment is to use a spare internal hard drive for daily backups, and an external USB or FireWire hard drive for weekly full backups. We have four external hard drives that we rotate for the weekly backups and store them off-site.

Backup Media

Whatever backup device you choose, you will need to have sufficient media for it to manage a full schedule of backups. Don't stint here by buying cheap media. If the price for a batch of DDS4 or DLT tapes seems too good to be true, it probably is. Hard drives, however, are quite reliable for the kind of duty cycles that a backup device sees.

Once you've decided on your backup strategy, you'll have a good idea of the number of media you'll need to support it, whether tapes or disks. Keep in mind that media *does* fail, and there will be times you want or need to do something special, so order accordingly. If your backup strategy calls for 25 tapes used in rotation, you'll probably want 30 or 35, plus a couple of cleaning tapes. Backup strategies are covered in the next section, "Designing a Backup Strategy."

Before you spend your money on a batch of tapes, buy one of the brand you are considering and test it. And test it some more. Some brands of tapes do have problems with some tape drives. You want to make sure there aren't any incompatibilities before you spend your money on a bunch of tapes.

If you're backing up to hard drive, and using multiple removable hard drives, buy one and test it thoroughly before you commit to this as a strategy. Choose a drive capacity to allow you plenty of room for growth—you can't easily swap hard drives in the middle of a backup if you run out of room. Once you've confirmed that a particular drive and case work well for your backup solution, order sufficient drives to handle your chosen rotational strategy, plus one extra. And while technically you could use one external case for all of your backup drives, we don't recommend it. The risk of damaging the cabling or wiring in some way is much higher if you're swapping drives every week.

Designing a Backup Strategy

To effectively back up a network, you must plan your approach to this complex task. Backups are more complicated than simply putting a tape in the drive and starting up the software. Your backup strategy should address all the following questions:

- How much data do you have to back up?

- How much time do you have to perform backups?

- How often should you back up the data?

- Who is going to be responsible for seeing that backups are completed?

- How many tapes (or other media) do you plan to use?

Even if you use a fairly simple and straightforward tape rotation schedule, you'll want to spend some time considering each of these questions to make sure your strategy answers them appropriately for your environment.

- **How much data**   With Windows Small Business Server, the standard backup strategy backs up *all* the files on your server. Make sure that you plan for the amount of growth you expect when you decide what backup hardware to use. Ideally, you want a tape type or hard-drive capacity that will store all your files on a single tape or drive. Or, if that's not possible, you'll need to buy a tape library that holds several tapes and can automatically change tapes as needed. If your backup hard drives prove too small, you'll have to replace them—there is no easy way to swap out hard drives in the middle of a backup.

- **How much time**   The total amount of data you need to back up, divided by the effective backup speed your backup device can support, yields the total time your backup will take. Ideally the backup should happen during a relatively quiet time on your network to reduce the overall load on the network and your server. Different tape technologies yield different speeds, but also have different costs. Balance your need for speed with your aversion to spending money to get the best tape drive you can afford. A hard-drive backup device is substantially faster than even the fastest tape drive.

- **How often**   This is simple, really. How much data can you and your business afford to lose? In the event of the death of a server, you'll need to restore from your most recent backup onto your new server. If the last time you did a backup was a week ago, you've just lost a week's worth of work. Realistically, most businesses should plan on a daily backup.

- **Who**   Who is responsible for doing backups? And more important, who is responsible when that person is out sick, on vacation, or out of town? Don't count on a single person being the only one who is responsible. Make sure that at least one other person knows the routine for changing tapes and handling the offsite backup plan, and so on.

- **How many tapes**   This will depend on how often you overwrite your tapes, and how many days are in your rotation. We'll go over some more details in the next section, "Backup Schedules."

Backup Schedules

It sometimes seems like there are as many different backup schedules as there are system administrators, but it really isn't quite that complicated. Your backup schedule should meet the needs of your company for data protection and disaster recovery, but should also recognize the reality of the resources available.

Frequency

For most businesses, a full *daily* backup is the core of their backup schedule. Once a week you should plan on archiving your backup tape—that is, removing it from the daily rotation and storing it someplace safe.

Why once a day? Because most businesses can't really afford to lose more than a day or two of work. In the event of a disaster, you might need to restore your most current backup, or even the one before that if there are problems. If you're comfortable with losing up to a week's work, you could do once-a-week backups. But if there's a problem with that most recent tape, you've lost two week's work.

Reusing Tapes

Magnetic tape is a reusable medium. You can write on it repeatedly and read it repeatedly without noticeable problems—up to the limits of the particular type of tape. Each type of tape has an expected life span. Most system administrators plan on throwing away their tapes at about half that life span. Nothing is more frustrating when you're in the middle of trying to restore a file or a whole directory than discovering that your backup has failed and you have to go to an earlier tape.

For most scenarios, a simple tape rotation of individual tapes for each day of the week, with a once-a-week archive tape, makes a reasonable compromise between simplicity and security. In this scenario you have a "Monday" tape, a "Tuesday" tape, and so on. Each week you put the Monday tape in the drive on Monday morning when you pull out the previous tape. Then on Tuesday morning, when you come in, you swap the Monday tape for Tuesday.

Whereas this simple one-week rotation is adequate for many scenarios, many businesses use a two-week or four-week rotation. This has the advantage of making it easier to keep the most current tapes readily available while still having an off-site archive set that is only a week old.

If you're using a hard drive for your backup, you'll either need to use a removable drive or make sure you have sufficient storage space on your target drive to handle as many backups as are in your standard rotation schedule.

Archive and Off-Site Storage

In addition to maintaining a daily backup, it is important to keep archival and off-site backups that allow you to recover in the event of a total disaster, or to recover to a point in time. You might well have legal requirements that require you to keep archival tapes also.

Why off-site storage? Well, if your business burns down, or is damaged by a hurricane or earthquake, it's a real mess. But if your only backup copies are in the burned-out server room, it's a disaster. There are commercial services that will pick up your backup tapes weekly (or as often as you want) and store them in a secure facility. They're not inexpensive, but they do provide a reliable, secure, and predictable service.

Note   Off-site storage is an essential part of any backup and recovery strategy. If your business really can't afford to use a commercial off-site storage service, you can get some of the same benefits by simply having someone take the archive tape home every week. It's not as good as having it in a secure storage facility, but it does protect from the most common disasters. It is essential, however, that you treat this as a serious responsibility and standardize how it is done if you're to be able to depend on it in an emergency.

Which tape should you send off-site? Well, not yesterday's! That's the one you're most likely to need, and need in a hurry. If your pickup day for tapes is Wednesday, send off the Wednesday tape, and put a new tape in your rotation on Wednesday. Keep at least a month's worth of weekly backups off-site, and then have the storage service bring back the tape from a month ago and put it back into your rotation.

Real World   A Combination Disk and Tape Strategy

Given the desire for both a reasonable disaster-recovery scenario, and simple and easy recovery in a non-disaster situation, one solution we've seen used by some small and medium businesses is a combination of hard-drive and tape backup. This isn't directly supported by the Backup Wizard in the Server Management GUI, but it's not hard to set up.

Daily backups are run from the Manage Small Business Server Backup page. They go to a dedicated, internal IDE hard drive that has enough capacity to hold at least three full backups. This drive has no other reason to exist, and nothing else is stored on it. It does *not* have volume shadow copying turned on. This drive can even be a group of several older hard drives that you just happen to have lying around unused. Combine them into a single drive letter using disk spanning, as covered in Chapter 6, "Disk Management."

Once a week, *after the normal disk backup has run*, have a separate backup task that writes the contents of the backup drive to tape. This doesn't have to be a particularly fast backup, since it is backing up files that are not being used and it can run during a quiet time on the network without affecting anything else. Use this tape for your off-site storage. It means that recovery in a disaster is a two-step process (restore the disk backup from the tape, then restore the operating system and data files from the disk backup), but it has the advantages of disk backup—speed and ease of restore—with the advantages of tape backup—inexpensive media and easy off-site and archival storage. The biggest disadvantage is that you'll have to use the Backup Utility (ntbackup.exe) directly, and then set the schedule task directly, since the Small Business Server Backup doesn't have the flexibility to handle more than a single-stage backup rotation.

Using Shadow Copies to Supplement Backups

Windows Small Business Server enables Volume Shadow Copy automatically on the drive that houses the Users share and sets save points or snapshots twice a day. You can enable Volume Shadow Copy on additional volumes as appropriate to your business. This allows users to quickly recover to a previous version of a lost, damaged, or deleted file without administrative involvement and without having to load up yesterday's backup tape and restore it.

If you have the disk space, and your comfort window for lost data is not very high, you can increase the frequency of scheduled snapshots to more often than twice a day. Keep in mind, however, that disk space is finite. For most situations, the default setting of twice a day is sufficient.

More Info   For more information about enabling and configuring volume shadow copies, see Chapter 7, "Storage Management."

Backing Up Your Data

Windows Small Business Server provides an excellent wizard that configures and executes backups. For most users and situations, using the provided wizard is definitely the way to go. You can also manually run Backup Utility (located by accessing Start, All Programs, Accessories, System Tools folder) for a greater set of options and choices. However, for daily full backups, automatically scheduled, using the wizard is easy and ensures that backup reports are fully integrated into the Windows Small Business Server reporting mechanism.

Real World   Test Your Backups!

A wise and perspicacious system administrator once explained to me that there were only two kinds of backups: ones that had been tested and verified, and ones that were worthless. Strong words, but worthy of some serious consideration. Magnetic tapes are not a perfect medium and they are subject to all kinds of possible errors and corruption. Until you have actually taken your backup tape and restored it, you don't actually know you can. Although in the real world not every single backup will get a full restore test, you really should test a full restore regularly, and a partial restore of a randomly selected set of files and folders more often—at least once a week and on a different day each week. Also check the Event Log and all your backup logs for any error messages that Backup Utility has generated. By carefully monitoring logs, and regularly checking the integrity of your tapes by restoring from them, you have at least reduced the likelihood of undetected problems causing a failed restore.

Configuring the Backup Utility

The first time you use the Backup Configuration Wizard for Windows Small Business Server, you will also be configuring your regular backup schedule. To get started, click Backup in the Server Management console. If you haven't yet configured Backup, your details pane will look like Figure 13-1.

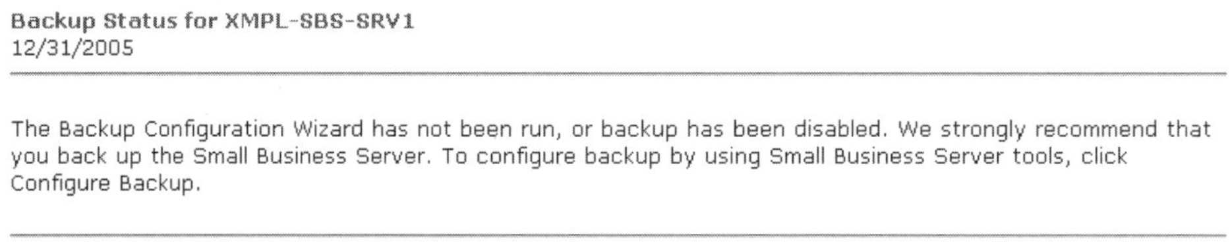

Backup Status for XMPL-SBS-SRV1
12/31/2005

The Backup Configuration Wizard has not been run, or backup has been disabled. We strongly recommend that you back up the Small Business Server. To configure backup by using Small Business Server tools, click Configure Backup.

Figure 13-1   The Backup Utility in Server Management console, before configuring.

To configure the Backup Utility, complete the following steps:

1. Click Configure Backup to start the Backup Configuration Wizard, shown in Figure 13-2.

Figure 13-2   The Backup Configuration Wizard.

2. On the Backup Location page, set the backup location, as shown in Figure 13-3. A tape drive is the preferred backup location. If you're backing up to a hard drive, you can browse to find the location, or simply type the location in the Store Backup Files At This Location box. Click Next.

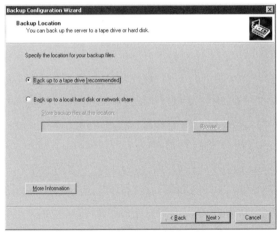

Figure 13-3   The Backup Location page.

3. On the Backup Data Summary page, the default is for everything to be backed up. If you want to exclude certain folders from the standard backup, click Exclude Folders to open the Exclude Folders dialog box, shown in Figure 13-4.

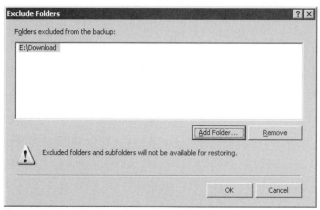

Figure 13-4   The Exclude Folders dialog box.

4. Add folders to the exclusion by clicking the Add Folder button, or highlight an existing exclusion and click Remove to add it back into the backup set. Click OK to return to the Backup Data Summary page. If you've excluded any folders, they will now show in the list.

5. Click Calculate Folder Sizes to update the display to show how much space you've excluded. Click Next.

6. On the Define Backup Schedule page, shown in Figure 13-5, the default schedule calls for backups to be performed Monday through Friday evenings at 11 p.m. Make any changes you need to here, and click Next.

7. If you are backing up to a tape, the Onsite Tape Changer page appears (Figure 13-6). (If you're backing up to a hard drive, you won't see this page, so skip to the next step.) Designate the person who will be responsible for changing tapes, known as the Onsite Tape Changer, and select the time when he or she will get an automatic reminder to change the tape. You can also send this person a monthly reminder to clean the tape drive by selecting the Send A Monthly Tape Drive Cleaning Reminder check box. Click Next.

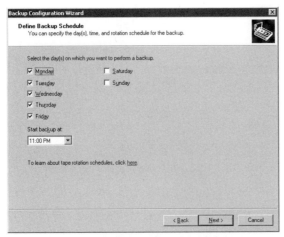

Figure 13-5   The Define Backup Schedule page.

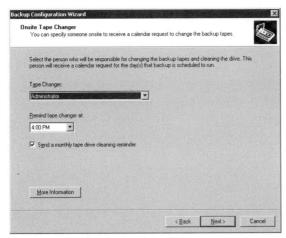

Figure 13-6   The Onsite Tape Changer page.

> **Note**   Windows Small Business Server will automatically remind you to do a monthly tape cleaning, which is good, but we prefer weekly cleanings. Cleaning tapes is cheap, but failed backups are potentially very expensive.

8. On the Storage Allocation For Deleted Files And E-Mail page (Figure 13-7), choose how long to retain copies of deleted e-mail messages, and how much space

to allocate for snapshots of the files in shared folders (Volume Shadow Copy). Clearing the check boxes will disable that functionality. Click Next.

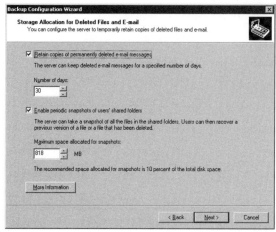

Figure 13-7   The Storage Allocation For Deleted Files And E-Mail page.

9. The final page of the wizard shows a summary of your backup configuration. If everything is OK, click Finish to implement the configuration.

Running a Backup Manually

Windows Small Business Server will schedule your backup for you, but there are often situations in which you want to manually execute a backup. You can use the Backup Utility directly, or if you prefer, use your already-configured selections for Windows Small Business Server.

Full Manual Backup

To use your already-configured backup selections, target, and so on, you can run the Backup Utility from within the Server Management console by clicking Backup and then clicking Backup Now.

Under the Hood   Backup Scripts

The Backup Utility uses backup scripts (*.bks) to control the backup process. Small Business Server creates a "Small Business Backup Script.bks" file in the %SystemDrive%\Program Files\Microsoft Windows Small Business Server\Backup directory to control the automated backups. When you run the configuration wizard, this script gets updated. But if you run the Backup Utility directly, the utility stores the scripts you create in user-specific directories—%USERPROFILE%\Local Settings\Application Data\Microsoft\Windows NT\NTBackup\Data. This is not terribly helpful when you have multiple users who might have responsibility for initiating a backup.

Back Up Selected Files and Folders

Rather than use the Windows Small Business Server Backup Configuration Wizard to change the standard backup selections, you can manually run the Backup Utility to make specific backups of important files or folders, or whenever you need to manually run a backup without backing up the entire server. To do this, start the Backup Utility by clicking Start, All Programs, Accessories, System Tools, Backup. Start the Backup Utility in Advanced Mode, as shown in Figure 13-8. From here you can use the Backup Wizard to select files, or click the Backup tab and manually select the files you want to back up.

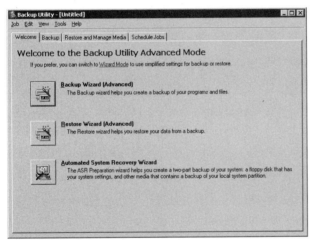

Figure 13-8   The Advanced Mode of the Windows Small Business Server 2003 Backup Utility.

Whether you use a wizard to help you select files or go straight to the Backup tab and select them yourself, you use a Microsoft Windows Explorer–like hierarchical display, as shown in Figure 13-9, to browse your drives and make selections using the check boxes. You can select entire drives or individual files and directories for backup. The System State item backs up the registry and the Active Directory database on the local machine, as well as other system elements required in a disaster-recovery situation.

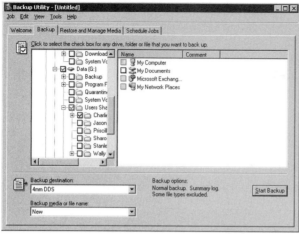

Figure 13-9   Choosing files and folders to back up.

Creating Selection Scripts

After you select the files and directories to back up, you can create a selection script that contains the job configuration you created. After choosing Save Selections from the Job menu, you specify a file name with a .bks extension for the selection script and the directory where the program should create it. You can use selection scripts to create an identical backup job during a subsequent session by loading the selection script from the Job menu. When you do this, the same system elements you selected before creating the script are selected again. You can then run the job as is or make additional selections. You can also use the script to execute the job from the command line using the ntbackup command.

Accessing Files and Folders for Backup

To back up any files and folders, the account used to run the job must have the appropriate permissions granting access to those files and folders. A user who is an Administrator is automatically granted permission to back up any and all files and folders on the server. Other users will have permission to back up their own files and folders.

Selecting the Backup Target

After you specify what you want to back up, you must tell the program where to write the data. In the Backup Destination drop-down list, the File option is the default. If you used the Backup Configuration Wizard to specify a tape device as a destination, you'll also have an option to use that tape device. After you make a selection, use the Backup Media Or File Name box to specify a tape or disk name or the path and file name the program should use to create a backup file.

When you select a tape device, you can then select one of the existing tapes already created by the Windows Small Business Server Backup Utility Wizard, or use the name New. When you have all your selections made, click Start Backup.

This opens the Backup Job Information dialog box shown in Figure 13-10. From here, type a description for the backup and a new name for the tape or disk file.

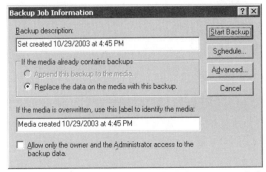

Figure 13-10   The Backup Job Information dialog box.

Now all you need to do is click Start Backup and the backup begins. If you want to set advanced backup options, click Advanced. The options that you can set are:

- Back Up Data That Is In Remote Storage
- Verify Data After Backup
- If Possible, Compress The Backup Data To Save Space
- Automatically Backup System Protected Files When Backing Up The System State
- Disable Volume Shadow Copy
- Backup Type

Some of these options might not apply to your selections or backup destination and will therefore be unavailable.

You can also schedule this backup to occur later by clicking Schedule. You'll have to save your selections before you can schedule the backup for later because the scheduler uses backup scripts to manage the backups. You'll be prompted for a name for the selection script, and for a user account and password to use to run the scheduled job. Finally, you can give the job a name, select the scheduled properties, and add the job to the schedule.

Important If you run a manual job that writes a backup to tape, make sure that the person responsible for changing tapes knows about the job and that the job doesn't interfere with the normal backup schedule. It's all too easy to have your job overwritten, and the nightly backup job fail as well.

Modifying the Backup Configuration

Instead of running the full Windows Small Business Server Backup Configuration Wizard to change one element of the backup configuration, you can run a shortened version of the Configuration Wizard to just change one portion. The options are listed on the left side of the Backup pane, as shown in Figure 13-11.

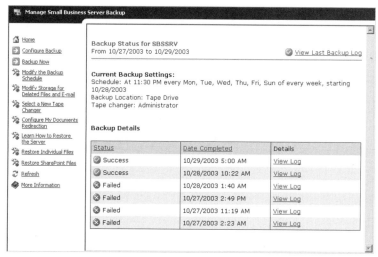

Figure 13-11 The Manage Small Business Server Backup pane.

To change an element of the backup configuration, click one of the following:

- **Modify The Backup Schedule** This allows you to modify the default backup schedule without affecting other configuration items. You'll see the Define Backup Schedule page shown in Figure 13-5.

- **Modify Storage For Deleted Files And E-Mail** This allows you to modify the storage and retention settings for deleted files and e-mail without affecting other configuration items. You'll see The Storage Allocation For Deleted Files And E-Mail page shown in Figure 13-7.

- **Select A New Tape Changer** If you are using a tape backup, this allows you to change the person designated to change tapes without affecting other configuration items. You can also set the notification options for the new designee. You'll see the Onsite Tape Changer page shown in Figure 13-6.

Restoring Data

Windows Small Business Server 2003 gives you two different and powerful tools for restoring lost, damaged, or corrupted data. The first tool is the traditional method of restoring files, folders, or the entire server using a tape or file system backup made with the Backup Utility. The second tool takes advantage of the Volume Shadow Copy feature to allow you to restore files or folders to a previous snapshot version of them. Since the two approaches use very different methods and technologies, we'll treat them quite separately.

> **Note**   In almost all cases, it's a lot quicker to restore a few files or folders using the Previous Versions client than to restore from tape. You should always use the Previous Versions client when the option is available.

Using the Backup Utility to Restore Files and Folders

The traditional method of backup and restore uses the Backup Utility we've discussed earlier in the chapter to make a backup of your Windows Small Business Server onto tape or a hard drive. This allows you to restore individual files or the entire server. The ability to restore files is not limited to files stored on a shared directory, and you can restore to the original location, or to a new location, giving you excellent flexibility.

> **More Info**   For details about how to restore in the event of a totally failed server, see Chapter 22, "Disaster Planning."

To restore individual files or folders with the Backup Utility, complete the following steps:

1. If you're restoring from a tape backup, insert the tape from the backup version of the file or folder that you want to restore into the tape drive and wait for any blinking lights to stop.

2. Open the Backup Utility by clicking Start, All Programs, Accessories, System Tools, Backup. Open in Advanced Mode.

3. Click the Restore And Manage Media tab to open the screen shown in Figure 13-12.

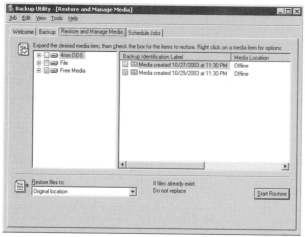

Figure 13-12   The Restore And Manage Media tab of the Backup Utility.

4. Highlight the media you will be restoring from and select the check box next to the file or folder you want to restore, as shown in Figure 13-13.

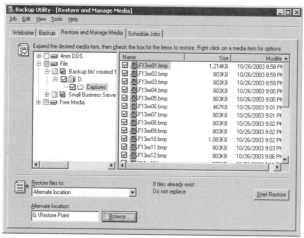

Figure 13-13   Selecting the files and folders to restore using the Backup Utility.

5. Choose whether to restore to the original location (not recommended) or to an alternative location or single folder.

6. Click Start Restore to open the Confirm Restore dialog box, shown in Figure 13-14. You can click Advanced in this dialog box to change mount point settings if you have mounted volumes to worry about; otherwise, click OK to restore your selected files and folders.

Figure 13-14   The Confirm Restore dialog box.

7.   Once the restore is complete, the Restore Progress dialog box will show that the restore is complete. You can click Close to exit the restore, or click Report to view a report of the restoration.

Real World   Restore to an Alternate Location

It's almost always best when restoring only a few files or folders to choose an alternative location to restore the files to. This prevents inadvertently overwriting files that you don't want to overwrite and makes sure that all the files from that restored point in time are available together. If the user who needs the restored file finds out that the version needed wasn't part of Wednesday's backup but rather Thursday's, for example, you're covered. And you don't have to worry about overwriting the current version of the file only to discover that the user has the wrong file name and it's really in a different file. Of course, if you're restoring an entire drive because you had to replace a failed drive, you'll simply restore to the original location.

Using the Previous Versions Client to Restore Files and Folders

Windows Small Business Server 2003 includes the new Volume Shadow Copy technology of Windows Server 2003 that allows the creation of shadow or snapshot copies of files that are shared to the network. This enables files and folders to be restored to a point in time when the snapshot was taken. By default, shadow copy snapshots are taken twice a day—at 7 a.m. and noon.

To restore files that have been saved by Volume Shadow Copy, you need to use the Previous Versions client. This client is installed by default on all Microsoft Windows XP and Windows 2000 (SP3 or later) client computers, and can be installed on earlier versions of the Windows operating system as well, as described in Chapter 11, "Managing Computers on the Network."

Real World   Test Your Restore Before You Need It

The procedure for restoring files and folders using the Previous Versions client is quite straightforward and seems pretty simple. And it is—until you realize that someone just deleted the payroll file for today's payroll, the CFO and CEO are standing in the server room looking over your shoulder wanting to know where it is, the telephone is ringing because the Finance Department just realized it's gone, and to top it off, you just spilled hot coffee on your lap. If you've never restored a file or folder using the Previous Versions client, you really don't want this to be your first attempt. Wouldn't you feel a lot more comfortable about the whole process knowing you'd tested and practiced the whole thing on some innocuous files you created for the purpose?

To restore snapshot copies of an individual file or folder using the Previous Versions client, complete the following steps:

1. Log on to a client workstation using an account with permission to view and restore the file or folder you want to recover. Generally this will be the owner of the missing or corrupted file.

2. In Windows Explorer, right-click the network share where the file or folder resided and choose Properties from the shortcut menu.

3. Click the Previous Versions tab, as shown in Figure 13-15.

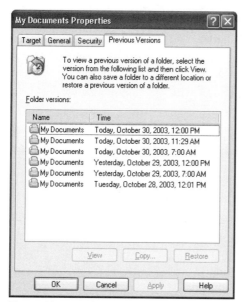

Figure 13-15   The Previous Versions client.

4. Select the folder version and then click View, Copy, or Restore.

   ❑ **View**   Opens the shadow copy in Windows Explorer. You can then open or copy the files just like in a normal folder (although you can't delete anything or save to these folders).

   ❑ **Copy**   Copies the shadow copy to the location you specify.

   ❑ **Restore**   Rolls back the shared folder to its state as of the snapshot image you selected.

Note   To access shadow copies from the Windows Small Business Server machine itself, connect to the shared folder using its UNC path (for example, \\sbssrv\Users) instead of using a local path.

As with the Backup Utility, we think it's a good idea to always restore files to a different location. With the Previous Versions client, this means using the Copy or View options and avoiding the Restore option. Restore will always restore the highlighted version of the file or folder over any existing version. It's much safer to copy it to a new location and inspect it there—you can always copy it back to its original location if that's what you want. But be sure. You can't undo a restore that has overwritten your current version.

Summary

In this chapter, we covered the essentials of backing up your server and the files and data on it. Backing up isn't exciting, but if you don't have a reliable backup of your system, you're betting your entire business that you won't have a hardware failure or other disaster that destroys your server. Windows Small Business Server 2003 provides an easy-to-use Backup Utility that, combined with the Volume Shadow Copy feature, can help protect your business from loss due to data corruption, server crash, or simple user error.

In Chapter 14, "Using Exchange Server," we'll cover e-mail and the Microsoft Exchange Server 2003, which is the e-mail engine of Windows Small Business Server.

Part IV
Performing Advanced Tasks

Chapter 14   Using Exchange Server 315

Chapter 15   Managing Connectivity. 363

Chapter 16   Using ISA Server 2004 409

Chapter 17   Using Group Policy. 443

Chapter 18   Customizing a SharePoint Web Site 465

Chapter 19   Managing an Intranet Web Server 495

Chapter 20   Using SQL Server 2005 515

Chapter 14
Using Exchange Server

Basic E-Mail Configuration. 315

POP3 E-Mail 322

Advanced E-Mail Configuration and Management 331

Managing E-Mail Delivery 342

Exchange 2003 SP2 359

Summary 361

One of the most used and most important parts of the Microsoft Windows Small Business Server 2003 package is Microsoft Exchange Server 2003. Installed as part of both the Windows Small Business Server 2003 Standard Edition and Premium Edition, Exchange Server provides a full-featured, flexible, and robust e-mail and collaboration infrastructure. Windows Small Business Server gives you the wizards and tools to make managing Exchange Server a straightforward process. This chapter covers basic e-mail configuration and goes on to address some of the advanced configuration options that allow you to tweak Exchange Server to your needs, including ways to block unwanted e-mail *before* it gets to your users.

Basic E-Mail Configuration

The default Exchange Server configuration is set up when you first run the CEICW, which was described in Chapter 5, "Completing the To Do List and Other Post-Installation Tasks." If you haven't yet run this wizard to connect to the Internet, you'll need to do that first. The first part of the wizard sets up your Internet connection. Once you configure the Internet connection, the wizard guides you through initial configuration of your Exchange server, starting with the Internet E-Mail page shown in Figure 14-1.

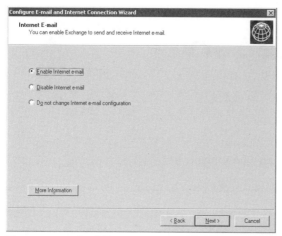

Figure 14-1   Enabling Internet e-mail as part of the CEICW.

If you've got the Exchange snap-in open when you click Next, you get a warning message about refreshing the snap-in when you're done so that you'll see any changes. Next, you need to decide how you want your outgoing e-mail configured. You can either use DNS to route outgoing e-mail or forward all your outgoing e-mail to a server specified by your ISP, as shown in Figure 14-2.

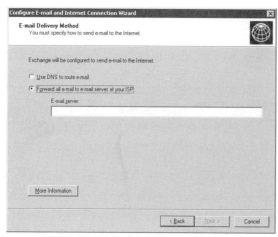

Figure 14-2   Choosing between DNS e-mail routing or forwarding through your ISP's server.

Real World   Use DNS E-Mail Routing

Choosing forwarding as your e-mail delivery mechanism has some serious drawbacks, not the least of which is that all e-mail from your Windows Small Business Server will show that it has been forwarded from your ISP. Because spam e-mails use this technique, often forwarding from unsuspecting and poorly configured mail servers, using a forwarder can result in undelivered e-mail. Some very fussy e-mail domains refuse to accept mail that has passed through a mail forwarder, and even those who are not that absolute can end up blocking your e-mail when your ISP gets on their block list—something you have no control over.

In the early days of e-mail on the Internet, forwarding was a sensible way to configure many Simple Mail Transfer Protocol (SMTP) servers. Configuring an SMTP server, most commonly one running Sendmail, was an arcane and difficult task even for experienced UNIX administrators. Many opted instead to use "smart hosts" that were configured to accept mail and send it on to the right place. Sadly, the flood of Unsolicited Commercial E-Mail (UCE, more commonly known as *spam*) has made that practice neither possible nor desirable. Fortunately, Exchange Server 2003 does most of the SMTP heavy lifting in the background, so you don't need to understand all the complexities.

Once you configure your sending method, click Next to open the E-Mail Retrieval Method page shown in Figure 14-3, where you define how e-mail gets delivered to you. Your ISP will have a preferred method, so make sure you consult with them before filling this page out. You can also configure Post Office Protocol version 3 (POP3) mailboxes at this point, but save that for later. Configuring POP3 e-mail will be discussed later in this chapter, in the "POP3 E-Mail" section. Click Next after you make your selections.

Note   Incorrectly configuring your e-mail retrieval method will result in e-mail not being delivered to your server. Your ISP's configuration will determine the correct method.

Under the Hood   E-Mail Retrieval Methods

There are two basic methods for e-mail retrieval: e-mail is directly delivered to your Exchange server, or e-mail is first delivered to your ISP, which holds it until your

Exchange server specifically asks for it. The method used is controlled by the DNS records for your domain—specifically the MX record.

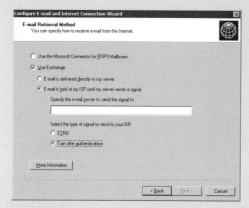

Figure 14-3   Configuring how your e-mail gets delivered to your server.

Direct Delivery

If you want e-mail delivered directly to your server, the MX record for your domain must point to your server. If you want it delivered first to your ISP, and to you only when you ask for it, the MX record must point to your ISP's server. Many ISPs support a mixture of the two methods—the primary MX record points to your server, but a secondary one points to your ISP. If for some reason your server is not available, your e-mail will go to your ISP. Once your e-mail server comes back online, you can either trigger delivery directly if your ISP supports that or wait until their automatic process recognizes that your e-mail server is back online.

***

Note   If your ISP wants to overcharge for the privilege of being your backup e-mail server, or won't do it at all, there are reasonably priced third-party alternatives. We like to use *ZoneEdit.com* for our DNS records, and they offer a very reasonably priced backup mail service. If for any reason our server isn't reachable, mail is automatically delivered to their server. When we come back online, they automatically send on the mail they've been holding. All for a fraction of what our ISP wanted to charge for maintaining our DNS records.

Indirect Delivery: ETRN

The Extended Turn (ETRN) command is used by most ISPs to initiate a download of queued e-mail messages that are stored while waiting for a server to be online to receive them. The ETRN command is documented in the Request for Comments (RFC) 1985, available at *http://www.ietf.org/rfc/rfc1985.txt*. The ETRN command is an extension of the TURN command, which had serious security issues and is generally no longer used.

Indirect Delivery: TURN After Authentication

The TURN After Authentication command gets around the most serious security issues of the TURN command by requiring your Exchange server to authenticate to your ISP's SMTP server before the SMTP server accepts a TURN command from it. This methodology is useful when your Exchange server doesn't have a fixed IP address but uses a dynamic IP address. Dynamic IP addresses are not supported for the ETRN method.

Manual ETRN Trigger

If you normally have e-mail directly delivered to your Exchange server and have secondary MX records that allow your ISP to hold e-mail when you're offline, once your server is back up and available, you can wait for normal processing to send your e-mail to you, or you can manually initiate the transfer if your ISP supports that. The following procedure starts a mail queue to send e-mail to your domain. It assumes that your ISP's SMTP server is smtp.example.com and your domain is microsoft.com.

```
telnet smtp.example.com 25
220 smtp.example.com ESMTP Mon, 3 Nov 2003 15:18:3 0 -0800 (PST)
ETRN @microsoft.com
250 2.0.0 Queuing for node @microsoft.com started
quit
221 2.0.0 smtp.example.com closing connection
```

The 220, 250, and 221 lines are the responses from the remote server.

If you're using TURN After Authentication as your retrieval method, you get prompted for an account name and a password, which are used to authenticate your Exchange server to your ISP, as shown in Figure 14-4. Fill in the authentication information you received from your ISP and click Next.

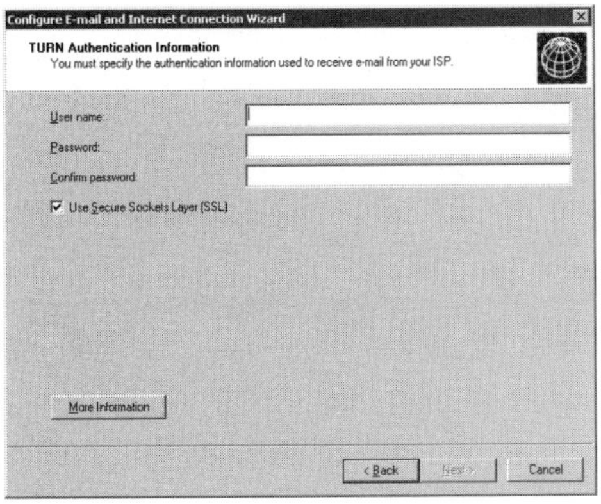

Figure 14-4   The TURN authentication information used to ensure that only your Exchange server can retrieve your e-mail.

The E-Mail Domain Name page is shown in Figure 14-5. Type your Internet domain name, which should be different from your internal domain name, and click Next.

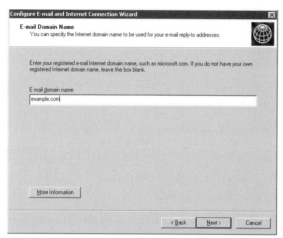

Figure 14-5 The E-Mail Domain Name page of the CEICW.

The Remove E-mail Attachments page of the CEICW, shown in Figure 14-6, lets you automatically strip certain attachments from incoming e-mail received from the Internet. E-mail that has an attachment removed will have a text note attached to it so that the recipient knows the attachment was stripped. You can edit this list to add additional extensions or to remove ones that your business routinely uses.

Security Alert If you routinely need to receive e-mail from the Internet with an attachment that can be used maliciously, don't simply enable that particular extension, but rather create a policy for how to change the extension so that both sender and recipient know what to use (for example, *.vb_* for *.vbs*). This strategy enables you to get your work done efficiently while still providing some protection.

Security Alert E-mail sent from one Exchange mailbox to another Exchange mailbox that does not go outside your internal network will neither be checked nor have attachments removed.

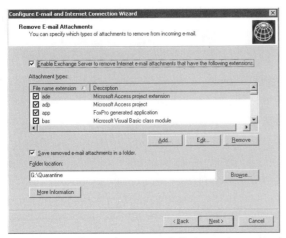

Figure 14-6   Removing potentially hazardous attachments is one way to help protect your network.

If you want any stripped attachments to be saved into a safe area for inspection, select the Save Removed E-Mail Attachments In A Folder check box and specify a location where the attachments will be saved.

Security Alert   Although automatically removing some attachments from your e-mail is a good thing to do, it just isn't enough these days. You should be running an antivirus suite that protects your network at multiple points of attack and includes at least file scanning and e-mail attachment scanning.

Click Next to display a final confirmation page that summarizes all your selections. If everything looks right, click Finish to implement them.

Note   You can run the CEICW again at any time if you need to change one or more of the configuration items. The wizard will start with your existing configuration and let you change just the items that need changing.

Under the Hood   Attachments

The SecAttsConfig.xml, located in the %SBSProgramDir%\Networking directory, controls which attachments are let through and which are blocked. By *carefully* editing this file, you can change which attachments are blocked. For example, to block .PNG files, just add the following line:

```
<Attachment Enabled="True" Extension="png" Description="Portable Network
Graphics file"/>
```

It's tricky to edit this file, since it doesn't contain normal line breaks, but if you're careful, this will make it much easier than rerunning the CEICW every time you want to make a change. If Attachment Enabled is set to True, the extension is blocked. If set to False, it is allowed. If the extension isn't in the file, it isn't on the drop-down list for the CEICW, and isn't blocked.

POP3 E-Mail

Many small businesses prefer their ISPs to handle all the configuration and maintenance of the public side of their e-mail. This responsibility can take the form of handling individual e-mail boxes for each employee or function within the company, or it can be managing a single, global e-mail box that receives all the mail for the entire domain. Windows Small Business Server can automatically download e-mail from POP3 e-mail boxes and distribute it to the correct Exchange mailbox using the Microsoft Connector for POP3 Mailboxes.

Configuring POP3 E-Mail

To configure and enable the Microsoft Connector for POP3 Mailboxes, you first need to add one or more POP3 mailboxes. If you haven't defined any POP3 mailboxes, the connector is disabled and the service doesn't start.

Adding, Removing, and Editing POP3 E-Mail Boxes

You can add, remove, and edit an existing POP3 e-mail box using the POP3 Connector Manager shown in Figure 14-7. To open the POP3 Connector Manager, open Server Management, expand Advanced Management in the console tree, click POP3 Connector Manager in the console tree, and then click Open POP3 Connector Manager in the details pane.

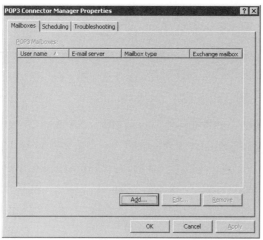

Figure 14-7   The POP3 Connector Manager, before any mailboxes have been created.

Adding a POP3 E-Mail Box

To add a POP3 e-mail box or to create your first one, complete the following steps:

1. Open the POP3 Connector Manager.

2. Click Add to open the POP3 Mailbox dialog box, shown in Figure 14-8.

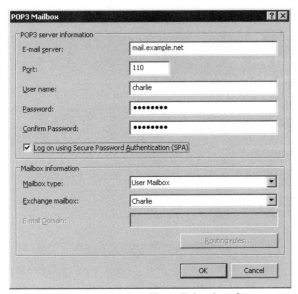

Figure 14-8 The POP3 Mailbox dialog box for a new mailbox.

3. Fill in the fields, which are:

   ❑ **E-Mail Server** Your ISP's e-mail server or the server of the e-mail hosting service you use.

   ❑ **Port** The TCP/IP port number your ISP uses. The default value of 110 should be correct unless your ISP specifies something else.

   ❑ **User Name** The ISP's account name for this POP3 e-mail box. This might not be the same as the user's name or Exchange mailbox.

   ❑ **Password and Confirm Password** Type the password used for this account.

   ❑ **Log On Using Secure Password Authentication (SPA)** Some ISP and e-mail hosting services permit or even require a secure logon to your POP3 account. If your ISP supports SPA, use it!

❑ **Mailbox Type**   Either a User Mailbox that is directly tied to a specific Exchange mailbox or a Global Mailbox that can contain e-mail for multiple users.

❑ **Exchange Mailbox**   If you selected User Mailbox as the mailbox type, you need to link it to a specific Exchange mailbox from the drop-down list.

❑ **E-Mail Domain**   If you selected Global Mailbox as the mailbox type, you need to specify the e-mail domain used as the return address for users of this e-mail box.

❑ **Routing Rules**   If each user of the Global Mailbox maps directly to an identical Exchange mailbox, you don't need to add routing rules. See the section "Routing POP3 E-Mail" for more information about routing rules.

4. Once you've filled in all the fields, click OK to return to the POP3 Connector Manager.

5. Click Add again to add additional mailboxes. When you're finished adding e-mail boxes, click OK. If this is the first POP3 e-mail box you've created, you get a message that the Microsoft Connector for POP3 Mailboxes service is not running. Click OK to start the service and create the mailbox.

Removing a POP3 E-Mail Box
To remove a POP3 e-mail box, complete the following steps:

1. Open the POP3 Connector Manager, shown in Figure 14-7.

2. Select the mailbox you want to remove and click Remove.

3. Confirm the removal. The POP3 e-mail box is removed. This action does not affect the regular Exchange mailbox—that's tied to the user account in Active Directory.

Editing an Existing POP3 E-Mail Box
To edit an existing POP3 e-mail box, complete the following steps:

1. Open the POP3 Connector Manager, shown in Figure 14-7.

2. Select the e-mail box you want to modify, and click Edit to open the POP3 Mailbox dialog box, shown in Figure 14-8.

3. Edit any fields you need to change. The fields are the same as above under Adding a POP3 E-Mail Box.

4. Click OK to return to the POP3 Connector Manager, and click OK again to exit.

Setting a POP3 Delivery Schedule

The default is for the Microsoft Connector for POP3 Mailboxes to download messages from POP3 mailboxes once an hour, every hour, seven days a week. You can change this as appropriate for your business, but the minimum time between download intervals is 15 minutes.

To change the default schedule, complete the following steps:

1. Open the POP3 Connector Manager and click the Scheduling tab, shown in Figure 14-9.

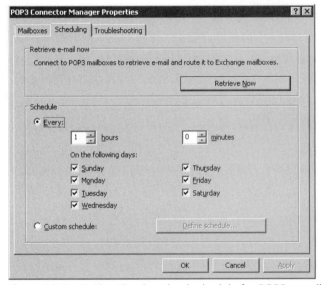

Figure 14-9   Setting the download schedule for POP3 e-mail boxes.

2. For a standard schedule, with the same frequency all day every day, select the appropriate check boxes and specify how often to schedule a download. Click OK when you're finished.

3. To define a custom schedule, select the Custom Schedule option and click Define Schedule to open the Define Schedule dialog box, shown in Figure 14-10.

4. Highlight a section of time and select from the download choices: None, Once Per Hour, Twice Per Hour, or Four Times Per Hour. You can select multiple periods and define each of the periods differently.

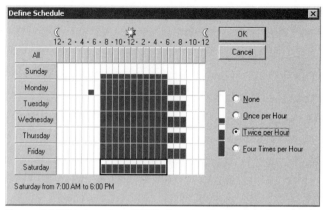

Figure 14-10   A custom POP3 download schedule for a business that doesn't operate much on the weekends.

5. When you're finished defining your schedule, click OK, and then click OK again to exit the POP3 Connector Manager.

To immediately download POP3 e-mail, complete the following steps:

1. Open the POP3 Connector Manager and click the Scheduling tab, as shown in Figure 14-9.

2. Click the Retrieve Now button. (This button is unavailable when the connector is in the midst of a download or the service is stopped.) You get an informational message.

3. Click OK to begin the download.

Routing POP3 E-Mail

Windows Small Business Server and Exchange Server support using a single, global POP3 mailbox for your domain. This allows you to have all e-mail that is sent to your domain automatically delivered to the same mailbox maintained by your ISP. There's no need to assign individual POP3 e-mail boxes to individual Exchange users, no worry about your customers getting bounced e-mail, and so on.

When mail is retrieved from the POP3 e-mail box by the Microsoft Connector for POP3 Mailboxes, it is automatically distributed to the corresponding Exchange mailboxes. So if there's a message with Charlie@example.com in the To field, and Wally@example.com and Priscilla@example.com are in the Cc field, each account gets a copy of the message.

If you get mail that is sometimes addressed to a particular function, such as sales@example.com or orders@example.com, you'll need to create a rule that routes them to the appropriate Exchange mailbox. Also, many mailing list servers hide the recipient's address, so mail to Security_List@TreyResearch.net might actually be intended for Stanley@example.com. But Exchange won't know that without an explicit routing rule.

Adding a Routing Rule

To add a routing rule, complete the following steps:

1. Open the POP3 Connector Manager.

2. Select the global mailbox you want to set routing rules for and click Edit to open the POP3 Mailbox dialog box.

3. Click Routing Rules to open the Routing Rules dialog box, shown in Figure 14-11.

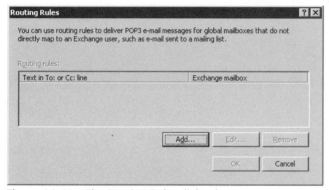

Figure 14-11   The Routing Rules dialog box.

4. Click Add to open the Routing Rule dialog box, shown in Figure 14-12.

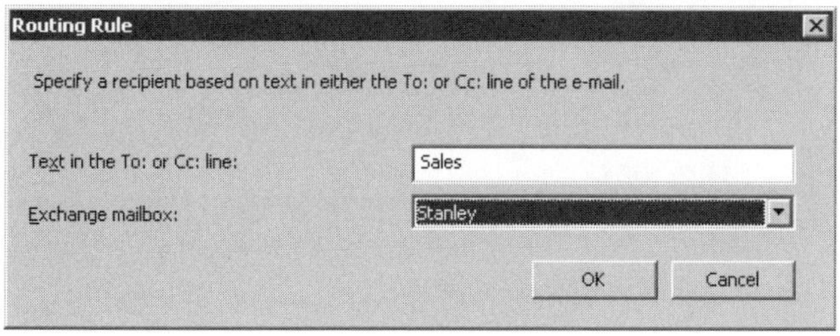

Figure 14-12   Determining how specific text in the To and Cc fields will be routed.

5. Type the text that will control the routing rule. This text will appear in either the To or Cc fields of the message. Rules based on Subject lines are not supported.

> **Note** For privacy reasons, some mailing lists and Outlook tools use the Bcc field to hide the recipient names when sending to multiple recipients. These e-mails will not be correctly routed by the POP3 Routing engine because this information is stripped off when the messages are delivered to the POP3 mailbox and are no longer available to Exchange. If you have users who need to be on this type of list, they will each need to have their own POP3 e-mail box.

6. Select the mailbox to route to from the Exchange Mailbox drop-down list, and then click OK to return to the Routing Rules dialog box. You can add additional rules here, modify existing rules, or delete rules that are no longer required. When you complete your changes, click OK again.

Changing a Routing Rule

To change a routing rule, complete the following steps:

1. Open the POP3 Connector Manager.

2. Select the global mailbox you want to modify the routing rules for, and click Edit to open the POP3 Mailbox dialog box.

3. Click Routing Rules to open the Routing Rules dialog box, shown in Figure 14-11.

4. Select the rule you want to modify, and then click Edit to open the Routing Rule dialog box, shown in Figure 14-12.

5. Make the necessary changes, and then click OK.

Removing a Routing Rule

To remove a routing rule, complete the following steps:

1. Open the POP3 Connector Manager.

2. Select the global mailbox you want to remove a routing rule from and click Edit to open the POP3 Mailbox dialog box.

3. Click Routing Rules to open the Routing Rules dialog box, shown in Figure 14-11.

4. Select the rule you want to remove, and click Remove. You get a confirmation dialog box. Click Yes and then click OK in the Routing Rules dialog box. The rule is removed.

Troubleshooting POP3

Windows Small Business Server includes several helpful features to enable you to troubleshoot POP3 problems. These features are available on the Troubleshooting tab of the POP3 Connector Manager, and include:

- Service Status

- Logging

- Undeliverable POP3 E-Mail

Microsoft Connector for POP3 Mailboxes Service Status

To view the current status of the Microsoft Connector for POP3 Mailboxes, open the POP3 Connector Manager and click the Troubleshooting tab. In the Service Status box, you'll see the number of messages in the Failed Mail Folder and the state of the connector service, as shown in Figure 14-13.

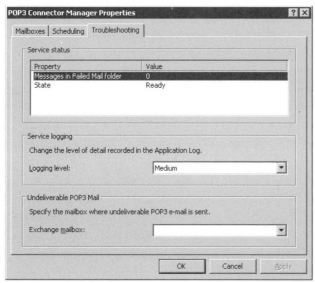

Figure 14-13   The Troubleshooting tab of the POP3 Connector Manager.

Messages that are in the Failed Mail Folder can be re-sent once the cause of the failure is identified. Before you try to resend the message, make sure that the other important Exchange Server services are running. At a minimum, the Microsoft Exchange Information Store, Microsoft Exchange Routing Engine, Microsoft Exchange System Attendant, and SMTP services should be up and running before attempting to retry delivery of the messages.

To try delivering failed messages again, complete the following steps:

1. Log on to the Windows Small Business Server machine with an account that has administrative privileges.

2. Open Microsoft Windows Explorer and navigate to the %SBSProgramDir%\Networking\POP3\Failed Mail folder.

3. Select the files you want to retry delivery for, and move them to the %SBSProgramDir%\\Networking\POP3\Incoming Mail folder.

4. The next time a POP3 connection is made—either a normal, scheduled connection or an immediate one—the delivery will be retried.

5. To trigger an immediate retry, open the POP3 Connector Manager, click Scheduling, and then click Retrieve Now.

Configuring Logging

Windows Small Business Server allows you to log connection information for the Microsoft Connector for POP3 Mailboxes service. Four levels of logging are supported:

- **None**   No logging at all is done.

- **Minimum**   Logs only critical error messages and security-audit success and failure messages.

- **Medium**   Logs additional informational messages beyond that of the Minimum setting.

- **Maximum**   Logs additional troubleshooting messages in addition to logging at the Medium setting.

Important   Enabling Maximum logging can fill up the Application Event Log quickly! You should enable Maximum logging only when actively trying to troubleshoot a connector problem. Once the problem is identified and resolved, return the logging level to your preferred normal level.

All logging messages are sent to the Application Event Log and can be viewed with the Event Viewer. Changes in logging level require stopping and restarting the Microsoft Connector for POP3 Mailboxes service.

Configuring Undeliverable POP3 E-Mail

When using a global POP3 mailbox, normal messages are routed to the Exchange Server mailbox for the recipients that appear in the To and Cc fields. Any messages that are retrieved by the Microsoft Connector for POP3 Mailboxes service and addressed to a recipient without an associated Exchange mailbox are delivered to the Administrator's mailbox. To change where undeliverable POP3 e-mail is sent, specify a different e-mail box on the Troubleshooting tab of the POP3 Connector Manager.

Advanced E-Mail Configuration and Management

There are a number of advanced e-mail configuration and management tasks available through the Server Management console. Click Advanced Management in the console tree, and then click Exchange Server in the details pane to open the Exchange Server console, which is shown in Figure 14-14.

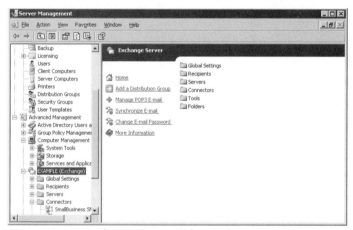

Figure 14-14   Exchange Server Advanced Management.

Changing E-Mail Password

If your e-mail is configured to use TURN After Authentication, to collect your e-mail, you must supply an account name and password to connect to the ISP's e-mail server. When you initially configure your e-mail using the CEICW, you supply this information, but if the data changes at any point in the future, you'll need to change the account information used by Exchange to connect and collect e-mail.

To change this information, complete the following steps:

1. Select your Exchange server in the Advanced Management section of the Server Management console, as shown in Figure 14-14.

2. Click Change E-Mail Password in the details pane to open the Change E-Mail Password dialog box, shown in Figure 14-15.

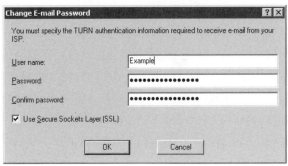

Figure 14-15   Changing the e-mail password for an Exchange server that uses TURN After Authentication.

3. Edit the user name if necessary, and type the new password provided by your ISP. Retype the password and select or clear the Use Secure Sockets Layer (SSL) check box as required by your ISP.

4. Click OK to make the change, and click OK again to acknowledge that the password was changed.

Synchronize E-Mail

E-mail is normally delivered according to the schedule you established when you initially configured your Exchange server using the CEICW. If your e-mail is delivered directly, without your ISP holding it for you, there's no need to synchronize e-mail. If your ISP holds your mail until you request it either using ETRN or TURN After Authentication, your e-mail is delivered only as often as you scheduled it initially. You can initiate an asynchronous connection at any time, however, by clicking Synchronize E-Mail in Exchange Server Advanced Management, as shown in Figure 14-14. When you click Synchronize E-Mail, you get an informational message. Click OK. Exchange Server connects to your ISP and downloads any pending messages while uploading any outgoing messages in your outgoing e-mail queue.

Managing E-Mail Distribution Lists

Windows Small Business Server uses distribution groups to manage how e-mail is delivered to various groups of users in your organization. These distribution groups are different from the security groups used to control access to specific features or directories, though there is often significant overlap, obviously.

When you initially run the CEICW, a distribution group is created that includes all users. The name of this group is based on your organization's name (such as Example.com for the fictitious organization we use in this book). Whenever a new user is created using one of the user templates, the user is automatically added to this distribution group. If you create a new user and do not use one of the default templates, make sure you include the user in this distribution group.

Creating a New Distribution Group (List)

Distribution groups, or distribution *lists*, as they are more commonly called when talking about e-mail, are a convenient mechanism for ensuring that e-mail gets consistently routed to the appropriate individuals without each user having to maintain his or her own individual list. For example, you might have one list that goes to Finance that your sales people use to send in their expense reports. Rather than sending e-mail to a specific individual—who might be on vacation or no longer with the company—the user sends the e-mail to the list. The list ensures that the e-mail gets routed as necessary, even when a key person is absent.

To create a new distribution list, complete the following steps:

1. Select your Exchange server in the Advanced Management section of the Server Management console.

2. Click Add A Distribution Group to open the Add Distribution Group Wizard.

3. Click Next to open the Distribution Group Information page, shown in Figure 14-16.

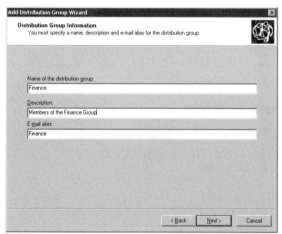

Figure 14-16   Specifying the information for a new distribution group.

4. Type the name of the distribution group. An e-mail alias for the group is automatically created based on that name, although you can modify the alias as needed. Also type a description for the group.

5. Click Next to display the Group Membership page, shown in Figure 14-17.

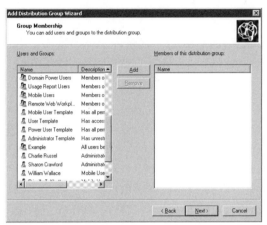

Figure 14-17   Add members to the new distribution group.

6. Select users or other groups from the left pane and click Add to add them to the new distribution group.

7. Click Next to display the Group Manager page, shown in Figure 14-18. The user or security group specified here will have permission to modify the membership of the group, regardless of whether that user or security group has any other administrative rights.

> **Note**   The group manager for a distribution group must be a member of the distribution group.

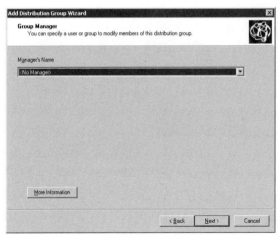

Figure 14-18   The Group Manager page of the Add Distribution Group Wizard.

8. Click Next to display the Group Options page, shown in Figure 14-19.

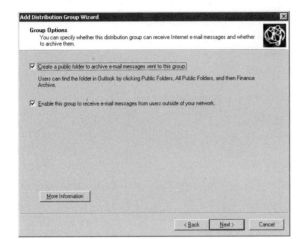

Figure 14-19   Setting options for a new distribution group.

9. Clear the appropriate check boxes if you do *not* want messages to this distribution group to be automatically archived in Public Folders, or if you want the group to be able to receive messages from the Internet.

10. Click Next to display the summary page, and then click Finish to create the distribution group.

Modifying a Distribution Group (List)

Inevitably, the membership of a distribution group changes over time. If you've assigned a group manager to the distribution group, that manager (along with Domain Admins) can modify the membership of the group, adding or removing members as needed using Microsoft Outlook.

Note   Modifying Exchange to run in native mode instead of the default mixed mode might prevent editing the membership of a group from within Outlook 2003, and can have issues with mail enablement of Public Folders.

Modifying Group Membership with Outlook 2003

To modify group membership, open Outlook 2003 on a client computer and complete the following steps:

1. If the distribution list isn't in your Contacts folder, add it.

Note   In Outlook, distribution groups are referred to as distribution lists.

---

2.   Open your Contacts folder and select the distribution list you want to modify. Double-click the list to open the Distribution List dialog box, as shown in Figure 14-20.

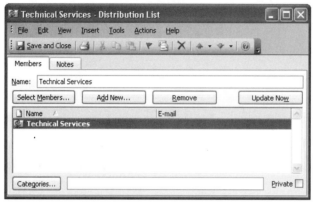

Figure 14-20   The Distribution List dialog box.

3.   Double-click the name of the distribution list to open the Properties dialog box, as shown in Figure 14-21.

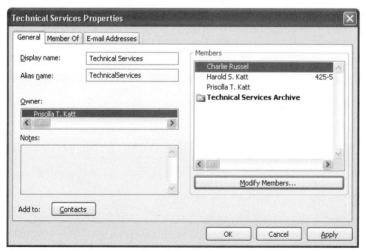

Figure 14-21   The properties of the Technical Services distribution list.

4.   Click Modify Members to open the Distribution List Membership dialog box, shown in Figure 14-22.

Figure 14-22   The Distribution List Membership dialog box lets you add or remove members from a distribution list.

5.   Click Add to add members or click Remove to remove members from the list. To see the properties of a current list member, highlight the member and click Properties. After you make the changes, click OK to return to the Properties dialog box, and click OK again to return to the Distribution List dialog box. Click Save and Close to save the changes and exit the dialog box.

Modifying Group Membership with the Server Management Console

Administrators can modify group membership, change the group's manager, and enable or disable group options using the Server Management console. To modify a distribution group using the Server Management console, complete the following steps:

1.   Select Distribution Groups from the Standard Management section of the Server Management console, as shown in Figure 14-23.

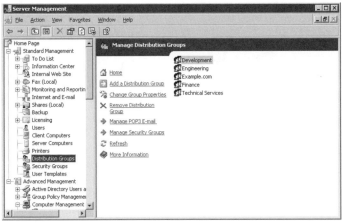

Figure 14-23   The Manage Distribution Groups pane of the Server Management console.

2. Double-click the group you want to modify to open the Properties dialog box for the Technical Services group, as shown in Figure 14-24.

Figure 14-24   The Properties dialog box for the Technical Services distribution group.

3. Modify the properties of the group as needed, and click OK when you're finished.

Deleting A Distribution Group (List)

To remove a distribution group from Windows Small Business Server, select Distribution Groups from the Standard Management section of the Server Management console and highlight the group you want to remove. Click Remove Distribution Group. A confirmation dialog box appears, as shown in Figure 14-25. If you also want to remove the public folder associated with the distribution group, select the check box and click Yes. You get a confirmation message that the group was removed, along with its public folder archive, if specified.

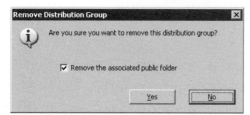

Figure 14-25   Deleting a distribution group, as well as its public folder archive.

Setting the Reply To Address

If you need to change the Reply To address on your outgoing e-mail, either for an individual user or for everyone, you can easily do it. You can also use this process to add e-mail domain addresses that Exchange Server will recognize as yours and accept e-mail for.

Changing the Reply To Address for All Users

To change the Reply To address for all users, complete the following steps:

1. Select your Exchange server in the Advanced Management section of the Server Management console.

2. Double-click Recipients, and then double-click Recipient Policies.

3. Double-click Default Policy to open up the Default Policy Properties dialog box. Click the E-Mail Addresses (Policy) tab, as shown in Figure 14-26.

Figure 14-26   Default Policy controls the SMTP Reply To address for all users.

4. To change the default SMTP Reply To address, highlight the current primary SMTP address. It is displayed in boldface (Figure 14-26). Click Edit and type the new domain address.

5. To add an additional SMTP address, click New.

6. Select SMTP as the address type for normal Internet e-mail addresses and click OK.

7. Type the new address you want to receive mail for in the form @domainname, as shown in Figure 14-27.

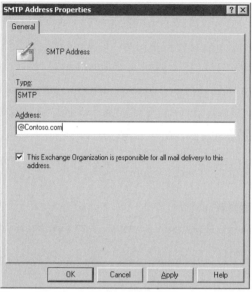

Figure 14-27   Adding a new SMTP address that Exchange will receive.

8. Click OK to return to the Default Policy Properties dialog box. To enable the new SMTP address, select the SMTP check box.

9. To make an address the primary address and appear as the Reply To address in outgoing e-mail, highlight the address and click Set As Primary.

10. Click OK when you are finished making changes.

Important   Always set your primary SMTP address field to a publicly reachable, official, SMTP domain name. When you send e-mail outside your company, this will be the e-mail address that is replied to. If you set the primary SMTP address field to your internal address (example.local in this book), external users won't be able to resolve the address correctly and e-mail sent to your company will bounce.

Changing the Reply To Address for a Specific User

To change the Reply To address for a specific user, complete the following steps:

1. Select Users from the Standard Management section of the Server Management console.

2. Double-click the user whose Reply To address you want to change; this opens the Properties dialog box for the user.

3. Click the E-Mail Addresses tab.

4. Click New to add an additional address. To change an existing address, highlight it and click Edit.

5. If the address is new, highlight the SMTP Address type (or other type, as appropriate) in the New E-Mail Address dialog box, as shown in Figure 14-28. Click OK.

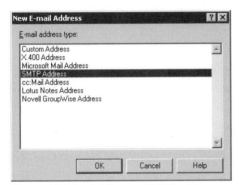

Figure 14-28   Adding an SMTP address type.

6. Type the new address in the Internet Address Properties dialog box, as shown in Figure 14-29. Click OK to return to the E-Mail Addresses tab.

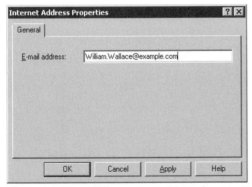

Figure 14-29   Adding a new address for user William Wallace.

7. If you want the new address set as the primary address (and have it used in the Reply To field), click Set As Primary.

8. Click OK to exit the user's Properties dialog box.

Managing E-Mail Delivery

The Advanced Management section of the Server Management console allows you to manage a number of Exchange Server features that affect the delivery and sending of e-mail. You can set default values for messages including the maximum size of individual messages—both sent and received—and the maximum number of individual recipients per message.

To set the message defaults, complete the following steps:

1. Select your Exchange server under the Advanced Management section of the Server Management console.

2. Double-click Global Settings in the details pane.

3. Right-click Message Delivery and select Properties to open the Message Delivery Properties dialog box.

4. Click the Defaults tab, shown in Figure 14-30. Set the maximum values for the size of incoming and outgoing messages, as well as the maximum number of recipients allowed for a message.

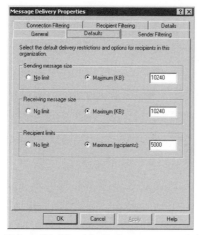

Figure 14-30   Managing message defaults and delivery options in the Message Delivery Properties dialog box

5. Click Apply or OK after you set the defaults.

Setting an Individual User's Message Properties

SBS gives you the ability to override the default values for messaging to handle special users and circumstances. Avoid the temptation whenever possible, however, because the default values are quite generous and it's much more work to try to manage multiple individual mailboxes. If the default values are inappropriate for many users, that's a good indication that it's time to change the defaults rather than override the values for many individual users.

To set message properties for users, complete the following steps:

1. Select Users from the Standard Management section of the Server Management console.

2. Double-click the user whose message limits you want to change; this opens the Properties dialog box for the user.

3. Click the Exchange General tab, shown in Figure 14-31.

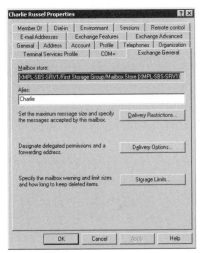

Figure 14-31   The Exchange General tab for user Charlie.

4. Click Delivery Restrictions to set the maximum sending and receiving message size for this user, as shown in Figure 14-32.

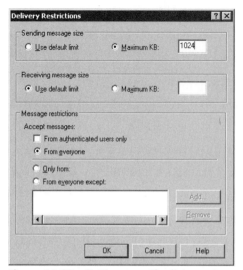

Figure 14-32 Setting user Charlie's maximum message sending size to 1MB.

5. Make the changes to the delivery restrictions, and then click OK to return to the Exchange General tab.

6. Click Delivery Options to open the Delivery Options dialog box, shown in Figure 14-33.

Figure 14-33 Setting the delivery options for an Exchange user.

7. Click Maximum Recipients and type the maximum number of recipients the user can send a message to. Use this dialog box to set a Send On Behalf permission as well.

8. Click OK to return to the Exchange General tab.

9. Click Storage Limits to open the Storage Limits dialog box. Here you can set the user's maximum mailbox size and the number of days a deleted message is retained.

Note   Setting the storage limits for users is one task that will come up again and again. There will always be users who insist, for all sorts of reasons, that they are special and the limits shouldn't apply to them. If it's the CEO, maybe. If it's your direct boss, certainly. Everyone else? No. Not without a seriously good justification, and confirmation from your boss.

Note   Deleted message retention is a very mixed blessing. It *can* save you if someone deletes an extremely important message, but it also creates potential legal problems around how long you choose to keep messages. You should have a clear, unambiguous message-retention policy that is provided to all employees and that has been agreed to by senior management. Unless there are legal constraints, we're strongly in favor of an extremely short retention policy and keeping deleted messages no more than just a few days. The vast majority of requests for recovery of deleted messages occur in the first 24 hours after the original deletion.

SMTP Filtering

Exchange Server 2003 has a rich set of filtering options to let you control what e-mail you allow. You can't stop all the spam sent to your organization with Exchange filtering, but you can definitely put a dent in it. Exchange Server supports five basic types of filtering:

- **Sender filtering**   Messages are blocked based on who the sender is.

- **Connection filtering**   Messages are blocked based on the connection the sender uses.

- **Recipient filtering**   Messages are blocked based on who the messages are sent to.

- **Intelligent Message filtering**   Messages are blocked based on the Spam Confidence Level (SCL) of the message.

- **Sender ID filtering**   Messages are blocked based on whether the sender has a valid Sender ID.

Sender Filtering

By default, no domains or senders are filtered. You can add individual senders or entire domains that will be blocked. You can also control how blocked messages are treated.

To modify sender filtering, complete the following steps:

1. Select your Exchange server under the Advanced Management section of the Server Management console.

2. Double-click Global Settings in the details pane.

3. Right-click Message Delivery and select Properties to open the Message Delivery Properties dialog box. Click the Sender Filtering tab, as shown in Figure 14-34.

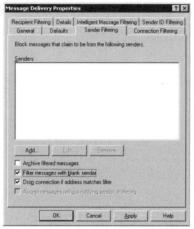

Figure 14-34 Automatically block messages from known bad senders.

4. Click Add to open the Add Sender dialog box, where you can type the sender's e-mail address. You can use wildcards to block an entire domain, as shown in Figure 14-35. After typing the new address, click OK to return to the Sender Filtering tab.

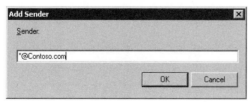

Figure 14-35 Blocking the entire contoso.com domain.

5. Click Edit to modify a current blocked sender, or click Remove to remove the sender from the list.

6. Select the Archive Filtered Messages check box if you want to archive messages that you've blocked.

> **Important** If you archive filtered messages, there is no automatic process to clean up the archive, which can grow very large very quickly. Make sure that cleaning up this archive is part of your regular Exchange maintenance.

7. Select the Filter Messages With Blank Sender check box to disallow messages that have a blank From field.

8. Clear the Drop Connection If Address Matches Filter check box if you don't want to automatically drop the SMTP connection when you recognize that a message should be blocked.

> **Note** The Drop Connection If Address Matches Filter check box is selected by default—and we think that's a good thing.

9. Click Apply to apply your filters. You get the message shown in Figure 14-36, warning you that the filtering won't actually happen until you enable it for specific SMTP virtual servers. (See "Enabling the Filters" later in this chapter for details on how to enable all the filters.) Click OK, and then click the Connection Filtering tab to configure filtering by IP address and block list service providers.

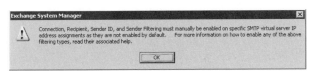

Figure 14-36 Warning indicating that filtering must be manually enabled.

Connection Filtering

By default, connection filtering is not configured. To configure blocking by block lists and by specific IP addresses, use connection filtering.

To configure connection filtering, complete the following steps:

1. Make sure the Message Delivery Properties dialog box is open and click the Connection Filtering tab, as shown in Figure 14-37.

Figure 14-37   Connection filtering can include block lists and specific blocks of IP addresses.

2. Click Add in the Block List Service Configuration box to add a new block list provider and configure the details for it.

3. After you add any block list providers you're going to use, click Exception to add exceptions for recipients who shouldn't be blocked regardless of what a block list says. Use this option to add addresses of any recipients who absolutely can't have an important message blocked.

4. Click Accept to specify an IP address or range of addresses that Exchange will always accept e-mail from.

5. Click Deny to specify an IP address or range of addresses that Exchange will always reject e-mail from.

Real World   **Block List Providers**

Block lists are an attempt to provide a central resource that accurately identifies known spammers and the IP addresses they use. These lists include real-time block lists (RBLs) and open relay lists. There are both free and commercial lists, and they range from those that contain only verified, known spam sources to those that are quite aggressive at deciding who and what is spam. Which type of list you choose will have a lot to do with how tolerant you are of false positives. One list of block lists you can start with is *http://www.email-policy.com/Spam-black-lists.htm*. Another useful resource is a list of resources related to spam and block lists: *http://dmoz.org/Computers/Internet/Abuse/Spam/Blacklists/*.

A word of caution, however: Using an RBL means that you are trusting someone else to make the decisions about what e-mail you will receive and what e-mail you will block. There are inherent problems with this approach, but it *does* make your decisions easier. If you do use an RBL, you should probably archive blocked messages to make sure you're not inadvertently blocking something you really want. But then make sure you actually check your archive and clean it up regularly.

Recipient Filtering

Use recipient filtering to filter messages sent to addresses that you know are only spam catchers. These filters will not apply to authenticated users or internal Exchange servers, so they won't interfere with any normal internal e-mail.

To configure recipient filtering, complete the following steps:

1. If you don't have the Message Delivery Properties dialog box open, open it, and click the Recipient Filtering tab, as shown in Figure 14-38.

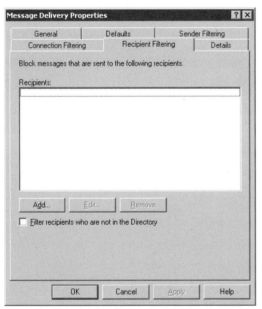

Figure 14-38   Using recipient filtering to catch e-mail sent to addresses that get only spam sent to them.

2. Click Add to type a recipient e-mail address to block (you can use wildcards here), and click OK after you type it in.

3. Click Edit to modify a currently blocked recipient, or click Remove to remove the recipient from the list.

4. Select the check box to filter recipients who are not in Active Directory.

> **Note** Although it might seem like a good idea to filter out any e-mail sent to nonexistent addresses in your domain, that filtering process is actually one way that spammers can tell what *is* a valid address. So we think it's probably not a good idea.

5. Click OK when you're finished.

Intelligent Message Filtering

Microsoft Exchange 2003 Service Pack 2 includes the Microsoft Intelligent Message Filter (IMF) v.2. If you've independently installed Exchange SP2, or you installed it as part of SBS 2003 R2, you can take advantage of this sophisticated junk-mail filtering to better manage and reduce your spam.

To configure Intelligent Message filtering, complete the following steps:

1. If you don't have the Message Delivery Properties dialog box open, open it, and click the Intelligent Message Filtering tab, as shown in Figure 14-39.

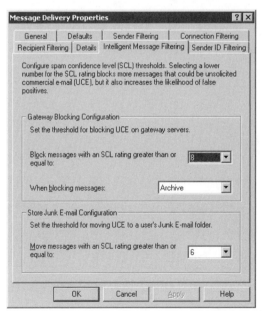

Figure 14-39   The Intelligent Message Filtering tab.

2.   In the Gateway Blocking Configuration section, set the spam confidence level (SCL) that you will completely block at the server level, before it gets to your users. The default value of 8 is a good starting point.

3.   Set the When Blocking Messages field to specify the action to take when the SCL is greater than or equal to that set in step 2. The choices are:

  ❑   **Archive**   Save blocked messages to the Archive folder for later inspection.

  ❑   **Delete**   Quietly delete blocked messages.

  ❑   **No Action**   Assign the SCL and modify the header of the messages with the SCL, but don't actually do anything with them.

  ❑   **Reject**   Messages that are blocked are rejected by the SMTP server and the sending SMTP server is responsible for any non-delivery report (NDR).

4.   In the Store Junk E-mail Configuration section, set the SCL threshold that will cause messages to be automatically moved to the Junk E-Mail folder. The default for this is also 8, but we think a lower value makes sense, since messages aren't being deleted, but simply moved to the Junk E-Mail folder.

5.   Click OK when you're finished.

Real World   Spam Confidence Levels

The IMF is based on the SCL technology Microsoft developed for its Hotmail accounts. The IMF assigns a value from 1 to 9 to each message, based on the deduced likelihood that the message is spam. The higher the number, the more likely that it is spam. A message that has a 9 assigned to it has a very high likelihood of being spam. In all the testing I've done, I've never had a false positive (a message identified as spam that is actually real) with an SCL of 9. For that matter, I've never had one with an SCL of 8, either.

On our SBS server, we set the SCL to 8 on the gateway. I then set the Junk E-Mail setting to a lower number (5 in our SBS environment) to move messages to our users' Junk E-mail folders. Users then have the responsibility of checking their Junk E-mail folders to make sure they don't contain any real messages. Setting the SCL to 5 is probably too low for most environments unless you're sure your users understand the implications. It *will* result in false positives. A setting of 6 or 7 is probably more appropriate in most environments.

Note   When you're first enabling IMF, it makes sense to set the SCL at the gateway to either No Action or Archive, and then closely monitor the behavior to make sure that you're not rejecting messages that you don't want to reject. Once you're confident that you've got it set to an appropriate level, change that action to either Reject or Delete. We prefer to reject messages to ensure that any real messages that are inadvertently blocked will at least tell the originator that their message didn't get through. Unfortunately, this can lead to some abuse by spammers, so you may need to change the setting to Delete if you experience problems.

Sender ID Filtering

Microsoft Exchange 2003 Service Pack 2 also includes the Sender ID filter. This filter uses the new Sender Policy Framework (SPF) to authenticate the sender of an e-mail using DNS records. The goal is to ensure that when a message says it comes from Microsoft.com, it really does come from Microsoft. Unfortunately, like the other filtering options available in Exchange, this doesn't work for mail retrieved from POP3 mailboxes. There's a secondary problem as well—SBS users who use a "smart host" to forward e-mail to will fail the Sender ID test. Since the use of a smart host is virtually a requirement for most POP3 accounts, this will create problems for SBS users. However, it probably makes sense to enable the Sender ID filtering, but leave it in an advisory role.

To configure Sender ID filtering, complete the following steps:

1. If you don't have the Message Delivery Properties dialog box open, open it, and click the Sender ID Filtering tab, as shown in Figure 14-40.

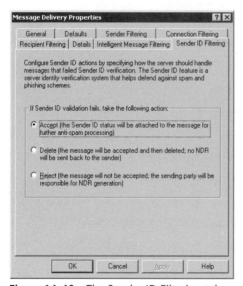

Figure 14-40   The Sender ID Filtering tab.

2. Select the action to take when a Sender ID fails. The choices are:

   ❑ **Accept**   The Sender ID status is attached to the message, but no other action is taken.

   ❑ **Delete**   Messages that fail the Sender ID validation are quietly deleted without an NDR.

   ❑ **Reject**   Messages that fail the Sender ID validation are rejected, and the sending SMTP server is responsible for generating an NDR.

3. Click OK when you've chosen the Sender ID filtering action. As with other filtering actions, nothing actually happens until the filters are enabled on the Virtual SMTP Server, as described in the next section.

Enabling the Filters

Before any of the filtering actions and settings that are configured in the Global Message Delivery section will actually do anything, they need to be enabled on the appropriate SMTP Virtual Server. For most SBS environments, where there is only a single Exchange server, and a single SMTP Virtual Server, this will be the Default SMTP Virtual Server.

To enable the filters, complete the following steps:

1. Select your Exchange server under the Advanced Management section of the Server Management console.

2. Double-click Servers, double-click *servername,* double-click Protocols, and then double-click SMTP in the details pane.

3. Right-click Default SMTP Virtual Server and select Properties to open the dialog box shown in Figure 14-41.

Figure 14-41   The General Properties tab of the Default SMTP Virtual Server.

4. On the General tab, click Advanced to open the Advanced dialog box shown in Figure 14-42.

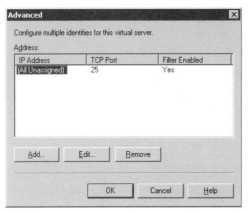

Figure 14-42   The Advanced dialog box of the Default SMTP Virtual Server general properties.

5. Highlight the IP address to configure (the default is All Unassigned) and click Edit to open the Identification dialog box, shown in Figure 14-43.

Figure 14-43   Choosing the filtering options to enable on the Default SMTP Virtual Server.

6. Check the boxes for each type of filtering you want enable on your SBS server, and click OK as necessary to exit.

    The next time Exchange and the SMTP Server are started the rules will be in effect.

7. The IMF Filter Manager is a very useful tool for managing archived messages created by the IMF. It's a simple little application, but it gets the job done. You can

download it from the releases section of its workspace on the "Got Dot Net" Web site: *http://www.gotdotnet.com/workspaces/workspace.aspx?id=e8728572-3a4e-425a-9b26-a3fda0d06fee.*

Managing Queues

Exchange Server uses queues to handle incoming and outgoing messages. Some of the things you can do with queues are:

- View and monitor queues

- Find messages that are in a queue

- Shut down all outgoing queues immediately

Viewing and Monitoring Queues

To view the queues on your server, open the Server Management console, expand Advanced Management, expand your Exchange server, expand Servers, expand your server name, and then click Queues to open the Queue Viewer, shown in Figure 14-44.

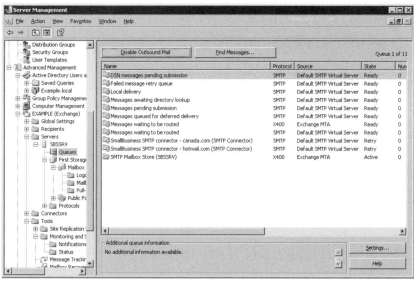

Figure 14-44   The Queue Viewer for Exchange Server.

From here you can see a number of queues, most of which you'll never have to do anything with. But if you see a queue with a bunch of messages in it, chances are there's a problem.

Finding the Messages In a Queue

If you have a queue with one or more messages in it, you can see what those messages are and take steps to either remove the messages or retry sending them once you've resolved the reason they got stuck. Sometimes the problem is simply a bad message and the only resolution is to remove it. Or, if the message is generated by spam, it might be trying to reach a nonexistent domain or addressee within a domain.

To find the messages in a queue, complete the following steps:

1. Open the Queue Viewer as described in the preceding section, "Viewing and Monitoring Queues."

2. Highlight the queue you want to view the messages in, as shown in Figure 14-45.

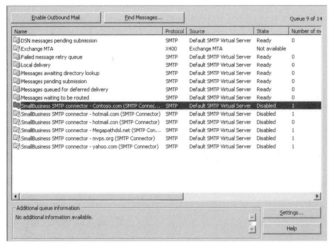

Figure 14-45   The Queue Viewer, with the SMTP connector to Contoso.com highlighted.

3. Double-click the queue to open the Find Messages dialog box, as shown in Figure 14-46.

4. You can specify search parameters, or to search for all messages in the queue, leave the fields blank and click Find Now.

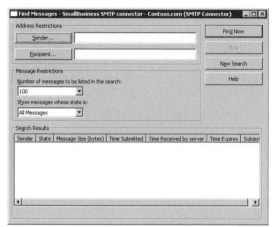

Figure 14-46   The Find Messages dialog box for an SMTP connector.

5. When the search returns, double-click any of the messages to see the message properties, as shown in Figure 14-47.

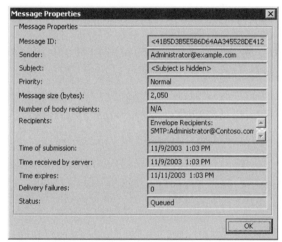

Figure 14-47   The message properties of a message in the Contoso.com SMTP connector queue.

6. To freeze, unfreeze, or delete a message in the queue, highlight the message in the Search Results window and right-click it, as shown in Figure 14-48.

7. If you delete the message, you can choose whether to send the sender an NDR.

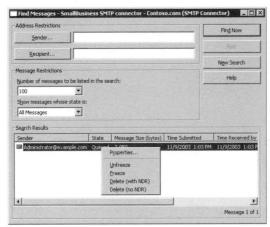

Figure 14-48   You can freeze, unfreeze, or delete a message—with or without a non-delivery report from the queue.

Shutting Down All Outgoing Queues Immediately

If you have a virus loose on the network that is trying to send itself to every e-mail address it can find in one or more of your client address books, you have a problem! Long term, you need to get to the root of why and how the virus got loose on your network and take steps to make sure it can't happen again. But first and foremost, you need to *stop the spread outside your organization—now.*

There are a number of ways to do that, up to and including pulling the power plug out of the back of your SBS server, but that's just a bit drastic. Probably the smartest and quickest way to make sure you don't create more problems is to quickly pull the network plug that connects your network to the outside world—if you have physical access to the server room. Once that is done, or if you don't have quick and ready access to the server room when the problem is discovered, you can stop all outgoing e-mail in its tracks on the server itself, without interrupting any other functions on the server—including incoming e-mail—by shutting down all outbound e-mail queues. To shut down all outgoing queues, complete the following steps:

1. Open the Queue Viewer as described in the section "Viewing and Monitoring Queues."

2. Click Disable Outbound Mail.

ZAP! That's it—the e-mail stops. Now you can deal with finding the virus, disabling and removing it, and removing the messages in the outbound queues that have the virus in them. Once you get all that sorted, and it's safe to start sending mail, click Enable Outbound Mail, and the queues will start sending mail again.

Exchange 2003 SP2

Windows Small Business Server 2003 R2 includes Service Pack 2 for Exchange 2003. You can also install Exchange SP2 independently on SBS 2003, as long as you've installed Service Pack 1 for SBS 2003 already. Exchange SP2 adds important functionality to Exchange and should definitely be installed, even if you're holding off installing R2. The three main features added by Exchange SP2 are the Intelligent Message Filter, the Sender ID Filter, and an increase in the size of supported message store from 16 GB to 75 GB–something SBS users have definitely been asking for.

We already covered the two new filters earlier in the chapter, but the change in the message store, as welcome as it is, shouldn't be made without some thought and planning. Increasing the maximum size of the Information Store to 75 GB can have a negative impact on hard disk space, backup times, and overall server performance. And it requires a bit of registry editing as well.

First, to modify the registry to support a larger Private Information Store, complete the following steps:

1. Open the registry editor by typing **regedit** at the Run prompt.

2. Navigate to HKEY_LOCAL_MACHINE\SYSTEM\CurrentControlSet\Services\ MSExchangeIS\<machinename>\Private-<GUID>, as shown in Figure 14-49.

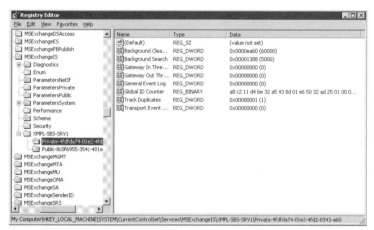

Figure 14-49   The registry key that controls the new database sizes for Exchange 2003 SP2.

Part IV   Performing Advanced Tasks

> **Note**   The actual registry key will vary depending on your SBS server
> name and the GUID that is assigned.

3. Insert a new DWORD value of Database Size Limit in GB, as shown in Figure 14-50.
    This will be a decimal value from 18 GB to 75 GB. I've chosen 25 GB as a good start-
    ing point.

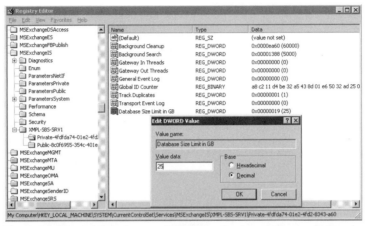

Figure 14-50   Adding the new DWORD value to set the maximum size of the Private
Information Store database.

4. Insert another new DWORD value, Database Size Buffer in Percentage, as shown in
    Figure 14-51. This controls what percentage of the maximum database size remains
    before warnings appear about running out of space. The default is 10 percent, and
    that seems like a reasonable number to us.

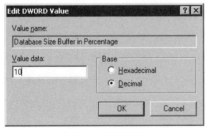

Figure 14-51   The DWORD value that controls when out-of-space warning messages are
issued.

5. While we're creating registry values, let's also set the time that Exchange checks the
    integrity of its database. The default is 5AM. Insert a new DWORD value of Data-

base Size Check Start Time in Hours From Midnight. We've set ours to 1 AM, just before the backup starts, as shown in Figure 14-52.

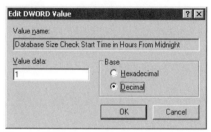

Figure 14-52 Setting the database check time.

6. Exit from the registry editor and restart the Microsoft Exchange Information Store with the following commands from the command line:

```
net stop MSExchangeIS
net start MSExchangeIS
```

Important Modifying the registry is dangerous and should be done with caution. You can make your system unbootable, or cause programs to not work as expected. Make backups and double-check all your changes before committing yourself.

Summary

In this chapter, we covered all the basics of setting up and maintaining Microsoft Exchanger Server 2003, which is a core component of Microsoft Windows Small Business Server 2003. We discussed connecting to your ISP to send and deliver e-mail, setting up and maintaining the Microsoft Connector for POP3 Mailboxes, changing e-mail passwords, managing distribution groups, changing the e-mail Reply To address, managing e-mail queues, and filtering e-mail to reduce spam.

In the next chapter, we'll cover the details of managing the connectivity of your Windows Small Business Server network.

Chapter 15
Managing Connectivity

Administering TCP/IP Services. 363
Administering Routing and Remote Access 370
Advanced Network Security. 372
Summary 407

Managing network connectivity is a complicated task that Microsoft SBS distills into a relatively simple process handled by two wizards—the Configure E-Mail and Internet Connection Wizard (the CEICW), and the Remote Access Wizard.

> **More Info** For more information about these wizards, see Chapter 5, "Completing the To Do List and Other Post-Installation Tasks."

These wizards are the preferred method of changing any settings that they cover—including all the standard connectivity issues. If your environment has special needs not covered by the wizards, however, you'll need to go beyond them to more direct management of the individual components that are part of connectivity. This chapter covers the most common and useful tasks, including managing Dynamic Host Control Protocol (DHCP), viewing Dynamic Name Service (DNS) and Windows Internet Naming Service (WINS) records, and changing virtual private network (VPN) settings using Routing and Remote Access(RRAS) and Internet Authentication Service (IAS).

This chapter also details three complex tasks that can increase network security and usability: creating a Public Key Infrastructure (PKI) to deploy certificates, setting up L2TP VPN connections, and implementing 802.1X authentication for wireless clients.

Administering TCP/IP Services

SBS manages DHCP, DNS, and WINS with no user intervention required. However, if clients experience trouble connecting to the server or other computers on the network, check DHCP, DNS, and WINS to verify that the clients are properly registered with each service.

> **More Info** See Chapter 21, "Monitoring and Fine-Tuning Performance," for additional network troubleshooting help. For an in-depth discussion about DHCP,

DNS, and WINS, see *Microsoft Windows Server 2003 Administrator's Companion*, 2nd Edition (Microsoft Press).

Managing DHCP

DHCP automatically provides computers on the local network segment with valid IP addresses and important additional configuration settings, including the addresses of DNS servers, WINS servers, and the default gateway, along with other configuration settings if needed. SBS manages the core DHCP settings automatically, but you can add additional settings as appropriate for your environment, as well as view and manage the current address leases and exclusions. If your network includes printers or other devices that require unchanging IP addresses, you can either exclude the address from use by DHCP and manually set the device, or configure DHCP for an address reservation to ensure that the device will always get the same address.

Viewing Current DHCP Address Leases

To view the addresses currently leased to clients, complete the following steps:

1. Open Server Management and expand Advanced Management, Computer Management, Services And Applications, and finally DHCP.

2. Expand the Scope container and then select Address Leases, as shown in Figure 15-1, to view a list of currently assigned IP addresses and their corresponding host names.

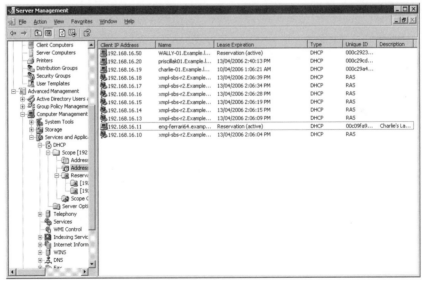

Figure 15-1   Viewing assigned IP addresses.

More Info   To set up a client computer to use DHCP, see Chapter 11, "Managing Computers on the Network."

Creating Exclusions in DHCP

The pool of addresses that a DHCP server can lease to clients is called a *scope*. For any device on the network that has a static IP address within the scope, you need to create an exclusion to prevent the DHCP server from handing out that address to a client.

To create an exclusion, complete the following steps:

1. Right-click Address Pool in the Server Management console and choose New Exclusion Range from the shortcut menu.

2. In the Add Exclusion dialog box, shown in Figure 15-2, use the Start IP Address and End IP Address boxes to specify the range of IP addresses you want to exclude. To exclude a single IP address, type it in the Start IP Address box.

3. Click Add to create the exclusion. Create any additional exclusions, and then click Close when you're finished.

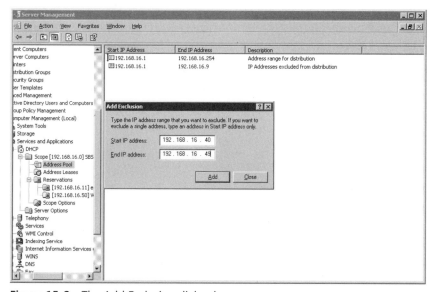

Figure 15-2   The Add Exclusion dialog box.

Adding a DHCP Reservation

As an alternative to manually setting and managing IP addresses for fixed IP devices, such as printers, you can use DHCP to assign an address and configuration settings to the device, and then use a DHCP reservation to ensure that the device always gets that address and that no other device or client is assigned that address. Because reservations inherit the Scope options and can be easily modified from a single point, it's much better to use a reservation instead of manually setting or managing IP addresses for devices that will support DHCP.

To create a DHCP reservation, complete the following steps:

1. Right-click Reservations in the Server Management console and choose New Reservation from the shortcut menu.

2. In the New Reservation dialog box, shown in Figure 15-3, fill in the fields for the new DHCP reservation:

    ❑ **Reservation name**   Usually the DNS name for the device or client. Choose a name that conforms to DNS naming requirements for best compatibility.

    ❑ **IP address**   The IP address that you are reserving for this device or client.

    ❑ **MAC address**   The Media Access Control or hardware address of the network card for the device or client. This is a hexadecimal number that is globally unique and is generally printed directly on the device.

    ❑ **Description**   A descriptive phrase that will make it easier to identify the specific device the reservation is assigned to.

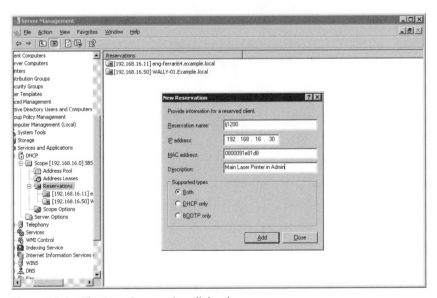

Figure 15-3   The New Reservation dialog box.

❑ **Supported types**   The choices are Both, DHCP only, or BOOTP only. BOOTP is an older protocol for automatically assigning IP addresses and configuration details that is no longer commonly used, but selecting the Both option is the best choice unless you have a specific reason not to.

3. Click Add and the reservation is added. The reservation will inherit the configuration options that have been set for the DHCP scope, and you can add specific options for each reservation.

Enabling DNS Updates

On an SBS server, the DHCP server is by default not configured to automatically update the DNS server when it assigns an IP address to a client. This is not a problem for Windows 2000 or Windows XP clients, since they will update their own records. But if you have other types of DHCP clients, you can configure DHCP to handle the DNS update automatically.

To enable DHCP to automatically update the DNS records, follow these steps:

1. Open Server Management and expand Advanced Management, Computer Management, Services And Applications, and finally DHCP.

2. Right-click DHCP, select Properties, and then click the DNS tab to bring up the DHCP Properties dialog box, shown in Figure 15-4.

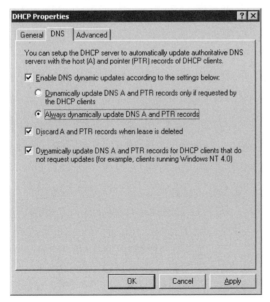

Figure 15-4   The DNS tab of the DHCP Properties dialog box.

3.   Select the Enable DNS Dynamic Updates According To The Settings Below check box. If you have dumb devices, such as printers, also select the Dynamically Update DNS A And PTR Records For DHCP Clients That Do Not Request Updates check box. Click OK when you've made your changes.

Viewing DNS Records

DNS is a TCP/IP service that maps IP addresses (192.168.16.2) to names (xmpl-sbs-r2.example.local). As such, it's an essential service for the Internet (the Web in particular) and for SBS-based networks (which rely on TCP/IP).

Under the Hood   Default DNS Settings

SBS uses the DNS server service for local name resolution only. If the name doesn't belong to the local domain, the DNS server forwards the query to your ISP's DNS server, which resolves the name on the Internet.

SBS automatically creates two types of zones for local name resolution. It creates a forward lookup zone for the domain (example.local), which allows you to use a DNS name to resolve an IP address. It also creates a reverse lookup zone (192.168.16.x Subnet or 16.168.192.in-addr.arpa if it uses the old naming conventions), which enables you to resolve the DNS name associated with a particular IP address (a useful trick for troubleshooting). Both zones use secure dynamic updates so that Microsoft Windows 2000, Windows XP, and Windows Server 2003 clients can automatically and securely update their own DNS records.

SBS manages DNS automatically for those clients that support dynamic updates, and there is usually no need to manually administer it. However, if you have non-Windows clients or legacy clients that don't automatically update their records, you'll need to manually create the A and PTR records for them. If they're DHCP clients, you'll need to enable DNS to automatically update their records, as described earlier in the chapter in the "Enabling DNS Updates" section. If you have trouble reaching hosts on the network by name (but can reach them by IP address), check their DNS resource records using the following steps:

1.   Open Server Management and expand Advanced Management, Computer Management, Services And Applications, and finally DNS.

2.   Expand the *XMPL-SBS-R2* container (where *XMPL-SBS-R2* is the name of the SBS computer), expand Forward Lookup Zones, and then select *example.local* (assuming the name of your SBS domain is *example.local*). This displays all resource records in the forward lookup zone. A Host (A) record for each computer in the domain, listing its current IP address and DNS name, should be visible.

3. To view records in the reverse lookup zone, expand the Reverse Lookup Zone container, and then 192.168.16.x Subnet (again, assuming that your SBS subnet is 192.168.16.x). All Pointer (PTR) records in the reverse lookup zone are displayed.

4. To create an A and a PTR record for a device that isn't listed, right-click the *example.local* container (where *example.local* is your internal SBS domain) and select New Host (A) from the Action menu, shown in Figure 15-5.

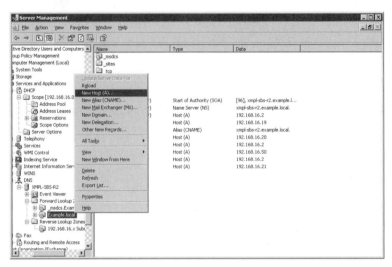

Figure 15-5   The Action menu for a forward lookup zone in DNS.

5. Fill in the name and IP address for the new host and check the Create Associated Pointer (PTR) Record box to also create the corresponding PTR record, as shown in Figure 15-6.

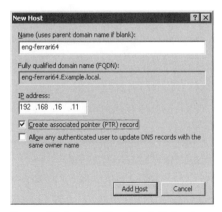

Figure 15-6   The New Host dialog box.

6. Click Add Host to create the record. You can continue to add hosts, or click Done to exit.

Under the Hood   WINS and NetBIOS Name Resolution

NetBIOS is an interface originally developed to allow applications to access network resources in the MS-DOS operating system. As such, it was the primary networking API and naming method for Microsoft networks until the release of Windows 2000, and it is still required by older operating systems and network applications.

NetBIOS host names are up to 15 characters long and part of a flat namespace, so all names on a given network must be unique. Normally, host names are resolved by broadcast—not the most efficient means in terms of either time or network bandwidth. Routers also usually do not forward NetBIOS broadcasts, requiring LMHOSTS files to handle name resolution on different subnets.

WINS was created to provide dynamic name mapping of NetBIOS names to IP addresses. Although many of us would like to do away with WINS, it is still used in SBS to provide NetBIOS name resolution services. If all your clients are Windows 2000 or later Windows clients, it is technically possible to run without WINS, and we know at least one SBS MVP who does so. But as much as we hate WINS, we leave it in there.

You can view the WINS records for your SBS network by following these steps:

1. Open Server Management and expand Advanced Management, Computer Management, Services And Applications, and then WINS.

2. Select the Active Registrations container.

3. Right-click Active Registrations and choose Display Records from the shortcut menu.

4. Click Find Now to display a list of all records in the WINS database along with their status.

According to Microsoft Knowledge Base article 837391 found at *http://support. microsoft.com/kb/837391*, WINS is still recommended for Microsoft Exchange.

Administering Routing and Remote Access

Routing and Remote Access serves as the router, firewall, and remote access (VPN and dial-up) server for a SBS, Standard Edition network. SBS, Premium Edition, uses Routing and Remote Access in combination with ISA Server 2004 for this functionality.

The primary configuration of Routing and Remote Access uses the CEICW and the Remote Access Wizard, both of which are covered in Chapter 5. To view connected remote access clients, increase the allowed number of VPN connections, or increase VPN security, read the following sections.

Viewing Remote Access Clients

To view the clients currently connected to the server via a VPN or dial-up connection, complete the following steps:

1. Open Server Management and expand Advanced Management, Computer Management, Services And Applications, and finally Routing And Remote Access.

2. Select Remote Access Clients to view a list of connected clients, as shown in Figure 15-7.

    a. Double-click a client to view detailed status information on the connection.

    b. Right-click a client and choose Disconnect from the shortcut menu to close the connection.

    c. Right-click a client and choose Send Message to send a pop-up message to the client, or choose Send To All to send a pop-up message to all connected clients.

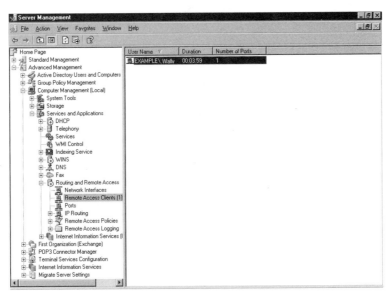

Figure 15-7   Remote Access clients.

Configuring Ports

SBS automatically creates VPN ports that clients can use to connect to the server: five Point To Point Tunneling Protocol (PPTP) ports and, if you've configured L2TP as described later in the chapter under "Creating L2TP VPN Connections," five Layer 2 Tunneling Protocol (L2TP) ports. If you need to support more simultaneous VPN connections, you can increase the number of ports available by following these steps:

1. In the Routing And Remote Access container of Server Management, right-click Ports and choose Properties from the shortcut menu.

2. In the Ports Properties dialog box, shown in Figure 15-8, select WAN Miniport (PPTP) or WAN Miniport (L2TP) and click Configure.

3. In the Configure Device dialog box, use the Maximum Ports box to specify the number of connections you want to allow and click OK when you're finished.

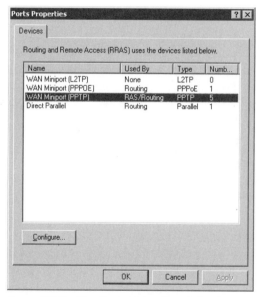

Figure 15-8 The Ports Properties dialog box.

Advanced Network Security

The default settings for an SBS server are quite secure, and for many installations the settings require no additional changes or configuration. However, if you're concerned about security, and you want to configure your SBS network to maximize the security as much as can reasonably be done, you can enable several additional features to strengthen the security. This includes adding a Remote Authentication Dial-In User Service (RADIUS) server and a Certificate server to enable additional authentication options for VPNs and wireless networking. Of course, since this is SBS, we'll be adding those two servers directly onto the main SBS server, though you always have the option of adding additional servers to your SBS network as necessary.

Even if you don't plan to set up Certificate services or configuring RADIUS on your network, you should read the two important sidebars in this chapter on wireless security: "WPA and WPA2" and "Wireless Security Strategies." These cover the basics that you *need* to know if you're using wireless on your network.

If you are interested in increasing the security of VPN clients and of wireless networking on your network, and you're willing to follow some fairly detailed steps to get it working, read on. In the following sections, we'll detail

- Using Internet Authentication Service to increase VPN security
- Deploying Certificate Services
- Creating L2TP VPN connections
- Using 802.1X authentication for wireless security
- Using Group Policy to automatically configure 802.11 and certificate settings

Using Internet Authentication Service to Increase VPN Security

For maximum compatibility, SBS uses PPTP as the default protocol for VPN connections. PPTP is widely supported and provides adequate security for most scenarios, but the default encryption settings in SBS are less than they should be, in our opinion. To increase the encryption level and also enable L2TP, you need to first install the Internet Authentication Service (IAS), Microsoft's implementation of a RADIUS server. IAS is also needed for 802.1X wireless authentication.

To install IAS, complete the following steps:

1. Open Add Or Remove Programs in Control Panel and then click Add/Remove Windows Components. The Windows Components Wizard opens.
2. On the Windows Components page, select Networking Services and click Details.
3. In the Networking Services dialog box, select the check box next to Internet Authentication Service, click OK, and then click Next. The Windows Components Wizard installs IAS. Click Finish when the installation is done.

Once IAS is installed, use the following steps to modify the SBS Remote Access Policy to disable the use of Microsoft Challenge Handshake Authentication Protocol (MS-CHAP) authentication and require 128-bit encryption:

1. From the Start menu, choose the Administrative Tools folder and then select Internet Authentication Service. This opens the Internet Authentication Service console.

2. Select Remote Access Policies and then double-click Small Business Remote Access Policy, shown in Figure 15-9.

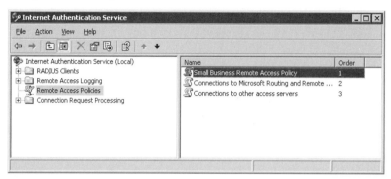

Figure 15-9   The Internet Authentication Service console.

3. In the Small Business Remote Access Policy Properties dialog box, click Edit Profile. (Be careful—there are two Edit buttons on this page. You want the Edit Profile button.) The Edit Dial-In Profile dialog box appears.

4. Click the Authentication tab and then clear the Microsoft Encrypted Authentication (MS-CHAP) check box, shown in Figure 15-10.

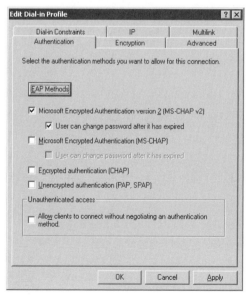

Figure 15-10   The Authentication tab of the Edit Dial-In Profile dialog box.

5. Click the Encryption tab, shown in Figure 15-11, clear all check boxes except Strongest Encryption (MPPE 128 bit), and then click OK twice.

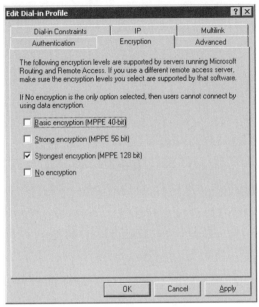

Figure 15-11   The Encryption tab of the Edit Dial-In Profile dialog box.

Deploying Certificate Services

Most networks use password-based authentication to secure network communications such as VPN and wireless connections. When used with secure authentication methods such as MS-CHAP v2 (for PPTP VPN connections) or WPA (for wireless connections), password-based security can be quite secure.

To increase security beyond the default level in SBS, you can add digital signing of communications using a digital certificate. This also enables clients to verify the identity of the server (reducing the risk of rogue servers), and to digitally sign and encrypt e-mails. Digital certificates are required by L2TP VPN connections and 802.1X authentication of wireless networks.

Installing Certificate Services

The first step in setting up 802.1X authentication or L2TP VPNs is to install Certificate Services and create an enterprise root Certificate Authority (CA), which can then be used to deploy certificates to users and computers on the network. To do so, complete the following steps:

1. Open Add Or Remove Programs in Control Panel and then click Add/Remove Windows Components. The Windows Components Wizard appears.

2. On the Windows Components page, select Certificate Services in the component list. The installer warns you that after the CA software is installed, you can't change the name of the server or move it into or out of an Active Directory domain. Click Yes, and then click Next.

3. On the CA Type page, shown in Figure 15-12, select Enterprise Root CA and then click Next.

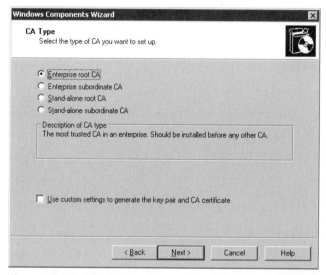

Figure 15-12   The CA Type page of the Windows Components Wizard.

4. On the CA Identifying Information page, shown in Figure 15-13, type a descriptive name for the CA in the Common Name field (most likely including the organization's name) and then click Next.

5. On the Certificate Database Settings page, accept the default storage location for the certificate database and log files and configuration information. Note that the location you specify *isn't* where issued certificates are stored—it's where the CA's own certificates are stored. Click Next.

> **Note**   If the computer acting as the Enterprise Root CA crashes and you lose the CA database, you must reissue every certificate. Consider this extra motivation to regularly back up your entire SBS installation.

6. Click Yes when prompted to stop Microsoft Internet Information Services. When prompted, insert the appropriate SBS CD or DVD and then click OK. The Windows Components Wizard completes the installation of Certificate Services. Click Finish when the installation is done.

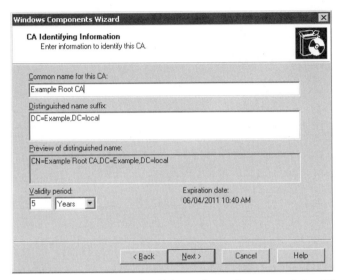

Figure 15-13   The CA Identifying Information page of the Windows Components Wizard.

Creating a Local Computer and Current User Certificates Console

Before you can request computer and user certificates for client computers, you need to create a console *on the client computer* that displays the Certificates (Local Computer) and Certificates (Current User) snap-ins. To do so, complete the following steps:

1. Log on to a client computer with the domain Administrator account.

2. Click Start, choose Run, type **mmc** in the Open box and then click OK. This opens a blank Microsoft Management Console (MMC).

3. Choose Add/Remove Snap-In from the File menu. The Add/Remove Snap-In dialog box appears.

4. Click Add, and select Certificates in the Add Standalone Snap-In dialog box, and then click Add again.

5. In the Certificates Snap-In dialog box, select Computer Account as shown in Figure 15-14, click Next, select Local Computer, and then click Finish.

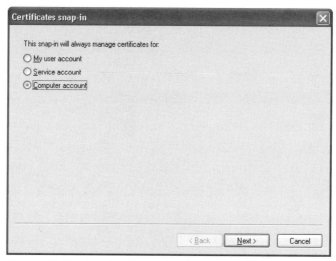

Figure 15-14   The Certificates Snap-In dialog box.

6. In the Add Standalone Snap-In dialog box, select Certificates again and click Add. The Certificates Snap-In dialog box appears.

7. Select My User Account and then click Finish. Click Close and then click OK. This displays the MMC console with the two Certificates snap-ins.

8. Choose Save As from the File menu and then save this to a network share so that you can use the console from any computer on the network.

Requesting Computer and User Certificates

After creating a console that displays the Certificates (Local Computer) and Certificates (Current User) snap-ins, use the following steps to request and install computer and user certificates on a client computer. You'll need to be connected to the SBS network to perform these steps.

> **Note**   The client computer should already be joined to the domain before you request and install certificates. If this is a new client and it hasn't yet been joined to the domain, see Chapter 11.

1. Open the console you created in the preceding section if it isn't already open. Expand the Certificates (Local Computer) container, right-click Personal, choose All Tasks from the shortcut menu, and then choose Request New Certificate.

2. Click Next on the first page of the Certificate Request Wizard. Select Computer on the Certificate Types page, shown in Figure 15-15, and then click Next.

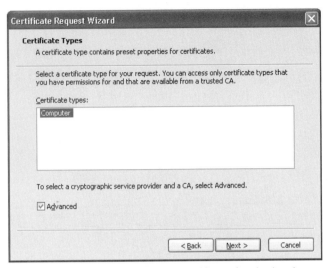

Figure 15-15   Requesting a new certificate for the local computer.

3. Accept the defaults and click Next until you get to the Certificate Friendly Name And Description page. Type a name and description for the certificate. Click Next and then click Finish. Click OK in the dialog box that appears if the request was successful. A new certificate is then created in the Certificates (Local Computer)\Personal\Certificates folder.

4. Expand the Certificates (Current User) container, right-click Personal, choose All Tasks from the shortcut menu, and then choose Request New Certificate.

5. Click Next on the first page of the Certificate Request Wizard, select User on the Certificate Types page, shown in Figure 15-16, and then click Next.

6. On the Certificate Friendly Name And Description page, type a name and description for the certificate, click Next, and then click Finish. Click OK in the dialog box that appears if the request was successful. A new certificate is then created in the Certificates (Current User)\Personal\Certificates folder.

> **Important**   If your DNS suffix isn't set correctly as part of the computer name, the creation of this certificate will fail. For example, if your computer is "xmpl-charlie-01" and the domain is "example.local", go to properties of My Computer and click the Computer Name tab. The Full Computer Name should be "xmpl-charlie-01.example.local." If it isn't, click the Change button and change the name. You'll have to reboot, but now the certificate request should succeed.

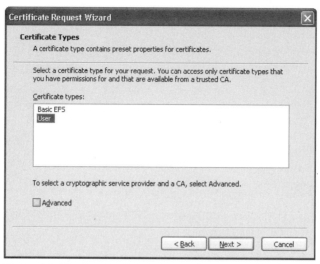

Figure 15-16   Requesting a new certificate for a user.

7. Just to be safe, expand the Trusted Root Certification Authorities container in either snap-in, select Certificates, and verify that the enterprise root CA that you created on the SBS computer appears in the list. (In our case, the enterprise root CA is Example Root CA, as shown in Figure 15-17.)

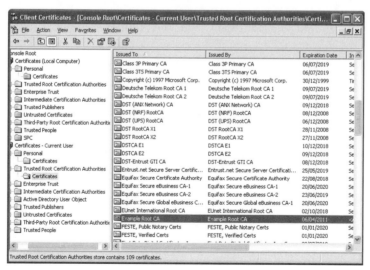

Figure 15-17   Verifying that the root CA has been added to the list of Trusted Root CAs.

Requesting a Certificate for the SBS Server

The SBS server needs to obtain a domain controller certificate so that it can validate its identity to clients for L2TP VPN connections and 802.1X authentication. To do so, first install Certificate Services as an enterprise root CA (as discussed earlier in this chapter), and then use the following procedure to request a certificate from the CA.

1. Open the Certificates (Local Computer) console on the server. See the "Creating A Local Computer and Current User Certificates Console" section earlier in this chapter if you have yet to create this console.

2. Right-click the Personal container, choose All Tasks from the shortcut menu, and then choose Request New Certificate. The Certificate Request Wizard opens.

3. Click Next on the first page of the Certificate Request Wizard, and on the Certificate Types page, select Domain Controller. Click Next to continue.

4. On the Certificate Friendly Name And Description page, type **SBS Server Certificate** in the Friendly Name box, type a description, and then click Next.

5. Review the settings and then click Finish. Click OK in the dialog box that appears, which states that the certificate request was successful. (If this doesn't appear, there's a problem with Certificate Services.)

Creating L2TP VPN Connections

Layer 2 Tunneling Protocol (L2TP) is currently the most secure VPN protocol available in SBS, offering significantly higher levels of security than PPTP. Unfortunately, setting up L2TP is a complex process involving a number of different services and tasks. The following sections reduce this complexity into a series of straightforward steps that make deploying L2TP almost easy.

Deploying Certificates

The first step in setting up L2TP is to deploy user and computer certificates to all VPN clients, and to request a computer certificate for the SBS computer. (Even though the computer already has several certificates, it needs a domain controller certificate signed by the certificate authority.) Follow the steps in the "Deploying Certificate Services" section earlier in this chapter to do this.

Modifying the Small Business Remote Access Policy

After deploying user and computer certificates to VPN clients and the SBS computer, edit the Small Business Remote Access Policy to allow authentication via certificates. You'll need to have already installed IAS, as described in "Using Internet Authentication Service to Increase VPN Security" earlier in this chapter. Then complete the following steps on the SBS server:

1. From the Start menu, choose the Administrative Tools folder and then select Internet Authentication Service. This opens the Internet Authentication Service console.

2. Select Remote Access Policies and then double-click Small Business Remote Access Policy.

3. In the Small Business Remote Access Policy Properties dialog box, click Edit Profile. The Edit Dial-In Profile dialog box appears.

4. Click the Authentication tab and then click EAP Methods. The Select EAP Providers dialog box appears.

5. Click Add, select Smart Card Or Other Certificate, and then click OK. The Select EAP Providers dialog box lists the newly added EAP type, as shown in Figure 15-18.

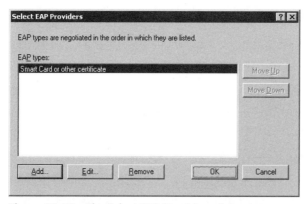

Figure 15-18   The Select EAP Providers dialog box.

6. Select Smart Card Or Other Certificate and click Edit. In the Smart Card Or Other Certificate Properties dialog box that appears, select the certificate named SBS Server Certificate, which you created earlier as the certificate that the server should use to authenticate itself with VPN clients, and then click OK. Click OK, and then click OK again to finish updating the profile.

> **Note**   Add the Protected EAP (PEAP) authentication method as well if you want to allow L2TP connections authenticated with MS-CHAP v2 instead of certificates. PEAP authentication provides a way of gradually moving to a certificate-based authentication—implement L2TP connections using certificates when possible, and PEAP when not. PEAP authentication also makes troubleshooting L2TP VPN connections easier.

Opening Ports in Routing and Remote Access

If you're using SBS 2003 Standard Edition, you can open the necessary ports on the built-in SBS firewall to allow L2TP VPN connections by completing the following steps:

1. Open Server Management, and expand Advanced Management, Computer Management, Services And Applications, and finally Routing And Remote Access.

2. Expand IP Routing, and then NAT/Basic Firewall. Right-click Network Connection and choose Properties from the shortcut menu. The Network Connection Properties dialog box appears.

3. Click the Services And Ports tab, shown in Figure 15-19, select the following protocols, specify 127.0.0.1 as the private address, and then click OK:

   ❑ IP Security (IKE)

   ❑ IP Security (IKE NAT Traversal)

   ❑ VPN Gateway (L2TP/IPSec–running on this server)

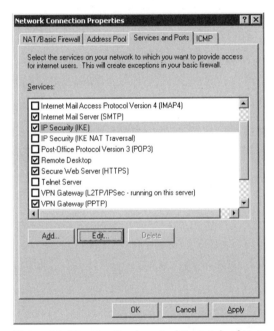

Figure 15-19   The Services And Ports tab of Network Connection Properties dialog box.

Note   For users of SBS 2003 Premium Edition with ISA Server 2004, see Chapter 16, "Using ISA Server 2004," for details on configuring firewall policies. The ISA Server wizards handle all the steps that configure Routing and Remote Access in this chapter.

Note   If you have a stand-alone firewall, open UDP port 500 for Internet Key Exchange (IKE), UDP port 4500 for IPSec NAT-Traversal traffic, and IP Protocol port 50 for IPSec ESP traffic.

Enabling EAP in Routing and Remote Access

The final step in preparing a server to accept incoming L2TP VPN connections is to enable Extensible Authentication Protocol (EAP) in Routing and Remote Access. To enable EAP in Routing and Remote Access, complete the following steps:

1. Open Server Management, and expand Advanced Management, Computer Management, Services And Applications, and finally Routing And Remote Access.

2. Right-click Routing And Remote Access and choose Properties from the shortcut menu. The Routing And Remote Access Properties dialog box appears.

3. Click the Security tab, and then click Authentication Methods. The Authentication Methods dialog box, shown in Figure 15-20, appears.

4. Select Extensible Authentication Protocol (EAP), clear Microsoft Encrypted Authentication (MS-CHAP), click OK, and then click OK again.

Figure 15-20   The Authentication Methods dialog box.

Important   Once you've configured the SBS server for L2TP connections, you also need to add L2TP ports for Routing and Remote Access. SBS 2003 does not create L2TP ports by default. See "Configuring Ports" earlier in this chapter for details on how to add ports.

Creating the VPN Connection

After the server is properly configured to accept incoming L2TP connections, manually create a VPN connection on the client computer using the following steps:

1. On the client computer, open the Network Connections (Windows XP) or Network and Dial-Up Connections folder (Windows 2000).

    Note   Any VPN connections you create using the Windows Small Business Server 2003 Connection Manager are PPTP connections by default. You can manually modify these connections to use L2TP.

    ---

2. Choose New Connection from the File menu. When the New Connection Wizard appears, click Next.

3. On the Network Connection Type page, choose Connect To The Network At My Workplace (Windows XP) or Connect To A Private Network Through The Internet (Windows 2000), and then click Next.

4. On the Network Connection page, choose Virtual Private Network Connection and then click Next. (This page doesn't appear in Windows 2000.)

5. On the Connection Name page, type the name for the connection and then click Next. (This page doesn't appear in Windows 2000.)

6. On the Public Network page, choose whether to establish a dial-up Internet connection before using the VPN connection and then click Next. (This page doesn't appear in Windows 2000 and won't appear in Windows XP if you don't have a modem or haven't installed Connection Manager.)

7. On the VPN Server Selection page (Windows XP) or Destination Address page (Windows 2000), type the Internet-accessible fully qualified domain name or IP address of the SBS server and then click Next.

8. On the Connection Availability page, choose whether to allow other users access to the VPN connection and then click Next. Type a name for the connection (if creating a connection in Windows 2000) and then click Finish to complete the wizard. The Connect dialog box appears.

    Note   If you will use this connection to VPN in to the SBS network before logging on to your computer, you need to make this connection available for anyone's use.

    ---

9. In the Connect dialog box, click Properties.

10. Click the Networking tab, shown in Figure 15-21, and choose L2TP IPSec VPN (Windows XP) or Layer-2 Tunneling Protocol (L2TP) (Windows 2000) from the Type Of VPN box.

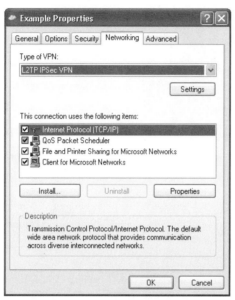

Figure 15-21   The Networking tab.

11. Click the Security tab, choose Advanced, and then click Settings. The Advanced Security Settings dialog box appears.

12. Choose Use Extensible Authentication Protocol (EAP), select Smart Card Or Other Certificate, as shown in Figure 15-22, and then click Properties. The Smart Card Or Other Certificate Properties dialog box appears.

13. Choose Use A Certificate On This Computer, as shown in Figure 15-23, select Validate Server Certificate, and then select the name of the SBS root CA in the Trusted Root Certification Authorities section of the dialog box. Click OK when you're finished. Click OK, and then click OK again. The VPN connection is then established.

14. In the Validate Server Certificate dialog box, click OK to accept the server's credentials and connect to the network.

> **Note**   Once you've got L2TP VPN connections working, automate the process of creating L2TP VPN connections for clients using the Connection Manager Administration Kit, which can be installed using the Windows Component Wizard, accessible from Add Or Remove Programs.

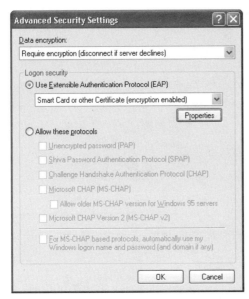

Figure 15-22   The Advanced Security Settings dialog box.

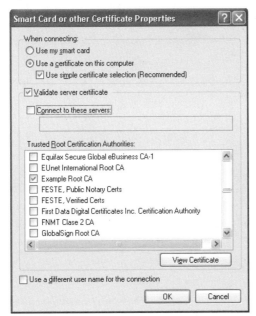

Figure 15-23   The Smart Card Or Other Certificate Properties dialog box.

Real World   L2TP Troubleshooting

If you have trouble connecting via L2TP, here are some troubleshooting steps:

- Try establishing an L2TP VPN connection from inside the internal network.
- Verify that there are available L2TP ports in Routing and Remote Access.
- If the client can connect from inside the network, but not from outside:
    1. Check the client firewall configuration.
    2. Verify that there isn't a NAT firewall between the client and the SBS server.
    3. Check Event Viewer and use Network Monitor to perform a network capture, if necessary.

If you receive Error 778 or Error 801 on the client when establishing a VPN connection, verify that the SBS enterprise root CA certificate appears in the list of Trusted Root Certification Authorities, and that the correct server certificate is used by IAS. (See the "Modifying the Small Business Remote Access Policy" section earlier in this chapter.) Clearing the Validate Server Certificate check box in the Advanced Security Settings dialog box on the client can also resolve these errors, though at the expense of mutual authentication.

Using 802.1X Authentication for Wireless Security

Securing 802.11 (Wi-Fi) networks is a subject of much debate and a myriad of options. (See the Real World sidebar, "Wireless Security Strategies," later in this chapter.) One of the most sophisticated methods of securing an 802.11 network is using 802.1X authentication in conjunction WPA or WPA2 encryption. Although setting up 802.1X authentication evokes panic in the hearts of many administrators because of its complexity, if you're careful and take your time, it is doable and worth the effort. We don't recommend trying to use 802.1X with EAP-TLS—frankly, we think that's just too much work for too little gain in any but the largest enterprise. But using 802.1X with PEAP and WPA or WPA2 encryption is both possible and has real benefits. The basic steps in the process are:

- Choosing an authentication protocol
- Deploying certificates
- Adding wireless access points as RADIUS clients
- Creating a remote access policy
- Configuring wireless access points
- Configuring wireless clients to use PEAP

Chapter 15   Managing Connectivity   389

In the following sections, we'll cover each of these steps. It's a complex process, but if you carefully follow along and do each step in the process without skipping anything, you'll succeed. We did, and we're now running our SBS network with full 802.1X authentication for wireless clients using self-signed certificates—and without buying a single additional piece of software or hardware (except for the wireless access points, but we had those already).

Under the Hood   WPA and WPA2

Because of the problems with the original WEP encryption algorithm and the time it takes to get a full IEEE standard adopted and agreed on, the Wi-Fi Alliance adopted an interim standard called Wi-Fi Protected Access (WPA). WPA increases security on three fronts: data encryption, data integrity, and user authentication.

The WPA standard has been absorbed into the 802.11i standard, but at the time of this writing, the products generally available on the market were a mix of those that implement the full 802.11i standard and those that only meet WPA certification.

Note   Products that are certified to support 802.11i are designated "WPA2" by the Wi-Fi Alliance.

Data Encryption

WPA replaces the flawed encryption algorithm of WEP with either Temporal Key Integrity Protocol (TKIP) or Advanced Encryption Standard (AES). TKIP changes the encryption key for each frame, but it can still run on existing hardware, while AES will likely require a new generation of hardware from wireless vendors.

Data Integrity

The original WEP standard had only a weak check for packet integrity—that is, there was no assurance that the packet you received was actually the packet that was sent, making WEP vulnerable to "Man in the Middle" attacks. WPA adds a Message Integrity Check (MIC), using the method known as "Michael." This MIC ensures that the packet received is the same as the packet sent. Additionally, Michael helps prevent replay attacks.

More Info   For more on MIC and other features of WPA, read this useful paper that we found at *http://iit-iti.nrc-cnrc.gc.ca/iit-publications-iti/docs/NRC-47460.pdf*

User Authentication

WPA supports the use of a RADIUS server for user authentication. In environments without a RADIUS server, WPA uses a preshared key for initial authentication of clients.

WPA2

The WPA2 is a product certification from the Wi-Fi Alliance signifying that a specific product meets the 802.11i standard. It replaces the encryption scheme (RC4) that was the basis of the WEP problems with a new and much more secure encryption scheme: Advanced Encryption Standard (AES). The AES used in WPA2 and 802.11i is the Counter Mode Cipher Block Chaining-Message Authentication Code (CBC-MAC) protocol (CCMP).

WPA/WPA2-Personal vs. WPA/WPA2-Enterprise

WPA comes in two flavors: WPA-Personal and WPA-Enterprise. (WPA2 has the same two types, WPA2-Personal and WPA2-Enterprise.) In WPA Personal, no RADIUS server is used. Instead, the access point and the client use a preshared key to initially authenticate. This is simple to implement, and since the key is only used for that initial session negotiation, it is quite secure if you use a complex and long key. For home users and many small businesses, WPA-Personal (or WPA2-Personal if your hardware supports it) is an acceptable and easy-to-implement security level for wireless security. However, by adding a RADIUS server (and there's a good one built into our SBS servers, of course), you can implement WPA-Enterprise. This uses the RADIUS server to authenticate clients and to manage key changes, eliminating the need for ever using a preshared key. And it has an added advantage: When an employee leaves, you don't have to change all the keys!

More Info   For more information on WPA2, 802.11i, and AES, an excellent starting point is the Cable Guy article titled "Wi-Fi Protected Access 2 (WPA2) Overview" found on Microsoft TechNet at *http://www.microsoft.com/ technet/community/columns/cableguy/cg0505.mspx*.

Real World   Wireless Security Strategies

A variety of security strategies for wireless networking have been suggested and used over the years—some useful and some not. The following list details our evaluation of several of these strategies.

- **MAC Address Filtering**   This strategy allows only a statically managed list of MAC addresses is access to the wireless network. It's a nice idea, but this strategy is easy to defeat with a sniffer as MAC addresses can be easily spoofed.

Plus, a static list of "allowed" MAC addresses is a hopeless mess to manually maintain. All in all, it's a complete waste of time.

- **SSID Hiding**   This strategy requires that the client know the name of the wireless network to be able to connect to it. And even if the network is known and configured into the Windows client, that client must continually probe to make sure that the network is present. This requirement causes all sorts of problems and limits the ability of Microsoft Windows to manage connections. The strategy is totally useless because anyone with access to the packets in the air can read the SSID from the commonly sent 802.11 management frames in a matter of seconds. Whereas broadcasting the SSID, when combined with appropriate security, makes the network easier to manage and easier for users as well. Hiding the SSID is another complete waste of time.

- **WEP Encryption**   The original encryption standard for wireless, this standard uses either a 40-bit or 104-bit key (along with a fixed 24-bit initialization vector). It is easily hacked by anyone with bad intentions and will keep only the most casually curious out of your network. WEP keys are static keys and must be manually maintained. Every time a user who has wireless access leaves the organization, the WEP keys need to be changed. A network protected with WEP alone should be considered completely unsecured.

- **WPA**   The WPA encryption standard is based on RC4, which can be compromised. However, because it changes keys with sufficient frequency and derives the new keys in an improved way as compared to WEP, it is generally considered secure. With 802.1X authentication and the appropriate authentication method, the initial encryption keys are automatically generated. Pre-shared key authentication generates new initial encryption keys for each authentication. Configuration of WPA preshared keys is simplified in Windows XP SP2 with the Wireless Network Setup Wizard. If your wireless hardware doesn't support at least WPA, don't let it inside your network.

- **WPA2**   The WPA2 encryption is based on AES and is much more secure than RC4, while the WPA2 standard incorporates additional security measures beyond just encryption. Both preshared key and RADIUS authentication scenarios are supported. All new wireless hardware that you buy should support WPA2.

- **IEEE 802.11i**   This is the underlying standard for WPA2, which is described in the preceding bullet point.

- **VPNs**   One solution to setting up secure wireless networks is to place the wireless network outside your main network and use a VPN connection to the main network. This approach has the advantage of getting around the insecurities of older equipment, but has inherent problems. If the external access point is open and unsecured, it leaves the client exposed to any other computer in range. It also imposes a performance hit and requires a VPN connection for every client. Machine group policies are not applied, and the overall reliability of the connection and the administrative overhead are significant issues as well. However, even with its problems, this can be a viable temporary solution when new equipment isn't in the budget and a limited number of clients need to be supported.

■ **IEEE 802.1X**   Using 802.1X as the authentication mechanism for WPA or WPA2 encryption is an excellent solution, and we'll detail how to implement it next.

Choosing Authentication Protocols

The 802.1X authentication standard requires the use of an authentication protocol. There are two commonly used with Microsoft clients and servers:

■ Protected Extensible Authentication Protocol (PEAP) combined with Microsoft Challenge Handshake Authentication Protocol version 2 (MS-CHAP v2)

■ Extensible Authentication Protocol-Transport Layer Security (EAP-TLS)

PEAP is the easiest protocol to implement—only the SBS server itself requires a certificate. However, because PEAP relies on user credentials for authentication, Group Policy computer configuration information won't work, nor will remote administration while the user is logged off.

EAP-TLS requires certificates for each user and computer, as well as the server, and is difficult to implement and fragile to maintain. Frankly, we think it's just too much pain and requires a level of IT support that just isn't feasible in most small businesses.

Note   A wireless client receives updated Computer Configuration policies every time it restarts while connected to the network via an Ethernet connection, including during the initial process of joining the computer to the SBS network. For companies that rarely change Group Policy settings, updating Computer Configuration policies in this manner might be satisfactory.

Under the Hood   802.1X Authentication Process

Here's a summary of the 802.1X authentication process for a client.

1. The client associates with an access point.

2. The client asks for the RADIUS server's certificate to authenticate the server.

3. The client sends its computer account credentials to the RADIUS server.

4. The RADIUS server contacts Active Directory to verify the computer account credentials, and checks any remote access policies to verify that the computer belongs to a group with access permissions.

5. If the client's computer account has the proper permissions, the client and RADIUS server generate keys and establish a secure session, logging the computer onto the domain.

6. The client sends user credentials, which the RADIUS server also checks in Active Directory.

7. If successful, the user is logged onto the domain and given network access.

Real World   PEAP and Group Policy Processing

Although PEAP provides great wireless security and is easier to implement than EAP-TLS authentication, there are two significant drawbacks. The first is that you won't be able to remotely administer wireless clients unless someone's logged on. The second is that Group Policy Computer Configuration won't work.

Group Policy Computer Configuration is used by SBS to apply the following Group Policies to computers in the network:

- Password policies

- Account lockout policies

- Tightened Kerberos policies

- Prohibit installation of Network Bridge on internal network

- Manage settings of Windows Firewall on internal network

- Prohibit use of Internet Connection sharing on internal network

- Enable Domain Admins to offer remote assistance without invitation

Deploying Certificates

The first requirement in setting up 802.1X on your wireless network is to request a domain controller certificate for the SBS server. See "Requesting a Certificate for the SBS Server" earlier in this chapter if you haven't already done this step. Because we're using PEAP, we don't need certificates on the clients.

Adding Wireless Access Points as RADIUS Clients

Once you've deployed the domain controller certificate to your SBS server, the next step is to configure IAS to recognize wireless access points as RADIUS clients. (If you haven't already installed IAS, described in the "Using Internet Authentication Service to Increase VPN Security" section, do that now.) To configure IAS, follow these steps:

1. Open Internet Authentication Service from the Administrative Tools folder.

2. Right-click the RADIUS Clients container and choose New RADIUS Client from the shortcut menu. This opens the New RADIUS Client Wizard.

3. On the Name And Address page, shown in Figure 15-24, type a descriptive name for the access point in the Friendly Name box. In the Client Address (IP or DNS) box, type the DNS name of the access point, and then click Next. (If you haven't added your access point to your DNS yet, just use the IP address here.)

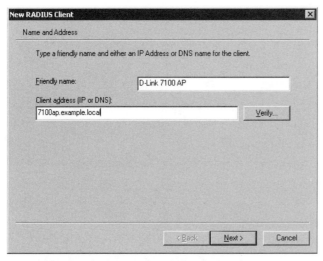

Figure 15-24   The New RADIUS Client Wizard.

> **Important**   The access point should use a static IP address or a DHCP reservation. We prefer a DHCP reservation for easier manageability. If you use a static IP address, make sure that the address is excluded from the DHCP scope, as discussed in "Managing DHCP" earlier in this chapter.

4. On the Additional Information page, accept the default of RADIUS Standard for the Client-Vendor field and type a complex password in the Shared Secret and Confirm Shared Secret boxes. You must type this password into each access point as well, as discussed in the "Configuring Wireless Access Points" section of this chapter. Leave the Request Must Contain The Message Authenticator Attribute field unchecked. Click Finish when you're done.

Note   A *shared secret* is a password or passphrase used between an IAS server and any wireless access points. The shared secret must be the same on both the IAS server and all access points and must follow general password rules: it's case sensitive, it can use alphanumeric and special characters, and it can be up to 255 characters long. See Chapter 8, "Managing Users and Groups," for a discussion of good passwords. Use a long (16 characters or longer) and complex string to maximize security. Because the shared secret is embedded in the software and is only typed once, you don't need to memorize it. But you do need to keep it in a safe but accessible place in case you ever need to add additional wireless access points.

Creating a Remote Access Policy

Next you need to create a remote access policy to allow clients to use 802.1X authentication, since it isn't enabled by default. To create the policy, follow these steps:

1. Open Internet Authentication Service from the Administrative Tools folder.

2. Right-click Remote Access Policies and choose New Remote Access Policy from the shortcut menu. This displays the New Remote Access Policy Wizard. Click Next on the first page.

3. On the Policy Configuration Method page, shown in Figure 15-25, select Use The Wizard To Set Up A Typical Policy For A Common Scenario, type in a policy name for this new policy, and click Next.

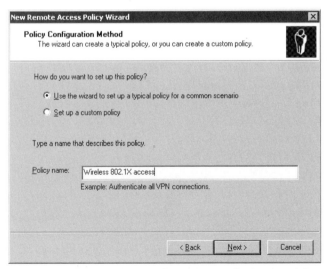

Figure 15-25   The Policy Configuration Method page of the New Remote Access Policy Wizard.

4. On the Access Method page, select Wireless, as shown in Figure 15-26, then click Next.

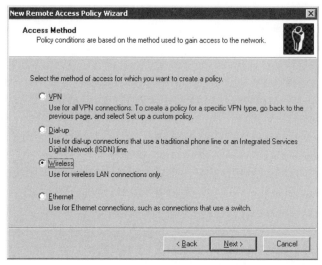

Figure 15-26 The Access Method page of the New Remote Access Policy Wizard.

5. On the User Or Group Access page, select Group and then click Add.

6. In the Select Groups dialog box, type **Domain Users; Domain Computers** and then click OK. The User Or Group Access page, shown in Figure 15-27, updates to show the Domain Users and Domain Computers groups . Click Next to continue.

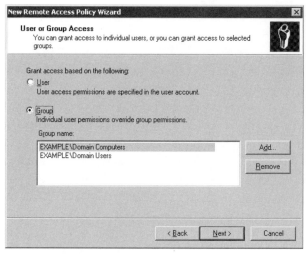

Figure 15-27 The User Or Group Access page of the New Remote Access Policy Wizard.

> **Note**   We actually prefer to explicitly limit wireless access to only those
> users (and their computers) that have signed our Acceptable Wireless Use
> policy. Instead of granting permission to all domain users and computers,
> we created a new security group called Wireless Users. We then add users
> and their computers to that group, and use that group in the Select Groups
> dialog box instead of Domain Users and Domain Computers. You can find
> samples of Acceptable Use policies in a variety of places, including *http://
> www.sans.org*.

7. On the Authentication Methods page, select Protected EAP (PEAP) as the type of
    authentication.

8. Click the Configure button to bring up the Protected EAP Properties page, shown in
    Figure 15-28. Select the domain controller certificate you created earlier, check the
    Enable Fast Reconnect box, click OK and then click Next.

> **Note**   The default certificate that is displayed here might be the certifi-
> cate we created for L2TP VPNs, not the domain controller certificate we
> want for wireless. Scroll down the list of certificates until you locate the
> domain controller certificate, and select that one.

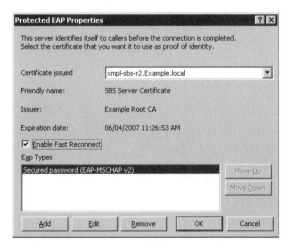

Figure 15-28   The Protected EAP Properties page.

9. Review the settings and then click Finish. If you have trouble getting to this page,
    check to make sure that the certificate was properly issued to the server.

10. In the Remote Access Policies container, double-click the remote access policy you
    just created and click Edit Profile in the Properties dialog box.

11. Click the Encryption tab and clear all check boxes except Strongest Encryption (MPPE 128 bit) to maximize the security of the connection. Click OK twice.

Configuring Wireless Access Points

Once the SBS server is properly configured for 802.1X authentication, it's time to set up the wireless access points. The procedure varies depending on your brand and model of wireless access point, so all we can offer are the basic guidelines, but here are the settings to configure:

- Set up the access points with static IP addresses or with DHCP reservations. If static addresses are used, they should be in a range that is excluded by your DHCP server. (If you've taken all the default settings for SBS, you can choose static addresses of 192.168.16.3 through 192.168.16.9, a subnet mask of 255.255.255.0, and a gateway address of 192.168.16.2. See the "Managing DHCP" section earlier in this chapter for information on setting up DHCP exclusions and DHCP reservations.)

- Disable the DHCP server feature of the access point.

- Change the SSID to one that's appropriate for the network but doesn't reveal the location or name of the business.

- Change all access point passwords to secure passwords.

- Enable Primary RADIUS Server and type the IP address of the SBS server in the Primary RADIUS Server IP Address field (most likely 192.168.16.2). In the Destination Port, type **1812**.

- Type the shared secret you typed when adding the access points as RADIUS clients. (See the "Adding Access Points as RADIUS Clients" section in this chapter for more information.)

- Enable WPA or WPA2 encryption.

- If you have the choice, enable WPA Enterprise (or WPA2 Enterprise) and specify the IP address of the SBS server as your RADIUS server.

- Enable 802.1X Authentication with 128-bit keys.

Configuring Clients to Use PEAP

To configure clients for 802.1X authentication using PEAP, complete the following steps.

1. Using a wired network connection, join the computer to the SBS network using the Network Configuration Wizard, if you haven't already. See Chapter 11 for help with this step.

2. While still connected via wired network connection, open the *xmpl-sbs-r2***CertEnroll** folder in Windows Explorer (where *xmpl-sbs-r2* is your SBS server name).

3. In the list of certificates, double-click the certificate corresponding to the new root CA you created earlier.

4. In the Certificate dialog box, shown in Figure 15-29, click Install Certificate. The Certificate Import Wizard appears.

Figure 15-29   The Certificate dialog box.

5. Click Next on the first page of the Certificate Import Wizard, click Next on the Certificate Store page, and then click Finish to install the certificate automatically. This places it in the root store.

6. Disconnect from the wired network (if you're connected), right-click the Wireless Network Connection icon in the system tray, and choose View Available Networks from the shortcut menu to open the Choose A Wireless Network dialog box, shown in Figure 15-30. Clients running operating systems other than Windows XP SP2 should follow the instructions provided with their wireless network cards.

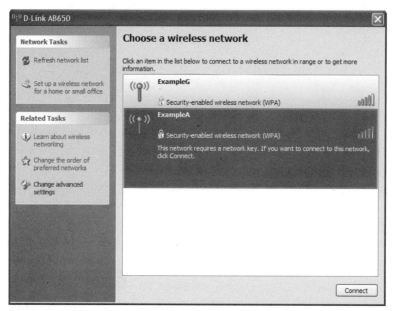

Figure 15-30   The Choose A Wireless Network dialog box of Windows XP Professional Service Pack 2.

7. Click Change Advanced Settings in the Related Tasks pane. and then click the Wireless Networks tab, shown in Figure 15-31.

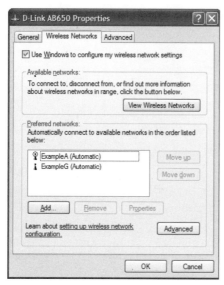

Figure 15-31   The Wireless Networks tab of the access point Properties.

8. In the Preferred Networks section, highlight the wireless network if it's visible and click Properties, or click Add to open the Wireless Network Properties page, shown in Figure 15-32. If you're adding a wireless network, enter the SSID of the network. Select WPA for Network Authentication, and TKIP for Data Encryption, as shown in the figure.

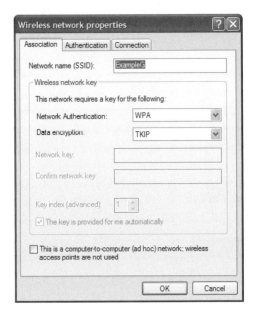

Figure 15-32   The Association tab of the Wireless Network Properties.

9. Click the Authentication tab and select Protected EAP (PEAP) in the EAP Type box, as shown in Figure 15-33.

10. Click Properties to open the Protected EAP Properties page. Select the Root Certificate Authority of your SBS network and check the Enable Fast Reconnect box, as shown in Figure 15-34. Click OK.

11. Back on the Authentication tab of the Wireless Network Properties dialog, ensure that the Authenticate As Computer When Computer Information Is Available check box is selected, click OK and then click OK again. The client should now connect automatically to your 802.1X authenticated wireless network.

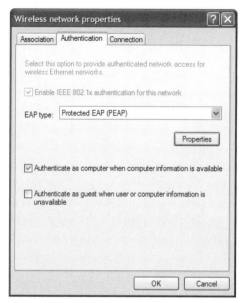

Figure 15-33   The Authentication tab of the Wireless Network Properties.

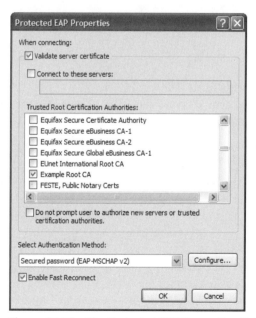

Figure 15-34   The Protected EAP Properties dialog box.

Real World Troubleshooting 802.1X Authentication

If clients can't connect using 802.1X authentication, check Event Viewer on the SBS computer for clues. Enable all encryption levels in the Remote Access Policy, and verify that the client computer has the SBS computer's certificate properly installed. Installing Network Monitor and performing a network capture while the client attempts to connect can also be helpful.

If the client loses a connection when roaming between access points in the same network, click Properties on the Authentication tab of the Wireless Network Properties dialog box and make sure to select the Enable Fast Reconnect check box.

Using Group Policy to Automatically Configure 802.11 and Certificate Settings

You can streamline the process of deploying computer certificates and 802.11 settings using Group Policy, making the deployment process for L2TP VPNs easier.

Use the following sections to create a new Group Policy Object (GPO) and configure it to automate computer certificate enrollment.

Note   You can automate the creation of L2TP VPN connections using the Connection Manager Administration Kit (CMAK).

Creating and Linking a New Group Policy Object

It's a good idea to create a new GPO any time you want to apply settings via Group Policy. This makes it easy to undo changes—simply disable the GPO.

Complete the following steps to create a new GPO and link it to the appropriate domain or organizational unit (OU):

1. From the Start menu, choose the Administrative Tools folder and then open the Group Policy Management console.

2. In the console tree, navigate to Domains, then to example.local (or whatever the domain is named), and then to Group Policy Objects.

3. Right-click Group Policy Objects (shown in Figure 15-35). Choose New from the shortcut menu, type a name for the GPO, and then click OK.

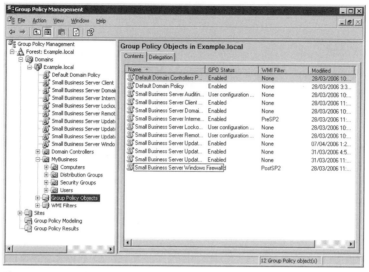

Figure 15-35   The Group Policy Objects container and the Group Policy Management console.

4. Link the new GPO by dragging it from the Group Policy Objects container to the appropriate OU or container:

    ❑ Use the Computers OU in the MyBusiness OU to link the GPO to all client and server computer accounts created with the Set Up Client Wizard and Set Up Server Wizard.

    ❑ Use the SBSComputers OU in the MyBusiness\Computers OU to link the GPO to all client computer accounts created with the Set Up Client Wizard.

    ❑ Use the SBSServers OU in the MyBusiness\Computers OU to link the GPO to all server computer accounts created with the Set Up Server Wizard.

    Note   Use the Group Policy Results and Group Policy Modeling tools to ensure that your GPO is being applied properly. For more information, see Chapter 17, "Using Group Policy."

Modifying Certificate Settings

After creating a new GPO for your settings, use the following steps to enable client computers to automatically obtain computer certificates and install the SBS computer's certificate in the Trusted Root Certificate Authorities certificate store.

1. Right-click the GPO you created in the Group Policy Management Console and choose Edit from the shortcut menu. This opens the Group Policy Object Editor.

2. Navigate to Computer Configuration, Windows Settings, Security Settings, and finally Public Key Policies, as shown in Figure 15-36.

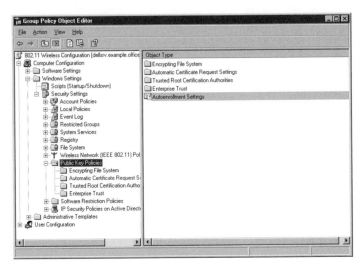

Figure 15-36   The Group Policy Object Editor displaying the Public Key Policies container.

3. Right-click Automatic Certificate Request Settings, choose New from the shortcut menu, and then choose Automatic Certificate Request. When the Automatic Certificate Request Setup Wizard appears, click Next.

4. On the Certificate Template page, select Computer, click Next, and then click Finish.

5. Right-click Trusted Root Certificate Authorities and choose Import from the shortcut menu. When the Certificate Import Wizard appears, click Next.

6. On the File To Import page, click Browse, select the certificate file for the SBS Certificate Authority (the root CA we created earlier), and then click Open, as shown in Figure 15-37. (The certificate should be located in the root directory of the C:\ drive.) Click Next.

7. On the Certificate Store page, click Next to place certificates in the Trusted Root Certification Authorities certificate store. Review the settings and then click Finish. If the import was successful, a message will appear.

8. In the Group Policy Object Editor, verify that the certificate appears in the Trusted Root Certification Authorities container.

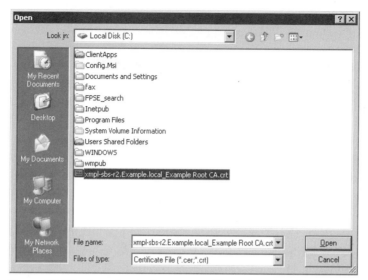

Figure 15-37   Browsing to the root certificate for use with 802.1X.

Creating a Wireless Network Policy

After creating a new GPO for your settings, complete the following steps to create a new wireless network policy that automates the deployment of 802.11 network settings to clients:

1. In the Group Policy Management Console, right-click the GPO you created and choose Edit from the shortcut menu. This opens the Group Policy Object Editor.

2. Navigate to Computer Configuration, Windows Settings, Security Settings, and finally Wireless Network (IEEE 802.11) Policies.

3. Right-click Wireless Network (IEEE 802.11) Policies and choose Create Wireless Network Policy from the shortcut menu. When the Wireless Network Policy Wizard appears, click Next.

4. On the Wireless Network Policy Name page, type a name and description for the policy, click Next, and then click Finish. The policy Properties dialog box appears.

5. Click the Preferred Networks tab and then click Add. The New Preferred Setting Properties dialog box appears, shown in Figure 15-38.

6. Type the SSID of your wireless network in the Network Name box.

7. Click the IEEE 802.1X tab and choose Protected EAP from the EAP Type box. Configure other settings as necessary and then click OK. Add other networks to which clients should automatically connect, and then click OK.

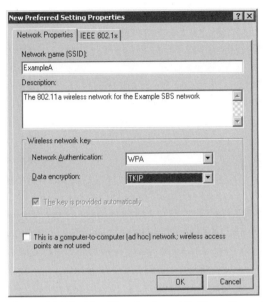

Figure 15-38   The New Preferred Settings Properties dialog box.

Summary

This chapter covered the many components that make up connectivity on an SBS network, including DHCP, DNS, WINS, and Routing and Remote Access on an SBS network. It also described the detailed steps required to use Internet Authentication Server, Certificate Server, and the higher-security features that they enable, including L2TP VPN connections and 802.1X authentication on your wireless network.

Chapter 16 discusses administering ISA Server 2004, a component of Windows Small Business Server 2003, Premium Edition.

Using ISA Server 2004

Concepts 410

Installing ISA Server 2004 414

Installing the Firewall Client 419

Administering ISA Server 2004 421

Advanced Configuration 429

Import, Export, Backup, and Restore 434

Monitoring ISA Server 437

Summary 441

Microsoft Windows Small Business Server 2003, Premium Edition, includes Microsoft Internet Security and Acceleration Server on the Premium Technologies CD. Beginning with the release of SBS SP1, the version of ISA Server included ISA Server 2004, Standard Edition. ISA Server is a full-featured, robust, and powerful firewall that can play an important role in:

- Securing your network from attacks
- Managing the use of your company's Internet resources
- Improving the effective bandwidth of your Internet connection

Real World Stand-Alone Firewall?

As with all components of SBS, the ISA Server software can only be installed on the main SBS server. Some argue that this is an inherently bad practice and violates the premise that your firewall should *only* be your firewall, and nothing else should be on the same computer, and definitely not your domain controller. And certainly when we're configuring enterprise environments, we'd specify a stand-alone ISA 2004 server, or even an array of ISA servers. But does this mean that ISA on SBS is inherently insecure? No. The SBS and ISA teams at Microsoft have done a good job of creating a viable, secure, and useable implementation of ISA server that will do an excellent job of securing your SBS network. If you really believe strongly that your firewall should not reside on the same computer as your domain, a good option is to buy a stand-alone ISA Server appliance. This is a special hardware and software bundle that includes the hardware, a specially hardened and locked-down Windows Server 2003, and ISA Server 2004 in a single package that is preconfigured and ready to just plug in to the perimeter of your network. Another option is a stand-alone firewall such as SonicWALL (*http://www.sonicwall.com*), but the disadvantage of any external firewall is that it isn't managed by the Configure E-Mail and Internet Connection Wizard (CEICW)—it must be separately managed. For a list of ISA appliance servers, see *http://www.isaserver.org/hardware/ISA-Appliances/*.

Concepts

The main goals of ISA Server are to insulate the network from attack, improve Internet performance for clients on the internal network, and control client access to the Internet.

ISA Server maintains control of connectivity and isolates the internal network by having two separate physical connections—one to the Internet and one to the internal network. Each network is connected to a different network card, and all packets must pass through the ISA Server software to get from one connection to the other.

The mechanisms that ISA Server uses to achieve these aims are fairly straightforward. The following four basic techniques are used:

- Network address translation
- Packet filtering and application-layer filtering
- Caching
- Firewall Policies

The following sections discuss each of these techniques, as well as the different methods available to support clients. They also describe some of the core concepts used with ISA Server.

Network Address Translation

Network Address Translation (NAT) hides your actual IP address from computers beyond the device doing the translation. Only the device doing NAT needs to have a valid Internet IP address; all clients and servers on the internal network are given private addresses from the address ranges reserved for private networks. (See the Real World sidebar, "IP Addresses for Internal Networks.")

To provide NAT, you can use a stand-alone router or firewall device, a proxy server or firewall software package such as ISA Server, or the built-in NAT functionality of Windows Small Business Server 2003.

Although NAT is the backbone of any Internet connection–sharing technique, and is also the first line of your security perimeter, by itself it isn't sufficient to truly protect your network. ISA Server supplements NAT with additional security measures, most notably application layer filtering.

Real World   IP Addresses for Internal Networks

Back when folks were deciding how to parcel out IP addresses (and long before anyone figured out how to perform NAT), the need for addresses that could be used for test networks was recognized. A special set of IP addresses called *private network addresses* was defined in RFC 1918 (*http://www.faqs.org/rfcs/rfc1918.html*) for test networks or other networks not physically connected to the Internet.

These private network addresses allow a much larger address space than would be possible with officially assigned addresses while protecting the integrity of the Internet. If a computer with one of these addresses were to connect to the Internet, it wouldn't cause a conflict with another computer because routers automatically filter out these addresses.

The following addresses are designated for private networks that won't be directly connected to the Internet. They can, of course, be connected to the Internet through ISA Server or another method that performs NAT:

- 10.0.0.0 through 10.255.255.255 (a single "Class A" network)

- 172.16.0.0 through 172.31.255.255 (16 contiguous "Class B" networks)

- 192.168.0.0 through 192.168.255.255 (256 contiguous "Class C" networks)

Quotation marks enclose the class in the preceding list because the Internet Assigned Numbers Authority (IANA) no longer uses classes to define IP address spaces. But the terminology is still commonly used to describe the size of the resulting address space.

One other block of addresses is important to NAT and internal networks: the "link local" block, 169.254.0.0 through 169.254.255.255. This block of addresses, defined in RFC 3330 (*http://www.faqs.org/rfcs/rfc3330 .html*), is self-configured by a network device whenever the device fails to get an assigned address from DHCP or by other means. As with the private networks defined in RFC 1918, these addresses are locally unique but not globally unique, and should never appear on the public Internet.

ISA Server automatically includes all of these addresses in its local address table (LAT) when you initially install the program.

Another byproduct of using NAT is that all the computers on a network *appear* to have the same single address to the outside world—the external address of the SBS server itself. This allows your entire organization to connect to the Internet using only a single public IP address.

Packet Filtering and Application Layer Filtering

Because every packet that passes to or from the Internet must first pass through ISA 2004, ISA 2004 is in a perfect position to act as a gatekeeper. Besides performing simple NAT, ISA 2004 can inspect each packet and permit only packets that use approved protocols and ports to enter or leave the internal network. (This process is called *packet filtering*.) When packet filtering is enabled, you can also restrict access to specific external sites or enable only certain external sites to be seen. In addition, third-party ISA 2004 plug-ins can add other controls and functionality.

In addition to basic packet filtering, ISA provides Stateful Packet Inspection (SPI), which analyzes the origin of every packet and allows only unaltered packets from approved hosts or networks to pass through the firewall. This prevents hackers from tampering with packets, and it provides the ability to block incoming packets that aren't specifically requested by network clients.

Stateful packet filtering is filtering that happens on layer 3 (the IP layer) of the OSI stack. As such, it is useful, but it can no longer be considered sufficient for all security needs because it must open ports based on a presumption that a packet is authorized, without being able to verify that the content isn't malicious. ISA 2004 adds intelligent application filtering—stateful application-layer inspection—that inspects the actual application frames to determine the content and can filter based on that content. SBS includes a number of intelligent application-layer filters, including HTTP, RPC, and SMTP as part of the ISA Server component.

Caching

Every organization has certain Web sites that users visit regularly. ISA 2004 can cache information from these frequently accessed sites so that when users connect to the site, much of the information is actually delivered by ISA 2004, not the remote site. Caching significantly improves the apparent speed of the connection to the Internet and leaves more Internet bandwidth available.

ISA 2004 can use off hours when few users are connected to the Internet to check frequently accessed sites to make sure the information it has stored for that site is current. This monitoring, called *active caching*, helps to balance and smooth out demand, providing improved throughput during busier times because fewer pages and images need to be downloaded.

ISA 2004 also performs fancy tricks such as splitting audio or video streams and sharing them with multiple users on the network, and performing reverse caching, which accelerates the perceived performance of Web servers to Internet clients.

Client Types

Clients can connect to the ISA Server using the Firewall Client, the SecureNAT client, or the Web Proxy client. For Windows clients, only the Firewall Client is a supported method with SBS, and the ISA Server installation will prompt you to add the Firewall Client to the automatically installed client software. For Macintosh and UNIX clients and for network devices, SecureNAT is used. Each client using SecureNAT should have its default gateway set to point to Windows Small Business Server. All systems should have their Web browsers configured to use the Web Proxy service. This is done automatically when installing the Firewall Client software, but needs to be done manually for SecureNAT clients.

Note   There is no publicly available 64-bit Firewall Client at the time of this writing, though one is expected "soon". If your SBS network includes Windows XP x64 Edition clients, you'll need to configure them as SecureNAT clients. This will mean creating special rules for these computers. The best way to do this is to use DHCP reservations to ensure that x64 clients are in a known IP address range, and then create rules that manage those specific IP addresses without having to have the Firewall Client on them, as described later in this chapter, under "Create Firewall Policy Rules."

ISA Server Firewall Policies

ISA Server uses firewall policies to define which sites and protocols can be accessed and by whom. Each policy is made up of several elements. These elements are:

- **Name**   The name doesn't actually do anything, but each policy has to have one, and you should choose a name that is descriptive.

- **Action**   Each firewall policy is either an allow rule or a deny rule.

- **Protocols**   The TCP/IP protocols and the direction that the rule will apply to. This can include all outbound traffic, all inbound traffic except specific protocols, or selected protocols in one or both directions.

- **Source**   The originating networks, clients, or groups of IP addresses that the rule applies to.

- **Destination**   The target networks, URLs, or groups of IP addresses that the rule applies to.

- **Users**   The specific SBS user or user group that the rule applies to. (Requires ISA Firewall Client to be installed on the user's computer.)

- **Schedule**   When the rule is in effect.

- **Content**   What type of traffic the rule applies to.

As you can see, firewall policies give the SBS administrator the ability to closely manage Internet access and protection. By default, SBS uses the CEICW to install and configure the basic firewall policies that you'll need. The exact number of policies that are configured will vary depending on the choices you make in the CEICW. You can also add specific additional policies based on the needs of your organization and environment.

Installing ISA Server 2004

You can install ISA Server either before you install the other elements of the Premium Edition, or after, and either before or after the rest of SBS 2003 R2. SBS 2003 SP1 included an upgrade to the ISA Server 2004 version of ISA Server, including SP1 for ISA Server 2004, and R2 includes that same version. We prefer to install ISA Server after we've installed the contents of CD6–WSUS, Microsoft Exchange SP2, and Windows Share-Point Services SP2–but the latest information available to us is that the installation order is not important.

Important   If you are adding ISA Server 2004 to an existing and established SBS network, you might encounter problems with the certificate used by SBS. To avoid any issues, read and carefully follow the instructions in the ISAInstall-Steps.HTM file in the root directory of the Premium Technologies CD1 disk to export the SBS certificate before installing ISA Server, and then import the certificate after the installation completes.

To install ISA Server 2004, insert the Premium CD1 into the SBS server's CD-ROM drive. The Windows Small Business Server 2003 R2 Premium Technologies Setup Wizard, shown in Figure 16-1, should appear. If it doesn't, run Setup.exe from the CD drive. Then follow these steps:

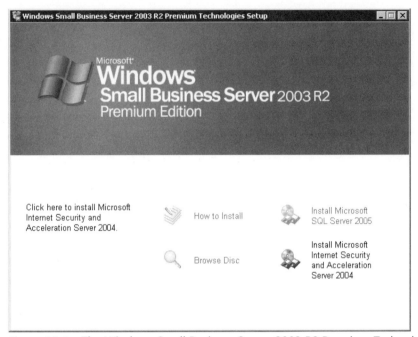

Figure 16-1   The Windows Small Business Server 2003 R2 Premium Technologies Setup Wizard.

1. Click the Install Microsoft Internet Security and Acceleration Server 2004 icon to start the ISA Setup for Windows Small Business Server 2003 Wizard. Click Next on the Welcome screen.

2. Read and agree to the End User License Agreement (EULA).

3. On the Installation Path page of the wizard, shown in Figure 16-2, specify where to install ISA Server and click Next.

4. If the settings are correct, click Finish and the installation will begin.

5. During the ISA installation, the wizard will start the CEICW, as shown in Figure 16-3.

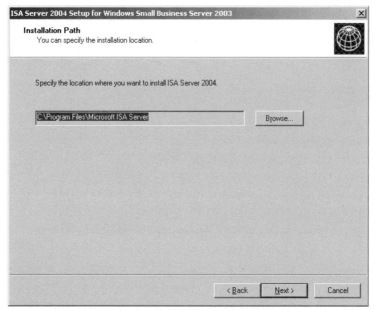

Figure 16-2 Setting the location to install ISA 2004.

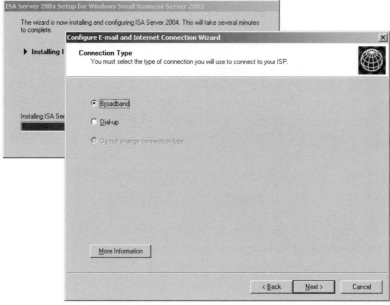

Figure 16-3 The ISA 2004 Setup program runs the CEICW.

6. Step through the CEICW, using the instructions from Chapter 5, "Completing the To Do List and Other Post-Installation Tasks." Once the CEICW completes, the installation will continue.

7. Click Close when the ISA Setup for Windows Small Business Server 2003 Wizard completes. You'll be prompted to restart the server. Click OK and the server will restart.

Important   If you're installing SBS 2003 R2, you must update ISA 2004 to at least the Service Pack 2 level. There is a known issue with ISA 2004 and MMC 3.0, which is included in SBS R2.

Real World   Enabling Caching

For reasons known only to Microsoft and the SBS team, the initial configuration of ISA Server 2004, which is completely automated for almost everything, does not automatically enable caching. If you want to provide Web site caching to your SBS network, you need to go in and enable it. The process is simple and straightforward, so we're not at all sure why it's not enabled by default. To enable ISA Server caching on your SBS server, follow these steps:

1. Open the ISA Management MMC if it isn't already open.

2. Navigate to the Cache configuration, shown in Figure 16-4.

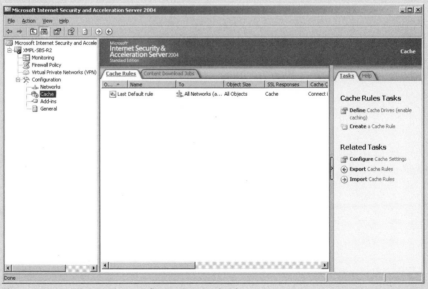

Figure 16-4   The Cache configuration and rules.

3. Click Define Cache Drives (Enable Caching) to open the Define Cache Drives dialog box.

4. Specify the size of the cache and its location. When you're finished, click OK to return to the Cache configuration section of the ISA Management console. As you can see in Figure 16-5, an Apply button is now available.

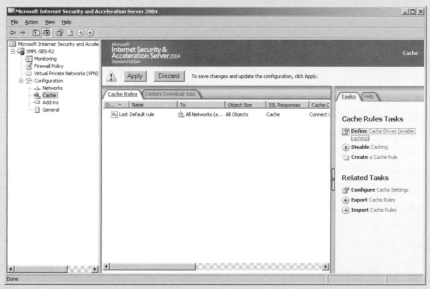

Figure 16-5 You must click Apply before any configuration changes actually happen.

5. Click Apply. The ISA Server Warning dialog box appears, shown in Figure 16-6. Choose to either restart the Microsoft Firewall service now or later, and then click OK.

Figure 16-6 Enabling caching requires a restart of the Firewall service.

> **Note**   Every configuration change you make to ISA Server requires a sep-
> arate Apply step, just as enabling the cache does. Some configuration
> changes require restarting one or more services; some do not. But resist
> the temptation to chain together several changes without doing the
> restarts—it's a lot harder to troubleshoot when you change more than one
> thing at a time.

Installing the Firewall Client

Once you've installed ISA Server on your SBS server, you need to add the ISA Firewall Client to any client computers that have already been configured and added to your network. Any new clients will automatically have the Firewall Client added to the list of
client applications that are installed.

Adding the Firewall Client to Client Applications

To assign the Firewall Client to client computers that are already configured, you need to
run the Assign Applications Wizard, as described in the following steps:

1. In the Server Management console, click Client Computers and then click Assign
   Applications To Client Computers to open the Assign Applications Wizard.

2. Click Next to open the Client Computers page, shown in Figure 16-7.

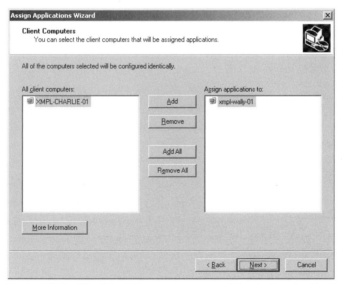

Figure 16-7   The Client Computers page of the Assign Applications Wizard.

3. Click Add All to assign the Firewall Client to all client computers. Remove any client computers that will never be allowed access to the Internet.

4. Click Next to open the Client Applications page, shown in Figure 16-8.

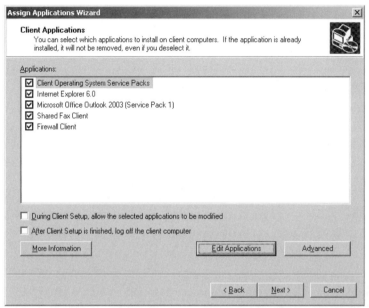

Figure 16-8   The Client Applications page of the Assign Applications Wizard.

5. Make sure the Firewall Client box is checked, and then click Next to open the Mobile Client And Offline Use page of the Assign Applications Wizard. You can add Connection Manager and ActiveSync here.

> **Note**   If the Firewall Client isn't listed as one of the applications to add, you'll need to add the application. For details on how to add client applications, see Chapter 11, "Managing Computers on the Network."

6. Click Next to display a summary of your settings, and then click Finish to complete the assignment.

> **Note**   If you have a previous version of the Firewall Client installed on client computers, you should uninstall it prior to deploying the ISA Server 2004 Firewall Client.

Deploying the Firewall Client

Once you assign the Firewall Client to client computers, the next time users log on to the computers, a shortcut is placed on the desktop to install the Firewall Client. All the users need to do to start the installation is double-click the shortcut.

If the shortcut isn't placed on your desktop, or you need to run the setup manually for some other reason, you can directly connect to the server to run the setup. To run the setup directly, log on to the client computer, click Start, click Run, and type *<sbssrv>* \Mspclnt\Setup.exe, where *<sbssrv>* is replaced by the SBS server's actual name or internal IP address.

Administering ISA Server 2004

The initial configuration of ISA Server is handled automatically as part of the CEICW, which is run as the final step of installing ISA Server. All the necessary protocol and publishing rules are set up, and if your installation never changes, you really don't need anything else. But inevitably there will be changes—there always are. If the changes are covered by the CEICW, your first step should always be to rerun the wizard. The tasks that you can use the CEICW to perform include:

- Changing your broadband or dial-up connection

- Enabling or disabling services through the ISA Server, specifically:
    - E-mail (enabled by default when you are running Microsoft Exchange)
    - Virtual Private Networking (VPN)
    - Terminal Services
    - File Transfer Protocol (FTP)

- Enabling or disabling Web publishing of internal Web site services, specifically:
    - Outlook Web Access
    - Remote Web Workplace
    - Server performance and usage reports
    - Outlook Mobile Access
    - Outlook via the Internet
    - Business Web site (your public Web site)

- Changing the Web server certificate
- Enabling or disabling Internet e-mail

Changing Your Broadband or Dial-Up Connection

You can use the CEICW to change your Internet connection type or to change the specific parameters of your current connection type. When you run the wizard, the wizard will make the necessary changes to ISA Server as well. See Chapter 5 for details about setting or changing your Internet connection type.

Enabling or Disabling Services Through the ISA Server

You can use the CEICW to control which services running on your SBS network are available directly from the Internet. When you run or rerun the CEICW, the wizard makes the necessary changes to firewall policy and publishing rules in ISA Server to support the changes you're making. The services you can enable for direct Internet access are:

- E-mail
- Virtual Private Networking (VPN)
- Terminal Services
- File Transfer Protocol (FTP)

To make changes to these services, complete the following steps:

1. In the Server Management console, click Internet And E-Mail, and then click Connect To The Internet to open the CEICW.

2. Click Next to open the Connection Type page. Select Do Not Change Connection Type and click Next to open the Firewall page.

3. Select Enable Firewall, and click Next to open the Services Configuration page, shown in Figure 16-9.

4. Select the check boxes of any service you want available directly through the Internet. Clear the others. If you enable Virtual Private Networking (VPN), these other services will be available to client computers once they have established a VPN connection to your network.

Important   Enabling VPN connections will not enable L2TP VPN connections, only PPTP. For details on how to enable L2TP VPN connections see "Enabling L2TP with ISA Server 2004." If you have already enabled L2TP, rerunning the CEICW will not disable it unless you disable all VPN connections.

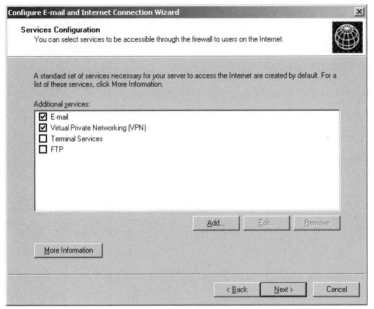

Figure 16-9   The Services Configuration page of the CEICW.

5. You can add custom services that are available directly from the Internet, or edit existing ones you created. If you click Add, you'll see the Add Or Edit A Service dialog box, shown in Figure 16-10. You need to know the port used by the service, the protocol type (TCP or UDP), and whether the service is an inbound or outbound service. Type and select the appropriate information, and then click OK to return to the Services Configuration page.

Figure 16-10   Adding or editing a custom service allows it to be used through the ISA Server.

6. After you make the necessary changes on the Services Configuration page, click Next.

7. Step through the rest of the CEICW without changing any additional settings. When you reach the end, click Finish to implement the changes.

8. Once the configuration is implemented, you'll see a confirmation message, shown in Figure 16-11. Click Close and you're finished.

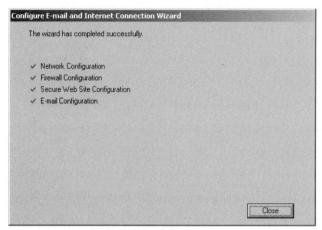

Figure 16-11   Confirmation message showing that the CEICW completed successfully.

Enabling or Disabling Web Services

You can use the CEICW to control which Web services running on your SBS server are available directly from the Internet through your firewall. When you run or rerun the CEICW, the wizard makes the necessary changes to the firewall policies in ISA Server to support the changes you're making. The Web services you can enable for direct Internet access are:

■ Outlook Web Access

■ Remote Web Workplace

■ Server performance and usage reports

■ Outlook Mobile Access

■ Outlook via the Internet

■ Business Web site (your public Web site)

To make changes to these Web services, complete the following steps:

1. In the Server Management console, click Internet And E-Mail, and then click Connect To The Internet to open the CEICW.

2. Click Next to open the Connection Type page. Select Do Not Change Connection Type, and click Next to open the Firewall page.

3. Select Enable Firewall, and click Next to open the Services Configuration page. Don't make any changes here, and click Next to open the Web Services Configuration page, shown in Figure 16-12.

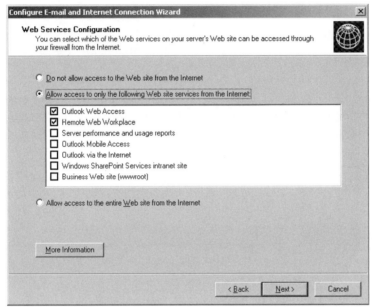

Figure 16-12   The Web Services Configuration page of the CEICW.

4. Select the check boxes of those Web services that you want available directly from the Internet.

5. After you make your changes, click Next.

6. Step through the rest of the CEICW without changing any additional settings. When you reach the end of the wizard, click Finish to implement the changes.

7. After the configuration is implemented, you see a confirmation message. Click Close and you're finished.

Enabling L2TP With ISA Server 2004

As we saw in Chapter 15, "Managing Connectivity," the default VPN configuration for SBS is to only use PPTP as the VPN protocol. Using L2TP requires extra configuration steps, and the addition of both Internet Authentication Service (IAS, the Microsoft implementation of a RADIUS server), and Certificate Services. Installing the ISA Server 2004 that is part of the Premium Technologies CD will not change those requirements, but it will disable the Routing and Remote Access portion of any existing L2TP VPN setup you may have made. Not to worry, configuring it is no more difficult in ISA Server than it was in Routing and Remote Access—in fact, it's a bit easier.

The first steps in enabling L2TP VPN connections are the same as those detailed in Chapter 15. Follow all the steps from Chapter 15 to install IAS and Certificate Services, and to create the necessary Domain Controller certificate, local client computer certificates and user certificates. Ignore any steps for configuring Routing and Remote Access—those are all handled inside the ISA Server 2004 management console.

Once you have your RADIUS server enabled, and you have assigned the necessary certificates to the SBS server, the client computers, and the users who will be using L2TP, follow these steps to finish the configuration and enable L2TP VPNs:

1. Open the Microsoft Internet Security and Acceleration Server 2004 Management console if it isn't already open, and navigate to the main Virtual Private Networks (VPN) section, as shown in Figure 16-13.

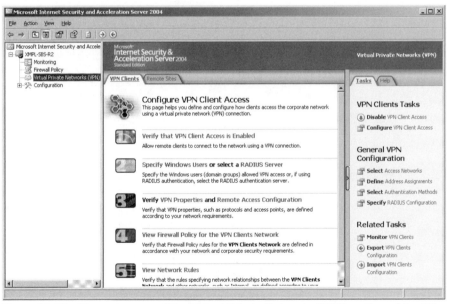

Figure 16-13   The main page of the Virtual Private Networks (VPN) section of the ISA Server 2004 management console.

2. In the Tasks pane, click Configure VPN Client Access to open the VPN Client Properties dialog box, shown in Figure 16-14.

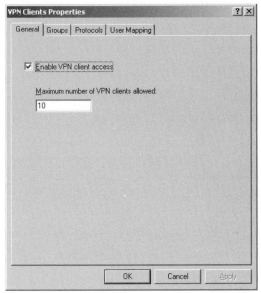

Figure 16-14 The General tab of the VPN Client Properties dialog box.

3. Select the Enable VPN Client Access check box, and set the maximum number of VPN clients allowed as appropriate for your network.

4. Click the Protocols tab, and select both PPTP and L2TP, as shown in Figure 16-15. (Once you have everything working, you can come back here and disable PPTP connections if you want to ensure that only L2TP connections are accepted.)

5. Click the User Mapping tab and select the Enable User Mapping check box, as shown in Figure 16-16. Also set the default domain to the internal DNS name of your SBS network. Ours is example.local, as shown in the figure.

6. Click OK to return to the main VPN page of the ISA Server management console. Click the Apply button and the changes will be applied. Your clients can start connecting using L2TP for their VPN protocol.

Note The configuration of clients to use L2TP is exactly the same whether you are using Routing and Remote Access, as in Chapter 15, or ISA Server 2004, as in this chapter. Follow the steps in Chapter 15 to configure your clients for L2TP.

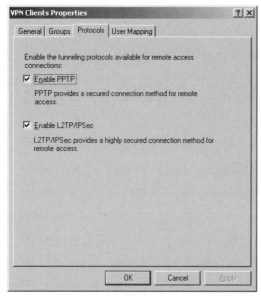

Figure 16-15   The Protocols tab of the VPN Client Properties dialog box.

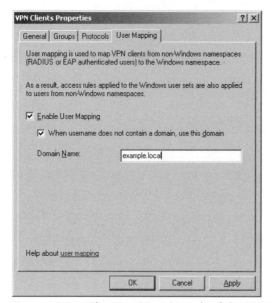

Figure 16-16   The User Mapping tab of the VPN Client Properties dialog box.

Advanced Configuration

While the CEICW will take care of most of the day-to-day tasks of configuring the ISA Server component of SBS, you might have a need to go beyond letting the wizard do all the work. One obvious need that isn't covered by the CEICW is creating a firewall policy that allows clients that aren't using the Firewall Client to access the Internet. If you have clients that are running Windows XP Professional x64 Edition, for example, or Mac or Linux clients, you'll need to create special firewall policy rules for those clients.

Create Firewall Policy Rules

As a way of describing the features and methods of ISA Server 2004, we'll create a firewall policy that allows Windows XP Professional x64 Edition clients to access the Internet. This is only one fairly simple example of the rich set of policies that you can configure ISA Server for, but one of the good things about ISA Server is that it is quite consistent. Once you know how to do one task, you're well on the way to discovering other tasks.

To allow basic Web browsing from x64 computers on our SBS network, we need to define an Allow policy to allow x64 computers on the Internal network to use standard Web protocols to access computers on the External network. We'll create just a simple "Allow All" rule that allows all computers within a specific address range on the Internal network to browse Web sites on the External network. But how will we know which computers are x64? Unfortunately, ISA doesn't have any way to do that natively. But what it *does* know is the IP address of the client, so the first step is to use DHCP reservations or DHCP exclusions and a fixed IP address to explicitly assign a known IP address to our x64 computers. (See Chapter 15 for details on how to configure DHCP.) For setting up this policy, we'll assume that the range of IP addresses from 192.168.16.200 to 192.168.16.225 are reserved for use by client computers that can't use the ISA Firewall Client. Meanwhile, we've set up a general DHCP exclusion for that range of IP addresses, and added a reservation at 192.168.16.200 for our x64 Ferrari laptop.

To create an Allow All x64 Browsing Rule, follow these steps:

1. Open the ISA management console if you haven't already done so.

2. Click the server name in the leftmost pane to open the Getting Started page, shown in Figure 16-17.

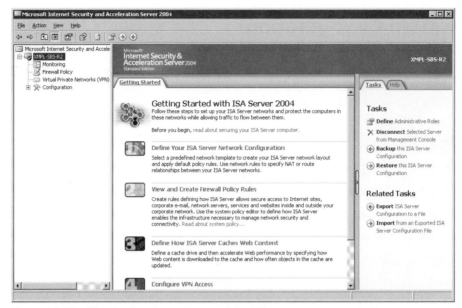

Figure 16-17   The Getting Started page of the ISA management console.

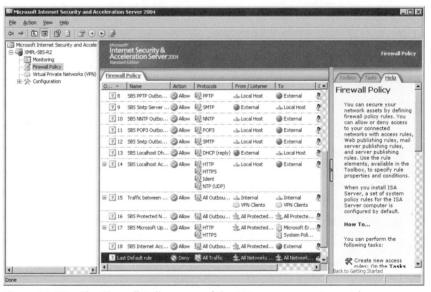

Figure 16-18   The Firewall Policy page of the ISA management console.

3. Select View And Create Firewall Policy Rules to open the Firewall Policy page, shown in Figure 16-18.

4. Click the Tasks tab in the rightmost pane and then click Create New Access Rule to start the New Access Rule Wizard.

5. Type in a name for the new rule, such as **Allow x64 Access All**, and click Next to open the Rule Action dialog box.

6. Select Allow and click Next. On the Protocols page, shown in Figure 16-19, select All Outbound Traffic from the drop-down list. Click Next.

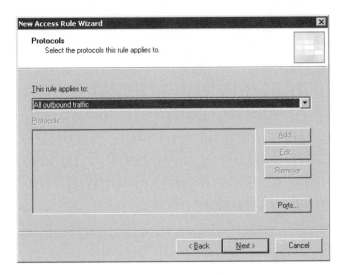

Figure 16-19   The Protocols page of the New Access Rule Wizard.

7. On the Access Rule Sources page, click Add to open the Add Network Entities dialog box, shown in Figure 16-20.

8. Click New, and select Address Ranges to open the New Address Range Rule Element dialog box, shown in Figure 16-21. Enter the address range for your x64 computers, as shown.

9. Click OK, highlight the element you just created, and click Add. Click Close to return to the Access Rule Sources page, shown in Figure 16-22 on page 433. Click Next.

10. On the Access Rule Destinations page, click Add to open the Add Network Entities dialog box again, and this time add the External network from the Networks section. Click Close.

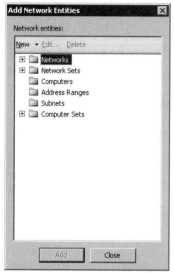

Figure 16-20   The Add Network Entities dialog box of the New Access Rule Wizard.

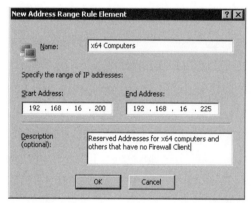

Figure 16-21   The New Address Range Rule Element dialog box.

11. Click Next. The User Sets page will show All Users already added. We'll leave that alone. Click Next and then click Finish to complete the New Access Rule Wizard.

12. Click Apply to enable the changes. The new firewall policy isn't actually enabled until you click the Apply button on the main ISA 2004 management page.

13. If you now try to connect to the Web from an x64 computer on your internal network, instead of getting the 403 Forbidden message, you'll be connected.

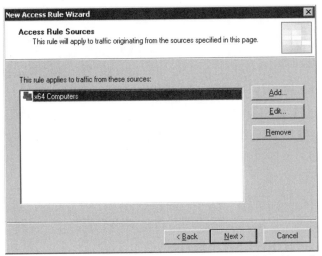

Figure 16-22   The Access Rule Sources page of the New Access Rule Wizard.

While we've created one rule here, we've actually used several features in the process. The Network Entities is part of the Toolbox. (Figure 16-18 shows the Toolbox tab.) This toolbox allows you to define protocols, users, content types, schedules, and network objects that you can then combine to create whatever rules you want or need to create.

ISA Server processes rules in the order they are seen on the Firewall Policy page. It checks each rule to see if the conditions are met. If it finds a rule that matches, and the rule is an allow rule, it allows the traffic. If the rule is a deny rule, it blocks the traffic. So the final rule is always a deny all rule that is created automatically by the initial installation.

Recommended Initial Configuration Steps

The CEICW does a pretty good job of setting up the basic rules for ISA Server 2004, but we've found the following configuration adjustments helpful:

- Ensure that the ISA Server 2004 Client Connection Limit is set to 160 or greater. The default for a fresh install is 160 connections per client, but if you've upgraded from ISA Server 2000, the default is 40, which is really too low.

    - Make this change in the ISA Server management console, under Configuration, General, Define Connection Limits.

    - You can set general limits and assign custom limits to specific client IP addresses.

- Configure firewall and Web proxy logging to retain logs for one month instead of the default of one week.

- Configure ISA Reporting.

  ❑ Make this change in the ISA Server management console, under Monitoring, Reports, Create and Configure Report Jobs

  ❑ If you publish these reports to a network share, they are easily accessible from clients without having to go into the ISA Server management console. You can restrict access to the share to appropriate users as necessary.

- Configure any specific ISA firewall policy rules. You'll find an excellent white paper on overall best practices for firewall policy rules at *http://www.microsoft.com/technet/prodtechnol/isa/2004/plan/firewall_policy.mspx.*

Backing Up the ISA Server Configuration

You should always run a full Windows Small Business Server backup as soon as practical after any major change, such as installing ISA Server. Follow the instructions in Chapter 13, "Backing Up and Restoring Data," for performing an immediate backup once you have your ISA Server installed and working correctly.

Import, Export, Backup, and Restore

ISA 2004 provides both export/import capability and full backup and restore capability. Both have their place in the defense and protection of your ISA 2004 server and should be performed regularly and on an as-appropriate basis.

Export and import can include the entire ISA 2004 configuration, but it's most appropriate to save the partial configuration information after you've made a change or where you want to be able to restore a configuration setting if you're concerned that the CEICW might overwrite it. (Our L2TP VPN rule is a good example of a configuration setting that it's a good idea to save.) During the export process, you can choose whether to include confidential information, and apply an encryption password to the resulting .xml file that contains the configuration information.

Backup and restore are used when you want to save a complete backup of the server configuration. It includes user permissions and all confidential information, and an encrypting password is required. Use backup and restore when you want to save the entire configuration of an ISA 2004 server to be able to restore in the event of a complete disaster.

To back up the configuration of an ISA 2004 server, follow these steps:

1. Open the ISA 2004 management console and navigate to the Getting Started page.

2. Click Backup The ISA Server Configuration in the rightmost pane to open the Backup Configuration dialog box, shown in Figure 16-23. Enter a descriptive file name for the backup, and click Backup.

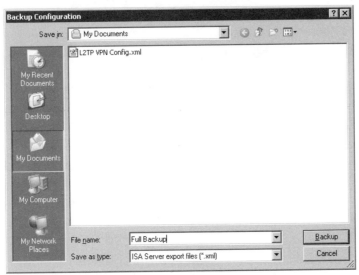

Figure 16-23 The Backup Configuration file dialog box.

3. The Set Password dialog box will open. Enter a password to encrypt the backup file. Passwords must be at least 8 characters and should follow strong password rules. Click OK, and the backup will start. When the backup is complete, click OK again.

To restore the configuration of an ISA 2004 server, follow these steps:

1. Open the ISA 2004 management console and navigate to the Getting Started page.

2. Click Restore The ISA Server Configuration in the rightmost pane to open the Restore Configuration dialog box. Navigate to the saved configuration file and click Restore.

3. Enter the encrypting password and click OK. If you type the wrong password, you'll see the dialog box shown in Figure 16-24, and the restore operation will terminate. If the restore operation is successful, you'll still need to click the Apply button on the main Getting Started page before the restored configuration will be implemented.

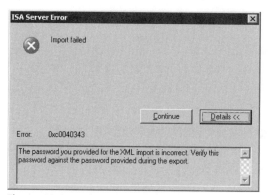

Figure 16-24   The ISA Server Error dialog box that appears when you enter the wrong password for a configuration restore.

To export the configuration of an ISA 2004 server, follow these steps:

1. Open the ISA 2004 management console and navigate to the main page of the portion of ISA 2004 configuration you want to export. To export the entire configuration, navigate to the Getting Started page. As an example of a partial export, navigate to the Virtual Private Networks (VPN) page.

2. Click Export VPN Clients Configuration on the Tasks tab in the rightmost pane to open the Export Configuration dialog box, shown in Figure 16-25. Enter a descriptive file name for the export. Select the Export Confidential Information box. If available, in this section, select the Export User Permission Settings box.

3. Click Export to open the Set Password dialog box if you've chosen to export confidential information. Enter and confirm the password to encrypt the information.

4. Click OK to begin the export. Click OK again when the export completes.

To import the configuration of an ISA 2004 server, follow these steps:

1. Open the ISA 2004 management console and navigate to the main page of the portion of ISA 2004 configuration you want to import. To import the entire configuration, navigate to the Getting Started page. As an example of a partial import, navigate to the Virtual Private Networks (VPN) page.

2. Click Import VPN Clients Configuration in the rightmost pane to open the Import Configuration dialog box. Highlight the policy you want to import. Select Import Cache Drive Settings and SSL Certificates if appropriate for the type of import.

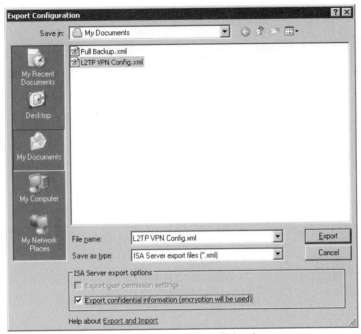

Figure 16-25   The Export Configuration dialog box.

3. Click Import. If the export was encrypted, you'll be prompted to enter the password for the file. Enter the password and click OK.

4. Once the import completes, click OK to close the dialog box. The actual changes to the ISA 2004 server configuration won't be implemented until you click the Apply button on the main System Policy page. If you decide you didn't really want to import your configuration, just click Discard.

Monitoring ISA Server

ISA 2004 provides a diverse set of monitoring tools. The main front end to the monitoring is the Dashboard, shown in Figure 16-26, which has a capsule summary of connectivity, services, reports, alerts, sessions, and the overall system performance all on a single page. The Dashboard's biggest weakness is that it's read-only. If you want more information or detail about a particular report, alert, and so on, you need to drill down to the tab related to the type of element it is. No double-clicking or right-clicking to get more information.

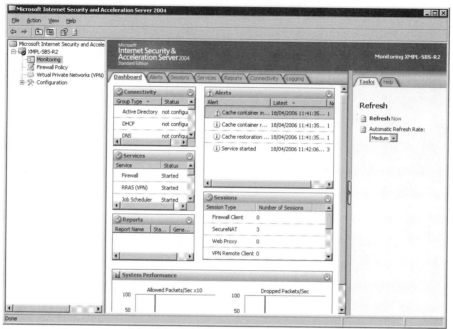

Figure 16-26   The Dashboard is a window onto the various reports and alerts of ISA 2004.

The default installation has some good reports, but they're not actually scheduled to run until you go in and create a reporting schedule. When you do that, you can also have reports e-mailed to you, publish them to a shared folder, and customize exactly which reports are generated how often. To add a new alert or report, change the filtering of sessions, or make other monitoring changes, click the tab in the center pane for the kind of monitoring you want to modify, and then click the Tasks tab in the rightmost pane. You'll have context-sensitive choices that are appropriate to the kind of monitoring you're configuring.

To create a reporting schedule, follow these steps:

1. Open the ISA Server 2004 Management console if it isn't already open.

2. Click Monitoring and then click the Reports tab in the center section.

3. Click Create And Configure Report Jobs to open the Report Job Properties dialog box, shown in Figure 16-27.

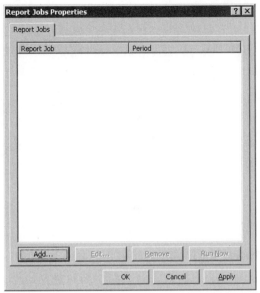

Figure 16-27   The Report Jobs Properties dialog box is empty on a fresh SBS installation.

4. Click Add to open the New Report Job Wizard. Type in a name for the report job and click Next to open the Report Content page of the New Report Job Wizard, shown in Figure 16-28.

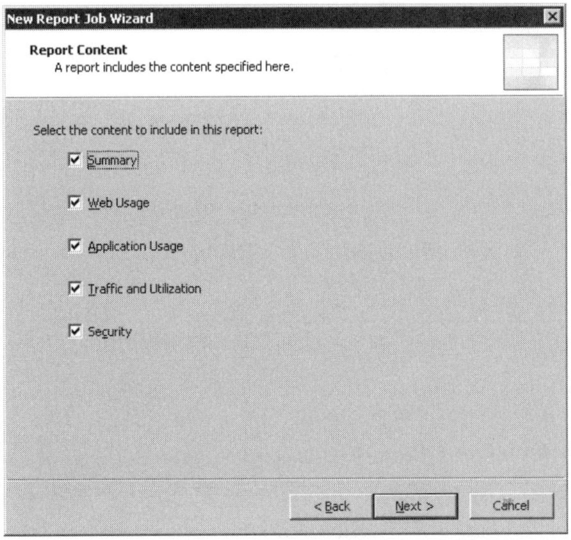

Figure 16-28   The Report Content page of the New Report Job Wizard.

5.   Select the check boxes for the kinds of reports you want to see as part of this sched-ule and then click Next.

6.   On the Report Job Schedule page, specify the reporting interval, and then click Next.

7.   On the Report Publishing page, shown in Figure 16-29, specify a folder to publish the report to, and (optionally) the account that does the publishing if you want to publish your reports to a folder on the server. Click Next.

Note   If you need to access the report from a client computer using an e-mail link, you should specify the publishing folder using a UNC path as shown in Figure 16-29.

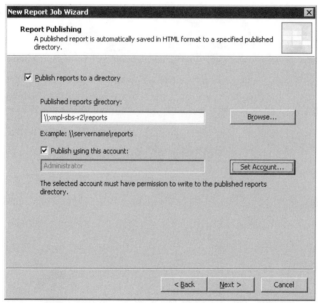

Figure 16-29   The Report Publishing page of the New Report Job Wizard.

8.   On the Send E-mail Notification page, you can specify the details to use for e-mail notification of reports, as shown in Figure 16-30.

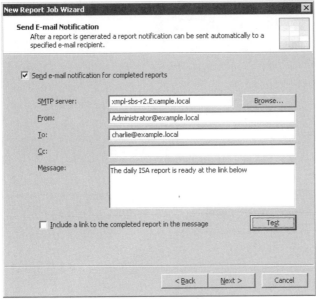

Figure 16-30   The Send E-mail Notification page of the New Report Job Wizard.

9. When you've got your details set for e-mail notification, click Test to verify that everything works as expected. If everything is working, click Next and then click Finish to create the report job schedule.

10. Click OK when you've added all the report jobs you want to add and then click Apply on the main Reports page when you're done to actually implement the schedule.

Summary

The ISA Server 2004 included as part of the Premium Edition gives Windows Small Business Server 2003 a full-featured, robust, and flexible Internet firewall. In this chapter, we covered configuring, administering, and monitoring your ISA Server installation.

In Chapter 17, "Using Group Policy," we cover how to use Group Policy to fine-tune the behavior and permissions of your SBS network.

Chapter 17
Using Group Policy

Group Policy Objects. 444
Managing Group Policies 444
Creating a Group Policy Object 450
Deleting a Group Policy Object. 451
Managing Group Policy Links 452
Refreshing Group Policy 455
Backing Up a Group Policy Object 456
Restoring a Group Policy Object 457
Delegating Permissions on a GPO. 457
Predicting Group Policy Outcomes. 459
Summary 463

In one form or another, Group Policy is all about security. The policies in place after installation include rules about logons, software installation, passwords, and other settings that have an effect on how safe your network will be. You probably won't need to change most of these settings. However, you do need to know how the policies work, how to make changes, and how to configure new policies for your particular circumstances.

The configuration of intelligent security policies has the serendipitous effect of potentially increasing productivity by providing a barrier against those great time-wasters: the accidental loss of vital folders, deletion of files, and the inadvertent introduction of viruses and other malicious software to the network. Group Policy also helps the cause of productivity by making it easier for users to find what they need to work efficiently.

Like many very powerful tools, Group Policy can be challenging to work with. It's often tricky to get the results you want without making unintended changes. Proceed with caution, and document every change so that you can undo it if necessary.

Group Policy Objects

A collection of policy settings is called a Group Policy Object (GPO). A GPO contains policies that affect computers and policies that affect users. Computer-related policies include computer security settings, application settings, and computer startup and shutdown scripts. User-related policies define application settings, folder redirection, assigned and published applications, user logon and logoff scripts, and user security settings. In cases of conflicting policies, the convention is that computer-related settings override user-related settings.

Note   Group Policy is the successor to the System Policy Editor in Windows NT and was first introduced in Windows 2000.

In a GPO, most settings have three possible states: enabled, disabled, and not configured.

Group policies are inherited and cumulative. When you associate a GPO with an Active Directory container, the Group Policy is applied to all computer and user accounts in the container.

Managing Group Policies

The Group Policy Management Console (GPMC) provides a comprehensive overview of Group Policy across the enterprise in a single console. All Group Policy management tasks can be performed in the GPMC except configuring individual policies in GPOs. When you want to configure individual policies, the GPMC will launch the Group Policy Object Editor with the policy loaded.

The GPMC adds the following features not available in the Group Policy Object Editor:

■ Back up and restore Group Policy objects.

■ Import and export GPOs and Windows Management Instrumentation (WMI) filters.

■ Copy and paste GPOs and Windows Management Instrumentation (WMI) filters

■ Manage Group Policy–related security more easily.

■ Generate HTML reports for GPO settings and Resultant Set of Policy (RSoP) data.

To start Group Policy Management Console, select Group Policy Management from the Administrative Tools menu.

Table 17-1 lists old and new ways to perform some common Group Policy tasks.

Table 17-1   Performing familiar tasks with and without the GPMC

Task	Before Group Policy Management Console	With the Group Policy Management Console
Create a Group Policy Object (GPO).	Click the Group Policy Properties tab for a site, domain, or organizational unit (OU) and select New.	Open the GPMC and navigate to Group Policy Objects in the console pane. Right-click Group Policy Objects and select New.
Create a GPO and a link to it.	On the Group Policy tab for a site, domain, or OU, click New.	In the GPMC, right-click the domain, site, or OU and select Create; And Link A GPO Here. For more information, see "Creating a Group Policy Object" later in this chapter.
Create an unlinked GPO.	Go to the Group Policy Properties tab for a site, domain, or OU and click Add.	Open the GPMC and navigate to Group Policy Objects, right-click Group Policy Objects and select New. For more information, see "Creating a Group Policy Object" later in this chapter.
Edit a GPO.	Navigate to the Group Policy Properties tab for the relevant domain, site, or OU. Select the GPO and then click Edit.	Open the GPMC, navigate to Group Policy Objects, right-click the GPO, and then click Edit. The Group Policy Object Editor will open with the GPO loaded. For more information, see "Creating a Group Policy Object" later in this chapter.
Link an existing GPO to a site, domain, or OU.	Go to the Group Policy properties tab for a site, domain, or OU, click Add and then select a GPO.	In the GPMC, navigate to a site, domain, or OU, right-click it, and then click Link An Existing GPO.

Table 17-1 Performing familiar tasks with and without the GPMC (Continued)

Task	Before Group Policy Management Console	With the Group Policy Management Console
Disable a branch of a GPO.	Navigate to the Group Policy Properties tab for the relevant domain, site, or OU. Make your selection on the General tab.	Open the GPMC and navigate to the GPO. Right-click on the GPO, point to GPO Status, and make your selection. See "Disabling a Branch of a GPO" later in this chapter for more information.
Use security groups to filter the scope of policy.	Open the GPO in the Group Policy Object Editor. Right-click the GPO, click Properties and then click the Security tab.	In the GPMC, click a GPO or GPO Link and click the Scope tab. Use the Add and Remove buttons to set the groups, users, and computers to which the GPO applies. For more information, see "Setting the Scope of the GPO" later in this chapter.
Delegate permission on a GPO.	Navigate to the properties of a GPO and click the Security tab. In the Permissions for Authenticated Users pane, select the permissions you want to grant.	In the GPMC, click the GPO, click the Delegation tab, and then click the Add or Remove buttons. For more information, see "Delegating Permissions on a GPO" later in this chapter.
Determine the results of current Group Policy settings on a computer.	In the Resultant Set of Policy snap-in, right-click Resultant Set Of Policy, then select Generate RSoP Data. Select Logging Mode or Planning Mode in the Resultant Set of Policy Wizard.	In the GPMC, right-click Group Policy Results, and then click Group Policy Results Wizard. For more information, see "Predicting Group Policy Outcomes" later in this chapter.

Under the Hood   Components of Group Policy

Group Policy is an abstraction consisting of two parts, a Group Policy Container (GPC) and a Group Policy Template (GPT). Both parts are contained in a Group Policy Object (GPO). The GPO is what we work with directly. The GPO contains all the settings that can apply to users and computers. When those settings are changed, the changes are made to the GPO. The two components of the GPO exist in different places.

The GPC is the Active Directory component of the GPO and includes subcontainers with version information, status information, and a list of which Group Policy extensions are employed in the GPO. It also contains some information used by clients, such as the software installation policy.

The GPT is a set of files in the SYSVOL folder on the server. When you create a GPO, the corresponding GPT folder structure is created automatically. The actual name of the folder for the GPT is the *globally unique identifier* (GUID) for the GPO—a number that is useful to the computer but is otherwise incomprehensible. To see the policy folder, look in %SystemRoot%\SYSVOL\sysvol\domain_name\policies. But *do not* change this folder in any way. Work on Group Policy through the Group Policy Management Console.

Order of Inheritance

As a rule, Group Policy settings are passed from parent containers down to child containers. This practice means that a policy that is applied to a parent container applies to all the containers—including users and computers—that are below the parent container in the Active Directory tree hierarchy. However, if you specifically assign a Group Policy for a child container that contradicts the parent container policy, the child container's policy overrides the parent Group Policy.

If policies are not contradictory, both can be implemented. For example, if a parent container policy calls for an application shortcut to be on a user's desktop, and the child container policy calls for another application shortcut, both appear. Policy settings that are disabled are inherited as disabled. Policy settings that are not configured in the parent container remain unconfigured.

Overriding Inheritance

Several options are available for changing how inheritance is processed. One option, called enforcing the GPO link, prevents child containers from overriding any policy setting set in a higher level GPO. This option is not set by default and must be turned on in each GPO where it's wanted.

Enforcing a GPO Link in the GPMC

To enforce a link, open the Group Policy Management Console, right-click the Group Policy Object link in the console tree, and select Enforced from the shortcut menu, as shown in Figure 17-1.

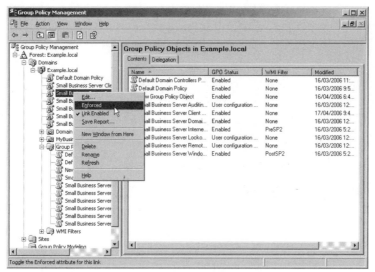

Figure 17-1   Preventing inheritance from overriding settings on a GPO.

A second option is Block Inheritance. When you select this option, the child container does not inherit any policies from parent containers. If there is a conflict between these two options, the Enforced option always takes precedence.

Simply stated, Enforced is a link property, Block Inheritance is a container property, and Enforced takes precedence over Block Inheritance.

Setting Block Inheritance

To enable Block Inheritance, open the Group Policy Management Console and right-click the domain or organizational unit (OU) for which you want to block inheritance. Select Block Inheritance, as shown in Figure 17-2.

Order of Implementation

Group policies are processed in the following order:

1. Local group policy object

2. GPOs linked to the site, in the order specified by the administrator

3. Domain GPOs, as specified by the administrator

4. OU Group Policy objects, from largest to smallest OU (parent to child OU)

The GPO with the lowest link order is processed last, and therefore has the highest precedence. If multiple GPOs attempt contradictory settings, the GPO with highest precedence wins.

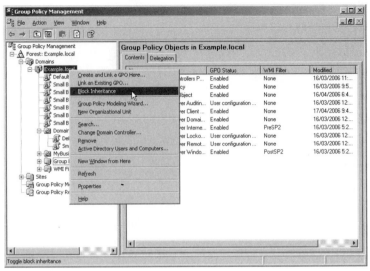

Figure 17-2   Setting Block Inheritance for a domain.

Exceptions to this order are GPOs with enforced or disabled links, GPOs with disabled user or computer settings, and OUs (or the whole domain) set to block inheritance.

To see the order of precedence for GPOs for a domain or OU, open Group Policy Management and in the console tree, select the domain name or the OU. In the details pane, click the Group Policy Inheritance tab, as shown in Figure 17-3.

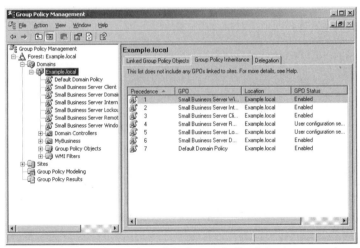

Figure 17-3   Viewing a domain's Group Policy inheritance order.

To change the order of precedence, click the Linked Group Policy Object tab, select the link you want to move, and use the up and down arrows to change the order.

Important Do not rename the OUs under Active Directory Users And Computers. In particular, be sure to avoid moving computers from SBSComputers and users from SBSUsers. If you do, Group Policy is only one of many processes that will not work properly afterward.

Creating a Group Policy Object

The installation of Windows Small Business Server creates an Active Directory domain that includes a default domain policy, a default Domain Controllers policy, and several policies specifically for Small Business Server. When you need to set up a GPO of your own, follow these steps:

1. Select Group Policy Management from the Administrative Tools menu and navigate to the container to which you want the new GPO to apply.

2. Right-click the domain, site, or OU and select Create And Link A GPO Here from the shortcut menu.

3. In the New GPO dialog box, enter a name for the Group Policy Object and click OK.

4. Right-click the new GPO and select Edit to launch the Group Policy Object Editor.

5. Specify settings for the GPO. When you're finished, close the Group Policy Object Editor.

6. In the Group Policy Management Console, right-click the domain name or the OU this GPO is to be associated with, and select Link An Existing GPO from the shortcut menu.

7. In the Select GPO dialog box, select the GPO to link and click OK.

   To shorten the process by one step, you can also right-click the domain or OU and select Create And Link A GPO Here.

Note Try to keep the total number of GPOs as low as possible. The processing of each GPO takes time, and too many objects can slow logons and logoffs. The number of settings within a GPO doesn't matter—it's the total number of GPOs.

Note   Avoid making changes to the default GPOs. Create new GPOs that can be enabled, disabled, or modified easily. If you do need to make changes to an existing policy, back it up first.

Under the Hood   Inside the Group Policy Object Editor

When you create a new GPO or edit an existing one, the Group Policy Object Editor is automatically launched. In the console tree, two nodes—Computer Configuration and User Configuration—display. Under each node are extensions for Software Settings, Windows Settings, and Administrative Templates.

Use the Computer Configuration folders to customize policies for computers on the network. These policies go into effect when the computer is turned on and the operating system starts. Settings in these folders apply to any user who logs on to the computer. For example, if you have computers in a training room for which you want to enforce a strict environment, the Computer Configuration node is where you configure those settings.

The User Configuration node contains settings for customizing environments or setting policies for users on the network. User Configuration policies come into play when a specific user logs on to the network.

Deleting a Group Policy Object

To delete a GPO, right-click it in the Group Policy Management Console and select Delete from the shortcut menu. When you delete a GPO, all links to the GPO will also be deleted. Be sure that you are logged on with an account that has sufficient permissions.

Neither the Default Domain Policy nor the Default Domain Controllers Policy can be deleted.

Real World   Using Group Policy Scripts

Scripts dealing with everyday tasks are included with Group Policy Management Console. They're located in Program Files\GPMC\Scripts. Although the script names are generally self-explanatory, enter *scriptname /?* at a command prompt to

see the parameters for using the script. For example, enter
SetGPOCreationPermissions /? at a command prompt and this dialog box opens:

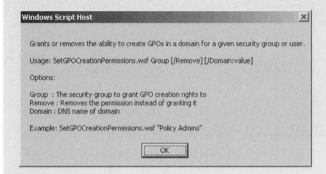

The scripts execute from the command line using Cscript.exe, so to run SetGPOCreationPermissions.wsf and thereby allow a designated group to create GPOs, you type

```
cscript \"program files"\GPMC\Scripts\SetGPOCreationPermissions.wsf
"Group Name"
```

Press Enter and the Command Prompt window displays the following output:

```
C:\>cscript \"program files"\gpmc\scripts\SetGPOCreationPermissions.wsf "Finance Operators"
Microsoft (R) Windows Script Host Version 5.6
Copyright (C) Microsoft Corporation 1996-2001. All rights reserved.

Added 'Finance Operators' as having GPO creation rights in example.local.

C:\>_
```

Many of the scripts require the library file Lib_CommonGPMCFunctions.js to operate. If you move or copy scripts to another location, move a copy of this file to the same location.

Managing Group Policy Links

With numerous GPOs on a network, it's important to keep track of GPO links within the domain. To find out what links exist for a particular GPO, follow these steps:

1. Select Group Policy Management from the Administrative Tools menu.

2. Right-click the domain name in the console tree and select Search from the shortcut menu.

3. In the Search Item drop-down list, select GPO-links.

4. Click Add and then click Search.

5. In the Search Results box shown in Figure 17-4, double-click a GPO to view its links and other settings.

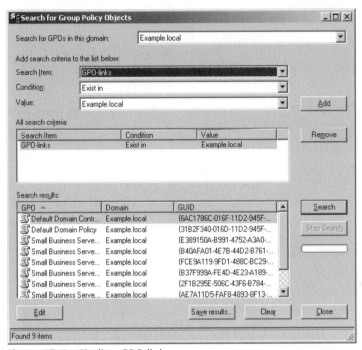

Figure 17-4   Finding GPO links.

Setting the Scope of the GPO

A GPO applies to all the users and computers in the container with which the GPO is associated. Most GPOs default to applying to Authenticated Users—namely, everyone who can log on to the network. Inevitably, there are GPOs that should apply only to some. To filter the application of a GPO, follow these steps:

■ Select Group Policy Management from the Administrative Tools menu.

■ Select the Group Policy Object you want to filter and click the Scope tab.

■ On the Scope tab in the Security Filtering section, click Add and locate the groups or users who should have the policy applied to them, as shown in Figure 17-5. Make your selection and click OK twice.

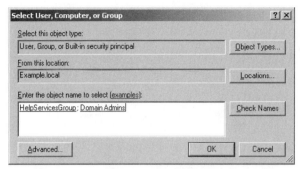

Figure 17-5   Selecting the groups or users to which the GPO applies.

■ If Authenticated Users appears in the Security Filtering list on the Scope page, select it and click Remove. This ensures that the GPO is applied only to the groups or users you added.

Enabling and Disabling GPO Links

To check or change the status of a GPO link, follow these steps:

1. Select Group Policy Management from the Administrative Tools menu.

2. In the console tree, navigate to the Group Policy Objects under your domain name and select the GPO.

3. On the Scope tab, links are listed and the status of the link is shown under Link Enabled. To change the status, right-click the link and select Link Enabled from the shortcut menu, as shown in Figure 17-6.

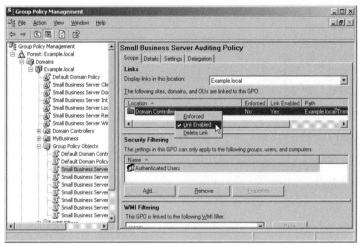

Figure 17-6   A check mark shows that the link is enabled.

Disabling a Branch of a GPO

If a GPO has an entire node under User Configuration or Computer Configuration that's not configured, disable the node to avoid processing those settings. This speeds startup and logon for all users subject to that GPO. To disable a node, open the Group Policy Management Console and follow these steps:

1. In the console tree, navigate to the domain or organizational unit which contains the GPO.

2. Double-click the domain or OU.

3. Right-click the GPO that contains the user or computer settings you want to disable, point to GPO Status, and then choose from the following actions:

   ❑ Click User Configuration Settings Disabled to disable user settings for the GPO.

   ❑ Click Computer Configuration Settings Disabled to disable computer settings for the GPO.

A check mark next to User Configuration Settings Disabled or Computer Configuration Settings Disabled indicates that the option is currently selected.

Refreshing Group Policy

Policy changes are immediate, but they are not instantly propagated to clients. Client computers request policy only when one of the following occurs:

■ The computer starts.

■ A user logs on.

■ An application requests a refresh.

■ A user requests a refresh.

■ A Group Policy refresh interval is enabled and the interval has elapsed.

By default, Group Policy refreshes in the background every 90 minutes with a random offset of 0 through 30 minutes added so that not all computers request a refresh at the same time.

To change the Group Policy refresh interval, follow these steps:

1. Select Group Policy Management from the Administrative Tools menu.

2. To add the setting to an existing GPO, right-click the GPO and select Edit. To create a new GPO, right-click the domain name or OU and select Create And Link A GPO

Here. Supply a name for the new GPO, right-click it in Group Policy Management Console, and select Edit.

3. In the console tree, expand Computer Configuration, Administrative Templates, System, and then select Group Policy.

4. In the details pane, double-click Group Policy Refresh Interval For Computers.

5. On the Settings tab, select Enabled, then supply the new settings. Click OK when finished.

Don't make the interval very short because of the large amount of network traffic generated by each refresh.

Because policy can be set at several levels, when you look at a policy object, what you see is both local policy and the policy in effect on the system. Local policy and actual policy in effect may not be synonymous if the computer is inheriting settings from domain-level policies. If you make a policy setting and it isn't reflected in effective policy, a policy from the domain is overriding your setting.

It's also possible that the policy change hasn't been refreshed since the change was made. To force a policy refresh for the local computer, open a Command Prompt window and type:

```
gpupdate [/target:{computer | user}] /force
```

Note   For details about the update parameters, open a Command Prompt window and type *gpupdate /?*.

Backing Up a Group Policy Object

A valuable feature, new in the Group Policy Management Console, is the ability to back up and restore GPOs. Include regular backup of all GPOs as part of your overall planning-for-disaster strategy. To back up a GPO, follow these steps:

1. Open Group Policy Management. In the console tree, navigate to Group Policy Objects in the domain that contains the GPO to be backed up.

   ❑ To back up a single GPO, right-click the GPO and select Back Up from the shortcut menu.

   ❑ To back up all GPOs in the domain, right-click Group Policy Objects and select Back Up All.

2. In the Back Up Group Policy Object dialog box, type the path to the backup location and then click Back Up.

3. After the operation completes, click OK.

Note Because the only reason to back up GPOs—or anything else, for that matter—is to protect data that might have to be restored one day, be sure that the backup folder is secure and can be accessed only by authorized administrators.

Restoring a Group Policy Object

Using the GPMC, you can restore GPOs that have been backed up. If you back up all the GPOs in a container, you can restore all of them, some of them, or one at a time.

To restore backed-up Group Policy objects, follow these steps:

1. Open the Group Policy Management Console. In the console tree, navigate to Group Policy Objects in the domain that contains the GPO that you want to restore.

2. To restore a previous version of an existing GPO or to restore a deleted GPO, right-click Group Policy Objects and select Manage Backups.

3. In the Manage Backups dialog box, select the GPO to restore and click Restore.

    When you have a lot of GPOs to sort through, select the check box that allows you to display only the latest versions of the backed-up GPOs. If you're unsure of which GPO to restore, highlight them one at a time and click View Settings.

Delegating Permissions on a GPO

Some very complex networks may require that part of the responsibility for Group Policy be delegated to others. If you're considering handing off some of the work, bear these issues in mind:

- If permission is set to inherit to all child containers, authority delegated at the domain level will affect all objects in the domain.

- Permissions granted at the OU level can affect only that unit or that unit plus its child OUs.

- Control delegated at the site level is likely to span domains and can influence objects in domains other than the domain where the GPO is located.

- Always assign control at the highest OU level possible.

Just about every chore connected with Group Policy can be delegated, including creating, editing, and managing Group Policy Objects. However, the right to edit, delete, or modify security is delegated separately from the right to link GPOs. And both of those are separate from permission to create GPOs.

Delegating Permission to Create

Open the GPMC and navigate to Group Policy Objects in the console tree. Click the Delegation tab, shown in Figure 17-7, and then click Add to identify the user or group you want to permit to create GPOs.

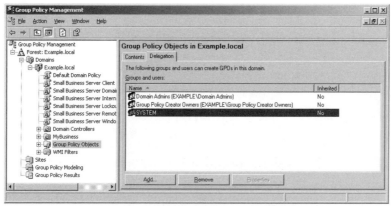

Figure 17-7   Viewing the delegation settings of a GPO.

Delegating Permission to Link

Open the GPMC and select the domain in the console tree. In the details pane, click the Delegation tab. In the drop-down list select Link GPOs and click Add to identify the user or group you want to give link permission to.

Delegating Permission to Edit, Delete, or Modify Security

Open the GPMC and navigate to the domain. In the console tree, select the specific GPO. In the details pane, click the Delegation tab. Click Add to locate the user or group. In the Add Group Or User dialog box, shown in Figure 17-8, select the range of permissions you want to delegate.

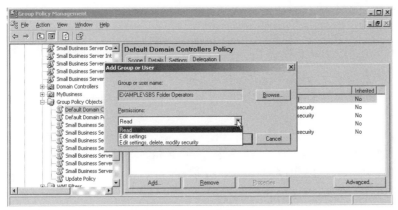

Figure 17-8   Choosing permissions to delegate.

Predicting Group Policy Outcomes

Because of the complexity of inheritances, user versus computer configuration, and a host of other variables, foreseeing the outcome of any policy change is usually not possible. Two tools in Windows Small Business Server can help you keep out of deep water: Group Policy Modeling and Group Policy Results.

Group Policy Modeling

The Group Policy Modeling tool lets you simulate a policy deployment and see the results. (Group Policy Modeling is essentially the same as Resultant Set of Policy planning mode on earlier versions of Windows Small Business Server).

To use Group Policy Modeling, complete the following steps:

1. Select Group Policy Management from the Administrative Tools menu.

2. Right-click Group Policy Modeling in the console tree and select Group Policy Modeling Wizard.

3. On the Domain Controller Selection page, your Windows Small Business Server domain controller is selected. Click Next.

4. On the User And Computer Selection page, you can select from the following combinations:

    ❑ A container with user information combined with a computer container

    ❑ A container with user information combined with a specific computer

    ❑ A single user and a computer container

    ❑ A single user and a specific computer

❑ A computer container alone

❑ A specific computer alone

❑ A user container alone

❑ A specific user alone

5. On the Advanced Simulation Options page, select any advanced simulation options to include.

6. If you specified a user or user container, the User Security Groups page appears, showing group membership. To see the results of changes to group membership, add or remove groups from the list.

7. On the Alternate Active Directory Paths page, you can simulate changes to the network location.

8. If you specified a computer or computer container, the Computer Security Groups page appears. You can change the security group memberships for the computer or computer container you're modeling.

9. WMI Filters For Users or WMI Filters For Computers page allows the specification of particular Windows Management Instrumentation filters to include.

10. Review the settings on the Summary Of Selections page, shown in Figure 17-9. Click Next. When Group Policy Modeling is complete, click Finish.

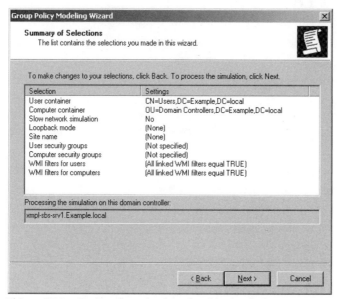

Figure 17-9 Review the selections for this simulation.

The report is generated and appears in the console tree under Group Policy Modeling. In the details pane, the Summary tab shows the applied and denied GPOs and the simulated group memberships.

Click the Settings tab to review the policies that apply to this simulation, what the settings are, and the GPO that determines each setting. The Query tab summarizes the settings that the report is based on.

Right-click the name of the saved report and select Rerun Query to run it again after you've made changes.

Under the Hood   WMI Filters

Windows Management Instrumentation (WMI) allows the dynamic checking of the scope of a GPO. When a GPO linked to a WMI filter is applied on a computer, the filter is evaluated. If the filter evaluates to false, the GPO is not applied. If the filter evaluates to true, the GPO is applied—except on Windows 2000 computers, which ignore the filter altogether and always apply the GPO.

WMI filtering applies only to computers running Windows Server 2003 and Windows XP and is really designed for very large networks, so using it in a Windows Small Business Server environment is like using a cannon to ring a doorbell.

If you want to read up on WMI filters, select Help And Support from the Start menu and search for WMI filters.

Group Policy Results

Use the Group Policy Results tool to determine current policy settings for a specific user or computer. To use Group Policy Results, complete the following steps:

1. Select Group Policy Management from the Administrative Tools menu.

2. Right-click Group Policy Results in the console tree and select Group Policy Results Wizard.

3. On the Computer Selection page, you must specify the computer to use. You can select the option to display only the user policy settings and not display the policy settings for the computer, as shown in Figure 17-10.

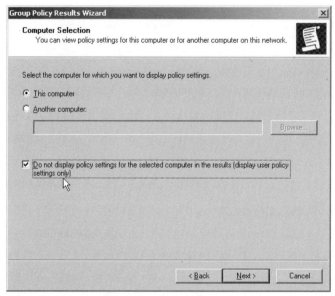

Figure 17-10   On the Computer Selection page, choose whether you want to view only user policy settings.

4. On the User Selection page, specify a user. On this page, you can select the option to report just the computer settings and not the user policy settings.

5. On the Summary Of Selections page, the summary of your selections is displayed. Click Next and then click Finish to generate a Group Policy Results report.

6. The report is generated and appears in the console tree under Group Policy Results. In the details pane, the Summary tab shows the applied and denied GPOs and the actual group memberships.

7. Click the Settings tab to review applied policies, what the settings are, and the GPO that determines each setting.

Real World   The MyBusiness OU

Much of the way SBS works, and the special GPOs that do the heavy lifting, are based around the special MyBusiness OU that SBS creates. Users and Groups are in the SBSUsers OU, which is part of the MyBusiness OU, client computers are part of SBSComputers OU, which is part of the MyBusiness OU, and server computers are part of SBSServers OU, which is part of the MyBusiness OU. Worse, the SBSUsers OU is actually nested inside the Users OU, which is nested inside the MyBusiness OU. SBSComputers and SBSServers are both nested within the Computers OU, which is nested in MyBusiness. Even distribution groups and security groups are in special OUs nested within the MyBusiness OU.

All this nesting and these special OUs can be disconcerting for system administrators who are more used to regular Windows Server 2003. If you are comfortable with regular Windows Server 2003 and Active Directory already, you might be inclined to want to start changing things around inside here. Resist the temptation! Changing the nesting, or renaming OUs or moving things around is likely to cause unexpected side effects. Because of the way SBS is so tightly integrated to this structure, you're far better off just leaving it alone.

The other part of that, of course, is that to fully take advantage of all the special GPOs and integration of SBS, you *need* to use the wizards to create users and computers. While it's certainly technically possible, for example, to manually create users directly from Active Directory Users and Computers, or even from the command line, it's hard to get all the settings where they should be and where SBS can take full advantage of them.

Summary

For a network to be considered successful, it must not only make needed information readily accessible, but also keep other information secure and protected. This chapter has explored some of the Group Policy options available for achieving those goals.

In the next chapter, we move on to editing, managing, and customizing a SharePoint site, which can be a valuable resource without requiring advanced Web skills.

Chapter 18

Customizing a SharePoint Web Site

Getting Familiar with Windows SharePoint Services 466

Changing the Appearance of the Site 471

Changing Home Page Content 472

Customizing Pages. 474

Administering a SharePoint Web Site. 477

Administering SharePoint Virtual Servers 482

Using FrontPage 2003 to Customize Windows SharePoint Services. . . . 485

Backup and Restore of a SharePoint Site 491

Summary 493

Microsoft Windows Small Business Server 2003 automatically creates a Microsoft Windows SharePoint Services Web site (*http://companyweb*) during installation. This Web site provides a central location for employees to collaborate and share information. Consider it a bulletin board, digitized and turbo-boosted.

You don't need to do anything special to get started using Windows SharePoint Services. By default, all domain users are given Web Designer privileges, which let them view the site, upload information, and change the design of the site. The site is accessible from the internal network and also from the Internet via the Remote Web Workplace (which requires a secure logon), if you enabled this when configuring your Internet connection.

This chapter gives you an overview of the default Windows SharePoint Services Web site, and then shows you how to edit, manage, and customize the site using Microsoft Office FrontPage 2003. For more sophisticated design work, you'll probably want to hire a professional developer.

Getting Familiar with Windows SharePoint Services

Familiarizing yourself with the default *http://companyweb* SharePoint site is helpful regardless of whether you're a company employee or an independent network consultant. (In fact, network consultants will be very happy about the Help Desk list.) Let's start by connecting to the default *http://companyweb* shown in Figure 18-1.

Figure 18-1 The default companyweb site.

Note The SharePoint Web site officially works best with Microsoft Internet Explorer 6 or later. It works fine in other browsers as well, though you should test your site first so that you understand where any differences are.

Under the Hood   Companyweb vs. SharePoint

The default SharePoint site on an SBS network is, of course, the *http://companyweb* site. At first glance it appears to be simply a default Windows SharePoint Services (WSS) Team site, but there are key areas of differences:

- Document libraries
- Photo libraries
- Lists

Document Libraries

The default WSS team site includes a basic Shared Documents library. For the companyweb site, we have General Documents, Projects, Presentations, and Archived Documents libraries. The difference, however, is purely superficial—you could create the exact same set of libraries on a WSS team site using the default Document Library template.

The document library that *is* a bit different is the Incoming Faxes library. This is a customized document library that the SBS Shared Fax feature works with.

Photo Libraries

The default WSS team site doesn't include any photo libraries. But it does include a default Photo Library template. On the SBS companyweb site, the default Company Photos library is built with the default Photo Library template.

Lists

The default WSS team site includes a Contacts list and a Tasks list. The companyweb site doesn't have either of these lists, but instead has a Help Desk and a Vacation Calendar. The Help Desk list is just a customized list based on the Issues List Template, and the Vacation Calendar is simply an Events List.

Understanding SharePoint Items

A SharePoint Web site contains several types of items:

- **Document and Picture Libraries** Web pages that make it easy to view, upload, and organize documents of all sorts (spreadsheets, presentations, pictures, faxes, and other Web pages), as shown in Figure 18-2.

- **Lists** Web pages that contain postings by users in the same way newsgroups do. (However, lists are not threaded for conversations as newsgroups are.) Some sample lists are Announcements, Help Desk, Links, and Vacation Calendar (which works a little differently from the other lists by also presenting the information in calendar form).

- **Discussion Boards** Web pages that are set up to very closely mimic newsgroups—users can carry on threaded conversations, as shown in Figure 18-3.

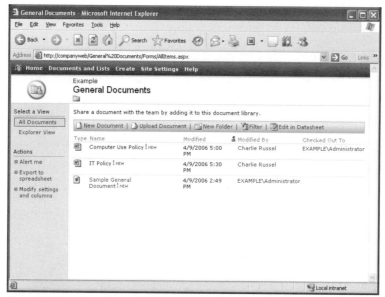

Figure 18-2   The General Documents page.

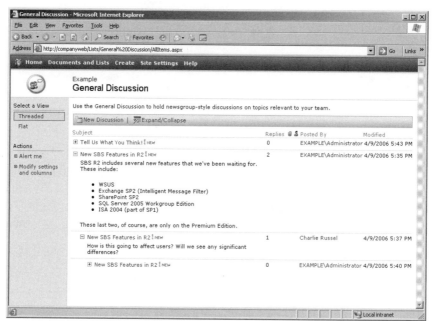

Figure 18-3   The General Discussion page.

■ **Surveys**   Web pages designed to poll users on topics of your choice.

Interacting with a SharePoint Site

You can interact with pages on a SharePoint site in a number of ways:

- **Change the view**   Each item on a SharePoint site can be viewed in a number of different ways, depending on the item (similar to the Views feature in Microsoft Windows Explorer). For example, documents can be viewed in the All Documents or Explorer View; Picture Libraries can be viewed in Details, Thumbnails, Filmstrip, or Explorer View. The Details view is shown in Figure 18-4.

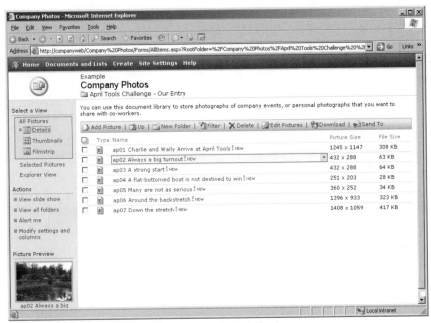

Figure 18-4   The Company Photos page in Details view.

- **Add items**   Create or upload new messages, documents, or pictures by using the New Document and Upload Document options, or by clicking the similarly named buttons prominently placed on each page of the site. When you create a new document from a SharePoint site, it will automatically open Microsoft Office Word, if it's installed, and save the document back to the SharePoint site when you close it.

- **Check out items**   Documents and pictures can be easily checked out, enabling multiple users to collaborate on a document. Checking out a document prevents other users from modifying it until the document is checked back in. To check out a file, move the mouse over the file name, click the down arrow next to the file name, and then choose Check Out from the pop-up menu. Check in documents the same way.

■ **Get alerted to changes**   Click the Alert Me link in the Actions section of a page to create alerts that notify you of changes made to the item.

■ **Import and export files**   Many pages in the SharePoint Web site allow you to export data to Microsoft Office Excel by clicking the Edit In Datasheet button or clicking the Export To Spreadsheet link. You must have Excel installed to use these options. You can also import Calendar items and Contacts from Outlook or export them to Outlook.

■ **Discuss pages and documents**   Click the Discuss toolbar button in Internet Explorer to write comments about the current page. These comments can then be viewed and replied to by other viewers of the site. (To view comments, the Discuss button must be toggled on, as shown in Figure 18-5.)

> **Note**   The Discussions feature stores comments in a database on the discussion server (the SharePoint Web site), not in the page or document itself.

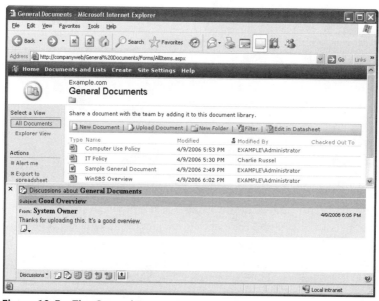

Figure 18-5   The General Documents page showing a comment and the Discussions toolbar, which appears at the bottom of the page.

Changing the Appearance of the Site

Once you're familiar with the default companyweb SharePoint site, you might want to change the way the overall site looks—the visual theme, title, and description. To do so, display the Site Settings page, shown in Figure 18-6, by clicking the Site Settings link at the top of a page in the SharePoint Web site.

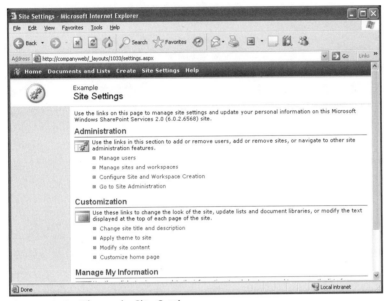

Figure 18-6   The main Site Settings page.

> **Note**   If you're a Value Added Reseller providing Small Business Server–based solutions to your customers, you can add additional features and a custom look and feel to the default companyweb site that you deploy. Once you've made the changes, use Stsadm.exe to save them off as a template for later reuse. See "Backup and Restore of a SharePoint Site" later in this chapter for details.

You can do the following to change the site's appearance:

- **Change the title and description**   Click the Change Site Title And Description link and type the new title and description in the Title and Description boxes. Click OK when you're finished. The title of the site (which is "Your Organization Name" by default) appears on all pages; the site description appears only on the home page.

■ **Apply a theme**   Click the Apply Theme To Site link, select a theme, and then click Apply to change the fonts and color scheme used for the site.

Note   You can add .pdf files to your site, but SharePoint doesn't automatically provide the correct icon for .pdf files. To fix that, check out Microsoft MVP Chad Gross's blog post at *http://msmvps.com/blogs/cgross/archive/2004/10/26/16679.aspx*.

Changing Home Page Content

After customizing the look of the overall SharePoint site, you might want to change the content of the home page to better suit the needs of your users. The home page is made up of several different parts: the Quick Launch link bar, which runs vertically down the left side of the page and contains links to commonly used pages on the site; a link bar across the top of the page, which appears on all pages of the site; and multiple Web Parts in the main body of the page.

Note   A Web Part is a single-purpose component that you can place on a Web page to present data such as images or the current contents of a SharePoint list, or to filter data such as announcements or links.

To change the content of the home page, display the SharePoint home page (*http://companyweb*) and then use the following list:

■ **Add a Web Part**   Click the Modify Shared Page link, choose Add Web Parts from the pop-up menu, and click Browse. Locate the desired Web Part from the Add Web Parts tool pane, shown in Figure 18-7, and then drag it to the desired location on the page. When dragging a Web Part on the page, acceptable locations will be indicated with a blue rectangle appearing around the Web Part. A thick blue line indicates where the top of the Web Part will be positioned. When finished, click the Close button in the top right corner of the Add Web Parts tool pane.

Note   Form Web Parts allow users to filter data from the SharePoint Web site, in essence acting as a search form. Once you have added a Form Web Part to the page, you can connect it to a data source. To connect the form to a data source, click the down arrow in the top right corner of the Web

Part, and then choose Connections, Provide Form Values To, and then the appropriate data source (such as Announcements or Links).

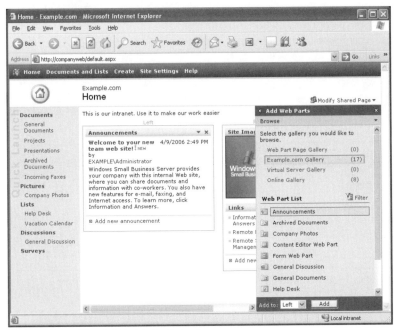

Figure 18-7   The Add Web Parts tool pane.

- **Move Web Parts around**   Switch the page into design mode by clicking the Modify Shared Page link and then selecting Design This Page from the menu. When you are in design mode, gray rectangles appear around each Web Part and a check mark will appear next to the Design This Page option in the pop-up menu. Drag each Web Part to the location you want. To switch off design mode, click Modify Shared Page link and click Design This Page again.

- **Minimize or close a Web Part**   Click the down arrow in the top right corner of the Web Part and choose Minimize or Close from the pop-up menu.

- **Modify a Web Part**   Click the down arrow in the top right corner of the Web Part and choose Modify Shared Web Part from the pop-up menu. A yellow dotted rectangle appears around the Web Part. Use the tool pane shown in Figure 18-8 to change the view, appearance, layout, and other settings related to the Web Part. When finished, click OK.

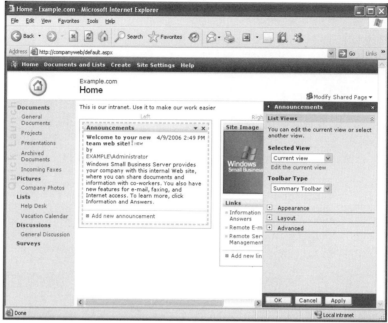

Figure 18-8   Modifying a Web Part.

Note   The Home Page has two views that you can customize. The Shared View is the home page view shared by all users of the site and is displayed by default. Any customizations to this view affect all users. The Personal View, on the other hand, can be customized to suit the preferences of each user because customizations are kept private to that user. To switch between the views, click the Modify Shared Page link and select Shared View or Personal View from the pop-up menu. When you switch to Personal View, some of the option names will change accordingly.

Customizing Pages

The home page isn't the only page on a SharePoint Web site that can be easily customized, though other pages have somewhat different options. To modify other pages, click the Site Settings link at the top of a page in the SharePoint Web site, click the Modify Site Content link, and then click the link corresponding to the item that you want to customize. This displays the Customization page for the specified item, as shown in Figure 18-9 for the General Documents library.

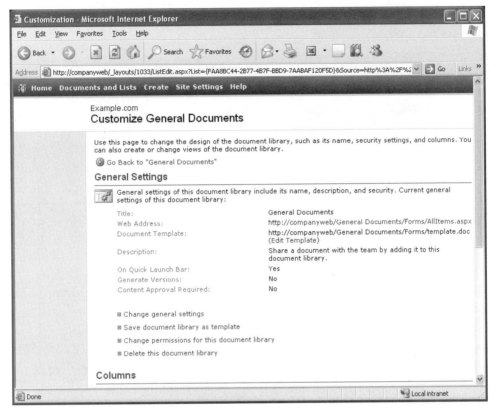

Figure 18-9   The Customization page for the General Documents library.

Note   To create a new item, click the Create link at the top of the SharePoint Web site, click the type of item you want to create, and then provide the general settings for the item.

On the Customization page, you can:

- **Modify settings on pages other than the home page**   Use the Change General Settings link to open the Document Library Settings page, shown in Figure 18-10, which you can use to change the following settings. (Not all settings are available for all item types.)

  ❑ Page name and description.

  ❑ Whether a link to the page appears in the Quick Launch bar.

❏ Whether user-submitted items and files require approval before being posted for general viewing on the site.

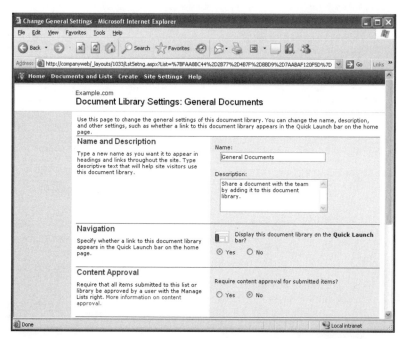

Figure 18-10   The Document Library Settings page for the General Documents library.

Note   Members of the Administrator site group or another site group with Manage Lists rights can accept or reject posted items in a SharePoint page for which content approval is enabled. To do so, open the page, click the Approve/Reject Items view, move the mouse over the item, click the down arrow to the right of the item, and choose Approve/Reject from the pop-up menu. Rejected and Pending items remain on the site until the creator of the items or an Administrator deletes them.

❏ Whether new versions of documents or pictures in the library are created with each edit. When versioning is enabled, users can access older versions of a file by clicking the down arrow next to the item name and choosing Version History. Office 2003 programs also support the Version History command directly from within files saved to a SharePoint library with versioning enabled.

❑   Whether users are allowed to attach files to posted items.

❑   Which permission levels users have for items created by other users.

❑   Which file is used as the template for new files created in the library.

■   **Create a template from the item**   Use the Save Item As Template link to create a template from the current SharePoint item. This allows users to create new items based on the settings from the template.

■   **Alter site group permissions for an item**   Use the Change Permissions For This Item link to alter the permissions each site group of users has for the item. You can also change which level of access to this item anonymous users have, if any, and whether to allow restricted users to request increased access privileges.

Note   Anonymous users can gain access to an item only when anonymous access is enabled on the *http://companyweb* site in Microsoft Internet Information Services (IIS) and anonymous access is enabled for the site in SharePoint Top-Level Site Administration. See the "Managing Site Groups and Access Permissions" section of this chapter for more information.

■   **Delete the item**   Use the Delete This Item link to delete the item and all data (posts, documents, and so on) stored within it. You probably don't need to be told to be careful with this.

■   **Make columns and views available for the item**   In the Columns and Views sections use the available links to modify which columns and views are available in the item.

Administering a SharePoint Web Site

Administrating a SharePoint Web site covers managing users and permissions, statistics and content management, the site collection galleries, and the administration of the site collection, as shown in Figure 18-11.

Note   You can also administer SharePoint from the command line using the Stsadm.exe command-line tool (C:\Program Files\Common Files\Microsoft Shared\Web server extensions\60\BIN\Stsadm.exe).

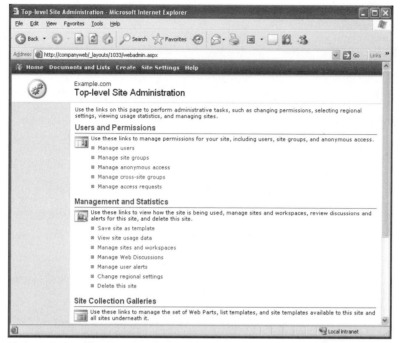

Figure 18-11   The Top-Level Site Administration page.

Managing Site Users

Active Directory user accounts are given differing levels of access and change permissions on a SharePoint Web site depending on their SharePoint site group membership. (You must have a user account in Active Directory to use a SharePoint site.) To manage users, click the Manage Users link in the Top-Level Site Administration page. This displays a list of users that you can administer, as described in the following list:

- To remove SharePoint site access permissions from a user, select the check box next to the user and click Remove Selected Users. (This doesn't delete the user's account in Active Directory.)

- To change the SharePoint site group memberships for the user, select the check box next to the user and click Edit Site Groups Of Selected Users.

- To add an Active Directory user account that doesn't have permissions on the SharePoint Site, complete the following steps:

    ❑ Click Add Users. This displays the Add Users page, shown in Figure 18-12.

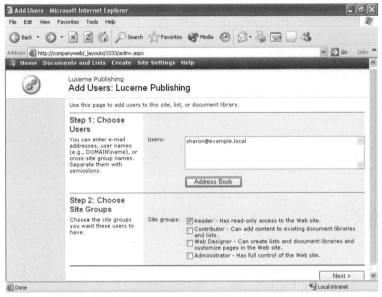

Figure 18-12   The Add Users page.

❑ Type the user's e-mail address (or click Address Book to find the user in your Address Book), specify which site groups the user should belong to, and then click Next.

❑ In the second Add User page, optionally modify the user name and display name of the user, and then customize the e-mail that is sent to the user inviting them to participate in the SharePoint Web site. Click Finish when you're finished.

Under the Hood   Site Groups and Rights

The groups used by SharePoint are called *site groups*. They are used to assign rights to users and have no direct comparison to Active Directory groups. The five site groups are:

- **Guest**   An implicit site group to which users are added by granting them access to an item or page without adding them to the list of site users. As such, they can only access the items to which they are explicitly given access. This site group is never seen and can't be deleted.

- **Reader**   This site group gives members read-only access to the site, though if Self-Service Site Creation is enabled on the virtual server (it's not by default), users with Reader rights can create new sites (in which they are given Administrator rights).

- **Contributor**   This site group gives members Reader rights plus the ability to add content to existing items.

- **Web Designer**   This site group gives members Contributor rights plus the ability to create new items and customize existing items. Active Directory Domain Users and Mobile Users are automatically members of this site group on an SBS SharePoint site.

- **Administrator**   This site group is the typical administrator group—members have full control of the site and can create and delete additional sites as well. Active Directory Domain Administrators and Domain Power Users are automatically members of this site group on an SBS SharePoint site.

Managing Site Groups and Access Permissions

To change SharePoint site group memberships, enable anonymous access, or deny users the ability to request access to items they don't have permission to access, use the Users And Permissions section of the Top-Level Site Administration page, as discussed in the following list:

- To add or delete site groups, click the Manage Site Groups link.

- To add or delete cross-site groups, which have permissions on all SharePoint sites created on the virtual server, click the Manage Cross-Site Groups link.

- To enable anonymous access to the site, first enable anonymous access to the *http://companyweb* site in IIS (as discussed in Chapter 19, "Managing an Intranet Web Server"), then click Manage Anonymous Access and use the Change Anonymous Access Settings page, shown in Figure 18-13, to control what anonymous users should be able to access. You'll still have to explicitly enable anonymous access on each item, as described in the "Customizing Pages" section of this chapter. Click OK when you're finished.

- To permit authenticated users on the network who aren't members of the Share-Point site access to the site, click Manage Anonymous Access to open the Change Anonymous Access Settings page. In the Allow All Authenticated Users To Access Site section of the page select Yes and choose a site group in which to place these users. Click OK when you're finished.

- To change whether users can request access to the site, click the Manage Access Requests link, enable or disable access requests, and specify an e-mail address to which requests should be sent. Click OK when you're finished.

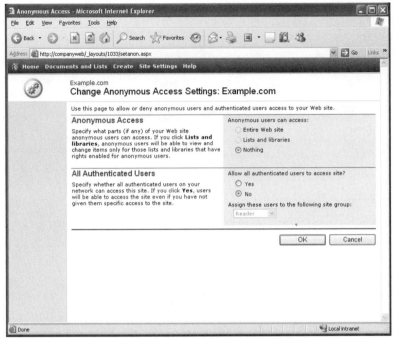

Figure 18-13   The Change Anonymous Access Settings page.

Managing Templates, Usage Data, and Other Settings

You can manage sites and templates, view usage data, manage alerts and Web discussions, delete a site, or change regional settings from the Management and Statistics section of the Top-Level Site Administration page. The choices are:

■ **Save the site as a template**   Click Save Site As Template to save the entire SharePoint site as a template for new sites. You can manage site templates and item templates by clicking the Manage Site Template Gallery and Manage List Template Gallery links in the Site Collection Galleries section of the page.

■ **See usage data for the site**   Click View Site Usage Data to see usage data for the site, including the number of hits and which users have been accessing the site. Use the View Site Collection Usage Summary and View Storage Space Allocation links in the Site Collection Administration section of the page for additional statistics.

■ **View a list of child sites and control creation of new sites**   Click Manage Sites And Workspaces to view a list of child sites, as shown in Figure 18-14, change which site groups can create new sites (by default, only the Administrator site group), as well as create new sites. This allows you to create extra sites for specific projects, while keeping a unified company site.

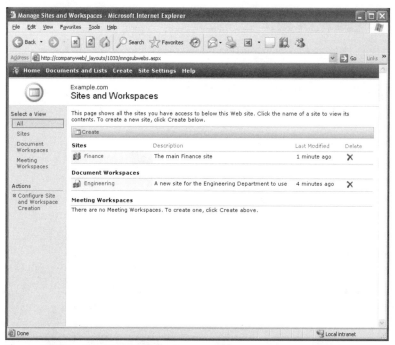

Figure 18-14 The Sites And Workspaces page.

- **View comments and delete discussions** Click the Manage Web Discussions link to view a list of pages with discussion comments and delete discussions as desired.

- **View and delete alerts** Click the Manage Users Alerts link to view all alerts set on the site, and optionally delete alerts.

- **Change regional settings** Click the Change Regional Settings link to change the time zone and format as well as other regional options.

- **Delete the site** Click Delete This Site to permanently delete the site, including all content. Once again, be careful with this link.

Administering SharePoint Virtual Servers

Besides administering SharePoint at the site level, you can also administer the IIS virtual server in which SharePoint sites run. This is useful for tweaking security settings and changing how SharePoint works with e-mail. To do so, open the SharePoint Central

Administration page, shown in Figure 18-15, from the Administrative Tools folder on the SBS computer.

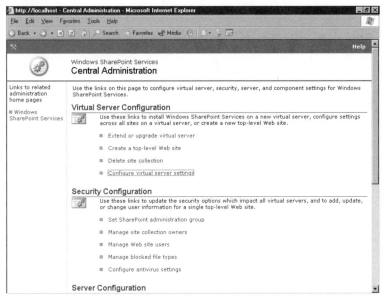

Figure 18-15   The Central Administration page.

You can change the following settings from the Central Administration page:

- **Change settings for a virtual server**   To change settings specific to a single virtual server, click the Configure Virtual Server Settings link, click companyweb (or the appropriate virtual server), and then use the following list:

  - To change which user rights are available to site groups on the virtual server, click Manage User Rights For Virtual Server, and then clear the check boxes next to any rights you want to prohibit. Click OK when you're finished.

  - To disable the ability to create connections between Web Parts, click Manage Security Settings For Web Part Pages. This generally breaks Web Parts that include forms; however, if you don't use any of these Web Parts, disabling this ability can improve site security by reducing the surface area open to attack.

  - To change general settings, such as the maximum size of uploaded files, or to permit properly configured document libraries on the virtual server to automatically publish attachments posted in Exchange public folders, click the Virtual Server General Settings link.

  - To enable Self-Service Site Creation, click the Configure Self-Service Site Creation link. This enables users with the Use Self-Service Site Creation right to create sites.

■ **Control ability to upload and download file types** To change which file types users are blocked from uploading or downloading, click Manage Blocked File Types.

■ **Control antivirus program interaction** To change how a third-party SharePoint antivirus program interacts with SharePoint, click Configure Antivirus Settings.

■ **Change how e-mail is sent** To change how e-mail is sent from SharePoint sites, click Configure Default E-Mail Server Settings. This configures such settings as the outbound SMTP server and the e-mail address used for the From and Reply-To fields.

■ **Enable full-text searching** To enable full-text search of Windows SharePoint Services sites, click the Configure Full Text Search link, select the Enable Full-Text Search And Index Component check box, and then click OK. Doing so places a search form on all SharePoint sites, utilizing Microsoft SQL Server 2005 for search results. To use this feature, you must be using the Premium Edition of SBS, with the Full-Text Search component of SQL Server installed. For information about SQL Server, see Chapter 20, "Using SQL Server 2005."

■ **Log usage data** To enable logging of usage data (which enables the viewing of site usage reports), click the Configure Usage Analysis Processing link, select the Enable Logging and Enable Usage Analysis Processing check boxes, optionally change the default settings, and then click OK.

Real World   The Microsoft Office HTML Viewer Service

The Configure HTML Viewer link leads to a page that you can use to enable on-the-fly, high-quality translations of .doc, .xls, .ppt, and .pps files in the Windows SharePoint Services site to .HTML files for clients who don't have appropriate Microsoft Office viewers installed. However, this nifty feature requires the use of a separate, dedicated HTML Viewer server running on Microsoft Windows XP Professional. This server runs Office 2003 and the Microsoft Office HTML Viewer Service. The good news is that because the HTML Viewer computer services only the SharePoint server, a server operating system is not required.

The Microsoft Office HTML Viewer Service won't work properly when installed on the SBS server, and doing so can cause significant security vulnerabilities and performance issues. For more information, download the Microsoft Office HTML Viewer from the Microsoft Office 2003 Resource Kit Web site (*http://www.microsoft.com/office/orkarchive/2003ddl.htm*) and read the HTML Viewer white paper included with the package.

Using FrontPage 2003 to Customize Windows SharePoint Services

FrontPage 2003 is a full-featured Web page editor that you can use to edit or create sophisticated Windows SharePoint Services sites as well as normal Web pages. Although entire books have been written about FrontPage, the coverage here focuses on accomplishing some select tasks on your SharePoint site. For a thorough grounding in FrontPage, see *Microsoft Office FrontPage 2003 Inside Out* (Microsoft Press, 2003).

Note   Microsoft FrontPage 2002 and earlier versions don't work with the version of Windows SharePoint Services installed on SBS. However, a single copy of FrontPage 2003 is included with the Premium Edition of SBS.

Customizing Existing SharePoint Sites

Although you can customize most aspects of a SharePoint Web site using a Web browser, as discussed earlier in this chapter, FrontPage provides the ability to exert complete control over the SharePoint site. From a client computer, you can easily modify the contents of link bars, work with Web Parts, create new pages, and do anything else you want.

Note   For security purposes, use a Web hosting company to host your public Internet site, and don't publish your default Web site to the Internet. Employees will still be able to access the SharePoint site from the Internet using the Remote Web Workplace, which is available on the Internet at *http://www.example.com/ remote*, if you configure your firewall appropriately (where *http://www.example.com* is the Internet domain name of the SBS computer).

Opening the SharePoint Site And Getting Comfortable

To open the SharePoint Web site (*http://companyweb*) in FrontPage 2003, complete the following steps:

1. In FrontPage, choose Open Site from the File menu.

2. In the Open Site dialog box, type **http://companyweb** in the Site Name box and then click Open. (To open the default Web site instead for the SBS computer, type **http://***sbssrv* where *sbssrv* is the computer name of the SBS computer).

3. The site is opened in Folders view, as shown in Figure 18-16. The Folders view has a listing of folders and pages on the site:

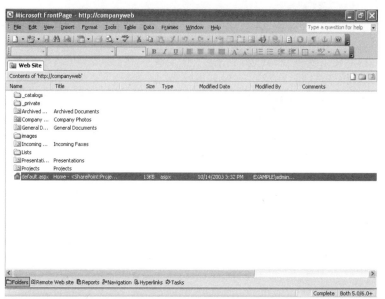

Figure 18-16   The *http://companyweb* site in FrontPage 2003.

❑ To open a folder, double-click it. To return to the previous folder, click the Up One Level button on the right side of the view.

❑ To open a page for editing, double-click it. This displays the page in Design view, a What You See Is What You Get (WYSIWYG) view that you can use to edit the page as if it were a normal Microsoft Office document.

❑ To change the Design view of a page to match a specific screen resolution, click the Page Size display on the Status bar and choose the desired resolution; 760 × 420 (800 × 600 Maximized) is usually a good choice.

❑ To change the Estimated Time To Download reading to reflect a different speed network connection, click the download time when it appears on the Status bar after you open a page, and choose the desired connection speed. As a rule, pages shouldn't take more than 15 seconds to download over the targeted connection speed, if possible.

❑ To disable tools that create pages incompatible with certain browser versions, choose Page Options from the Tools menu and then use the Authoring tab, shown in Figure 18-17, to specify Web browser compatibility options.

Figure 18-17   The Page Options dialog box.

❑ To select a specific area of a Web page by using an HTML tag (a trick Macromedia Dreamweaver users are accustomed to), click the desired tag at the top of the page in Design view.

❑ To change the view to show HTML code or view the page as it would appear rendered in Internet Explorer 6, click the Split, Code, and Preview buttons at the left side of the Status bar.

❑ To preview a page in the Web browser of your choice, click the down arrow next to the Preview toolbar button and select the desired browser and resolution. To add browsers to the list, choose Edit Browser List.

Note   To back up the entire Web site, choose Server and then Backup Web Site from the Tools menu. To package a group of pages and all dependent files into a Web Package that can be imported into any other site, choose Packages and then Export from the Tools menu.

Adding Links and Customizing the Link Bar

Two essential tasks that you can't perform using the SharePoint Web interface are adding links to pages and customizing the link bar that appears across the top and left side of a SharePoint site. These are easy to accomplish in FrontPage—just open the page in FrontPage 2003 and follow this list of options:

- To add a link to a link bar, click + Add Link on the appropriate link bar, as shown in Figure 18-18. This opens the Add To Link Bar dialog box, which you can use to link to another item in the site or a page anywhere on the Internet.

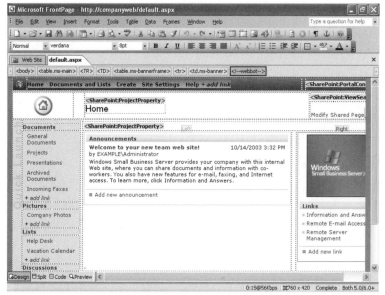

Figure 18-18   The *http://companyweb* Home page in FrontPage.

- To edit a link bar, right-click a link bar and choose Link Bar Properties. This displays the Link Bar Properties dialog box, shown in Figure 18-19. Select the link bar you want to edit from the Choose Existing box, and use the following list:

  - Click Create New to make a new link bar.

  - To add, remove, or edit links, click the Add Link, Remove Link, and Modify Link buttons, respectively.

  - To rearrange links, click the Move Up and Move Down buttons.

  - Click the Style tab to change the link bar style, orientation, and appearance.

Figure 18-19   The Link Bar Properties dialog box.

- To add a bookmark in a page so that you can create hyperlinks to that specific location in the page (such as the top of the page), place the cursor at the location to which you want to link, choose Bookmark from the Insert menu, type a name for the bookmark, and then click OK.

- To add a normal hyperlink, place the cursor in the desired location or select the desired element, and click the Insert Hyperlink toolbar button. Use the Insert Hyperlink dialog box to specify where the hyperlink should send users. To send users to a bookmark in the current page, click Place In This Document on the Link To bar, select the appropriate bookmark, and then click OK.

Adding Web Parts

To add Web Parts to a Windows SharePoint Services page with FrontPage, complete the following steps:

1. Open the SharePoint page and place the cursor in the location you want to insert a Web Part.

2. Choose Insert Web Part from the Data menu to display the Web Parts task pane.

3. If you want the Web Part to be customizable using the SharePoint Web site, first create a new Web Part zone in which to place the Web Part. To do so, click New Web Part Zone.

4. Select the Web Part that you want to insert and then click Insert Selected Web Part. The new Web Part is placed on the page (in the newly created Web Part zone, if you made one), as shown in Figure 18-20.

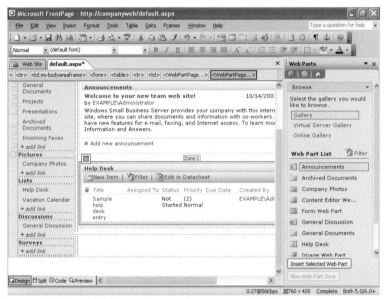

Figure 18-20   A Web Part in a newly created Web Part zone.

5.   To connect a Web Part to a data source (for those Web Parts that support connections), right-click the newly inserted Web Part and choose Web Part Connections from the shortcut menu. This displays the Web Part Connections Wizard, which walks you through the connection process.

Note   You don't have to create all your Web Parts yourself—lots of them are already created and available for download. A good place to start is the Microsoft Download Center—just do a search on the term SharePoint (*http:// www.microsoft.com/downloads/results.aspx?pocId=&freetext=SharePoint&Display-Lang=en*) or check out these links on Chad Gross's blog: *http://msmvps.com/blogs/ cgross/archive/2005/08/03/61320.aspx.*

Note   To change whether a user can customize a Web Part zone, right-click the zone and choose Web Part Zone Properties from the shortcut menu.

Creating New SharePoint Web Sites

FrontPage 2003 makes it easy to create powerful SharePoint Web sites from templates or from scratch. Here's how to get started:

1.   In FrontPage, choose New from the File menu.

2.   In the New task pane, click More Web Site Templates.

3. In the Web Site Templates dialog box, shown in Figure 18-21, click the SharePoint Services tab.

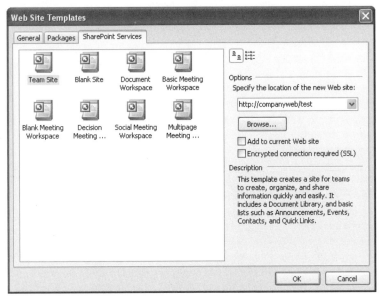

Figure 18-21   The Web Site Templates dialog box.

> **Note**   You can use the Packages tab of the Web Site Templates dialog box to create a News And Reviews Site or a Web Log (blog) site.

4. Select the desired template, specify where to save the new site, and then click OK. FrontPage creates the new site and displays it.

Backup and Restore of a SharePoint Site

The normal SBS Backup will back up all the files that comprise your companyweb site. But finding and restoring just the SharePoint files is more pain than absolutely necessary. Instead, use one of two tools to handle the task: Stsadm.exe or Smigrate.exe. Both of these tools are a bit hard to find—they're in the "%CommonProgramFiles%\Microsoft Shared\web server extensions\60\bin" directory. Both are command-line tools, so you can easily automate their running with a little script and then use the Windows Task Scheduler to run the backup script automatically.

Using Stsadm

The most complete backup of a SharePoint site is done with Stsadm.exe. The command line to backup the companyweb site is

```
cd /d %CommonProgramFiles%\"Microsoft Shared"\"web server extensions"\60\bin
stsadm -o backup -url http://companyweb -filename fullpath\filename.dat
```

Restoring files *should* be this easy, but there can be problems. You can't restore to a different computer, or restore to a fresh new computer in disaster recovery situation without also restoring the STS_Config database and also doing a System State restore. But assuming you are simply restoring to your SBS server, the restore command would be

```
cd /d %CommonProgramFiles%\"Microsoft Shared"\"web server extensions"\60\bin
stsadm -o restore -url http://companyweb -filename fullpath\filename.dat -
overwrite
```

> **Note**   For additional options, including a script to automate daily backups of companyweb, see Microsoft Knowledge Base article 829112 found at *http://support.microsoft.com/kb/829112/*.

Using Smigrate

Stsadm.exe is good, and it does restore all the security settings during the backup. Smigrate.exe is much more flexible, allowing you to restore to a different computer entirely, which makes Smigrate.exe an excellent tool for using one SharePoint Web site as a template for additional sites. The one thing Smigrate.exe doesn't do, however, is restore all of the security settings for a site, so if you've customized those, you'll need to go back and make any necessary changes.

The beauty of using Smigrate.exe to back up a SharePoint site, including companyweb, is that you can restore the site to any SharePoint server without having to worry about STS_Config databases or System State. The command line to back up the companyweb site using Smigrate.exe is

```
cd /d %CommonProgramFiles%\"Microsoft Shared"\"web server extensions"\60\bin
smigrate -w http://companyweb -f fullpath\filename.fwp
```

The matching restore would be

```
cd /d %CommonProgramFiles%\"Microsoft Shared"\"web server extensions"\60\bin
smigrate -r -w http://companyweb -f fullpath\filename.fwp
```

Note An excellent community resource for SharePoint on SBS is Microsoft SBS MVP Chad Gross' blog at: *http://msmvps.com/blogs/cgross/default.aspx*.

Summary

This chapter showed you how to use the *http://companyweb* SharePoint Web site created by Windows SBS, as well as how to customize and administer it. The chapter also discussed administering SharePoint virtual servers and how to use FrontPage 2003 to perform more sophisticated authoring of SharePoint sites.

In the next chapter, you will move on to performing common Web server administration tasks using SBS's built-in Web server—Internet Information Services (IIS).

Chapter 19

Managing an Intranet Web Server

Creating New Virtual Directories. 496

Using Web Sharing 498

Changing Security Settings 499

Limiting Network Usage by Web Sites. 508

Setting Up an FTP Server 509

Configuring the Indexing Service 511

Backing Up and Restoring the IIS Configuration 512

Reinstalling IIS 513

Summary 514

Microsoft Windows Small Business Server 2003 automatically installs and configures Microsoft Internet Information Services (IIS) 6.0 to serve as an intranet Web server. This intranet Web site includes the *http://companyweb* SharePoint intranet site (discussed in Chapter 18, "Customizing a SharePoint Web Site"), the Network Configuration Wizard, Remote Web Workplace, and Outlook Web Access (all discussed in Chapter 11, "Managing Computers on the Network").

Normally, you'll find that the installed defaults of SBS's intranet site are perfectly adequate. However, in this chapter we'll cover some of the customizations and changes you can easily make to fit your particular environment. These changes include additional virtual directories, anonymous access, bandwidth and CPU limits, the FTP server, and indexing

---

More Info Sources for more information about IIS include *Microsoft IIS 6.0 Administrator's Companion* by William Stanek (Microsoft Press, 2003) and the *Microsoft Internet Information Services (IIS) 6.0 Resource Kit* (Microsoft Press, 2004).

Real World   Hosting Your Own Internet Web Site

Internet-accessible Web servers sit on the front lines of a virtual battlefield, exposed to continual assault by hackers and automated exploit engines that are continually looking for Web sites to deface or use for their own purposes. For this reason, you should use a commercial Web hosting company to host your public Web site. Commercial Web hosting companies have the staff and the expertise to properly protect their sites. If you really want to host your own public Web site, do *not* do it on your SBS server. Install a dedicated Windows Server 2003 Web Edition server for this purpose and then lock it down completely. Always keep this server completely updated with the latest patches. The one exception to this recommendation we'd make is to enable Remote Web Workplace (RWW). You should configure SBS and your firewall to publish only the Remote Web Workplace, not the default Web site. You may even consider adjusting your firewall to only expose ports 443 and 4125 (for RWW) as an example of a way to keep a minimum exposure point to the Web.

Creating New Virtual Directories

If you want to create a new Web site or a series of Web pages on the internal network, the best way to do this is to create a new virtual directory in IIS. A *virtual directory* is a directory name or alias that corresponds to a physical directory on the server. Virtual directories appear as subfolders on a Web site but in reality can point to a folder located anywhere on the network.

Real World   Creating New Web Sites

It's usually more convenient to create new virtual directories in an existing site such as the Windows SharePoint Services site (*http://companyweb*) or the Default Web Site instead of creating a completely new site in IIS. Creating new sites requires managing host headers as well as manually adding alias (CNAME) records to the DNS reverse lookup zone, which is a nuisance and unnecessary for most small businesses. If you need to create a new site, right-click the Web Sites container in the Internet Information Services console, and choose New Web Site from the shortcut menu to start the Web Site Creation Wizard—just remember to create the alias record in DNS corresponding to the Web site's host header.

To create a new virtual directory, complete the following steps:

1. Open the Server Management console, expand the Advanced Management container, and then expand Internet Information Services.

2. Expand the SBSSRV (local computer) container (assuming your server is named SBSSRV), and select the Web Sites container, as shown in Figure 19-1.

3. In the details pane, right-click Default Web Site, and choose New, Virtual Directory from the shortcut menu. The Virtual Directory Creation Wizard appears.

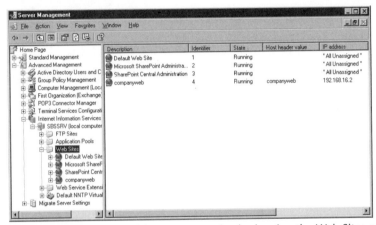

Figure 19-1   The Server Management console showing the Web Sites container.

> **Note**   You can also publish from Microsoft Office FrontPage directly into a new virtual directory without first creating the directory in IIS if you publish with a user account that has the appropriate permissions.

4. On the first page of the Virtual Directory Creation Wizard, click Next.

5. On the Virtual Directory Alias page, type a folder name and then click Next.

6. On the Web Site Content Directory page, specify the path to the real folder that will contain the Web site content (for example, **c:\inetpub\training**), and then click Next.

> **Note**   Placing content in a subfolder of the c:\inetpub folder is usually the most convenient approach because this folder already has the proper NTFS permissions applied to it, and the Windows Small Business Server default and *http://companyweb* sites are located here as well.

7. On the Virtual Directory Access Permissions page, make sure the Run Scripts check box is cleared (unless you plan to use scripts or dynamic Web pages in the virtual directory). Click Next and then click Finish.

Using Web Sharing

You can make any folder on an SBS server directly accessible from your Web site by using the Web Sharing feature. This feature provides a handy way to quickly make a virtual directory for a folder that stores a Web site or to simulate an FTP site. To do either, complete the following steps:

1. In Windows Explorer, right-click the folder you want to share on your Web site and choose Properties from the shortcut menu.

2. Click the Web Sharing tab (Figure 19-2), and then select the Web site on which you want to share the folder (most likely Default Web Site).

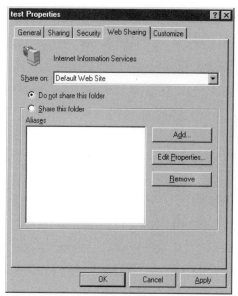

Figure 19-2   The Web Sharing tab.

3. Choose Share This Folder. This opens the Edit Alias dialog box, shown in Figure 19-3.

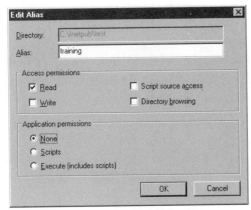

Figure 19-3   The Edit Alias dialog box.

4. Type the virtual directory name you want to use in the Alias box.

5. Specify the Access Permissions and Application Permissions for the folder.

    ❑   To use the folder as a standard Web site with the home page (Default.htm or Index.htm) linking to all relevant files, select the Read check box for the Access Permissions and the None option for the Application Permissions.

    ❑   To use server-side scripting or dynamic Web pages in the virtual directory, select both the Read check box and Scripts option.

    ❑   To allow users to browse the folder as if it were an FTP site, select the Directory Browsing check box.

Security Alert   Directory Browsing is usually disabled on Web sites to improve security—visitors can view only those linked pages or files for which they know the exact URL. Although this is arguably of less concern on an internal Web site, it's still best to leave this feature disabled. There are other ways to provide access to the folder to internal clients if necessary.

6. Click OK when you're finished.

7. Click Add to create any additional aliases, and click OK when you're finished.

Changing Security Settings

Windows Small Business Server 2003 does a pretty good job of locking down IIS while still allowing all its relevant features to work. Nonetheless, there are several security settings that you might want to change, such as which sites are externally accessible or which allow anonymous users, as well as which server certificate is used for secure communications.

Changing Which Sites Are Externally Accessible

There are three ways to control whether a site hosted by SBS is accessible to external users who don't have a Virtual Private Network (VPN) connection to your network:

- Change the firewall settings to prohibit or allow access to the Remote Web Workplace, Microsoft Outlook Web Access, the Default Web Site, or the *http:/ /companyweb* site. This permits or denies all external users (though some sites such as *http://companyweb*, Remote Web Workplace, and Outlook Web Access are still password-protected).

- Change the IP addresses to which a Web site responds in the Internet Information Services console. Configuring the Web site (Default Web Site or http://company-web) to respond only to the internal IP address blocks all external users to the site and all virtual directories within it.

- Change the Directory Security for a Web site or a virtual directory to block or allow a range of IP addresses or a specific domain. For example, you could block all external IP addresses.

The first method is covered in Chapter 5, "Completing the To Do List and Other Post-Installation Tasks." To use the other two methods, follow these steps:

1. Open the Server Management console, expand the Advanced Management container, and then expand Internet Information Services.

2. Expand the SBSSRV (local computer) container (assuming your server is named SBSSRV), select the Web Sites container, right-click the Web site or virtual directory with which you want to work, and then choose Properties from the shortcut menu.

   If you chose a Web site, complete Step 3. If you chose a virtual directory, continue with Step 4.

3. If you chose a Web site, use the Web Site tab of the Properties dialog box (Figure 19-4) to identify the IP address or addresses on which you want the Web site to be available.

   Important   Choosing an internal IP address for a Web site blocks external access to all virtual directories hosted by the Web site. Doing this on the Default Web Site will block external access to the Remote Web Workplace and Outlook Web Access, even if the firewall is configured to allow it.

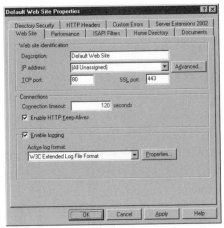

Figure 19-4   The Web Site tab of the Properties dialog box.

4. To specify access permissions by IP address, which is the only way to change access to virtual directories, click the Directory Security tab of the Properties dialog box. Click the Edit button in the IP Address And Domain Name Restrictions section of the dialog box. This displays the IP Address And Domain Name Restrictions dialog box shown in Figure 19-5.

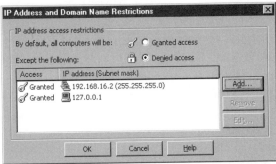

Figure 19-5   The IP Address And Domain Name Restrictions dialog box.

5. Choose Granted Access or Denied Access to allow or block all computers by default.

6. Click the Add button to create a rule allowing or denying a computer, group of computers, or all computers belonging to a specific domain name.

   Depending on the default condition you chose, either the Grant Access (Figure 19-6) or the Deny Access dialog box is displayed.

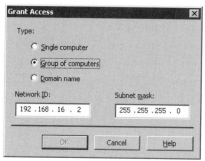

Figure 19-6   The Grant Access dialog box.

7. In the Grant Access or Deny Access dialog box, choose Single Computer or Group Of Computers. To block or allow a single computer, type the computer's IP address in the Network ID box. To block or allow a group of computers, type the IP address of the first computer in the group in the Network ID box and then type a subnet mask indicating how many computers are in the group, as shown in Figure 19-6. Click OK when you're finished.

8. Add any additional rules and then click OK when you're finished.

Important   Don't allow or block computers by Domain Name—doing so requires that a reverse DNS lookup be performed on every visitor, which can generate excessive network traffic. And since reverse DNS records are notoriously unreliable, it can cause legitimate traffic to be blocked.

Real World   What Subnet Mask to Use

When including or excluding a group of computers by IP address and subnet mask, use the following subnet masks to include or exclude entire Class A, B, or C networks:

- Use the 255.255.255.0 subnet mask to include all computers in a Class C network (for example, 192.168.16.0 through 192.168.16.255).

- Use the 255.255.0.0 subnet mask to include all computers in a Class B network (for example, 172.16.0.0 through 172.16.255.255).

- Use the 255.0.0.0 subnet mask to include all computers in a Class A network (for example, 10.0.0.0 through 10.255.255.255).

To include or exclude a subset of these networks, you need to use a variable length subnet mask such as 255.255.255.192 (which includes 62 addresses starting with the IP address you type in the Network ID box). For in-depth information about subnet masks, hop on the Web and download a custom subnet mask calculator, or try the free one at *http://www.subnet-calculator.com/*.

Enabling or Disabling Anonymous Access

You can enable or disable anonymous (unauthenticated) users, controlling access to particular Web sites. This is probably most significant with the *http://companyweb* Share-Point site—anonymous users won't be able to access the site even when you give them permission within Windows SharePoint Services, unless you enable anonymous access in Internet Information Services. Why you'd want to do this is something we have trouble figuring out, however. Do you really want just anyone to be able to get on your company's internal SharePoint site?

To enable or disable anonymous access to a Web site or virtual directory, complete the following steps:

1. Open the Server Management console, expand the Advanced Management container, and then expand Internet Information Services.

2. Expand the SBSSRV (local computer) container (assuming your server is named SBSSRV), select the Web Sites container, right-click the Web site or virtual directory with which you want to work, and then choose Properties from the shortcut menu.

3. Click the Directory Security tab, and then click Edit in the Authentication And Access Control section of the dialog box.

4. In the Authentication Methods dialog box (Figure 19-7), select or clear the Enable Anonymous Access check box depending on whether you want to allow or prohibit anonymous access.

5. Use the Authenticated Access section of the dialog box to control which methods are available for client authentication. These methods are used when anonymous access is disabled, or when the NTFS permissions on the folder storing the content don't give Read permissions to the anonymous user account IUSR_SBSSRV. Click OK when you're finished.

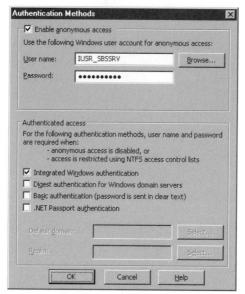

Figure 19-7   The Authentication Methods dialog box.

More Info   See the Under the Hood sidebar "Anonymous Access and NTFS Folder Permissions," appearing later in this chapter, for more information about how anonymous access works.

Security Alert   Integrated Windows Authentication and .NET Passport Authentication are the only authentication methods that don't have significant security problems. .NET Passport Authentication is complex and outside the scope of this book. Digest Authentication, although secure over the network, requires that passwords be stored in plaintext unencrypted form on the Windows Small Business Server computer; and Basic Authentication sends passwords in clear text (unencrypted form) over the network.

Under the Hood   Anonymous Access and NTFS Folder Permissions

Anonymous access is controlled using the IUSR_SBSSRV user account (where SBSSRV is the name of the Windows Small Business Server computer), which is a member of the Guests and Domain Users groups.

To determine whether anonymous users can access a folder with NTFS permissions applied, right-click the folder in Windows Explorer, choose Properties from the shortcut menu, and then click the Security tab and look for the Users or

Domain Users groups. To explicitly check on IUSR_SBSSRV permissions, click Advanced, click the Effective Permissions tab, and then click Select. In the Select User, Computer, Or Group dialog box, type **IUSR_SBSSRV** (where SBSSRV is the NetBIOS name of the Windows Small Business Server computer), and then click OK. This displays the Effective Permissions for anonymous Web site users, as shown in Figure 19-8.

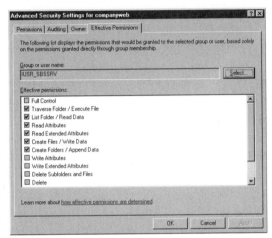

Figure 19-8   The Advanced Security Settings dialog box.

Note   Note that when you buy a server from one of the major OEMs, complete with a preinstalled OEM version of SBS, the IUSR account will not accurately reflect the name of the computer. This is an annoying artifact of the OEM imaging process.

Changing Server Certificates and SSL Settings

When you run the Configure E-mail and Internet Connection Wizard, the Web Server Certificate page lets you create a new self-signed certificate used to authenticate the Web server for Secure Sockets Layer (SSL) communication, or you can use an existing certificate obtained from a trusted Certificate Authority (such as VeriSign or a locally installed CA). Rerunning the wizard is the easiest way to change the certificate used by Internet Information Services, but doing so is cumbersome for viewing and choosing certificates, and the wizard can't create certificate requests to send to commercial or locally hosted CAs. For these tasks, complete the following steps:

1. Open the Server Management console, expand the Advanced Management container, and then expand Internet Information Services.

2. Expand the SBSSRV (local computer) container (assuming your server is named SBSSRV), select the Web Sites container, right-click the Web site or virtual directory with which you want to work, and then choose Properties from the shortcut menu.

3. Click the Directory Security tab. In the Secure Communications section of the dialog box, click View Certificate to view the currently assigned certificate, or click Edit to enable or disable SSL.

Important Don't enable SSL on the http://companyweb site—doing so makes the site inaccessible. This is because SSL encrypts host headers, preventing IIS from sending users to sites that make use of host headers, including the *http://companyweb site.*

---

4. To manage certificates, click Server Certificate on the Directory Security tab, and then click Next on the first page of the IIS Certificate Wizard.

5. If a certificate is currently installed, use the Modify The Current Certificate Assignment page (Figure 19-9) to choose the action that you want to perform and then click Next. You can choose from the following actions:

   ❑ Renew The Current Certificate

   ❑ Remove The Current Certificate

   ❑ Replace The Current Certificate

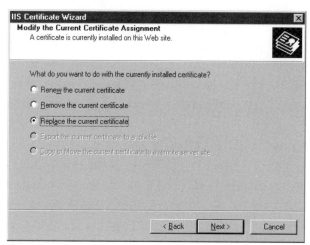

Figure 19-9 The Modify The Current Certificate Assignment page of the IIS Certificate Wizard.

6. If no certificate is currently installed, the Server Certificate page (Figure 19-10) appears instead of the Modify The Current Certificate Assignment page. Choose one of the following actions and then click Next:

    ❑ Create A New Certificate

    ❑ Assign An Existing Certificate

    ❑ Import A Certificate From a .pfx File

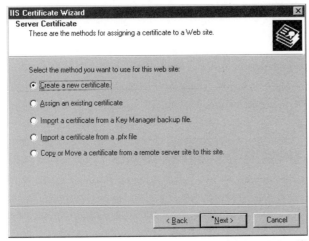

Figure 19-10   The Server Certificate page of the IIS Certificate Wizard.

7. If you chose to assign an existing certificate or replace the current certificate, click Next, select a certificate (only certificates that have been installed on the computer are displayed), click Next, accept the default SSL port, click Next, verify the settings, and then click Next to install the certificate for use with IIS.

8. If you chose to create a new certificate, click Next and, on the Delayed Or Immediate Request page, select whether to send the request later or send it immediately to a local CA. Click Next.

> **More Info**   For more information about installing Certificate Services and creating your certificate authority, see Chapter 15, "Managing Connectivity."

9. On the Name And Security Settings page, type a descriptive name for the certificate and then click Next.

10. On the Organization Information page, type the name of your company and organizational unit, and then click Next.

11. On the Your Site's Common Name page, type the DNS name of the Web site and then click Next. (If this is a publicly accessible Web site, make sure to use the public DNS name of the site.)

12. On the Geographical Information page, type the country, state, and city in which the server is located, and then click Next.

13. If you chose to submit the certificate request later, type a file name for the certificate request and click Next. Review the settings and click Next to complete the request.

14. If you chose to submit the request immediately, click Next on the SSL Port page to accept the default SSL port (443).

15. On the Choose A Certificate Authority page, select the internal CA, click Next, review the settings, and then click Next again to submit the certificate request. Click Finish when prompted.

Limiting Network Usage by Web Sites

By default, IIS allows Web site visitors to consume as much network bandwidth as is available. When you have a lot of remote users or a slow Internet connection, visitors can consume all available bandwidth, preventing users of the internal network from accessing the Internet for Web browsing and e-mail. This is yet another good reason to have your public Web site hosted by a commercial Web hosting service. While it is easy to place limits on the maximum number of people who can concurrently connect to the Web site and the maximum amount of network bandwidth a Web site (virtual server) can consume, there is a catch—internal and external (Internet) users are treated the same. Therefore, it's best not to apply this feature to the *http://companyweb* site, and you should think about your usage patterns before applying it to the Default Web Site as well.

Important IIS must install QoS Packet Scheduler to enable *bandwidth throttling,* which will drop all currently connected users of the server—not just Web site users. Make sure you do *not* do this while users are connected to the Windows Small Business Server computer.

To limit network bandwidth or the number of concurrent connections, complete the following steps:

1. Open the Server Management console, expand the Advanced Management container, and then expand Internet Information Services.

2. Expand the SBSSRV (local computer) container (assuming your server is named SBSSRV), select the Web Sites container, right-click the Web site on which you want to limit bandwidth, and then choose Properties from the shortcut menu.

3. Click the Performance tab (Figure 19-11), select the Limit The Network Bandwidth Available To This Web Site check box, and specify the maximum bandwidth that IIS should allow the Web site and all virtual directories on the virtual server to use.

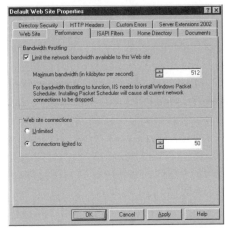

Figure 19-11   The Performance tab of the Default Web Site Properties dialog box.

4. To limit the number of concurrent users who can use the site, select the Connections Limited To option and type the maximum number of connections to allow.

5. Click OK when you're finished.

Setting Up an FTP Server

Although it might seem like a throwback to the days of Archie, Gopher, and Mosaic, File Transfer Protocol (FTP) is still occasionally useful as a quick and efficient way of sharing large files with external users. It contains no security worth using (passwords are sent in plaintext), so enable FTP on an as-needed basis, and disable it while not in use.

Note   Unfortunately, some scanners require the use of FTP for their network scanning functionality. If this is the case in your environment, you'll need to enable FTP and leave it enabled. But then make sure you block port 21 (the FTP port) on your firewall to ensure that only internal users can connect via FTP.

FTP in SBS is a component of IIS and is administered using the standard IIS consoles. It is not installed by default. Therefore, before you can use it, you must install it.

Installing FTP

To install the FTP service, complete the following steps:

1. Click Add Or Remove Programs in Control Panel, and then click Add/Remove Windows Components. This opens the Windows Components Wizard.

2. Select Application Server, click Details, select Internet Information Services (IIS), and then click Details again.

3. Select the File Transfer Protocol (FTP) Service check box, click OK twice, and then click Next to install the service. Click Finish when it's done. Windows Small Business Server installs the FTP service and creates the default FTP site in the C:\Inetpub\FTProot directory.

Security Alert   Once FTP is installed, to allow external users to access FTP, you must rerun the Configure E-Mail and Internet Connection Wizard to open the firewall. If you have a non-UPnP external firewall in addition to Windows Small Business Server, make sure you open port 21 as well. Once you're finished transferring files, close the port again to prevent hackers from attacking your server over this port.

Configuring FTP

Although Windows Small Business Server sets up FTP with no additional help, you will probably want to change some settings, such as the welcome messages and directory security. To do so, complete the following procedure:

1. Open the Server Management console, expand the Advanced Management container, expand Internet Information Services, and finally expand the SBSSRV (local computer) container (assuming your server is named SBSSRV). Then expand the FTP Sites container.

2. Right-click Default FTP Site and choose Properties from the shortcut menu. This displays the Default FTP Site Properties dialog box.

3. On the FTP Site tab, click the Current Sessions button to view currently connected users and optionally disconnect them.

4. Click the Security Accounts tab and select the Allow Only Anonymous Connections check box. This increases security by preventing users with valid accounts from sending their credentials in clear text over the Internet.

5. Click the Messages tab to type welcome messages that appear to visitors when they enter the site.

6. Click the Home Directory tab to specify where the FTP site should be stored.

7. Click the Directory Security tab to selectively block or enable access to certain IP addresses. This is useful for enabling the FTP site for a small number of users with known IP addresses. Click OK when you're finished.

> **Note**   For maximum security, when you're finished using the FTP site, temporarily disable it by right-clicking it and choosing Stop from the shortcut menu. If you won't be using it regularly, disable the FTP Publishing Service using the Services application.

Configuring the Indexing Service

The Indexing Service is a built-in service that builds a searchable catalog of files on the server. This service significantly increases the speed of search operations as long as you perform the search locally on the SBS server or use a search form created on a Web page hosted by SBS. (Web page search forms hosted by IIS won't work until the Indexing Service is enabled.)

Although the Indexing Service is installed by default, it's not turned on because it reduces overall server performance a small amount because of its background indexing of files.

> **Note**   Windows SharePoint Services can't use the Indexing Service—it requires the full version of Microsoft SQL Server to perform searches. The SQL Server Desktop Engine included with Windows Small Business Server 2003 Standard Edition won't work either—you need the full version included with Windows Small Business Server 2003, Premium Edition.

If you want to enable a search form on a non-SharePoint Web site, complete the following steps to enable the Indexing Service:

1. Open the Server Management console, expand Advanced Management, Computer Management, Services And Applications, and then select Services.

2. Right-click Indexing Service in the Services container and choose Properties from the shortcut menu.

3. Choose Manual in the Startup Type box, click Apply, and then click Start to start the service. Click OK when you're finished.

To view what the Indexing Service is cataloging, select the Indexing Service container (located under the Services And Applications container in the Advanced Management section of the Server Management console) and then use the following list:

■ To view a list of folders included in and excluded from the catalog, expand the System or Web containers and then select Directories.

■ To add rules including folders in or excluding folders from the catalog, right-click the Directories container, and choose New, Directory from the shortcut menu. Then use the Add Directory dialog box to specify which folder or network share to include or exclude.

■ To perform a search against the catalog, select the Query The Catalog object and use the search form to perform your query.

When including network shares not located on the Windows Small Business Server computer, you should be aware that catalog searches will show all matches on the network share, even if the user isn't permitted access to the files.

Backing Up and Restoring the IIS Configuration

IIS has a couple of backup and restoration features that can complement a regular system and data backup schedule. Specifically, IIS lets you save configuration data for Web sites to XML files, which can be used to re-create the Web site settings. IIS also performs general configuration backups automatically. Neither of these features restores Web site data—you'll still need a full-fledged backup program for that, but they can help protect your IIS configuration.

To use these features, use the following list as a guide:

■ To save the configuration of a Web site to a file, right-click the Web site in the Internet Information Services console, and choose All Tasks, Save Configuration To File from the shortcut menu.

■ To restore a previously saved Web site configuration, right-click the Web Sites container, and choose New, Web Site (From File) from the shortcut menu.

■ To back up or restore the IIS configuration, right-click the computer name in the Internet Information Services console, and choose All Tasks, Backup/Restore Configuration from the shortcut menu.

Reinstalling IIS

Windows Small Business Server 2003 is much more than the sum of its parts—it is a synthesis of many discrete features. This is especially true with regard to IIS, which is closely integrated with Windows SharePoint Services, the Microsoft SQL Server Desktop Engine, Exchange Server, Routing and Remote Access, client deployment, remote access, and even Internet Security and Acceleration (ISA) Server.

The downside to this high level of integration is that fixing things can be a delicate operation. If IIS, Windows SharePoint Services, or a related product becomes corrupted, do some research on the Microsoft Knowledge Base and in the SBS online community, and contact Microsoft Product Support, if necessary. Before attempting to fix things, make a current backup, save your IIS configuration to a file, and try creating a duplicate Web site to experiment with.

If your problems persist, here's a last-ditch approach you can attempt before resorting to a complete reinstall or restore from backup. Proceed with caution.

1. Launch Windows Small Business Server Setup by selecting Windows Small Business Server 2003 in the Add Or Remove Programs tool and clicking Change/Remove.

2. Use the Microsoft Window Small Business Server Setup Wizard to remove intranet support.

3. Use Add Or Remove Programs to uninstall Microsoft Window SharePoint Services 2.0 and, possibly, uninstall Microsoft SQL Server Desktop Edition. It will appear in the Add Or Remove Programs list as Microsoft SQL Server Desktop Edition (SHAREPOINT).

   > **Note** If the automatic uninstall doesn't work, see the Microsoft Knowledge Base Article 320873 for the lengthy procedure to manually uninstall Microsoft SQL Server Desktop Edition. Also, the Microsoft Knowledge Base Article 829114 covers the uninstallation and reinstallation of companyweb.

4. Open the Server Management console, expand Advanced Management, Internet Information Services, and then expand the SBSSRV (local computer) container (assuming your server is named SBSSRV). Expand the Web Sites container, select companyweb, and click Delete.

5. Open Registry Editor, export the following keys to backup files, and then delete them:

```
HKEY_LOCAL_MACHINE\SOFTWARE\Microsoft\SmallBusinessServer\Intranet
HKEY_LOCAL_MACHINE\SOFTWARE\Microsoft\Microsoft SQL Server\SHAREPOINT
```

> **Important**   Editing the registry can cause serious damage to your Windows Small Business Server software installation, which might be fixable only by reinstalling Windows Small Business Server. Use extreme caution.

6. Open Windows Explorer and delete C:\Program Files\Microsoft SQL Server\MSSQL$SHAREPOINT folder. (You might have to reboot into Safe Mode to do this.)

7. Reboot the computer and use Windows Small Business Server Setup to reinstall the intranet feature.

Summary

This chapter covered how to create new virtual directories, share folders on a Web site directly from within Windows Explorer, change security settings and network usage, and set up an FTP server, as well as how to configure the Indexing Service. You've also learned to back up and restore the IIS configuration and what to do in the event of major troubles.

In the next chapter, you'll learn how to use SQL Server 2005, included in Windows Small Business Server 2003 R2, Premium Edition.

Chapter 20
Using SQL Server 2005

Installing SQL Server 2005 515

Upgrading Windows SharePoint Services to SQL Server 2005 522

Architecture 532

Administration 532

Summary 538

The Premium Edition of Microsoft Windows Small Business Server 2003 R2 includes Microsoft SQL Server 2005 Workgroup Edition. SQL Server 2005 is a set of components, based around a relational database, that work together to meet the data storage and analysis needs of some of the largest Web sites and enterprise data-processing systems. SQL Server 2005 can meet the day-to-day business needs of the small business equally well.

In this chapter, we will *not* pretend to tell you everything you need to know about SQL Server 2005–frankly, that's the subject of many books already out there and beyond the scope of what we can do in this book. But what we will do is give you a quick overview of some of the features of SQL Server 2005.

One important new feature of SBS 2003 R2 is that the licensing of SQL Server has been changed. As part of your R2 license, you have the right to use a stand-alone copy of SQL Server 2005 Workgroup edition on an additional server within your SBS domain without having to purchase additional SQL CALs, up to the number of SBS CALs you have.

Installing SQL Server 2005

SBS 2003 R2 Premium Edition includes two additional CDs that are not part of the Standard Edition: Premium Technologies CD1 and Premium Technologies CD2. Both CDs are required for installing Microsoft SQL Server 2005. The installation process for SQL Server 2005 includes the installation of the SQL Server 2005 native client application, and the configuration of an initial database.

To install SQL Server 2005, follow these steps:

1. Insert the SBS 2003 R2 Premium Technologies CD1 into your CD-ROM drive. If SBS R2 Premium Technologies Setup, shown in Figure 20-1, doesn't automatically start, double-click Setup.exe in the root of the CD-ROM drive using Windows Explorer.

Figure 20-1   The opening screen of SBS 2003 R2 Premium Technologies Setup.

2. Click Install Microsoft SQL Server 2005 to begin the installation program.

3. Accept the EULA and click Next.

4. The Installing Prerequisites page, shown in Figure 20-2, will open. This will install any missing prerequisites required for SQL Server 2005 to successfully install. Click Install.

5. Once the prerequisites have installed successfully, click Next and the setup program will check your system configuration. When this check is complete, the Welcome page of the actual SQL Server installation will open. Click Next.

6. On the System Configuration Check page of the Microsoft SQL Server 2005 Setup Wizard, shown in Figure 20-3, you'll see the results of the system configuration check. You can filter this screen on errors, warnings, success, or all actions by clicking Filter. You can view, save, copy, or e-mail a report on the results by clicking Report. Once you're ready to proceed, click Next.

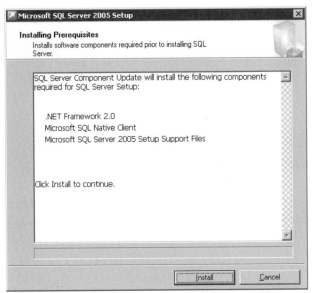

Figure 20-2   The Installing Prerequisites page of the Microsoft SQL Server 2005 Setup Wizard.

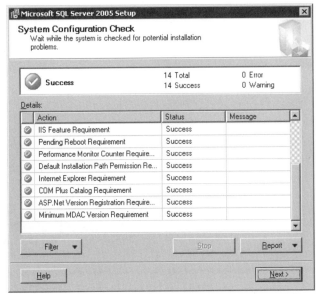

Figure 20-3   The System Configuration Check page of the Microsoft SQL Server 2005 Setup Wizard.

7. Fill in the Registration Information and click Next.

8. On the Feature Selection page, shown in Figure 20-4, choose the features of SQL Server 2005 that you want to install. The default selections are minimally appropriate for SBS environments, but you can add any additional features you'll need. (We like to add the Management Tools, as well.) Define the installation path here and then click Next.

Note   You should install the Management Tools even though they aren't part of the default installation. If you decide to use SQL Server 2005 as your SharePoint database engine later, you'll need them, and it can be a nuisance to install them after the initial installation.

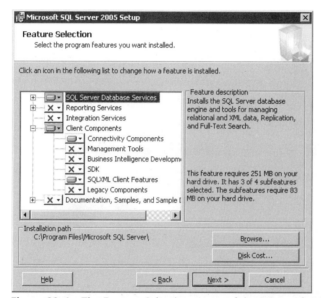

Figure 20-4   The Feature Selections page of the Microsoft SQL Server 2005 Setup Wizard.

9. On the Instance Name page, shown in Figure 20-5, you can choose to install the Default Instance or a new Named Instance. To see the existing installed instances, click the Installed Instances button to open the Installed Instances page, shown in Figure 20-6. To upgrade one of the installed instances, select it and click OK. To return to the Instance Name page, click Cancel.

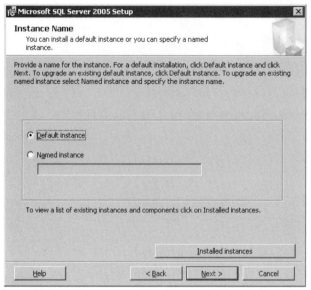

Figure 20-5   The Instance Name page of the Microsoft SQL Server 2005 Setup Wizard.

Important   Do not attempt to upgrade either the Monitoring database (MSSQL$SBSMONITORING) or the WSUS database (MSSQL$WSUS) to SQL Server 2005—this is not a supported configuration. If you want to upgrade the companyweb SharePoint database (MSSQL$SHAREPOINT), follow the instructions later in this chapter, in the section titled "Upgrading Windows SharePoint Services to SQL Server 2005."

---

10. Once you've decided which instance to install or upgrade, click Next to open the Service Account page shown in Figure 20-7. On this page, you can select the account to use for starting and stopping each of the SQL Server services. You can use different accounts for each, or use the same account for all services. See the Under the Hood sidebar "Service Accounts," or the built-in Help file for security considerations for service accounts. Click Next.

Note   If you've taken the default set of features, you'll have three services showing, as in Figure 20-7. If you've selected all the available features, you'll have two additional accounts: the Analysis Service and the Report Server.

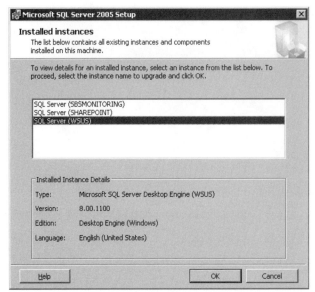

Figure 20-6 The Installed Instances page of the Microsoft SQL Server 2005 Setup Wizard.

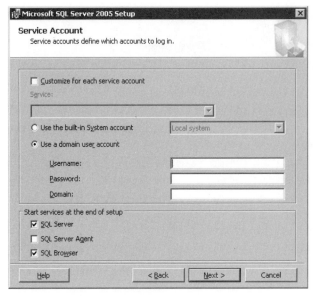

Figure 20-7 The Service Account page of the Microsoft SQL Server 2005 Setup Wizard.

11. On the Authentication Page, you can choose between Windows Authentication Mode or Mixed Mode for authentication. Windows authentication mode is strongly recommended and provides significantly greater security. Click Next.

12. On the Collation Settings page, shown in Figure 20-8, you can choose the sort order and type. Unless you have a known need and understand why you are changing this, we suggest taking the default, which is to use SQL collations in case-insensitive dictionary order, which maintains compatibility with previous versions of SQL Server. Click Next.

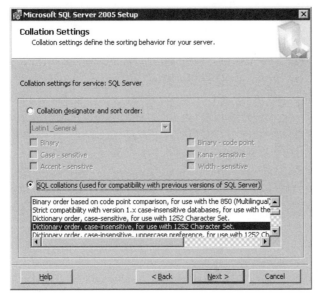

Figure 20-8   The Collation Settings page of the Microsoft SQL Server 2005 Setup Wizard.

13. On the Error and Usage Report Settings page, you can elect to automatically send error and usage reports to Microsoft. This is purely voluntary, and does help to improve the product. All collection is done anonymously. However, error reports might unintentionally contain personally identifiable information. In the event that such information is transmitted to Microsoft, it will not be used. Click Next.

14. The Ready to Install page shows which components will be installed. Click Install to begin the actual installation.

15. The progress of the installation is displayed on the Setup Progress page. During setup, you will be prompted to insert the second Premium Technologies CD. When setup completes, click Next.

16. Click Finish to complete the Microsoft SQL Server 2005 Setup Wizard.

Under the Hood   Service Accounts

SQL Server 2005 requires several service accounts to run its various services. Choosing which account to use for a service account is always a tradeoff between simplicity and security. The simplest solution is to select the Local System account. You never need to worry about the password changing, and this account always has sufficient privileges. Unfortunately, running your SQL Server services under that account is not the best solution from a security standpoint. The Local System account is a powerful account, especially when it's running on your SBS server: If your security in SQL Server is breached, the entire network is compromised.

Using a regular user domain account is a possibility for the SQL Server service—it does not require any administrative privileges. But the SQL Server Agent process *does* require administrative privileges if your SQL Server environment uses CmdExec or ActiveScript jobs, or if you use the AutoRestart feature. If this is the case in your SQL Server environment, you should use separate service accounts for the SQL Server service and the SQL Server Agent.

Whatever domain accounts you use for SQL Server, you should use strong (long and complex) passwords. Also, when entering the domain name for a domain user account, you must use the NetBIOS name, not the DNS name. (In our environment this means that the domain must be entered as "EXAMPLE" or "example," but not "example.local.")

Upgrading Windows SharePoint Services to SQL Server 2005

You can upgrade the companyweb SharePoint site to use SQL Server 2005 instead of the Windows Microsoft SQL Server Desktop Engine (WMSDE) instance (MSSQL$SHARE-POINT). You can do this as part of the original SQL Server 2005 installation, or after installing a default database by running the SQL Server 2005 Setup program.

Before You Upgrade

You should perform a cold backup of the existing companyweb SharePoint site before attempting to upgrade it. A cold backup is a file-system backup of the files while all activity and services that connect to it are stopped.

To do a cold backup of the companyweb site, follow these steps:

1. Log on to the console of the SBS server with the Administrator account or an account in the Domain Admins group.

2. Find the companyweb site by opening the Internet Information Services (IIS) Manager and navigating to the Web Sites container, as shown in Figure 20-9.

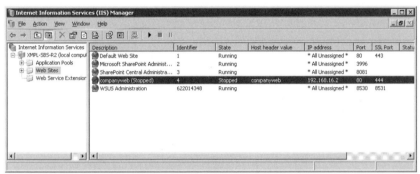

Figure 20-9   The Internet Information Services (IIS) Manager.

3. Right-click companyweb and select Stop.

4. Open the Services application, stop the SharePoint Timer Service, and set its startup type to Manual, as shown in Figure 20-10.

5. While in the Services application, stop the MSSQL$SHAREPOINT service. Close the Services application.

6. Copy the SharePoint database files to a backup location. The files are located in the "%ProgramFiles\Microsoft SQL Server\MSSQL$SHAREPOINT\data" directory. The four files are:

   ❑ STS_*xmpl-sbs-r2*_1.mdf (where *xmpl-sbs-r2* is your server name)

   ❑ STS_*xmpl-sbs-r2*_1.mdf_log.ldf (where *xmpl-sbs-r2* is your server name)

   ❑ STS_Config.mdf

   ❑ STS_Config_log.ldf

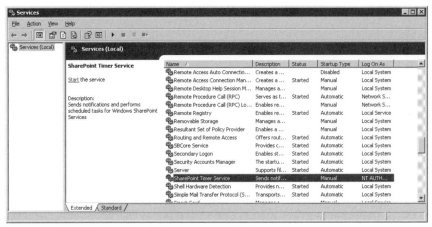

Figure 20-10 The Services application with SharePoint Timer Service stopped and set to Manual.

7. Remove the SharePoint WMSDE instance by opening the Add/Remove Programs application from Control Panel and selecting Microsoft SQL Server Desktop Engine (Sharepoint), as shown in Figure 20-11. Click Remove and then click Yes in the Add Or Remove Program confirmation dialog box.

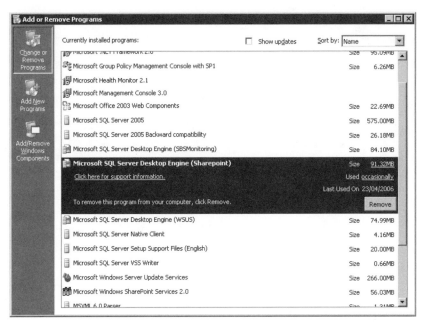

Figure 20-11 Removing the Microsoft SQL Server SharePoint instance.

Upgrading Companyweb to SQL Server 2005

Once you've ensured that you have a sound backup of the existing configuration to fall back to, and that all the existing files are quiescent, you're ready to upgrade by following these steps:

1. Restart your server. Yes, we know it didn't prompt you for a reboot, but do it anyway.

2. Log on to the console of the SBS server with the Administrator account or an account in the Domain Admins group.

3. Insert the Premium Technologies CD1. If Autorun doesn't automatically start the Setup program, manually start it by double-clicking Setup.exe in Windows Explorer.

4. Follow the steps to install SQL Server 2005—as described previously in the section "Installing SQL Server 2005"—until you get to the Feature Selection page. If this is not the first SQL Server 2005 database instance you're installing, you might see slightly different steps.

5. On the Feature Selection page, verify that SQL Server Database Services is set to Entire Feature Will Be Installed Local Hard Drive, as shown in Figure 20-12.

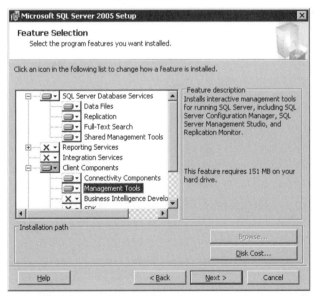

Figure 20-12   The Feature Selection page of the Microsoft SQL Server 2005 Setup Wizard with all SQL Server Database Services selected.

6. Select Management Tools and Connectivity Components from the Client Components feature.

7. On the Instance Name page, select Named Instance and type **SHAREPOINT** (all uppercase) in the Named Instance field, exactly as shown in Figure 20-13. Click Next.

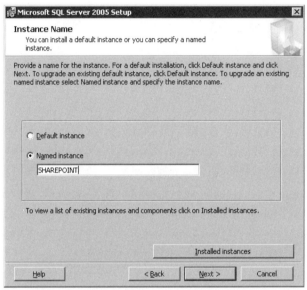

Figure 20-13   Adding the SharePoint named instance on the Instance Name page of the Microsoft SQL Server 2005 Setup Wizard.

8. If this is not the first instance installed on the SBS server, you might see an Existing Components page. Click Next if you do.

9. On the Service Account page, select Use The Built-In System Account, as shown in Figure 20-14.

10. Follow the rest of the steps from the previous section, "Installing SQL Server 2005," and click Finish when the installation has finished.

11. Open SQL Server Management Studio. Select *XMPL-SBS-R2*\SHAREPOINT (where *XMPL-SBS-R2* is the name of your SBS server) from the drop down list of Server Names, as shown in Figure 20-15. Click Connect.

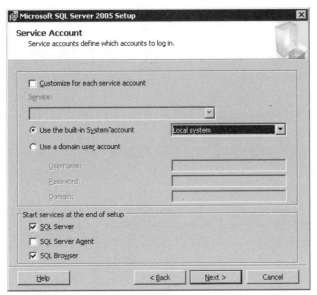

Figure 20-14   Use the Local System account on the Service Account page of the Microsoft SQL Server 2005 Setup Wizard.

Figure 20-15   Connecting to the SHAREPOINT instance using Microsoft SQL Server Management Studio.

12.   In the Object Explorer pane, navigate to the Security folder, right-click Logins and then select New Login, as shown in Figure 20-16.

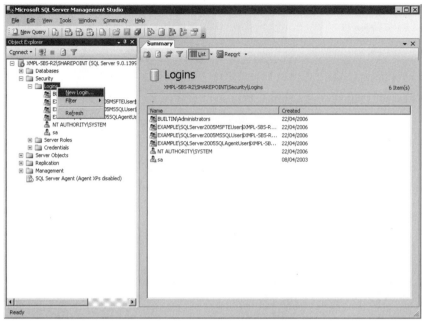

Figure 20-16   Creating a new login for the SHAREPOINT instance.

13. In the Login – New dialog box, shown in Figure 20-17, type **NT Authority\Network Service** and click OK.

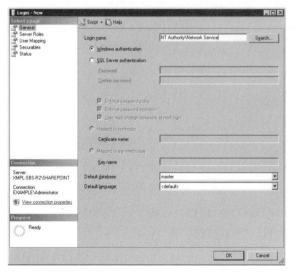

Figure 20-17   Specifying a login account.

14. Repeat the previous two steps to create a login for *EXAMPLE*\SBS SP Admins (where *EXAMPLE* is your SBS NetBIOS domain name).

15. Right-click the NT Authority\Network Service login you just created and select Properties to open the Login Properties – NT AUTHORITY\Network Service dialog box. Click Server Roles in the right-hand pane and select dbcreator and securityadmin from the list of roles, as shown in Figure 20-18. Click OK.

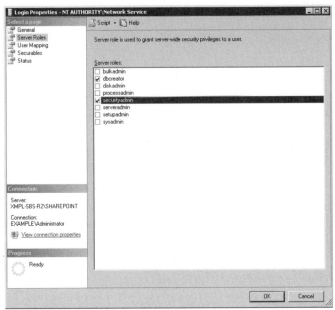

Figure 20-18   The Server Roles page of the Login Properties dialog box.

16. In the left-hand pane of Microsoft SQL Server Management Studio, right-click Databases and select Attach to open the Attach Databases dialog box, shown in Figure 20-19.

17. Click Add and then browse to %ProgramFiles%\Microsoft SQL Server\MSSQL$SHAREPOINT\data directory, as shown in Figure 20-20. Select STS_*XMPL-SBS-R2*_1.mdf and click OK twice.

18. Repeat the previous two steps to add the STS_Config.mdf database files.

19. Close Microsoft SQL Server Management Studio.

20. Open the Services application, start the Windows SharePoint Timer Service, and change it back to Automatic.

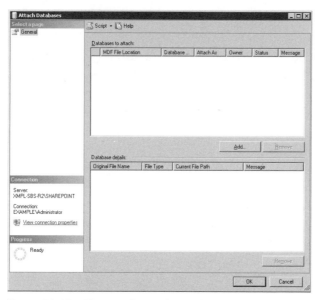

Figure 20-19   The Attach Databases dialog box.

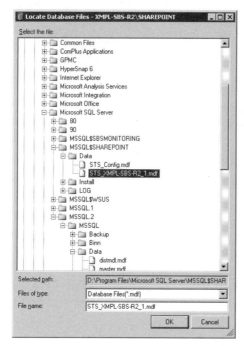

Figure 20-20   The Locate Database Files dialog box.

21. Restart the companyweb Web Site in the Internet Information Services (IIS) console.

Finally, turn on full-text search in Windows SharePoint Services by following these steps:

1. Open Administrative Tools, SharePoint Central Administration.

2. Scroll down to Component Configuration, as shown in Figure 20-21.

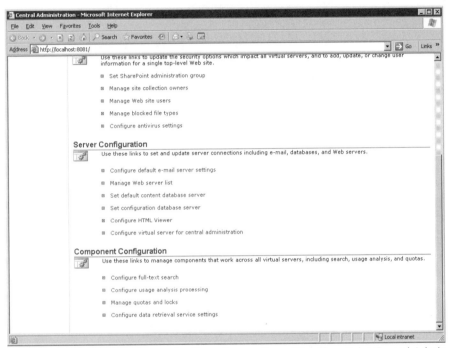

Figure 20-21 The Component Configuration section of the SharePoint Central Administration page.

3. Click Configure Full-Text Search, select the Enable Full-text Search and Index Component check boxes, and then click OK. Voila! You're now using SQL Server as your repository for companyweb.

> **Note** The main advantage to using full SQL Server 2005 for your companyweb is the full-text search capability that SQL Server 2005 gives you. This will significantly speed up your SharePoint site.

Architecture

At the core of Microsoft SQL Server 2005 is the relational database, which is made up of the actual database files that store the data and the database management system (DBMS) that both manages the structure of the database—including the relationship between various portions—and maintains the integrity of the data, including handling system failures by restoring the data to a point in time when it was consistent.

In addition to the DBMS components, at the core of the database are communications components that ensure that the database can communicate with clients, manage encryption, and accept or provide streaming data as required. There are also additional server components that help integrate the database into the overall Microsoft .NET architecture.

Administration

Microsoft SQL Server 2005 administration is not integrated into the Server Management console, but instead uses its own management console—SQL Server Management Studio (SqlWb.exe), shown in Figure 20-22.

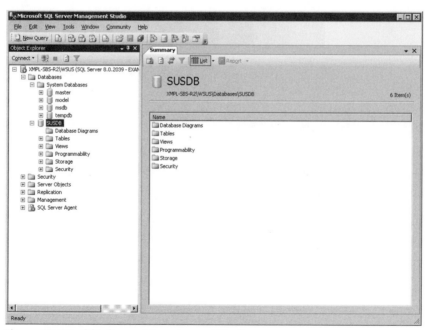

Figure 20-22   SQL Server Management Studio.

In addition to SQL Server Management Studio, SQL Server 2005 includes other management tools, including the SQL Server Configuration Manager, the SQL Server Profiler, the Database Engine Tuning Advisor, the Reporting Services Configuration Manager, the Deployment Wizard, and the SQL Server Service Manager. Many of these can be launched directly from within SQL Server Management Studio.

SQL Server Management Studio works with the WMSDE databases on your SBS server as well as databases you've migrated to SQL Server 2005. Figure 20-22 shows SQL Server Management Studio with the Object Explorer connected to the WSUS instance that uses WMSDE.

Important   The SBSMONITORING and WSUS databases should not be migrated to SQL Server 2005, but remain on WMSDE. Using SQL Server 2005 for these databases is not a supported configuration.

Start, Stop, and Pause

Although it's easy enough to start or stop instances on your local machine using SQL Server Management Studio or even the Net Start and Net Stop commands from a command line, using the SQL Server Service Manager (Sqlmangr.exe), shown in Figure 20-23, enables you to start, stop, or pause a database on a remote server as well. You can also set a service to automatically start by selecting the Auto-Start Service When OS Starts check box.

Figure 20-23   The SQL Server Service Manager lets you start, stop, and pause the services for both local and remote databases.

Backup

Backing up your SQL Server databases should be done on a regular schedule as part of a comprehensive backup and disaster recovery program. The SQL Server 2005 database backup is *not* integrated into the Windows Small Business Server Backup utility and so must be run separately. SQL Server 2005 supports both standard tape and file backups and logical backups using the export utility covered in the section "Import and Export Data" later in this chapter.

More Info   For more information about backups in general, see Chapter 13, "Backing Up and Restoring Data." For detailed information about off-site backups and disaster recovery scenarios, see Chapter 22, "Disaster Planning."

Defining a Backup Device

To simplify backing up your SQL Server 2005 database, you can define a backup device before you actually back up the database. That backup device can be a tape drive or a file.

To define a backup device, open SQL Server Management Studio and follow these steps:

1. Connect the Object Explorer to the database you want to define a backup device for.

   Note   You can connect the Object Explorer to more than one SQL Server database concurrently. Once SQL Server Management Studio is open, select Database Engine from the Connect drop-down list to connect to additional databases.

   ---

2. Navigate to Server Objects, Backup Devices in the left-hand pane.

3. Right-click Backup Devices and select New Backup Device, as shown in Figure 20-24.

4. In the Backup Device dialog box, shown in Figure 20-25, type a descriptive name for the device in the Device Name field and then specify the target destination.

5. Click OK and the device is added. You can predefine multiple backup devices, or define a device when creating the backup.

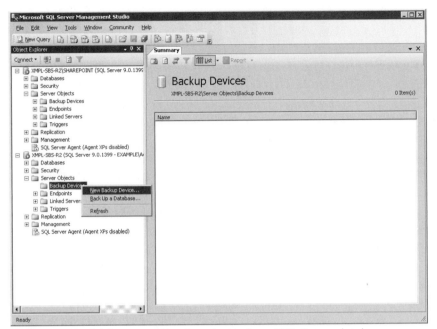

Figure 20-24   Adding a new backup device for a SQL Server database.

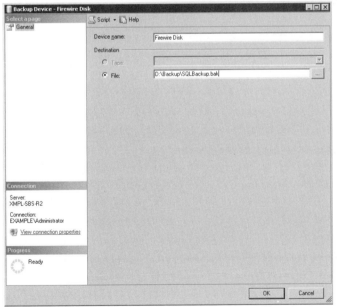

Figure 20-25   The Backup Device dialog box in SQL Server Management Studio.

Backing Up a Database

Even if you haven't yet defined a backup device, you can add a backup device as part of the backup process when you are doing your backup from SQL Server Management Studio. When you back up using SQL Server Management Studio, you can use existing backup devices or specify new ones.

To back up a database from SQL Server Management Studio, complete the following steps:

1. Open Microsoft SQL Server Management Studio if it isn't already open.

2. Navigate to Server Objects, Backup Devices in the left-hand pane.

3. Right-click the backup device you want to use and select Backup A Database. (To define a new device as part of the backup process, right-click Backup Devices and select Back Up A Database.)

4. In the Back Up A Database dialog box, shown in Figure 20-26, select the database to back up from the drop-down list.

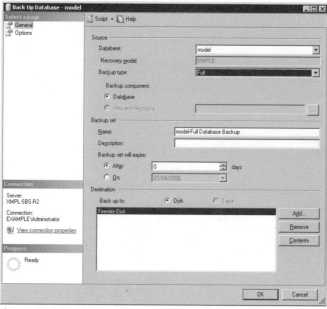

Figure 20-26   The Back Up A Database dialog box in SQL Server Management Studio.

5. Type a name for the database backup in the Name field.

6. Choose a Backup Type—either Full or Differential.

7. Type a name and a description for the backup.

8. Set an expiration date for the backup, either in number of days or an absolute date. An expiration of zero days means that the backup will never expire.

9. Select the backup destination. If the destination you want to use is not shown, click Add to add an additional destination to the list.

10. You can set additional options, including appending to the backup media or overwriting, and verification of the backup by clicking Options in the left-hand pane of the Back up A Database dialog box, as shown in Figure 20-27.

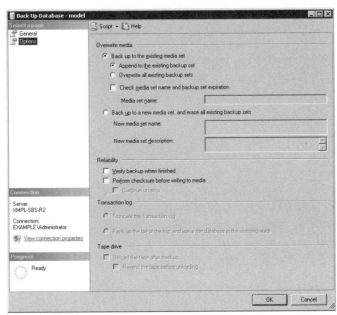

Figure 20-27   The Options page of the Back up a Database dialog box.

11. Click OK and the backup will begin.

Viewing the Contents of a Backup Device

Because a backup device might contain more than one backup, it is useful to be able to see the contents of the device. To view the contents of a backup device, follow these steps:

1. Open Microsoft SQL Server Management Studio if it isn't already open.

2. Navigate to Server Objects, Backup Devices in the left-hand pane.

3. Double-click the backup device to open the Backup Device dialog box.

4. Click Media Contents in the left-hand pane to see a list of the backups on the device, as shown in Figure 20-28.

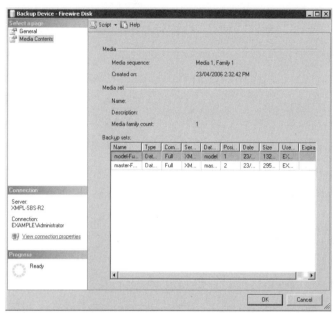

Figure 20-28   The Backup Device page of the Firewire Disk backup device.

Summary

In this chapter, we've taken a brief look at the Microsoft SQL Server 2005 component of Microsoft Windows Small Business Server 2003 Premium Edition, including detailing how to convert your companyweb SharePoint site to use SQL Server 2005 as the repository for the site.

In the next chapter, we'll examine the tools and techniques for monitoring and troubleshooting your Microsoft Windows Small Business Server 2003 network.

Part V
Maintenance and Troubleshooting

Chapter 21   Monitoring and Fine-Tuning Performance 541

Chapter 22   Disaster Planning 581

Chapter 23   Planning Fault Tolerance and Avoidance 601

Chapter 21
Monitoring and Fine-Tuning Performance

Enabling Auditing And Monitoring 541

Selecting A Monitoring Method 546

Using System Monitor. 546

Performance Logs and Alerts. 553

Using Alerts. 558

Permissions for Counter Logs, Trace Logs, and Alerts 561

Monitoring Memory Usage 562

Monitoring Processor Activity 565

Monitoring Disk Activity. 567

Using Health Monitor 568

Summary 579

For a network to operate at its best, you must be able to recognize bottlenecks and take action to eliminate them. This chapter covers the system and network monitoring tools in Microsoft Windows Small Business Server 2003 that enable you to detect problems and tune your system to its optimum performance level.

Enabling Auditing And Monitoring

If you haven't already set up Monitoring on your SBS server, now is a good time. SBS gives you daily reports of the overall health of your network, along with weekly usage reports. The two reports give you an excellent overview of the status of your network; any security events that you need to be aware of; and a snapshot of the e-mail, fax, and file system usage patterns of your users. For details on enabling Monitoring on your SBS server, see Chapter 5, "Completing the To Do List and Other Post-Installation Tasks."

Predefined Performance and Usage Reports

Windows Small Business Server 2003 includes two predefined monitoring reports: One is a daily performance monitoring report that includes all the critical events in your system, including security events, and the other is a weekly usage report that shows the fax, e-mail, and file system usage patterns for your users and helps you highlight issues before they get out of hand or you run out of space. If you haven't already enabled these reports, do so now. They're both excellent reports and can help you maintain your network health and availability. See Chapter 5 to learn how to enable them.

Auditing Events

Auditing is a necessary part of network administration. By reviewing reports and event logs, you can track usage patterns, security problems, and network traffic trends. Beware of the impulse to audit everything, however. The more events you audit, the bigger the logs. Reviewing huge event logs is a painful chore, and eventually no one looks at them anymore. Therefore, it's critical to decide on an auditing policy that protects your network without creating a large administrative burden. Also bear in mind that every audited event results in a small increase in performance overhead.

Customizing Auditing

Every audited event tells you something, but it's not always something you need to know. For example, auditing successful logons and logoffs might reveal the use of a stolen password, or it might just produce countless pages showing that your duly authorized users are logging on and off as expected. Auditing logon failures, however, can definitely be rewarding when someone is trying a random password hack.

Table 21-1 lists the categories of events that can be audited.

Table 21-1 Auditing categories

Event Category	Activated When
Account logon events	A domain controller receives a logon request.
Account management	A user account or group is created or changed.
Directory service access	An Active Directory object is accessed.
Logon events	A user logs on or logs off.
Object access	An object is accessed.
Policy change	A policy affecting security, user rights, or auditing is modified.
Privilege use	A user right is used to perform an action.
Process tracking	An application executes an action that is being tracked.
System events	A computer is rebooted or shut down, or another event occurs that affects security.

You need to use Group Policy Management to change the settings for auditing events. To do this, complete these steps:

1. Select Group Policy Management from the Administrative Tools menu.

2. In the console tree under Group Policy Objects, right-click Default Domain Controllers Policy and select Edit.

3. In the console tree of the Group Policy Object Editor, expand Computer Configuration, Windows Settings, Security Settings, and Local Policies to reach Audit Policy, as shown in Figure 21-1.

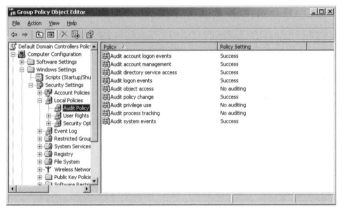

Figure 21-1   Auditing categories in the GPO for domain controllers.

4. Double-click an auditing category in the details pane to change a policy definition. Click OK when you are finished.

Viewing Event Logs

Event logs must be viewed with regularity for auditing to be useful. To view the security log, open Event Viewer from the Administrative Tools folder and then click Security. Double-click any entry to see more information about it. The security entries in Figure 21-2 occurred over a couple of minutes because the object being audited was set to audit successful events. Of course, you'll generally learn more from auditing failed events than from auditing successful ones, but this does demonstrate the need to choose your auditing battles carefully.

Searching Event Logs

No matter how selective you are, the event logs mix all sorts of information together, making searches for specific information difficult. To search for a specific type of event, select the log in Event Viewer, and choose Filter from the View menu. In the Properties dialog box, shown in Figure 21-3, select the type or types of events you want returned. Table 21-2 describes the filtering options in the Properties dialog box.

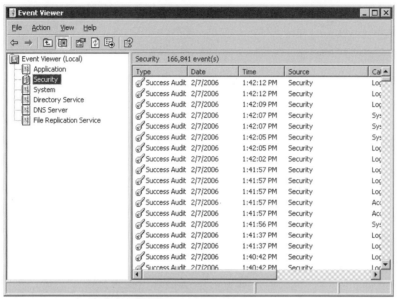

Figure 21-2   Viewing the Security Event Log.

Figure 21-3   Filtering event information using Event Viewer.

Table 21-2   Options for filtering event logs

Option	Use to Search or Filter for
Information	Notification that some major operation has been performed successfully.
Warning	Notification of some problem or potential problem. Warnings might or might not be significant. For example, an "unexpected" reboot of the server with the reason "other" generates a warning.
Error	Notification of an important event. Errors signify a loss of data or a loss of function. For example, failure of a service to start during bootup generates an error.
Success Audit	Events audited for success.
Failure Audit	Events audited for failure.
Event Source	A source for an event, such as a system component or a program.
Category	Events by category, such as logon/logoff, policy change, or process tracking.
Event ID	The specific ID number assigned to each logged event.
User	A specific user.
Computer	A specific computer.
From	Events after a specific date. The default is the first date in the log. You can click the drop-down box to select events on a specific date.
To	Events before a specific date. The default is the last date in the file.

Setting the Size of Event Logs

When an event log is full, a dialog box pops up to notify you. If this happens often, you might want to reduce the number of items being reported or increase the size of the log. To set event log options, complete the following steps:

1. Select Event Viewer from the Administrative Tools menu.

2. Right-click the log you want to configure and choose Properties.

3. On the General tab, select the options you want. Under When Maximum Log Size Is Reached, there are three options:

   ❑ If you don't archive this log, select Overwrite Events As Needed.

   ❑ If you archive this log at regular intervals, you can select the Overwrite Events Older Than option. Fill in the appropriate number of days.

   ❑ Do Not Overwrite Events, the last option, means that the log must be cleared manually. When the maximum log size is reached, new events are simply not recorded.

4. Click OK when you're finished.

> **Important** While SBS will allow you to create event logs larger than 64 MB, resist the temptation. Having event logs larger than that will cause backup problems, and realistically won't help you manage your SBS network. If you *must* keep all event logs for legal reasons, set the size at a reasonable level and create a scheduled script task that automatically archives off the logs and clears them.

Selecting A Monitoring Method

If you need to observe a system event as it's happening, use a graph in System Monitor. Graphs are helpful for real-time, short-term monitoring of a remote or local computer. Choose an update interval that best captures the data for the type of activity you are observing. Performance logs are better suited for long-term monitoring and record keeping. You can export logged data and use it to generate reports, and you can also view the information as graphs or histograms using System Monitor. Logging in this manner is also more practical when you need to monitor several computers at once.

Health Monitor can track just about everything that System Monitor and performance logs can, plus it includes a preconfigured set of alerts that are only for Windows Small Business Server.

> **Planning** This is a good place to repeat the adage that just because something *can* be done, it doesn't mean it *should* be done. Many counters, logs, and alerts are quite esoteric and of no practical use in an SBS environment. Keep the number of counters and logs you have to manage to a bare minimum. Reduce the number of conditions that generate alerts so that you are using only those conditions that are genuinely critical.

Using System Monitor

System Monitor tracks various processes on a Windows Small Business Server system in real time, returning the results in a graphical display. Use the data from System Monitor to target processes and components that need to be optimized, check the results of your tuning and configuration, and understand trends in workloads and their effect on resource usage.

System Monitor Items

System Monitor uses three types of items to monitor the system:

- **Counter** A component within an object that represents data for a specific aspect of the system or service.

- **Instance** A single occurrence of multiple-performance objects of the same type on a computer. If a particular object has multiple instances, you can track the statistics for each instance by adding a counter for each. You can also add a counter to track all instances at once. An instantaneous counter, such as Process\Thread Count, is an example of an instance. It displays the most recent count of the number of threads for a particular process. An instance can also be an average of the last two values for a process over a period of time between samples.

- **Object**   A collection of counters associated with a resource or service that generates data you can evaluate. Each time an object performs a function, its corresponding counters are updated. A range of objects typically corresponding to major hardware components is built into the operating system. Some programs that you install add other components and their corresponding objects. Table 21-3 lists some of the more common objects and what each type monitors.

Table 21-3   Objects tracked in System Monitor

Object	What It Monitors
Browser	The Browser service for a domain or workgroup
Cache	Disk cache usage
Memory	Memory performance for physical and virtual memory
Objects	The number of events, mutexes, processes, sections, semaphores, and threads on the computer at the time of data collection
Paging File	Pagefile usage
PhysicalDisk	Hard disks with one or more partitions
Process	All processes running on a computer
Processor	Each processor on the system
Server	Bytes, sessions, certain system errors, pool nonpaged usage, and pool paged usage
System	Counters that affect all the hardware and software running on the system
Thread	All threads running in the system

Running System Monitor

To launch System Monitor, select Performance from the Administrative Tools menu. By default, System Monitor displays the system's current processor utilization as a line graph. Most functions are performed using the System Monitor toolbar shown in Figure 21-4.

Adding Counters

You can add counters by clicking the Add button to display the Add Counters dialog box shown in Figure 21-5. System Monitor compresses the data as necessary so that it fits into the details pane, and you can display dozens of counters at a time, more than you can comfortably view on a single screen.

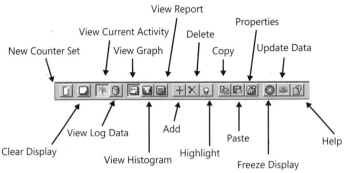

Figure 21-4   System Monitor toolbar.

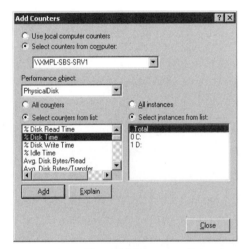

Figure 21-5   The Add Counters dialog box.

Selecting Counters

In the Add Counters dialog box, select either the Use Local Computer Counters option or the Select Counters From Computer option. If you're monitoring the computer on which System Monitor is running, you'll want to select Use Local Computer Counters. If you want to monitor a different computer, select the Select Counters From Computer option, and then choose the name of the computer to be monitored from the list box.

In the Performance Object list, specify an object to monitor. The Processor object is selected by default. For each object, you can choose to monitor all the available counters or only those you specify. To monitor all the available counters for a particular object, select the All Counters option. To monitor only the counters you specify, select the Select Counters From List option. For a description of any counter, select the name of the counter and then click Explain.

Note   When you monitor multiple instances of the same counter, the instance index number assigned to a particular instance might change over time. This happens because the instance starts and stops and in the process is assigned a different instance index number.

Matching Counters to Graph Lines

A color and bar thickness is assigned to each counter within the legend. If you aren't monitoring many counters, you can easily match the color to the counter. However, there are certainly occasions when several counters bunch together on the graph, making it difficult to visually separate them. When that happens, click a counter in the list below the graph and then click Highlight. As you can see in Figure 21-6, the selected line is heavily traced to make it more visible.

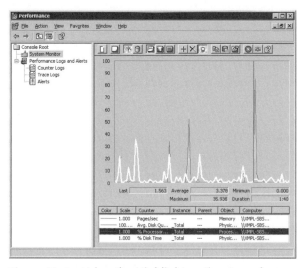

Figure 21-6   Using the Highlight option to make a graph line more visible.

Deleting Counters

To stop monitoring one or more counters, you can delete only specific counters or delete all counters. Open System Monitor, select the name of a counter in the legend in the System Monitor details pane, and click the Delete button on the toolbar. To delete all the counters currently being monitored so that you can monitor a new set of counters, click New Counter Set on the toolbar.

Determining How Often to Monitor

How often you monitor a particular data set is important because if the interval is too short, the resulting log is large and unwieldy. If the interval is too long, the event might not be captured. For routine data logs, start out by setting the value in the Sample Data

Every box in the Properties dialog box for the log to 15 minutes. To find this option, display the Properties dialog box of the specific counter log. You can adjust this interval to fit the type of data you are monitoring. If you have a slow memory leak, for example, use a longer time interval. Another consideration is the overall length of time you monitor a system. If you are monitoring for fewer than 4 hours, a 15-minute interval is acceptable. If you are monitoring a system for 8 hours or more, don't set a time interval that is shorter than 5 minutes (300 seconds). Monitoring at a frequent rate causes the system to generate a lot of data, producing large log files. It also greatly increases the overhead.

Modifying the Display

Change the way System Monitor displays information by using the System Monitor Properties dialog box (Figure 21-7). Click Properties on the toolbar or right-click in the details pane and choose Properties from the shortcut menu.

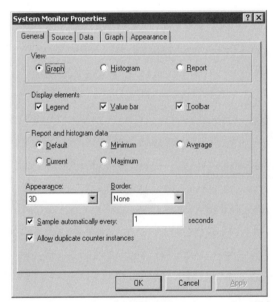

Figure 21-7   The System Monitor Properties dialog box.

Choosing a View

On the General tab, choose to view the data in the form of a graph, a histogram, or a report:

- **Graph view**   Presents information in a traditional line graph format. Each counter and instance is displayed in a different color and line thickness. Although the graph view is the most versatile, it's better to use the histogram or report view because the graph view increases monitoring overhead, particularly when a large number of counters is being monitored.

- **Histogram view**   Presents information in a bar graph format as shown in Figure 21-8. As in graph view, each of the counters and instances is presented in a different color. You can track up to 100 counters using this view because System Monitor adjusts the bars to fit the display.

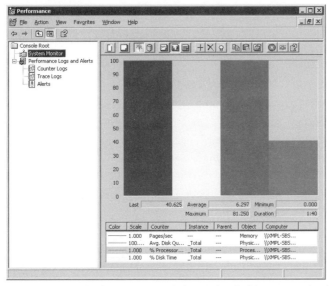

Figure 21-8   Displaying system information in histogram view.

- **Report view**   Objects are listed in alphabetical order, as are each of the chosen counters for each object. The data itself is displayed numerically. Each object displays the total percentage of processor time in use for the chosen counters. (See Figure 21-9.) This view is best when you need to track a large number of counters.

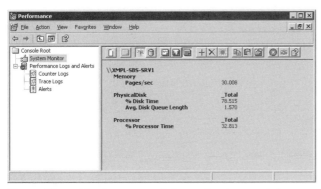

Figure 21-9   Viewing system information in report view.

Choosing Display Elements

On the General tab, you can also choose the following display options in the Display Elements area:

- **Legend**   At the bottom of the details pane, shows the data scale used for each counter, the counter name, the instance, the parent object (if applicable), the object the counter belongs to, the computer being monitored, and the color used to draw the line for the counter. The legend is available for the graph and histogram views. You must display the legend to see the counter name associated with the data line.

- **Value Bar**   Provides a quick way to see the values for a specific counter. Click a counter in the legend or double-click a data line to display the last, average, minimum, and maximum values recorded. The values are calculated from the number of samples and time period displayed in the graph. The duration value is based on the update interval time and is calculated to show the total elapsed time displayed in the graph. This display element is available for the graph and histogram views and is helpful for monitoring a specific value that you want to keep a close watch on.

- **Toolbar**   Displays the toolbar across the top of the details pane.

Choosing the Time Interval for Monitoring

You can sample data for all three views at regular intervals. To set the time interval option, click the Properties button on the toolbar, and on the General tab, select the Sample Automatically Every *n* Seconds check box. The default interval is 1 second, but consider specifying a longer interval to reduce the size of log files. Select the update interval that is best for capturing the type of activity you want to view.

Selecting Additional Properties

Add vertical and horizontal grid lines to the graph and histogram views on the Graph tab of the System Monitor Properties dialog box. You can also change the maximum and minimum vertical scale values on the Graph tab; the defaults are 100 for the maximum value and 0 for the minimum value. The highest value you can specify is 999999999, and the lowest value is 0. Both values must be a positive integer. Determine the vertical scale range from the ranges of values for the counters you are monitoring. Change the display colors on the Data tab and the background and font display on the Appearance tab shown in Figure 21-10.

On the Source tab, select the log file or database to view as part of configuring your monitoring plan.

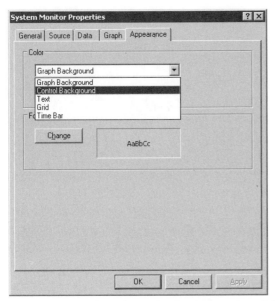

Figure 21-10   Changing color, background, and font used for System Monitor.

Monitoring Another Computer

By default, System Monitor displays information about the local system, but you can also configure it to monitor another computer on the network. To do so, click Add Counters, select the Select Counters From Computer option, and, in the text box, type the name of the computer to be monitored. You can choose and delete counters and modify the display as described in the previous sections.

You need administrative permissions on the other computer to monitor that computer through System Monitor. If you don't have administrative permissions, an error message is generated. The counter appears in the display, but no data or graph lines are associated with it. If a particular counter that you want to monitor does not appear in the counter list, it is likely that the service or feature providing the counter has not been installed or enabled on that computer.

Performance Logs and Alerts

Performance Logs and Alerts expands the monitoring capabilities of System Monitor to include features for logging counter and trace data and for generating performance alerts. Logged counter data information can be exported to spreadsheets or databases for analysis and report generation. The data can be stored as a text file (comma- or tab-delimited), a binary file, a binary circular file where the log file is a set size and new data overwrites old data, or a SQL database.

Performance logging runs as a service. As a result, a user doesn't have to be logged on to the monitored computer for data collection to occur. You can manage multiple logging sessions from a single console window and view data as it is collected as well as after collection has stopped. Automatic log generation enables the defining of parameters such as file name, file size, and start and stop times. An alert can be set on a counter to cause a specific action to occur, such as starting a specified program, sending a notification message, or starting a log when the value of a selected counter falls below or exceeds a specified setting.

Counter Logs

A counter log collects data at a predefined interval. Counter logs are helpful for recording data about system services activities and hardware usage from the local computer or a remote computer. You can log data manually on demand or schedule logging to start and stop automatically. The system can also perform continuous logging, depending on the file size and duration limits you set. The logged data can be viewed through the System Monitor display or exported to spreadsheets or databases.

You can view the counters configured in the counter log dynamically through System Monitor by saving log settings such as counters as an HTML page. The resulting page hosts the System Monitor control through an Active X control that provides the interface for the monitoring user.

Trace Logs

Rather than measure samples at a predefined interval, as counter logs do, a trace log monitors data continuously and waits for specific events such as page faults to occur. That data is then recorded into a binary trace log file. Developers can use the tools in the Microsoft Platform SDK to translate binary trace logs into human-readable form.

Creating Counter and Trace Logs

To create a counter log or a trace log, complete the following steps:

1. Launch Performance from the Administrative Tools menu, and in the console tree, expand Performance Logs And Alerts.

2. In the console tree, select Counter Logs to create a counter log, or select Trace Logs to create a trace log. Existing logs are listed in the details pane. A red icon indicates a log that is not running or has been stopped; a green icon indicates a log that is running.

3. Right-click in a blank area of the details pane and choose New Log Settings (Figure 21-11).

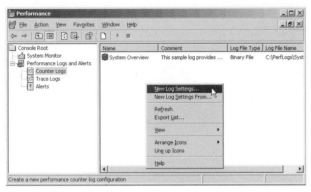

Figure 21-11   Creating new log settings.

4. In the Name text box, type the name of the counter or trace log you are creating and click OK. A Properties dialog box for configuring the counter or trace log you are creating is displayed.

5. Configure the counter or trace log to monitor your local or remote computer by choosing the proper counters for the resources to be monitored, selecting log file properties, and choosing the desired scheduling options. The sample data interval for counter logs is set on the General tab of the Properties dialog box for the log.

More Info   For guidelines about setting time intervals, see the "Determining How Often to Monitor" section earlier in this chapter.

Adding Counters to Counter Logs

Counters are added on the General tab of a log's Properties dialog box. When you create a counter log file, the Properties dialog box is displayed automatically. If you need to add counters later, you can display the Properties dialog box by right-clicking the name of the log file, choosing Properties from the shortcut menu, clicking Add on the General tab, and then choosing the desired counters. The procedure for selecting counters is identical to that described earlier this chapter in the section titled "Selecting Counters."

Saving Log and Alert File Settings

To save the settings for a log or an alert file, right-click the name of the log or alert file in the details pane, and then choose Save Settings As from the shortcut menu. Type the name you want to give to the log or alert file, and save it as an .htm file. You can use the saved settings for a new log or alert by right-clicking in the details pane, choosing New

Log Settings From, and then selecting the .htm file containing the settings you want to reuse.

Selecting System and Nonsystem Providers for Trace Logs

-Events in trace logs are monitored not by counters but by providers. You can choose to log events by system or nonsystem providers. The default system provider, the Windows Kernel Trace Provider, monitors threads, processes, disk I/O network TCP/IP, page faults, and file details. The default system provider uses the most overhead to monitor events. Only one trace log at a time can be run using the system provider. If you attempt to run more than one, you receive an error message.

To choose providers, right-click the name of the trace log file and choose Properties from the shortcut menu. On the General tab, as shown in Figure 21-12, select the Events Logged By System Provider option and then choose the events you want to monitor, or select the Nonsystem Providers option and then add the nonsystem providers of your choice (for example, Active Directory) by clicking Add.

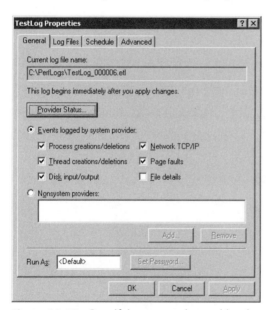

Figure 21-12 Specifying events logged by the system provider.

Remember that trace logging of page fault and file details generates a huge amount of data. Microsoft recommends that you limit trace logging using these fault options to a maximum of two hours; otherwise, you might run out of disk space on your computer.

Choosing nonsystem providers to monitor the system incurs less overhead. With nonsystem providers, you can select the data providers of your choice. You cannot run concurrent multiple trace logs using the same nonsystem provider, but you can do so using different nonsystem providers. Some of the nonsystem providers available in SBS 2003 include ACPI Driver Trace Provider; Active Directory: Kerberos; Active Directory: NetLogon; Active Directory: SAM; DNS Trace; Local System Authority (LSA); NTLM Security Protocol; and Exchange Information Store.

Setting File Parameters for Counter and Trace Logs

To set file parameters for counter and trace logs, complete the following steps:

1. Open Performance and expand Performance Logs And Alerts.

2. In the console tree, select Counter Logs to set file parameters for counter logs, or select Trace Logs to set file parameters for trace logs.

3. Double-click the name of the log for which you want to set the file parameters. A dialog box displaying the properties of the log appears.

4. Click the Log Files tab, and set the desired parameters for the log file. (The available parameters are described in the next section.)

Understanding the Log File Parameters

The Log Files tab of the Properties dialog box for a counter or trace log allows the setting of a number of file parameters, such as the file type and whether to end the file name with a set of sequential numbers or a date to keep track of multiple log files. To specify a folder other than the default chosen by Windows (the PerfLogs folder at the root directory), click Configure.

The Configure Log Files dialog box also has a log file size option to allow the log file to become as large as disk quotas or the operating system permits or to limit the size to a specific size. Limit the size of a log file if you want to use one of the circular logging options. In conjunction with limiting the size of a log file, you can use the When The Log File Is Full option on the Schedule tab to run a command if you want a particular action to occur when the log file reaches its limit. You can choose from among five file types for a counter log:

- **Text File - Comma Delimited** Used to export data to a spreadsheet program. The data is stored as a comma-delimited log file with the file extension .csv.

- **Text File - Tab Delimited** Can also be used to export data to a spreadsheet program. The data is stored as a tab-delimited log file with the file extension .tsv.

- **Binary File** Used for intermittent instances (instances that stop and start after the log has been started). The data is stored as a sequential, binary-format log file with the file extension .blg.

- **Binary Circular File**   Records data continuously to the same log file where the new records overwrite the previous ones. The data is stored in binary format as a circular file with the file extension .blg.

- **SQL Database**   Records data into an existing SQL database.

Trace logs can be either of two file types:

- **Circular Trace File**   Records data continuously to the same log file where the new records overwrite the previous ones. The data is stored in a circular file with the file extension .etl.

- **Sequential Trace File**   Collects data until a user-defined limit is reached. When the limit is reached, the current file is closed and a new one is started. The data is stored as a sequential file using the file extension .etl.

The default file type for counter logs is Binary File (with the extension .blg), and the default file type for trace logs is Sequential Trace File (with the extension .etl).

Using Alerts

An alert notification is sent to the user by means of the Messenger service when a pre-defined counter value reaches, falls below, or rises above a defined threshold. The Messenger service must be running for alert notifications to be sent to the user.

Creating an Alert

To create an alert, complete the following steps:

1. Open Performance, and expand Performance Logs And Alerts.

2. In the console tree, select Alerts. Existing alerts are listed in the details pane. A red icon indicates an alert that is not running or has been stopped; a green icon indicates an alert that is running.

3. Right-click Alerts and select New Alert Settings from the shortcut menu.

4. In the Name text box, type the name of the alert you are creating and click OK. A Properties dialog box for configuring the alert (in this case named High Level Activity) opens.

5. Click Add on the General tab to open the Add Counters dialog box (Figure 21-13).

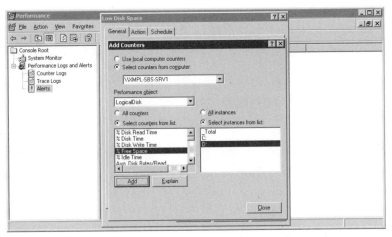

Figure 21-13   The Add Counters dialog box for new alert settings.

6. Configure the alert by specifying whether to monitor the local computer or a remote computer, choosing one or more counters, and setting threshold values for the counters. Click Add to add the alerts, and then click Close to close the Add Counters dialog box.

7. On the Action tab, select an action to perform when an alert is triggered.

8. On the Schedule tab, choose when and how the Alert log starts. (These settings are described in the next section.)

Configuring an Alert

You must choose threshold values for each counter on which you set an alert. This is done on the General tab of the Properties dialog box for the alert. When you create an alert, the Properties dialog box is displayed automatically. If you need to add counters at a later date, you can access the Properties dialog box by right-clicking the name of the alert file, choosing Properties from the shortcut menu, and clicking Add on the General tab.

> **More Info**   For information about specifying a computer to monitor and on selecting counters for the alert, see the section titled "Selecting Counters" earlier in this chapter.

Thresholds trigger an alert when the value of the counter falls either above or below a baseline you've chosen. To establish a baseline, determine the acceptable level of system performance when your system is experiencing a typical workload and running all required services. You do this by reviewing logged data graphed by System Monitor or by exporting the data and generating reports for analysis.

On the Action tab of the Properties dialog box, as shown in Figure 21-14, you can specify actions that should occur when a threshold is exceeded.

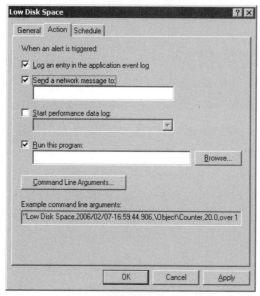

Figure 21-14   Specifying actions to take when a threshold is crossed.

Four options are available:

- **Log An Entry In The Application Event Log**   Causes the alert to log an entry that is visible to you in Event Viewer.

- **Send A Network Message To**   Triggers the Messenger service to send an alert message to a specified computer.

- **Start Performance Data Log**   Runs an existing counter log.

- **Run This Program**   Specifies a program to run when an alert is triggered. Click the Command Line Arguments button to add command-line arguments that provide additional information. For example, in Figure 21-15, selecting Alert Name, Counter Name, Measured Value, and Limit Value adds the details shown in the Example box.

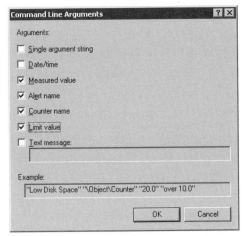

Figure 21-15   Adding arguments to the alert to produce additional information.

Permissions for Counter Logs, Trace Logs, and Alerts

To create or modify a log or alert, you must have Full Control permission for the registry entry HKEY_LOCAL_MACHINE\SYSTEM\CurrentControlSet\Services\SysmonLog\ LogQueries. Administrators are assigned this permission by default, and they can grant this permission to users by using Regedit.exe.

To run the Performance Logs and Alerts service, you must have permission to configure or start services on the system. Administrators are assigned this permission by default and can grant this permission to others using Group Policy. (The built-in groups Performance Log Users and Performance Monitor Users are useful for this.) To log data for a remote computer, the Performance Logs and Alerts service must run under an account that has access to that remote system. The service runs in the background after a log or alert is configured and running.

Real World   Tuning and Testing Strategies

Before starting System Monitor or Performance Logs and Alerts on the computer you are monitoring, turn off screen savers and stop services that are not essential to monitoring the system. Other best practices include the following:

- Set up Performance Logs and Alerts to monitor and report data on counters at regular intervals, such as every 10 to 15 minutes.

- Make only one change at a time. Bottlenecks can be caused by one component, or they can be the result of a series of faults. Making multiple changes at once can make it impossible to assess the impact each change has on the system.

■ Keep a record of changes you make, and repeat the monitoring process after every change. Changes can affect other resources, and keeping records helps to determine the effect of each change and whether additional changes are necessary.

■ Compare programs that run over the network against those that run locally. This tells you whether network components might be playing a part in performance problems.

■ Pay regular attention to event logs. Some performance problems generate output into Event Viewer.

■ When logging data through Performance Logs and Alerts, exclude times that include start-up events. Start-up events tend to skew overall performance results because they show temporarily high values.

■ Find out what your baseline memory usage is on a freshly booted server. Use this to compare against when you want to see who the memory hog is.

■ If you have a server with more than 2 GB of RAM, you will almost certainly need to adjust the thresholds of several memory usage alerts to avoid false alerts.

Monitoring Memory Usage

Memory usage is usually the first item to look at when experiencing performance problems. If you find that your system is paging frequently, you probably need more memory. Some paging is expected to expand memory, but too much paging is a drain on system performance. Since hard disks are the slowest component of your system, anything that increases the need to read or write from the hard disk will have a negative impact on performance.

> **Note** Paging is used to free memory for other uses by moving fixed-size blocks of data and code from RAM to your disk in units called *pages*.

Before monitoring memory usage, perform a few checks. For example, verify that your system has the recommended amount of memory for running SBS plus any additional applications or services you are running on your server. If you don't know what the memory requirements are for a process, you can discover its working set within System Monitor. Shut the process down and observe the effect on paging activity. The amount of memory that is freed when you terminate a process is the amount of memory the process was using.

Note   A *working set* is the portion of physical memory allocated to each program running on the computer.

Recommended Counters

To check for possible memory leaks or bottlenecks, monitor these counters:

- **Memory\Pages/Sec**   Displays the number of pages written to or read from disk to resolve hard page faults. A *hard page fault* occurs when a process requires code or data that must be retrieved from disk rather than from its working set or elsewhere in physical memory. If this value is above 20 per pagefile, you need to research paging activity and make adjustments as necessary. A high value for this counter might be more indicative of a paging problem than a memory problem.

- **Memory\Committed Bytes**   Displays the number of committed bytes of virtual memory on your system and is an instantaneous counter. Monitor this counter, along with Memory\Available Bytes, over a period of time if you suspect a memory leak.

- **Memory\Pool Nonpaged Bytes**   Displays the number of bytes allocated to the nonpaged pool for objects that cannot be written to disk but must instead remain in physical memory as long as they are allocated. If this value is high, you need additional memory on your system. Use this counter in conjunction with Memory\ Pool Nonpaged Allocs if you suspect that a kernel-mode process is the cause of a memory leak.

- **Memory\Pool Nonpaged Allocs**   Shows the number of calls to allocated space in the nonpaged pool. Use this counter in conjunction with Memory\Pool Nonpaged Bytes to determine whether you have a memory leak.

- **Server\Bytes Total/Sec**   Monitors the number of bytes the computer has received from and sent to the network. The value is indicative of how busy the server is. You need to add memory if you have a sustained, dramatic increase in this value.

- **Server\Pool Paged Bytes**   Monitors the number of bytes of pageable computer memory currently in use by the system. Use this information to determine values for the MaxPagedMemoryUsage entry in the Windows registry.

- **Server\Pool Nonpaged Bytes**   Monitors the number of bytes of nonpageable computer memory in use by the system. Use this information to determine the values for the MaxNonpagedMemoryUsage entry in the Windows registry.

To monitor for a low memory condition, use these counters:

- **Memory\Available Bytes**   When free bytes fall into short supply (4 MB or fewer), the shortage is replenished by taking memory from the working sets of less active programs. As a result, you see an increase in the working set value for one program and a steady decrease in the values of other programs, causing an increase in paging that causes performance to suffer. You'll need to add memory to solve the problem.

- **Memory\Cache Bytes**   Monitors the number of bytes being used by the file system cache. Use this counter in conjunction with Memory\Available Bytes.

- **PhysicalDisk\% Disk Time and PhysicalDisk\Avg. Disk Queue Length**   Indicates a memory shortage when used in conjunction with Memory\Page Read/Sec. If an increase in queue length is not accompanied by a decrease in the Memory\Page Read/Sec value, a shortage does exist.

To check for excessive paging, monitor these counters:

- **Paging File\% Usage (all instances)**   Paging files are shared by every process and are used to store pages of memory on your system. If you suspect that paging is to blame for your bottleneck, it is helpful to review this value, along with Memory\Available Bytes and Memory\Pages/Sec. The acceptable threshold for this value is 99 percent. Enlarge Pagefile.sys if the value increases to 100 percent.

- **Paging File\% Usage Peak**   If the value for this counter approaches the maximum paging file setting, the size of Pagefile.sys needs to be increased.

- **PhysicalDisk\Avg. Disk Sec/Transfer and Memory\Pages/Sec**   The PhysicalDisk\ Avg. Disk Sec/Transfer counter displays the average disk transfer in seconds. The Memory\Pages/Sec counter displays the number of pages written to or read from the disk when a process requires information that is no longer in its working set and must be retrieved from disk. To determine whether the system is paging excessively, multiply the values of these two counters. If the result exceeds 0.1, paging is taking up more than 10 percent of disk access time. If this condition persists over a period of time, you need additional memory.

Under the Hood   Tips for Memory Troubleshooting

For most SBS servers, memory is the primary limiting factor to performance. If you are experiencing problems with memory, try checking these areas:

- **Paging file**   Verify that the paging file is the correct size. You can also split the paging file between multiple physically separate disks (not multiple volumes on the same physical disk) of similar speeds to increase performance.

When the paging file reaches the maximum limit assigned to it, a warning is displayed and the limit is increased. Programs might become unstable while the limit is increased, and the system might crash if there isn't enough disk space for additional virtual memory.

- **Physical memory**   Increase the physical memory above the required minimum. The limit for SBS is 4 GB of RAM.

- **Memory settings**   Confirm that memory settings are configured properly.

- **Memory-intensive programs**   If possible, run memory-intensive programs when your system workload is lightest, or run them on another server.

Monitoring Processor Activity

High processor values can mean either that your computer is handling the workload in a very efficient manner or that it is struggling to keep up. When a bottleneck occurs because a process's threads need more processor cycles than are available, long processor queues build up, causing the system response to suffer. The two common causes of processor bottleneck are excess demand placed on the processor by CPU-bound programs and excess interrupts generated by drivers or subsystem components, such as disk or network components.

Minimum Recommended Counters

The minimum recommended counters for monitoring the server's processor component for possible bottlenecks are the following:

- **System\Processor Queue Length (all instances)**   A sustained queue length of more than 10 items per processor indicates a bottleneck.

- **Server Work Queues\Queue Length**   A queue length of greater than four over a sustained period of time indicates possible processor congestion.

- **Processor\Interrupts/Sec**   Use this counter to determine whether interrupt activity is causing a bottleneck. A dramatic increase in this counter value without a corresponding increase in system activity indicates a hardware problem. To resolve this problem, you need to find the network adapter or other device that is the source of the interrupts. Refer to the manufacturer's specifications for the acceptable processor threshold; use 1000 interrupts per second as a starting point.

- **Processor\% Interrupt Time**   Displays the percentage of time the processor spends receiving and servicing hardware interrupts during the sample interval. This value provides an indirect indication of the activities of devices that generate interrupts, such as disk drives, network adapters, and other peripheral devices. These devices interrupt the processor when they require attention or complete a task. Look for a dramatic increase in the value without a corresponding increase in system activity.

To monitor possible usage problems, use these counters:

- **Processor\% Processor Time (all instances)** Use this counter to discover a process that is using more than 85 percent of processor time. You might need to install an additional processor or upgrade to a faster one.

- **Processor\% User Time** Monitors the percentage of nonidle processor time that is spent in user mode. A high rate could indicate a need to upgrade or install additional processors. Use this counter in conjunction with Processor\% Processor Time (all instances).

- **Processor\% Privileged Time** Monitors the percentage of nonidle processor time designated for hardware-manipulating drivers and operating system components. A high rate might be attributed to a large number of interrupts being generated by a device that is failing. Use this counter in conjunction with Processor\% Processor Time (all instances).

Under the Hood   Tips for Processor Monitoring

Try the following to resolve problems with the processor:

- **Upgrade the processor** Upgrade to a faster processor, replace a failing one, or add another processor to the computer, especially if you are running multithreaded programs. In computers that only support a single processor, you can often upgrade to a dual-core processor and gain a substantial improvement.

- **Adjust the workload of the system** Distribute programs more efficiently among servers, or schedule programs to run at off-peak hours.

- **Manage processor affinity on multiprocessor computers** Managing the processor affinity with respect to interrupts and process threads can improve performance because it reduces the number of processor cache flushes during thread movement from one processor to another.

You set affinity for a particular process or program when you assign it to a single processor to improve its performance, at the expense of the other processors. Be warned that when you dedicate a process or program to a processor, your other program threads might not be permitted to migrate to the least busy processor. You can set affinity in Task Manager, and it is available only on multiprocessor systems.

Monitoring Disk Activity

Monitoring disk usage helps to balance the load of servers. When monitoring disk performance, log the performance data to another disk or computer to prevent it from skewing the data for the disk you are testing.

Note   Disk counters are permanently enabled in Windows Small Business Server 2003 and Microsoft Windows XP. To enable disk counters for Microsoft Windows 2000, use the Diskperf command. (Type **diskperf -?** at a command prompt for additional information.)

Minimum Recommended Counters

The following list shows the minimum recommended counters for monitoring the server's disk performance for possible bottlenecks:

- **PhysicalDisk\Current Disk Queue Length (all instances)**   Monitors the number of system requests that are waiting for disk access. This number should remain steady at no more than 1.5 to 2 times the number of spindles that make up the physical disk. Most disks have one spindle. The exception is Redundant Array of Independent Disks (RAID) devices, which usually have more than one spindle. You need to observe this value over several intervals because it is an instantaneous counter.

- **PhysicalDisk\% Disk Time**   Indicates how busy your server's disk drives are by displaying the percentage of time that a drive is active. If the value of this counter rises to more than 90 percent or if you are using a RAID device, check the PhysicalDisk\ Current Disk Queue Length (all instances) counter to see how many disk requests are queued for disk access. RAID devices can cause the PhysicalDisk\% Disk Time value to exceed 100 percent and thus give an incorrect reading.

- **PhysicalDisk\Avg. Disk Sec/Transfer**   Monitors the amount of time a disk takes to fulfill a request. A high value might indicate that the disk controller is continually trying to access the disk as a result of failures. For most systems, a value of 0.3 seconds or higher indicates a high average disk transfer time.

To monitor possible usage problems, use these counters:

- **PhysicalDisk\Avg. Disk Bytes/Transfer**   Monitors the average number of bytes that are transferred from or to a disk during read or write operations. A value less than 20 KB indicates that an application is accessing the disk drive inefficiently.

■ **PhysicalDisk\Disk Reads/Sec and Disk Writes/Sec** If these counters show that actual usage is near the specified transfer rate of the physical disks, consider reducing the server's workload or upgrading to a RAID setup.

Under the Hood   Tuning and Upgrading Tips for Disks

If you are experiencing problems with disk performance, try the following solutions:

■ Verify that you have installed the latest driver software for your host adapters.

■ Install additional disks, or upgrade your hard disk to a faster disk. Update the bus and the disk controller at the same time.

■ On servers, create striped volumes on several physical disks to increase throughput.

■ Distribute applications among your servers to help balance the workload.

■ Optimize disk space by running Disk Defragmenter.

■ To help in balancing the server workload, isolate tasks that use disk I/O heavily to separate disk controllers or physical disks.

■ Relocate the Windows pagefile to a separate physical disk.

See Chapter 6, "Disk Management," for more information about disk management and optimization.

Using Health Monitor

Health Monitor is the easiest tool for checking current conditions on the server. To launch this tool, select Health Monitor from the Administrative Tools menu. In the console tree, expand Health Monitor and All Monitored Computers to the name of your server. Under the server name, expand Small Business Server Alerts and then Core Server Alerts (Figure 21-16).

Select an alert in the list to display details about it in the right panes. On the Thresholds tab, shown in Figure 21-17, the name and status of the alert rule are displayed. In the Alerts pane (lower pane) are the alerts that have been generated by the rule.

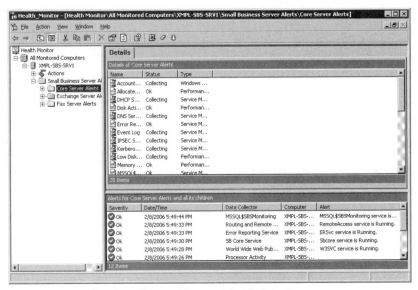

Figure 21-16   The Core Server Alerts in Health Monitor.

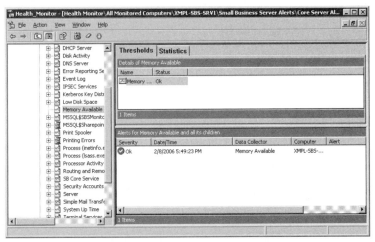

Figure 21-17   Display of the Memory Available alert.

To see the actual settings for the alert, right-click the name in the details pane and select Properties from the shortcut menu. As you can see in Figure 21-18, the status for Memory Available changes to Critical if the average available memory is less than 4 MB for 10 minutes (10 samplings).

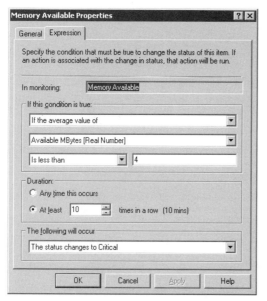

Figure 21-18   Settings to generate an alert.

Under Small Business Server Alerts in the console tree, there are also folders for Exchange Server Alerts and Fax Server Alerts. In general, the preconfigured settings are optimal for all the Alerts, but you can modify the settings or add another threshold to the existing one.

Modifying an Existing Threshold

To change the conditions that trigger an alert, select the alert in the console tree. Right-click the threshold and select Properties from the shortcut menu. Make changes on the Expressions tab and click OK when you finish.

Real World   Servers with > 2GB of RAM

One example of a threshold you might want to change is the Allocated Memory threshold, shown in Figure 21-19. If your server has more than 2 GB of RAM, you will need to modify the threshold values in your memory monitoring to avoid annoying alerts telling you that your server has "a large amount of memory allocated to applications and processes." The default values were set and defined when a typical SBS server rarely had more than 1 GB of RAM. They're simply wrong if you have more than 2 GB of RAM, and will generate false reports. On our server, with 3GB of RAM, we find that setting this value to 3000000000 (just under 3 GB) avoids annoying false alerts, while still warning us if our server is getting memory starved.

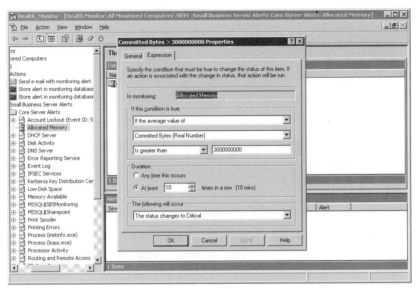

Figure 21-19   Setting the Allocated Memory alert.

Adding a Threshold

To add a threshold that triggers an alert, right-click the alert in the Health Monitor console tree and select New and then Threshold from the shortcut menu. Click the Expression tab and make your settings.

If you select an average value condition, the status of the threshold always shows as Collecting.

Configuring Actions

When an alert is generated because a threshold is crossed, the response is an action. Actions can take the form of an e-mail sent to specified recipients, a specific Windows event recorded to an event log, and several other forms. Once you configure an action, you can select it when setting up the Action tab of a data collector's Properties. (See the section titled "Creating a Data Collector" later in this chapter.)

Command-Line Action

A command-line action runs a program and parameters in response to a threshold being crossed.

To create a command-line action, complete the following steps:

1. In the console tree, right-click Actions, select New, and then select Command Line Action to open the Properties dialog box.

2. On the Details tab, click the Browse button next to the File Name box. In the Browse For File dialog box, locate the program you want to run.

3. To specify a directory the program should run in, browse for a folder by clicking the Browse button next to the Working Directory box.

4. In the Command Line box, type the parameters for the program. Or click the > button and select one of the strings (Figure 21-20).

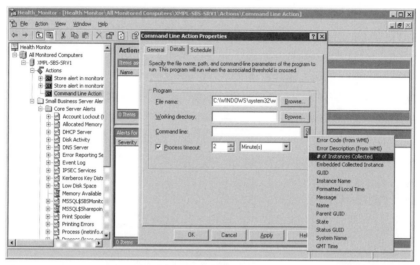

Figure 21-20 Setting command-line options.

5. Set a Process Timeout, which refers to the amount of time to allow the program to run before being automatically terminated.

6. Select the Schedule tab to set days and times the action can be taken. (The default is to run all the time.) On the General tab, you can give the action a descriptive name and also type in comments, a description, or other information.

7. Click OK when finished.

E-Mail Action

An e-mail action sends e-mail to specified recipients in response to a threshold being crossed.

To create an e-mail action, complete the following steps:

1. Right-click Actions in the console tree, select New, and then select E-Mail Action to open the Properties dialog box.

2. On the Details tab, specify the SMTP mail server and the recipients.

3. Click the > button next to the Subject field and select the message parameters to be shown in the e-mail's subject line. Or type in your own subject.

4. Click the > button next to the Message field to specify the variables included in the message, or modify the message by typing directly in the Message text field.

5. Select the Schedule tab to set days and times the action can be taken. (The default is to run all the time.) On the General tab, you can give the action a descriptive name and also type in comments, a description, or other information.

6. Click OK when finished.

Text Log Action

A text log action writes to a specified log in response to a threshold being crossed.

To create a text log action, complete the following steps:

1. In the console tree of Health Monitor, right-click Actions, select New, and then select Text Log Action to open the Properties dialog box.

2. Click the Browse button for the File box. In the Browse For File dialog box, find the text log file you want to use.

3. Specify the maximum size for the log file.

4. Click the > button next to the Text box to specify the variables included in the text to be logged, or modify the text by typing directly in the text field.

5. Select the Schedule tab to set days and times the action can be taken. (The default is to run all the time.) On the General tab, you can give the action a descriptive name and also type in comments, a description, or other information.

6. Click OK when finished.

Windows Event Log Action

A Windows event log action launches a specified Windows event in response to a threshold being crossed.

To create a Windows event action, complete the following steps:

1. Right-click Actions in the console tree, select New, and then select Windows Event Log Action to open the Properties dialog box.

2. On the Details tab, select the Event type:

   ❑ **Information** Report on a successful event such as when a service starts.

   ❑ **Warning** Event that is not in itself important but suggests future problems.

❑ **Error**   A problem that must be heeded. Signifies a failure such as loss of data or a loss of function. For example, if a printer driver fails to load successfully, an Error is reported.

3. Click the > button next to the Text box to select insertion strings or modify the text.

4. Select the Schedule tab to set days and times the action can be taken. (The default is to run all the time.) On the General tab, you can give the action a descriptive name and also type in comments, a description, or other information.

5. Click OK when finished.

Script Action

A script action runs a specified script in response to a threshold being crossed.

To create a script action, complete the following steps:

1. Right-click Actions in the console tree, select New, and then select Script Action to open the Properties dialog box.

2. Select the script type. Type the Path for the script or click the Browse button and navigate to the script file.

3. After you locate the file, you can click the Edit button to edit the script text.

4. Select a process timeout.

5. Select the Schedule tab to set days and times the action can be taken. (The default is to run all the time.) On the General tab, you can give the action a descriptive name and also type in comments, a description, or other information.

6. Click OK when finished.

Using Data Collectors

Data collectors are objects that collect and hold information about counters, events, states, and instances. When you create data collectors, you specify when the data is collected and from which computer it is collected.

Creating a Data Collector

Data collectors are gathered in data groups under the name of the computer from which data is being collected. To create a new data group, right-click the computer name in the Health Monitor console tree, select New, and then Data Group. To add a collector to an existing data group, right-click the group in the Health Monitor console tree. Next, select New, Data Collector, and then select the type of data collector (Figure 21-21).

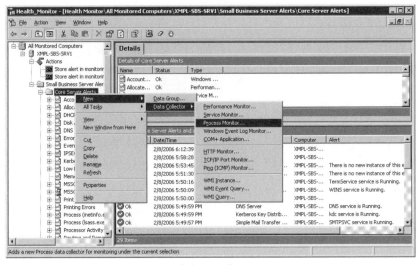

Figure 21-21   Selecting a type of data collector to create.

The available data collectors are:

- Performance Monitor

- Service Monitor

- Process Monitor

- Windows Event Log Monitor

- COM+ Application Monitor

- HTTP Monitor

- TCP/IP Port Monitor

- Ping (ICMP) Monitor

- WMI Instance

- WMI Event Query

- WMI Data Query

If you use Health Monitor, you're likely to use only the first four types of data collector, possibly the next three, and the last three not at all. Not that the various monitors can't be helpful, but most of them are surplus to requirements in the context of Windows Small Business Server.

After you select a data collector, the Properties dialog box for the collector opens. Supply the information required on the Details tab, which varies according to the data collector chosen. The following sections describe the options for the most commonly used data collectors.

In addition to the Details tab, all Properties dialog boxes include a tab to configure the message sent with a report and a Schedule tab to select collection days, times, and interval. On the General tab, you can rename the data collector from its default name and also type in comments, a description, or other information. The Actions tab specifies the actions for the system to take when the status of the data collector changes.

Performance Monitor

On the Details tab of a Performance Monitor data collector, you can specify the object to monitor.

- **Object** Click the Browse button next to the Object field. In the Browse For Objects On *Computer_Name* dialog box (Figure 21-22), select the object to monitor and click OK.

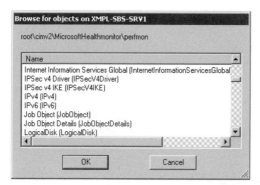

Figure 21-22 Selecting an object to monitor.

- **Counter** Select one or more counters to monitor.
- **Instance** Click Browse to select an instance or leave blank to monitor all instances.

By default, one threshold is set:

- Change the state to Critical if the error code is not equal to zero. A nonzero return points toward a data collection error.

To manually configure thresholds, select the data collector in the console tree, right-click the threshold in the details pane, and then select Properties from the shortcut menu. Click the Expression tab and set the conditions that trigger a change in state alert. To add a new threshold, right-click the data collector in the console tree, select New, and then click Threshold.

Real World   Requires Manual Reset Option

A data collector that exceeds its configured threshold automatically resets to an OK state when the collected information shows that the values have fallen to *below* the threshold. The logic behind this default behavior is that Health Monitor is intended to display the most current status of the objects being monitored. And most of the time, that's what you use Health Monitor for.

However, there are times when this default behavior is not what you want—for example, when you're having intermittent problems that are proving hard to substantiate, or you want to be sure that when the state of a given object changes, the change is reflected in the console tree.

For those objects, select the option for Requires Manual Reset To Return To OK Status on the Details tab of the data collector's Properties dialog box.

To perform a manual reset, right-click the data collector in the console tree and select All Tasks, and then select Reset & Check Now.

Service Monitor

On the Details tab of a Service Monitor data collector, you can specify the service to monitor.

- **Service**   Click the Browse button next to the Service field. In the Browse For Services On *Computer_Name* dialog box, select the service to be monitored and click OK.

- **Properties**   Select the properties you want to monitor.

By default, services have two thresholds already set:

- Change the state to Critical if error code is not equal to zero. A nonzero return signifies a data collection error.

- Change the state to Critical if the service is not started.

You can right-click either of the thresholds in the details pane and select Properties to make changes. Add a threshold by right-clicking the data collector in the console tree, selecting New, and then clicking Threshold.

Process Monitor

On the Details tab of a Process Monitor data collector, you can specify the process to monitor. Use Process Monitor to monitor applications and processes that are not Windows services. You can monitor only one process at a time.

- **Process** Click the Browse button next to the Process field. Select the Process to be monitored and click OK.

- **Properties** Select the properties to be monitored.

By default, a single threshold is set:

- Change the state to Critical if error code is not equal to zero. A nonzero return points toward a data collection error.

You can right-click the threshold in the details pane and select Properties to make changes. Add a threshold by right-clicking the data collector in the console tree, selecting New, and then clicking Threshold.

Windows Event Log Monitor

On the Details tab of a Windows Event Log Monitor data collector, you can specify the Windows events to monitor.

- **Types** The types of events to monitor.

- **Information** Report on a successful event such as when a service starts.

- **Warning** Event that is not in itself important but suggests future problems.

- **Error** A problem that must be heeded. Signifies a failure such as loss of data or a loss of function. For example, if a printer driver fails to load successfully, an error is reported.

- **Success Audit** An audited security access event that is successful. For example, a user successfully logs on to the network.

- **Failure Audit** An audited security access try that is unsuccessful. For example, a user's failed attempt to logon generates a Failure audit event.

- **Log file** Select the log file to use.

- **Application** Records events reported by applications.

- **Security** Records changes to the security settings and reports on possible security breaches.

- **System** Records events reported by Windows system components. For example, a service fails to start.

- **Source, Category, Event ID, User** To monitor all sources, categories, event IDs, and users, clear these check boxes. To monitor specifics, select the option and type the event source, event category, event ID, or particular user.

By default, two thresholds are set:

- Change the state to Critical if error code is not equal to zero. A nonzero return points toward a data collection error.

- Change the state to Critical if the number of instances collected is greater than zero.

You can right-click either of the thresholds in the details pane and select Properties to make changes. Add a threshold by right-clicking the data collector in the console tree and selecting New and then Threshold.

Other Monitors

Other monitors are available in addition to those just described. For information about how they're used, right-click Data Group in the console tree and select Help from the shortcut menu. Click the Index tab, type **data collection**, and then click the Display button.

Summary

In this chapter, you learned about the many ways to monitor virtually everything that happens on your network. Most of these monitors won't be used in the typical Windows Small Business Server environment, but making an acquaintance with the more accessible methods is time well spent. Chapter 22, "Disaster Planning," covers planning for the inevitable day when disaster—in one form or another—strikes, with a special emphasis on the unique needs of small businesses.

Chapter 22
Disaster Planning

Planning for Disaster. 581

Preparing for a Disaster 590

Summary. 600

Smart SCUBA divers dive with a "buddy" and carry an alternate air source, even though they've trained extensively and checked their equipment thoroughly. Schools and businesses have fire drills even though the vast majority of buildings never burn down. Similarly, system administrators sincerely hope they'll never need the verified backups and Automated System Recovery disks they have spent so much time creating. Nevertheless, we keep them because there are only two types of networks: those that have experienced disaster and those that haven't—yet.

Disaster can take many forms, from the self-inflicted pain of a user or administrator doing something really, really unwise, to the uncontrollable, unpreventable results of a natural disaster such as a flood or an earthquake. In any case, your business will depend on how well you were prepared for the disaster and how well you and your team responded to it and recovered from it.

This chapter covers emergency preparedness. It discusses creating a disaster recovery plan, with standardized procedures to follow in the event of a catastrophe. It also describes how to prepare for a disaster, including how to make an Automated System Recovery disk, how to make a boot disk, how to install the Recovery Console, how to specify recovery options in Microsoft Windows Server 2003, and how to create an external recovery drive.

Planning for Disaster

Some people seem to operate on the assumption that if they don't think about a disaster, one won't happen. This is similar to the idea that if you don't write a will, you'll never die—and just about as realistic. No business owner or system administrator should feel comfortable about their degree of preparedness without a clear disaster recovery plan that has been thoroughly tested. Even then, you should continually look for ways to improve the plan—it should only be your starting point. A good disaster recovery plan is one that you are constantly examining, improving, updating, and testing. But understand your disaster plan's limitations: It isn't perfect, and even the best disaster recovery plan needs to be constantly examined and adjusted or it quickly gets out of date.

Planning for disaster or emergencies is not a single step, but an iterative, ongoing process. Systems are not mountains, but rivers, constantly moving and changing, and your disaster recovery plan needs to change as your environment changes. To put together a good disaster recovery plan—one you can bet your business on—you need to follow these steps:

1. Identify the risks.

2. Identify the resources.

3. Develop the responses.

4. Test the responses.

5. Iterate.

Real World   Size Does Matter

Disasters happen to businesses of all sizes and types. Small businesses are no more insulated from them than large businesses are, but generally don't have the same levels of resources to respond to them and recover from them. A large, multinational corporation with an IT staff of several hundred worldwide certainly has more resources than a small accounting firm with an IT staff of one. As you work through the steps to build your disaster recovery plan, how you plan and implement it will vary depending the size of your company and the resources available.

Some of the steps we suggest here may be substantially more informal in a small business, but don't ignore them. No matter how small your business, if it uses and depends on Windows Small Business Server 2003, you have valuable and business-critical assets on your server, so take the steps to protect them and your business *before* you have a disaster. You'll save money, time, and, most important, business reputation by being able to withstand and even grow in the face of disaster.

We've been through fires, earthquakes, crashed servers, and just plain egregious error, and we've learned the hard way that disaster recovery is something that you can do a lot better if you've planned for it ahead of time. It's not sexy, and it's sometimes hard to sell to upper management, but it *is* worth the effort. If you're lucky, you'll never need to use all of your worst-case scenarios, but if you do need them, you'll really, really be glad you have them.

Identifying the Risks

The first step in creating a disaster recovery plan is to identify the risks to your business and the costs associated with those risks. The risks vary from the simple deletion of a critical file to the total destruction of your place of business and its computers. To properly prepare for a disaster, you need to perform a realistic assessment of the risks, the potential costs and consequences of each disaster scenario, the likelihood of any given disaster scenario, and the resources available to address the risks. Risks that seemed vanishingly remote a few years ago are now part of our everyday lives.

Identifying risks is not a job for a single person. As with all the tasks associated with a disaster recovery plan, all concerned parties must participate. There are two important reasons for this: You want to make sure that you have commitment and buy-in from the parties concerned, and you also want to make sure you don't miss anything important.

No matter how carefully and thoroughly you try to identify the risks, you'll miss *at least* one. You should always account for that missing risk by including an "unknown risk" item in your list. Treat it just like any other risk: Identify the resources available to address it and develop countermeasures to take should it occur. The difference with this risk, of course, is that your resources and countermeasures are somewhat more generic, and you can't really test your response to the risk, because you don't yet know what it is.

Start by trying to list all the possible ways that your system could fail. Solicit help from everyone with a stake in the process. The more people involved in the brainstorming, the more ideas you'll get and the more prevention and recovery procedures you can develop and practice. Be careful at this stage in the process to not dismiss *any* idea or concern as trivial, unimportant, or unlikely.

Next, look at all the ways that some external event could affect your system. (The current buzz word for this is "threat modeling," if you care.) The team of people responsible for identifying possible external problems is probably similar to a team looking at internal failures, but with some important differences. For example, if your business is housed in a large commercial office building, you'll want to involve that building's security and facilities groups even though they aren't employees of your business. They will not only have important input into the possible threats to the business, but also information on the resources and preventative measures already in place.

The risk identification phase is really made up of two parts—*identification* and *assessment.* *They are different tasks.* During the identify portion of the phase, you need to identify *every possible risk, no matter how remote or unlikely.* No risk suggested should be regarded as silly—don't limit the suggestions in any way. You want to identify every possible risk that anyone can think of. Then, when you have as complete a list as you can create, move on to the assessment task. In the risk-assessment task, you will try to understand and quantify just how likely a particular risk is. If you're located in a floodplain, for example, you're much more likely to think flood insurance is a good investment.

> **Note** Even in a very small business, where there may only be one person involved in disaster planning, it's a really good idea to get others involved somehow in at least the identification task of risk identification. Different people think up different scenarios and risk factors, and getting more and different viewpoints involved will improve the overall result of the process.

Identifying the Resources

Once you've identified the risks to your network, you need to identify what the resources are to address those risks. These resources can be internal or external, people or systems, hardware or software.

When you're identifying the resources available to deal with a specific risk, be as complete as you can, but also be specific. Identifying everyone in the company as a resource to solve a crashed server might look good, but realistically only one or two people are likely to actually be able to rebuild the server. Make sure you identify those key people for each risk, as well as the more general secondary resources they have to call on, such as Microsoft Product Support Services (PSS) and local Microsoft partners. So, for example, the primary resources available to recover a crashed server might consist of your hardware vendor to recover the failed hardware, and your own IT person or primary system consultant to restore the software and database. General secondary resources could include Microsoft Support (*http://support.microsoft.com/oas/default.aspx?gprid=3208*), Microsoft Partners in your area, and even newsgroups such as the microsoft.public.windows.server.sbs newsgroup.

An important step in identifying resources in your disaster recovery plan is to specify both the first-line responsibility *and* the back-end or supervisory responsibility. Make sure everyone knows who to go to when the problem is more than they can handle or when they need additional resources. Also, clearly define *when* they should escalate. The best disaster recovery plans include clear, unambiguous escalation policies. This takes the burden off individuals to decide when and whom to notify and makes it simply part of the procedure.

Developing the Responses

An old but relevant adage comes to mind when discussing disaster recovery scenarios: When you're up to your elbows in alligators, it's difficult to remember that your original objective was to drain the swamp. This is another way of saying that people lose track of what's important when they are overloaded by too many problems that require immediate attention. To ensure that your swamp is drained and your network gets back online, you need to take those carefully researched risks and resources and develop a disaster recovery plan. There are two important parts of any good disaster recovery plan:

- Standard operating procedures (SOPs)
- Standard escalation procedures (SEPs)

Making sure these procedures are in place and clearly understood by everyone involved *before* a disaster strikes puts you in a far better position to recover gracefully and with a minimum of lost productivity and data.

Standard Operating Procedures

Emergencies bring out both the best and worst in people. If you're prepared for the emergency, you can be one of those who come out smelling like a rose, but if you're not prepared and let yourself get flustered or lose track of what you're trying to accomplish, you can make the whole situation worse than it needs to be.

Although no one is ever as prepared for a system emergency as they'd like to be, careful planning and preparation can give you an edge in recovering expeditiously and with a minimal loss of data. It is much easier to deal with the situation calmly when you know you've prepared for this problem and you have a well-organized, *tested* standard operating procedure (SOP) to follow.

Because the very nature of emergencies is that you can't predict exactly which one is going to strike, you need to plan and prepare for as many possibilities as you can. The time to decide how to recover from a disaster is *before* the disaster happens, not in the middle of it when users are screaming and bosses are standing around looking serious and concerned.

Your risk assessment phase involved identifying as many possible disaster scenarios as you could, and in your resource assessment phase you identified the resources that are available and responsible for each of those risks. Now you need to write up SOPs for recovering the system from each of the scenarios. Even the most level-headed system administrator can get flustered when the system has crashed, users are calling every 10 seconds to see what the problem is, the boss is asking every 5 minutes when you'll have it fixed, and your server won't boot. And that's the easy case compared to the mess that can be caused by an external disaster.

Reduce your stress and prevent mistakes by planning for disasters before they occur. Practice recovering from each of your disaster scenarios. Write down each of the steps, and work through questionable or unclear areas until you can identify exactly what it takes to recover from the problem. This is like a fire drill, and you should do it for the same reasons—not because a fire is inevitable, but because fires do happen, and the statistics demonstrate irrefutably that those who prepare for a fire and practice what to do in a fire are far more likely to survive it.

Even where you know you're the only resource the company has to recover from a disaster scenario, write down the basic steps to do it. You don't need to go into minute detail, but at the very least, outline the key steps. This may be something you do for real only once in your life, so don't count on being able to remember everything. Disasters, by their very nature, raise the overall stress level and cause people to forget important steps.

Your job as a system administrator is to prepare for disasters and practice what to do in those disasters—not because you expect the disaster, but because if you do have one, you want to be the hero, not the goat. After all, it isn't often that the system administrator or IT consultant gets to be a hero, so be ready when your time comes.

The first step in developing any SOP is to outline the overall steps you want to accomplish. Keep it general at this point—you're looking for the big picture here. Again, you want everyone to be involved in the process. What you're really trying to do is make sure you don't forget any critical steps, and that's much easier when you get the overall plan down first. There will be plenty of opportunity later to cover the specific details.

Once you have a broad, high-level outline for a given procedure, the people you identified as the actual resources during the resource assessment phase should start to fill in the blanks of the outline. You don't need every detail at this point, but you should get down to at least a level below the original outline. This will help you identify missing resources that are important to a timely resolution of the problem. Again, don't get too bogged down in the details at this point. You're not actually writing the SOP, just trying to make sure that you've identified all of its pieces.

When you feel confident that the outline is ready, get the larger group back together again. Go over the procedure and smooth out the rough edges, refining the outline and *listening* to make sure you haven't missed anything critical. When everyone agrees that the outline is complete, you're ready to add the final details to it.

The people who are responsible for each procedure should now work through all the details of the disaster recovery plan and document the steps thoroughly. They should keep in mind that the people who actually perform the recovery might not be who they expect. It's great to have an SOP for recovering from a failed router, but if the only person who understands the procedure is the IT person, and she's on vacation in Bora Bora that week, your disaster recovery plan has a big hole in it.

When you create the documentation, write down *everything*. What seems obvious to you now, while you're devising the procedure, will not seem at all obvious in six months or a year when you suddenly have to follow it under stress.

Real World   Multiple Copies, Multiple Locations

It's tempting to centralize your SOPs into a single, easily accessible database. And you *should* do that, making sure everyone understands how to use it. But you'll also need to have alternative locations and formats for your procedures. Not only do you *not* want to keep the only copy in a single database, you also don't want to have only an electronic version—how accessible is the SOP for recovering a failed server going to be when the server has failed? Always maintain hard-copy versions as well. The one thing you don't want to do is create a single point of failure in your disaster recovery plan!

Every good server room should have a large binder, prominently visible and clearly identified, that contains all the SOPs. Each responsible person should also have one or more copies of at least the procedures he or she is either a resource for or likely to become a resource for. We like to keep copies of all our procedures in several places so that we can get at them no matter what the source of the emergency or where we happen to be when one of our pagers goes off.

Even if you're the only resource, keep multiple copies of your procedures and key phone numbers of external resources. Don't rely entirely on electronic storage, since even external electronic storage may be difficult to access if the disaster is major. But don't ignore electronic storage either. Most of the time, it's the fastest and easiest to get to, and the most likely to be completely up to date.

Once you have created the SOPs, your job has only begun. You need to keep them up to date and make sure that they don't become stale. It's no good having an SOP to recover your ISDN connection to the Internet when you ripped the ISDN line out a year ago and put in a DSL line with three times the bandwidth at half the cost.

You also need to make sure that all your copies of an SOP are updated. Electronic ones should probably be stored in a database or in a folder on the Windows Small Business Server that is available off-line. However, hard-copy documents are notoriously tricky to maintain. A good method is to make yet another SOP that details who updates what SOPs, how often, and who gets fresh copies whenever a change is made. Then put a version control system into place and make sure everyone understands his or her role in the process. Build rewards into the system for timely and consistent updating of SOPs—if 10 or 20 percent of someone's bonus is dependent on keeping those SOPs up to date and distributed, you can be sure they'll be current at least as often as the review process.

Standard Escalation Procedures

No matter how carefully you've identified potential risks, and how detailed your procedures to recover from them are, you're still likely to have situations you didn't anticipate. An important part of any disaster recovery plan is a standardized escalation procedure. Not only should each individual SOP have its own procedure-specific SEP, but you should also have an overall escalation procedure that covers everything you haven't thought of—because it's certain you haven't thought of everything.

An escalation procedure has two functions—resource escalation and notification escalation. Both have the same purpose: to make sure that everyone who needs to know about the problem is up to date and involved as appropriate, and to keep the overall noise level down so that the work of resolving the problem can go forward as quickly as possible. The *resource escalation procedure* details the resources that are available to the people who are trying to recover from the current disaster so that these people don't have to try to guess who (or what) the appropriate resource might be when they run into something they can't handle or something doesn't go as planned. This procedure helps them stay calm and focused. They know that if they run into a problem, they aren't on their own, and they know exactly who to call when they do need help.

The *notification escalation procedure* details who is to be notified of serious problems. Even more important, it should provide specifics regarding *when* notification is to be made. If a particular print queue crashes but comes right back up, you might want to send a general message only to the users of that particular printer letting them know what happened. However, if your e-mail has been down for more than half an hour, a lot of folks are going to be concerned. The SEP for e-mail should detail who needs to be notified when the server is unavailable for longer than some specified amount of time, and it should probably detail what happens and who gets notified when it's still down some significant amount of time after that.

This notification has two purposes: to make sure that the necessary resources are made available as required, and to keep everyone informed and aware of the situation. If you let people know that you've had a server hardware failure and that the vendor has been called and will be on site within an hour, you'll cut down the number of phone calls exponentially, freeing you to do whatever you need to do to ensure that you're ready when the vendor arrives.

Testing the Responses

A disaster recovery plan is nice to have, but it really isn't worth a whole lot until it has actually been tested. Needless to say, the time to test the plan is at your convenience and under controlled conditions, rather than in the midst of an actual disaster. It's a nuisance to discover that your detailed disaster recovery plan has a fatal flaw in it when you're testing it under controlled conditions. It's a bit more than a nuisance to discover it when every second counts.

You won't be able to test everything in your disaster recovery plans. Even most large organizations don't have the resources to create fully realistic simulated natural disasters and test their response to each of them under controlled conditions, and even fewer small businesses have those kinds of resources. Nevertheless, there are things you can do to test your response plans. The details of how you test them depend on your environment, but they should include as realistic a test as feasible and should, as much as possible, cover all aspects of the response plan. The other reason to test the disaster recovery plan is that it provides a valuable training ground. If you've identified primary and backup resources, as you should, chances are that the people you've identified as backup resources are not as skilled or knowledgeable in a particular area as the primary resource. Testing the procedures gives you a chance to train the backup resources at the same time.

You should also consider using the testing to cross-train people who are not necessarily in the primary response group. Not only will they get valuable training, but you'll also create a knowledgeable pool of people who might not be directly needed when the procedure has to be used for real, but who can act as key communicators with the rest of the community.

Iterating

When you finish a particular disaster recovery plan, you might think your job is done, but in fact it has just begun. Standardizing a process is actually just the first step. You need to continually look for ways to improve it.

You should make a regular, scheduled practice of pulling out your disaster recovery plan with those responsible and making sure it's up to date. Use the occasion to actually look at it and see how you can improve on it. Take the opportunity to examine your environment. What's changed since you last looked at the plan? What equipment has been retired, and what has been added? What software is different? Are all the people on your notification and escalation lists still working at the company in the same roles? Are the phone numbers, including home phone numbers, up to date?

Real World   Understand and Practice Kaizen

Kaizen is a Japanese word and concept that means "small, continuous, improvement." Its literal translation is, "Change (*kai*) to become good (*zen*)."

So, why bring a Japanese word and concept into a discussion about disaster recovery? Because a good disaster recovery plan is one that you are constantly Kaizening. When you really understand Kaizen, it becomes a way of life that you can use in many ways.

The first thing to understand about Kaizen is that you are *not* striving for major change or improvement. Small improvements are the goal. Don't try to fix or change everything all at once. Instead, focus on one area, and try to make it just a little bit better.

The second part of Kaizen is that it is continuous. You must constantly look for ways to improve and implement those improvements. Because each improvement is small and incremental, you can easily implement it and move on to the next one.

Kaizen is very much about teamwork. Good Kaizen balances the load on a team and finds ways to build the strengths of the team as a whole. If you practice Kaizen and continually look for small, incremental ways to improve your work, you will soon have a better and more enjoyable workplace. As a manager, if you find ways to encourage and reward those who practice Kaizen, your team and you will grow and prosper.

Another way to iterate your disaster recovery plan is to use every disaster as a learning experience. Once the disaster or emergency is over, get everyone together *as soon as possible* to talk about what happened. Find out what they think worked and what didn't in the plan. What tools did you not have that would have made the job go quicker or better? Actively solicit suggestions for how the process could be improved. Then make the changes and test them. You'll not only improve your responsiveness to this particular type of disaster, but you'll also improve your overall responsiveness by getting people involved in the process and enabling them to be part of the solution.

Preparing for a Disaster

As Ben Franklin was known to say, "Failure to prepare is preparing to fail." This is truer than ever with modern operating systems, and although Windows Small Business Server 2003 includes a number of exceptionally useful recovery modes and tools, you still need to prepare for potential problems. Some of these techniques are covered in detail in other chapters and are discussed here only briefly, whereas others are covered here at length.

Setting Up a Fault-Tolerant System

A fault-tolerant system is one that is prepared to continue operating in the event of key component failures. This technique is very useful for servers running critical applications. Here are a few of the many ways to ensure fault tolerance in a system:

- Use one or more RAID arrays for system and data storage, protecting you from hard-disk failure. If a hard disk in the array fails, only that disk needs to be replaced—and no data is lost. See Chapter 6, "Disk Management," for information about using Windows Small Business Server 2003 to implement software RAID.

- Use multiple SCSI adapters to provide redundancy if a SCSI controller fails.

- Use an uninterruptible power supply (UPS) to allow the server to shut down gracefully in the event of a power failure.

- Use multiples of everything that is likely to fail, including power supplies.

- Buy hardware that is listed in the Windows Server Catalog at:
  http://www.microsoft.com/windows/catalog/server/

Backing Up the System

Back up the system and system state regularly using a good Windows Small Business Server 2003 backup program. If a hard disk fails and must be replaced, and you're not using some sort of RAID array, the data and system can be restored from backup. See Chapter 13, "Backing Up and Restoring Data," for details about using the Windows Small Business Server 2003 backup program.

Creating an Automated System Recovery Disk

Whereas earlier versions of Windows Small Business Server created an emergency repair disk (ERD) to help rescue the system in the event of a disaster, Windows Small Business Server 2003 creates an Automated System Recovery (ASR) disk. The ASR disk contains important information that can be used to fix system files, the boot sector, and the startup environment. The ASR disk is easy to make, and it is *very* useful in the event of a disaster.

> **Note** In Windows Small Business Server 2003, you might have noticed that you didn't get prompted to create an ERD during installation, as you did during the setup of earlier versions. In fact, the entire procedure has changed. Now, instead of an ERD, you run the Backup program in Windows Small Business Server 2003 to create an ASR disk and backup. To make a fresh ASR disk, you need a floppy disk that you don't mind being formatted and sufficient space on your backup hard drive (or a fresh tape for your tape drive). Always use a freshly formatted floppy disk to create an ASR disk. It's also a good idea to have a backup of your

ASR disk, so always keep at least one generation back. We also like to keep an original ASR disk created immediately after the installation process as a kind of ultimate fallback position.

Note   Many servers today are bought without a floppy drive. If your server doesn't have a floppy drive, get an inexpensive USB floppy drive that you can use when you need one.

Important   ASR does *not* support write-enabled DVD or CD devices when those devices are used as a hard drive. Yet another reason we strongly suggest that DVD drives are not an appropriate backup device.

To make an ASR disk, complete the following steps:

1. Open the Windows Small Business Server Backup program. From the Start menu, point to All Programs, Accessories, System Tools, and then click Backup.

2. Switch to the Advanced Mode as shown in Figure 22-1 if you get a wizard prompt.

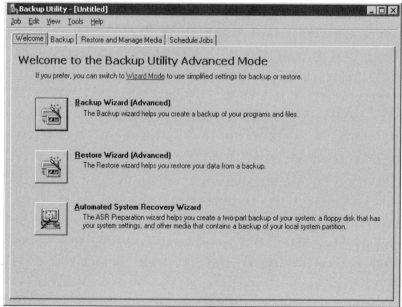

Figure 22-1   The Advanced mode of the Windows Small Business Server utility.

3. Click Automated System Recovery Wizard to open the Automated System Recovery Preparation Wizard. Click Next.

4. On the Backup Destination page shown in Figure 22-2, select the backup type and destination you'll be using. Click Next.

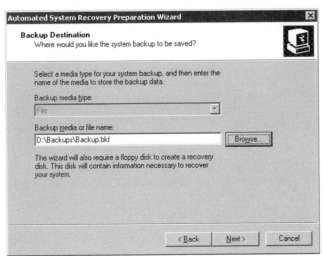

Figure 22-2   The Backup Destination page of the Automated System Recovery Preparation Wizard.

5. Click Finish to complete the wizard. The backup starts automatically when you exit the wizard, as shown in Figure 22-3.

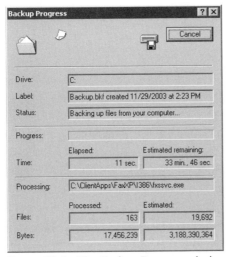

Figure 22-3   The Backup Progress window during Automated System Recovery Preparation.

6. Once the backup has completed, you'll be prompted to insert a blank floppy disk to create the ASR disk, as shown Figure 22-4.

Figure 22-4 The Create Automated System Recovery Disk prompt.

7. Insert a blank floppy disk in drive A, and click OK.

8. Backup writes the necessary files to the floppy disk and confirms that the process has been successful, as shown in Figure 22-5. Label the disk and the backup media used as requested and store them in a safe place.

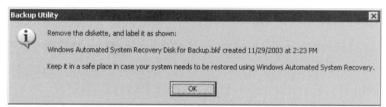

Figure 22-5 Always carefully label each ASR disk exactly as requested.

Note The ASR disk is not bootable; it must be used in conjunction with the Windows Small Business Server 2003 installation media. Also, each ASR is viable only with the specific backup set it was created as part of, so make sure you label the ASR carefully.

Under the Hood   Using the ASR Set Effectively

What, exactly, is on the ASR disk? Well, certainly not all the stuff that used to be there in Microsoft Windows NT. Instead of trying to fit all of the files necessary to recover your system onto a single floppy disk, a task that had become more than a little problematic, Windows Small Business Server now copies only three files to the floppy:

- **Setup.log**   Points to the location of system files on your server

- **Asr.sif**   Contains information on disk, partitions and volumes on the system, and the location of the backup media used

- **Asrpnp.sif**   Contains information on the various plug-and-play devices on the system

With this change to the ASR disk, it's easy to maintain multiple generations of repair information, because each ASR disk points to a specific system backup. You should always keep the ASR disk with the specific backup that it was made with.

Whenever you make a major change to your system, it's a good idea to make a fresh ASR set *before* you make the change. This gives you a fallback position if something goes wrong. If something doesn't work right, you can quickly restore the previous configuration. After you confirm that the new configuration is stable and working, then and only then should you update your ASR set for that server.

What constitutes a major change? Adding, removing, or otherwise modifying the hard disks or their partitions, formats, configurations, and so on, for one. Any time you make a change to the hard disk configuration, you'll definitely want to make a fresh ASR set just before you make the change. Another major change would be the addition of a new component to the server, such as adding the components of the Premium Technologies Disk - Microsoft ISA Server or Microsoft SQL Server. Any changes made from Control Panel are candidates for redoing the ASR set as well.

Creating a Boot Disk

With Windows Small Business Server 2003, you can still create a useful boot disk that can help with recovery in the event something corrupts a critical file on your hard disk. Although this is less important these days, because you can add the Recovery Console to your boot menu or run it from the Windows Small Business Server 2003 installation CD-ROM, we're the cautious type; we like to have available every possible way to recover. Although a Windows Small Business Server 2003 boot disk doesn't get you to a command prompt, as a Microsoft Windows 95 or Microsoft Windows 98 boot disk does, it does permit you to boot the system under the following circumstances (provided that your actual Windows Small Business Server installation isn't damaged in any other way):

- Corrupted boot sector
- Corrupted master boot record (MBR)
- Virus infections of the MBR
- Missing or corrupt Ntldr or Ntdetect.com files

The boot disk can also be used to boot from the shadow drive of a broken mirror set, although you might need to edit the Boot.ini file on the boot disk for this to work.

Under the Hood   Why MS-DOS Boot Disks Won't Help

More than one person new to Windows Small Business Server 2003 has acciden-
tally deleted or corrupted a key file required to boot the system and tried to recover
by digging out an old MS-DOS or Windows boot floppy disk. Alas, it doesn't work.

The files you need to get your hard disk back to booting condition aren't even on an
MS-DOS floppy disk. When you install Windows Small Business Server 2003, the
software modifies the system's boot sector to look for and run a file called Ntldr.
When you format a floppy disk under MS-DOS, even when you make it a system
disk, this file doesn't get created, because MS-DOS doesn't know anything about
Windows Small Business Server 2003 and doesn't know anything about NTFS file
systems, either.

As such, a boot disk is occasionally useful, and because it's easy to make and floppy disks
grow on trees (although these trees are rarely seen outside of the Microsoft campus), you
might as well make one. To create a boot floppy disk, complete these steps:

1. Insert a blank floppy disk into your floppy drive.

2. At a command prompt, type the command **format a:** /**u** and follow the instructions
   that appear.

3. Copy the Ntdetect.com and Ntldr files from the \i386 folder on the first Windows
   Small Business Server 2003 CD-ROM to the floppy disk.

4. Create a Boot.ini file or copy the file from the boot drive to the floppy disk.

Under the Hood   ARC Naming Conventions

Understanding how the hard disks and partitions are named on your system is not
a trivial task, unfortunately. To provide a uniform naming convention across multiple platforms, Microsoft uses a fairly arcane designation for all the disks and partitions on your computer. Called ARC—short for Advanced RISC Computing—this is
a generic naming convention that can be used in the same way for both x86-based
and RISC-based computers. Which is nice, but since Windows Small Business
Server only runs on x86-based computers, we'd prefer something that was a bit easier to understand.

The convention describes the adapter type and number, the disk number, the rdisk
number, and finally the partition number. The format is as follows, where <**adaptertype**> can be SCSI, multi, or signature:

$<adaptertype>(x)disk(y)rdisk(z)partition(n)$

Use multi for all non-SCSI adapters and for SCSI adapters that use a BIOS—as most adapters used with x86-based processors do. The (**x**) is the adapter number, starting at 0. If <**adaptertype**> is signature, (**x**) is an 8-character drive signature.

The value for (**y**) is the SCSI ID of the disk for SCSI adapters. For multi, this is always 0. The number for (**z**) is 0 for SCSI, and is the ordinal number of the disk for multi, starting with 0. Finally, the partition number (**n**) is the number of the partition on the target disk. Here the partitions start at 1, with 0 reserved for unused space.

Installing the Recovery Console

One of the most useful recovery features in Windows Small Business Server 2003 is the Recovery Console. This is basically an enhanced, NTFS-enabled, secure command prompt that can be used to copy files, start and stop services, and perform other recovery actions when you can't boot the system using Windows Small Business Server 2003's safe mode. The Recovery Console is always available for use through the first Windows Small Business Server 2003 CD-ROM; however, you can also install it as an option on the Boot menu for use in those instances when you can't boot using safe mode. You'll still need to use the boot disk if you can't get to the Boot menu or the Recovery Console is damaged.

To install the Recovery Console, complete the following steps:

1. Insert the first Windows Small Business Server 2003 CD-ROM.

2. Close the autorun dialog box if one appears.

3. At a command prompt or in the Run dialog box, type the command **d:\i386\winnt32 /cmdcons**, replacing **d** with the drive letter of the Windows Small Business Server 2003 CD-ROM or network share.

4. Click Yes to install the Recovery Console, as shown in Figure 22-6.

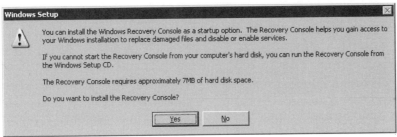

Figure 22-6   The Windows Setup window, installing the Recovery Console.

5. If a Getting Updated Setup Files page appears, select an appropriate option and click Next. The Copying Installation Files page appears and copies the necessary files from the CD.

6. A message box appears indicating that Recovery Console was successfully installed. Click OK. The next time you reboot, one of the boot options will be Microsoft Windows Recovery Console.

Specifying Recovery Options

You can specify how you want Windows Small Business Server 2003 to deal with system crashes by changing a few options in the System tool in Control Panel. To do so, complete the following steps:

1. Open the System tool from Control Panel and click the Advanced tab.

2. Click Settings in the Startup And Recovery box to display the Startup And Recovery dialog box, shown in Figure 22-7.

Figure 22-7   The Startup And Recovery dialog box.

3. If you have multiple operating systems on the machine, from the Default Operating System list box, select the operating system you want to have boot by default.

4. If you want to boot the default operating system automatically, without waiting, clear the Time To Display List Of Operating Systems check box. Otherwise, specify how long you want to display a list of options in the box provided.

5. If you want recovery options automatically displayed in the event of problems, select the Time To Display Recovery Options When Needed check box, and set the time for it.

6. Select the Write An Event To The System Log check box, if available, to record an entry in the event log when the system experiences a crash.

7. Select the Send An Administrative Alert check box to send an alert to administrators over the network when the system crashes.

8. Select the Automatically Restart option to instruct Windows Small Business Server to reboot the system in the event of a crash. Otherwise the system remains at a blue screen until an administrator manually reboots it.

9. From the Write Debugging Information list box, select how much debugging information you want to record. Note that if you have a large amount of RAM, you need the same amount of free disk space if you want to use the Complete Memory Dump option.

10. Enter the file name for the dump file in the Dump File text box, and select the Overwrite Any Existing File check box to maintain only a single dump file.

Creating and Using a Recovery Drive

An excellent way to recycle an old, small SCSI drive that's not good for much else is to use it as an external recovery drive. This drive needs to be only about 2 GB or so, smaller than you could even buy today. Using a recovery drive in this way offers a somewhat cheaper alternative to mirroring the drive.

To create the recovery drive, perform a minimal install of Windows Server 2003 on the drive, configuring your paging file to be on that drive. Do not install all of Windows Small Business Server, but stop after the initial operating system installation, before additional CDs are requested. Create a bootable Windows Small Business Server 2003 floppy disk, following the procedure outlined earlier in the section entitled "Creating a Boot Disk," and edit the Boot.ini file on it to point to the SCSI address of the recovery drive.

If you have a completely failed system drive, for example, you can simply cable the recovery drive to the server and boot from the boot disk that points to the recovery drive. You won't have any of Windows Small Business Server's features on the drive, such as Exchange or all the wizards, but you will have enough of an operating system to run the

Backup utility to restore your server from tape or hard drive. And it will take a *lot* less time than reinstalling from scratch.

Note   Using a recovery drive in this way presents some interesting licensing and activation issues. Because of the licensing and activation of Windows Server 2003, you're going to need to install, license, and activate a copy of Windows Server 2003 for this recovery drive. Consult your Microsoft Account Manager or other licensing resource for how to do this most effectively.

Summary

Assume that disaster will eventually occur, and plan accordingly. Create standardized recovery procedures and keep them up to date. When there's a lot of turmoil, as always happens in the case of a major failure, people forget important steps and can make poor decisions. Standardized procedures provide a course of action without the need for on-the-spot decisions. In the next chapter, we cover some of the technologies you can use to improve your fault tolerance.

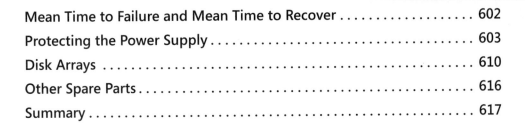

Chapter 23
Planning Fault Tolerance and Avoidance

Mean Time to Failure and Mean Time to Recover 602

Protecting the Power Supply 603

Disk Arrays 610

Other Spare Parts 616

Summary 617

Even the most optimistic system administrator knows that sooner or later she or he will be faced with a major problem. In Chapter 22, "Disaster Planning," we covered disaster recovery planning in depth, and you should refer to that chapter for information on how to prepare for major problems and build a disaster recovery plan to respond quickly and efficiently to major trouble. But as exhilarating as it may be to work through a major problem and successfully recover from it, it's far better to avoid major problems as much as possible.

This chapter focuses on the hardware and software tools that help you to build a highly available and fault-tolerant Windows Small Business Server 2003 environment. Remember, however, that hardware and software are only a small part of the equation—building and deploying for fault tolerance requires time, a clear understanding of the necessary tradeoffs, and—most important—discipline. Yes, you can avoid most computer downtime, but you'll need to be realistic about what your resources are, and what you can reasonably afford to spend. Because SBS does not support clustering, your options for high availability are somewhat limited, but you can still take some important steps to improve your availability and fault tolerance. Your primary focus needs to be on building fault tolerance into your server and network infrastructure.

Building fault-tolerant systems doesn't come without costs, in both effort and money. In this chapter, we'll try to help you make informed decisions about where building fault tolerance into your SBS environment is most cost (and resource) effective. To most effectively use this information, you should have a clear understanding of the business needs you're trying to resolve, and a realistic assessment of the resources available to meet those requirements. When planning for a highly available and fault-tolerant deployment, you should consider all points of failure and work to eliminate any single point of failure. Redundant power supplies, dual disk controllers, multiple network interface cards (multihoming), and fault-tolerant disk arrays (RAID) are all strategies that you can and should employ.

Mean Time to Failure and Mean Time to Recover

The two most common metrics used to measure fault tolerance and avoidance are the following:

- **Mean time to failure (MTTF)**   The mean time until the device will fail
- **Mean time to recover (MTTR)**   The mean time it takes to recover once a failure has occurred

Although a great deal of time and energy is often spent trying to lower the MTTF, it's important to understand that even if you have a finite failure rate, an MTTR that is zero or near zero may be indistinguishable from a system that hasn't failed. Downtime is generally measured as MTTR/MTTF, so increasing the MTTF *will* reduce the downtime—but at a significant cost. Trying to increase the MTTF beyond a certain point can be prohibitively expensive. A more cost-effective and realistic strategy is to spend both time and resources on managing and reducing the MTTR for your most likely and costly points of failure.

Most modern electronic components have a distinctive "bathtub" curve that represents their failure characteristics, as shown in Figure 23-1. During the early life of the component (referred to as the "burn-in" phase), it's more likely to fail; once this initial phase is over, a component's overall failure rate remains quite low until it reaches the end of its useful life, when the failure rate increases again.

Under the Hood   Hard Disk Reliability

The typical commodity hard disk of 10 years ago had an MTTF on the order of 3 years. Today, a typical MTTF for a commodity hard disk is more likely to be 35 to 50 years, with MTTF ratings of server-oriented hard drives hitting 134 years! At least part of that difference is a direct result of counting only the portion of the curve in the normal aging section while taking externally caused failure out of the equation. Therefore, a hard disk that fails because of an improperly filtered power spike doesn't count against the MTTF of the disk, nor does a disk that fails in its first week or two. This might be nice for the disk manufacturer's statistics, but it doesn't do much for the system administrator whose system has crashed because of a disk failure.

As you can see, it's important to look at the total picture and carefully evaluate all the factors and failure points on your system. Only by looking at the whole system, including the recovery procedures and methodology, can you build a truly fault-tolerant system.

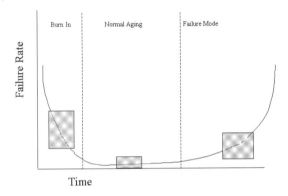

Figure 23-1   The normal statistical failure rates for mechanical and electronic components: a characteristic "bathtub" curve.

Protecting the Power Supply

The single biggest failure point for any network is its power supply. If you don't have power, you can't run your computers. It seems pretty obvious, and most of us slap an uninterruptible power supply (UPS) on the order when we're buying a new server. However, this barely scratches the surface of what you can and should do to protect your network from power problems. You need to protect your network from four basic types of power problems:

- **Local power supply failure**   Failure of the internal power supply on a server, router, or other network component

- **Voltage variations**   Spikes, surges, sags, and longer-term brownouts

- **Short-term power outages**   External power failures lasting from fractions of a second to several minutes

- **Long-term power outages**   External power failures lasting from several minutes to several hours or even days

Each type of power problem poses different risks to your network and requires somewhat different protection mechanisms. The level of threat that each poses to your environment varies depending on the area where you are located, the quality of power available to you, and the potential loss to your business if your computers are down.

Local Power Supply Failure

Computer power supplies have made substantial gains in the last 10 years, but they are still one of the greatest risk points. All the power conditioning, uninterruptible power supplies, and external generators in the world won't help much if your server's power supply fails. Most servers these days either come with a redundant power supply or have the option of including one. Take the option! The extra cost associated with adding a redundant power supply to a server or critical piece of network hardware is far less than the cost of downtime should the power supply fail.

If your server, router, or other piece of network hardware doesn't have the option of a redundant power supply, order a spare power supply for it when you order the original hardware. Don't count on the hardware manufacturer's "4-hour response" time, especially when you consider the cost to your business even if they actually repair the equipment in four hours. If you have a spare power supply in a well marked cabinet where you can find it, you can quickly, and with minimal disruption, replace the failed power supply and return the equipment to full functionality. *Then* you can afford to wait patiently for the manufacturer's service response.

Note   Most major manufacturers use proprietary components in their servers. This usually means that you can't count on using an off-the-shelf component, such as a power supply, but must use one specifically designed to fit the particular brand and model of server you have.

Real World   It's Only Useful if You Can Find It!

Having a good supply of critical spares is a great idea, but sometimes reality intrudes. Storage can be the weak link here. Most server rooms are not nearly as spacious as we would like them to be, and in the SBS world a server room may be little more than a lockable closet. If that's the case, make sure the closet has adequate, filtered, ventilation and cooling – servers produce a significant amount of heat and a poorly ventilated environment will greatly shorten the life of your server.

Dust is the enemy of your server – it will impede cooling, and can actually short out electrical components. Server rooms should not have carpet. And remove any printers from the area – printers are dust generators.

All too often the spare parts end up jammed into a bin or shoved up onto an upper shelf with inadequate or nonexistent identification. If your network is down and you need a power supply to get it back up, you don't want to be pawing through a jumble of spare parts looking for the right power supply.

Make every effort to develop a single, central, secure location for all spare parts. At least then there's only a single place to search. Then make sure the manufacturer's part number is visible, and clearly label the machine or machines each part is for. Protect the part from dust and spilled coffee by keeping it in a sealed plastic storage bag.

We like to tape a list of the manufacturer's part numbers, details of the installed hardware, and the list of spare parts we have right inside the case cover of the server itself. It's easy to find and doesn't end up getting lost. It does you no good to have a spare power supply if you can't find it or don't know you have it. And don't forget to include the location of any special tools required. It never ceases to amaze us how many different and apparently unique screwdriver bits we need to get into our various computers! We started our toolkit with an inexpensive computer toolkit, and add tools to it as needed.

Finally, *practice*! If you've never replaced a power supply before, and you don't have clear and detailed instructions, it will take you orders of magnitude longer to replace it when the server is down and everyone is yelling and the phone keeps ringing. By practicing the replacement of the power supplies in your critical hardware, you'll save time and reduce the stress involved.

Ideally, document the steps you need to perform and include well illustrated and detailed instructions on how to replace the power supplies of your critical hardware as part of your disaster recovery standard operating procedures. If you can swap out a failed power supply in 10 minutes, rather than waiting hours until an outside technician arrives, you've saved more than enough money to pay for the spare part several times over.

Voltage Variations

Even in areas with exceptionally clean power that is always available, the power that is supplied to your network inevitably fluctuates. Minor, short-term variations merely stress your electronic components, but major variations can literally fry them. You should never, ever simply plug a computer into an ordinary wall socket without providing some sort of protection against voltage variations. The following sections describe the types of variations and the best way to protect your equipment against them.

Spikes

Spikes are large but short-lived increases in voltage. They can occur because of external factors, such as lightning striking a power line, or because of internal factors, such as a large motor starting. The most common causes of severe voltage spikes, however, are external and outside your control. The effects can be devastating. A nearby lightning strike can easily cause a spike of 1,000 volts or more to be sent into equipment designed to run on 110 to 120 volts. Few, if any, electronic components are designed to withstand large voltage spikes of several thousand volts, and almost all will suffer damage if they're not protected from them.

Protection from spikes comes in many forms, from the $19.95 power strip with built-in surge protection that you can buy at your local hardware store to complicated arrays of transformers and specialized sacrificial transistors that are designed to die so that others may live. Unfortunately, those $19.95 power strips just aren't good enough. They *are* better than nothing, but barely, because they have a limited ability to withstand really large spikes.

More specialized (and more expensive, of course) surge protectors that are specifically designed to protect computer networks are available from various companies. They differ in their ability to protect against really large spikes and in their cost. There's a fairly direct correlation between the cost of these products and their rated capacity and speed of action within any company's range of products, but the cost for a given level of protection can differ significantly from company to company. As always, if the price sounds too good to be true, it is.

In general, these surge protectors are designed to work by sensing a large increase in voltage and creating an alternate electrical path for that excessive voltage that doesn't allow it to get through to your server. In the most severe spikes, the surge protectors should destroy themselves before allowing the voltage to get through to your server. The effectiveness of these stand-alone surge protectors depends on the speed of response to a large voltage increase and the mechanism of failure when their capacity is exceeded. If the surge protector doesn't respond quickly enough to a spike, bad things will happen.

Most UPSs also provide some protection from spikes. They have built-in surge protectors, plus isolation circuitry that tends to buffer the effects of spikes. The effectiveness of the spike protection in a UPS is not directly related to its cost, however—the overall cost of the UPS is more a factor of its effectiveness as an alternative power source. Your responsibility is to read the fine print and understand the limitations of the surge protection a given UPS offers. Also remember that just as with simple surge protectors, large voltage spikes can cause the surge protection to self-destruct rather than allow the voltage through to your server. That's the good news; the bad news is that instead of having to replace just a surge protector, you're likely to have to repair or replace the UPS.

Finally, one other spike protection mechanism can be helpful—the constant voltage transformer (CVT). You're not likely to see one unless you're in a large industrial setting, but they are often considered to be a sufficient replacement for other forms of surge protection. Unfortunately, they're not really optimal for surge protection. They do filter some excess voltage, but a large spike is likely to find its way through. However, in combination with either a fully protected UPS or a good stand-alone surge protector, a CVT can be quite effective. They also provide additional protection against other forms of voltage variation that surge protectors alone can't begin to manage.

Surges

Voltage surges and spikes are often discussed interchangeably, but we'd like to make a distinction here. For our purposes, a *surge* lasts longer than most spikes and isn't nearly as large. Most surges last a few hundred milliseconds and are rarely over 1,000 volts. They can be caused by many of the same factors that cause voltage spikes.

Providing protection against surges is somewhat easier than protecting against large spikes. Most of the protection mechanisms just discussed also adequately handle surges. In addition, most CVTs are sufficient to handle surges and might even handle them better if the surge is so prolonged that it threatens to overheat and burn out a simple surge protector.

Sags

Voltage *sags* are short-term reductions in the voltage delivered. They aren't complete voltage failures or power outages and are shorter than a full-scale brownout. Voltage sags can drop the voltage well below 100 volts on a 110- to 120-volt normal line and cause most servers to reboot if protection isn't provided.

Stand-alone surge protectors provide no defense against sags. You need a UPS or a very good CVT to prevent damage from a voltage sag. Severe sags can overcome the rating of all but the best constant voltage transformers, so you generally shouldn't use constant voltage transformers as the sole protection against sags. A UPS, with its battery power supply, is an essential part of your protection from problems caused by voltage sag.

Brownouts

A *brownout* is a planned, deliberate reduction in voltage from your electric utility company. Brownouts most often occur in the heat of the summer and are designed to protect the utility company from overloading. They are *not* designed to protect the consumer, however.

In general, a brownout reduces the available voltage by 5 to 20 percent from the normal value. A CVT or a UPS provides excellent protection against brownouts, within limits. Prolonged brownouts might exceed your UPS's ability to maintain a charge at the same time that it is providing power at the correct voltage to your equipment. Monitor the health of your UPS carefully during a brownout, especially because the risk of a complete power outage increases if the power company's voltage reduction strategy proves insufficient.

The best protection against extended brownouts is a CVT of sufficient rating to fully support your critical network devices and servers. If you live in an area that is subject to brownouts, and your budget can afford it, a good CVT is an excellent investment. This transformer takes the reduced voltage provided by your power company and increases it to the rated output voltage. A good constant voltage transformer can handle most brownouts for an extended time without problems, but you should still supplement the CVT with a quality UPS and surge protection between the transformer and the server or network device. This extra protection is especially important while the power company is attempting to restore power to full voltage because during this period you run a higher risk of experiencing power and voltage fluctuations.

Short-Term Power Outages

Short-term power outages last from a few milliseconds to a few minutes. They can be caused by either internal or external events, but you can rarely plan for them even if they are internal. A server that is unprotected from a short-term power outage will, at the very least, reboot or, at the worst, fail catastrophically.

The best protection against a short-term power outage is a UPS in combination with high-quality spike protection. Be aware that many momentary interruptions of power are accompanied by large spikes when the power is restored. Further, a series of short-term power outages often occur consecutively, causing additional stress to electronic components.

Long-Term Power Outages

Long-term power outages, lasting from an hour or so to several days, are usually accompanied by other, more serious problems. Long-term power outages can be caused by storms, earthquakes, fires, and the incompetence of electric power utilities, among other things. As such, plans for dealing with long-term power outages should be part of an overall disaster recovery plan. (See Chapter 22 for more on disaster planning.)

Protection against long-term power outages really becomes a decision about how long you want or need to function if all power is out. If you need to function long enough to be able to gracefully shut down your network, a simple UPS or a collection of them will be sufficient, assuming that you've sized the UPS correctly. However, if you need to be sure that you can maintain the full functionality of your SBS network during an extended power outage, you're going to need a combination of one or more UPSs and an auxiliary generator. But before you start spending money on generators and failover switches, evaluate the overall infrastructure supplying your power. If you're dependent on Internet connectivity to do business, it does you no good to be up and running in the middle of a two-day power outage if your Internet is also down.

Real World   Generators Require Serious Expertise and Maintenance

We've been involved with more than one operation that depended on—and implemented—auxiliary generators to support their operations during extended power outages. The results have been rather mixed, however. The one lesson we've learned the hard way is that simply buying and installing an auxiliary generator will do little, if anything, to keep you up and running when the power goes out. Generators are complex mechanical and electrical machines that require specialized expertise and consistent, conscientious processes, and maintenance.

If your situation requires an auxiliary generator to supplement your UPSs, you should carefully plan your power strategy to ensure that you provide power to all of the equipment that the network will require in the event of a long-term power outage. You'll need the expertise of a licensed electrician who has experience installing and configuring generator failover switches. Test your solution to make sure you didn't miss anything! Further, you should regularly test the effectiveness of your disaster recovery plans and make sure that all key personnel know how to start the auxiliary generator manually in the event it doesn't start automatically. Finally, you should have a regular preventive maintenance (PM) program in place that services and tests the generator and ensures that it is ready and functioning when you need it. This PM program should include both static tests and full load tests on a regular basis, and should also call for periodically replacing the fuel to the generator. One of the best ways to do all of this is to plan and execute a "disaster day" for testing your entire disaster recovery plan in as close to real-world conditions as possible, including running your entire operation from the backup generator.

Disk Arrays

The most common hardware malfunction is probably a hard disk failure. Even though hard disks have become more reliable over time, they are still subject to failure, especially during their first month or so of use. They are also vulnerable to both catastrophic and degenerative failures caused by power problems. Fortunately, disk arrays have become the norm for servers, and good fault-tolerant RAID systems are available in Windows Small Business Server 2003 and RAID-specific hardware supported by SBS. The choice of software or hardware RAID, and the particulars of how you configure your RAID system, can significantly affect the cost of your servers. To make an informed choice for your environment and needs, you must understand the tradeoffs and the differences in fault tolerance, speed, configurability, and so on.

Hardware vs. Software

RAID can be implemented at the hardware level, using RAID controllers, or at the software level, either by the operating system or by a third-party add-on. Windows Small Business Server 2003 supports both hardware RAID and its own software RAID.

Hardware RAID implementations require specialized controllers and cost significantly more than an equal level of software RAID. However, for that extra price, you get a faster, more flexible, and more fault-tolerant RAID. When compared to the software RAID provided in SBS 2003, a good hardware RAID controller supports more levels of RAID, on-the-fly reconfiguration of the arrays, hot-swap and hot-spare drives (discussed later in this chapter), and dedicated caching of both reads and writes.

Software RAID requires that you convert your disks to dynamic disks. Converting your boot disk (C drive) is probably not a good idea. Dynamic disks can be more difficult to access if a problem occurs, and the SBS setup and installation program provides only limited support. For maximum fault tolerance, we recommend using hardware mirroring (RAID 1) on your boot drive; if you do use software mirroring, make sure that you create the required fault-tolerant boot floppy disk and test it thoroughly before you need it (see Chapter 22).

RAID Levels for Fault Tolerance

Except for level 0, RAID is a mechanism for storing sufficient information on a group of hard disks such that even if one hard disk in the group fails, no information is lost. Some RAID arrangements go even further, providing protection in the event of multiple hard disk failures. The more common levels of RAID and their appropriateness in a fault-tolerant environment are shown in Table 23-1.

Table 23-1   RAID levels and their fault tolerance

Level	Number of Disks*	Speed	Fault Tolerance	Description
0	N	+++	- - -	Striping alone. Not fault-tolerant—it actually increases your risk of failure—but does provide for the fastest read and write performance.
1	$2N$	+	++	Mirror or duplex. Slightly faster read than single disk, but no gain during write operations. Failure of any single disk causes no loss in data and minimal performance hit.
3	$N+1$	++	+	Byte-level parity. Data is striped across multiple drives at the byte level with the parity information written to a single dedicated drive. Reads are much faster than with a single disk, but writes operate slightly slower than a single disk because parity information must be generated and written to a single disk. Failure of any single disk causes no loss of data but can cause a significant loss of performance.
4	$N+1$	++	+	Block-level parity with a dedicated parity disk. Similar to RAID-3 except that data is striped at the block level.
5	$N+1$	+	++	Interleaved block-level parity. Parity information is distributed across all drives. Reads are much faster than a single disk but writes are significantly slower. Failure of any single disk provides no loss of data but results in a major reduction in performance.

Table 23-1   RAID levels and their fault tolerance (Continued)

Level	Number of Disks*	Speed	Fault Tolerance	Description
0+1 and 10	2N	+++	++	Striped mirrored disks or mirrored striped disks. Data is striped across multiple mirrored disks or multiple striped disks are mirrored. Failure of any one disk causes no data loss and no speed loss. Failure of a second disk could result in data loss. Faster than a single disk for both reads and writes.
Other	Varies	+++	+++	Array of RAID arrays. Different hardware vendors have different proprietary names for this RAID concept. Excellent read and write performance. Failure of any one disk results in no loss of performance and continued redundancy.

*In the Number of Disks column, N refers to the number of hard disks required to hold the original copy of the data. The plus and minus symbols show relative improvement or deterioration compared to a system using no version of RAID. The scale peaks at three symbols.

When choosing the RAID level to use for a given application or server, consider the following factors:

■ **Intended use**   Will this application be primarily read-intensive, such as file serving, or will it be predominantly write-intensive, such as a transactional database? SBS servers are heavily write-intensive, at least on the disks that Exchange uses.

■ **Fault tolerance**   How critical is this data, and how much can you afford to lose?

■ **Availability**   Does this server or application need to be available at all times, or can you afford to be able to reboot it or otherwise take it offline for brief periods?

■ **Performance**   Is this application or server heavily used, with large amounts of data being transferred to and from it, or is this server or application less I/O intensive? If this is your main SBS server, it's heavily used.

■ **Cost**   Are you on a tight budget for this server or application, or is the cost of data loss or unavailability the primary driving factor?

You need to evaluate each of these factors when you decide which type of RAID to use for a server or portion of a server. No single answer fits all cases, but the final answer requires you to carefully weigh each of these factors and balance them against your situation and your needs. The following sections take a closer look at each factor and how it weighs in the overall decision-making process.

Intended Use

The intended use, and the kind of disk access associated with that use, plays an important role in determining the best RAID level for your application. Think about how write-intensive the application is and whether the manner in which the application uses the data is more sequential or random. Is your application a three-square-meals-a-day kind of application, with relatively large chunks of data being read or written at a time, or is it more of a grazer or nibbler, reading and writing little bits of data from all sorts of different places?

If your application is relatively write-intensive, you'll want to avoid software RAID if possible and avoid RAID 5 if other considerations don't force you to use it. With RAID 5, any application that requires more than 50 percent writes to reads is likely to be at least somewhat slower, if not much slower, than it would be on a single disk. You can mitigate this to some extent by using more but smaller drives in your array and by using a hardware controller with a large cache to offload the parity processing as much as possible. RAID 1, in either a mirror or duplex configuration, provides a high degree of fault tolerance with no significant penalty during write operations—a good choice for the system disk.

If your application is primarily read-intensive, and the data is stored and referenced sequentially, RAID 3 or RAID 4 might be a good choice. Because the data is striped across many drives, you have parallel access to it, improving your throughput. And because the parity information is stored on a single drive, rather than dispersed across the array, sequential read operations don't have to skip over the parity information and are therefore faster. However, write operations are substantially slower, and the single parity drive can become an I/O bottleneck during write operations.

If your application is primarily read-intensive and not necessarily sequential, RAID 5 is an obvious choice. It provides a good balance of speed and fault tolerance, and the cost is substantially lower than the cost of RAID 1. Disk accesses are evenly distributed across multiple drives, and no one drive has the potential to be an I/O bottleneck. However, writes require calculation of the parity information and the extra write of that parity, slowing write operations down significantly. Windows Small Business Server file shares are a good fit for RAID 5, but avoid RAID 5 for the volume that holds your Exchange database.

If your application provides other mechanisms for data recovery or uses large amounts of temporary storage, which doesn't require fault tolerance, a simple RAID 0, with no fault tolerance but fast reads and writes, is a possibility—but we strongly advise against RAID 0 on an SBS server.

Fault Tolerance

Carefully examine the fault tolerance of each of the possible RAID choices for your intended use. All RAID levels except RAID 0 provide some degree of fault tolerance, but the effect of a failure and the ability to recover from subsequent failures can be different.

If a drive in a RAID 1 mirror or duplex array fails, a full, complete, exact copy of the data remains. Access to your data or application is unimpeded, and performance degradation is minimal, although you do lose the benefit gained on read operations of being able to read from either disk. Until the failed disk is replaced, however, you have no fault tolerance on the remaining disk. Once you replace the failed disk, overall performance is significantly reduced while the new disk is initialized and the mirror is rebuilt.

In a RAID 3 or RAID 4 array, if one of the data disks fails, a significant performance degradation occurs because the missing data needs to be reconstructed from the parity information. Also, you'll have no fault tolerance until the failed disk is replaced. If it is the parity disk that fails, you'll have no fault tolerance until it is replaced, but also no performance degradation. Once you replace the failed disk, overall performance is significantly reduced while the new disk is initialized and the parity information or data is rebuilt.

In a RAID 5 array, the loss of any disk results in a significant performance degradation, and your fault tolerance will be gone until you replace the failed disk. Once you replace the disk, you won't return to fault tolerance until the entire array has a chance to rebuild itself, and performance is seriously degraded during the rebuild process.

RAID systems that are arrays of arrays can provide for multiple failure tolerance. These arrays provide for multiple levels of redundancy and are appropriate for mission-critical applications that must be able to withstand the failure of more than one drive in an array.

Real World   Multiple Disk Controllers Provide Increased Fault Tolerance

Spending the money for a hardware RAID system increases your overall fault tolerance, but it can still leave a single point of failure in your disk subsystem: the disk controller itself. Although failures of the disk controller are certainly less common, they do happen. Many hardware RAID systems are based on a single multiple-channel controller—certainly a better choice than those based on a single-channel controller—but an even better solution is a RAID system based on multiple identical controllers. In these systems, the failure of a single disk controller is not catastrophic but simply an annoyance. In RAID 1 this technique is known as *duplexing*, but it is also common with many of the proprietary arrays of arrays that are available from server vendors and in the third-party market.

Availability

All levels of RAID, except RAID 0, provide higher availability than a single drive. However, if availability is expanded to also include the overall performance level during failure mode, some RAID levels provide definite advantages over others. Specifically, RAID 1, mirroring/duplexing, provides enhanced availability when compared to RAID levels 3, 4, and 5 during failure mode. There is minimal performance degradation when compared to a single disk if one half of a mirror fails, whereas a RAID 5 array has substantially compromised performance until the failed disk is replaced and the array is rebuilt.

In addition, RAID systems that are based on an array of arrays can provide higher availability than RAID levels 1 through 5. Running on multiple controllers, these arrays are able to tolerate the failure of more than one disk and the failure of one of the controllers, providing protection against the single point of failure inherent in any single-controller arrangement. RAID 1 that uses duplexed disks running on different controllers—as opposed to RAID 1 that uses mirroring on the same controller—also provides this additional protection and improved availability.

Hot-swap drives and hot-spare drives (discussed later in this chapter) can further improve availability in critical environments, especially hot-spare drives. By providing for automatic failover and rebuilding, they can reduce your exposure to catastrophic failure and provide for maximum availability.

Performance

The relative performance of each RAID level depends on the intended use. The best compromise for many situations is arguably RAID 5, but you should be suspicious of that compromise if your application is fairly write-intensive. Especially for relational database data and index files where the database is moderately or highly write-intensive, the performance hit of using RAID 5 can be substantial. A better alternative is to use RAID 0+1 or RAID 10.

Whatever level of RAID you choose for your particular application, it will benefit from using more small disks rather than a few large disks. The more drives contributing to the stripe of the array, the greater the benefit of parallel reading and writing you'll be able to realize—and your array's overall speed will improve.

Cost

The delta in cost between RAID configurations is primarily the cost of drives, potentially including the cost of additional array enclosures because more drives are required for a particular level of RAID. RAID 1, either duplexing or mirroring, is the most expensive of the conventional RAID levels, because it requires at least 33 percent more raw disk space for a given amount of net storage space than other RAID levels.

Another consideration is that RAID levels that include mirroring or duplexing must use drives in pairs. Therefore, it's more difficult (and more expensive) to add on to an array if you need additional space on the array. A net 36 GB RAID 0+1 array, comprising four 18 GB drives, requires four more 18 GB drives to double in size, a somewhat daunting prospect if your array cabinet has bays for only six drives, for example. A net 36 GB RAID 5 array of three 18 GB drives, however, can be doubled in size simply by adding two more 18 GB drives, for a total of five drives.

Hot-Swap and Hot-Spare Disk Systems

Hardware RAID systems can provide for both hot-swap and hot-spare capabilities. A hot-swap disk system allows failed hard disks to be removed and a replacement disk inserted into the array without powering down the system or rebooting the server. When the new disk is inserted, it is automatically recognized and either will be automatically configured into the array or can be manually configured into it. Additionally, many hot-swap RAID systems allow you to add hard disks into empty slots dynamically, automatically or manually increasing the size of the RAID volume on the fly without a reboot.

A *hot-spare* RAID configuration uses an additional, preconfigured disk or disks to automatically replace a failed disk. These systems usually don't support hot-swapped hard disks so that the failed disk can't be removed until the system can be powered down, but full fault tolerance is maintained by having the hot spare available.

Even where you don't have a hot-swap or hot-spare drive already configured into your array, it makes sense to always keep a matching spare drive available in your replacement-parts cabinet. Hard drives aren't all that expensive, and it will save you time if you have a drive failure in your array. Plus, with drive sizes and technology changing rapidly, it can be annoying to try to find a matching drive two or three years after you buy the original array.

Other Spare Parts

So, you've got a spare power supply, and a spare hard drive for your array, but are there any other parts that you should keep a spare of around? Yes. Any other peripheral or card that you couldn't run your business without is a good candidate for a spare. An obvious choice is a spare network card, ideally of the same type as is in your server. That gets a bit more difficult when the network interface is on the motherboard, as is common these days, but even if it's not the same type as your existing network interfaces, having a server-quality network card available and ready to drop into the server in the event of a failure can make it much quicker to recover.

Another candidate is a spare video card, though this is less critical. You can, after all, always Remote Desktop into the server if you need to, and replacement video cards are easy and quick to come by.

Any other cards or peripherals that you would have problems doing without for the time it takes to get a new one to replace a failure is a good candidate for your spare-parts cabinet. We like to keep a spare network switch with a few spare network cables available. Another smart choice is to keep a spare of your DSL modem or boundary router.

Summary

Building a highly available and fault-tolerant system requires you to carefully evaluate both your requirements and your resources to eliminate single points of failure within the system. You should evaluate each of the hardware subsystems within the overall system for fault tolerance, and ensure that recovery procedures are clearly understood and practiced to reduce recovery time in the event of a failure. UPSs, redundant power supplies, and RAID systems are all methods for improving overall fault tolerance.

Part VI
Appendices

Appendix A   Introduction to Networks 621

Appendix B   Partially Automating Installation 627

Appendix C   Using the Transition Pack. 637

Appendix D   Using File Server Resource Manager 647

Appendix A
Introduction to Networks

Features of the Windows Operating System 622

Domains and Workgroups 623

If you've ever made a phone call or used a bank ATM, you've already experienced using a network. After all, a *network* is simply a collection of computers and peripheral devices that can share files and other resources. The connection can be a cable, a telephone line, or even a wireless channel. The Internet itself is a network—a global network made up of all the computers, hardware, and peripherals connected to it.

Your bank's ATM consists of hardware and software connected to central computers that know, among other things, how much money you have in your account. When you call cross-country or just across town, telephone company software makes the connection from your phone to the phone you're calling through multiple switching devices. It's something we do every day without thinking about the complicated processes behind the scenes.

Both the telephone and the ATM networks are maintained by technicians and engineers who plan, set up, and maintain all the software and hardware; however, the assumption underlying Windows Small Business Server is that there isn't anyone dedicated to maintaining the network and its operating system full time. Instead, Windows Small Business Server provides the Manage Your Server interface—a unified administrative interface designed to meet the needs of small businesses and simplify your choices.

Servers

A *server* is a computer that provides services. It's really just that simple. The difficulty comes when people confuse the physical box that's providing the service with the actual service. Any computer or device on a network can be a server for a particular service. A server doesn't even need to be a computer in the traditional sense. For example, you might have a "print server" that is nothing more complicated than a device that's connected to the network on one side and to a printer on the other. The device has a tiny little brain with just enough intelligence to understand when a particular network packet is intended for it, and to translate those packets into something that the printer can understand.

In Windows Small Business Server 2003, usually a single computer acts as the physical server box (though you can have secondary servers), but that box provides a variety of services to the network beyond the usual file and print services. These services meet your core business needs, including authentication and security; e-mail and collaboration; an Internet connection; sharing; faxing; and, even database services and a full-featured firewall in Premium Edition.

Clients

A *client* is anything on the network that avails itself of a server's services. Clients are usually the other computers on the network. The client machines typically print to network printers, read e-mail, work on shared documents, connect to the Internet, and generally use services that aren't available on their local machines. Clients aren't usually as powerful as servers, but they're perfectly capable computers on their own.

Media Connecting Servers and Clients

Another portion of a network is the actual network media that connects the various servers and clients to each other. This media includes both the network cards that are part of the server or client and the physical wire (or wireless connection) between them, and the various other components involved, such as hubs, routers, and switches. When all these media components work as they should, we pretty much forget about this portion of the network and take it for granted. But when a failure of one component of the network media occurs, we face troubleshooting and repairs that can be both frustrating and expensive—a good reason to buy only high-quality network components from vendors and dealers who support their products.

Features of the Windows Operating System

The Windows Server 2003 operating system that underlies Windows Small Business Server is a proven, reliable, and secure operating system with the features to run a business of virtually any size. With Windows Small Business Server, the operating system and server components have been specifically tuned to support from 5 to 75 users in a small business environment, with all the server functions residing on a single machine.

Some of the features that make Windows Server 2003 ideal for a small business server include:

- Easy installation that is almost fully automated in Windows Small Business Server
- A robust yet easy-to-administer security model using Active Directory

- The NTFS file system that fully supports long file names, dynamic error recovery, shadow copies, user space limitations, and security
- Support for a broad range of hardware and software

Domains and Workgroups

Microsoft provides for two different networking models in their operating systems: workgroups and domains. Windows Small Business Server supports only the domain model of Microsoft networking, but it's worthwhile to go over why this decision makes sense, even in a very small business.

Do Workgroups Work?

Microsoft introduced the concept of the workgroup in 1992 with Microsoft Windows for Workgroups. The *workgroup* is a logical grouping of several computers whose work or users are connected and who want to share their resources with each other. Usually, all the computers in a workgroup are equal, which is why such setups are referred to as *peer-to-peer networks*.

Workgroup networks are appealing because they're easy to set up and maintain. Individual users manage the sharing of their resources by determining what will be shared and who will have access. A user can allow other users to use a printer, a CD-ROM drive, an entire hard drive, or only certain files. The difficulty arises when it's necessary to give different levels of access to different users. Passwords can be used for this purpose in a limited way, but as the network gets larger, passwords proliferate and the situation becomes increasingly complicated. Users who are required to have numerous passwords start using the same one over and over or choose passwords that are easy to remember and therefore easy to guess, and there is no way to enforce a minimum password quality level. If someone leaves the company to work for your biggest competitor, passwords have to be changed and everyone in the workgroup has to be notified of the new passwords. Security, such as it is, falls apart.

Another problem that occurs when a workgroup becomes too large is that users have difficulty locating the resources they need. The informal nature of workgroups also means that centralized administration or control is nonexistent. Everything has to be configured computer by computer. This lack of central administration and control, along with the limited security, makes the workgroup model a bad choice for all but the home network.

Defining Domains

To provide a secure and easy-to-manage environment that takes full advantage of Active Directory and the collaborative features of Microsoft Exchange 2003 and the other components of Windows Small Business Server, Microsoft made the decision to use a domain-based networking environment. Management is simplified and centralized on the server, reducing the complexity and security problems caused by having to manage users, resources, and passwords across multiple clients.

A *domain* is really just a type of workgroup that includes a server – but a server that manages and administers all of the users and computers in the network. It is a logical grouping of users who are connected by more than the cables between their computers. The goal of a domain is to let users share resources within the group and to make it easier for the group to work. However, the key difference is that Active Directory, and the Server it runs on, manages, catalogs, and secures the users, groups, computers and resources for the entire network, providing a single point of administration and control.

Additional Users

When adding a new user to the domain, you won't need to go around to each computer and enter all the information. As the administrator, you can simply connect to the server and add the new user, using the Server Management application. You can create the user's mailbox, set up a home folder, add the user to security and distribution groups, configure his or her Share Point access, set up disk quotas, and even configure a client computer—all with only a few clicks and the entering of the user name and password. The change will be immediately seen across the entire domain.

All users, including the newest, can get at their resources, no matter which machine is being used. Permission to access resources is granted to individual users (or a group of users), not to individual computers. And when you need to restrict access to a sensitive document or directory, you need to log on to only a single workstation to make the change across the entire domain. You can easily and quickly grant or restrict access by individual user or by groups of users.

Access Control

In a workgroup, there are limitations on sharing your machine's resources with the rest of the workgroup. At the simplest level, you can either share the resource or not share it. Beyond that, you can require a password for a particular level of access to the resource. This enables only a very limited ability to control access to the resource, and virtually none if your machine is physically accessible to anyone but yourself.

Windows Small Business Server provides *discretionary access control*, which allows, for example, some users to create a document or make changes to an existing one while other users can only read the document and still other users can't even *see* it. You can set access for:

■ An individual file or files within a directory

■ The entire directory

Windows Small Business Server lets you make selection as fine or as coarse as needed and makes the administration of security easy to manage.

Domain Components

An SBS domain has at least two main components and an optional third component:

■ Domain controller

■ Member server (optional)

■ Workstations or clients

Let's take a look at these components.

Domain Controller

The main computer in the SBS domain is the *domain controller*. In many, if not most, SBS domains, the domain controller will be the only server. It hosts Active Directory and all the components of SBS, as well as acts as the file and print server for the domain. All computers in the domain must authenticate to the domain controller, and all domain security is controlled by it.

Member Servers

In some larger SBS domains, additional Windows Server 2003 computers might be in the domain. These computers can be used to spread some of the network's resource load around so that the domain controller doesn't carry the whole load, and they can even be the Exchange or SQL Server host if you buy separate, stand-alone versions of these products. Unfortunately, the bundling and licensing of Windows Small Business Server 2003 allows the installation of the Windows Small Business Server CD versions on only the main Windows Small Business Server computer.

Another reason you might have an additional member server in your SBS domain is to host Windows Terminal Services. Terminal Services allows you to use inexpensive, easily managed desktop computers and terminals whose only function is to run applications directly on the Terminal Server computer. The Terminal Server provides the disk space and all the applications that the user has, while the terminal or computer of the user is merely a display and console (keyboard and mouse). Centralizing applications onto a Terminal Server can dramatically reduce costs and simplify administration in some scenarios. However, for security reasons, Terminal Services can not be run from the main SBS server, so if you'll be using Terminal Services, you'll need at least one additional server on your network.

Workstations or Clients

All the Windows clients of an SBS network must be running Windows 98 or later, but in most networks they will be running Windows XP Professional or a version of Windows Vista. Since Windows 98 and Windows Me are no longer supported operating systems, it is more than time to upgrade any of them you still have on your network. You can also have Mac and even UNIX or Linux clients, but their ability to integrate fully with the SBS network will be limited.

Appendix B
Partially Automating Installation

Automating CD-Based Installations 627

Using the System Preparation Tool to Image Windows Server 2003 . . . 633

Those who install SBS often can save a good deal of time by automating Setup. There are two significant ways to automate SBS Setup: using answer files and using the System Preparation Tool (Sysprep) in conjunction with a disk imaging program to make a copy of SBS halfway through Setup.

Note You can automate only the installation of the underlying operating system—you can't automate the Microsoft Windows Small Business Server Setup Wizard, which is run in the second major phase of Windows Small Business Server Setup. (See Chapter 3, "Installing Windows Small Business Server 2003.")

Automating CD-Based Installations

During a normal installation of Windows Small Business Server, Setup stops a number of times to prompt the user for information. This process can be automated by using an *answer file*, which is a text file with answers to the questions Setup asks. You can create answer files manually using any text editor, or by using the handy Setup Manager tool, as described in the following steps:

1. From any Windows computer, insert SBS CD 1, or download updated Support Tools from the Microsoft Web site. Support Tools are usually upgraded with each Service Pack. Navigate to the \Support\Tools folder and extract the contents of the Deploy.cab file to a location on the hard drive.

2. Launch the Setupmgr.exe file from the location on the hard drive to which you copied the contents of the Deploy.cab file. The Setup Manager Wizard appears.

3. Click Next to begin using the wizard.

4. On the New Or Existing Answer File page, choose Create New and then click Next.

5. On the Type Of Setup page, choose Unattended Setup and then click Next.

6. On the Product page, shown in Figure B-1, choose Windows Server 2003, Standard Edition, and then click Next.

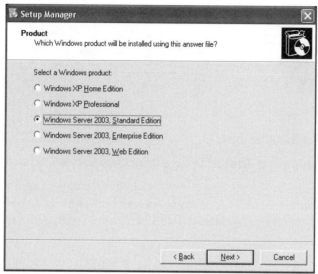

Figure B-1   The Setup Manager Product page.

7. On the User Interaction page, shown in Figure B-2, choose the level of interaction that will be available during Setup, and then click Next.

> **More Info**   For more information about determining user interaction during Setup, see the Real World sidebar "Choosing an Interaction Level" in this appendix.

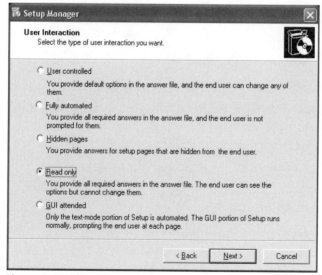

Figure B-2   The Setup Manager User Interaction page.

Real World   Choosing an Interaction Level

The level of user interaction determines how much the person running the installation needs to attend to the process. Here's a more detailed explanation of the interaction levels:

- **User Controlled**   Uses the information in the answer file as default answers during the Windows installation. The user still has to confirm the defaults or make changes as the installation progresses.

- **Fully Automated**   Completely automates Setup by using the answer file. This option is best for quickly setting up multiple systems with identical configurations. If any settings don't work properly (such as might happen when the product key is wrong), Setup will prompt for the correct information.

- **Hidden Pages**   Automates the parts of Setup for which you provide information, and prompts the user to supply any information not included in the answer file. The user sees only the parts of Setup that aren't covered in the answer file. Use this option to standardize some aspects of installation but not others (such as the product key, the computer name, and user information).

- **Read Only**   Hides the parts of Setup for which you provide information, just like the Hidden Pages option. However, if a window with only partial answers is supplied in the answer file (and therefore not hidden from the user), the user can complete only the unanswered portion of the window. Settings provided by the answer file can't be changed during installation.

- **GUI Attended**   Automates the text-based portion of Setup. The person running Setup supplies answers for the Windows Setup Wizard. Use this level when you want to automate the text-based portion of Setup and allow the person running the installation to provide the settings during the graphical user interface (GUI) portion.

8. On the Distribution Share page, select Set Up From A CD and then click Next.

> **More Info**   SBS can be installed from a network distribution share, but this requires the client to have network connectivity before running Setup, which often is impractical for SBS installations. For information about distribution shares, refer to *Microsoft Windows Server 2003 Administrator's Companion*, 2nd Edition, (Microsoft Press).

9. If you chose to fully automate the first phase of Windows Small Business Server Setup, on the License Agreement page, accept the terms of the End User License

Agreement (EULA), and then click Next. OEMs aren't permitted to use this step, and must use the OEM Preinstallation Kit (OPK) instead of Setup Manager. If you've chosen one of the other levels of automation, the setup process will prompt for acceptance of the EULA during installation.

10. On the Name And Organization page, supply the name and organization you want to use, and then click Next. A name and organization are required for a fully automated answer file.

11. On the Display Settings page, select the display settings for the computer, as shown in Figure B-3, and then click Next.

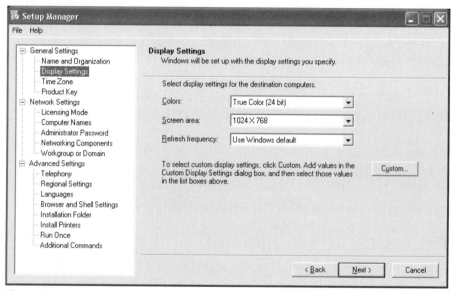

Figure B-3   Specifying display settings.

Important   Although the Windows default display—640 × 480, 60 Hz, and 16 colors—is hopelessly dated, use caution here. A usable setting that is mostly safe is 1024 × 768 × 60 Hz and High Color (16-bit) or True Color (24-bit), but you should know your hardware well enough to make an informed choice. If the screen area (*resolution*), colors, or refresh frequency is too high for the monitor plugged into the computer, the monitor could be damaged, though most are smart enough these days to simply refuse to do something they can't do. But if your choice can't be displayed, you'll be forced to reboot using the Safe Mode or Enable VGA Mode boot options and adjust the display settings to something safer.

12. On the Time Zone page, specify the time zone in which the servers will be placed and then click Next.

13. On the Product Key page, type the product key and then click Next. You'll have to edit the answer file for each installation to update the product key. Or leave this blank and you'll be prompted for the key during the install.

14. On the Licensing Mode page, click Next to accept licensing Per Server with 5 CALs. (SBS licensing is configured after Setup, as discussed in Chapter 5, "Completing the To Do List and Other Post-Installation Tasks.")

15. On the Computer Names page, create a list of computer names to use for the systems on which you will be installing Windows Small Business Server, as shown in Figure B-4. Type a computer name in the Computer Name text box, and then click Add. Setup Manager takes the names (if you have two or more) and creates a Uniqueness Database File (.UDF) that Setup then queries for computer names, using each name only once. Click Next to continue.

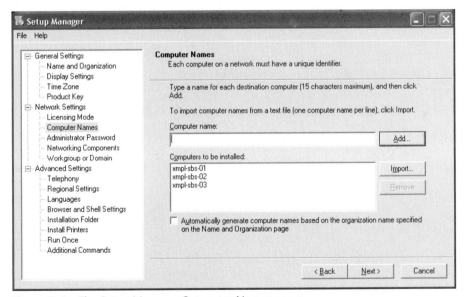

Figure B-4   The Setup Manager Computer Names page.

16. On the Administrator Password page, you can specify an administrator account password for the systems and other settings. If you choose to specify a password now, select the Encrypt The Administrator Password In The Answer File check box, as shown in Figure B-5. If you don't select this check box, the password is stored in plain text for anyone with Microsoft Notepad to read. Select the When A Destination Computer Starts Automatically Log On As Administrator, and set

the value to 1. This will bypass the first logon screen and take you straight to the Microsoft Windows Small Business Server Setup Wizard. Click Next to continue.

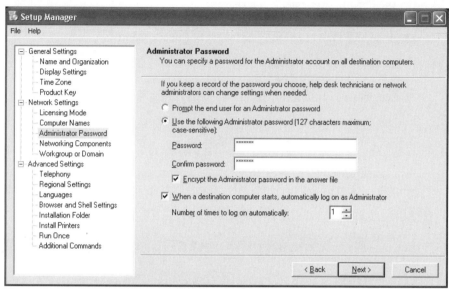

Figure B-5   Setting the Administrator password.

17. Click Next on the Networking Components page, and then click Next again on the Workgroup Or Domain page. (Typical settings will be used for Networking Components and the computer will belong to a Workgroup. These settings get handled during the Microsoft Windows Small Business Server Setup Wizard stage anyway.)

18. Use the rest of the pages to customize other settings such as Telephone, Regional, and Internet Explorer settings. On the Additional Commands page, click Finish.

19. In the Setup Manager dialog box, type the folder path in which you want to store the answer file, and name the answer file Winnt.sif (or Unattend.txt if you want to use the answer file with a distribution folder). Click OK and then click Cancel to exit Setup Manager.

20. Copy the Winnt.sif and Winnt.udb files to a floppy disk. (The Winnt.udb file exists only if you enter more than one computer name.) To use the disk, insert it immediately after the computer boots from the SBS CD-ROM, before Setup prompts you to press F2 to start the Automated System Recovery process.

More Info   For detailed information about the parameters in the answer file, see the Microsoft Windows Corporate Deployment Tools User's Guide help file, Deploy.chm, which is located in the \Support\Tools\Deploy.cab file on SBS CD 1.

Real World   Storage Drivers

Running an automated installation requires that all the drivers that Windows needs to install on your hardware are part of the distribution media and integrated into Windows Setup. If your servers require specialized RAID or other storage drivers, however, you will need to take this process further to integrate those drivers into the Windows Setup process. The alternative, as described in Chapter 3, is to press F6 during the initial CD-ROM boot process and then load the drivers from a floppy disk. This is actually the simplest method if you only need to do a few servers, especially if each one might have different hardware. It adds one more step you need to interact with the setup process, but the tradeoff is that it's simple to do.

Using the System Preparation Tool to Image Windows Server 2003

Running the first phase of SBS Setup using a fully automated answer file usually takes from 30 to 60 minutes, depending on hardware. This does not, of course, include the Microsoft Windows Small Business Server Setup Wizard which can't be automated. You can achieve the same results in about 5 or 10 minutes using the System Preparation Tool (Sysprep) in conjunction with a hard-drive imaging program.

However, this process has a few restrictions that make it useful only to consultants and OEMs who frequently install SBS on identical or nearly identical hardware. First of all, you must use a third-party drive imaging tool such as Acronis True Image or Symantec Ghost. Second, the computers must have identical mass storage controllers (SCSI controller or IDE chipset), and share the same HAL—no mixing ACPI systems with non-ACPI systems or uniprocessor systems with multiprocessor systems. Third, the system must be imaged before running the Microsoft Windows Small Business Server Setup Wizard (the second major phase of Setup).

> **More Info**   For information about the Microsoft Windows Small Business Server Setup Wizard, see Chapter 3.

Imaging makes sense for deploying tens to hundreds of identical servers—not all that common in the SBS world. If you do need to do that, however, we strongly recommend setting up a test environment and thoroughly testing your imaging and deployment process before rolling out to production servers. The following steps summarize how to image and deploy a partially installed SBS computer (the process also works for Windows Server 2003).

1. Install SBS on the reference system, but do not run the Microsoft Windows Small Business Server Setup Wizard. (If you're an OEM, contact Microsoft for information about imaging computers after running the Microsoft Windows Small Business Server Setup Wizard.)

2. Create a folder named Sysprep in the root directory of the system partition (for example, C:\Sysprep).

3. Extract Sysprep.exe and Setupcl.exe from the \Support\Tools\Deploy.cab file on the SBS CD 1 to the newly created \Sysprep folder.

4. Empty the Recycle Bin, delete any temporary files (including Temporary Internet files and cookies), and if the computer is a member of a domain, remove it from the domain.

5. Defragment the hard disk, check for viruses, and scan for hard-drive errors.

6. Clear the Event View log files and clear the Administrator account password so that there is no password. (Otherwise, all computers will use the same password.)

7. Right-click the Start button, choose Properties, click Customize, and then click Clear List to reset the Recently Used Programs listing. Then click the Advanced tab and click Clear List to reset the Recent Documents list.

8. Run Sysprep.exe. A message box appears indicating that Sysprep can modify security settings and that after you run Sysprep, Windows will automatically shut down. Click OK. The Sysprep tool appears, as shown in Figure B-6.

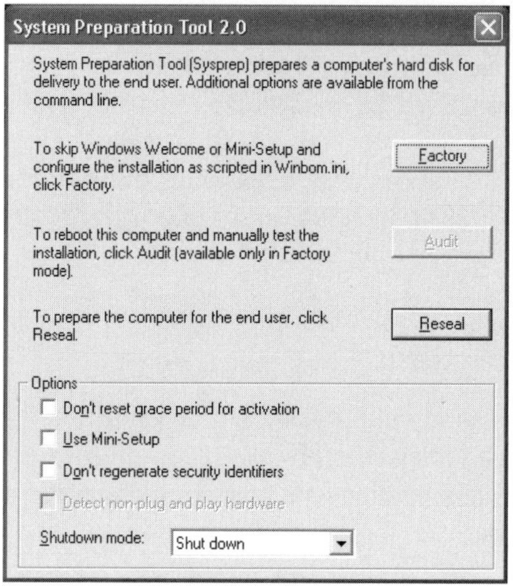

Figure B-6 Running Sysprep.

9. To force a full hardware detection that can take up to 20 minutes to complete during the Mini-Setup Wizard (Step 14), select Detect Non-Plug And Play Hardware.

10. Click Reseal, and then click OK in the message box to remove all identity information from the computer. The computer is automatically shut down.

11. Use a drive imaging program to create an image of the hard-drive partition, and save it to a network share, CD, DVD, or external hard drive.

12. On a new computer, use your drive imaging boot disk (created with the drive imaging program) to boot the computer on which you want to deploy SBS.

13. Connect to the network share, CD, DVD, or hard drive on which the image file is located and restore it onto the new computer's hard drive.

14. Restart the computer. A Mini-Setup Wizard runs (which is nothing more than an abbreviated version of Setup), personalizing the software, detecting any additional Plug and Play (PnP) devices, and hiding any missing devices. The system is now fully functional.

> **Note**   You can also provide an answer file to modify system configurations without recreating the disk image. To do this, use Setup Manager to create a Sysprep answer file (choose Sysprep Setup on the Type Of Setup page), save it to a floppy disk as Sysprep.inf, and insert the disk right after booting the new computer, before the Mini-Setup Wizard opens.

Using the Transition Pack

What's in a Transition Pack?. 637

Why Convert?. 638

Preparing to Run the Transition Pack. 640

Performing the Transition. 641

Post-Transition 644

So what do you do when you need to leave SBS and move to "regular" Windows Server 2003? Do you have to completely start over, build a new domain, and reinstall all your applications? Do you lose your e-mail? And what about all the special features of SBS, like Remote Web Workplace (RWW), the pre-built monitoring reports, and all those wizards?

Scary questions, but the good news is that the answers are all pretty much what you might hope they'd be. Microsoft has two transitions packs—one for SBS Standard and one for SBS Premium—that not only do the conversion, but also convert the server licenses to Windows Server 2003 Standard Edition, Microsoft Exchange Server, Microsoft Internet Security and Acceleration (ISA) Server, and Microsoft SQL Server.

What's in a Transition Pack?

Transition Packs come in two versions: a Standard Edition and a Premium Edition. Each includes a CD that does the actual conversion and five Client Access Licenses (CALs) for users or devices for the underlying server applications. There are specific Transition Packs that include Windows Server 2003 SP1, and the expectation is that there will be an R2 pair of Transition Packs as well, though they aren't available as of this writing. The Microsoft part numbers for the SP1 Transition Packs are as follows:

- **T72-00634** Microsoft Windows Small Business Server 2003 Standard Edition Transition Pack with SP1 and 5 CALS

- **T75-00752** Microsoft Windows Small Business Server 2003 Premium Edition Transition Pack with SP1 and 5 CALS

Why Convert?

You might need to convert for several reasons, but the two most common ones are: Your business has outgrown the 75-user limit of SBS, or you need to be able to support multiple domains in your Active Directory forest. This second reason can be the result of the merging of two or more businesses, each of which already has its own domain structure.

As your business grows and the number of users or devices connecting to SBS approaches the maximum of 75, you should start actively planning your conversion. Don't wait until you're already there. The conversion process is fairly straightforward, but like any software installation, it's a complex process that has real risks. By preparing your environment and your users for the conversion, you'll limit your risks and your downtime.

Handling Business Growth

One problem that your business will face as it grows is the load on your main SBS server. Long before you reach the maximum of 75 users, you'll have an ever-increasing load on the SBS server. Running the Transition Pack to convert from SBS won't solve that problem—it doesn't move your applications off of the SBS server. But it does convert the licenses so that they are no longer tied to the single server. To quote from the End User License Agreement (EULA) for the Transition Pack:

"You may install a single copy of each of the Server Software Components for use on more than one Server, provided you do not install more than one copy of each Server Software Component and you do not further separate individual portions of the Server Software Components for use on separate Servers. For each computer onto which a Server Software Component is installed, you will need a Microsoft Windows Server 2003 license. This agreement includes one Windows Server 2003 license."

This means that you can now offload Exchange, for example, onto a different server, move your ISA server to be stand-alone—which it should be for optimal security anyway—and move SQL Server to a separate server as well. While it's certainly true that you could offload these functions without removing SBS, you would then have to buy additional Server Software Component licenses, because the SBS license can't be split among multiple computers.

Handling Multiple Domains

The second main reason that businesses need to transition off of SBS is that they need to be able to support multiple domains. Maybe your business has gone global and you really need to have a separate domain (and a separate security policy) for your new international office. Or perhaps you've merged with another company that has its own domain, e-mail, and environment. Or you need to spin off a subsidiary company that will have its own name, security policy, and domain, but will still need to have a special relationship with your main business. Any of these reasons can make you wish that SBS supported multiple domains—as well as the domain trust relationships that make them work. By using the Transition Pack, you convert to Windows Server 2003, Standard Edition, and you can have multiple domains in your forest. You can even have cross-forest trust relationships.

Will I Lose RWW?

And what about all the other cool things that are part of SBS? Well, the answer is a bit of yes and a bit of no. Once you've run the Transition Pack and converted your SBS network to Windows Server 2003, all the features and wizards of SBS are still there, and they still work. Sounds good to us, but there is a catch—these features and wizards are no longer supported. As long as they work, you're welcome to use them. But if something breaks them, you can't call support to get a fix. You're on your own. That said, there's no particular reason to expect them to break. You can use the SBS wizards or you can use the conventional Windows Server tools—whatever works best for what you're trying to do. Figure C-1 shows both the SBS Server Management page and the Windows Server 2003 Manage Your Server page open at the same time. I'm impressed.

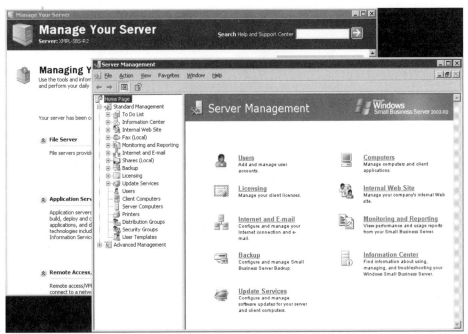

Figure C-1   Manage Your Server and SBS Server Management together!

But what about Remote Web Workplace? After all, it's *the* single most-envied feature of SBS that Windows Server folks wish they had. Yup, as you can see in Figure C-2, it's still there, and works just fine.

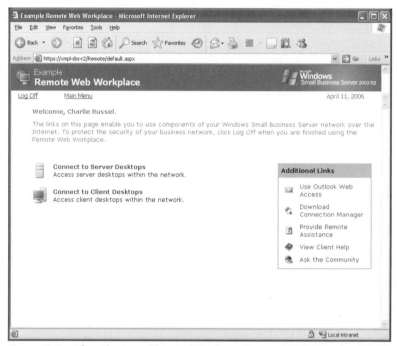

Figure C-2   After the transition to Windows Server 2003, Standard Edition, Remote Web Workplace still works.

Preparing to Run the Transition Pack

Before you run the Transition Pack against your SBS server, you need to do some basic maintenance and backups—both to protect yourself from disaster and to make the whole process run smoother, with a smaller risk of problems. You'll need to take the following preparation steps:

- Do a thorough, complete backup. And *verify* the backup.

- Clean up the hard drive on the SBS server. Remove temporary files, old log files, and so forth. Run Disk Cleanup (Cleanmgr.exe).

- Defragment the hard disk, using the built-in Windows defragmentation utility, or a third-party utility such as our favorite, PerfectDisk from Raxco.

- Disconnect the server from the Internet completely. The easiest way to do this is simply to unplug the network connector from the back of the server.

- Stop any third-party services that are running as a system account and set them to disabled or uninstall them. This includes antivirus programs, backup agents, disk utilities, and any real-time monitoring programs.

- Remove Veritas Backup Exec if you have installed it on the SBS server (see Microsoft Knowledge Base Article 914990 found at *http://support.microsoft.com/kb/914990/*).

- Run Regedit.exe and check for the presence of a key called HKLM\Software\Microsoft\Small Business. If this key is present, export it and remove it. (This is not the same as the HKLM\Software\Microsoft\SmallBusinessServer key. That key is expected.)

If this all seems a bit daunting , don't worry. Just make sure that you allocate sufficient time for the transition and that you've done all your preparation ahead of time.

Note   You should always match your Transition Pack version to your SBS version carefully. If your SBS is at Service Pack 1 level, you *must* have a Service Pack 1 Transition Pack.

One final note: You should order media kits for your individual server software packages to have them on hand during the transition. The Transition Pack does not include media for Exchange, ISA, or SQL Server, so if your goal is to move any of these servers off of the main SBS server, you'll need media to accomplish that. Purchasing the Transition Pack explicitly enables you to order media for the underlying server applications. You'll probably have to pay a small media-fulfillment cost, but you shouldn't be charged anything else.

Performing the Transition

Once you've done all the preparation and are ready to actually perform the transition, make sure that all your users are offline and that the server is disconnected from the Internet. If you have additional domain controllers in your SBS network, you should leave them powered up and connected if they're local to the main SBS server. Then insert the Transition Pack CD and follow these steps:

1. The Setup.exe program from the root of the CD drive should autorun, opening the Microsoft Windows Small Business Server Transition Pack Wizard, as shown in Figure C-3. If it doesn't, start the Setup.exe program manually. Click Next.

Figure C-3   The Microsoft Windows Small Business Server Transition Pack Wizard.

2. Agree to the End User License Agreement (EULA) and click Next.

3. Read the Upgrade Information, shown in Figure C-4, and then click Next.

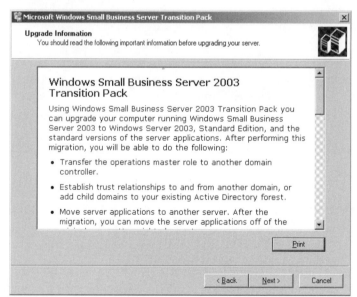

Figure C-4   The Upgrade Information page of the Microsoft Windows Small Business Server Transition Pack Wizard.

4. Enter the Product Key. This key is located inside the CD case of the Transition Pack. Click Next.

5. The Logon Information page, shown in Figure C-5, lets you provide the logon password for the Administrator account. If you don't provide this information, you'll have to log on each time the Transition Pack reboots, which is at least seven times by my count. But we might have missed one or two.

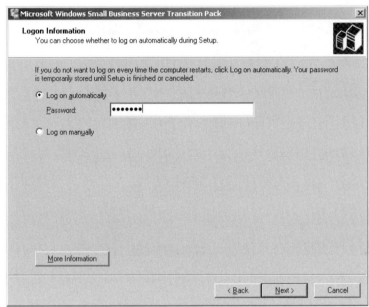

Figure C-5   The Logon Information page of the Microsoft Windows Small Business Server Transition Pack Wizard.

6. The Transition Pack should now complete automatically, without further intervention if you've provided the logon password. The full process takes anywhere from an hour and a half to two hours on typical SBS hardware.

> **Note**   In writing this appendix, I ran the Transition Pack six times. Four of those times—in no particular pattern—the first reboot required me to log on to the server because the password I had provided was not accepted. But all future logons happened automatically. So don't walk away from the Transition Pack installation until at least that first logon has taken place.

Post-Transition

Once you've completed the transition, you have the full capabilities of Windows Server 2003 Standard Edition, and you can upgrade to Enterprise Edition if you need to. The normal Windows Server 2003 administrative tools, including the Manage Your Server Wizard shown in Figure C-6, are there, and are the officially supported method for administering your server.

Figure C-6   The Manage Your Server Wizard.

You also still have the familiar SBS wizards and features, including Remote Web Workplace, Server Management, Monitoring and Reports, and so on. However, though these features are still there, and they still work, they are no longer supported. You can also no longer run the SBS Installation Wizard to add or remove components.

Post-Transition Tasks

Once your transition is complete, there's one *very important* task you should do immediately: a full, complete backup. Do this now, before you do anything else. This is your baseline for moving forward, and provides your fallback position if you encounter any problems at all. You can use the SBS Backup Wizard, or you can manually run NTBackup from Start, All Programs, Accessories, System Tools, Backup. Whichever way you run it, you'll want a full backup, including system state.

If you are transitioning from the Premium Edition of SBS, and you intend to leave ISA Server 2004 on the same server, you must run a repair installation of ISA Server 2004 after you complete the Transition Pack.

To do a repair installation of ISA Server 2004, follow these steps:

1. Open Add/Remove Programs and select Microsoft Internet Security and Acceleration Server 2004, as shown in Figure C-7.

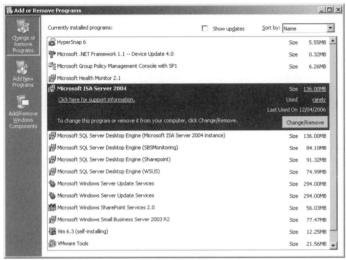

Figure C-7   Add/Remove Programs.

2. Click Change/Remove and select Repair. Click Next.

3. When the repair process completes, you'll need to reboot the server.

> **Note**   You will not normally require media for the ISA Server repair process, but you should be prepared ahead of time with the correct media, just in case.

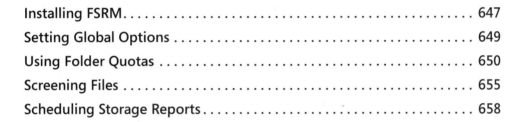

Appendix D
Using File Server Resource Manager

Installing FSRM. 647

Setting Global Options 649

Using Folder Quotas 650

Screening Files 655

Scheduling Storage Reports. 658

File Server Resource Manager (FSRM) is a last-minute addition to the feature set for the R2 release of Microsoft Windows Small Business Server 2003. FSRM is a collection of tools that enable Quota Management, File Screening Management, and Storage Reporting beyond what the Server Management–based SBS reporting provides.

Quota Management enables the managing of quotas on folders or directories instead of only on entire volumes–something SBS administrators have been definitely been asking for.

File Screening Management enables the SBS administrator to restrict the types of files that are stored in a folder or directory path. Restrictions are based on the extension of the file, not the content.

Storage Reporting provides preconfigured and custom reporting on the use (and abuse) of the storage resources of your SBS server. Reports can be generated on demand or on a regular schedule.

> **Note** FSRM was added late in the release process for SBS 2003 R2, and the authors have had to write this appendix based on a preliminary build. While we fully expect the version of FSRM described below to be identical, or nearly so, in the final released product, it is possible that some screens might change slightly.

Installing FSRM

Once you install the R2 Technologies CD into SBS, you enable the addition of FSRM to your SBS server, but it isn't actually installed yet. (See Chapter 12, "Patch Management," for details on how to install the contents of the R2 Technologies CD.) Installation is done through Add/Remove Programs, and requires you to have both CD1 and the R2 Premium Technologies CD available.

Important If you're installing SBS 2003 R2, you must update ISA 2004 to at least the Service Pack 2 level. There is a known issue with ISA 2004 and MMC 3.0, which is included in SBS R2.

Tip Check the Release Notes for SBS R2 for any late-breaking news about installing FSRM.

To install FSRM, follow these steps:

1. Open Add/Remove Programs from Control Panel and click Windows Components.

2. Click Management and Monitoring Tools and then click Details to open the Management and Monitoring Tools dialog box, as shown in Figure D-1.

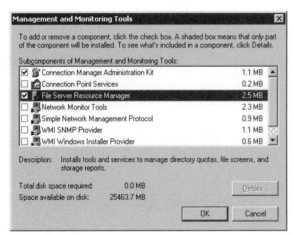

Figure D-1   The Management and Monitoring Tools dialog box of the Windows Components Wizard.

3. Select the File Server Resource Manager check box and click OK. Click Next to begin the actual installation. You will be prompted for the location of files if they're not found where SBS expects them.

Note The functions of FSRM are only available locally on the server they are installed on. If you have additional servers in your SBS network, and you want them to have FSRM functionality, they will need to be running Windows Server 2003 R2. Earlier versions of Windows Server did not include FSRM.

Setting Global Options

Before you can create notifications in FSRM, you need to specify the e-mail settings. This is also a good time to configure other global options, such as where Windows stores storage reports and whether to audit file screening.

To set global options, follow these steps:

1. Open File Server Resource Manager from the Administrative Tools folder.

2. Click File Server Resource Manager (Local) and click Configure Options in the Actions pane (the far-right pane) to open the File Server Resource Manager Options dialog box, shown in Figure D-2.

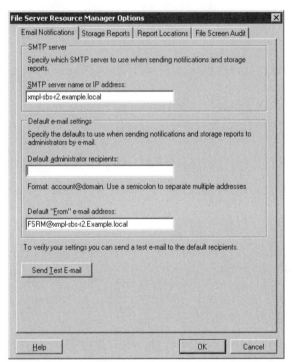

Figure D-2   The Email Notifications tab of the File Server Resource Manager Options dialog box.

3. Enter your SBS server name in the SMTP Server Name or IP address box.

4. Enter an administrative e-mail address or addresses to send notifications to, and adjust the From e-mail address if required. Click Send Test E-mail to verify that everything is working.

5. You can also configure the various reports by clicking the Storage Reports tab, change the storage locations for reports by clicking the Report Locations tab, and enable auditing of file screening activity by clicking the File Screen Audit tab.

6. Click OK when you've set the options you want to change at this time.

Using Folder Quotas

While the price of disk storage is certainly less than it was a few years ago, it's equally true that the amount of storage required has grown enormously. One way to manage that growth is through the use of quotas. There are two ways of doing this in SBS 2003 R2— disk quotas and folder or directory quotas. Disk (or volume) quotas allow you to create storage limits on each volume for individual users, and are covered in Chapter 7, "Storage Management."

Folder or directory quotas are new to the R2 release of SBS 2003 and are enabled only through FSRM. FSRM can set "hard" limits, which prevent users from exceeding their quotas, or "soft" limits, which merely serve as a warning and notification method. Unlike disk quotas, limits are set exactly the same for all users.

Creating Quotas

You can create individual quotas, auto quotas that are automatically applied to subfolders of the original folder, or quotas based on a template. In general, you should use templates to create quotas. When you change a quota template, all the quotas that are based on that template are automatically updated to the new template properties. SBS 2003 R2 comes with several predefined templates, and you can also easily create your own template in FSRM.

To create a quota from an existing template, follow these steps:

1. Open FSRM if it isn't already open. Click Quotas in the Quota Management container, as shown in Figure D-3.

2. Click Create Quota in the Actions pane to open the Create Quota dialog box, shown in Figure D-4. This dialog box offers you the following choices for the quota:

    ❑ Create Quota On Path *or* Auto Apply Template And Create Quotas On Existing And New Subfolders

    ❑ Derive Properties From This Quota Template (recommended) *or* Define Custom Quota Properties (not available for auto quotas)

3. You'll see a summary of the quota properties at the bottom of the dialog box. Once you're satisfied with the settings, click Create to enable the new quota.

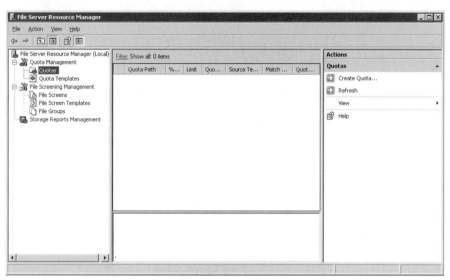

Figure D-3   The Quotas section of FSRM.

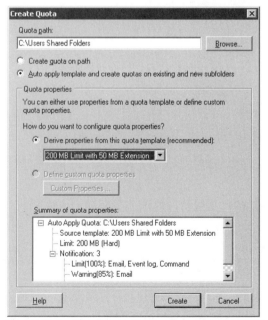

Figure D-4   The Create Quota dialog box in FSRM.

Under the Hood   Automatic Quota Extensions

FSRM has the ability to set hard quotas that can be automatically extended. How does it do that, you ask? A careful look at the "200 MB Limit with 50 MB Extension" quota template shows us how it's done. The template creates a hard quota of 200 MB, with warnings at 85 percent and 95 percent. Pretty ordinary. But take a look at the limit properties, as shown in Figure D-5, and you'll see how it's done.

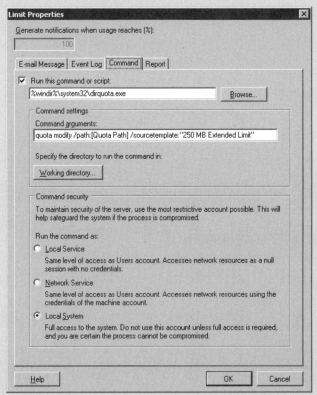

Figure D-5   The Command tab of the Limit Properties for the 200 MB Limit with 50 MB Extension quota template.

When the quota limit is reached, it causes a command to be executed. The command uses the command-line interface to quotas to generate an extension to the quota hard limit from 200 MB to 250 MB.

You can use the command features of quota templates to extend the properties and behavior of quotas beyond their default. Type **dirquota /?** from the command line to see a list of options and switches that dirquota supports.

Creating and Editing Quota Templates

Quota templates enable you to quickly apply standardized quota settings, as well as simultaneously update all quotas that make use of a template. When you edit a quota template, SBS gives you the option to update all quotas based on the template. To create or edit a quota template, follow these steps:

1. In the File Server Resource Manager console, right-click Quota Templates and choose Create Quota Template, or right-click an existing quota template and choose Edit Template Properties.

2. To create a quota template based on an existing quota, right-click the quota and choose Create Template From Quota.

3. To base the template on an existing template, in the Create Quota Template dialog box, shown in Figure D-6, choose a template from the Copy Properties From Quota Template box and then click Copy.

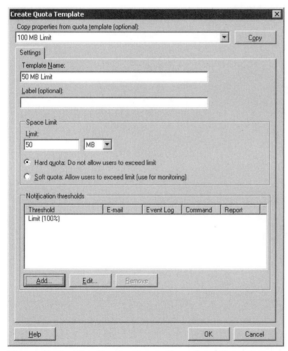

Figure D-6 The Create Quota Template dialog box.

4. Type a name and label for the template in the Template Name and Label boxes.

5. In the Limit box, type the maximum amount of disk space each user can use in the specified folder.

6. Choose Hard Quota to prevent users from exceeding the limit you specify, or choose Soft Quota to use the quota only for monitoring.

7. In the Notification Thresholds section of the dialog box, click Add to create a new notification, or select an existing notification and then click Edit. The Add Threshold dialog box, shown in Figure D-7, appears.

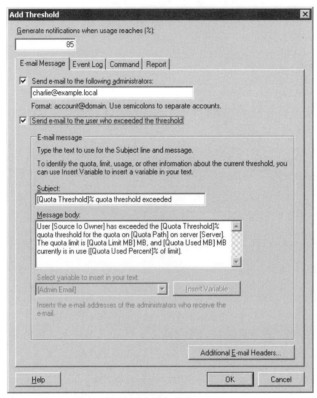

Figure D-7   The Add Threshold dialog box.

8. In the Generate Notifications When Usage Reaches box, specify when to notify users.

9. Specify which of the following actions to take when a user exceeds the threshold you specify, and click OK when you are finished:

    ❑   Use the E-mail Message tab to send an e-mail notification to a user who exceeds the threshold and/or an administrator. Use the E-mail Message section of the tab to customize the message that Windows generates.

❑ Use the Event Log tab to record a log entry on the server when a user exceeds the threshold.

❑ Use the Command tab to run a command or script when a user exceeds the threshold.

❑ Use the Report tab to generate a storage report when a user exceeds the threshold. See the "Scheduling Storage Reports" section earlier in this appendix for more information about storage reports.

10. Click OK when you are finished. If you are editing an existing template, the Update Quotas Derived From Template dialog box appears. Choose one of the following options and then click OK:

❑ **Apply Template Only To Derived Quotas That Match The Original Template** Updates quotas based on the quota template only if you have not customized them

❑ **Apply Template To All Derived Quotas**   Updates all quotas based on the quota template

❑ **Do Not Apply Template To Derived Quotas**   Does not update any quotas based on the template

Screening Files

Administrators who use a storage reporting tool for the first time—such as the one included in FSRM—are often surprised, and occasionally outraged, by how many audio and video files they find on file servers. We're not quite sure why, since—with or without an automatic tool—administrators should have a pretty good idea of who has stored what on their server, but apparently many operate under the "ignorance is bliss" premise. At least until they find they've suddenly run out of disk space on the server at a critical time.

There are also legal implications attached to the files stored on your server. It is prudent and wise to both know what is stored there and take reasonable steps to manage and limit that storage to acceptable types of files.

Real World   Controlling Types of Files on the SBS Server

If you are serious about blocking users from saving specific types of files on the SBS server, you should have two things:

■ An acceptable-use policy that clearly states what users can and cannot place on file shares

■ A file screen that implements this policy

The file screening in SBS's FSRM can be circumvented by changing the extension of prohibited file types to one that isn't blocked, since file screening works strictly by file name pattern matching. But if you have a clear and unequivocal acceptable-use policy, as well as a file screen, anyone discovered circumventing the policy has clearly changed the "terms of engagement." No longer can a wayward employee pretend innocence and beg forgiveness—a clear company policy has deliberately been circumvented, and the violator is subject to the sanctions laid out in that policy.

Creating File Screens

To create a file screen, follow these steps:

1. In the File Server Resource Manager, click File Screening Management.

2. Click the File Screens container and then click Create File Screen in the Actions pane. The Create File Screen dialog box appears, as shown in Figure D-8.

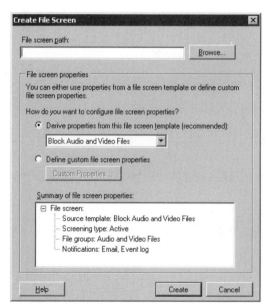

Figure D-8   The Create File Screen dialog box.

3. Enter the path for the screen in the File Screen Path field.

4. Select the file screen template you want to apply and click Create to create the screen.

Real World   Using Exceptions to Control Location

FSRM works at the level of the folder that is screened, which includes all subfolders. So if you put an audio and video file screen at the root of a volume, no one will be able to save any audio or video files on that entire volume. But suppose you want to distribute officially sanctioned audio or video files without having to remove the overall file screen? Create an exception to the screen on a subfolder, and then change the permissions of that subfolder to allow only authorized users to write to the folder. By combining file screening, share permissions, and NTFS permissions, you can fine-tune the permissions and file types you allow on the server. Figure D-9 shows this type of configuration, with an overall file screen on C:\Public that prohibits audio and video files, but a "Company Videos" exception below it that can serve as a repository for official videos.

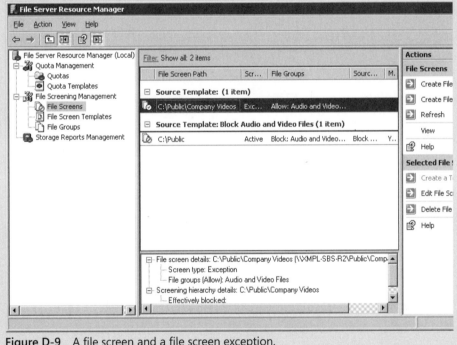

Figure D-9   A file screen and a file screen exception.

Under the Hood   File Screens Are Flexible

While the most obvious use of file screens is to block particular types of files by their extension, file screens actually are far more flexible than that. The screening works by matching a file name pattern, so you can create file types that match any kind of pattern at all, not just by the file extension. Use this flexibility wisely, though, as you can easily get carried away.

Another feature is the passive file screen. This doesn't actually prevent someone from saving a particular file type on the server, but you use it with the Storage Reporting to allow easy monitoring of files that meet the passive file screening criteria. We actually prefer this type of file screening when possible—it imposes less overhead on the server, it doesn't encourage creative file renaming, and it still provides managers with the tools they need to encourage appropriate behavior.

Scheduling Storage Reports

FSRM supports reporting in Dynamic Hypertext Markup Language (DHTML), HTML, Extensible Markup Language (XML), Comma-Separated Values (CSV) text, or plain text, making it easy to view reports or process them using scripts, Microsoft Office Excel, or other applications.

FSRM includes the following preconfigured storage reports:

- Duplicate files
- File screening audit
- Files by file group
- Files by owner
- Large files
- Least recently accessed files
- Most recently accessed files
- Quota usage

To schedule a storage report, follow these steps:

1. In File Server Resource Manager, click Storage Reports Management.

2. Choose Schedule A New Report Task from the Actions pane. The Storage Reports Task Properties dialog box appears, as shown in Figure D-10.

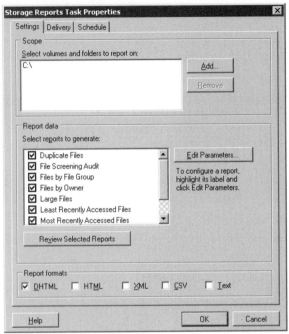

Figure D-10   The Storage Reports Task Properties dialog box.

3. In the Scope section of the dialog box, click Add to select the local folders that you want to monitor.

4. In the Report Data section of the dialog box, select the reports that you want to generate.

   To view the settings for all selected reports, click Review Selected Reports. To adjust the settings for a report, select the report and then click Edit Parameters.

5. In the Report Formats section of the dialog box, select the formats in which you want to generate the reports.

6. Click the Delivery tab, select the Send Reports To The Following Administrators check box if you want to send the reports via e-mail. Enter the addresses to send the report to, separating them with semicolons.

7. Click the Schedule tab, and then click Create Schedule. The Schedule dialog box appears, which you can use to schedule the storage reports.

8. After you finish creating the scheduled report task, click OK in the Storage Reports Task Properties dialog box.

Note You must create at least one schedule for the report before you can save it or run it interactively.

---

9. To run the scheduled report immediately, right-click it and choose Run Report Task Now. The Generate Storage Reports dialog box appears, asking whether you want to view the reports immediately or whether File Server Resource Manager should generate the reports in the background for viewing later.

Note When viewing a storage report in DHTML format, you can sort the listing by columns, as long as Microsoft Internet Explorer can display active content. (You might need to use the Information Bar in Internet Explorer to allow blocked content.)

Under the Hood Storage Reports, Snapshots, and Performance

To create a storage report, Windows creates a Scheduled Task in the Scheduled Tasks folder that uses the Volume Shadow Copy Service to take a snapshot of the specified storage volumes. Windows then creates the storage report from this snapshot using XML style sheets stored in the %WINDIR%\system32\srm\xslt folder. This process minimizes the performance impact on the server but does degrade file server performance temporarily.

To minimize the performance impact of storage reports, schedule storage reports outside of normal business hours or during times when few users need to access the server. Consolidate storage report tasks to minimize the number of snapshots Windows must take. (All storage reports in a storage report task use the same snapshot.)

Glossary

Numbers and Special Characters

802.11   Refers to a family of specifications for wireless networking.

802.11a   An extension to 802.11 that applies to wireless LANs and provides up to 54 Mbps in the 5-GHz band.

802.11b   An extension to 802.11 that applies to wireless LANs and provides 11-Mbps transmission (with a fallback to 5.5, 2, and 1 Mbps) in the 2.4-GHz band. 802.11b is a 1999 ratification to the original 802.11 standard, allowing wireless functionality comparable to Ethernet. Also called Wi-Fi.

802.11g   An extension to 802.11 that applies to wireless LANs and provides 54 Mbps transmission in the 2.4-GHz band. Compatible with 802.11g.

802.11i   An extension to 802.11 that applies to wireless LANs and provides security protocols for wireless networks. Includes different levels and support for WPA and WPA2, along with RADIUS.

802.11n   An extension to 802.11 that applies to wireless LANs. The next major speed jump for the 802.11 networks. Just now starting to be implemented.

A

Access control entry (ACE)   An entry in an access control list (ACL) that defines the level of access for a user or group.

Access control list (ACL)   A set of data associated with a file, directory, or other resource that defines the permissions users or groups have for accessing it. In Active Directory, the ACL is a list of access control entries (ACEs) stored with the object it protects. In Microsoft Windows Server 2003, Windows 2000, and Windows NT, an ACL is included in a data structure called a security descriptor.

Access point   A hardware device or software that acts as a communication hub for users of a wireless device to connect to a wired LAN.

Account lockout   A security feature that disables a user account if failed logons exceed a specified number in a specified period of time. Locked accounts cannot log on and must be unlocked by an administrator.

Active Directory   Beginning in Microsoft Windows 2000 Server and continuing in Windows Server 2003, Active Directory replaces the Windows NT collection of directory functions with an integrated implementation that includes DNS, DHCP, LDAP, and Kerberos.

ActiveX   A loosely defined set of technologies that allows software components to interact with each other in a networked environment.

ActiveX component   Reusable software component that adheres to the ActiveX specification and can operate in an ActiveX-compliant environment.

Address   A precise location where a piece of information is stored in memory or on disk. Also, the unique identifier for a node on a network. On the Internet, the code by which an individual user is identified. The format is *username@hostname*, where username is your user name, logon name, or account number and hostname is the name of the computer or Internet provider you use. The host name might be a few words strung together with periods.

Address Resolution Protocol (ARP)   A TCP/IP and AppleTalk protocol that provides IP-address-to-MAC (media access control) address resolution for IP packets.

Administrative credentials   Logon information used to verify the identity of a member of the administrators group.

Advanced Configuration Power Interface (ACPI)   An industry specification defining power management on a range of computer devices. ACPI compliance is necessary for devices to take advantage of Plug and Play and power management capabilities.

Allocation unit   The smallest unit of managed space on a hard disk or logical volume. Also called a cluster.

Anonymous FTP   A way to use the FTP program to log on to another computer to copy files when you do not have an account on that computer. When you log on, type **anonymous** as the user name and your address as the password. This gives you access to publicly available files. See *File Transfer Protocol (FTP)*.

AppleTalk   A local area network architecture built into Macintosh computers to connect them with printers and other devices. A network with a Windows Server 2003 server and Macintosh clients can function as an AppleTalk network with the use of AppleTalk network integration (formerly Services for Macintosh). Now mostly deprecated.

Associate   To connect files having a particular extension to a specific program. When you double-click a file with the extension, the associated program is launched and the file you clicked is opened. In the Windows operating system, associated file extensions are usually called registered file types.

Asynchronous Digital Subsciber Line (ADSL)   *See* Digital Subscriber Line.

Asynchronous Transfer Mode (ATM)   A network technology based on sending data in cells or packets of a fixed size. It is asynchronous in that the transmission of cells containing information from a particular user is not necessarily periodic.

Attribute   A characteristic. In Windows file management, it is information that shows whether a file is read-only, hidden, compressed, encrypted, ready to be backed up (archived), or should be indexed.

Audit policy   Defines the type of security events to be logged. It can be defined on a server or an individual computer.

Authentication   Verification of the identity of a user or computer process. In Windows Server 2003, Windows 2000, and Windows NT, authentication involves comparing the user's security identifier (SID) and password to a list of authorized users on a domain.

B

Backup Domain Controller   On a Windows NT4 or earlier network, a secondary and less powerful domain controller. On an SBS network, an additional domain controller that distributes the authentication load.

Bandwidth   On a network, the transmission capacity of a communications channel stated in megabits per second (Mbps). For example, Ethernet has a bandwidth of 10 Mbps. Fast Ethernet has a bandwidth of 100 Mbps, and Gigabit Ethernet has a bandwidth of 1000 Mbps.

Binding   A software connection between a network card and a network transport protocol (such as TCP/IP).

BOOTP   Boot Protocol. Used on TCP/IP networks to enable a diskless workstation to learn its own IP address, the location of a BOOTP server on the network, and the location of a file to be loaded into memory to boot the machine. This allows a computer to boot without a hard disk or a floppy disk.

Bottleneck   A condition in which one resource is preventing another resource from functioning at its best. For example, when one application monopolizes the system processor to the exclusion of all other operations, there is a bottleneck at the processor.

Broadband   A type of data communications channel in which the medium (such as a wire or fiber-optic cable) carries multiple messages at a time.

Broadcasting   To simultaneously send a message to everyone on a network. See *multicasting.*

Browser service   The service that maintains a current list of computers and provides the list to applications when needed. When a user attempts to connect to a resource in the domain, the Browser service is contacted to provide a list of available resources.

C

Certificate   A credential used to prove the origin, authenticity, and purpose of a public key to the entity that holds the corresponding private key.

Certificate authority (CA)   The service that accepts and fulfills certificate requests and revocation requests and that can also manage the policy-directed registration process a user completes to get a certificate.

Certificate revocation list (CRL)   A digitally signed list (published by a certificate authority) of certificates that is no longer valid.

Child domain A domain located directly beneath another domain name (parent domain). For example, *engineering.example.com* is a child domain of *example.com*, the parent domain. Also called a subdomain. Child domains are not supported in Windows Small Business Server 2003.

Child object An object based on another object or inside another object. For example, a file is a child object inside a folder, which is the parent object.

Counter A component within an object that represents data for a specific aspect of the system or service.

Counter log A recorder of data at predefined intervals.

D

Digital Subsciber Line (DSL) A technology that uses existing copper telephone lines to provide high-speed Internet access. ADSL is Asynchronous DSL and has faster download speeds than upload speeds. SDSL is synchronous DSL and has the same speeds in both directions.

Directory service A means of storing directory data and making it available to network users and administrators. For example, Active Directory stores information about user accounts, such as names, passwords, and phone numbers, and enables other authorized users on the same network to access this information.

Disk quota A limitation, set by an administrator, on the amount of disk space available to a user.

Distinguished name (DN) In the context of Active Directory, "distinguished" means the qualities that make the name distinct. The distinguished name identifies the domain that holds the object, as well as the complete path through the container hierarchy used to locate the object.

Distributed file system (DFS) A file management system in which files can be located on separate computers but are presented to users as a single directory tree. Not supported on Windows Small Business Server 2003.

DNS name servers Servers that contain information about part of the Domain Name System (DNS) database. These servers make computer names available to queries for name resolution across the Internet. Also called domain name servers.

Domain A group of computers that share a security policy and a user account database.

Domain controller A server in a domain that accepts account logons and initiates their authentication. In an Active Directory domain, a domain controller controls access to network resources and participates in replication.

Domain local group A local group used on ACLs only in its own domain. A domain local group can contain users and global groups from any domain in the forest, universal groups, and other domain local groups in its own domain.

Domain name   In Active Directory, the name given to a collection of networked computers that share a common directory. On the Internet, the unique text name that identifies a specific host. A machine can have more than one domain name, but a given domain name points to only one machine. Domain names are resolved to IP addresses by DNS name servers.

Domain Name System (DNS)   A service on TCP/IP networks (the Internet included) that translates domain names into IP addresses. This allows users to employ friendly names like Companyweb or example.com when querying a remote system instead of using an IP address, such as 198.45.233.59.

Dynamic Data Exchange (DDE)   Communication between processes implemented in the Windows family of operating systems. When programs that support DDE are running at the same time, they can exchange data by means of conversations. Conversations are two-way connections between two applications that transmit data alternately. Mostly deprecated now and replaced with more robust and powerful communications mechanisms.

Dynamic DNS   Domain Naming System service that allows for dynamically changing name to IP address changes. See http://en.wikipedia.org/wiki/Dynamic_dns.

Dynamic Host Configuration Protocol (DHCP)   A TCP/IP protocol used to automatically assign IP addresses and configure TCP/IP for network clients.

Dynamic-link library (DLL)   A program module that contains executable code and data that can be used by various programs. A program uses the DLL only when the program is active, and the DLL is unloaded when the program closes.

E

Environment variable   A string of environment information, such as a drive, path, or filename, associated with a symbolic name. The System option in the Control Panel or the Set command from the command prompt can be used to define environment variables.

Ethernet   A local area network protocol. Ethernet supports data transfer rates of 10 Mbps and uses a bus topology and thick or thin coaxial, fiber-optic, or twisted-pair cabling. A newer version of Ethernet called Fast Ethernet supports data transfer rates of 100 Mbps, and an even newer version, Gigabit Ethernet, supports data transfer rates of 1000 Mbps.

Extended partition   A nonbootable portion of a hard disk that can be subdivided into logical drives. There can be only a single extended partition per hard disk.

Extensible Authentication Protocol (EAP)

An extension to the Point-to-Point Protocol (PPP) that allows the use of arbitrary authentication methods for validating a PPP connection.

Extensible Markup Language (XML)   A text format derived from the Standard General Markup Language (SGML). It allows the flexible development of user-defined document types and provides a non-proprietary, persistent, and verifiable file format for the storage and transmission of text and data both on and off the Web.

F

Failover   An operation that automatically switches to a standby database, server, or network when the primary system fails or is temporarily shut down for servicing. In server clusters, the process of taking resources off one node in a prescribed order and restoring them on another node.

Fault tolerance   The ability of a system to ensure data integrity when an unexpected hardware or software failure occurs. Many fault-tolerant computer systems mirror all operations—that is, all operations are done on two or more duplicate systems, so if one fails, the other can take over.

File Transfer Protocol (FTP)   A method of transferring one or more files from one computer to another over a network or telephone line. Because FTP has been implemented on a variety of systems, it's a simple way to transfer information between usually incongruent systems, such as a PC and a minicomputer.

Firewall   A protective filter for messages and logons. An organization connected directly to the Internet uses a firewall to prevent unauthorized access to its network. See *proxy server*.

Folder redirection   An option in Group Policy to place users' special folders, such as My Documents, on a network server.

Fully qualified domain name (FQDN)   A domain name that includes the names of all network domains leading back to the root to clearly indicate a location in the domain namespace tree. Examples of an FQDN are sbssrv.example.local or sales.europe.microsoft.com.

G

Global group   A group that can be used in its own domain and in trusting domains. However, it can contain user accounts and other global groups only from its own domain.

Globally unique identifier (GUID)   Part of the identifying mechanism generated by Active Directory for each object in the directory. If a user or computer object is renamed or moved to a different name, the security identifier (SID), relative distinguished name (RDN), and distinguished name (DN) will change, but the GUID will remain the same.

Group Policy   Setting of rules for computers and users. Group Policy stores policies for file deployment, application deployment, logon/logoff scripts, startup/shutdown scripts, domain security, Internet Protocol security (IPSec), and so on.

Group Policy Object (GPO) A collection of policies stored in two locations: a Group Policy container (GPC) and a Group Policy template (GPT). The GPC is an Active Directory object that stores version information, status information, and other policy information (for example, application objects). The GPT is used for file-based data and stores software policy, script, and deployment information. The GPT is located in the system volume folder of the domain controller.

H

Host Any device on the network that uses TCP/IP. A host is also a computer on the Internet you might be able to log on to. You can use FTP to get files from a host computer and use other protocols (such as Telnet) to make use of the host computer.

Hosts file A local ASCII text file that maps host names to IP addresses. Each line represents one host, starting with the IP address, one or more spaces, and then the host's name.

Hypertext A system of writing and displaying text that enables the text to be linked in multiple ways, available at several levels of detail. Hypertext documents can also contain links to related documents, such as those referred to in footnotes.

Hypertext Markup Language (HTML) A system used for writing pages for the World Wide Web. HTML allows text to include codes that define fonts, layout, embedded graphics, and hypertext links.

Hypertext Transfer Protocol (HTTP) The method by which Web pages are transferred over a network.

I

Integrated Services Digital Network (ISDN) An international communications standard for sending voice, video, and data over regular or digital telephone wires. ISDN supports data transfer rates of 64 Kbps (64,000 bits per second).

Internet Authentication Service (IAS) The Microsoft implementation of Remote Authentication Dial-In User Service (RADIUS), an authentication and accounting system used by many Internet Service Providers (ISPs). When a user connects to an ISP using a user name and password, the information is passed to a RADIUS server, which checks that the information is correct and then authorizes access to the ISP system.

Internet Control Message Protocol (ICMP)

A protocol used to report problems encountered with the delivery of data, such as unreachable hosts or unavailable ports. ICMP is also used to send a request packet to determine whether a host is available. The receiving host sends back a packet if it is available and functioning. See *ping*.

Internet Protocol (IP) The inter-network layer protocol used as a basis of the Internet. IP enables information to be routed from one network to another in packets and then reassembled when they reach their destination.

Internet Protocol Security (IPSec)   An Internet Engineering Task Force (IETF) standard for creating Virtual Private Networks (VPNs).

IP number or IP address   In IPv4, a four-part number separated by periods (for example, 165.113.245.2) that uniquely identifies a machine on the Internet. Every machine on the Internet has a unique IP number.

K

Kerberos   An identity-based security system that authenticates users at logon. It works by assigning a unique key, called a ticket, to each user who logs on to the network. The ticket is then embedded in messages to identify the sender of the message. The Kerberos security protocol is the primary authentication mechanism in Windows Server 2003 and Windows 2000 Server.

L

Layer 2 Tunneling Protocol (L2TP)   An extension to the PPP (Point-to-Point Protocol) allowing ISPs to operate Virtual Private Networks (VPNs).

Lightweight Directory Access Protocol (LDAP)   A protocol used to access a directory service. LDAP is a simplified version of the Directory Access Protocol (DAP), which is used to gain access to X.500 directories. LDAP is the primary access protocol for Active Directory.

LISTSERV   A family of programs that manage Internet mailing lists by distributing messages posted to the list and adding and deleting members automatically.

Lmhosts   An ASCII text file, such as Hosts, but used to associate IP addresses to host names inside a network.

Local area network (LAN)   A group of connected computers, usually located close to one another (such as in the same building or the same floor of the building) so that data can be passed among them.

Log   A record of transactions or activities on a computer. See also *counter log, trace log.*

Log on   The act of entering into a computer system; for example, "Log on to the network and read your e-mail." Also log in.

Logon   The account name used to gain access to a computer system. Unlike a password, the logon name is not a secret. Also login, especially in UNIX networks.

Logon or logoff script   Typically, a batch file set to run when a user logs on or logs off a system. A logon script is used to configure a user's initial environment. A logoff script is used to return a system to some predetermined condition. Either script can be assigned to multiple users individually or through Group Policy.

M

Master boot record (MBR)   The first sector on a hard disk where the computer gets its startup information. The MBR contains the partition table for the computer and a small program called the master boot code.

Media access control (MAC) address A unique 48-bit number assigned to network interface cards by the manufacturer. MAC addresses are used for mapping in TCP/IP network communication.

Media pool A logical collection of removable media sharing the same management policies.

Member server A server that is part of a domain but is *not* a domain controller. Member servers can be dedicated to managing files or printer services or other functions. A member server does not verify logons or maintain a security database.

Mirror 1. Two partitions on two hard disks configured so that each will contain identical data to the other. If one disk fails, the other contains the data and processing can continue. 2. Web site that is a replica of an already existing site, used to reduce network traffic or improve the availability of the original site.

Mount To make a physical disk or tape accessible to a computer's file system.

Multicasting Simultaneously sending a message to more than one destination on a network. Multicasting is distinguished from broadcasting in that multicasting sends to only selected recipients.

Multilink dialing Combining two or more physical communication links into a single logical link to increase available bandwidth.

Multithreading The simultaneous processing of several threads inside the same program. Because several threads can be processed in parallel, one thread does not have to finish before another one can start. See *thread*.

N

Name resolution The process of mapping a name to its corresponding address.

Namespace A name or group of names defined according to a naming convention; any bounded area in which a given name can be resolved. Active Directory is primarily a namespace, as is any directory service. The Internet uses a hierarchical namespace that partitions names into categories known as top-level domains, such as .com, .edu, and .gov.

NetBIOS Enhanced User Interface (NetBEUI) A small and fast protocol that requires little memory but can be routed only by using token ring routing. Remote locations linked by routers cannot use NetBEUI to communicate. Not supported by Windows Server 2003.

Net Logon service A service that accepts logon requests from any client and provides authentication from the Security Accounts Manager (SAM) database of accounts.

Network Two or more computers connected for the purpose of sharing resources.

Network Access Server (NAS) A server that accepts Point-to-Point Protocol connections and places them on the network served by NAS.

Network Address Translation (NAT)

Enables a local area network (LAN) to use one set of IP addresses for internal traffic and a second set of addresses for external traffic.

Network News Transfer Protocol (NNTP) A protocol defined for distribution, inquiry, retrieval, and posting of news articles on the Internet.

Newsgroup On the Internet, a distributed bulletin board system about a particular topic. USENET News (also known as Netnews) is a system that distributes thousands of newsgroups to all parts of the Internet.

Node A location in a tree structure with links to one or more items below it. On a LAN, a device that can communicate with other devices on the network. In clustering, a computer that is a member of a cluster.

NTFS file system The native file system for Windows Server 2003, Windows 2000, and Windows NT. Supports long filenames, a variety of permissions for sharing files, encryption, compression and a transaction log that allows the completion of any incomplete file-related tasks if the operating system is interrupted.

O

Object A particular set of attributes that represents something concrete, such as a user, a printer, or an application. The attributes hold data describing the thing that is identified by the object. Attributes of a user might include the user's given name, surname, and e-mail address. The classification of the object defines which types of attributes are used. For example, the objects classified as users might allow the use of attribute types such as common name, telephone number, and e-mail address, whereas the object class of organization allows for attribute types such as organization name and business category. An attribute can take one or more values, depending on its type.

Object identifier (OID) A globally unique identifier (GUID), which is assigned by the Directory System Agent (DSA) when the object is created. The GUID is stored in an attribute, the object GUID, which is part of every object. The object GUID attribute cannot be modified or deleted. When storing a reference to an Active Directory object in an external store (for example, a database), you should use the object GUID because, unlike a name, it will not change.

Organizational unit (OU) A container object in Active Directory used to separate computers, users, and other resources into logical units. An organizational unit is the smallest entity to which Group Policy can be linked. It is also the smallest scope to which administration authority can be delegated.

P

Packet   The basic unit of information sent over a network. Each packet contains the destination address, the sender's address, error-control information, and data. The size and format of a packet depend on the protocol being used.

Page   A document, or collection of information, available over the World Wide Web. A page can contain text, graphics, video, and sound files. Also, a portion of memory that the virtual memory manager can swap to and from a hard disk.

Paging   A virtual memory operation in which pages are transferred from memory to disk when memory becomes full. When a thread accesses a page that is not in memory, a page fault occurs and the memory manager uses page tables to find the page on disk and then loads the page into memory.

Partition   A portion of a memory device that behaves as if it were a physically separate unit.

Ping   A network management utility that checks to see whether another computer is available and functioning. It sends a short message to which the other computer automatically responds. If the other computer does not respond to the ping, you usually cannot establish communications.

Point of presence (POP)   A physical site in a geographic area where a network access provider, such as a telecommunications company, has equipment to which users connect. The local telephone company's central office in a particular area is also sometimes referred to as their POP for that area.

Point-to-Point Tunneling Protocol (PPTP)

A protocol that provides router-to-router and host-to-network connections over a telephone line (or a network link that acts like a telephone line). See *Serial Line Internet Protocol (SLIP)*.

Post Office Protocol (POP)   A protocol by which a mail server on the Internet lets you access your e-mail and download it to a PC or Macintosh. Most people refer to this protocol with its version number (POP2, POP3, and so on) to avoid confusing it with points of presence (POPs).

Primary partition   A portion of the hard disk that has been marked as a potentially bootable logical drive by an operating system. MS-DOS can support only a single primary partition. Master boot record disks can support four primary partitions. Computers with the Intel Itanium processor use a GUID partition table that supports up to 128 primary partitions.

Profile   Loaded by the system when a user logs on, the profile defines a user's environment, including network settings, printer connections, desktop settings, and program items.

Protected Extensible Authentication Protocol (PEAP)   A protocol developed jointly by Microsoft, RSA Security, and Cisco for transmitting authentication data, including passwords, over 802.11 wireless networks.

Protocol   A set of rules for transferring data between two devices.

Proxy server   A server that receives Web requests from clients, retrieves Web pages, and forwards them to clients. Proxy servers can dramatically improve performance for groups of users by caching retrieved pages. Proxy servers also provide security by shielding the IP addresses of internal clients.

Public-key cryptography   A method of secure transmission in which two different keys are used—a public key for encrypting data and a private key for decrypting data.

Q

Quality of Service (QoS)   A set of standards for ensuring the quality of data transmission on a network.

R

Redundant array of independent disks (RAID)   A range of disk management and striping techniques to implement fault tolerance.

Relative distinguished name (RDN)   Active Directory uses the concept of a relative distinguished name (RDN), which is the part of the distinguished name that is an attribute of the object itself.

Relative identifier (RID)   The part of the security identifier (SID) that is unique to each object.

Remote Access Service (RAS)   Allows users to connect from remote locations and access their networks for file and printer sharing and e-mail. The computer initiating the connection is the RAS client; the answering computer is the RAS host.

Remote Authentication Dial-In User Service (RADIUS)   A security authentication system used by many Internet service providers (ISPs). A user connects to the ISP and enters a user name and password. This information is verified by a RADIUS server, which then authorizes access to the ISP system.

Remote Installation Services (RIS)   Allows clients to boot from a network server and use special preboot diagnostic tools installed on the server or to automatically install client software.

Replication   On network computers, enables the contents of a directory, designated as an export directory, to be copied to other directories, called import directories.

Requests for comments (RFCs)   An evolving collection of material that details the functions within the TCP/IP family of protocols. Some RFCs are official documents of the Internet Engineering Task Force (IETF), defining the standards of TCP/IP and the Internet, whereas others are simply proposals trying to become standards, and others fall somewhere in between. Some are tutorial in nature, whereas others are quite technical.

Router   A special-purpose device, computer, or software package that handles the connection between two or more networks. Routers look at the destination addresses of the packets passing through them and decide which route to use to send them.

RSS (Really Simple Syndication) An XML-based method of providing Web content to clients automatically.

S

Scope In DHCP, the range of IP addresses available to be leased to DHCP clients by the DHCP service. In groups, scope describes where in the network permissions can be assigned to the group.

Security Accounts Manager (SAM) Manager of user account information, including group membership. A service used at logon.

Security Identifier (SID) A unique number assigned to every computer, group, and user account on a Windows Server 2003, Windows 2000, or Windows NT network. Internal processes in the operating system refer to an account's SID, rather than to a name. A deleted SID is never reused.

Serial Line Internet Protocol (SLIP) A protocol used to run IP over serial lines or telephone lines using modems. Rapidly being replaced by Point-to-Point Tunneling Protocol (PPTP). SLIP is part of Windows remote access for compatibility with other remote access software.

Server A computer that provides a service to other computers on a network. A file server, for example, provides files to client machines.

Shadow copies Point-in-time copies of files on network shares. With shadow copies of shared folders, you can view the contents of shared folders as they existed at specific times in the past.

Simple Mail Transport Protocol (SMTP) A TCP/IP protocol for sending e-mail messages between servers.

Simple Object Access Protocol (SOAP) An XML/HTTP–based protocol that provides a way for applications to communicate with each other over the Internet, independent of platform.

SIP (Session Initiation Protocol) An Internet protocol used for instant messaging.

Smart card A credit card–sized device that securely stores user credentials and other personal information, such as passwords, certificates, and public and private keys.

Socket An end point to a connection. Two sockets form a complete path for a bidirectional pipe for incoming and outgoing data between networked computers. The Windows Sockets API is a networking API for programmers writing for the Windows family of products.

Subnet The portion of a TCP/IP network in which all devices share a common prefix. For example, all devices with an IP address that starts with 198 are on the same subnet. IP networks are divided using a subnet mask.

Superscope A collection of scopes grouped into a single administrative whole. Grouping scopes together into a superscope makes it possible to have more than one logical subnet on a physical subnet.

Synchronous Digital Subsciber Line (SDSL)
See *Digital Subscriber Line.*

SystemRoot   The path and folder where the Windows system files are located. The variable %SystemRoot% can be used in paths to replace the actual location. To identify the SystemRoot folder on a computer, type **echo %SystemRoot%** at a command prompt. The same location can also be identified as **%windir%**.

T

Telnet   The protocol and program used to log on from one Internet site to another. The Telnet protocol/program gets you to the login prompt of another host.

Terminal   A device that allows you to send commands to another computer. At a minimum, this usually means a keyboard, a display screen, and network connectivity. You usually use terminal software in a personal computer—the software pretends to be, or emulates, a physical terminal and allows you to type commands to another computer. Also used to describe a thin client to Windows Terminal Services.

Thread   An executable entity that belongs to one (and only one) process. In a multitasking environment, a single program can contain several threads, all running at the same time.

Threshold   A configured baseline. When a counter falls above or below the baseline, an action is triggered.

Thin Client   A client application or device that has little or no processing power or responsibilities. Provides a display and input facilities only, with all processing power relegated to the server. Can be used with both software applications and hardware terminals, such as Windows Terminals or XWindows Terminals.

Token ring   A type of computer network in which the computers are connected in a ring. A token, which is a special bit pattern, travels around the ring. To communicate to another computer, a computer catches the token and attaches a message to it. The token continues around the network, dropping off the message at the designated location.

Trace log   A record of data monitoring for a specific event, such as page faults.

Transmission Control Protocol/Internet Protocol (TCP/IP)   A set of protocols that networks use to communicate with one another. The native suite of protocols used on the Internet.

Transport Layer Security (TLS)   A protocol ensuring privacy and data reliability between client/server applications communicating over the Internet.

Tree   A tree in Active Directory is just an extension of the idea of a directory tree. It is a hierarchy of objects and containers that demonstrates how objects are connected or the path from one object to another. End points on the tree are usually objects.

U

Uniform Resource Locator (URL)   The standard way to give the address of any resource that is part of the World Wide Web. For example, *http://*

www.microsoft.com/info/cpyright.htm. The most common way to use a URL is to enter it into a Web browser program.

Universal Naming Convention (UNC) A PC format for indicating the location of resources on a network. UNC uses the following format: \\ServerName\Share-Name\ResourcePath. To identify the Ample.txt file in the Sample folder in the Docs share on the server named Example, the UNC would be \\Example\Docs\Sample\Ample.txt.

User account A user's access to a network. Each user account has a unique user name and security ID (SID).

User profiles Information about user accounts. See *profile*.

V

Virtual Private Network (VPN) A network constructed by using public wires to connect nodes. VPNs use encryption and other security mechanisms to make sure only authorized users can access the network and that the data cannot be intercepted.

Voice over Internet Protocol (VoIP) A method for using the Internet as a transmission medium for telephone calls.

W

Web part A module of information that is the basic building block of a Sharepoint site.

Well connected Sufficiently fast and reliable for the needs of Active Directory clients and servers. The definition of "sufficiently fast and reliable" for a particular network depends on the work being done on the specific network.

Wide area network (WAN) Any Internet or network that covers an area larger than a single building or campus.

Windir The path and folder where the Windows system files are located. The variable %windir% can be used in paths to replace the actual location. Also identified as **%SystemRoot%**.

Windows Internet Name Service (WINS) A name resolution service that converts computer names to IP addresses in a routed environment.

Windows Sockets (Winsock) Winsock is a standard way for Windows-based programs to work with TCP/IP. You can use Winsock if you use SLIP to connect to the Internet.

Workstation In Windows NT, a computer running the Windows NT Workstation operating system. In a wider context, used to describe any powerful computer optimized for graphics or computer-aided design (CAD) or any of a number of other functions requiring high performance.

X

X.500 A standard for a directory service established by the International Telecommunications Union (ITU). The same standard is also published by the International Standards Organization/International

Electro-technical Commission (ISO/IEC). The X.500 standard defines the information model used in the directory service. All information in the directory is stored in entries, each of which belongs to at least one object class. The actual information in an entry is determined by attributes that are contained in that entry.

Z

Zone   A part of the DNS namespace that consists of a single domain or a domain and subdomains managed as a single, separate entity.

Index

A

Acceptable Wireless Use policy, 397
Access control, 624–625
Access Method page, 396
Access permissions, 480
Access points (APs), 19, 23–26
Access Rule Destinations page, 431
Access Rule Sources page, 431, 433
Account logon events, 542
Account management, centralized
    user, 15
Account management event, 542
Account Operators, 150–151
ACPI systems, 633
Acronis True Image, 633
Actions, configuring
    command-line action, 571–572
    e-mail action, 572–573
    script action, 574
    text log action, 573
    Windows event log action, 573–
        574
Active caching, 413
Active Director Domain Users, 480
Active Directory
    in Microsoft Exchange 2003, 624
    in Windows Operating System,
        622
    installation, 41
    swing migration and, 58–59
    use Windows Small Business
        Server Setup Wizard, 48
Active Directory database, 303
Active Directory directory service,
    147
Active Directory Domain
    Administrators, 480
Active Directory Installation Wizard,
    64
Active Directory Migration Tool
    (ADMT), 57
Active Directory object, 542
ActiveScript job, 522
Add Counters dialog box, 547–548,
    558–559
Add Directory dialog box, 512
Add Distribution Group Wizard,
    154–155, 333–334
Add Drive Letter Or Path dialog box,
    129
Add Exclusions dialog box, 365

Add Group Or User dialog box,
    458–459
Add License Wizard, 89–90
Add LPR Compatible Printer dialog
    box, 215
Add Mirror dialog box, 123
Add Multiple Users, 90
Add Network Entities dialog box,
    431–432
Add Or Edit A Service dialog box,
    423
Add Or Remove Program
    confirmation dialog box, 524
Add Or Remove Programs, 63
Add Port page, 212
Add Printer Driver Wizard, 219, 225
Add Printer Wizard, 209, 211–212,
    232
Add Recovery Agent Wizard, 199
Add/Remove Programs, 645
Add/Remove Snap-In dialog box,
    377
Add Security Group Wizard, 153
Add Sender dialog box, 346
Add ShadowStorage, 145
Add Standalone Snap-In dialog box,
    377–378
Add Standard TCP/IP Printer Port
    Wizard, 211–212
Add Template Wizard, 5–6
Add Threshold dialog box, 654
Add To Link Bar dialog box, 488
Add a User, 90
Add User Wizard, 5–6, 90, 156–159,
    236
Add Users page, 478
Add Web Parts tool pane, 472–473
Additional Commands page, 632
Additional Drivers dialog box, 218
Additional Information page, 394
Additional Port Information
    Required page, 213
Additional properties, selecting, 552
Address Information page, 158
Administration, for SQL Server
    2005, 532–538
Administrative templates, 150
Administrator, 151
Administrator Password page, 47,
    631
Administrator Template, 157

ADMT. See Active Directory
    Migration Tool (ADMT)
Adobe Acrobat, 289
ADSL. See Asynchronous Digital
    Subscriber Line (ADSL)
Advanced Attributes dialog box,
    138, 202
Advanced dialog box, 354
Advanced Encryption Standard
    (AES), 243, 390
Advanced Intelligent Tape (AIT),
    292
Advanced Management, 513
Advanced Management container,
    500, 503, 505, 508
Advanced network security. See
    Network security, advanced
Advanced RISC Computing (ARC),
    596
Advanced Security Settings dialog
    box, 192, 195, 386–388, 505
Advanced Simulation Options page,
    460
Advanced Technology Attachment
    (ATA), 102
AES. See Advanced Encryption
    Standard (AES)
AES encryption, 35
AIT. See Advanced Intelligent Tape
    (AIT)
Alert file settings, saving, 555–556
Alert Me Link, 470
Alerts
    configuring, 559–561
    creating, 558–559
    permissions for, 561–562
    saving file settings, 555–556
    settings to generate, 570
    See also Health Monitor;
        Performance Logs And Alerts
Alerts page, 94
All Authenticated Users to Access
    Site, 480
All Documents, 469
All Standard Mail in Plain Text, 275
Allocated Memory threshold, 570–
    571
Allocation unit, 100
Allow All x64 Browsing Rule, 429–
    433

Allow Inheritable Permissions From The Parent To Propagate To This Object And All Child Objects, 186–187
Allow Only Anonymous Connections, 610
Alternate Active Directory Paths page, 460
Alternate clients, connecting, 249
Analog telephone line. *See* Dial-up
Analysis Service, 519
Announcements, 467
Anonymous access, 503–505
Answer file, 627
Antispyware software, 35
Antivirus software, 34–35, 259
AP Client, 25
Application event log, 330, 560–561
Application Information dialog box, 262
Application layer filtering, 412
Application Setup Progress page, 247
Applications, 259–263
Apply Template Only To Derive Quotas That Match The Original Template, 655
Apply Template To All Derived Quotas, 655
Apply Theme To Site link, 472
Apply These Permissions To Objects And/Or Containers Within This Container Only, 190–191
Approve/Reject Items view, 476
APs. *See* Access points (APs)
ARC. *See* Advanced RISC Computing (ARC)
Archie, 509
Architecture, for SQL Server 2005, 532
Archive and off-site storage, 296
Archived Document libraries, 467
Arrays, 610, 612. *See also* RAID arrays
ASR. *See* Automated System Recovery (ASR) Disk
Asr.sif, 594
Asrpnp.sif, 594
Assess phase, 272–273
Assign Applications Wizard, 260–262, 419–420
Assign Drive Letter Or Path page, 112, 115, 119
Assign Users To This Computer And Migrate Their Profiles page, 245

Assigned Applications page, 247
Asynchronous Digital Subscriber Line (ADSL), 18
ATA. *See* Advanced Technology Attachment (ATA)
Attach Databases dialog box, 530
Auditing, 542–543
Authenticated Users, 153
Authentication Methods dialog box, 384, 503–504
Authentication Methods page, 397
Authentication Page, 521
Authentication protocols, choosing, 392
Auto Apply Template And Create Quotas On Existing And New Subfolders, 650
Automated System Recovery (ASR) Disk, 591–5995
Automated System Recovery Preparation Wizard, 592–593
Automated System Recovery Wizard, 592
Automatic Certificate Request Setup Wizard, 405
Automatic Logon Information page, 247
Automatic quota extensions, 652
Automating CD-based installations, 627–633
Autorun dialog box, 597
Auxiliary generator, 609–610
Available Applications page, 262

B

Back up system, 591
Background display, 552–553
Backing up data
    configure backup utility, 298–302
    modify backup configuration, 306–307
    running backup manually, 302–306
    test backups, 298
Backup
    accessing files and folders for, 304
    centralized, 16
    configuring, 95
    of selected files and folders, 303–306
    test, 298
    using shadow copies to supplement, 297
Backup Configuration, modifying, 306–307

Backup Configuration dialog box, 435
Backup Configuration Wizard, 6, 298–299, 303–306
Backup a Database dialog box, 536–537
Backup Data Summary page, 300
Backup Destination drop-down list, 304
Backup Destination page, 593
Backup device, 291–293, 534–535
Backup Device dialog box, 534–535, 537–538
Backup domain controller (BDC), 64
Backup Internet connection, 19
Backup Job Information dialog box, 305
Backup Location page, 299
Backup media, 291, 293
Backup Operations, 152
Backup schedule
    archive and off-site storage, 296
    combination disk and tape strategy, 296–297
    frequency, 295
    modify, 306
    reusing tapes, 295–296
Backup scripts, 302–303
Backup strategy, designing, 294–295
Backup target, selecting, 304
Backup Utility
    backup scripts, 303
    configuring, 298–302
    running manually, 298, 305
    using, to restore files and folders, 307–309
Backup Wizard, 297
Bandwidth, determining baseline level requirements, 16–17
Bandwidth throttling, 508
Basic Authentication, 504
Basic disk, 101, 105
Bathtub curve, 602–603
BDC. *See* Backup domain controllers (BDC)
Binary circular file, 554, 558
Binary file, 554, 557
BIOS, 41, 597
.bks extension, 304
Black-and-white laser printer, 207
Blaster, 33
Block inheritance, 448–449
Block-level parity, 611

Block list provider, 348–349
Boot disk, 595–596
Boot drive, 611
Boundary router, 617
Bradley, Susan, 246
Broadband connect, change, 422
Broadband connection
    set up, with local router, 76–77
    set up, with user authentication
        (PPPoE), 78
    set up direct, 77
Brownout, 608
Browse For File dialog box, 571–573
Browser, 547. *See also* Web browser
Built-in groups, managing
    domain local groups, 152–153
    global groups, 153
    local groups, 151–152
    overview, 149
    universal groups, 150–151
    view list of, 150
Built-in surge protectors, 607–609
Built-in wireless access point, 28
Business growth, handling, 638
Business inkjet printer, 207
Business Owner Usage Report page,
    94
Business Web site, 424
Byte-level parity, 611

C
CA. *See* Certificate Authority (CA)
CA Identifying Information page, 36
Cable, network, 20–21. *See also*
    individual cable types
Cable connection, 18
Cable Guy article, 390
Cable modem, 23, 75
Cache, 547
Caching, 412–413, 417
CAIDA. *See* Cooperative Association
    for Internet Data Analysis
    (CAIDA)
CALs. *See* Client Access Licenses
    (CALs)
Cancel All Documents, 226
Cat 3 Unshielded Twisted Pair
    (UTP) cable, 21
Cat 5 cable, 20–21
Cat 5e, 21
Cat 6, 21
Cc field, 327–328, 330
CD-based installations, automating,
    627–633

CEICW. *See* Configure E-mail And
    Internet Connection Wizard
    (CEICW)
Centralized update management, 15
Centralized user account
    management, 15
Certificate Authority (CA), 375, 505
Certificate Database Settings page,
    376
Certificate dialog box, 399
Certificate Export Wizard, 200
Certificate Friendly Name And
    Description page, 379, 381
Certificate Import Wizard, 203, 399,
    405
Certificate Request Wizard, 378–
    381
Certificate server, 373
Certificate Services
    creating local computer and
        current used certificates
        console, 377–378
    enabling L2TP with ISA Server
        2004, 426
    installing, 375–377
    request certificate for SBS server,
        381
    requesting computer and user
        certificates, 378–380
    to create digital IDs, 35
Certificates
    deploying, 381, 393
    modifying settings for, 404–406
    requesting, for SBS Server, 381
Certificates (Current User) snap-in,
    377–378
Certificates (Local Computer) snap-
    in, 377
Certificate Store page, 399, 405
Certificate Template page, 405
Certificate Types page, 378–379,
    381
Certificates MMC snap-in, 200, 203
Certificates Snap-in dialog box,
    377–378
Certification Authority, 83
CF_TEXT, 136
CF_UNICODETEXT, 136
Change Anonymous Access Settings
    page, 480–481
Change Drive Letter And Paths
    dialog box, 128
Change E-Mail Password dialog box,
    332
Change General Settings link, 475

Change Permissions For This Item
    link, 477
Change Regional Settings link, 482
Change Site Title And Description
    link, 471
Change Update Group Membership
    dialog box, 289
Change User Permissions Wizard,
    69–70, 162–163
Channels, 21
Choose A Certificate Authority page,
    508
Choose A Wireless Network dialog
    box, 242, 399–400
Circular trace file, 558
Client Access Licenses (CALs), 11,
    63, 89–90
Client Addressing page, 86–87
Client Applications page
    adding single user, 158
    assigning applications to client
        computers, 260–262
    creating computer accounts for
        client computers, 237–238
    installing Firewall Client, 420
Client Computer Names page, 159,
    236–237
Client computers
    assigning applications to, 259–
        262
    creating computer accounts for,
        236–238
    prepare, for upgrade, 64
    secure, 33–35
    setting applied to, 265–266
    update, 96
    viewing and modifying, settings,
        265–266
    See also Clients
Client Computers container, 259–
    260, 266
Client Computers page, 260, 263,
    419
Client deployment, 513
Client Document Redirection dialog
    box, 166
Client hardware, 29–30
Client limit, 11–12
Client set up and local
    administrator, 246–247
Client Setup Wizard, 244, 246–247
Client software, 29–30
Client/server-based network, 14
Clients
    connecting alternate, 249–254

media connecting servers and, 622
set up, to use, 143
See also Client computers
Clustering, 601
Clusters, 117
CmdExec job, 522
Coaxial (thinnet) Ethernet, 21
Code button, 487
Code Red, 33, 271
Collation Settings page, 521
Color laser printer, 207
Color management, in Windows, 220
Color profile, specify, 220
Columns and Views sections, 477
COM+Application Monitor, 575
Combination disk and tape strategy, 296–297
Comma Separated Value, 136
Command line
manage printers from, 228
manage quotas from, 135
Command-line action, 571–572
Command-line interface, 107–108
Commercial certificate, 83
Commercial Web hosting companies, 496
Company Information page, 49, 67
Company Photos Library, 467
Company Photos page, 469
Companyweb
SharePoint *vs.*, 466–467
upgrade, to SQL Server 2005, 525–531
Completing The Network Configuration Wizard page, 246
Component Message page, 52, 69
Component Selection page, 51, 68, 278, illus.
Component Summary page, 52, 68
Compression, 117
Computer accounts, creating, 236–238
Computer Configuration node, 451
Computer Configuration policies, 392
Computer Management console, 266
Computer Management snap-in, 232–233, 248
Computer Name And Administration Password page, 47

Computer Name Changes dialog box, 268
Computer Name page, 246, 631
Computer Security Groups page, 460
Computer Selection page, 461
Computers
add, 90–91
assigning applications to client, 259–262
connecting, to network, 236–254
monitoring another, 553
naming, 32
prepare client computers for upgrading, 64
remotely managing, 266
removing from, 267–268
secure client, 33–35
update, 96
Computers With Update Installation Errors page, 283–284
Configure Antivirus Settings, 484
Configure Default E-Mail Server Settings, 484
Configure Device dialog box, 372
Configure E-Mail And Internet Connection Wizard (CEICW)
E-Mail Domain Name page of, 320–321
function of, 4
Remote Web Workplace (RWW), 255
run to open firewall, 510
To Do List, 69, 73
See also E-mail configuration
Configure firewall and Web proxy, 434
Configure Full Text Search link, 484
Configure HTML Viewer link, 484
Configure ISA Reporting, 434
Configure Log Files dialog box, 557–558
Configure My Documents Redirection, 167
Configure Password Policies dialog box, 160
Configure Remote Access Wizard, 88
Configure Self-Service Site Creation link, 484
Configure Standard TCP/IP Port Monitor dialog box, 213
Configure Usage Analysis Processing link, 484

Configure Virtual Server Settings link, 483
Confirm Attributes dialog box, 139
Confirm Network Key, 242
Confirm Password text box, 47
Confirm Restore dialog box, 308–309
Confirmation dialog box
delete distribution group (list), 338
remove routing rule, 328
Confirmation message
CEICW completed successfully, 424
for deleting partition, 120
for overwriting quota entry with imported entry, 136
Connect dialog box, 385
Connect To Client Desktop, 257
Connect To Computer Via Terminal Services, 284
Connect To Small Business Server window, 264
Connect To The Internet, 73
Connection Availability page, 385
Connection filtering, 345, 347–349
Connection Manager, 6, 88, 158
Connection Name page, 385
Connection Type page, 76–79, 422, 425
Constant voltage transformer (CVT), 607–608
Consumer inkjet, 207
Contact Method page, 89
Contacts in Exchange, 154
Content filtering, 27
Contributor rights, 480
Conventional migration
choosing between upgrading and migrating, 56
problems with process, 57
steps in process, 57–58
Convert To Dynamic Disk dialog box, 120–121
Cooperative Association for Internet Data Analysis (CAIDA), 33
Copy Properties From Quota Template box, 653
Core Server Alerts, in Health Monitor, 569
Corrupted boot sector, 595
Corrupted master boot record (MBR)
Cost
of drivers, 615–616

of printers, 207
Counter log
    add counters to, 555
    creating, 554–558
    permissions for, 561–562
    setting file parameter for, 557
    types of, 557–558
Counter Mode Cipher Block
    Chaining-Message
    Authentication Code (CBC-
    MAC) protocol (CCMP), 390
Counters
    adding, 547–548
    adding, to counter logs, 555
    as system monitor item, 546
    deleting, 549
    matching, to graph lines, 549
    minimum recommended, 565–
    566
    recommended, 563–565
    selecting, 548–549
Create Automated System Recovery
    Disk prompt, 594
Create File Screen dialog box, 656
Create Quota dialog box, 650–651
Create Quota On Path, 650
Create Quota Template dialog box,
    653
Create Remote Connection Disk
    Wizard, 263
Create Shadow, 145
Critical update, 270
Cscript, 228
Customization page, 474–475
Customized roaming profiles, 170–
    171
CVT. *See* Constant voltage
    transformer (CVT)
Cybertrust, 27

D
Darwin, 251
Dashboard, 437–438
Data
    encrypting sensitive, 198–204
    restoring, 307–311
Data collection, 579
Data collectors
    available, 575
    creating, 574–576
    other monitors, 579
    performance monitor, 576
    process monitor, 577–578
    service monitor, 577

Windows event log monitor, 578–
    579
Data Collector's Properties dialog
    box, 577
Data encryption, 389
Data Folders page, 52, 68
Data integrity, 389
Data management, 8
Database Engine Tuning Advisor,
    533
Database management system
    (DBMS), 532
Database Size Buffer in Percentage,
    360
Database storage, using Microsoft
    SQL Server, 16
Date And Time Settings page, 48
DBMS. *See* Database management
    system (DBMS)
DDS. *See* Digital Data Storage (DDS)
Default DNS settings, 368
Default Domain Controllers Policy,
    253, 451
Default FTP Site Properties dialog
    box, 510
Default password, 35
Default Policy Properties dialog box,
    339–340
Default Server Folder, redirecting
    My Documents to, 165
Default SMTP Virtual Server dialog
    box, 353–354
Default SSL port, 443, 508
Default Web Site, 496–497, 500, 508
Default Web Site Properties dialog
    box, 500–501, 509
Define Backup Schedule page, 300–
    301
Define Cache Drives dialog box, 417
Define Schedule dialog box, 325–
    326
Defragmentation, 141, 640
Delayed Or Immediate Request
    page, 507
Delete message, 357–358
Delete Shadow, 145
Delete ShadowStorage, 145
Delete This Item link, 477
Deleted message retention, 345
Delivery Options dialog box, 344
Denial-of-service (DoS) attack, 26
Deny Access dialog box, 501
Deploy phase, 276
Deployment Wizard, 533

Derive Properties From This Quota
    Template, 650
Design This Page, 473
Design view, 486–487
Desktop, 266
Destination Address page, 385
Details dialog box, 283–284
Details view, 469
Detect Non-Plug And Play
    Hardware, 635
DHCP. *See* Dynamic Host
    Configuration Protocol
    (DHCP)
DHCP address leases, 364–365
DHCP Administrators, 152
DHCP Properties dialog box, 367
DHCP reservations, 365–367
DHCP Server service, 152
DHCP Users, 152
Dial-up connection, 18, 74
    change, 422
    providing logon information for,
    79, illus.
    remote access via, 87–88
    setting up, 79–80
Dial-Up Phone Numbers page, 88
Dialing Location, 48
Differential backup, 292
Digest Authentication, 504
Digital certificate, 375. *See also*
    Certificate services
Digital Data Storage (DDS), 292
Digital Linear Tape (DLT), 292
Digital Subscriber Line (DSL), 74
Digitally Sign Communications
    (Always) dialog box, 254
Direct Broadband Connection page,
    77–78
Directory Browsing, 499
Directory Security, 500
Directory service access event, 542
Disable Outbound Mail, 358
Disaster planning
    developing responses, 585–588
    integrating, 589–590
    multiple copies, multiple
    locations, 587
    overview, 581–582
    resource identification, 584
    risk identification, 583–584
    standard escalation procedures
    (SEPs), 585, 588
    standard operating procedures
    (SOPs), 585–588
    testing responses, 589

Disaster preparation
  backing up system, 591
  creating and using recovery
    driver, 599–600
  creating Automated System
    Recovery (ASR) disk, 591–595
  creating boot disk, 595–596
  installing recovery console, 597
  setting up fault-tolerant system,
    591
  specifying recovery options, 598–
    599
Disaster protection, search for, 100
Discretionary access control, 624–
  625
Discussion boards, 467
Disk(s)
  convert to dynamic disk, 120–121
  tuning and upgrading tips for,
    568
Disk arrays, 610–616
Disk cache usage, 547
Disk Cleanup Wizard, 65
Disk defragmentation, 141, 143
Disk Defragmenter, 568
Disk full message, 132
Disk I/O network TCP/IP, 556
Disk management
  adding mirror, 123–124
  adding partition or volume, 108,
    111–114
  break mirror, 127
  choosing storage solution for
    network, 103–104
  converting disk to dynamic disk,
    120–121
  disk terminology, 100–103
  drive failure in mirrored volume,
    124–126
  dynamic disks, 107
  extending volume, 121–123
  managing disks, 105
  mounting volume, 128–129
  overview, 99–100
  RAID-5 volumes, 127–128
  remove mirror, 126–127
  search for disaster protection, 100
  using, 105–129
Disk Management console, 110
Disk Management snap-in, 105–106
Disk mirroring, 101
Disk partition, choosing, 46, illus.
Disk quotas
  avoid individual quotas, 135–136
  creating quota reports, 136–137

  enabling, 132–133
  exporting and importing quotas,
    136
  managing quotas from command
    line, 135
  Quota tab of Properties window,
    133
  setting quota entries for users,
    134–136
Disk Quotas page, 158
Disk terminology, 100–103
Diskpart.exe, 107
Disks To Convert dialog box, 120
Display, modifying, 550
Display colors, 552–553
Display elements, choosing, 552–
  553
Display Settings page, 630
Distribution Group Information
  page, 154, 333
Distribution groups, 148
  creating, 154–155
  deleting, 338
  modifying, 335–338
Distribution Groups page, 158
Distribution List dialog box, 336
Distribution List Membership dialog
  box, 336–337
DLT. *See* Digital Linear Tape (DLT)
Dmoz, 349
DNS. *See* Domain Name System
  (DNS)
DNS domain name, 274
DNS e-mail routing, 317
DNS records, viewing, 368–370
DNS reverse lookup zone, 496
DNS settings, default, 368
DNS updates, enabling, 367–368
Do Not Apply Template To Derived
  Quotas, 655
Do Not Redirect My Documents
  Folder, 167
Document libraries, 466–467
Document Library Settings page,
  475–476
Document Library template, 467
Domain(s)
  defining, 624–625
  domain controller, 625
  handling multiple, 638–639
  member server, 625
  workstations or clients, 625–626
Domain Admin, 153, 335, 393
Domain Computers, 153

Domain Controller Selection page,
  459
Domain controllers, 153, 625
  additional, 11
  single, 10–11
Domain Controllers container, 253
Domain local groups, built-in, 152
Domain local scope, 149
Domain master, 63
Domain name
  don't allow or block computers
    by, 502
  internal vs. Internet, 31–32
Domain Name System (DNS), 41, 50
Domain Power Users, 150, 480
Domain profile, 169
Domain Users, 153
Drive failure, in mirrored volume,
  124–126
Driver Properties dialog box, 225
DSL. *See* Digital Subscriber Line
  (DSL)
DSL, in network diagram, 23
DSL modem, 617
Dual-WAN support, 27
Duplex, 611. *See also* Mirroring/
  duplexing
Duplicate files storage report, 658
Dust, 605
DWORD value, 360–361
Dynamic disk
  converting disk to, 120–121
  defined, 101
  hardware vs. software, 611
  introduction of, 105
  overview, 107
  storing shadow copies, 140–141
Dynamic DNS Service, 19
Dynamic error recovery, 623
Dynamic Host Configuration
  Protocol (DHCP), 50, 52
  adding reservation, 365–367
  configuring Windows 2000 to
    use, 241
  creating exclusions in, 365
  enabling updates, 367–368
  network adapter for Internet has
    dynamically assigned IP
    address via, 82
  viewing current address leases,
    364–365
Dynamic Host Configuration
  Protocol (DHCP) database, 59

Dynamic Host Configuration Protocol (DHCP) Server, 50–52, 57
Dynamic Host Control Protocol (DHCP), 239–240
Dynamic IP address, 52, 319

E

E-mail, 264, 422
access for employees, 16
advanced configuration and management, 331–341
DNS for delivering, 80
finding messages in queue, 356–358
freeze, unfreeze, or delete, 357–358
modify storage for, 306
queued, messages, 318
sign and encrypt, 35
synchronize, 332
E-mail action, 572–573
E-mail attachments, 321–322
E-mail configuration
attachments, 321–322
direct delivery, 318
e-mail retrieval methods, 317–318
indirect delivery: Extended Turn (ETRN) command, 318
indirect delivery: TURN After Authentication, 319
manual ETRN trigger, 319–321
overview, 315–316
use DNS E-mail routing, 317
E-mail delivery
Exchange 2003 SP2, 359–361
managing message defaults and delivery options, 342
managing queues, 355–358
setting individual user's message properties, 343–345
SMTP filtering, 345–355
E-Mail Delivery Method page, 83
E-mail distribution lists
creating new distribution group (list), 333–335
deleting distribution group (list), 338
managing, 332
modifying distribution group (list), 335–338
E-Mail Domain Name page, 83, 320
E-mail message properties, setting individual user's, 343–345
E-mail Notifications tab, 649

E-Mail Options page, 94
E-mail password, changing, 331–332
E-Mail Retrieval Method page, 83, 317–318
EAP. *See* Extensible Authentication Protocol (EAP)
EAP-TLS. *See* Extensible Authentication Protocol-Transport Layer Security (EAP-TLS)
Edit Alias dialog box, 498–499
Edit Browser List, 487
Edit Dial-In Profile dialog box, 374–375, 382
Edit In Datasheet, 470
Edit Site Groups Of Selected Users, 478
EFS. *See* Encrypting File System (EFS)
802.11, 403–407
802.11a, 20–21
802.11b, 21
802.11b (WiFi), 18
802.11g, 18, 20–21
802.11i (WPA2), 20, 23–24, 35
802.1x, 20, 24, 35–36
802.1x Authentication, 36, 375, 381
process, 392–393
troubleshooting, 403
using, for wireless security, 388–403
Emergency repair disk (ERD), 591
Enable Advanced Printing Features, 223, 232
Enable Full-Text Search And index Component, 484
Enable Logging, 484
Enable Outbound Mail, 358
Enable Shadow Copies dialog box, 142
Enable Usage Analysis Processing, 484
Encrypting File System (EFS), 34, 137, 198–203
Encrypting files, 137–139, 202
Encrypting sensitive data, 198–204
Encryption
Advanced Encryption Standard (AES), 389
availability of, 137
best practices, 201
enabling, 138
restoring, 137
Temporal Key Integrity Protocol (TKIP), 389

End User License Agreement (EULA), 415, 629–630, 638, 642
Enterprise Root CA, 376, 381
Entire Feature Will Be Installed Local Hard Drive, 525
Entourage, 249
ERD. *See* Emergency repair disk (ERD)
Error 778, 388
Error 801, 388
Error and Usage Report Settings page, 521
eSATA. *See* External Serial Advanced Technology Attachment (eSATA)
Estimated Time To Download reading, 486
Ethernet, 18
Ethernet network segment, 26
ETRN, 80, 332
EULA. *See* End User License Agreement (EULA)
Evaluate phase, 275–276
Event logs
check for error messages, 298
options for filtering, 545
remotely managing computers and viewing, 266–267
searching, 543–545
setting size of, 545–546
viewing, 543–544
Event Reports and Activity Logging, 93
Event View log files, 634
Event Viewer, filtering event information using, 544
Events Logged By System Provider option, 556
Everyone group, 153
Excel, 136–137
Exceptions, using, to control location, 657
Exchange, 249, 641
Exchange Chat Service, 63
Exchange Connector for Lotus cc:Mail, 63
Exchange e-mail, 254
Exchange Information Store, 329
Exchange Installation Wizard, 277–279
Exchange Instant Messaging Service, 63
Exchange Key Management Service, 63

Exchange mailbox, 69, 320, 322–324

Exchange Mailbox Merge Wizard (ExMerge.exe), 57–58

Exchange Migration Wizard, 57

Exchange MSMail Connector, 63

Exchange Routing Engine, 329

Exchange server, 27, 29, 258, 266
  advanced e-mail configuration and management, 331–341
  basic e-mail configuration, 315–322
  Exchange 2003 SP2, 359–361
  managing e-mail delivery, 342–358
  POP3 e-mail, 322–331
  Queue Viewer for, 355
  using Windows Small Business Server Setup Wizard, 48

Exchange Server 2003, 3–4

Exchange Server Advanced Management, 331–332

Exchange Server Alert, 570

Exchange SP2, 350

Exchange System Attendant, 329

Exchange 2000 Service Pack 3, 62

Exchange 2003, 624

Exchange 2003 SP2, 359–361

Exclude Folders dialog box, 300

Existing Components page, 526

ExMerge.exe. *See* Exchange Mailbox Merge Wizard (ExMerge.exe)

Explicit permissions, 185–187

Explorer View, 469

Export Configuration dialog box, 436–437

Exporting and importing quotas, 136

Extend Volume Wizard, 121

Extended partition, 100, 117–119

Extended Turn (ETRN) command, 318

Extended volume, 101. *See also* Spanned volume

Extending volume, 121–123

Extensible Authentication Protocol (EAP), 384

Extensible Authentication Protocol-Transport Layer Security (EAP-TLS), 392

External firewall device, 26

External Serial Advanced Technology Attachment (eSATA), 104

External USB, 293

F

F6 key, 43

Failed Mail Folder, 329–330

Fas Server Alert, 570

Fast Ethernet, 19–21, 24

FAT, 114, 117

FAT32, 114, 117, 131

Fault tolerance
  multiple disk controllers provide, 614–615
  RAID levels for, 611–616

Fault-tolerant boot floppy disk, 611

Fault-tolerant disk arrays (RAID), 602

Fault-tolerant system, 591, 601–602

Fax, delivered through e-mail, 7

Fax Configuration Wizard, 91

Fax Operators, 150–151

Fax printers, 266

Fax Properties dialog box, 92–94, illus.

Fax server, centralized, 16

Fax services
  changing fax sending and receiving, 92–93
  configuring, 91–94
  setting properties for, 93–94
  shared, 7

Fax settings, 266

Feature pack, 270

Feature Selection page, 518, 525

Fiber Channel, 104

50 MB Extension quota template, 652

File Access Table (FAT) file system, 131. *See also* FAT; FAT32

File detail, 556

File parameters, setting, 557

File permissions, share permissions vs., 183–189

File screening audit storage report, 658

File screens. *See* Screening files

File Server Resource Manager (FSRM), 3–4, 9
  installing, 647–648
  scheduling storage reports, 658–660
  screening files, 655–658
  setting global options, 648–649
  using folder quotas, 650–655

File Server Resource Manager Options dialog box, 649

File storage, centralized, 16

File Transfer Protocol (FTP), 422, 509–511

Files
  decrypting, 201–202
  encrypting, 137–139, 200–201
  recovering, 202–203
  sharing, 16
  sharing encrypted, 202
  special permissions for, 185

Files And Setting Transfer Wizard, 245

Files by file group storage report, 658

Filmstrip, 469

Filters, enabling, 353–355

Find Messages dialog box, 356–357

Firewall
  choosing device for, 26–28
  configuring, 80–85
  external device, 26
  in network diagram, 23
  internal, 8
  securing Internet, 36
  selecting service to pass through, 81, illus.
  stand-alone, 409–411

Firewall Client, 413
  adding, to Client Applications, 419–420
  deploying, 421
  installing, 419–421

Firewall page, 80, 422, 425

Firewall policies, 413–414

Firewall Policy page, 430–431, 433

Firewall Policy rules, 429–433

Firewire Disk backup device, 538

FireWire hard drive, 293

Flexible Single Master Operation (FSMO) roles, 59

Folder Operators, 150–151

Folder permissions, 184–185

Folder quotas
  automatic quota extension, 652
  creating and editing quota templates, 653–655
  creating quotas, 650–652

Folders
  blocking inheritance on, 186
  decrypting, 201–202
  encrypting, 200–201
  sharing, 176–177
  special permissions for, 184–185
  view NTFS permissions for new, 191

Folders Path page, 180

Font display, 552–553
Format Partition page, 116, 119
Format Volume page, 113
Formatting options, 117
403 Forbidden message, 432
FQDN. *See* Fully qualified domain name (FQDN)
Fractional T1, 75
Frame relay/T1, 18
FreeBSD, 251
Freeze message, 357–358
FrontPage, 485–487, 497
  add Web Parts with, 489–490
  create new SharePoint Web sites using, 490–491
  for creating advanced Web pages, 9
  home page in, 488
FrontPage Server Extensions, 19
FSMO roles, 63
FSRM. *See* File Server Resource Manager (FSRM)
FTP, 8. *See also* File Transfer Protocol (FTP)
FTP Server, setting up, 509–511
Full backup, 291
Fully automated interaction level, 629
Fully qualified domain name (FQDN), 210, 214, 216

G

Gateway Building Configuration, 351
General Discussion page, 467–468
General Documents library, 474–476
General Documents page, 467–468, 470
Generate Storage Reports dialog box, 660
Generator, auxiliary, 609–610
Geographical Information page, 508
Geosynchronous satellite, 18
GeoTrust, 83
Getting Started page, 429–430, 435–436
Gigabit Ethernet, 19–21
Gimp-Print, 252
Global Catalog server, 59
Global groups, built-in, 153
Global Mailbox, 324
Global Message Delivery, 353
Global options, setting, 648–649
Global scope, 149

Globally unique identifier (GUID), 447
Gopher, 509
GPC. *See* Group Policy Container (GPC)
GPO. *See* Group Policy Object (GPO)
GPT. *See* Group Policy Template (GPT)
Grant Access dialog box, 501–502
Graph lines, matching counters to, 549
Graph view, 550
Graphical User Interface (GUI), 42, 629
Gross, Chad, 472, 493
Group Manager page, 154, 334
Group membership, 335–338
Group Membership page, 154, 334
Group Options page, 154–155, 335
Group Policy, 8, 259
  components of, 446–447
  determine results of current, settings on computer, 446
  managing, 444–450
  managing Group Policy links, 452–455
  order of implementation, 448–450
  order of inheritance, 447
  overriding inheritance, 447–448
  overview, 443
  predicting, outcomes, 459–463
  refreshing, 455–456
  Software Installation And Maintenance feature of, 263
  using, to automatically configure 802.11 and Certificate settings, 403–407
Group Policy Computer Configuration, 393
Group Policy Container (GPC), 446
Group Policy Management console, 57, 252–253, 444–447
Group Policy Modeling, 459–460
Group Policy Object (GPO), 57, 252–253
  backing up, 456–457
  create, 445
  create unlinked, 445
  creating, 450–451
  creating and linking new, 403–404
  defined, 444
  delegate permission on, 446

  deleting, 451–452
  disable branch of, 446, 455
  edit, 445
  Group Policy Container (GPC) and Group Policy Template contained in, 446
  link, 445
  link existing, to site, domain, or organizational unit (OU), 445
  setting scope of, 453–454
Group Policy Object Editor, 253–254, 404–405, 444, 446, 450–451, 543
Group Policy Object (GPO) link
  delegating permissions on, 457–459
  enabling and disabling, 454
  enforcing, in Group Policy Management console, 447
  managing, 452–455
  restoring, 457
Group Policy outcomes, 459–463
Group Policy Results report, 462
Group Policy Results Wizard, 446, 461
Group Policy scripts, 451–452
Group Policy Template (GPT), 446
Group printer priorities, 221–222
Group projects, facilitation of, 16
Group scope, 148–149
Groups
  assigning group scopes, 149
  create distribution, 154–155
  create security, 153–154
  logon rights assigned to, by default, 196
  privileges assigned to, by default, 197–198
  reasons for, 148
  types of, 148
  understanding, 147–149
  view list of, 150
Groups dialog box, 188
Guests, 152
GUI Attended interaction level, 629
GUID. *See* Globally unique identifier (GUID)

H

Hackers
  Internet, 33
  security against, 8
  wireless, 33
HAL, 633
Hard disk reliability, 602–603

Hard quota, 132
Hard-disk failure, 591
Hardware
    arranged for direct broadband
        connection, 77
    client, 29–30
    server, 28–29
    See also Client hardware; Server
        hardware
Hardware RAID, 106–107, 121–123,
    610–611
Health Monitor
    adding threshold, 571
    configuring actions, 571–574
    Core Server Alerts in, 569
    defined, 568
    Display of Memory Available alert,
        569
    modifying existing threshold,
        570–571
    settings to generate alert, 570
    using data collectors, 574–579
Help Desk, 467
Help file, for connecting to Internet,
    73
Hewlett-Packard JetDirect, 211
Hidden pages interaction level, 629
High-quality color laser printer, 207
Highlight option, 549
Histogram view, 550–551
HKLMSoftwareMicrosoftSmall
    Business, 641
HKLMSoftwareMicrosoftSmall
    BusinessServer key, 641
Hold Mismatched Documents, 223
Home page, in FrontPage, 488
Home page content, change, 472
Hosting, Web, 19
Hot-spare drive, 106, 610
Hot-spare RAID configuration, 616
Hot-swap disk system, 616
Hot-swap drive, 106, 610
Hotfix, 270
Hotmail, 351
HTTP. *See* HyperText Markup
    Language (HTTP)
HTTP Monitor, 575
Hub, 622
Hub and spoke, 23
HyperText Markup Language
    (HTTP), 8

I
IANA. *See* Internet Assigned
    Numbers Authority (IANA)
IAS. *See* Internet Authentication
    Service (IAS)
ICM. *See* Integrated Color
    Management (ICM)
ICSA certification, 27
ICSA Labs, 27
IDE. *See* Integrated Device
    Electronics (IDE)
IDE chipset, 633
IDE hard drives, 293
Identification dialog box, 354
Identify phase, 273–175
IEEE. *See* Institute of Electrical and
    Electronics Engineers (IEEE)
IIS. *See* Internet Information
    Services (IIS)
IKE. *See* Internet Key Exchange
    (IKE)
IMF. *See* Intelligent Message
    Filtering (IMF)
IMF Filter Manager, 355
Import Configuration dialog box,
    436
Importing quotas, 136
Inbound Fax Routing page, 91
Incoming Faxes library, 467
Incremental backup, 292
Indexing service, configuring, 511–
    512
Individual quotas, avoid, 135–136
Infrastructure master, 63
Inherit From Parent The Permission
    Entries That Apply To Child
    Objects, 194
Inheritance, 447–448
Inherited permissions, 185–187,
    192
Initialize and Convert Disk Wizard,
    108–110, 114–117
Inkjet photo printer, 207
Insert Hyperlink dialog box, 489
Install Printer Software page, 210,
    214, 216
Installation, review status of
    updates, 286–287
Installation Path page, 415
Installation Summary page, of
    Microsoft Exchange
    Installation, 279
Installed Instances page, 516, 520
Installing Prerequisites page, 516–
    517

Installing Windows Small Business
    Server 2003
    Active Directory and domain
        name system (DNA), 41
    configuring network settings, 48–
        49
    dividing storage, 40
    Dynamic Host Configuration
        Protocol (DHCP), 50, 52
    operating system, 42–48
    overview, 39
    planning partitions, 40
    preparing server, 41–42
    RAID controllers and F6, 43
    text-mode and graphical setup, 42
    using Windows Small Business
        Server Setup Wizard, 48–52
Instance, 546–547
Instance Name page, 518–519, 526
Institute of Electrical and
    Electronics Engineers (IEEE),
    242
    802.11i, 391
    802.1X, 392
Integrated Color Management
    (ICM), 220
Integrated Device Electronics (IDE),
    102, 104
Integrated Services Digital Network
    (ISDN), 18, 74
Integrated Windows
    Authentication, 504
Intelligent Message Filtering (IMF),
    259, 285–286, 345, 350–352,
    359
Interleaved block-level parity, 611
Internal domain, 50
Internal Domain Information page,
    50, 67
Internal domain name, *vs.* Internet
    domain name, 31–32
Internal firewall, 8
Internal networks
    in network diagram, 23
    IP addresses for, 411–412
    network adapter connects to local
        network, 48
    remote access to, via Internet, 16
Internal Web site. *See* Intranet
Internet, Outlook via, 424
Internet Address Properties dialog
    box, 341
Internet Assigned Numbers
    Authority (IANA), 411

Internet Authentication Service
  (IAS), 35, 381, 426
  using, to increase VPN security,
    373–375
Internet Certificate Authority, 35
Internet connection
  backup, 19
  bandwidth needs, 16–17
  broadband connection with local
    router, 76–77
  broadband connection with user
    authentication (PPPoE), 78
  choices, 74–75
  client hardware and software, 29–
    30
  configuring firewall, 80–85
  e-mail delivery and retrieval, 80
  help file, 73, illus.
  in network diagram, 23
  ISPs, 19
  network device, 22–28
  network speed, 17
  network type, 19–21
  server hardware, 28–29
  setting up dial-up connection, 79–
    80
  setting up direct broadband
    connection, 77–78
  types, 18, 73–74
Internet Connection sharing, 393
Internet Connection Wizard, 244
Internet domain name, vs. internal
    domain name, 31–32
Internet E-Mail page, 83, 315–316
Internet Explorer, 172, 266
Internet Explorer 6, 261
Internet firewall, securing, 36
Internet hackers, 33
Internet Information Services (IIS),
    57, 477, 503, 505, 508, 510,
    513–514
  Certificate Wizard, 506–507
  Configuration, 512
  console, 496–497, 500, 512, 531
  Manager, 523
  6.0 Migration Tool, 57
Internet Key Exchange (IKE), 384
Internet Printing support, 227
Internet Protocol (TCP/IP)
    Properties dialog box, 240–241
Internet SCSI (iSCSI), 104
Internet Security and Acceleration
    (ISA) Server, 8, 513, 641
  2004, 4, 426

Internet service provider (ISP), 16–
    19
Intranet, 5, 16
Intranet Web Server
  anonymous access and NTFS
    folder permissions, 504–505
  backing up and restoring IIS
    configuration, 512
  change security settings, 499–508
  configuring indexing service,
    511–512
  creating new virtual directories,
    496–498
  hosting Internet Web site, 496
  limiting network usage by Web
    sites, 508–509
  overview, 495–496
  reinstalling IIS, 513–514
  setting up FTP server, 509–511
  subnet masks, 502–503
  using Web sharing, 498–499
IP address, 274, 500
  network adapter for Internet has
    dynamically assigned, via
    Dynamic Host Configuration
    Protocol (DHCP), 82
  static and dynamic, 52
  viewing assigned, 364
IP Address And Domain Name
    Restrictions dialog box, 501
IP Address Configuration page, 239
IP Spoofing, 26, 36
IPSec, 27
ISA. See Internet Security and
    Acceleration (ISA) Server
ISA firewall policy rules, 434
ISA management console, 430
ISA Server 2000 Required Updates
    for Windows Server 2003, 62
ISA Server 2000 Service Pack 1, 62
ISA Server 2004, 645
  administer, 421–428
  advanced configuration, 429–434
  backup, 434–435
  change broadband or dial-up
    connection, 422
  client types, 413
  concepts, 410–414
  enable L2TP with, 425–428
  enable or disable services
    through, 422–424
  enable or disable Web services,
    424–425
  export, 434, 436
  goals of, 410

  import, 434, 436–437
  install, 414–419
  install Firewall Client, 419–421
  monitor, 437–441
  restore, 434–436
  stand-alone firewall, 409–410
ISA Server 2004 Client Connection
    Limit, 433
ISA Server caching, 8
ISA Server Configuration, back up,
    434
ISA Server Error dialog box, 435–
    436
ISA Server Firewall Client, 237, 262
ISA Server Warning dialog box, 418
ISA Setup for Windows Small
    Business Server 2003 Wizard,
    415, 417
iSCSI. See Internet SCSI (iSCSI)
ISDN. See Integrated Services Digital
    Network (ISDN)
Items to Synchronize dialog box,
    182

J

JBOD. See Just a bunch of disks
    (JBOD)
Just a bunch of disks (JBOD), 102

K

Kaizen, 590
Kbps. See Kilobits per second
    (Kbps)
KBps. See Kilobytes per second
    (KBps)
Keep Printed Documents, 223
Kilobits per second (Kbps), 17
Kilobytes per second (KBps), 17
Knowledge Base (KB) article, 270,
    274, 285–286, 455, 513, 641

L

.lan, 50
LAN Network Adapter, 28
LAND Attack, 26
Large files storage report, 658
Laser printer, 208
LAT. See Local address table (LAT)
Layer 2 Tunneling Protocol (L2TP),
    27, 372, 375
  enabling, with ISA Server 2004,
    425–428
  troubleshooting, 388

Least recently accessed files storage report, 658

Legend, 552

Let's Activate Windows, 88–89

Level 2 driver, 229–230

Level 3 driver, 229–230

License Agreement page, 66, 89, 629

License Code Information page, 89

Licensing, online, 9–10

Licensing Mode page, 631

Limit The Network Bandwidth Available To This Web Site, 509

Line Printer Daemon (LPD), 206, 215

Line Printer Remote (LPR) service, 206, 214

Link Bar Properties dialog box, 488–489

Linked Group Policy Objects, 253

Links, 467, 488–489

Linux, 206, 215, 235, 249

Linux clients, 626

List Providers, 145

List ShadowStorage, 145

List Volumes, 145

List Writers, 146

Lists, 467, 647

.local, 50, 249

Local address table (LAT), 412

Local Area Connection Properties dialog box, 240–241

Local computer objects, 147

.local domain, can't connect to, 251

Local group, built-in, 151

Local Network Adapter Configuration page, 51, 68

Local Network Adapter Information page, 67 (illus.)

Local Network Connection page, 78–79

Local Or Network Printer page, 209, 215

Local power supply failure, 603–605

Local printer, vs. network printer, 208

Local profiles, 167–169

Local router, setting up broadband connection with, 76–77

.local syntax, 249

Local users and groups MMC snap-in, 248

Local(internal)network, 50, illus.

Locally attached printer, 208–211

Locate Database Files dialog box, 530

Location, using exceptions to control, 657

Location And Comment page, 10, 214, 216

Log file parameters, 557–558

Log file setting, saving, 555–556

Logging, configure, 330

Logical drive, 101, 117–120

Logical printer, 206

Logical volume, 101

Login Properties dialog box, 529

Logon events, 542

Logon Information page, 68, 643

Logon rights, 164, 196–197

Logon script, 171–172

Logs. See Performance logs

Long-term power outages, 604, 609

LPD. See Line Printer Daemon (LPD)

LPR. See Line Printer Remote (LPR) service

LPR Port Monitor, 211

LPR printer port, add printers on, 215–216

L2TP. See Layer 2 Tunneling Protocol (L2TP)

L2TP VPN Connection, 381–388

  creating certificates, 381

  creating VPN connection, 385–388

  disable Routing and Remote Access with existing, 426

  enabling EAP in Routing and Remote Access, 384

  modifying Small Business Remote Access Policy, 381–382

  opening ports in Routing and Remote Access, 382–384

M

MAC address. See Media Access Control (MAC) address

MAC address filtering, 390–391

Machine group policies, 392

Mac OS/X, 30, 235, 249–254

Mac OS/X 10.3, 253

Mac Rendezvous automatic network configuration, 249

Macromedia Dreamweaver, 487

Mail Operators, 150–151

Mail Schedule page, 84

Malware, 258–259

Manage Access Requests link, 480

Manage Anonymous Access, 480

Manage Blocked File Types, 484

Manage Cross-Site Groups link, 480

Manage Distribution Groups pane, 337

Manage List Template Gallery links, 481

Manage Security Settings For Web Part Pages, 483

Manage Site Groups link, 480

Manage Site Template Gallery, 481

Manage Sites And Workplaces page, 481–482

Manage Small Business Server Backup, 297, 306

Manage User Rights For Virtual Server, 483

Manage Users Alerts, 482

Manage Users link, 478–480

Manage Web Discussions link, 482

Manage Your Server Wizard, 644/

Managed switches, 24

Management and Monitoring Tools dialog, 648

Management Tools, 518

Mandatory profiles, 167, 171

Manual ETRN trigger, 319

MAPI applications, 266

Master boot record (MBR), 595

Mbps. See Megabits per second (Mbps)

MBps. See Megabytes per second (MBps)

MBR. See Master boot record (MBR)

McAfee, 35

Mean time to failure (MTTF), 602–603

Mean time to recover (MTTR), 602–603

Media, connecting servers and clients, 622

Media Access Control (MAC) address, 366

Megabits per second (Mbps), 17

Megabytes per second (MBps), 17

Member server, 625

Memory, 562–565

Memory Available alert, 569

Memory performance, 547

MemoryAvailable Bytes, 564

MemoryCache Bytes, 564

MemoryCommitted Bytes, 563

Memory-intensive programs, 565

MemoryPage/Sec, 563

MemoryPages/Sec, 564

MemoryPool Nonpaged Allocs, 563

MemoryPool Nonpaged Bytes, 563

Memory settings, 565

Message Delivery Properties dialog box, 342, 346, 352
Message Integrity Check (MIC), 389
Messages. *See* E-mail
MFM. *See* Modified Field Modification (MFM)
MIC. *See* Message Integrity Check (MIC)
Microsoft Baseline Security Analyzer version 2.0 (MBSA2), 34
Microsoft Challenge Handshake Authentication Protocol (MC-CHAP), 373, 375
Microsoft Challenge Handshake Authentication Protocol version 2 (MS-CHAP v2), 392
Microsoft Connector for POP3 Mailboxes, 324, 326
  logging levels, 330
  service status, 329–330
Microsoft Defender, 259
Microsoft Download Center, 490
Microsoft Encrypted Authentication (MS-CHAP), 384
Microsoft .NET architecture, 532
Microsoft Network Server, 254
Microsoft Office FrontPage 2003 Inside Out, 485
Microsoft Office HTML Viewer Service, 484–485
Microsoft Product Support, 270, 513
Microsoft SmartPhone, 261
Microsoft TechNet, 390
Microsoft Update, 276
Microsoft Windows Server 2003 Administrator's Companion, 30, 629
Microsoft XP Tablet PC Edition, 235
Microsoft-defined migration, 56
Microwave wireless, 18
Middleton, Jeff, 60
Migrating
  choosing between upgrading and, 55–56
  Microsoft-defined, 56
  using permissions, 69–70
  See also Conventional migration; Swing migration
Migrating profiles, from existing domain, 248
Migrator print server, 229–230
Mini-Setup Wizard, 635
Mirror, 611
  add, 123–124
  break, 127
  remove, 126–127

Mirror striped disk, 612
Mirrored (RAID-1), 111
Mirrored volume, 101, 124–126
Mirrored volumes, 105
Mirroring (RAID-1), 106
Mirroring/duplexing, 615
Mixed Mode for authentication, 521
Mobile Client And Offline Use page, 158, 237, 261
Mobile devices, services for, 6
Mobile User template, 157
Mobile users, 150, 480
Mobile Users group, 148
Mobile users of Remote Web Workplace, 256
Modem Selection page, 88
Modified Field Modification (MFM), 102
Modify Share Page link, 473–474
Modify Share Web Part, 473–474
Modify Shared Page link, 472
Modify Site Content link, 474
Modify The Current Certificate Assignment page, 506–507
Monitor threads, 556
Monitoring
  another computer, 553
  configuring, 94–95
  frequency of, 549–550
  memory usage for, 562–565
  selecting method of, 546
Monitoring and Reports, 644
Monitoring Configuration Wizard, 7, 94
Monitoring disk activity, 567–568
Monitoring processor activity, 565–566
Mosaic, 509
Most recently accessed files storage report, 658
Mounted volume, 114
MS-CHAP. *See* Microsoft Challenge Handshake Authentication Protocol (MC-CHAP)
MS-CHAP v2. *See* Microsoft Challenge Handshake Authentication Protocol version 2 (MS-CHAP v2)
MTTF. *See* Mean time to failure (MTTF)
MTTR. *See* Mean time to recover (MTTR)
Multihoming. *See* Multiple network interface cards (multihoming)
Multiple disk controllers, 614–615

Multiple domains, handling, 638–638
Multiple network interface cards (multihoming), 602
Multiple user accounts, add, 148
Multiprocessor, 633
MX records, 318–319
My Documents, 165–167
My Network Places, 266
My Private Stuff, 191–194
MyBusiness OU, 462–463

N

Name And Address page, 394
Name And Organization page, 630
Name And Security Settings page, 507
Name Your Printer page, 210, 214, 216
Naming computers, 32
Naming conventions
  benefits of, 30
  choosing domain name for network, 31
  internal domain name *vs.* Internet domain name, 31–32
  naming computers, 32
NAS. *See* Network Attached Storage (NAS)
NAT. *See* Network Address Translation (NAT)
NetBIOS, 370
NetBIOS name, 50, 522
.NET Passport Authentication, 504
Net Start command, 533
Net Stop command, 533
Net 36 GB RAID 0+1 array, 616
Network(s)
  choosing domain name for, 31
  choosing storage solution for, 103–104
  clients, 622
  connecting computers to, 236–254
    connecting alternate clients, 249–254
    creating computer accounts for client computers, 236–238
    creating computer accounts for server computers, 238–239
    establishing basic network connectivity, 239–243
    migrating profiles from existing domain, 248

using Small Business Server Network Configuration Wizard, 243–247
defining domains, 624–625
domain components, 625–626
features of Windows Operating System, 622–623
media connecting servers and clients, 622
removing computers from, 267–268
servers, 621–622
workgroups, 623
Network Address Translation (NAT), 26, 410–412
Network appliance. *See* Print servers
Network Attached Storage (NAS), 23, 103–104, 106–107
Network Bridge, 393
Network cable, 20–21, 617
Network card, 616, 622
Network Configuration page, 245
Network Configuration Wizard, 244, 248, 398
Network Connection page, 77
Network Connection Properties dialog box, 383
Network Connection Type page, 385
Network connectivity, 239–243
Network devices
diagramming network, 22–23
firewall device or router, 26–28
network switch, 23–24
placing access points for best coverage, 25–26
wireless access points (WAPs), 24–25
Network diagram, 22–23
Network File System (NFS), 114
Network Folder, 165–167
Network infrastructure, planning
client hardware and software, 29–30
determine needs, 15–16
Internet connection, 16–19
network devices, 22–28
network operating system (NOS), 13–15
network type, 19–21
server hardware, 28–29
Network interface, add printers with, 211–216
Network key, 242

Network operating system (NOS), 13–15
Network printer, 23, 208
Network security, advanced
create L2TP VPN connections, 381–388
create local computer and current user certificates console, 377–378
deploying certificate services, 375–381
requesting certificate for SBS server, 381
requesting computer and user certificates, 378–380
using 802.1x authentication for wireless security, 388–403
using group policy to automatically configure 802.11 and certificate settings, 403–407
using Internet Authentication Service to increase VPN security, 373–375
Network settings, configure, 48–49
Network speed, 17
Network switch, 23–24, 617
Network type, choosing
network cable, 20–21
types, 19–20
wireless standard 802.11a/b/g, 21
Networked printers, connecting to, 251–252
New Access Rule Wizard, 431–433
New Address Range Rule Element dialog box, 431–432
New Connection Wizard, 385
New dialog box, 528
New E-Mail Address dialog box, 341
New Hardware Found dialog box, 209
New Host dialog box, 369
New Logical Drive, 117
New Or Existing Answer File page, 627
New Partition Wizard, 114–115, 117–118
New Preferred Setting Properties dialog box, 406–407
New RADIUS Client Wizard, 394
New Remote Access Policy Wizard, 395–396
New Report Job Wizard, 439–441
New Reservation dialog box, 366
New Volume Wizard, 111

NFS. *See* Network File System (NFS)
NFTS. *See* NT File System
Nimda, 271
Non-ACPI systems, 633
Nonsystem provider, selecting, 556–557
NOS. *See* Network operating system (NOS)
Notepad, print test document from, 231
Notification escalation procedure, 588
Notification Settings page, 95–96
Notification Thresholds section, 654
Notify Computer, Not User, When Remote Documents Are Printed, 225
Notify When Remote Documents Are Printed, 225
NT AUTHORITYNetwork Service dialog box, 529
NT File System (NFTS), 34, 117, 131, 596, 623
NT File System (NFTS) folder, 187–188
NT File System (NFTS) Full Format, 46
NT File System (NFTS) permissions, 183–185, 188–189, 191, 504–505
NT File System (NFTS) Quick Format, 46
Ntdetect.com files, 595–596
Ntldr, 595–596

O

Object access event, 542
Object Explorer, 533–534
Object Explorer pane, 527
OEM Preinstallation Kit (OPK), 630
Office 2003 Resource Kit Web site, 485
Office 2004, 249
Office Excel, 470
Offline files, 180–182
Offline Settings dialog box, 181
Off-site storage, 296
OMA. *See* Outlook Mobile Access (OMA)
Online licensing, 9–10
Onsite Tape Changer page, 300–301, 307
Open Site dialog box, 486

Operating system
  choosing client hardware and
    software, 29–30
  installing, 42–48
OPK. *See* OEM Preinstallation Kit
  (OPK)
Options page, 537
Organization Information page, 507
Organizational unit (OU), 403,
  448–449
OU. *See* Organizational unit (OU)
Outbound Fax Device page, 91
Outgoing queues, shut down, 358
Outgoing Routing, 93
Outlook, 335, 424
Outlook Mobile Access (OMA), 82–
  83, 424
Outlook Profile Settings, 266
Outlook 2003, 4, 30, 244, 258–259,
  262, 274–275
  modifying group membership
    with, 335–337
Outlook Via The Internet, 82
Outlook Web Access (OWA), 19,
  82–83, 254, 256–257, 266,
  424, 500
OWA. *See* Outlook Web Access
  (OWA)
Ownership, 191–194

P

Packet filtering, 26, 412
Page fault, 556
Page Options dialog box, 487
Paging file, 564–565
Paging file usage, 547
Paging File% Usage (all instances),
  564
Paging File% Usage Peak, 564
Partition, 100
  adding, 108, 111–114
  create, 114–116
  create logical drives in extended,
    117–119
  delete, 119–120
  planning, 40
Passive file screen, 658
Passphrase, 161
Password, 504
  change e-mail, 331–332
  default, 35
  set Administrator password, 632
Password policy
  conditions, 160
  configure, 159–161

enable, 34
minimum password length, 160
privacy, 161
rules for good passwords, 161
Patch management
  importance of, 270–271
  installing SBS 2003 R2 WSUS,
    277–280
  patch cycle, 272–277
  terminology, 269–270
  third-party solutions, 269
  using WSUS, 280–289
Patch Tuesday, 271, 276
Patching cycle
  assess phase, 272–273
  deploy phase, 276
  evaluate and plan phase, 275–276
  identify phase, 273–275
  repeat phase, 276–277
PatchLink, 289
Pause Printing, 226
PCL. *See* Printer Control Language
  (PCL)
PEAP. *See* Protected Extensive
  Authentication Protocol (PEAP)
Peer-to-peer network, 14
PerfectDisk, 640
Performance, 660
Performance logs
  counter logs, 553–554
  creating counter an trace logs,
    554–558
  trace logs, 554
Performance Logs And Alerts, 554,
  557–558, 562
Performance Monitor, 575–576
Performance monitoring report, 542
Performance Object list, 548
Performance Properties dialog box,
  555
Performance Report, 94–95
Perimeter network, in network
  diagram, 23
Permission Entry dialog page, 166
Permissions, 148, 163–164
  assign NTFS permissions to file,
    188–189
  configure NTFS folder, 187–188
  configure special, 189–191
  delegating, on Group Policy
    Object (GPO), 457–459
  determine effective, 195–196
  explicit, 185–187
  how permissions work, 183–184
  inherited, 185–187

remove inheritance from, 192
rules for, 184
view NTFS for new folder, 191
working with NTFS file and
  Folder, 184–185
Permissions Entry dialog box, 189–
  190
Permissions for Authenticated Users
  pane, 446
Permissions page, 181
Personal Information Exchange or
  PFX format, 203
Personal View, 474
Personalize Your Software, 47
PFM. *See* Pulse Frequency
  Modulation (PFM)
PGP Key, 274
Phishing attack, 274
Phone And Modem Options tool, 48
Photo libraries, 467
Photo Library template, 467
Physical drive, 100
Physical memory, 565
Physical security, ensuring, 33
Physical wire, 622
PhysicalDisk, 547
PhysicalDisk% Disk Time, 564
PhysicalDiskAvg. Disk Queue
  Length, 564
PhysicalDiskAvg. Disk Sec/Transfer,
  564
Pico local, 251
Picture libraries, 467, 469
Ping command, 231
Ping (ICMP) Monitor, 575
Ping of Death, 26, 36
PJL. *See* Printer Job Language (PJL)
PKCS #12, 203
Plain Old Telephone Service
  (POTS), 18. *See also* Dial-up
Plan phase, 275–276
Plenum-grade cable, 21
Plug and Play (PnP) devices, 209,
  635
Plug-and-Play mechanism, 45
PM. *See* Preventative maintenance
  (PM) program
.PNG files, 321
PnP. *See* Plug and Play (PnP) devices
Pocket PC, 242, 261
Point to Point Protocol over Ethernet
  (PPPoE) connection, 78
Point To Point Tunneling Protocol
  (PPTP), 27, 372–373
Point-to-Point, 25

Policy change event, 542
Policy Configuration Method page, 395
POP Mailbox Accounts, 83
POP3. *See* Post Office Protocol 3 (POP3)
POP3 Connector Manager, 322–331
POP3 E-Mail
  adding, boxes, 322–323
  configuring, boxes, 317, 322
  configuring undeliverable, 330–331
  delivery schedule, 325–326
  editing, boxes, 322, 324–325
  removing, boxes, 322, 324
  routing, 326–328
  troubleshooting, 329–331
  undeliverable, 329
POP3 Mailbox dialog box, 323–325, 328
Port settings, change, 222
Ports
  configuring, 372
  opening, in Routing and Remote Access, 382–384
Ports Properties dialog box, 372
Post Office Protocol 3 (POP3), 80, 317
PostScript, 206
PostScript printer, 224
Post-transition, 644–645
POTS. *See* Plain Old Telephone Service (POTS)
Power supply
  local power supply failure, 603–605
  long-term power outages, 604, 609
  overview of types of, 603
  short-term power outages, 604, 608–610
  Simple Network Management Protocol (SNMP), 606
  spare, 616
  voltage variations, 603, 606–608
Power User Templates, 151
PPPoE Connection page, 78
PPPoE. *See* Point to Point Protocol over Ethernet (PPPoE) connection
PPTP. *See* Point To Point Tunneling Protocol (PPTP)
Preconfigured storage reports, 658
Premium Technologies Disk, 595
Presentations, 467

Preventative maintenance (PM) program, 610
Preview button, 487
Primary domain controller (PDC) emulator, 63
Primary partition, 100
Primary Rate ISDN, 74
Principal name, 155
Principal name suffix, 155
Print Directly To The Printer, 223
Print drivers, level 2 and level 3, 229–230
Print management, 225
  from command line, 228
  from Web browser, 227
  from Windows, 226–227
  using print migrator to back up or migrate print servers, 229–230
Print migrator, 229–230
Print Operators, 150, 152
Print queue window, 226
Print Server Properties dialog box, 224
Print servers
  defined, 205
  printer terminology, 206–207
  use print migrator to back up or migrate, 229–230
Print Services For Unix, 251
Print Spool service, 232–233
Print Spooled Documents First, 223
Print test document, from Notepad, 231
Print Test Page, 211, 215–216
Printer(s), 266
  add, 90
  add, on LPR printer port, 215–216
  add, on standard TCP/IP printer port, 211–215
  add, with network interface, 211–216
  adding locally attached, 208–211
  change share name, 217–219
  choosing, 207
  connecting to networked, 251–252
  costs of, 207
  defined, 206
  installing, 208–216
  local vs. networked, 208
  managing, 225–230
  networked, 23
  share, 16
  terminology for, 206–207
Printer availability, 221

Printer Control Language (PCL), 206
Printer driver settings, change
  change printer availability and priorities, 221
  change spool settings, 223–224
  determine group printer priorities, 221–222
  set up printer pools and change port settings, 222
  share printer and add client drivers, 217–219
  specify color profile, 220
  support x64 clients, 219–220
Printer Job Language (PJL), 224
Printer List dialog box, 252
Printer Migrator utility, 229–230
Printer pool, 206–207, 222
Printer priorities, 221, 227
Printer server options, setting, 224–225
Printer Sharing page, 210, 214, 216
Printing problems, troubleshooting, 230–233
Privacy, password, 161
Private Information Store, 359
Private network, 48
Private network addresses, 411–412
Privilege use event, 542
Privileges, 164, 196–198
Process Monitor, 575, 577–578
Process Timeout, 572
Process tracking event, 542/ Process% Processor Time (all instances), 566
Processor, 547
  monitoring activity, 565–566
  tips for monitoring, 566
Processor object, 548
Processor% Interrupt Time, 565–566
Processor% Privileged Time, 566
Processor% User Time, 566
ProcssortInterrupts/Sec, 565
Product Key page, 66, 631
Product page, 627
Profile(s)
  defined, 167
  domain, 169
  local, 167, 169–171
  mandatory, 167, 171
  migrating, from existing domain, 248
  roaming, 167, 169–171
  specify color, 220

what's stored in, 168
See also User profiles
Projects, 467
Properties dialog box, 544
    Advanced tab of, 230
    Advanced tab of printer's, 221
    General tab of, 559–560
    Sharing tab of printer's, 217
    to change ownership of folder,
        193–194
    to change permissions and access
        folder, 194
    to create customized roaming
        profiles, 170–171
    to set up roaming profiles, 169–
        170
Protected EAP (PEAP)
    authentication method, 382
Protected EAP (PEAP) Properties
    page, 397, 401–402
Protected Extensive Authentication
    Protocol (PEAP)
    and group policy processing, 393
    configuring clients to, 398–403
    overview, 392
Provide Company Information page,
    91
Public Key Policies, 405
Public Network page, 385
Pulse Frequency Modulation (PFM),
    102

Q

QoS Packet Scheduler, 508
Query The Catalog object, 512
Queue Viewer, 355–356, 358
Queued e-mail message, 318
Queues
    finding messages in, 356–358
    shutting down all outgoing, 358
    viewing and monitoring, 355–356
Quota Entries window, 134–136
Quota extensions, 652
Quota reports, creating, 136–137
Quota template, creating and
    editing, 653–655
Quota usage storage report, 658
Quotas
    creating, 650–652
    exporting and importing, 136

R

RADIUS. *See* Remote Authentication
    Dial-In User Service (RADIUS)

RADIUS authentication, 391
RADIUS client, adding wireless
    access point as, 393–395
RADIUS server, 35–36, 390, 392–
    393, 426
RAID (redundant array of
    independent disks), 40, 101
RAID 0, 101, 106, 121, 613–614
RAID 1, 106, 611, 613–615
RAID 3, 613–615
RAID 4, 613–615
RAID 5, 102, 105, 111, 121–122,
    127–128, 613–614
RAID 10 (RAID 0+1), 106, 615
RAID arrays, 591, 612
RAID controller, 43, 60, 610
RAID levels, for fault tolerance
    array of RAID array, 612
    availability, 612, 615
    block-level parity, 611
    byte-level parity, 611
    cost, 612, 615–616
    fault tolerance, 612, 614
    intended use, 612–613
    interleaved block-level parity, 611
    mirror or duplex, 611
    performance, 612, 615
    striped mirrored disks or
        mirrored striped disks, 612
    striping, 611
RAID solution, 103–104
RAID-specific hardware, 610
RAW, 214
Raxco, 640
RBLs. *See* Real-time block lists
    (RBLs)
Read All Digitally Signed Mail in
    Plain Text, 275
Read Only interaction level, 629
Ready to Install page, 521
Real-time block lists (RBLs), 348–
    349
Recipient filtering, 345, 349–350
Recovery agent certificates,
    protecting, 204
Recovery Console, 595, 597–598
Recovery drive, creating and using,
    599–600
Recovery key, 203
Recovery options, specifying, 298–
    299
Recovery policy, create, 199–200
Recycle Bin, 634
Regeneration, 124

Regional And Language Options
    page, 46–47, illus.
Registry editor, 359–361
Registry key, 359–360
Regredit.exe, 61
Relative identifier (RID) master, 63
Remote access, 27, 513
    configuring, 85–88
    internal network to Internet, 16
    via dial-up, 87–88
    via Virtual Private Networking
        (VPN), 85–87
    viewing clients, 371
Remote Access Method page, 86–87
Remote Access Policy, 373, 395–
    398, 403
Remote Access Wizard, 86–88
Remote Assistance, 266–267
Remote Authentication Dial-In User
    Service (RADIUS), 372–373
Remote Connection CD, 264
Remote Connection Disk, 263–264
Remote Connection Wizard, 261
Remote Desktop Connection, 249,
    254, 265–267
Remote domain controllers,
    upgrade, 64
Remote Operators, 150
Remote procedure calls (RPC), 8
Remote Storage service, remove, 63
Remote Web Workplace (RWW),
    249, 424, 485, 496, 500
    access of, 254–258
    Connection Manager and, 6
    defined, 6
    migrating user permissions, 69
    Mobile Users of, 256
    Outlook Mobile Access and, 82–
        83
    overview of how to use, 255–256
    post-transition, 644
    Security Groups page, 157
    Transition Pack and, 639–640
    in universal groups, 151
    Virtual Private Networking or, 85–
        86
    for Windows XP clients, 243
Remote Web Workplace (RWW)
    page, 255
Remove E-Mail Attachments page,
    84, 320
Remove Mirror dialog box, 126
Remove Selected Users, 478
Remove share, 177
Rendezvous, 251

Repeat phase, 276–277

Replace Permission Entries On All Child Objects With Entries Shown Here That Apply To Child Objects, 186

Reply To address
change, for all users, 339–340
change, for specific user, 340–341

Report Content page, 439

Report Job Properties dialog box, 438–439

Report Job Schedule page, 440

Report Publishing page, 440

Report Server, 519

Report view, 550–551

Reporting Options page, 94

Reporting Services Configuration Manager, 533

Request for Comments (RFC) 1985, 318

Required Components page, 67

Required Information For Connecting To The Internet, 73

Requires Manual Reset TO Return To OK Status, 577

Resize ShadowStorage, 146

Resource escalation procedure, 588

Restore And Manage Media tab, 307–308

Restore Configuration dialog box, 435

Restore Progress dialog box, 309

Restoring data
test before you need it, 309–310
to alternate location, 309
using Backup Utility to restore files and folders, 307–309
using Previous Versions Client to restore files and folders, 309–311

Resultant Set of Policy (RSoP) data, 444

Resultant Set of Policy planning mode, 459

Resultant Set of Policy snap-in, 446

Resynching, 124

Review Pending Updates link, 284

RFC 1918, 411–412

Rich Text Format, 136

Rights, 163–164, 479–480

RISC-based computer, 596

Roaming profiles, 167, 169–171

Router, 622
choosing, 26–28
with built-in access points, 24

Router Connection page, 77

Routing and Remote Access (RRAS), 80, 426, 513
enabling EAP in, 384
opening ports in, 382–384

Routing and Remote Access Properties dialog box, 384

Routing Rule dialog box, 327–328

RPC. See Remote procedure calls (RPC)

RRAS. See Routing and Remote Access (RRAS)

Rule Action dialog box, 431

Rules, set offline file, 180–182

Run As, 172–174

Run As dialog box, 173

Run Assigned Applications Wizard, 265

Run dialog box, 597

Run Disk Cleanup (Cleanmgr.exe), 640

Run This Program, 560–561

RWW. See Remote Web Workplace (RWW)

S

Safe Mode, 65

Sags, 608

SAN. See Storage Area Network (SAN)

SAS. See Serially Attached SCSI (SAS)

SATA. See Serial ATA (SATA)

SATA controller driver, 43

SATA RAID, 102

Satellite, 75

Save Items As Template link, 477

Schedule dialog box, 659

Scheduled Tasks folder, 660

Schema master, 63

SCIS. See Small Computer System (or Serial) Interface (SCSI)

SCL. See Spam confidence level (SCL)

Scope page, 454

Screening files, 655–658
controlling types of files on SBS Server, 655–656
create file screens, 656–658
file screens are flexible, 657–658
using exceptions to control location, 657

Script action, 574

Scriptomatic Tool, 267

SCSI adapter, 597

SCSI controller, 591, 633

SCSI ID, 597

SDSL. See Synchronous DSL (SDSL)

SecAttConfig.xml, 321

Secure Sockets Layer (SSL), 83, 332
changing settings, 505–508

Security, 623
against hackers, 8
best practices, 72
of client computers, 33–35
planning for, 32–36
client computers, 33–35
Internet firewalls, 36
physical security, 33
wireless networks, 35–36

Security Alert, 83

Security basics, 95

Security Event Log, viewing, 544

Security Groups, 150, 153–154

Security Groups page, 157

Security Options, 253–254

Security principal name, 155

Security settings
change externally accessible sites, 500–503
change server certificates and SSL settings, 505–508
changing, 499–508
enable or disable anonymous access, 503–505

Security update, 270

Security Warning dialog box, 245

Select A Printer Port page, 209–212, 215

Select Disks page, 111, 121–122

Select Disks To Convert page, 109–110

Select Disks To Initialize page, 109–110

Select EAP Providers dialog box, 382

Select GPO dialog box, 450

Select Partition Type page, 114–115, 118

Select User, Computer, O Group dialog box, 505

Select Volume Type, 111

Selection scripts, creating, 304

Self-assigned certificate, 83

Self-Service Site Creation, 479

Send E-Mail Notification page, 440–441

Send Network Message To, 560

Sender filtering, 345–347

Sender ID Filter, 359

Sender ID filtering, 345, 352–353

Sender Policy Framework (SPF), 352
Sendmail, 317
Sensitive data, encrypting, 198–204
Separator Page, 223–224
SEPs. *See* Standard escalation procedures (SEPs)
Sequential trace file, 558
Serial ATA (SATA), 102, 104
Serially Attached SCSI (SAS), 103–104
Server(s)
  activating, 88–89
  clients, 622
  disk technologies for, 102–103
  introduction to, 621–622
  managing computers from, 258–268
  media connecting, and clients, 622
  prepare, for installation, 41–42
  preparing, for upgrading, 62–64
  with more than 2GB of RAM, 570–571
Server Certificate page, 507
Server certificates, manage, 505–508
Server Computer Name page, 239
Server computers, creating computer accounts for, 238–239
Server Computers container, 266
Server configurations, 28–29
Server hardware, 28–29
Server loads, 28–29
Server Management, 164, 282
Server Management console, 259–260, 263, 266–267, 280–281, 298–299, 500, 503, 505, 508, 510–511, 513
  Disk Management snap-in, 105–106
  for changing fax sending and receiving, 92–93
  Manage Distribution Groups pane of, 337
Server Management GUI, 297
Server Message Blocks (SMBs), 251
Server Operators, 152
Server Performance And Usage Report, 82
Server performance and usage reports, 424
Server Roles page, 529
Server Work Queue Length, 565
ServerBytes Total/Sec, 563

ServerPool Nonpaged Bytes, 563
ServerPool Paged Bytes, 563
Service, 547
Service Account page, 519–520, 526–527
Service Configuration page, 80, 422–423
Service Monitor, 575, 577
Service Pack, 270
Service Pack 2 for Microsoft Exchange 2003, 259
Services and Ports tab, 383
Set Password dialog box, 435–436
Set Up Client Applications Wizard, 5
Set Up Client Computer page, 158, 159
Set Up Client Wizard, 404
Set Up Computer Wizard, 5, 6, 236–238, 246
Set Up Server Wizard, 238–239, 404
Setting dialog box, 142
Setup Manager Computer Name Page, 631
Setup Manager dialog box, 632
Setup Manager Product page, 627–628
Setup Manager user Interaction page, 628
Setup Manager Wizard, 627
Setup Progress page, 522
Setup Requirements page, 49, 66–67, 280
Setup.exe program, 641–643
Setup.log, 594
Shadow copies, 623
Shadow copy
  assessing, 143–144
  configure, 140
  defined, 140
  disabling, 145
  disk defragmentation and volume, 143
  enabling, 140–142
  of shared folder, 140–146
  setting storage location and limits for, 142
  setting up clients to use, 143
  using, to supplement backups, 297
  volume, command line, 145–146
Share, 177, 179–180
Share a Folder Wizard, 180
Share name, change, 217–219

Share permissions, 175–176, 183–189
Shared Fax Client, 261
Shared fax service, 7
Shared Fax Service, 3
Shared folder, 140–146, 178–180
Shared resources, 175
Shared secret, 395
Shared View, 474
SharePoint Access page, 158
SharePoint Administrators, 150–151
SharePoint Central Administration page, 482–483, 531
SharePoint intranet site, 254, 257, 266
SharePoint library, 477
SharePoint Services, 5, 7, 9, 503, 513, 522–531
  facilitation of group projects via, 16
  Web site for, 496
SharePoint Services Intranet Site, 82
SharePoint Services site, 484
SharePoint Services Team site, 466–467
SharePoint site, 503
SharePoint Timer Service, 523–524, 529
SharePoint Web site
  administering, 477–482
  administering SharePoint virtual servers, 482–485
  backup and restore, 491–493
  changing appearance of, 471–472
  changing home page content, 472–474
  company web site *vs.*, 466–467
  customizing pages, 474–477
  interacting with, 469–470
  items contain in, 467–469
  opening, 485–487
  overview, 465–467
  using FrontPage 2003 to customize Windows SharePoint Services, 485–491
SharePoints Services, 3
SharePoint-specific antivirus software, 259
Sharing
  files, 16
  folders, 176–177
  making, available offline, 182
  Web, 498–499
Shavlik's HFNetChkPro, 289

Short-term power outages, 604, 608–609

Simple Mail Transport Protocol (SMTP), 8

Simple Mail Transfer Protocol (SMTP) server, 317

Simple Network Management Protocol (SNMP), 214, 606–608

Simple volume, 100, 111

Single domain, 11

Single large expensive disk (SLED), 102

Single server, 106

Site groups, 479–480

Site Settings link, 474

Site Settings page, 471

Slammer, 271

SLED. *See* Single large expensive disk (SLED)

Small Business Remote Access Policy, 381–382

Small Business Remote Access Policy Properties dialog box, 374, 382

Small Business Server, 622, 624–625
    Backup Wizard, 644
    Computers OU, 462
    controlling types of files on, 655–656
    Installation Wizard, 644
    monitoring, 533
    R2 Premium Technologies Setup, 516
    Remote Access Policy, 373
    Server Certificate, 381
    Shared Fax feature, 467
    Shared Fax service, 266
    To Do List. *See* To Do List
    Transition Pack, 10
    Update Services, 287
    updating, 95–93
    usage reports, 254

Small Business Server 2000, 60

Small Business Server 2000 Service Pack 1, 62

Small Business Server (SBS) 2003, 3
    Premium Edition additional features with, 4, 8
    restrictions on, 10–12
    Standard Edition features, 3–10

Small Business Server 2003 R2 Premium Technologies Setup Wizard, 415

Small Business Server Alerts, 570

Small Business Server Backup utility, 534

Small Business Server Network Configuration Wizard, 236, 243–247, 267

Small Business Server Setup
    Update Services page, 281
    Welcome page of, 282

Small Business Server Setup Wizard, 66–67, 513, 632–634, illus.
    configure network settings, 48–49
    Dynamic Host Configuration Protocol (HDCP), 50, 52
    Setup Requirements page, 280

Small Business Server Transition Pack Wizard, 641–643

Small Computer System (or Serial) Interface (SCSI), 102–104

Smart Card Or Other Certificate Properties dialog box, 382, 386–387

SMB/CIFS Filesystem Authentication dialog box, 251

SMBs. *See* Server Message Blocks (SMBs)

Smigrate, using, 492–493

SMTP. *See* Simple Mail Transport Protocol (SMTP)

SMTP address type, add, 341

SMTP connector, 356–357

SMTP filtering
    connection filtering, 345, 347–349
    intelligent filtering, 345, 350–352
    recipient filtering, 345, 349–350
    sender filtering, 345–347
    sender ID filtering, 345, 352–353

SMTP Services, 329

SMTP Virtual Server, 353

Smurg, 36

Snapshot, 140, 660

Sniff, 26

SNMP. *See* Simple Network Management Protocol (SNMP)

Software, 623
    antivirus, 34–35, 259
    client, 29–30

Software Installation And Maintenance feature, of Group Policy, 263

Software RAID, 610–611

Software update, 270

SOHO method, 35

Sophos, 35

SOPs. *See* Standard operating procedures (SOPs)

Source volume, 140–141

SPA, 324

SPA2-Enterprise, 243

Spam, 317, 348

Spam confidence level (SCL), 351–352

Spam strategies, 258–259

Spanned volume, 101, 105, 111

Spare parts, 616–617

Special permissions, configure, 189–191

Specify Additional Device, 44, illus.

Specify Partition Size page, 115–116, 118

SPF. *See* Sender Policy Framework (SPF)

SPI. *See* Stateful Packet Inspection (SPI)

Spikes, 606–607

Split button, 487

Spool Print Documents So Program Finishes Printing Faster, 223

Spool settings, change, 223

SQL Configuration Manager, 533

SQL database, 558

SQL Server, 8–9, 16, 641

SQL Server 2000, 4

SQL Server 2000 Service Pack 3a, 62

SQL Server 2005
    administration, 532–538
    architecture, 532
    install, 515–522
    upgrade Windows SharePoint Services too, 522–531

SQL Server 2005 Setup Wizard, 516–522, 525–526

SQL Server database, 58

SQL Server Desktop Engine, 512

SQL Server Management console, 534–536

SQL Server Management Studio, 532–533, 537

SQL Server Profiler, 533

SQL Server Server Manager, 533

SQL Services Manager, 533

SSID, 35

SSID hiding, 391

SSL. *See* Secure Sockets Layer (SSL)

SSL Port page, 508

St. Bernard Software's UpdateEXPERT, 289

Stand-alone surge protector, 607–608

Stand-alone wireless bridges, 25
Standard escalation procedures (SEPs), 584
Standard operating procedures (SOPs), 584
Standard TCP/IP printer port, add printers on, 211–215
Star network topology, 23
Start Performance Data Log, 560
Startup And Recovery dialog box, 598
Stateful Packet Inspection (SPI), 26, 36, 412
Static IP address, 19, 52
Storage
    as weak link during power failure, 604–605
    choosing solution for, 103–104
    drivers for, 45
    shadow copies, 140
Storage Allocation For Deleted File And E-Mail page, 301–302, 306
Storage Area Network (SAN), 103–104, 106
Storage connection technologies, 104
Storage drivers, 633
Storage Limits dialog box, 345
Storage management
    disk quotas, 132–137
    encrypting files, 137–139
    NTFS, 131
    shadow copies of shared folders, 140–146
Storage reports, scheduling, 658–660
Storage Reports Task Properties dialog box, 658–659
Storage resources, management of, 9
Storage space
    centralized file storage, 16
    dividing, 40
    See also Partition
Store Junk E-mail Configuration, 351
Streaming media, 8
Stripe set, 101
Striped (RAID-0), 111
Striped mirrored disk, 612
Striped Volumes (RAID-0), 101, 105
Striping, 106, 611
STS_Config database, 492
Stsadm.exe, 492
Stuck documents, print, 232
Subnet mask, 502–503

Summary Of Selections page, 460, 462
Surge, 607
Surge protectors, 606–608
Swing migration
    advantages of, 59–60
    as preferred migration strategy, 55–56
    steps in, 58
Switches, 622. See also Network switch
Symantec, 35
Symantect Ghost, 633
SYN Flood, 26
Synchronize E-Mail, 331–332
Synchronous DSL (SDSL), 18
Sysprep answer file, 634–635
Sysprint.sep, 224
System, 547
System Configuration Check page, 516–522
System events, 542
System Monitor
    choosing display elements, 552–553
    choosing time interval for monitoring, 552
    choosing view, 550–551
    deleting counters, 549
    determining how often to monitor, 549–550
    items, 546–547
    matching counters to graph lines, 549
    modifying display, 550
    monitoring another computer, 553
    objects tracked in, 547
    running, 547–553
    selecting additional properties, 552–553
    selecting counters, 548–5549
System Monitor Properties dialog box, 550, 552–553
System Monitor toolbar, 548
System Policy page, 437
System provider, 556–557
System State restore, 492
SystemProcessor Queue Length (all instances), 565
SYSVOL folder, 447

T

Tape, strategy, 296–297
Tape changer, select new, 307

Tapes, reusing, 295–296
TCP/IP. See Transmission Control Protocol/Internet Protocol (TCP/IP)
Technical Services Properties dialog box, 336–338
Telephone Information page, 90
Template Selection page, 69, 157–159, 163
Templates
    managing, 481–482
    managing user, 162–164
Temporal Key Integrity Protocol (TKIP), 389
Terminal Servers, 30, 625–626
Terminal Services, 422
Text file (comma- or tab-delimited), 553, 557
Text log action, 573
Text-mode mechanism, 45
Text-mode setup, 42
Thawte, 35, 83
Thread, 547, 556
Threshold
    adding, 571
    modify existing, 570
Thumbnails, 469
Time interval, for monitoring, 552
Time Zone page, 631
TKIP. See Temporal Key Integrity Protocol (TKIP)
To Do List
    activating server, 88–89
    adding client access licenses, 89–90
    adding printers, 90
    adding users and computers, 90–91
    configuring backup, 95
    configuring fax service, 91–94
    configuring monitoring, 94–95
    configuring remote access, 85–88
    connecting to Internet, 73–85
    if not displayed, 71–72
    overview, 69
    security basics, 95
    strategies for security, 72
    updating Windows Small Business Server, 95–96
To field, 327–328, 330
Token Ring equipment, 21
T1 line, 75
Toolbar, 552
Top-level domain, 50

Top-Level Site Administration, 477–478, 480–481
Trace logs
  creating, 554–558
  permissions for, 561–562
  setting file parameters for, 557
Transfer limitations, 19
Transition Pack
  handling business growth, 638
  handling multiple domains, 638–639
  included in, 637
  media not included in, 641
  performing transition, 641–643
  post-transition, 644–645
  prepare to run, 640–641
  Remote Web Workplace, 639–640
Transmission Control Protocol/Internet Protocol (TCP/IP), 48, 364–370
Transmission Control Protocol/Internet Protocol (TCP/IP) Port Monitor, 575
Trend Micro, 35
Trojan horse attacks, 172
Troubleshooting
  POP3 e-mail, 329–331
  printing problems, 230–233
  tips for memory, 564–565
Trusted Root Certification Authorities, 380, 388, 405
T72-00634, 637
T75-00752, 637
Tuning and test strategies, 561–562
Tuning and upgrading tips for disks, 568
TURN After Authentication, 80, 319, 331–332
TURN command, 318–319
255.0.0.0 subnet mask, 502
255.255.0.0 subnet mask, 502
255.255.255.0 subnet mask, 502
255.255.255.192 subnet mask, 503
Type Of Setup page, 627, 635

U

UCE. *See* Unsolicited Commercial E-Mail (UCE)
.UDF. *See* Uniqueness Database File (.UDF)
UNC path, 311
Undeliverable POP3 E-Mail, 329–331
Unencrypted files, 138

Unfreeze message, 357–358
Uninterruptible power supply (UPS), 41, 591, 603, 607–609
Uniprocessor, 633
Uniqueness Database File (.UDF), 631
Universal groups, 150–151
Universal Plug and Play (UPnP), 27, 36, 52
Universal scope, 149
Universal Serial Bus (USB), 104
UNIX, 114, 215, 626
Unpatched Web browser, 35
Unsolicited Commercial E-Mail (UCE), 317
Update Details dialog box, 285
Update Details page, 285
Update management, centralized, 15
Update rollup, 270
Update Services, 286–288
Update Services Home page, 284
Update Services page, 280, 282
Update Services Status page, 280–281
Updates installation, review status of, 286–287
Upgrade
  backing up existing server, 56
  choosing between upgrading and migrating, 55–56
  enhancing performance of current server with, 56
  performing, 66–69
  preparation for
    checking for compatibility issues, 60–61
    fallback plan, 61
    final preparation, 65–66
    preparing for, 60–66
    preparing client computers, 64
    preparing server, 62–64
    upgrading remote domain controller, 64
  remote domain controllers, 64
Upgrade Information page, 642
UPnP. *See* Universal Plug and Play (UPnP)
UPS. *See* Uninterruptible power supply (UPS)
Usage Report, 94–95, 542
Usage Report Users, 151
USB. *See* Universal Serial Bus (USB)
USB key, 264

Use Custom Share And Folder Permissions, 181
Use Security Groups page, 460
Use The Following ISP Address, 77
User Account And Password Information page, 245
User Account Information page, 156
User accounts, 164
  add multiple, 159
  add single user, 156–158
  configure password policy, 159–161
  create, 155–159
  naming, 155–156
  redirecting My Documents to Default Server Folder, 165
  redirecting My Documents to Network Folder, 165–167
User and Computer Selection page, 459–460
User authentication, 390
User Configuration node, 451
User controlled interaction level, 629
User Information page, 159
User interaction, choosing, 629
User Mailbox, 324
User Or Group Access page, 396
User Password page, 159
User profiles, 167–172
User rights, 148
User Selection page, 163, 462
User space limitations, 623
User templates, 162–164
Users, 90–91, 152

V

Vacation Calendar, 467
Validate Server Certificate dialog box, 386
Value Bar, 552
VeriSign, 35, 83, 505
Veritas Backup Exec, 641
Version History, 476
Video card, 617
View Installation Status page, 286–287
View Or Change Client Computer Settings dialog box, 265
View Security Best Practices, 72
Virtual directories, 498, 500
Virtual Directory Access Permissions page, 498
Virtual Directory Alias page, 497

Virtual Directory Creation Wizard, 497
Virtual Private Network (VPN), 16, 19, 391–392, 426, 436, 500
Virtual Private Networking (VPN), 81, 85–87, 422
Virtual Server General Settings link, 483
Virus, 258–259
  from e-mail attachments and infected documents, 33
  infections of master boot record (MBR), 595
  security against, 8
  upgrade definitions, 65
Virus scan, 65
Voltage variations, 603
  brownouts, 608
  sags, 608
  spikes, 606–607
  surges, 607
Volume, 100
  adding, 108, 111–114
  assign names, 128
  create, 111–112
  delete, 119–120
  enabling shadow copies on, 141
  extend, 121–123
  mirror, 123–124
  mount, 128–129
Volume Shadow Copy, 6, 143, 297, 302, 307, 309
  command line, 145–146
Volume Shadow Copy Service, 660
VPN. *See* Virtual Private Network (VPN)
VPN Client Properties dialog box, 427–428
VPN connection, 69
  connecting clients across, 244
  creating, 385–388
  Layer 2 Tunneling Protocol (L2TP), 375, 381
  using Remote Connection disk, 264
VPN pass-through, 27
VPN security, 373–375
VPN Server Name page, 87
VPN Server Selection page, 385
VPN tunnels, 27
Vsadmin command, 145–146

W

WAN Network Adapter, 28

Warning message
  filtering must be manually enabled, 347
  refreshing snap-in, 316
Web browser, managing printers from, 227
Web hosting, 19
Web page
  create advanced, 9
  customizing, 474–477
Web page editor, 485
Web Part Connections Wizard, 490
Web Part zone, 489–490
Web Parts, adding, 489–490
Web Server Certificate page, 83
Web services, enabling or disabling, 424–425
Web Services Configuration page, 81, 255, 425
Web sharing, 498–499
Web site
  access for employees, 16
  and static IP address, 19
  create new, 496
  facilitation of group projects via Windows SharePoint Services intranet, 16
  hosting, 496
  limit network usage by, 508–509
Web Site Content Directory page, 497
Web Site Creation Wizard, 496–497
Web Site Templates dialog box, 491
Welcome page, of Windows SBS 2003 R2 Setup, 278
WEP. *See* Wired Equivalent Privacy (WEP)
WEP encryption, 391
What You *See* Is What You Get (WYSIWYG) view, 486
Wi-Fi Alliance, 389
Wi-Fi Protected Access (WPA), 242–243, 375, 391–392
Wi-Fi Protected Access (WPA) encryption, 35
Wi-Fi Protected Access 2 (WPA2), 390–392
Window x64 Edition drivers, 219
Windows, managing printers from, 226–227
Windows 2000, 29–30, 34, 64, 244, 249
  configuring, to use DHCP, 241
Windows 2000 Professional, 30, 235, 259

Windows 2000 Server, 60
Windows 2000 Service Pack 4, 62
Windows Authentication Mode, 521
Windows Automatic Updates, 96
Windows clients, connecting older, 249
Windows Components Wizard, 63, 252, 376–377, 510, 648
Windows Corporate Deployment Tools User Guide, 632
Windows defragmentation utility, 640
Windows event log action, 573–574
Windows event log monitor, 575, 578–579
Windows Explorer, 303
Windows file share, connecting, 250–251
Windows Firewall, 393
Windows Kernel Trace Provider, 556
Windows Management Instrumentation (WMI), 267, 444, 461
Windows Management Instrumentation Console (WMIC), 267
Windows ME, 61, 235, 249
Windows Mobile Pocket PC Phone Edition, 158
Windows 95, 61, 249
Windows 98, 61, 235, 249, 626
Windows NT, 61
Windows NT 4, 64, 235, 249
Windows Operating System, features of, 622–623
Windows SBS Server 2003 R2 Setup Wizard, Welcome page of, 278–279
Windows Server 2003, 60, 244, 622–623
  configuring, to use DHCP, 240
  using system preparation tool to image, 633–635
Windows Server 2003 Hotfix Q832880, 48
Windows Server 2003 Manage Your Server page, 639
Windows Server 2003 POP3 Service, 63
Windows Server 2003 SP1, 242
Windows Server 2003 Web Edition, 496
Windows Server Catalog, 60, 591

Windows Server Update Services
      (WSUS), 3, 34, 69, 96, 235,
      258, 533
   installing SBS 2003 R2, 277–280
Windows Setup Wizard, 42
Windows Update Web site, 84
Windows Vista, 29–30, 34, 235, 626
Windows XP, 30, 34
   configuring, to use DHCP, 240
Windows XP Home Edition, 249
Windows XP Professional, 29, 34,
      64, 235, 242, 244, 249, 259,
      626
Windows XP Professional x64
      Edition, 242
Windows XP Tablet PC Edition,
      244, 259
WINS, 370
WinZip, 289
Wired Equivalent Privacy (WEP),
      35, 242
Wireless access points, 24
   adding, as RADIUS client, 393–
      395
   associating with, 241–242
   built-in, 28
   configuring, 398
Wireless bridge, 26
Wireless Ethernet bridge, 25
Wireless hackers, 33
Wireless network card antennas, 25
Wireless Network Connection
      dialog box, 242
Wireless Network Policy, creating,
      406–407
Wireless Network Policy Name page,
      406
Wireless Network Policy Wizard,
      406
Wireless Network Properties dialog
      box, 401–403
Wireless Network Setup Wizard,
      391
Wireless networks, 35–36, 375
Wireless Protected Access (WPA),
      20, 23–24
Wireless security, 388–403
WMI. See Windows Management
      Instrumentation (WMI)
WMI data query, 575
WMI event query, 575
WMI Filters For Users or WMI
      Filters for Computers page, 460
WMI Instance, 575

WMIC. See Windows Management
      Instrumentation Console
      (WMIC)
Workgroup, 14, 248, 623
Workstation operating system,
      clients use, 15
Workstations, 625–626
Worms, security against, 8, 33
WPA. See Wi-Fi Protected Access
      (WPA)
WPA. See Wireless Protected Access
      (WPA)
WPA encryption, 35, 389
WPA-PSK (Pre-Shared Key), 35
WPA/WEP key, 239
WPA2, 242–243. See also Wi-Fi
      Protected Access 2 (WPA2)
WPA2-Personal, 243
WSUS. See Windows Software
      Update Services (WSUS)

X

x86-based computers, 596
XML response file, 263
XML style sheets, 660

Y

Your Product Key, 47
Your Site's Common Name page,
      508

Z

Zero Configuration Wi-Fi, 242
ZoneEdit, Inc., 41, 318

Charlie Russel and **Sharon Crawford** are co-authors of numerous books on operating systems. Their titles include *Microsoft Windows Server 2003 Administrator's Companion 2nd Edition*, *Microsoft Windows XP Resource Kit, 3rd Edition*, and *Upgrading to Windows 98*. Their server is, of course, Microsoft Windows Small Business Server 2003.

Charlie Russel is a chemist by education; an electrician by trade; a UNIX sysadmin and Oracle DBA because he raised his hand when he should have known better; an IT Director and consultant by default; and a writer by choice. Charlie is a Microsoft MVP for Windows Server, Security, and Tablet PC, and is the author of more than two dozen computer books on operating systems and enterprise environments, including *Microsoft Windows Server 2003 Administrator's Companion*, *Microsoft Windows XP Resource Kit, 3rd Edition* and (with Robert Cordingley), the *Oracle DBA Quick Reference Series*. He has also written numerous white papers and case studies on Microsoft.com and is a regular columnist for the Windows Expert Zone.

Sharon Crawford began writing computer books in 1991 and hasn't tired of it yet. She also writes about using Windows XP at home for the Microsoft Windows XP Expert Zone at *http://www.microsoft.com/windowsxp/expertzone*.

Sharon and Charlie live in beautiful British Columbia with one dog, varying numbers of cats, and a delightful, if somewhat distracting, view of Pender Harbour.

Additional Windows (R2) Resources for Administrators

Published and Forthcoming Titles from Microsoft Press

Microsoft® Windows Server™ 2003 Administrator's Pocket Consultant, Second Edition

William R. Stanek ● ISBN 0-7356-2245-0

Here's the practical, pocket-sized reference for IT professionals supporting Microsoft Windows Server 2003—fully updated for Service Pack 1 and Release 2. Designed for quick referencing, this portable guide covers all the essentials for performing everyday system administration tasks. Topics include managing workstations and servers, using Active Directory® directory service, creating and administering user and group accounts, managing files and directories, performing data security and auditing tasks, handling data back-up and recovery, and administering networks using TCP/IP, WINS, and DNS, and more.

MCSE Self-Paced Training Kit (Exams 70-290, 70-291, 70-293, 70-294): Microsoft Windows Server 2003 Core Requirements, Second Edition

Holme, Thomas, Mackin, McLean, Zacker, Spealman, Hudson, and Craft ● ISBN 0-7356-2290-6

The Microsoft Certified Systems Engineer (MCSE) credential is the premier certification for professionals who analyze the business requirements and design and implement the infrastructure for business solutions based on the Microsoft Windows Server 2003 platform and Microsoft Windows Server System—now updated for Windows Server 2003 Service Pack 1 and R2. This all-in-one set provides in-depth preparation for the four required networking system exams. Work at your own pace through the lessons, hands-on exercises, troubleshooting labs, and review questions. You get expert exam tips plus a full review section covering all objectives and sub-objectives in each study guide. Then use the Microsoft Practice Tests on the CD to challenge yourself with more than 1500 questions for self-assessment and practice!

Microsoft Windows® Small Business Server 2003 R2 Administrator's Companion

Charlie Russel, Sharon Crawford, and Jason Gerend ● ISBN 0-7356-2280-9

Get your small-business network, messaging, and collaboration systems up and running quickly with the essential guide to administering Windows Small Business Server 2003 R2. This reference details the features, capabilities, and technologies for both the standard and premium editions—including Microsoft Windows Server 2003 R2, Exchange Server 2003 with Service Pack 1, Windows SharePoint® Services, SQL Server™ 2005 Workgroup Edition, and Internet Information Services. Discover how to install, upgrade, or migrate to Windows Small Business Server 2003 R2; plan and implement your network, Internet access, and security services; customize Microsoft Exchange Server for your e-mail needs; and administer user rights, shares, permissions, and Group Policy.

Microsoft Windows Small Business Server 2003 R2 Administrator's Companion

Charlie Russel, Sharon Crawford, and Jason Gerend ● ISBN 0-7356-2280-9

Here's the ideal one-volume guide for the IT professional administering Windows Server 2003. Now fully updated for Windows Server 2003 Service Pack 1 and R2, this *Administrator's Companion* offers up-to-date information on core system administration topics for Microsoft Windows, including Active Directory services, security, scripting, disaster planning and recovery, and interoperability with UNIX. It also includes all-new sections on Service Pack 1 security updates and new features for R2. Featuring easy-to-use procedures and handy work-arounds, this book provides ready answers for on-the-job results.

MCSA/MCSE Self-Paced Training Kit (Exam 70-290): Managing and Maintaining a Microsoft Windows Server 2003 Environment, Second Edition

Dan Holme and Orin Thomas ● ISBN 0-7356-2289-2

MCSA/MCSE Self-Paced Training Kit (Exam 70-291): Implementing, Managing, and Maintaining a Microsoft Windows Server 2003 Network Infrastructure, Second Edition

J.C. Mackin and Ian McLean ● ISBN 0-7356-2288-4

MCSE Self-Paced Training Kit (Exam 70-293): Planning and Maintaining a Microsoft Windows Server 2003 Network Infrastructure, Second Edition

Craig Zacker ● ISBN 0-7356-2287-6

MCSE Self-Paced Training Kit (Exam 70-294): Planning, Implementing, and Maintaining a Microsoft Windows Server 2003 Active Directory® Infrastructure, Second Ed.

Jill Spealman, Kurt Hudson, and Melissa Craft ● ISBN 0-7356-2286-8

For more information about Microsoft Press® books and other learning products, visit: **www.microsoft.com/mspress** *and* **www.microsoft.com/learning**

Additional SQL Server Resources for Administrators

Published and Forthcoming Titles from Microsoft Press

Microsoft® SQL Server™ 2005 Reporting Services *Step by Step*
Hitachi Consulting Services • ISBN 0-7356-2250-7

SQL Server Reporting Services (SRS) is Microsoft's customizable reporting solution for business data analysis. It is one of the key value features of SQL Server 2005: functionality more advanced and much less expensive than its competition. SRS is powerful, so an understanding of how to architect a report, as well as how to install and program SRS, is key to harnessing the full functionality of SQL Server. This procedural tutorial shows how to use the Report Project Wizard, how to think about and access data, and how to build queries. It also walks the reader through the creation of charts and visual layouts to enable maximum visual understanding of the data analysis. Interactivity (enhanced in SQL Server 2005) and security are also covered in detail.

Microsoft SQL Server 2005 Administrator's Pocket Consultant
William R. Stanek • ISBN 0-7356-2107-1

Here's the utterly practical, pocket-sized reference for IT professionals who need to administer, optimize, and maintain SQL Server 2005 in their organizations. This unique guide provides essential details for using SQL Server 2005 to help protect and manage your company's data—whether automating tasks; creating indexes and views; performing backups and recovery; replicating transactions; tuning performance; managing server activity; importing and exporting data; or performing other key tasks. Featuring quick-reference tables, lists, and step-by-step instructions, this handy, one-stop guide provides fast, accurate answers on the spot, whether you're at your desk or in the field!

Microsoft SQL Server 2005 Administrator's Companion
Marci Frohock Garcia, Edward Whalen, and Mitchell Schroeter • ISBN 0-7356-2198-5

Microsoft SQL Server 2005 Administrator's Companion is the comprehensive, in-depth guide that saves time by providing all the technical information you need to deploy, administer, optimize, and support SQL Server 2005. Using a hands-on, example-rich approach, this authoritative, one-volume reference book provides expert advice, product information, detailed solutions, procedures, and real-world troubleshooting tips from experienced SQL Server 2005 professionals. This expert guide shows you how to design high-availability database systems, prepare for installation, install and configure SQL Server 2005, administer services and features, and maintain and troubleshoot your database system. It covers how to configure your system for your I/O system and model and optimize system capacity. The expert authors provide details on how to create and use defaults, constraints, rules, indexes, views, functions, stored procedures, and triggers. This guide shows you how to administer reporting services, analysis services, notification services, and integration services. It also provides a wealth of information on replication and the specifics of snapshot, transactional, and merge replication. Finally, there is expansive coverage of how to manage and tune your SQL Server system, including automating tasks, backup and restoration of databases, and management of users and security.

Microsoft SQL Server 2005 Analysis Services *Step by Step*
Hitachi Consulting Services • ISBN 0-7356-2199-3

One of the key features of SQL Server 2005 is SQL Server Analysis Services—Microsoft's customizable analysis solution for business data modeling and interpretation. Just compare SQL Server Analysis Services to its competition to understand/grasp the great value of its enhanced features. One of the keys to harnessing the full functionality of SQL Server will be leveraging Analysis Services for the powerful tool that it is—including creating a cube, and deploying, customizing, and extending the basic calculations. This step-by-step tutorial discusses how to get started, how to build scalable analytical applications, and how to use and administer advanced features. Interactivity (which is enhanced in SQL Server 2005), data translation, and security are also covered in detail.

Microsoft SQL Server 2005 Express Edition
Step by Step
Jackie Goldstein • ISBN 0-7356-2184-5

Inside Microsoft SQL Server 2005:
The Storage Engine
Kalen Delaney • ISBN 0-7356-2105-5

Inside Microsoft SQL Server 2005:
T-SQL Programming
Itzik Ben-Gan • ISBN 0-7356-2197-7

Inside Microsoft SQL Server 2005:
Query Processing and Optimization
Kalen Delaney • ISBN 0-7356-2196-9

For more information about Microsoft Press® books and other learning products,
visit: **www.microsoft.com/mspress** *and* **www.microsoft.com/learning**

Prepare for Certification with Self-Paced Training Kits

Official Exam Prep Guides—
Plus Practice Tests

Ace your preparation for the skills measured by the MCP exams—and on the job. With official *Self-Paced Training Kits* from Microsoft, you'll work at your own pace through a system of lessons, hands-on exercises, troubleshooting labs, and review questions. Then test yourself with the Readiness Review Suite on CD, which provides hundreds of challenging questions for in-depth self-assessment and practice.

- **MCSE Self-Paced Training Kit (Exams 70-290, 70-291, 70-293, 70-294): Microsoft® Windows Server™ 2003 Core Requirements.** 4-Volume Boxed Set. ISBN: 0-7356-1953-0. (Individual volumes are available separately.)

- **MCSA/MCSE Self-Paced Training Kit (Exam 70-270): Installing, Configuring, and Administering Microsoft Windows® XP Professional, Second Edition.** ISBN: 0-7356-2152-7.

- **MCSE Self-Paced Training Kit (Exam 70-298): Designing Security for a Microsoft Windows Server 2003 Network.** ISBN: 0-7356-1969-7.

- **MCSA/MCSE Self-Paced Training Kit (Exam 70-350): Implementing Microsoft Internet Security and Acceleration Server 2004.** ISBN: 0-7356-2169-1.

- **MCSA/MCSE Self-Paced Training Kit (Exam 70-284): Implementing and Managing Microsoft Exchange Server 2003.** ISBN: 0-7356-1899-2.

For more information about Microsoft Press® books, visit: **www.microsoft.com/mspress**

For more information about learning tools such as online assessments, e-learning, and certification, visit: **www.microsoft.com/mspress** *and* **www.microsoft.com/learning**

Microsoft Windows Server 2003 Resource Kit
The *definitive* resource
for Windows Server 2003!

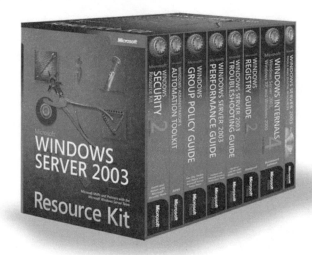

Get the in-depth technical information and tools you need to manage and optimize Microsoft® Windows Server™ 2003—with expert guidance and best practices from Microsoft MVPs, leading industry consultants, and the Microsoft Windows Server team. This official *Resource Kit* delivers seven comprehensive volumes, including:

- **Microsoft Windows® Security Resource Kit, Second Edition**
- **Microsoft Windows Administrator's Automation Toolkit**
- **Microsoft Windows Group Policy Guide**
- **Microsoft Windows Server 2003 Performance Guide**
- **Microsoft Windows Server 2003 Troubleshooting Guide**
- **Microsoft Windows Registry Guide, Second Edition**
- **Microsoft Windows Internals, Fourth Edition**

You'll find 300+ timesaving tools and scripts, an eBook of the entire *Resource Kit*, plus five bonus eBooks. It's everything you need to help maximize system performance and reliability—and help reduce ownership and support costs.

Microsoft Windows Server 2003 Resource Kit
Microsoft MVPs and Partners with the Microsoft Windows Server Team
ISBN: 0-7356-2232-9

For more information about Microsoft Press® books, visit: **www.microsoft.com/mspress**

For more information about learning tools such as online assessments, e-learning, and certification, visit: **www.microsoft.com/learning**

What do you think of this book?
We want to hear from you!

Do you have a few minutes to participate in a brief online survey? Microsoft is interested in hearing your feedback about this publication so that we can continually improve our books and learning resources for you.

To participate in our survey, please visit:

www.microsoft.com/learning/booksurvey

And enter this book's ISBN, 0-7356-2280-9. As a thank-you to survey participants in the United States and Canada, each month we'll randomly select five respondents to win one of five $100 gift certificates from a leading online merchant.* At the conclusion of the survey, you can enter the drawing by providing your e-mail address, which will be used for prize notification *only*.

Thanks in advance for your input. Your opinion counts!

Sincerely,

Microsoft Learning

Learn More. Go Further.